Cambridge Studies in Medieval Life and Thought

THE RISE AND DECLINE OF AN IBERIAN BOURGEOISIE

The Rise and Decline of an Iberian Bourgeoisie is one of the first long-term studies in English of an Iberian town during the late medieval crisis. Focusing on the Catalonian city of Manresa, Jeff Fynn-Paul expertly integrates Iberian historiography with European narratives to place the city's social, political, and economic development within the broader context of late medieval urban decline. Drawing from extensive archival research, including legal and administrative records, royal letters, and a cadastral survey of more than 640 households entitled the 1408 *Liber Manifesti*, the author surveys the economic strategies of both elites and non-elites to a level seldom achieved for any late medieval town. In a major contribution to the series, *The Rise and Decline of an Iberian Bourgeoisie* reveals how a combination of the Black Death, royal policy, and a new public debt system challenged and finally undermined, urban resilience in Catalonia.

JEFF FYNN-PAUL is a lecturer in History at Leiden University.

Cambridge Studies in Medieval Life and Thought
Fourth Series

The series *Cambridge Studies in Medieval Life and Thought* was inaugurated by G.G. Coulton in 1921; Professor Rosamond McKitterick now acts as General Editor of the Fourth Series, with Professor Christine Carpenter, Dr Magnus Ryan and Dr Len Scales as Advisory Editors. The series brings together outstanding work by medieval scholars over a wide range of human endeavour extending from political economy to the history of ideas.

This is book 103 in the series; a full list of titles in the series can be found at:
www.cambridge.org/medievallifeandthought

THE RISE AND DECLINE OF AN IBERIAN BOURGEOISIE

Manresa in the Later Middle Ages, 1250–1500

JEFF FYNN-PAUL

CAMBRIDGE
UNIVERSITY PRESS

CAMBRIDGE
UNIVERSITY PRESS

University Printing House, Cambridge CB2 8BS, United Kingdom

Cambridge University Press is part of the University of Cambridge.

It furthers the University's mission by disseminating knowledge in the pursuit of education, learning and research at the highest international levels of excellence.

www.cambridge.org
Information on this title: www.cambridge.org/9781107091948

First published 2016

Printed in the United States of America by Sheridan Books, Inc.

A catalogue record for this publication is available from the British Library

Library of Congress Cataloguing in Publication data
Fynn-Paul, Jeff.
The rise and decline of an Iberian bourgeoisie : Manresa in the later Middle Ages, 1250-1500 / Jeff Fynn-Paul (Leiden University).
pages cm. – (Cambridge studies in medieval life and thought. Fourth series)
Includes bibliographical references and index.
ISBN 978-1-107-09194-8 (hardback : alkaline paper)
1. Manresa (Spain) – History. 2. Middle Ages. 3. City and town life – Spain – Manresa – History. 4. Middle class – Spain – Manresa – History. 5. Black Death – Spain – Manresa – History. 6. Debts, Public – Spain – Manresa – History. 7. Manresa (Spain) – Politics and government. 8. Manresa (Spain) – Social conditions. 9. Manresa (Spain) – Economic conditions. 10. Spain – History – 711–1516. I. Title.
DP402.M25F96 2015
946.7′2 – dc23 2015012663

ISBN 978-1-107-09194-8 Hardback

CONTENTS

ILLUSTRATIONS

MAPS

FIGURE

TABLES

ACKNOWLEDGEMENTS

This book has been a long time in the making. During the nearly fifteen years since the project's genesis the manuscript has been thoroughly rewritten with an eye to incorporating secondary literature from across Europe, and during that process enough material on Manresa has been analysed and produced to fill a second volume. (This additional matter will be published under a separate title, by a different publisher.) I am most grateful to Cambridge University Press for taking up this project when my original publisher balked at its size; thanks particularly to Elizabeth Friend-Smith, Amanda George, and Jonathan Shepard for their kindness and patience. I wish also to thank the series editors and anonymous readers for Cambridge, whose commentary was immensely valuable.

The nature of this project was largely determined by the guidance and enthusiasm of Mark Meyerson and John Munro. It was Mark who encouraged my desire to produce an urban history of an Iberian city in the later Middle Ages, and John who encouraged me to provide as much quantitative data as possible. Their exacting standards of archival research, logic, and writing set the bar at the level which I have ever since attempted to achieve. I regret that John did not live to see this project reach fruition, but I hope that he would be proud of the result. Paul Freedman, a veteran of the archives of the neighbouring city of Vic, helped point me towards the archival riches that I discovered in Manresa. The Arxiu Històric de la Ciutat de Manresa was still being converted to the Arxiu Comarcal del Bages when I first arrived. Marc Torras, the archivist, showed kindness and good humour when I began to make requests in less-than-fluent Spanish and Catalan for his assistants to make hundreds of copies from the fourteenth- and fifteenth-century tomes which he had painstakingly reorganized and re-catalogued. His archival efforts and generosity were essential prerequisites to the genesis of this project.

It was my admiration for David Herlihy, especially his classic book on Pistoia, which most determined the structure of this book, although David Nicholas and Charles Phythian-Adams, Stephen Bensch, James

Amelang, Benjamin Kedar, Jaume Aurell, Flocel Sabaté, Philip Daileader, Katherine Reyerson, Christian Guilleré, Manuel Sánchez, Jan Dumolyn, Samuel Cohn, Maryanne Kowaleski, and Christian Liddy have also been very influential role models. I thank Maryanne in particular for reading parts of this manuscript.

I graduated from Toronto with a Ph.D. in 2005, at about the time that the managerial class in American universities had discovered that they could cut each tenure-track position into several adjuncting positions and thus 'save money'. Within a few years, the ratio of tenure to non-tenure jobs went from roughly 80/20 to 20/80. The powers that be would have us believe that this is an economic necessity. On the contrary it is an ideological, cultural, and institutional phenomenon, which can be reversed as easily as it was created, if sufficient will, knowledge, and organization can only be brought to bear. I daresay that one of the purposes of this study is to teach us just how susceptible economic phenomena are to political, institutional, cultural, and ideological influence. A goal of this book is to help empower, by means of wisdom and understanding, that majority of even the smartest and wisest people who have been taught to believe that accepting less as a middle class is somehow economically inevitable, when history can readily teach us that it is not.

As a result of these managers' overzealous application of supply-side economic theory, I spent three years from 2005 to 2008 as an adjunct professor. During my time as an adjunct, Warren Goldstein of the University of Hartford recognized my teaching and research talent, and strove to provide me with a stable platform and income that might enable me to pursue a career as an historian. He was humane beyond the call of duty, and it is department chairs such as him on whom much of the burden now falls for safeguarding the future of the historical profession in the United States, until saner times return. A turning point came when Jan Luiten van Zanden helped to arrange a postdoc position at the University of Utrecht in the Netherlands. Although the 2008 financial crisis hit hard, I was lucky enough to be given another postdoc position, partly by the efforts and guidance of Marjolein 't Hart, Griet Vermeesch and Hugo Soly. This stint at the Free University of Brussels enabled me to undertake a thorough revision of this manuscript, and it was the dialogue with these historians, as well as with Frederik Buylaert, Wouter Ryckbosch, Jan Dumolyn, and others, that kept my eye on the state of the literature.

Meanwhile, my contacts with the Iberian world have been maintained through conversations with Lluís To Figueras, Aurelia Martín Casares, Carme Batlle, Manuel Sánchez Martinez, Flocel Sabaté, Pere Orti Gost, Antoni Furió, James Amelang (long since an Iberian), and others; special thanks must go to Jose Roman Diaz de Durana and Fabrizio Titone of the Universidad del País Vasco bringing me to Vittoria, and to Alfonso Herranz Loncán for inviting me to deliver a Jaime Vicens Vives lecture at the University of Barcelona. I wish also to thank the generosity of the Spanish Ministerio de Economía y Competitividad for co-awarding me a MINECO grant, which will enable to me to do further research on Manresa.

In 2012 I came to Leiden, and since that time have been fortunate to have discovered one of the more vibrant, collegial, and enthusiastic departments of which an historian could hope to be part. The size of the department, coupled with its complement of world-class researchers, provides a very stimulating environment for doing scholarship, and this work has benefited immensely from the scholarly conversation which has been possible at many colloquia, and simply during lunchtime conversation and after-hours drinks. The vibrant managerial style of Leo Lucassen has done much to foster this environment, and he has been a great support while I became established at Leiden. To Cátia Antunes I owe a lasting debt of gratitude; and Jeroen Touwen has been likewise wonderfully supportive. My fellow hispanists at Leiden, especially Raymond Fagel and Maurits Ebben, have been welcoming and supportive; additional thanks must go to André Gerritts, Jeroen Duindam, Judith Pollmann, Peter Hoppenbrouwers, Luuk de Ligt, Jaco Zuiderduijn, Chris Quispel, Marlou Schrover, Manon van der Heijden, Damian Pargas, Jessica Roitman, and Karwan Fatah-Black, just to name a few of the many scholars who have provided support and collegiality. Janet Hunter of the London School of Economics and Roey Sweet of the University of Leicester have likewise provided particularly helpful advice and support at various junctures.

Cutbacks in institutional support such as we have seen occurring across the globe inevitably necessitate a fallback on private means, and it might be the case that the next generation of Ph.D. students will be recruited largely from that minority of people whose families possess enough resources to provide them with the leisure to study without the necessity of earning bread through labour. I am no gentleman scholar; my parents' middle-class means were gained largely by dint of my father's ability to get and hold a tenured professorship at Lehigh University, which was itself facilitated by a US Navy scholarship programme at Cornell University. Anxiously dipping into their retirement savings, my parents have spent nearly two decades 'on call', stepping in to help with moves, conference flights, and job interview expenses, when my own adjuncting and postdoc wages were insufficient for these necessities of the scholarly lifestyle. Thus, I thank my parents, John W. and Revelly Paul, without whom this book would never have been possible. I suspect that my own generation will find it much more difficult to provide for our children in the way that my parents' generation has been able to do for us. My wife's parents Jerry and Ingrid Stevens have likewise helped us in many small and not-so-small ways since we made the fateful, yet wonderful and vitally important decision to pursue careers in the humanities. My wife's grandmother Anne Chrapko and her uncle Chuck Chrapko were particularly generous in helping us to make more than one international move, with children, when our own savings were exhausted.

Finally, this book is dedicated to my wife Jennifer Fynn, my companion of more than fifteen years. Scholar, friend, poet, philosopher, idealist, musician, art critic, gardener, travel enthusiast, and immensely talented and energetic chef, her ability to make domestic life sparkle wherever we have found ourselves in the world has continually astonished me, and kept me in awe of her powers of mind and spirit. Our children Persephone and Patrick have grown up alongside this Manresa project, and I can only hope that when they visit Manresa for the first time, someday soon, they will find a city as delightful and intriguing as Jennifer and I did when we first stepped off the platform in the shadow of Montserrat over fifteen years ago.

ABBREVIATIONS

ACA	Arxiu de la Corona d'Aragon (Archive of the Crown of Aragon in Barcelona).
ACB	Arxiu Capitular de Barcelona (Archive of the Cathedral of Barcelona).
AHCB	Arxiu Històric de la Ciutat de Barcelona (Archive of the City of Barcelona).
AHCM	Arxiu Històric de la Ciutat de Manresa (Archive of the City of Manresa). When most of the medieval volumes were catalogued by Marc Torras Serra in the 1980s and 1990s, the designation given in his guides was AHCM, and the system is still in use. Thus, volumes are referred to by these letters, as opposed to the new appellation: Arxiu Comarcal del Bages (ACBG).
AHPM	Arxiu Històric de Protocols de Manresa. Now part of ACBG.
BT	Berenguer de Talamanca (Notarial register). AHCM Tr. 175 (1335–1370).
Cortes	*Cortes de los Antiguos Reinos de Aragón y de Valencia y Principado de Cataluña.* (Madrid, 1896–1920). As of initial writing, the first three tomes of the new edition, ed. Sesma Muñoz, covering the period before the 1370s, had not yet appeared.
EPLV	Marc Torras i Serra. *Els privilegis del 'Llibre verd' de Manresa.* Manresa, 1998.
FS	Familia Sarta (Notarial register). AHPM a. 4054. (1313–75).
FT1	Familia Talamanca, I (Notarial register). No reg. number (1317–69).
FT2	Familia Talamanca, II (Notarial register). AHCM Tr. 343 (1369–1433).
JS	Jaume Sarta (Notarial register). AHCM Tr. 224 (1351–88).
LM	*Liber Manifesti*, 1408–11. AHCM/AM I-165.

LV	*Llibre Verd*. Josep M. Gasol and Marc Torras Serra. *El Llibre Verd de Manresa: 1218–1902*. Barcelona, 1996.
MC	*Manuales Concilii*. AHCM I-series. Most of these, as with other Manresan primary sources used for this volume, are unfoliated. Thus, it was necessary to refer to documents by date. Since dating is regular and generally in good order, this should present no problems in finding entries quickly. Scribal entries were dated in Roman form prior to May 1351, when Manresan scribes changed over to 'modern' dating. Thus, 1333 pi3 means *Pridie Idus Martii*, 1335 15k6 is 15th *kalends* of June, and n7 is *nones* of July. 1363.10.7 is 7 October 1363. In a few instances a question mark (?) has been placed after the dates of certain entries which are either undated, or where it is uncertain whether the entry in question is a continuation of a previous dated entry. Individual I-series volumes are listed in the Bibliography.
MCOA	Thomas Bisson. *The Medieval Crown of Aragon*. Oxford, 1991.
PS	Pere Sarta (Notarial register). AHCM Tr. 113 (1324–56).
RS	Ramon Sarta (Notarial register). AHCM Tr. 323 (1351–93).
RT	Ramon de Talamanca (Notarial register). AHCM Tr. 120 (1328–81).

GLOSSARY

Bages — The region around Manresa, centered on the Pla de Bages (plain of the Bages), which offers a rare spot of relatively level ground in the otherwise rugged lower Pyrenean foothills, as the rivers Cardoner and Llobregat approach their confluence some 5km south of Manresa. Long demarcated by the borders of the *vegueria* (q.v.) of the Bages.

Batlle — Bailiff. Royal bailiffs were low-level crown officials who nonetheless had significant executive and fiscal powers at the local level.

Castellan — A 'feudal' lord who, by right of his status as a member of the gentry, the lowest order of nobility, had a right to monopolize violence on his estate, acting as judge and legislator for his tenants, except where such rights were expressly reserved to the king. In the fourteenth century, castellans could be either *donzells* (squires) or knights. *Persons generoses*, as they were known, were represented by the *braç armada* (noble estate) in the Catalan Parliament.

Censal — Originally any annual rent, including 'emphyteusis', or quit-rent on land. In its most influential form, this was a perpetual, transferable instrument of public debt secured on civic revenues and paying between 5 and 10 per cent interest. These became widely available after 1359, and their widespread acceptance and contractual legality resulted in the subsequent spread of 'private *censals*', guaranteed by the government, as a means of transferring capital between individuals on a long-term basis. A relatively conservative investment which nonetheless proved both stable and popular with holders of capital throughout the later fourteenth and fifteenth centuries.

Conseller — The terms *conseller* and 'consul' are used interchangeably to indicate a member of the city's highest body, the Council of Four (or, from 1323–55, the Council of Six). This council was never known in any official document as the Council of Four (or Six); the term is only used here for clarity. This body was almost always attended by a larger body of *jurats*, whose powers, except perhaps during a brief revolutionary spell in the 1360s, were distinctly inferior to those of the *consellers*. The term 'councillors' as used in the text usually indicates the larger governing group of consuls and *jurats*. *Consellers* served for one year and were elected every 1 April. Election conferred the lifetime title *venerabilis* on a *conseller*, giving them titular parity with knights and *donzells,* until knights were awarded the superior title *honorabilis* in 1354.

Corts — Catalan Parliament. This consisted of the *braç ecclesiastic* (representing the clergy) the *braç armada* (representing the nobility and the knighthood), and the *braç reial* (representing the citizens of the royal cities and towns). Beginning in the early fourteenth century, Manresa, like most royal cities, sent two representatives to the *Corts*. Barcelona customarily sent five.

Diputació — The 'permanent arm' of the Catalan *Corts*, which began its existence in 1359, at the time that the public debt became permanent as a result of the massive borrowing (facilitated by sales of *violaris* and *censals*) that occurred as a result of the Castilian War (commonly known as the War of the Two Peters, 1356–75). The formation of the *Diputació* was the result of a compromise between the *Corts* and the Crown over the management of the newly expanded funded public debt.

Jurat — One of between sixteen and thirty men who sat as an advisory body to the *consellers*. They sat for one year and received no title. Together with the *consellers*, the *jurats* made up the *Consell Special*, which was most often entrusted with voting on the legislative decisions of civic government. *Jurats* were drawn from a more economically diverse background than the generally much wealthier *consellers*.

Mas — Manse. An isolated, usually fortified farmhouse held by a (frequently prosperous) tenant family, who were subject to the jurisdiction of a lord, usually a castellan.

Rentier — A term usually reserved in the Catalan context for a non-noble, urban-dwelling male householder who identified himself by his not having to work or engage in active entrepreneurial activity due to his ability and inclination to live off the income from rents. In the early fourteenth century such *rentiers* sought to base their claims on descent from a castellan family. By the fifteenth century, *rentier*-ism was increasingly identified with the emergent urban 'class' known as '*ciutadans honrats*' (honoured citizens).

Sèquia — An ambitious irrigation system begun by Manresan civic authorities after the droughts of 1333 and complete under private contract towards 1400. One of the most extensive engineering projects of late medieval Catalonia. It includes 26km of canals and many aqueducts, and brought ample irrigation to many parts of the *Pla de Bages*.

Veguer — Catalan rendering of the Latin *Vicarius*, or 'lieutenant.' This was the name given to the high-level royal officials appointed to administer royal justice in Catalonia, whose functions were expanded from the late twelfth century until about the mid-fourteenth century, when the system reached maturity.

Vegueria — A substantial territory administered by a *veguer*; often more than 50×50km in extent. The *vegueria* of the Bages also included for much of the fourteenth century a *sotsvegueria* (sub-*vegueria*) whose capital was Berga, a smaller royal town to the north.

Violari — An annuity secured on civic revenues, paying between 14 per cent and 17 per cent interest, which paid only for the duration of the life of the buyer and a named heir. The principal was not repaid. These were promulgated in large numbers in Catalonia only between 1359 and about 1370, when they were phased out of government finance due to their high interest rates compared with *censals*. Private *violaris* also spread from this time, and continued to exist after the phase-out of their public cousins.

NOTES ON CITATIONS, MONEY, NAMES, AND ACCENTUATION

CITATIONS

With the notable exception of the *Liber Manifesti*, few of the Manresan volumes utilized in this study contain page numbers, that is, they were unfoliated. It has therefore been necessary to cite Manresan sources using the dating of the entry. In almost all cases, the registers followed a strict chronological order, so that references should be almost as easy to locate as if folio numbers were present. After 1352, Catalan scribes used the 'modern' system of noting the date, and these have been converted to the modern system, using the notation yyyy.mm.dd. For earlier references, the scribes used the Roman system, and these have been abbreviated for easy reference. 3i6 means the third day before the ides of June, 3k6 means the third day before the kalends of June, and 3n6 means the third day before the nones of June. Data for certain *Liber Manifesti* householders have been cited according to the folio upon which their entry begins. In cases where data from many householders have been compiled, individual citations have been omitted.

MONEY

The primary Catalan money of our period was the *diner de tern* of Barcelona. This was derived from the old Carolingian system where a pound (*librum*) comprised 20 shillings (*solidi*) with each shilling valued at 12 pence (*denarii*), making a total of 240 pence per pound. The Catalan names were *lliura*, *sou*, and *diner*, abbreviated £ / s / d. In 1346, Pere III ordered the creation of a gold Aragonese Florin, in deliberate imitation of a recent Florentine issue that itself followed earlier Genoese and Venetian issues. After several devaluations these were fixed at a rate of 11 *sous* per florin from 1366.[1] These florins were never much used or quoted in our sources, however. Similarly uncommon was the old judicial money

[1] ACA, Real Patrimonio, *Maestre Racional*, Reg. 347, unfoliated, final (summary) page.

of account, mostly used in our period for the purpose of levying fines, which was also reckoned in gold and known as the *morabatí*. By the 1370s this was valued at 9 *sous*.[2] In Aragon proper the basic coinage after 1197 was not the Catalan sou but the *dinar* of Jaca.[3] Valencia also had its own silver *diner*, from 1247.

CATALAN NAMES

The rulers of the House of Barcelona (to 1410) are given in their Catalan form whenever possible, since Catalan was their primary language. These are followed by regnal dates at the first mention in a chapter. The Counts of Barcelona are referred to as kings, because with very few exceptions this is how they were known in contemporary Catalan documents. Furthermore, the Trastámara kings who came to the Aragonese throne from 1412 are called by their Castilian names, since the family was, and remained, more Castilian than Catalan. Later medieval Manresan sources give personal names in both Catalan and Latin; where possible, these have been Catalanized to reflect vernacular practice. The Catalan official known as the *veguer* presents some difficulties in translation. While Stephen Bensch and Philip Daileader use 'vicar' for *veguer*, I have opted here to keep the Catalan term '*veguer*' for the most part, since the term 'vicar' has other connotations in English. In a similar vein, while '*batlle*' translates quite nicely as bailiff, both terms are used for variety. The terms *consellers* and 'consuls' are used interchangeably to indicate a member of the city's highest body, the Council of Four (or, from 1323–55, the Council of Six). The term 'councillors' as used in the text usually indicates the larger governing group of consuls and *jurats*. The *sèquia* of Manresa is usually spelled using modern Catalan spelling, although early twentieth-century Catalan spelled it '*cequia*', and there were several medieval variations. Zaragoza, which is an Aragonese (as opposed to Catalan) city, is spelled as per modern Aragonese spelling. The names of Spanish historians, whether Catalan or Castilian, are increasingly subject to a movement to use only a single surname (the *primer apellido*); in this book both surnames are generally used in bibliographical entries and when authors are first introduced; sometimes, particularly with repetition, only the *primer apellido* is used.

2 MC 1372.5.21.

3 Thomas N. Bisson, *Conservation of Coinage: Monetary Exploitation and its Restraint in France, Catalonia, and Aragon (c.A.D.1000–c.1225)* (Oxford, 1979), p. 86.

ACCENTUATION

Regarding accentuation: fourteenth-century Manresan sources in Catalan do not regularly utilize accents, but, rather, the medieval system of abbreviation carried over from Latin (in which the 'i' looks like an *accent agut*); transcriptions of medieval texts, including names, will sometimes lack accents where modern Catalan usage would so dictate. Meanwhile, while efforts have been made to utilize correct accentuation, there are increasingly frequent cases in which modern databases (Iberian and otherwise) have dropped accents from the names of Iberian authors, or where transliteration from one Iberian language to another has occurred, or where there has been a change of accepted practice in Castilian or Catalan since the publication date of older works, or indeed, a simple inability to agree on the part of native speakers, all of which result in a plurality of acceptable representations. French is likewise problematic, as when some older spellings of Moyen Age insist upon a circumflex over the A (thus Â), while others (seemingly the majority now) drop it.

THE KINGS OF CATALONIA-ARAGON

Dates	Catalan name and regnal number	Aragonese name and regnal number	Name in English
1162–96	Alfons I	Alfonso II	Alphonse
1196–1213	Pere I	Pedro II	Peter
1213–76	Jaume I	Jaime I	James
1276–85	Pere II	Pedro III	
1285–91	Alfons II	Alfonso III	
1291–1327	Jaume II	Jaume II	
1327–36	Alfons III	Alfonso IV	
1336–87	Pere III	Pedro IV	
1387–96	Joan I	Juan I	John
1396–1410	Martí I	Martín I	Martin
1412–16	(Ferran I)[4]	Fernando I	Ferdinand
1416–58	(Alfons IV)	Alfonso V	
1458–79	(Joan II)	Juan II	
1479–1516	(Ferran II)	Fernando II	

4 The native Catalan House of Barcelona, which could trace its ancestry back to Count Guifré el Pelos (Geoffrey the Hairy) in the late ninth century, perished with King Martí I in 1410. Parentheses indicate that from the time of the first Trastámara king of Aragon (1412), the Aragonese monarchs were largely Castilian (or in the case of Alfonso V, Italian) in language and outlook.

Chapter 1

INTRODUCTION

Catalan urban institutions, the Catalan bourgeoisie, and the late medieval crisis

This is a work of medieval urban history. Its fundamental purpose is to tell the tale of a particular city and its inhabitants over the course of the long fourteenth century. The city is Manresa, in Catalonia. During the period covered by this history, Catalonia was the dominant province of the Crown of Aragon. The core patrimony of this dynastic polity lay in the north and east of the Iberian Peninsula, in an area defined by the geographical contours of the greater Ebro River basin. Manresa was one of approximately a dozen royal towns which regularly sent electors to the Catalan parliament during the era of King Pere III (1336–87).[1] Pere's half-century reign as the sovereign of the Crown of Aragon, and thus of Catalonia and the city of Manresa, forms the temporal backbone of our study. This study is based on a rich treasure trove of archival material, which yields unusually detailed information regarding the society, politics and economy of late medieval Manresa. Our sources shed light on the history of individual Manresan families, as well as on many subgroups of Manresan townspeople, including a number of occupational groups, women of all socio-economic strata and urban officeholders. They also enable a detailed reconstruction of Manresa's political institutions, and an in-depth exploration of the interaction between royal and urban political power as the so-called 'crisis' of the later medieval period unfolded.[2] The

[1] Following Catalan practice, King Peter IV of Aragon ('Pedro' in Aragonese, 'Pere' in Catalan), will be known as Pere III, since he held Catalonia by dint of his title Count of Barcelona, and he was the third count of the ancient House of Barcelona with that name. For a list of towns which sent representatives to the Catalan *Corts* during the fourteenth and fifteenth centuries, see José Ángel Sesma Muñoz, 'La oblación urbana en la Corona de Aragón (siglos XIV–XV)', in *Las sociedades urbanas en la España medieval: XXIX semana de estudios medievales, Estella, 15 a 19 de Julio de 2002* (Pamplona, 2003), pp. 151–93; p. 165. This table indicates that Barcelona, Lleida, Girona, Manresa, Cervera, and Vilafranca del Penedes were regular participants after 1323. Perpignan participated regularly from 1353. Tortosa, Vic, and Montblanc were also fairly regular participants. They were joined by a number of smaller centres such as Besalú, Camporodón, Puigcerdá, and Berga.

[2] In Catalonia, the tradition of 'decline' hearkens back to a seminal article by Pierre Vilar, entitled 'Le déclin catalan du bas Moyen Age: Hypothèses sur sa chronologie', *Estudios de Historia Moderna*, 6 (1956–9), 1–68. This is elaborated upon in Claude Carrère, *Barcelone centre économique 1380–1462*,

economic data which may be teased from a variety of Manresan records lend themselves to an analysis of the far-reaching social and political implications of the fourteenth-century Catalan 'financial revolution', as well as to an analysis of quantitative socio-economic indices such as demographic trends, wages, prices, investment returns, rates of home ownership, food storage and living standards.[3]

The urban community conjured to life in the following pages was particularly vibrant during the long fourteenth century – not least because it was represented by leaders who exercised a considerable measure of political autonomy. The heart of the urban government after 1315 was a consulate consisting of an executive council of four or six *consellers*, and a group of some two dozen *jurats*, or 'sworn men', who served as an extended deliberative body.[4] These men were the political voice of the city, which had about 7000 inhabitants prior to the Black Death of 1348, and about half as many afterwards. Even then, Manresa remained large enough to support a reasonably broad panoply of late medieval occupational types. Its grandest streets and plazas were home to wealthy lawyers, *rentiers*, merchants, and the capitalist chiefs of the cloth and leather industries, who lived side by side with notaries, grocers and apothecaries of middling means. Concentrated in the less fashionable parts of town were the modest homes of laboring craftsmen such as carpenters, weavers, and fullers; these men lived alongside many poorer householders who eked out livings as hunters, agricultural hands, porters, or guards. Manresa was also home to a substantial number of widow-householders of all socio-economic strata. Indeed, women headed nearly one sixth of the city's households in 1408. Less visible to us were substantial numbers of servants and dependants whose presence must for the most part be guessed at, rather than glimpsed directly.

vol. II (Paris, 1967), Part III, pp. 655–954; and Carmen Batlle, *La crisis social y económica de Barcelona a Mediados del siglo XV*, 2 vols. (Barcelona, 1973). Other influential works on this theme include J. N. Hillgarth, *The Problem of a Catalan Mediterranean Empire 1229–1327* (London, 1975), and Ramon d'Abadal i de Vinyals, *Pere el cerimoniós i els inicis de la decadència politica de Catalunya* (Barcelona, 1987). Many of these sentiments are echoed in Thomas Bisson, MCOA; Donald J. Kagay, 'War Financing in the Late-medieval Crown of Aragon', *Journal of Medieval Military History*, 6 (2008), 119–48; Maria Teresa Ferrer i Mallol, *Entre la paz y la guerra: La Corona Catalano-aragonesa y Castilla en la baja edad media*, Anuario de estudios medievales, Anejo, 59 (Barcelona, 2005), esp. ch. 6; and Alan Ryder, *The Wreck of Catalonia: Civil War in the Fifteenth Century* (Oxford, 2007). A crisis of the mercantile elites is proposed in Jaume Aurell i Cardona, *Els mercaders Catalans al quatre-cents: Mutacio de valors i proces d'artistocratitzacio a Barcelona, 1370–1470* (Barcelona, 1996). This topic is treated further in Chapter 4.

3 For a recent overview of the notion of a fourteenth-century Catalan 'financial revolution' see the introduction to Manuel Sánchez Martínez, *La deuda pública en la Cataluña bajomedieval* (Madrid, 2009), pp. 7–20. For more literature, see also Chapter 6, n. 1.

4 The government officials introduced here, including *consellers*, *jurats*, the bailiff, and the *veguer* are discussed and referenced at length in the next chapter.

Despite the evident power of the consuls, all of these inhabitants remained subject to the royal bailiff, who represented the will of the king in the city, and whose jurisdiction was coterminous with the 'parish' of Manresa. The parish included the city itself plus the land within about two kilometers of its walls. But the Manresan community did not stop at the parish bounds; indeed the city was highly integrated with a wider hinterland, known as the Bages. By the fourteenth century the Bages was roughly coterminous with a royal administrative unit known as the *vegueria* of Manresa. This extended about 20 to 30 kilometers from Manresa in all directions, until it met the boundaries of neighbouring *veguerias*, which also corresponded with the urban 'catchment areas' of neighbouring regional capitals and the greater market towns, such as Cervera, Vilafranca and Vic. The *veguer* (Catalan for 'vicar' or 'lieutenant') was a royal official responsible for adjudicating property disputes involving royal subjects, particularly those arising in rural regions which did not have their own bailiff. The court of the *veguer* also acted as a chamber of appeals for the local bailiffs' courts. The *veguer*, as the royal lieutenant in a given region, was also responsible for the levy and command of all royal troops in his jurisdiction. For these reasons, the limits of the *veguer*'s territory came to represent a watershed for local investment and other legal ties beyond which the costs of trade became significantly higher.

Outside the parish of Manresa, and a few other enclaves of royal and clerical power including the monastery of St Benet de Bages, the majority of the land in the Bages belonged by feudal tenure to a few dozen castellans. These were castle-lords whose small stone fortresses sat perched on high ground above the more substantial villages. As '*generoses*', these castellans and their families maintained the legal right to be represented, and taxed, only with the consent of the second estate of the nobility, the *braç militar*, in parliament.[5] Ancient traditions ascribed a further right to the private monopoly of jurisdiction and of violence in their territories, and although the latter right was being actively challenged during the fourteenth century by royal bailiffs, *veguers*, and urban officials, these rights proved highly resilient.

These 'class' differences between nobles and non-nobles in Catalonia led to the exclusion of nobles from political power in the cities. While nobles enjoyed many privileges, they were firmly barred by custom from

[5] While commoners could sometimes hope to enter the ranks of the 'gentry' in late medieval England through lifestyle choices and economic gain, in Catalonia, the group of '*persons generoses*' was much more strictly limited to people related to a knight or squire by birth or marriage. For England see Rosemary Horrox, 'The Urban Gentry in the Fifteenth Century', in John A. F. Thomson (ed.), *Towns and Townspeople in the Fifteenth Century* (Gloucester, 1988), pp. 22–44.

holding urban office in the royal vills, and this custom remained in force until the sixteenth century.[6] In part because of this stricture, the nobles of the Bages generally preferred to live outside the city walls, within their own patrimonies. However, the many services available within Manresa's city limits, its increasingly important status as a seat of royal administration, and the increased wealth of its urban elites, helped to ensure that regional castellan families nonetheless became enmeshed in a web of economic, political, and even familial bonds connecting them to the town and its inhabitants during the fourteenth century. And despite their noble status, the castellans were not clearly dominant in all these transactions. Meanwhile, many urban inhabitants maintained strong ties with the wider urban hinterland – especially so in the earlier decades of the fourteenth century. A significant fraction of Manresan householders were agricultural workers, many of whom held or rented small plots of land within walking distance of the walls. Urban elites, for their part, found it expedient to invest in rural land, or to lend money to rural people, since these activities provided an avenue to both profit and honour. Outside this regional economy and society, the Manresans were also very much a part of the wider world beyond the Bages. They imported animal skins and other raw materials from all over Catalonia; and they produced leather products, particularly shoes, for export to Barcelona, whence they would be shipped throughout the Mediterranean. Long-standing ties to the episcopal seat of Vic provided the impetus for a continual stream of interactions with the inhabitants of that town, which was in many regards a sister city to Manresa. Leading Manresan merchants built trade networks which stretched to Valencia, Mallorca, and beyond, and urban representatives regularly sat in council with the king himself, helping to deliberate on matters of international import during parliamentary sessions.

As part of the royal patrimony of Catalonia, Manresa belonged to that amalgam of feudal principalities known to historians as the Crown of Aragon. Although the union is named after the small, landlocked Kingdom of Aragon whose capital is Zaragoza on the Ebro River, by the later Middle Ages the Principality of Catalonia had emerged as the dominant territory in the union, in terms of demography, culture, politics, and economy. The origins of Catalonia can be traced to the genesis of the County of Barcelona in 801 CE, when Charlemagne's son Louis the Pious added the city and its surrounding territory to the 'Spanish March' of the Carolingian Empire. By the twelfth century, the Counts of Barcelona had succeeded in asserting dominance over a number of neighbouring Carolingian 'counties', forming the nucleus of the territory since known

[6] More precise definitions of 'class' are introduced below, pp. 15–17.

Map 1.1 The Crown of Aragon in 1410

as Catalonia. In 1137, Count Ramon Berenguer IV of Barcelona married the then-infant queen Petronilla of Aragon, thus uniting the two regions under a single house. The House of Barcelona, which had been ruling its eponymous county in an unbroken line since 878, was to rule these two territories until the line went extinct in 1410. Although fourteenth-century monarchs of Catalonia such as Pere III ruled by virtue of their title 'Count of Barcelona', we will follow fourteenth-century Manresan practice by calling the Catalan rulers kings, rather than counts, or count-kings.[7]

By the reign of Pere III, the Crown of Aragon had expanded to include not only Catalonia and Aragon, but also the Kingdoms of Valencia and Mallorca; the latter included the trans-Pyrenean counties of Cerdanya and Roussillon. While the inhabitants of Aragon proper spoke Aragonese, a version of Castilian, the majority of the inhabitants of the Crown of Aragon, including those of Catalonia, Valencia, and Mallorca, spoke Catalan, which is more closely related to Occitan than to Castilian or French. According to some estimates, the landlocked kingdom of Aragon contained about 250,000 inhabitants in the early fourteenth century.[8] The Kingdom of Valencia was home to about 200,000 inhabitants, including many Muslims known as *mudéjares*, who had remained after the Christian conquest of their capital in 1238.[9] The Principality of Catalonia, with its capital at Barcelona, was home to about 500,000 inhabitants, and was thus more populous than Aragon and Valencia combined.[10] In Catalonia, whose eastern half had long been far from the frontier, there were very few resident Muslims by the fourteenth century.[11] Beyond the

7 Manresan documents almost invariably refer to fourteenth-century rulers of Catalonia and Aragon as 'El Senyor Rey'. Modern Catalan has changed the spelling of 'Rey' to 'Rei'.

8 The spelling is Aragonese; but Catalan forms will be used for Catalan cities.

9 For a brief overview see David Nirenberg, 'Muslims in Christian Iberia, 1000–1526: Varieties of Mudejar', in Peter Linehan and Janet L. Nelson (eds.), *The Medieval World* (London, 2001), pp. 60–76. For a synopsis of the historiography on this group from a Valencian perspective, see Isabel A. O'Connor, *A Forgotten Community: The Mudejar Aljama of Xàtiva, 1240–1327* (Leiden, 2003), pp. 6–27.

10 These are from MCOA, pp. 163–4.

11 One major cause of social friction, however, was the *mals usos*, or 'bad customs', which gave the feudal lords of Old Catalonia a number of resented rights, such as the baldly named *ius maletractandi* or the 'right of maltreatment'. The tenants subject to these rights were known as *remenças*. In 1388, due to heightened economic pressures on seigneurial incomes after the Black Death, social tensions between lords and *remenças* broke out into a conflict which in various forms would last for the better part of a century. Urban disturbances in that year might well have been related, but little has been done to confirm or deny such a link. Although the boundary between Old and New Catalonia was generally understood to be the Llobregat River, the peasants of the Bages region (even those slightly east of the Llobregat) were not subject to the *mals usos*, and thus the region was spared the worst excesses of the *remença* conflict. See Paul Freedman, *The Origins of Peasant Servitude in Medieval Catalonia* (Cambridge and New York, 1991).

peninsular realms, Mallorca had been forcibly reunited to the Crown of Aragon by Pere III in 1344 after some fifty years of independence under a junior branch of the House of Barcelona. Sardinia was taken into the federation beginning in 1323, although it remained troublesome until 1409. Sicily had been ruled by another cadet branch since 1282, and the island kingdom remained formally independent until it reverted to the senior branch in 1409. But in 1410, King Martí I 'the Humane' of Aragon died unexpectedly, with his last surviving heir the King of Sicily having predeceased him in the previous year. After a lengthy judicial arbitration, resulting in the so-called Compromise of Caspé, the Castilian-born Fernando de Antequera was installed as King Fernando I of Aragon in 1412. This marked the inauguration of the new Aragonese House of Trastámara. Fernando's son and successor, Alfonso V of Aragon (1416–58), was never easy with the idea of a Catalan lifestyle; he saw the Catalans as too protected by constitutional rights, and regarded them as somewhat ungovernable. In 1442, after a long struggle, he added the Kingdom of Naples to his dynastic realms. Alfonso became smitten with his new territory and moved his court to Naples, where he would become famous as a patron of a (distinctly absolutist) form of humanism.[12]

The Barcelona elite, for their part, had long enjoyed certain privileges stemming from their city's position as the de facto capital of the Crown of Aragon, and as the 'golden goose' of the Aragonese monarchy. These privileges served as a model which was spread to other Catalan royal cities. Due in large measure to the commercial successes of the Barcelona merchants, and helped by the fact that the successful Barcelona institutions were spread to other regional urban centres, the Catalans had for centuries been the most prosperous people of the Crown of Aragon in per capita terms. Even in the mid-fifteenth century, after a period of palpable decline in Catalan mercantile fortunes, Alfonso V could expect to receive three times more revenue from Catalonia than from Valencia, and five times more from Catalonia than from Aragon.[13] But Alfonso's absentee reign aggravated fault lines in the social fabric at Barcelona, and tensions boiled over during the reign of his successor, the strongly Castileophile King Juan II (1458–78). A civil war, in which the principal adversaries were the king and the city of Barcelona, raged for the decade between 1462 and 1472. After several vicissitudes, the war ended in a royal victory. Perhaps the greatest casualty of the war was the prosperity of the Catalan cities, many of whom allied with

[12] For Alfonso's career see Alan Ryder, *Alfonso the Magnanimous: King of Aragon, Naples, and Sicily, 1396–1458* (Oxford, 1990).

[13] The figures are taken from a royal subsidy. See MCOA, p. 163.

Barcelona.[14] Although Manresa was destined to share this fate, and undoubtedly fared much worse than the capital itself, one goal of the present study is to ameliorate what has traditionally been a negative, even fatalistic reading of the late medieval history of the Catalan cities.

THE SOURCES

Manresa was chosen as the basis of this study because it provides a number of definite methodological advantages. Because it was medium-sized, it was both large enough to be a full participant in the 'urban' culture of the Catalan royal cities, and yet small enough so that its society can be analysed with a reasonable sense of 'completeness' – although one would like to know more about the city's poor, and our records say relatively little about the lives of those in clerical orders. Because Manresa was a fairly typical royal town, evincing economic practices, laws, and social mores similar to those found at cities such as Cervera, Vilafranca, Girona, Vic, Tarragona, and Lleida, one can be reasonably sure that, broadly speaking, the experience of Manresa was similar to that experienced by these other royal vills. And if the fourteenth-century history of Barcelona is still in want of a definitive history, the existence of a study of contemporary Manresa will make the experience of the capital and its burgher-citizenry that much more intelligible and meaningful.

But the most important methodological reason for studying Manresa as opposed to some better-known royal vill is undoubtedly the richness of its sources. One of the crown jewels of the rich legacy stored in the archives of Catalonia is the *Liber Manifesti* of 1408–11, a cadastral survey of 640 Manresan households, which is a particularly complete and detailed exemplar of a fiscal document that was relatively common in the cities of later medieval Catalonia and parts of Italy.[15] The only survey which has been studied in a manner comparable to that presented in the following pages is the Florentine Catasto of 1427, as studied by David Herlihy and Christiane Klapisch-Zuber in their famous monograph *Tuscans and their*

[14] See Alan Ryder, *The Wreck of Catalonia: Civil War in the Fifteenth Century* (Oxford, 2007).

[15] For an overview of the *estim* in Catalonia, see Max Turull Rubinat and Jordi Morelló Baget, 'Estructura y tipología de les "*Estimes-Manifests*" en Cataluña (siglos XIV–XV)', *Anuario de Estudios Medievales*, 35:1 (2005), 271–326. For the phenomenon in Italy, see David Herlihy and Christiane Klapisch-Zuber, *Tuscans and their Families: A Study of the Florentine Catasto of 1427* (New Haven, CT, 1985), pp. 6–25. See also Donald E. Queller, 'The Venetian Family and the "Estimo" of 1379', in Bernard S. Bachrach and David Nicholas (eds.), *Law, Custom, and the Social Fabric in Medieval Europe: Essays in Honor of Bryce Lyon* (Kalamazoo, NJ, 1990), pp. 185–210.

Families.[16] The Manresan survey is perhaps, after the Catasto, the most detailed source for the patrimonies of individual urban households to survive from later medieval Western Europe. It was compiled on the order of the Manresan town councillors for the purpose of assessing the total worth of all citizens, between 4 November 1408 and 13 February 1411.[17] Because it was the first complete *estim* document to survive at Manresa, it had to be compiled from scratch, like the 1427 Catasto, rather than through the utilization of existing documentation. While tallying gross worth, citizens' tax liabilities were figured on a formula which counted half of the value of their home, real estate and moveable goods. Money and investments, including interpersonal loans and money placed in *censals* and *violaris*, were however assessed at full value, as were slaves (see Figure 1.1). Unfortunately, the age of householders, and the number and age of their dependants, is not recorded, meaning that studies of marriage cohorts, household size, and sex ratios are not possible. But the names, occupations, and a detailed breakdown of assets and asset values enables us to detail the economic strategies of Manresan householders, 15 per cent of whom were women, to a degree unprecedented outside Tuscany.

Of singular importance is the fact that the *Liber Manifesti* contains entries relating to nearly all of Manresa's householders, including the very poorest.[18] There is no cutoff point for householder wealth, and the entries at the low end of the economic spectrum include an ex-slave named Marta, whose worldly wealth amounted to about £15, and a number of destitute widows, including Guillmonetta, widow of Romeu Redon, whose total worth was £8.[19] Many wealthy householders, by contrast, were worth between £1,000 and £4,000. That the list of householders is nearly complete may be deduced from the fact that the city's householders in the *fogatge* of 1365 numbered 691, while the 1408 survey counts 640 households. This represents only an 8 per cent reduction after years of plague, when much of Europe was losing at a much more rapid rate.[20] The social inclusiveness of the survey is also asserted by the Manresan archivist and historian Marc Torras Serra, whose brief but illuminating study of the *Liber Manifesti* independently serves to

16 Originally, David Herlihy and Christiane Klapisch-Zuber, *Les toscans et leurs familles: Une étude du "catasto" florentin de 1427* (Paris, 1978); later published in English as Herlihy and Klapisch-Zuber, *Tuscans and their Families*.

17 These dates are inscribed in LM.

18 Of 640 entries, 39 were entries for the estates of the recently deceased, which were being kept for minor wards by executors.

19 For Marta LM 43r, for Guillmonetta, LM 144r.

20 See Table 7.1.

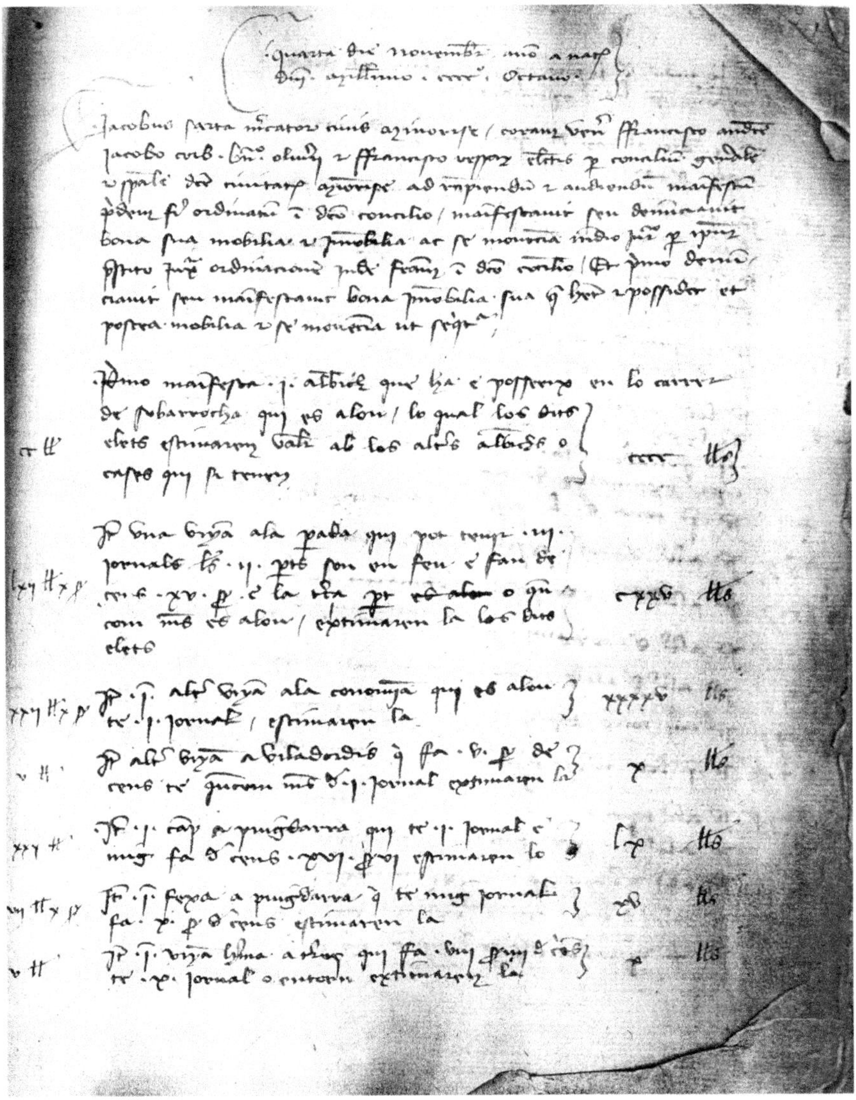

Figure 1.1 1408 *Liber Manifesti*. Entry of Jaume Sarta

corroborate many of the findings presented here.[21] The survey did, however, exclude clerics and knights. We know from several sources that the

[21] Marc Torras Serra, *La crisi del segle XV a Manresa: Una aproximació a partir dels Llibres de Manifests* (Angle, 1996). See p. 74 for his calculations on the total worth of Manresan patrimony. While Torras calculated a total gross wealth from the 1408 *Liber Manifesti* of £175,270, the

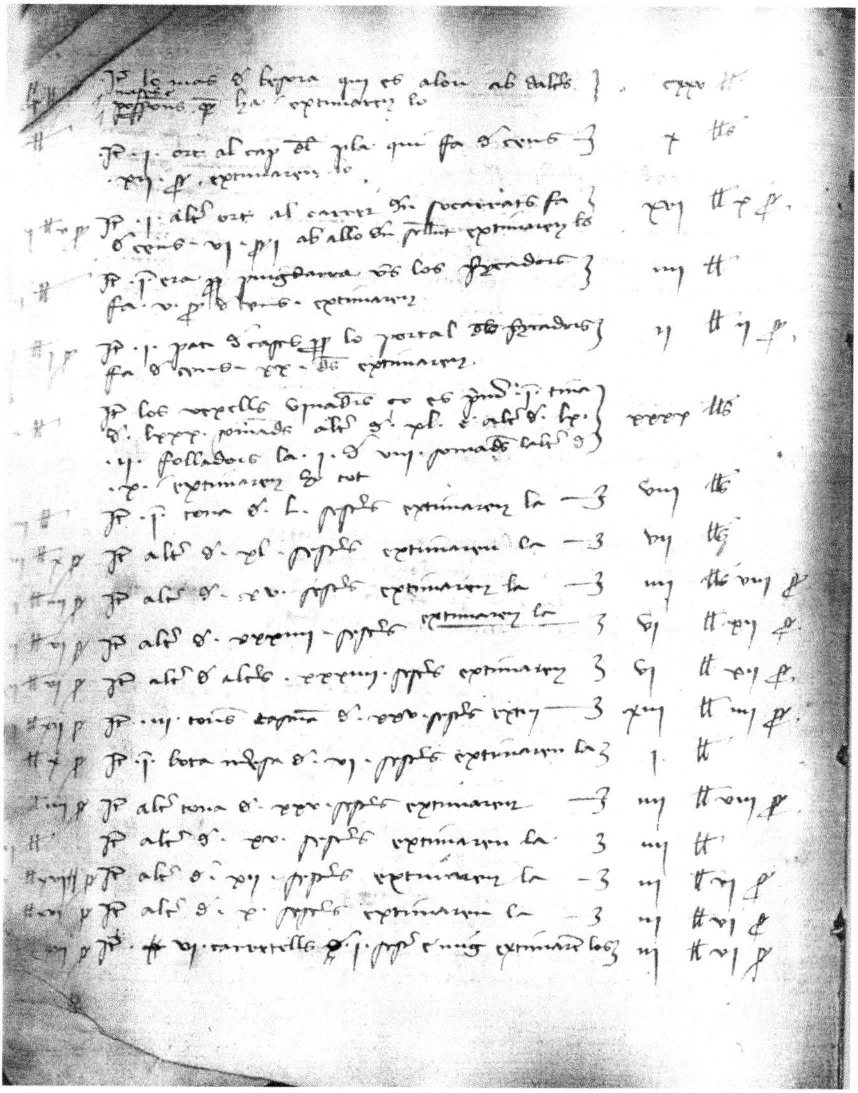

Figure 1.1 (*cont.*)

latter, at least, were almost non-resident in the city, and the former probably amounted to fewer than two or three dozen canons, apart from

calculations used in this study came to a total gross wealth of £171,037. The difference of 2.4 per cent, arrived at by the tallying of thousands of handwritten entries, should be taken as proof of the robustness of both sets of calculations.

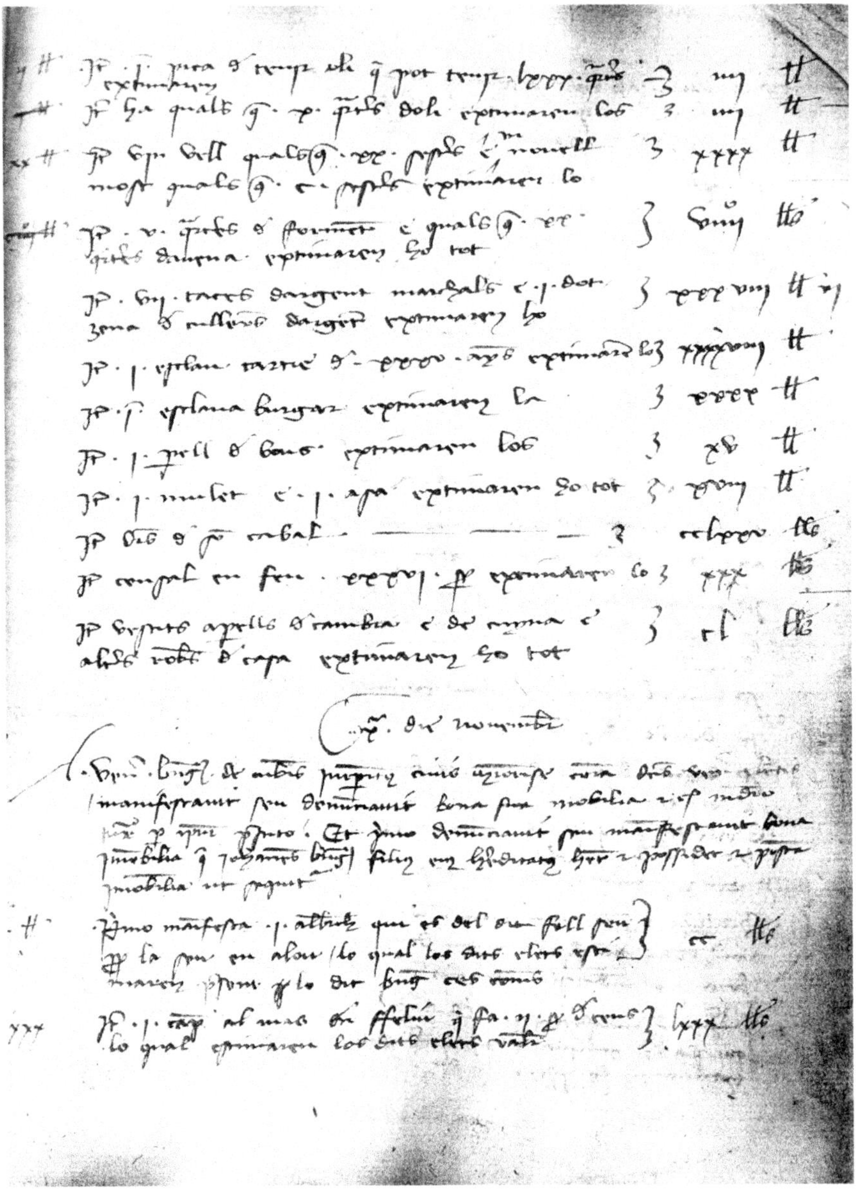

Figure 1.1 (*cont.*)

a larger number of cloistered monks.[22] One of the more persuasive arguments for the inclusiveness of the Manresan document, however, is the broadly similar distribution of wealth and debt which is arrived at by tallying the Manresan figures and those of similarly-sized Tuscan cities, as described in Chapter 8. Thus, any argument that the Manresan figures were not complete, would necessarily imply a similar criticism of the Florentine Catasto – something which has not been seriously entertained during the past three decades since Herlihy's studies on the Catasto were introduced. Another important indicator of the completeness of the *Liber Manifesti* is the fact that – unlike with the Florentine Catasto – many of the Manresan householders' occupations can be known, and the resultant sample is in accord with what other studies have led us to expect regarding a late medieval town of Manresa's size and function.[23] As the evidence mounts from such distinct lines of enquiry, therefore, it becomes increasingly difficult to impugn the sample provided for us by the *Liber Manifesti.*

As can be seen from the entry in Figure 1.1, the types of goods listed in a *Liber Manifesti* entry included the value, location, and rent paid on homes, other edifices owned, descriptions, values and rent paid on real estate, the value of a wide variety of household goods, feudal properties and rights held, money loaned or invested, to whom or in what it was invested, and often the amount of interest received, and also debts owed, to whom, and sometimes the rate of interest. The *Liber Manifesti* entries are written in a combination of Latin (for the introductions) and Catalan (for the inventories proper). The entry in Figure 1.1 is that of Jaume Sarta. It shows that the redactors actually entered the house of each citizen, and catalogued their belongings, after the manner of a contemporary bailiff's inventory *post mortem.*[24] In the early entries, including that of Jaume Sarta shown here, the redactors went so far as to label the contents of each storage vessel in the householder's cellar.

22 There were probably fewer than ten knightly households owning property in Manresa in 1370, split up amongst three or four families. See Chapter 5. In 1497, after a massive population decline, Manresa contained 272 common households, 8 households maintained by '*persons generoses*', 15 canons' households, and 10 other ecclesiastical households. Thus, of a total population of 305 households, the castellanate made up less than 3 per cent, and ecclesiastics just over 8 per cent of the population. It is likely that these figures would have been lower prior to 1420, since the number of commoners would been higher relative to the other groups. For the survey, see Josep Iglésies, *El fogatge de 1497: Estudi i transcripció*, vol. I (Barcelona, 1991), p. 18.

23 On the poor showing of the Catasto regarding urban occupations, see Herlihy and Klapisch-Zuber, *Tuscans and Their Families*, pp. 122–5. For a synopsis of expected occupational structures in later medieval cities, see David Nicholas, *The Later Medieval City: 1300–1500* (London, 1997), pp. 203–7.

24 Such inventories can be found in e.g. AHPM Tr. 475 (*Inventariorum, sentenciarum, compromissorum I*), and 1353–1358 AHPM Tr. 476 (*Inventariorum, sentenciarum, compromissorum II*) 1358–1365.

As the process became more streamlined, however, the contents of the cellar and similar entries were lumped together in a single value estimate. And of course, the entries for poorer people could be quite brief: that of Marta the freedwoman consisted of one small house on the Carrer d'en Talamanca, and a small quantity of clothing and household furnishings lumped together in a single estimate.[25] The nature of the *Liber Manifesti*, derived as it was from contemporary Italian fiscal practice, makes its data highly comparable with the data presented by David Herlihy and Christiane Klapisch-Zuber in *Tuscans and their Families*, and by Herlihy in *Medieval and Renaissance Pistoia*.[26] Consequently, much of the material in Chapter 8 relates to a comparison of these two sources. Many readers will be surprised to find that living standards in Manresa compared quite favourably with those in the contemporary cities of the Florentine *contado*, and much of the material in this book provides insight into why this might have been so.

But the *Liber Manifesti* by itself can only present a static picture – albeit a particularly rich one – of the state of the town and its inhabitants at the beginning of the fifteenth century.[27] In order to understand how the society which emerges from the folio of the *Liber Manifesti* came to be, a number of other record series were utilized. It is fortunate that the Manresan archives have come down to us highly intact, and have benefited from the attentions of a number of gifted archivist–historians.[28] The Manresan city archive was until recently known as the Arxiu Històric de la Ciutat de Manresa (AHCM), but is now known as the Arxiu Comarcal de Bages (ACB). The abbreviation AHCM is still used for our primary source referencing, since the volumes we refer to were catalogued under the old name. In any event, the archive formerly known as the AHCM contains a nearly complete set of town council records for fourteenth-century Manresa, and it has been possible to read these alongside the *Liber Manifesti* in order to gain many insights on the composition and strategies of the Manresan political elite, particularly in the years around 1400. The existence of a large book of royal letters addressed to the city, now published as the *Llibre Verd* de Manresa, sheds further light on the interaction between town and royal government throughout our period. Particularly in the fourteenth century, nearly every royal letter addressed to the town was dutifully copied into the *Llibre Verd*.[29] Substantial (though

25 LM 43r.

26 For the fiscal practise which led to the creation of the Catasto, see Herlihy and Klapisch-Zuber, *Tuscans and their Families*, pp. 1–19.

27 For a list of the individual sources consulted, see Bibliography.

28 These include Joaquim Sarret i Arbós (1853–1935) and Marc Torras i Serra (1962–).

29 LV, 9.

incomplete) series of administrative volumes from the *veguer*, the royal bailiff of Manresa, and of the urban *clavaria* or fiscal administration help to round out our picture of the political and economic life of the city. The city also contains a series of guild records, which are however of limited use, and which in any event were employed for this project only sparingly due to the need to limit time and space. In addition, the Manresan civic archive is home to an enviable collection of notarial books, many of which were kept for individual families who did business at Manresa. Thus, the notarial paper trail of many of the city's prominent families, including sales, purchases, dowry agreements, estate valuations, inventories *post mortem*, and similar details has been preserved in a format which makes the pursuit of family history eminently practicable.

THEORIES OF CLASS IN THE LATE MEDIEVAL URBAN CONTEXT: A NEW TYPOLOGY

This book's title, *The Rise and Decline of an Iberian Bourgeoisie*, is clearly predicated upon the notion that something like what used to be understood as 'class divisions' are germane to its argument. This idea remains controversial, although recent historiography suggests that it is becoming less so.[30] Therefore, it is imperative that our definitions of 'bourgeoisie', and more generally of 'class' be taken up – and their usefulness asserted – in order to make these long out of fashion terms palatable to the modern reader.

In a recent article, the author has put forward a new typology of class in the cities of pre-modern Europe, and since this typology will be utilized in the following chapters, it ought briefly to be spelled out here.[31] The principal idea is that the term 'class' remains useful to the point of irreplaceability for making certain horizontal political and economic divisions in pre-modern urban society, but that, understandably, historians have been wary of utilizing the term class for fear of the many theoretical baggages with which it has been saddled. For a long time, this fear of theoretical plethora was enough to drive the term 'class' almost entirely out of usage, but it is increasingly apparent that this was done to the detriment of analytical clarity. A workable solution can be arrived at by noticing that, in practice, historians tend to use the term 'class' or something akin to it only in a handful of meaningful ways; thus, an

[30] The relevant historiography, and the typology set out in this section, have been presented in J. Fynn-Paul, 'Let's Talk about Class: Towards an Institutionalist Typology of Class Relations in the Cities of Pre-modern Europe c.1200–c.1800', *Urban History* 41:4 (2014), 582–605.

[31] See previous note.

inductive model of class can be arrived at, based on historians' actual usage, which suggests the following typology. Notice also that 'class' will always denote a distinction between two horizontal groups:

Material usages

A. Classical (i.e., Marxist, or pseudo-Marxist, interpretations, which suggest that access to means of production such as land or capital leads to 'classes' of exploiters and exploited, and which focuses also on occupation as a form of class division).
B. Economic (i.e., simple economic divisions such as lower, middle and upper, which depend entirely on the size of a household's or an individual's fortune).

Institutional usages

C. A distinction between nobles and non-nobles.
D. A distinction between groups of non-nobles, particularly, in our context, created by access to urban office. Sometimes based on legally and politically defined occupational status.
E. A distinction between slave and free.

This typology suggests that in all societies, there will be class divisions based on material wealth, caused by differing access to means of production, and legal control of property. Probably more interesting is the fact that there are also what our model calls 'class-determining institutions' within each society, which may differ from one political or cultural region to the next. Thus, the three institutional distinctions mentioned above, C, D and E, suggest the principal class-determining institutions which were operational in later medieval Catalonia. Since this study does not deal at length with slavery, our Type E is suggested mostly for completeness.[32] Type C encompasses the fact that the nobility in Catalonia were possessed of certain privileges that most commoners did not, as outlined above. (The status of 'clergy' was arguably not as class-determining as that of

32 The author has dealt with this topic in some detail elsewhere. See J. Fynn-Paul, 'Tartars in Spain: Renaissance Slavery in the Catalan City of Manresa, c. 1408.' *Journal of Medieval History*, 34:4 (Dec. 2008), 347–59; 'Empire, Monotheism, and Slavery in the Greater Mediterranean Region from Antiquity through the Early Modern Era,' *Past and Present*, 205:1 (Dec. 2009), 3–40; and 'Reasons for the Limited Scope and Duration of "Renaissance Slavery" in Southern Europe (ca. 1348–ca. 1750): A New Structuralist Analysis', in Simonetta Cavaciocchi, ed., *Schiavitù e servaggio nell'economia europea, secc. XI–XVII: Serfdom and Slavery in the European Economy, 11th–18th Centuries. Atti delle 'Quarantunesima Settimana di Studi', 14–18 aprile 2013* (Florence, 2014), 337–50.

nobility, since access to high ecclesiastical office with high incomes was, in Manresan practice, often reserved for scions of noble families.)

Since Catalan civic government in our period was only open to non-nobles, this meant that the Type C nobility also suffered a certain debility insofar as they could not hold civic office (which in any event they generally held to be beneath them). This means that, in Catalonia, any palpable class distinction granted by the holding urban office would be qualified as a Type D class division. Briefly put, our focus in this book is on those non-noble urban dwellers who lived within this Type D realm. This group also conveniently serves as our working definition of 'bourgeoisie', whose parameters will be revealed in much greater detail in the following chapters.

HISTORIOGRAPHICAL CONTEXTS: OVERVIEW

The length of this volume precludes a lengthy discussion here of the key historiographical trends in Iberian and European later medieval urban history with which this work engages. The main contours of these trends will probably be known to most readers of this work, and in any event they tend to be addressed at some length in the chapters to which they are relevant. For both of these reasons, it is only necessary here to point out the fact that, as the history of a later medieval Iberian town, this study stands at the intersection of three main historiographical traditions which have long been distinct, but which have recently shown increasing signs of cross-pollination. The first strand is the later medieval urban historiography of the cities of the Crown of Aragon which has been written in Catalan, Castilian, and French. In this tradition, urban history was long written in a 'Structuralist' fashion, which tended to single out individual groups or institutions, and then describe them statically, with less regard to chronological developments and interactions – though as will be noted in subsequent chapters, this trend has thankfully been put to rest in recent years.

The second tradition is the English-language historiography of the Crown of Aragon. Since there is very little in English on the later medieval cities of the Crown of Aragon per se, the present work will have to settle itself into a host of historiographical traditions in which the city features in a more or less tangential fashion. This Anglograph literature is a distinct mix of Iberian subject matter, blended with some of the issues which have been the particular province of Anglophone scholarship. By far the greatest focus has been on social, rather than economic or political history; this has created a deficit that the current work hopes to redress somewhat.

Thirdly, this book should ideally integrate the extant history of Catalan-Aragonese cities in English and continental languages with wider Anglograph traditions of late medieval urban history. This is especially important, since there is so little English historiography for the cities of the later medieval Crown of Aragon with which this study can naturally dialogue. The issue is more pressing for the later medieval period than for the high medieval centuries studied by the likes of S. Bensch and P. Daileader, since, in part due to a greater abundance of sources, the Anglograph literature on late medieval urban history is vast, and encompasses a much larger population of historiographical sub-threads. Since the Anglograph literature is particularly strong with regard to the cities of England, Italy, and the Low Countries, particular recourse has been made to these literatures. One aim of this is to enable urban historians of all European regions to gain a better sense of where Catalonia fits in the larger puzzle of late medieval urban history. Furthermore, this approach enables us to help break down the decades-long segregation of 'northern' and 'southern' medieval urban historiography, and to construct a more universal picture of what precisely were the similarities and differences possible within the Western European 'polyarchal zone'.[33]

PRINCIPAL ARGUMENTS

We are now in a position to briefly summarize the principal arguments and themes to be introduced in the following pages. From a global and theoretical perspective, this work posits that the polyarchal urban consulate was critical in providing increased opportunity to Manresan inhabitants, but that the relative lack of Type C or Type D class distinctions in fourteenth-century Manresa also provided a number of additional benefits. Royal policy favouring urban elites vs. Type-C nobles also played a key role. Together, this institutional configuration helped to create a distinct urban culture in the Catalan royal cities, which, had it been allowed to continue into the early modern period, would likely have resulted in Catalonia becoming one of the most 'modern' societies in

[33] The term 'polyarchy' has been coined by the author to encompass the distinctive type of urban regime which, having antecedents in the Roman *municipium*, began to spread across Latin Europe from the later eleventh century, and which in many places has remained normative until the present day. The term is useful because during the later medieval centuries these urban regimes ranged from narrow oligarchies to broad democracies, and yet, as a group, they have certain characteristics which distinguish them from any 'monarchical' regime (local or otherwise) headed by a single lord or ruler. For this see J. Fynn-Paul, 'Political Institutions and the Great Divergence Debate: The Role of 'Democratic' Institutions in Birthing Capitalism, Science, Human Rights, and Modern "Global" Culture', in Cátia Antunes and Karwan Fatah-Black, eds., *The Routledge Handbook for History and Globalization* (London, 2015).

southern Europe. Its urban society might easily have developed, economically and intellectually, on a par with that of the Low Countries. At the international and interregional levels, this study will highlight differences between a relatively smooth-running, egalitarian Catalan urban system, and the cities of the neighbouring regions of Valencia, Aragon, Castile, and southern France. The Catalan cities arguably produced more in the way of intellectual and economic capital than these neighbouring systems.

Zooming further in to the regional level, this study argues that the medium-sized royal town became a crucial island of 'bourgeois' culture in a Catalan society which, when later deprived of these regional capitals, fell back into a refeudalized stagnancy. At the local level, this system provided a good deal of political, economic, and social opportunity to a large number of the city's inhabitants, which was not available to those who did not live in similarly sized and similarly privileged royal cities. The Manresans faced the fourteenth-century 'crisis' brought on by the Black Death, war, and fiscal change with a good deal of energy and resourcefulness. The demise of this vibrant urban society and the ways of life it enabled was anything but inevitable, even in the face of economic decline and eventual civil war. Rather than blaming these 'usual suspects', this study will argue that, while economic stagnation and demography played a part, some of the most important factors in the demise of this Manresan urban system were related to the nature, rights, and boundaries of urban social classes. While Manresa's medium size influenced, for example, the relative ease with which wealthy men could enter the urban patriciate, the precise methods by which the city 'civilized' the countryside, and, ultimately, the city's vulnerability to seigneurial encroachments in the absence of royal support, the fact that Manresa and Barcelona shared so many institutional characteristics meant that size created a difference between metropolis and satellite which was more a question of degree, than kind. All of these issues are explored through an accumulation of specific arguments over the course of this book.

The present work also moves beyond the older 'decline' narratives, found in sources as disparate as Vives, Vilar, and Bisson, by attempting to portray the fourteenth-century situation as something more than a prelude to fifteenth-century decline and eventual implosion.[34] It moves beyond d'Abadal, Ferrer, and Hillgarth's interpretations of Pere III as a

[34] These are found in Jaume Vicens Vives, *Els trastàmares: El segle XV* (Barcelona, 1961); Pierre Vilar, 'Le déclin catalan du bas Moyen Age: Hypothèses sur sa chronologie', *Estudios de Historia Moderna*, 6 (1956–9), 1–68; MCOA.

'weak king' by incorporating the newer researches of Sánchez Martínez, which show that Pere's government presided over a vastly improved and highly successful fiscal machinery, which was on the cutting edge of European fiscal innovation.[35] It also moves beyond the earlier decline narratives by establishing that certain groups of average Manresans, both men and women, were better off than contemporary urban-dwelling Italians in terms of food storage, housing and debt levels.[36] In sum, this work seeks to stimulate further exploration of the importance of political institutions in creating the conditions for economic growth. It does this by attempting, as thoroughly as possible for a study of its size, to discuss the intersection between political institutions both with macroeconomic factors and with more specifically economic institutions such as the public debt system.

POSTSCRIPT: A BOURGEOISIE WITHOUT BURGHERS?

One point which might be found missing from the following discussion of the rise and fall of an Iberian bourgeoisie, is a detailed description of the individual, family, household, and occupational lives of the townsmen themselves, or of the lives of the feudal lords who lived in the Manresan hinterland. In fact the author has been involved with a detailed analysis of these very subjects, to the extent that they have now filled enough pages to calve another full-sized monograph. It is expected that these studies will be published soon.

A summary of what has been discovered during these social researches is not however out of order here. The presence in Manresa of what might be called 'family' notarial volumes, that is, which pertain to a particular family, has made it possible to trace the fortunes of a single burgher family, the Sartas, in great detail, between roughly 1310 and 1420.[37] Likewise, the fortunes of a knightly family, the Talamancas, have also proved traceable. The difference in lifestyles between these two families is marked: one pursued a strategy of castle-ownership and estate management, bolstered by broad judicial and fiscal immunities, and banal power; while the other pursued a much more 'bourgeois' economic

35 d'Abadal, *Pere el cerimoniós;* Hillgarth, *Problem;* María Teresa Ferrer Mallol, 'El patrimoni reial i la recuperació dels senyorius jurisdiccionals en les estats Catalano-Aragonesos a la fi del segle XIV', *Anuario de Estudios Medievales*, 7 (1970–1), 351–491.

36 This has not been treated in the Iberian literature, but must be drawn particularly from other, older continental sources such as David Herlihy, *Medieval and Renaissance Pistoia: The Social History of an Italian Town, 1200–1430* (New Haven, CT, 1967), and Herlihy and Klapisch-Zuber, *Tuscans and their Families,* and from Nicholas, *The Metamorphosis of a Medieval City: Ghent in the Age of the Arteveldes, 1302–1390* (Leiden, 1987).

37 For the Sarta and Talamanca papers, see Bibliography.

strategy of entrepreneurialism and civic office-holding. The differences between Talamanca and Sarta lifestyles, and opportunities, therefore goes far towards strengthening our case for the existence of a distinct 'bourgeoisie', which was indeed often at odds with, and which defined itself against, the lower feudal classes who held most of the land and controlled most of the households in the Bages. Interestingly, the feudal and bourgeois classes intermarried more in the early fourteenth century, before the crisis decades, than afterwards, when they succumbed for various reasons to a Europe-wide stiffening of social boundaries. Other findings in this vein include a discovery that what might be called Type A (material) class divisions were quite weak at Manresa prior to the 1390s. Thus, groups of families did not strongly identify with a particular occupation, for example, with rentierism, or with merchanting, or with craftsmanship. This helped to keep Type D class divisions, based on access to urban office, weak as well. The occupational topography of Manresa, whose economy was based on leatherworking (approaching 20 per cent of households) and cloth-making (about 10 per cent), in that order, is likewise explored. The role of women in the Manresan economy, which does seem to have become stronger after the Black Death, as per the arguments of Jeremy Goldberg for England, is likewise addressed in forthcoming work, as there was no space for inclusion of this material here. In all, however, the arguments made above, while they are nuanced and strengthened by the social material, stand very well on their own. Thus, the pages which follow will begin at the beginning, with a discussion of the evolution of later medieval Manresa's most important political institutions, and how these 'created' the Manresan bourgeoisie.

PART I

Politics

Chapter 2

THE CREATION OF A REGIONAL CAPITAL

Town government and royal policy

THE TOPOGRAPHY OF MANRESA TO 1400

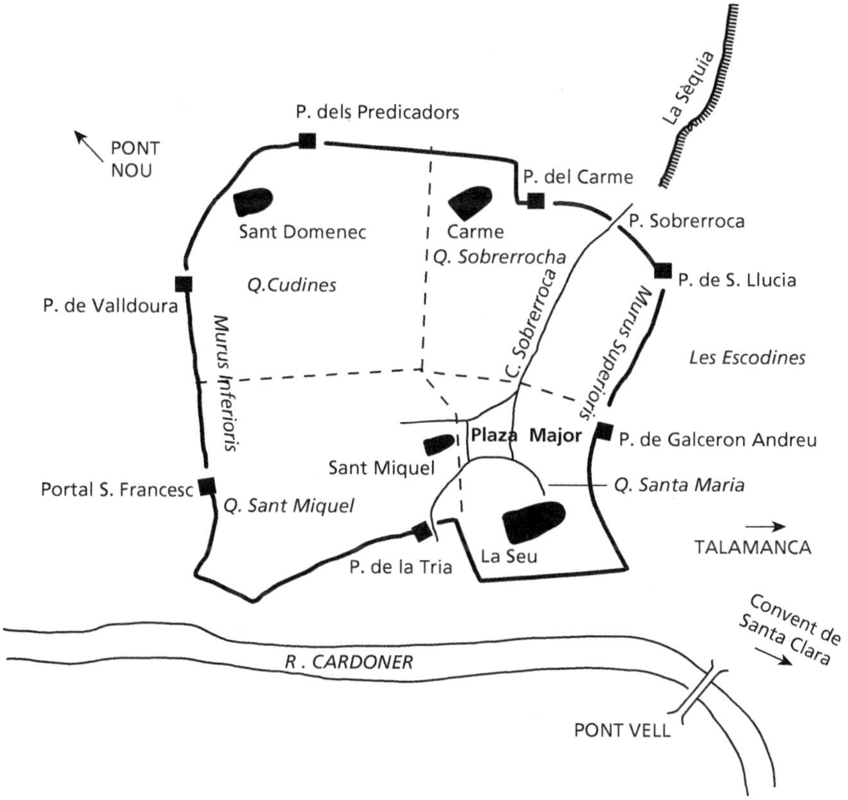

Map 2.1 Manresa *c.* 1400

Before the political institutions that shaped late medieval Manresa can be properly introduced, the situation and physical shape of the city must be sketched. Despite local traditions to the contrary, which may date from the later Middle Ages, there is no evidence to suggest that Manresa shares the Roman pedigree of its episcopal neighbour Vic, which had been known in ancient times as *Ausa*. Instead, the city of Manresa probably began its existence during the Dark Ages as a fortified hilltop settlement. Its location above the confluence of the Llobregat and the Cardoner rivers, which flow southward from the high Pyrenees, made it a natural meeting place for people living in or travelling through the region.[1] By the tenth century at least, the site contained a monastery on the present site of Santa Maria, near the Col Cardoner.[2] A tiny area immediately around the monastery was by this time enclosed by a wall.[3] To the north, the Puigmercadal remained unenclosed by these first city walls, but it is believed already to have held a small castle or tower, in addition to serving as the town's fairgrounds.[4] Much has been made of a reference to the city of Manresa lying in ruins as late as 1056: it is possible that the city had been destroyed during the famous raid of Al-Mansur on Catalonia in 985, and had not yet been fully repaired.[5] In any event this evocative reference serves as a reminder of the continuing proximity of the perilous frontier with Islam. In 1118, Alfonso the Battler captured Zaragoza and opened the plain of the Ebro to the Christians; Aragon and Catalonia were united by dynastic marriage in 1137, and in 1149 Lleida, in western Catalonia fell.[6] From this point onwards, Manresa ceased to be a frontier town in any way, and it was not seriously menaced by Islamic

1 The classic local study of Manresan history, which is based on an extensive knowledge of the city's medieval archives, is Joaquim Sarret i Arbós, *Historia de Manresa*, Monumenta Historica Civitatis Minorise, 5 vols. (Manresa, 1910–24). For a somewhat whimsical account of the city's early history, see Sarret i Arbós, *Historia de Manresa,* vol. I, pp. 16–21. See also Albert Benet i Clarà, *Història de Manresa: Dels origins al segle XI* (Manresa, 1985).

2 See Josep M. Gasol i Almendros, 'Les esglésies medievals de Manresa', in *Manresa medieval* (Manresa, 2001), pp. 135–58, and Anna Orriols i Alsina, 'El romànic a Manresa: La seu,' in *ibid.*, pp. 31–60.

3 Raquel Valdenebro i Manrique, 'L'Evolutió Urbana de Manresa i les seves muralles', in *Manresa medieval* (Manresa, 2001), pp. 170–1.

4 By 1045, the Castle of Manresa belonged to the lord of Balçereny. This family would retain interests in the castle and court of the city until the 1270s. Pere Català i Roca (ed.), *Els castells Catalans*, vol. V (Barcelona, 1976), pp. 654, 658. Another document mentions the *ecclesiam Sanctae Mariae, intra Minorisam civitatis menia constructae* ('. . . the church of Santa Maria, which stands inside the fortifications of the city of Manresa'), Català i Roca, *Els castells Catalans*, vol. V, p. 657.

5 '. . . *cum civitate dirute que dicitur Minorisa.*' Sarret i Arbós, *Historia de Manresa*, vol. I, p. 35.

6 The fact that the Bages had been in Christian hands almost continuously since Carolingian times means that the region was not home to any significant settlements of Muslims, i.e., the *mudéjars* whose history in the Ebro valley has been chronicled by Brian Catlos in *The Victors and the Vanquished: Christians and Muslims of Catalonia and Aragon, 1050–1300* (Cambridge, 2004).

incursion. The Bages prospered as a result of this new stability. By the later twelfth century, Manresa had become established as a regional trading and production centre, and the city walls were extended to enclose the spine of higher ground which runs north of the Col Cardoner, including the Puigmercadal. The Plaça Maior and the main thoroughfare of the Calle Sobrerrocha formed the nucleus of the newly expanded settlement. By the end of the thirteenth century, a combination of factors led to the rapid accumulation of elite fortunes at Manresa. A relatively weak system of royal taxation meant that the *nouveaux riches* of Manresa felt possessed of disposable income; they decided to spend some of this on civic architecture which would assert their city's emergence as a regional power. As a result, between about 1290 and 1330 the city elite embarked upon the construction or rebuilding of no fewer than four gothic churches, and a new stone bridge. A number of impressive new church spires now began to assert the increasing ambitions of the Manresan elites.[7] In the 1330s, after a drought-induced famine, the town leaders reacted by inaugurating a similarly ambitious irrigation project, known as the *sèquia*, which was designed to enhance the agricultural productivity of the city's hinterland. During this period the city grew well beyond the old twelfth-century circuit, and two significant suburbs were established to the east and west of the city. By the 1320s, Manresa's suburbs were nearly as large as the area enclosed by the old walls.[8]

Also by about 1300, a tradition had emerged which divided the city into four quarters. These were used for the purpose of levying troops for the *veguer*'s militia, for assessing and paying taxes, and sometimes for electing ad hoc councils for the purpose of making civic decisions.[9] Two of the city's quarters lay within the old twelfth-century walls, and two quarters consisted of the eastern and western suburbs. The quarters within the walls were Santa Maria to the south and Sobrerrocha to the north. The western suburb was known as the quarter of Sant Miquel, and the eastern suburb was known as Les Cudines (now referred to as Les Escodines or Codines).[10] The Castilian invasion threats of the 1360s led Pere III to order the construction of new walls; a statement from 1362 indicates that the city '*non est clausa*', meaning probably that its ancient defences, such as they might have been, were now wholly inadequate.[11]

7 This is chronicled in Joaquim Sarret i Arbós, *Història religiosa de Manresa: Iglésies i convents*, Monumenta Historica Civitatis Minorisae, vol. IV (Manresa, 1924).

8 See Map 2.1.

9 See for example MC 1370.1.19; MC 1370.7.17; for a meeting of city representatives called by quarter, see MC 1358.4.27.

10 See Map 2.1 11 MC 1362.8.1.

From 1368, after several false starts, the fortification programme was begun in earnest. The new circuit of walls completely enclosed the quarter of St Miquel, and was largely complete by about 1375. Work continued until about 1400.[12] The Cudines suburb to the east and its adjoining neighbourhoods of St Andreu northeast of the old city were left unenclosed by the new fortifications. This was done not only for financial reasons, but also because these easternmost parts of the city were strategically indefensible, lying as they do between the high ground of the Santa Maria and Sobrerrocha quarters, and the hill of Santa Clara to the east. Even though the new walls did not enclose all of Manresa's householders, everyone within the parish was assessed for taxes in order to pay for their construction.[13] In contrast to the relatively common use of quarters to distinguish the different parts of the city, parishes figure infrequently in our sources.[14] The available evidence suggests that Manresa itself was considered to be a single parish during the fourteenth century, and the 'parish' included the city itself plus some territory up to about five kilometres from the walls.[15] Subdivisions of the city proper were therefore referred to in terms of quarter or street, rather than by parish, as was common in larger cities such as Ghent and Bologna.[16] The relative weakness of neighbourhood and 'parish' in Manresa is therefore due in part to the city's medium size. But it also reflects a prevailing casualness, with discernible overtones of egalitarianism, which pervaded Catalan urban life in the fourteenth century, and militated against the creation of too many hard and fast boundaries.[17] This stands in contrast to the more rigidly hierarchical culture that would creep into the Catalan cities by 1500.

12 Valdenebro, 'L'evolutió urbana', p. 178. 13 MC 1370.7.19.

14 For the jurisdiction of the town council of Barcelona outside the city walls, see Pere Orti i Gost, 'El municipi de Barcelona i les parròquies del seu entorn al segle XIV', *Anuario de Estudios Medievales*, 31:1 (2001), 33–48.

15 For a reference to the parish, see MC 1359.9.20.

16 E.g., MC 1371.3.2 for usage suggesting the parish and bailiwick were coterminous. However, the 'city limits' seem by the mid-fourteenth century to have included some outlying villages and towns, whose territories were called 'parishes'; this included settlements such as Sant Fruitós de Bages, Navarcles, and (disputedly) St Benet de Bages. MC 1357.12.8. For an enlightening discussion of neighbourhood and parish in contemporary Bologna, see Shona Kelly Wray, *Communities and Crisis: Bologna during the Black Death* (Leiden, 2009), pp. 194–222. For this in Ghent, see David Nicholas, *The Metamorphosis of a Medieval City: Ghent in the Age of the Arteveldes, 1302–1390* (Leiden, 1987), pp. 67–119; esp. p. 119.

17 For a further discussion of this egalitarian ethos, see Chapter 8, *passim*. For an assertion of the variety that could be found in a single neighbourhood or block of a medieval town, see Nicholas A. Eckstein, 'Addressing Wealth in Renaissance Florence', *Journal of Urban History*, 32:5 (July 2006), 711–28.

ROYAL INSTITUTIONS IN MANRESA: THE *VEGUER* AND THE BAILIFF

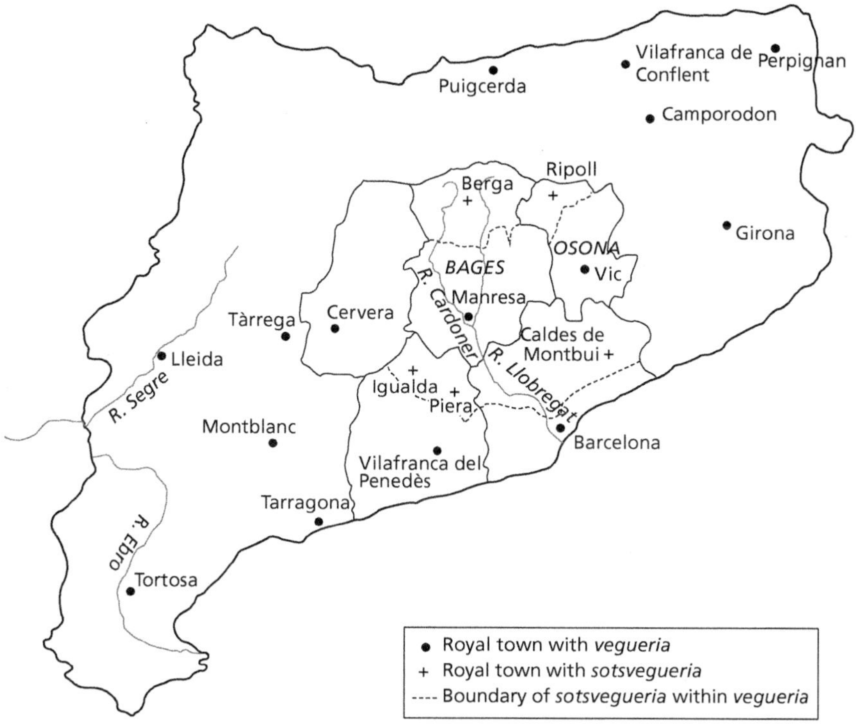

Map 2.2 The *vegueria* of the Bages with neighbouring *veguerias*, *c.* 1350

During the feudal devolutions of the eleventh and twelfth centuries, royal officials at all levels, from viscounts to bailiffs, became more and more independent of royal authority.[18] This was the result, amongst other things, of a trend towards the heritability of previously appointed

[18] The idea of a 'feudal devolution' was made famous by Georges Duby in e.g., *The Chivalrous Society*, trans. C. Postan (Berkeley, CA, 1977); this was taken up and turned into a 'Feudal Revolution' by Thomas Bisson; see Thomas N. Bisson 'The "Feudal Revolution"', *Past and Present: A Journal of Historical Studies*, 142 (1994), 6–42; and Thomas N. Bisson, The *Crisis of the Twelfth Century: Power, Lordship and the Origins of European Government* (Princeton, NJ, 2009); see also R. I. Moore, *The First European Revolution 900–1215* (Oxford, 2000), and Charles West, *Reframing the Feudal Revolution: Political and Social Transformation between Marne and Moselle, c.800–c.1100* (Cambridge, 2013). For the effects of this in Perpignan, see Daileader, *True Citizens*, pp. 73–9.

offices. Although the kings of Catalonia-Aragon did not definitively regain title to the local administration of Manresa until 1315, the process of reclaiming royal control over the countryside had begun much earlier, most notably during the reign of Alfons I (1162–96). This king and his successors pursued several overlapping strategies in their centuries-long struggle against seigniorial usurpations. Their most direct strategy was to strengthen the already-existing regional royal officials known as *veguers*.[19] Ironically, the *veguers* had been appointed in order to combat the pretensions of the nobles, many of whom had originally served the Counts of Barcelona as royal officials. The long-term royal strategy was to augment the *veguers*' powers by assigning them a role as the keepers of the king's 'peace and truce' (Catalan '*pau i treva*').[20] Between 1180 and 1230, and with the Church's blessing, the Catalan monarchs undertook a progressive strengthening of the old *pau i treva* statutes, which had originally begun as an episcopal initiative designed to protect church property. After an initial reliance on the bishops, the kings began to focus on the coercive powers of their *veguers* as enforcers of the peace. During the first *Corts* of his majority in 1225, Jaume I (1213–76) definitively separated the roles of the *veguers* and bishops, which had remained indistinct in previous proclamations of the *Corts*. The *veguers* now had sole executive power in cases of infraction against the king's peace, and the bishops were relegated to the spiritual role of excommunicating offenders. In the event, the latters' power proved too unwieldy for regular judicial use and it was allowed to lapse. As the powers of the *veguers* were strengthened, the scope of the peace and truce was extended to encompass almost everyone and everything in Catalonia, including the knights who most often broke it. The knights' wives were also singled out as being covered by the newly extended peace and truce statutes. Almost the only thing not included were knights' castles, which remained fair game as objects of feudal violence.[21] Much had been accomplished since 1131, when the only things covered under the peace and truce were buildings within thirty paces of an unfortified church, travelling merchants and plough

19 See definition p. xviii.

20 Flocel Sabaté comes to similar conclusions about the origins of the *veguer*; see Sabaté, 'El veguer a Catalunya', pp. 147–59, at p. 149.

21 *Cortes de los antiguos reinos de Aragón y de Valencia y Principado de Cataluña*, vol. I-i (Madrid, 1896), pp. 115–16 (1228). These *Corts* stipulated that *veguers* could in fact make a '*cavalcatum*', into the honours of knights and the church, but only for the express purpose of arresting the person presumed responsible for breaking the peace ('*nisi in domino feudi prius inventa fuerit fatica de directo racione illius qui pacem dicitur violasse*'). *Cortes*, I-i, 121.

beasts.[22] By 1235, when the 1225 and 1228 statutes were confirmed, most of the legal foundations for the later medieval *vegueria* were in place.[23]

Manresa was under the nominal jurisdiction of the *veguer* of Barcelona until 1276, when the records of the Manresan *vegueria* begin.[24] The history of this *vegueria* is tied to a grant made by King Jaume I to Ramon Folc V, viscount of Cardona in 1254. In that year, the king granted Manresa, Vilafranca, and several smaller jurisdictions as a fief to the viscount of Cardona for life. In return Cardona was to provide the king with the service of thirty knights.[25] The viscount died in 1276, the same year as Jaume, and within months the new king Pere II (1276–85) had established a *vegueria* in the Bages with Manresa as its capital. The process of strengthening the vicariate, and especially of crystallizing its territorial jurisdictions, continued under Pere, Alfons II (1285–91), and Jaume II (1291–1327), until by the 1320s the system had largely attained the form it would retain throughout the early modern period.[26]

The *veguer* and his local counterparts the bailiffs wielded a broad range of judicial and executive powers in the fourteenth century.[27] While

22 *Cortes*, I-i, 50. Also by these *Corts*, 'no one' was to 'dare to burn the house of another, unless a written order has been given on the advice of the bishop, who considers the burning necessary for the fulfillment of justice'.

23 *Cortes*, I-i, 125.

24 The earliest records of the *veguer* of Manresa are AHCM V-1 (9.7.1276–12.4.1277). The ubiquitous authority of the crown in Catalan cities is similar to the situation in contemporary English towns; the English analogy is perhaps the closest, since Catalonia and England were both relatively compact units with resident and interested royal administrations. See for example, Edward Miller, 'English Town Patricians, c. 1200–1350', in Annalisa Guarducci (ed.), *Gerarchie economiche e gerarchie sociali secoli XII–XVIII: Atti della 'dodicesima settimana di studi', 18–23 Aprile 1980* (Florence, 1990), pp. 217–40, at p. 228.

25 Ambrosio Huici Miranda and María Desamparados Cabanes Pecourt, *Documentos de Jaime I de Aragon*, vol. III (Valencia, 1978), pp. 154–5.

26 For the process of territorial delineation, see Sabaté, 'El veguer a Catalunya', pp. 158–9. For the notion that this was part of a deliberate royal strategy, as is also argued in the following pages, see Christian Guilleré, 'Les élites urbaines Catalanes à la fin du Moyen Age: L'Exemple Géronais', in *Les élites urbaines au moyen age: Actes du XXVIIe congrès de la société des historiens médiévistes de l'enseignement supérieur public (Rome, Mai 1996)*, (Paris, 1997; Rome, 1997), pp. 269–85, at p. 271. See also Turull and Verdés, 'Gobierno municipal y fiscalidad en Cataluña durante la baja edad media', though I am not sure that such a direct causality between the Crown's economic desires and political realignment can be posited. If Turull's thesis is correct in the main, it should be emphasized that the format taken by Catalan political reforms were, in my estimation, a principal generator of the levels of prosperity and cultural achievement that can be found in the fourteenth- and early fifteenth-century Catalan cities. For a similar process in Zaragoza see Enrique Mainé Burguete, 'Infanzones contra ciudadanos: Luchas por el poder en la parroquia de la Magdalena (Zaragoza)' in *Homenaje a la professora Carmen Orcástegui Gros*, Aragón en la edad media 14–15 (Zaragoza, 1999), pp. 941–53, at p. 943.

27 The classic study on this subject is Jesús Lalinde Abadía, *La jurisdicción real inferior en Cataluña* (Barcelona, 1966); for a recent synthesis of governmental evolution during this period which suggests that these political realignments often occurred in response to fiscal problems, see Turull

the *veguer*'s jurisdiction was regional, it overlapped with those of the bailiffs, who were each responsible for a particular royal locality, such as Manresa, or its satellite city of Sant Pedor. Both the *veguer* and the bailiffs held regular sessions of court, in which they heard disputes involving royal subjects throughout their jurisdictions. At Manresa, each of the two officials maintained a lieutenant, who could function as a virtual double of themselves.[28] The lieutenants were called in Catalan *sotsveguer* and *sotsbatlle* respectively, and in Latin *subvicarius* and *subbaiulus*. After the lieutenants, the third most important officer in each administrative hierarchy was the *assessor*. An *assessor* was often a lawyer, usually in the case of Manresa a native Manresan, and they seem to have served as judges during routine court sessions. Occasionally the assessorships of the *veguer* and bailiff were held by the same man, just as at times the offices of *veguer* and bailiff, or those of *sotsveguer* and *sotsbatlle*, were held by the same man. For most of the fourteenth century, however, the offices of *veguer* and bailiff together with the subordinate offices were held by separate individuals. Both the *veguer* and the bailiff were appointed by the king for three year terms that began in late winter or early spring. The cycle of these offices was surprisingly regular: in Manresa it remained unbroken between at least 1324 and 1399.[29]

Of the two principal royal officials who operated from Manresa, the bailiff had a more direct hand in the daily affairs of the city, but the *veguer* was by far the senior official within the overall royal administration of Catalonia. A *vegueria* was a much more extensive and important jurisdiction than a bailiwick: the *vegueria* of Manresa consisted of more than fifty royal bailiwicks alone, leaving aside the ecclesiastical and seigniorial lands that were also encompassed by it.[30] One of the earliest vicarial books extant at Manresa, dating from 1298, makes clear that the *veguers* were firmly in control of the rural bailiffs within their jurisdiction by this time. Many of the entries in this book record the *veguer*'s orders to various rural bailiffs that they are to compel certain men to pay someone else a quantity of money, as had been settled in the vicarial court. A typical entry runs: 'We have written to the bailiff[s] of Sorisa that he [they] should make the following people pay the following quantities to

and Verdés, 'Gobierno municipal'. See also various works by Flocel Sabaté Curull, including "El veguer" a Catalunya: Anàlisi del funcionament de la jurisdicció reial al segle XIV', *Butlletí de la Societat Catalana d'Estudis Històrics*, 6 (1995), 147–59; and Flocel Sabaté Curull, 'El veguer i la vegueria de Tortosa i de la ribera d'Ebre al segle XIV', in *Les darreres investigacions històriques del antic territori de Tortosa* (Tortosa, 1997), pp. 113–52.

28 On the lieutenant *veguers*, see Sabaté, 'El veguer a Catalunya', p. 150.

29 These observations are taken from MC.

30 The names of over fifty bailiwicks, both rural and based upon small towns, appear in AHCM V-4 (1298.6.1 to 1298.8.1).

Berenguer Jonquera within twenty days.' In this example there follows a list of men and women together with the amounts payable by each, such as: 'Ramon dEspoler, 50s. Pere ça Sabrega, 19s. Agnetis *muller* den Guillem dAmbric, 2s.' The people so listed may have been tenants of Berenguer Jonquera who owed him back rents.[31]

In terms of social class and remuneration the *veguers* were also pointedly superior to the bailiffs of Manresa. At least six of the twelve known *veguers* of Manresa during the period 1329 to 1390 were knights, and one was a *donzel*, or noble squire.[32] In contrast, only two of twenty-one known bailiffs of Manresa were knights or *donzels*. The crown appointed members of the castellan class or lower nobility, rather than wealthy commoners, to vacant *veguerias* for a number of reasons. First, the *veguer* led the royal army of the Bages, and in the eyes of contemporaries knighthood and military leadership were seen as highly complementary.[33] A more pressing reason for ensuring that *veguers* were knights had to do with the overlapping jurisdictions within his *vegueria*. In the performance of his duties, the *veguer* frequently came into conflict with noble seigniors and ecclesiastical lords whose lands were nominally under his jurisdiction. The affront created by a commoner pursuing this difficult agenda would have been that much greater than that created by a member of the castellanate, and so the appointment of knights remained the most practical course of action. The salaries of the *veguer* and the bailiff of Manresa also showed a large disparity: at 2,000 *sous* per year, the *veguer* was paid one of the highest salaries in the land.[34] By 1380, this amount was comparable to the annual income of the wealthiest Manresan *rentiers*.[35] At 500 *sous* per year, the bailiff's salary was respectable, but not aristocratic.[36]

In addition to his judicial powers, the *veguer* acted as the executor of his court's sentences. Like the local bailiff, he maintained a small police force and a jail for the apprehension and detention of criminals.[37] He was also responsible for maintaining order on all royal thoroughfares within the *vegueria*. As stated above, one of his most conspicuous executive functions

31 *Scripsimus bayulis d sorisa quod infra XX dies faciat solvi Berengerii Jonquera quantitates infrascriptis per homines scriptos*. AHCM V-4, 1298.5.9.

32 Source: MC.

33 For the *veguer*'s responsibility for keeping the standard (*vexillum*) of the city's militia, see e.g., MC 1365.7.31.

34 The *veguer*'s salary is listed in Table 7.7.

35 For the income of Manresan *rentiers*, see Table 7.8.

36 See Table 7.7 and relevant discussion.

37 For the *veguer*'s *saigs* (guards) keeping the city's flag, see MC 1370.3.5. The *saigs* of the bailiff appear much more frequently in Manresan records; e.g. MC 1357.12.19; MC 1361.8.10; MC 1372.6.7. For a brief description and definition of the late fourteenth-century Catalan *saig*, see Josefina Mutge Vives, 'Preocupacions del govern municipal Barceloní en el 1371 a través dels testaments dels consellers', *Acta Historica et Archaeologica Mediaevalia*, 23–4 (2003), 331–51.

was to lead the army of the *vegueria*. One of the few examples of civic ritual that come to light in the Manresan council manuals involved the transfer of the standard to the *veguer*. When the army of the Bages was summoned by royal order, the banner of the City of Manresa was taken from its sanctuary on the altar of Sant Miquel – the church in which the town council routinely met – and entrusted to the *veguer* by two of the councillors during a public ceremony held in the *plaça maior*.[38] The form of this ceremony clearly symbolizes the continual competition for power between royal and municipal officials, even as it leaves us in no doubt as to the ultimate superiority of the crown.

The bailiff's function was an ancient one in Catalonia, and the counts of Barcelona had been employing *batlles* as their local estate managers since Carolingian times.[39] Prior to the re-establishment of the royal bailiwick in 1315, the primary organs of government in the city included the castellany, whose executive functions provided physical protection as well as a base for repression, and the court of justice, about whose legal functions the same observations can be made.[40] In the eleventh century the city had been dominated by the lords of Balçereny, a larger-than-average fortress town to the north of the city, but by the mid-twelfth century a local family, the de Manresas, had established a firm claim over the city's jurisdictions.[41] By the mid-thirteenth century, the de Manresa family had established itself as dominant feudatories in the town, a fact further attested by their patronym. This family dominated the town into the early fourteenth century, although like other urban lords at this time, who at Manresa included the dean and chapter of Santa Maria, the de Manresas were losing ground to the increasing power of the townsmen.[42] It was from Bernat de Manresa that Jaume II purchased the rights to the castle and civic court in 1315. It is known that in 1252 there was a castellan at Manresa in addition to a bailiff. This means that two separate officers administered the city's government, although both of them were appointed by the same feudal lord.[43]

38 For an instance of the *veguer* handing the banner back to the councillors, see MC 1368.7.18. For an instance in which the *councillors* accused the *veguer* of misplacing the banner, MC 1373.1.28.

39 For early references to the Catalan royal bailiffs, see MCOA, 34–5, at p. 28.

40 For the establishment and regulation of the bailiwick, see LV, 93–6. For these functions, see Torras, EPLV, pp. 121–6. See also Joaquim Sarret y Arbós, *Historia De Manresa*, vol. I (Manresa, 1921), pp. 27–73.

41 Català i Roca (ed.), *Els castells Catalans*, vol. V, p. 658.

42 For evidence of this struggle in Cervera, including the sale to townsmen of the rights to various feudal exactions by the de Cervera family, and for the later confirmation of these sales by the king, see Max Turull (ed.), *El Llibre de Privilegis de Cervera*, Documents 1, 3, 4, 5, and 6 (pp. 25–35).

43 This can be deduced by the 1315 purchase, in which the king bought both the 'castlania' and the 'feu' from Bernat de Manresa, attested in Català i Roca, *Els castells Catalans*, vol. V, p. 660.

The bailiff of Manresa was responsible for judicial and executive functions within the parish, whose boundaries not unsurprisingly went through a process of definition in the first half of the century.[44] The bailiwick took a more definitive form after its boundaries were enlarged in 1359, during the fiscal crisis brought about by the Castilian war and the rapid expansion of the *censal* system.[45] Some of our first records of the functions of the bailiff's office come from the mid-thirteenth century, when a grant of immunity from judicial extradition granted by Jaume I in 1252 helped to secure the importance of the bailiff's court for all litigation between Manresan residents.[46] Even after 1315, however, the bailiff's authority was limited by the local ambit of his bailiwick, and also by his subordination to the *veguer*. Already by 1315, the *veguer* of Manresa heard appeals from cases in all of his bailiwick courts including that of Manresa.[47] In civil cases, the *veguer*'s court was normally the highest court of appeals, while in criminal cases appeals from the *veguer*'s court went directly to the king.[48] While the bailiff served as the court of first redress for local grievances, his primary function, particularly as the fourteenth century advanced, was to oversee and enforce the increasingly sophisticated local tax collection system. Generally, warnings were sufficient. These could be followed up by the imposition of judicial fines, called *terçs*, on delinquent taxpayers. Only very rarely was physical force threatened, let alone used, by the bailiff and his men. That being said, the bailiff did maintain some sort of jail, and provided full-time employment for at least one guard.[49] Thus the threat of violence was omnipresent. Other important functions of the bailiff included being the guarantor of urban real estate transactions and ensuring that the estates of Manresan citizens were divided according to the laws of testament and inheritance. As a witness to this latter function, the majority of the folios of the extant bailiffs' books are taken up by inventories *post mortem*, lists of property held by the recently deceased. As evidenced by the case of the Sarta family, these were drawn up as soon as possible after death to reduce fraud.[50] A further function of the bailiff was the largely symbolic but nonetheless crucial power to 'approve' all the acts of the Manresan town council.

44 The relationships between bailiffs and urban governments in the fourteenth century Crown of Aragon have received some scholarly attention. See Daileader, *True Citizens*, *passim*, and Mark Meyerson, *Jews in an Iberian Frontier Kingdom: Society, Economy, and Politics in Morvedre, 1248–1391* (Leiden, 2004), esp. pp. 18–23; pp. 25–30.

45 MC 1359.1.20. 46 LV, 29–31. 47 AHCM, V-4.

48 This is evidenced in the Talamanca papers, e.g., FTII 1372.9.25, in which local knights are seen appealing directly to the Duke of Girona, over the head of the local *veguer*.

49 MC 1372.6.7.

50 For the bailiff's inquest see AHCM Tr. 224 (Jaume Sarta) 1351–81 (actually 1389), entry dated 1388.7.15.

In practise, this approval was made as often as not by the *sotsbatlle*; one can imagine that the bailiffs were generally happy to delegate the duty of attending town council meetings to their lieutenants. Throughout the fourteenth century, there were only a handful of times, again mostly during the Castilian war crisis, that the town council showed any inclination to chafe at this royal oversight.[51] Generally, the town councillors were aware that the royal authority's ability to lend power to their actions in the Bages outweighed what they might have lost in terms of autonomy.

THE CREATION OF FORMAL MUNICIPAL INSTITUTIONS AT MANRESA

In addition to buying back the rights to local bailiwicks and strengthening the *veguers*, another contra-feudal strategy pursued by the late twelfth- and early thirteenth-century Catalan kings was to harness the bourgeoning energies of the Catalan townsmen to aid in the pursuit of their own political ends. The legitimization of town armies, such as can be seen in a 1218 act from the *Llibre Verd* of Manresa, was a phenomenon stemming from this period.[52] Of course, this royal strategy could also have the effect of increasing the power, wealth, and prestige of the Catalan townsmen in proportion to its success. Another aspect of this royal policy involved the legitimization and elevation of urban governments. Between 1175 and 1200 consulates were created in Barcelona, Cervera, Perpignan and Lleida, and another attempt was made at Vic.[53] If a consulate was created

[51] These are discussed at length in Chapter 5.

[52] For the creation of civic armies, see Philip Daileader, *True Citizens: Violence, Memory, and Identity in the Medieval Community of Perpignan, 1162–1397* (Leiden, 2000), pp. 79–87. For the 1218 privilege at Manresa, see LV, 27–9.

[53] For a chronology which sees the appearance of an early form of consulate in the cities of Catalonia during the late twelfth century, their 'disappearances' in the early thirteenth century, followed by resurgences in Perpignan and elsewhere that were consolidated in the early fourteenth century, see Philip Daileader, 'The Vanishing Consulates of Catalonia', *Speculum: A Journal of Medieval Studies*, 74:1 (1999), 65–94; for Vic, see Paul H. Freedman, 'An Unsuccessful Attempt at Urban Organization in Twelfth-century Catalonia', *Speculum: A Journal of Medieval Studies*, 54 (1979), 479–91.

Regarding the second (permanent) wave of consiliar foundations, Batlle gives much of the credit for the creation and strengthening of consulates to Pere el Gran, but in many towns (such as Cervera and Manresa), the consulates were not consolidated until the reign of Jaume II. Batlle and Vilar, *Historia De Catalunya*, p. 81. In this wave, the *paers* (consuls) of Cervera appear relatively early, in 1267, although their powers were strengthened over the succeeding two generations and their late medieval–early modern format really emerged after 1311. For the 1267 consulate, see Max Turull i Rubinat, *La configuració juridica del municipi baix medieval: Regim municipal i fiscalitat a Cervera entre 1182–1430* (Barcelona, 1990), pp. 126–30; for the consolidation of a regime of 'paers' and the provision of *jurats* at Cervera in 1311, see Max Turull i Rubinat, *El règim municipal de paeria. Cervera, 1331–1333: Dinàmica social i politica* (Lleida, 1986), p. 19, and *La configuració*, pp. 130–6.

at Manresa in this early period, no trace of it has been discovered by local researchers. It has long been known that Catalan cities created organized urban governments much later than their Italian and southern French counterparts; many cities in the latter regions had formed communes with consulates by 1100 or 1150 at the latest.[54] At Manresa, a formal government consisting of four *consellers* and a larger advisory body of *jurats* was not created until 1315, in the same year that the bailiwick was recovered and reorganized by the Crown. Even so, no foundation charter survives for the Manresan government, so that the foundation must be inferred from the change of terminology in extant documents.[55]

One of the earliest privileges that evinces signs of a corporate identity in Manresa is Jaume I's 1252 grant of immunity from judicial extradition. Tellingly, this letter is addressed merely to 'every man of Manresa', and even fails to make mention of any *probi homines,* or distinguished men.[56] While it used to be held that this terminology was a sign of a 'primitive democracy' on the part of the burghers, the fact that burghers of the twelfth and early thirteenth centuries were hemmed in on all sides by feudal rights and exactions, exercised by rapacious lords, that there was little law or order to be had outside of a resort to violence, and that burghers were relatively poor in comparison with their later descendants, means that the functioning of any such 'democracy' happened in conditions which strip them of much of their idealistic appeal.[57] Likewise, there was almost certainly some sort of de facto hierarchy amongst the burghers, which does not appear in contemporary documents. Even at this early stage, it is probable that the influence of the wealthiest townsmen was more than equal to the influence of humbler men in communal affairs. Still, the effects of an earlier 'primitive democracy' should not be discounted in fostering a sense of *esprit de corps* in the town's militia, or of fostering a sense of belonging, pride, and responsibility that would have drawn artisans and residents of all economic strata into a

[54] The term 'communal revolution' has long been employed to describe the creation of republican institutions in the cities of Latin Europe between about AD 1050 and about 1300. The term is most often employed in Italian history, but is understood to have occurred in cities throughout Latin Europe over the two and a half centuries after 1050. For the phenomenon as whole, see Peter Clark, *European Cities and Towns: 400–2000*, reprint (New York, 2009), pp. 91–6. One of the most comprehensive treatments of the Italian scenario remains Philip Jones, *The Italian City-State* (Oxford, 1997), pp. 103–51. Other detailed analyses can be found in Lauro Martines, *Power and Imagination: City-States in Renaissance Italy* (New York, 1979), and J. K. Hyde, *Society and Politics in Medieval Italy: The Evolution of the Civil Life, 1000–1350* (London, 1973).

[55] See n. 86, below.

[56] Turull, *La configuració juridica*, pp. 119–20, notes that Cervera moved from an earlier consular system to a use of the term *universitas* during the 1260s. The 1252 accord has already been cited.

[57] This argument stems primarily from J. M. Font Rius, *Orígines del regimen municipal de Cataluña*: see discussion in Daileader, *True Citizens*, pp. 80–1.

certain solidarity, even with the town's wealthiest members. As has been observed for England, oligarchy might have been present in this earlier period, but at a time when there were more conflicts with local lords, oligarchs had a vested interest in ensuring that their regime was more 'friendly, discreet, and useful to all' than it would later become.[58] Just as in England, the relative practicality and 'friendliness' which characterized the Manresan oligarchy lasted well into the fourteenth century, despite the ongoing process of legal definition, economic downturn, and indeed a pacification of society which led to increasing social ossification.[59]

Returning to our evidence regarding the early development of civic status and corporate identity, a 1262 accord between the *universitas hominum de Minorisa* and the dean and chapter of the Seu does not distinguish any citizens or *probi homines.* This may indicate that through the 1260s, Manresa was not considered large or important enough that its leading men should be distinguished with the title that had been used by powerful citizens of Barcelona since at least 1203.[60] The failure to distinguish *probi homines* may have to do with the 1254 grant of the city to the viscount of Cardona mentioned above. Despite that retrograde step, the 1262 accord with the dean and chapter shows that the Manresan civic elite continued to move towards greater self-assertion.[61] The act freed the townsmen from a number of feudal exactions that had been demanded by the chapter, exactions which amounted to marks of servitude. These included fees for reading the service of the dead (*lectis mortuorum*), a fee taken from the estates of the deceased (*legatis mortuorum*), and fees exacted for performing marriages (*nubentibus ratione nuptiarum* or elsewhere *eorum que consuevistis dare pro nuptiis*).[62] The document also states that the struggle between the townsmen and the chapter over these exactions had been going on for some time. Now, as it turned out, the dean and chapter were forced to give up their feudal pretensions over the townsmen once and for all. The townsmen were gracious in victory; they admitted that they might wish to contribute to their church on the occasions of death, burial, and marriage, but they made plain that they would do so voluntarily. After renouncing his and his successors' rights

58 David Gary Shaw, 'Social Networks and the Foundations of Oligarchy in Medieval Towns', *Urban History*, 32:2 (2005), 200–22, at 222.

59 On a 'defeudalizing' of society in the Crown of Aragon from the fourteenth through the fifteenth centuries, see Flocel Sabaté Curull, 'Ejes vertebradores de la oligarquía urbana en Cataluña', *Revista d'Història Medieval*, 9 (1998), 127–53.

60 Stephen Bensch, *Barcelona and its Rulers*, 181.

61 For the use of the term 'patriciate', which some used to find objectionable, but which has lately become less tendentious in the post-theory age, see the discussion in Stephen Bensch's *Barcelona and its Rulers, 1096–1291* (Cambridge, 1995), pp. 174–6.

62 LV, 31–4.

to make legal petitions for money on the strength of feudal prerogative, the dean for his part was careful to keep the right to pursue legally whatever might be offered as a pious gift: 'We [the dean], however, retain for ourselves the right to sue for whatever goods may be bequeathed to this church by a man or woman of their own free will.'[63]

For this privilege the town paid 5,000 *sous* (£250), a modest sum that in 1318 amounted to only one third of the fortune of a single moderately wealthy Manresan, Pere Sarta.[64] The small size of this settlement suggests that the church had really little choice in the matter: the city's power was increasing, and the canons presumably realized that future offers might be even less, and made with less goodwill.

In 1276 Ramon Folc V of Cardona died, Manresa returned to the royal orbit, and the city was almost immediately established as the centre of a new *vegueria*. All the evidence points to a rapid rise in Manresa's demographic and economic fortunes between 1280 and 1320. This trend is in accord with the assessment of Bisson, who has noted a similar phenomenon across Catalonia as a whole.[65] In documents of 1284, 1288, 1292, 1300, 1311, and 1315, the city's leading men were now routinely distinguished by the title *probi homines*.[66] Manresa's importance as a regional economic centre grew as well. In 1284, Pere II conceded that the city could celebrate an eight-day fair beginning on the feast of the Ascension, a moveable feast usually occurring between 4 and 31 May; and in 1311, Jaume II added a second fair to the city's calendar; this one was to last for ten days beginning in the late autumn on the feast of St Andrew, which is celebrated on 30 November.[67] This propagation of regional fairs was part of a wider royal policy which affected other royal towns as well.[68]

While it is true that demographic and economic trends were favourable to elites with capital in the years around 1300, Manresa's elite in particular took extra benefit from their evolving relationship with the *veguer*. Instead of resorting to violence on a regular basis, townspeople could be reasonably sure that business transactions could be conducted between townsmen, knights, and seigniorial tenants, under the guarantee of effective judicial and executive power. The *veguer* quickly and effectively moved

63 *Salvo tamen et retento nobis quod si aliquis vel aliqua voluerit aliquid dare vel legare gratis dicte ecclesie quod nos possimus illus petere et exigere*. LV, 32.

64 This figure is given in SF 1320 10k1.

65 MCOA, 169.

66 LV, 70–96.

67 For the Manresan fairs, see LV, 70–1, 85–6.

68 For a similar situation in Cervera which suggests that the pheonomeon was Catalan-wide and the product of a deliberate royal policy, see Turull, 'Intercanvi comercial, fira i mercat a Cervera entre 1136 i 1392'. For fairs also being established by Jaume II in the small market town of Santa Coloma de Queralt, outside of Cervera, see Gregory Milton in *Market Power: Lordship, Society, and Economy in Medieval Catalonia (1276–1313)*, (Basingstoke, 2012).

to secure property rights throughout the Bages, thus driving down transaction costs and interest rates, with the result that it became much more profitable for non-nobles to do business in the countryside.[69] An examination of the early vicarial court records shows that the majority of the *veguers*' business was concerned with collecting rents and debts owed to prominent Manresans. Crucially, these cases could even involve tenants living on land belonging to clerics and seigneurs.[70] In a typical month in the summer of 1298, some 8,200s were awarded in the *vicarial* court, and over 62 percent of this went to fifteen prominent Manresans.[71] During a three-month period over the same summer, the Manresan Jaume Sarta, ancestor of the Jaume Sarta who was the city's richest merchant in 1408, was the recipient of over 200 *sous*, awarded by the *veguer* in six different judgments.[72] The *veguers*' books provide clear evidence that the power of their court was a foundation of the land boom which took place in the Bages in the 1310s.[73]

Unsurprisingly given this state of affairs, the Manresan patriciate began to regard the *vegueria* as synonymous with their collective power; this is illustrated by the keen interest they took in increasing both the *veguer*'s jurisdictions and the boundaries of the *vegueria*. Disputes in 1311, 1315, and 1336 each resulted in the assignment of disputed castles and territories to the *vegueria*, and each dispute served to settle boundaries with a separate neighbouring *vegueria*. The dispute in 1311 was with the *vegueria* of Cervera, which lay to the west of the *vegueria* of the Bages, that of 1315 was with Berga to the north, and a further dispute in 1336 settled boundaries with Vilafranca to the south.[74] The Manresan patricians' concern with the boundaries of their *vegueria* was not purely a point of honour, as may be seen from a debate held in 1359, when the king had recently sold or leased certain royal jurisdictions within the *vegueria*. After a contentious deliberation, the Manresan council decided to buy the jurisdictions back for the crown, specifically citing financial interests that certain of their number had in the disputed territories. Clearly, the investors felt that the removal of these territories from the *vegueria* would place their assets in considerable jeopardy.[75] Likewise, in 1362, the king authorized the city to collect tolls on all roads within the *vegueria* as a

69 For an anti-magnate policy being pursued in thirteenth- and early fourteenth-century Italian communes for similar reasons, see Dale Kent, 'The Power of the Elites: Family, Patronage, and the State', in John M. Najemy (ed.), *Italy in the Age of the Renaissance, 1300–1550*, The Short Oxford History of Italy (Oxford, 2004) at pp. 165–83, 175–7.

70 See FT 1324 3n5; FT 1343 15k9; MC 1375.2.27.

71 AHCM V-4, 1298.5.11 to 1298.8.23.

72 AHCM V-4, 1298.5.16 to 1298.6.11.

73 For the land boom see n. 8 below.

74 For the 1311 Dispute see LV, 89; For 1315, see LV, 90; and for 1336, LV, 105.

75 MC 1359.1.30.

means of defraying the public debt payments which were mushrooming as a result of the war with Castile.[76] In this instance, the patricians directly exploited the *vegueria* for its tax revenue.

Although the Manresan civic elite showed many signs of increased self-assertion during the half century between 1250 and 1300, it was the policies of Jaume II (1291–1327) that gave them the tools they needed in order to challenge the castellanate for dominance in both the city and its region.[77] The Manresan royal scrivany began keeping regular records during the time of Pere el Gran; but the record house blossomed into a major institution, which touched the lives of many inhabitants of Manresa and the Bages during the reign of Jaume II. Not only were the records of the *veguer* and the bailiff now housed in the scrivany, so also were the various record series of the town government, the private notarial books of the city's principal families, the transactions of the city's Jews, and a series of general notarial books to accommodate those who did not maintain private books. While it is possible for an historian who benefits from these records to exaggerate the importance of this change, in fact, it did create a permanent central repository for many of the legal documents made in the city, and it established the important idea that institutions and even individual families were meant to keep long-term, organized, centralized and consultable record series. The records in the scrivany, many of which were produced by Manresan citizens for their own benefit, gave them new forms of control over their own lives, their environment, and their interactions with other townsmen, churchmen, crown officials, and nobles alike.[78] The scrivany also gave the town's elites a prominent record of the city's past, and provided governors with a corresponding sense of perspective. As a result, the scrivany encouraged citizens to think more concretely about the future greatness of their city, a speculation which is corroborated by the ambitious building projects and career paths pursued by Manresan elites during these decades.

Between 1311 and 1315, Jaume II took a number of decisive steps to increase the legal status of Manresa and its citizens in the Bages. A charter of 1311 gave Manresans a monopoly on intramural wine sales; henceforth all wine sold in Manresa was to come from vineyards within the parish of Manresa. An important corollary was that vineyards outside the parish but owned by Manresan citizens could also sell inside the city.[79]

76 MC 1362.3.14.

77 Jaume's policy of elevating his cities into regional commercial and political centres has been amply chronicled at Cervera by Turull in *La configuració juridical.*

78 See Gregory B. Milton, 'The Transition from Ecclesiastical Scribania to Professional Notariate in Santa Coloma de Queralt', *Journal of Medieval History*, 39 (2013), 1–19.

79 LV, 87–8.

This new monopoly represented a serious blow to the seigneurs in the vicinity of Manresa, who thereby lost their principal market, while the landowning elites of the city were now in a position to charge a premium on their own vintages.[80] This privilege was especially important to the city's patricians because wine growing was a principal capital investment for them at this time.[81] Such a monopoly encouraged the elite to invest in the seigneurial lands in the countryside, which thanks to the legal protection granted by the *veguers* now became practicable. However, by creating a strong economic barrier between seigneurial lands and lands held by royal citizens, one can imagine that this sort of monopoly would not stimulate the rural economy as a whole; rather it would tend, in the long run, to dampen the growth of both the rural and the urban economies by keeping them separate. In this way, the Manresan-Bages economic model might have become closer, in the fourteenth century, to what Stephan Epstein described for Florence and its *contado*, rather than for Lombardy with its weaker urban privileges.[82]

Another royal privilege of 1311 shows that the crown's concern for the economic well-being of its citizens was part of a broader plan to increase royal revenue: in that year Jaume also granted Manresans the right to collect taxes from everyone who had property within the territory of Manresa.[83] The wording of this privilege is significantly vague. The types or quantities of property are not specified, so that anyone possessing the least amount of movable goods could theoretically be made to contribute to all royal and civic taxes in full. Likewise the phrase *in eius territorio* is less precise than the terms 'parish' and 'bailiwick' which were employed in other documents, possibly in order to leave open an avenue for the Manresans' taxation of the *vegueria*, which is known to have taken place from the 1360s, but perhaps had been done earlier.[84] Taken together,

80 On the development of the municipal wine tax in early fourteenth-century Catalonia, see Manuel Sánchez Martínez, 'Vino y fiscalidad en la edad media: El caso de los municipios Catalanes', in Javier Maldonado Rosso (ed.), *Actas del i simposio de la asociación internacional de historia y civilización de la vid y el vino, 1999* (Madrid and Barcelona, 2001), pp. 403–19.

81 This is briefly argued for Girona in Josep Fernández Trabal, 'De mercaders a terratinents. Formació del patrimoni rural de la família Bell-lloc de Girona, 1302–1398', *L'Avenç: Història del Països Catalans*, 94 (1986), 42–7. Detailed discussions of this can be found in Josep Fernández i Trabal, *Una família catalana medieval: Els Bell-lloc de Girona, 1267–1533* (Barcelona, 1995), and in Christian Guillere, *Girona medieval: L'Etapa d'apogeu, 1285–1360*, Quaderns d'historia de Girona (Ajuntament de Girona, 1991). For the sense that the land around Barcelona had already been saturated with vineyards during the thirteenth century, indicating a 'land boom', see Stephen P. Bensch, *Barcelona and its Rulers, 1096–1291* (Cambridge, 1995), pp. 304–5.

82 For this model, see Stephan R. Epstein, 'Town and Country: Economy and Institutions in Late Medieval Italy', *Economic History Review*, 46:3 (1993), 453–77.

83 LV, 88–9.

84 See e.g., MC 1362.3.14; See also discussion of this point in Chapter 5.

the privileges of 1311 set the stage for a fundamental realignment of the power relationships between Manresa and the Bages, a realignment whose momentum would make the fourteenth century one of the most dynamic in the city's history.[85]

In 1315, Jaume decided to up the ante even further, and promulgated a series of institutional innovations which were arguably the most momentous in the entire history of the city. The erection of the royal bailiwick in this year has already been discussed. This was accompanied by two further actions: first, the elevation of the city from the legal status of a *villa*, or town, to the status of a *civitas*, or city. Also in that year, Manresa received permission to form a conciliar government.[86] To take the former development first. The circumstances and significance of Manresa's elevation to *civitas* have long remained an intriguing problem for Catalan urban historians. The text of the document of elevation, preserved in the *Llibre Verd*, in fact provides some clue as to why this unusual step was taken. One of the phrases in this document runs: 'Because many ancient and authentic writings have been found, in which the place of Manresa was formerly called *civitas* . . . '[87] This sentence shows that the Manresan citizens had been conducting an archival search of their city's records, and that they had discovered this ancient usage. Why would this title have meant so much to them? The answer probably lies in the fact that in contemporary Catalan Latin usage, the title *civitas* was reserved for a bishopric.[88] It is therefore quite likely that the Manresans had been searching their archives for evidence that the city had once contained a bishop, but the closest they could come was to discover that it had once been designated by the title *civitas*. This might have been taken as evidence of Roman heritage, which itself might also support the notion that the city, as a Roman *municipium*, had once held a bishop. The motive behind such an archival search is not hard to guess. First,

[85] For a similar change in Flanders, see David M. Nicholas, 'Town and Countryside: Social and Economic Tensions in Fourteenth-century Flanders', *Comparative Studies in Society and History*, 10 (1968), 458–85.

[86] Although no charter has survived, the change is apparent from the terminology used in documents in LV. Note that through 22 May 1315, royal letters are addressed to the '*universitas*' or the '*probi homines et universitas*'. From 18 February 1316, however, all letters are addressed to the *consellers* and *universitas*, or the *consellers*, *jurats*, and *universitas*. See LV, 94–7.

[87] LV, 92. '*Attendes quod plures et diverse scripture antique ac publice et autentice reperiuntur et alia quamplurima legittima documenta, ex quibus manifesti colligitur et aperte quod locus de Minorisa, in Bagiis situatus, ab antiquo est et consuevit nominari civitas et describi . . .* '

[88] Philip Daileader notes that Perpignan, although it had perhaps four times the population of Manresa, was never called by the title of *civitas*, because it had no bishop. Daileader, *True Citizens*, p. 2. For this usage becoming common across Europe by the sixth century, see David Nicholas, *The Growth of the Medieval City: From Late Antiquity to the Early Fourteenth Century* (Boston, MA, 1997), p. 17.

the tradition that Manresa once had its own bishop is a very old one, enshrined in the nickname of the city's principal church, *La Seu*, which means 'the seat', that is, the cathedral. The legend can also be found in the third chapter of Joaquim Sarret i Arbós' 1921 *Historia de Manresa*, which argues quite unequivocally for the historical existence of a Bishop of Manresa.[89]

Apart from the obvious prestige, the city's elevation to a bishopric would pay significant economic and political dividends to an increasingly self-assertive patriciate that must have chafed at being beholden to the Bishop of Vic. That bishop was seen as the lord of a rival city, which was the same size or slightly smaller than Manresa, and throughout the fourteenth century he would continue to place many obstacles in the way of the Manresan government. This was most notable during the construction of the irrigation canal known as the *sèquia*, which caused serious land disputes in the Bages, and led the Bishop of Vic in 1341 to excommunicate the Manresan consuls and place the populace under interdict. This situation would continue until a new bishop came to the episcopal throne in 1345.[90] An increasingly significant difficulty, also, was that Vic lay in the neighbouring *vegueria* of Osona. Thus it seems that the city's request to be elevated to the status of *civitas*, which corresponded with its massive church-building programme, was part of a larger ambition to be granted its own bishop. Although such a plan never came to fruition, such an ambition is not out of keeping with the civic spirit of the time.

Even if the status of *civitas* was not intended as a step towards 'reviving' a Manresan bishopric, it provided some immediate benefits as well. One of the most important was the right that this title conferred on Manresa to be represented in *Corts* by two procurators, instead of the single procurator that was allowed to a *villa*.[91] The capitals of the *Corts* of 1311 are addressed first to the cities of Lleida, Tortosa, Terragona and Girona, and then to the towns of Manresa, Vilafranca, Cervera, Tarraga, Montblanch, and so forth. In 1315, however, there were not one but two new additions to the list of cities: Manresa and its rival city of Vic were both elevated at the same time.[92] Left behind, however, were similarly

89 Sarret i Arbós, *Historia de Manresa*, vol. I, p. 21.

90 This was done because the Bishop feared for his revenue from the parish of Sallent. The incident is described in EPLV, 174–5. The best modern description of the construction of the *sèquia* is to be found in EPLV, 173–84. Sarret devoted an entire volume to elaborating on its construction. Joaquim Sarret i Arbós, *La cequia de Manresa* (Manresa, 1906).

91 For Manresa as firmly established as a member city of the Catalan *braç reial* by 1323, see Sesma Muñoz, 'La población urbana en la Corona de Aragón', p. 165.

92 For 1311: *Cortes*, I-1, 208; for 1315: *Cortes*, I-1, 237.

Table 2.1 *The number of officials in municipal government posts*[93]

	1315	1323	1356	1365	1369	1393
Consellers	4	6	4	4	4	4
Jurats	?	30	?	16	30	25
Consellers Special	?	36	?	20	34	29
Consellers General	?	?	?	?	?	75

sized cities, such as Vilafranca and Cervera.[94] Although Vic's elevation to a *civitas* at this time has not been generally remarked upon, it seems clear that the citizens of Vic would not have tolerated the elevation of Manresa unless their own city, which after all did have a bishop, was granted a similar status. It may have been the case that the elevation of Manresa had begun with a request by the citizens of Vic to have their city elevated, which in turn prompted a furious archival search and a string of similar petitions from Manresa itself.[95] All the same, the citizens of Vic must have resented Manresa's elevation more than most Catalans, since the elevation implied some loss of honour to Vic.

Finally, along with the elevation, Jaume granted to Manresan citizens the right not to be stripped of their horses, weapons, beds, strongboxes, or other important items because of indebtedness.[96] This right to bear arms even in poverty was a quasi-noble privilege, one which now distinguished the citizens from the mass of commoners in Catalonia and the Bages. This unprecedented mark of distinction was further bolstered by the creation of the Manresan consulate, to which we shall now turn.

THE STRUCTURE OF THE MANRESAN COUNCIL, 1315–1415

Table 2.1 shows the evolution of the Manresan town council over the course of the fourteenth century. All of these offices and councils will

93 Sources: 1315: LV, 414. 1323: EPLV, 99–100. MC 1354.3.31 lists five *consellers*, presumably of six. By the next list, in MC 1356.10.6, there were only four *consellers*. 1365: MC 1365.4.1. 1369: MC 1369.4.1(?). 1393: LV, 322–45.

Notes: The numbers of officeholders in the 1323 system were confirmed in 1346. See EPLV, 414.

94 Note that the much larger city of Perpignan was at this time part of the Kingdom of Mallorca, and was only reincorporated into Catalonia after 1344.

95 For example, the elevation is not mentioned in Eduardo Junyent, *La ciutat de Vic i la seva historia*, (Vic, 1976).

96 LV, 91–2.

be addressed in the succeeding pages, but it is worth enumerating their relationships to one another at the outset. The highest municipal office was that of the consul (Catalan *conseller*); there were between four and six of these at various times during the century. In addition, there was a larger number of *jurats*, whose primary function was to assist the consuls; they were also present to mitigate against the creation of too closed an oligarchy amongst the consuls, and to render the entire governing process somewhat more participatory, democratic, and legitimate in the eyes of the citizenry. Together, the consuls and *jurats* made up a body known as the *consell special*. It was legally required, at least after 1323, that a quorum of consuls and *jurats* must be present in order for civic business to be addressed. The *consell special* handled the vast majority of civic business during the fourteenth century, with the consuls serving as the chief executives and chief representatives of the town both in internal and external business. In addition to the *consell special*, there was also a '*consell general*'. This was the survival of an older tradition, which held that civic business was only truly legitimate if it was approved by a large body of the citizens of Manresa – perhaps even the entire body of citizens. The issue of citizenship is taken up in the next chapter, but by 1400, at least, only about 16 per cent of the wealthiest male inhabitants of Manresa were accorded the title 'citizen'.[97] During the fourteenth century, the authority of the *consell general* was seldom invoked, and it is likely that men in the *consell special* were for the most part inclined to see the notion of a *consell general* settle into desuetude. The concept of a *consell general* was however given a boost in the 1393 reforms of Joan I, which for the first time in a century mandated a specific number of men be appointed to a *consell general* – in this case seventy-five.[98] This number, which was supposed to be in addition to the twenty-nine men in the

[97] Source: LM.

[98] These reforms are found in LV, 322–45. They were part of a series of urban reforms promulgated soon after Joan I came to the throne in 1387, as part of the King's attempt to deal with urban unrest resulting from social and economic problems between contending groups of urban elites. These stemmed from the crisis of the 1360s and 1370s, but became more pronounced after the economic difficulties of the 1370s and early 1380s in particular. Vilar tied these too closely to the pogroms of 1391. Pierre Vilar, 'Le déclin catalan du bas Moyen Age: Hypothèses sur sa chronologie', *Estudios de Historia Moderna*, 6 (1956–9), 5–48, at 20–1. For another overview of these difficulties, see Claude Carrère, *Barcelone: Centre économique à l'époque des difficultés 1380–1462* , vol. II, (Paris, 1967), pp. 655–724. The best modern treatment of these are found in Carme Batlle, *Historia de Catalunya*, vol. III: *L'Expansio baixmedieval (segles XIII–XV)*, Historia de Catalunya 3 (Barcelona, 1998), pp. 271–3, esp. pp. 242–3. The effects of the *censal* system on similar reforms are argued for Valencia in Rafael Narbona Vizcaíno and Enrique Cruselles Gómez, 'Espacios económicos y sociedad política en la Valencia del siglo XV', *Revista d'Història Medieval*, 9 (1998), 193–214. For these reforms at Manresa, see LV, 322–45, and for a discussion of this see EPLV, 411–36.

consell special, theoretically placed nearly one-fifth of all male Manresan householders in an official government capacity. In reality, however, the newly reconstituted *consell general* hardly ever met as a body, and effective power continued to be monopolized primarily by the consuls, and to a lesser degree by the *consell special* as a whole.

The creation of the Manresan consulate in 1315, then, was no mere change in form, but a move away from the collective egalitarianism of the *prohoms*, which in itself had been a step beyond the earlier concept of the *universitas*. From 1315 the existence of the consulship gave elites a platform from which they could challenge the powers and prestige of the regional lower nobility such as the Talamancas. The *consellers* were now distinguished by the title *venerabilis*, the same title used by knights, and this honour was retained by ex-*consellers* for life. The issue of knightly and consular parity would have been especially piquant because, as was the case in Barcelona and the other Catalan cities, knights were customarily banned from holding public office in Manresa.[99] The origins of this custom remain obscure, but not one fourteenth-century *conseller* or *jurat* was a knight, with the exception of one member of the de Talamanca family, who appears on a conciliar list during the chaotic months succeeding the Black Death.[100] This custom was long one of the strongest bulwarks of the Catalan 'bourgeoisie', which enjoyed a monopoly of urban consulates across the province until the early sixteenth century.[101] In addition, there can be found relatively little intramural struggle between knights and burghers in Manresa during the fourteenth century.[102] Part of the reason for this lies in the fact that very few knights lived within the city walls at all: only two families, the de Talamanca and the de Manresa, figure in the *Manuales Concilii* as property holders within the city.[103] The property taxes levied for the construction of the city walls in the late 1360s and

[99] No direct evidence for the banning of knights from Catalan urban government during the later medieval period has come to light, but the fact that no knights participated in the Barcelona government prior to the end of the fifteenth century, or in Manresa, Cervera, Girona, or other towns that have been studied, means that such a custom was definitely enforced. For the eventual introduction of knights into the Barcelona *Consell de Cent*, see Josep Fernández Trabal, 'De "prohoms" a "honrats": Orígenes y justificación de la nobleza de los ciudadanos honrados de Catalunya', *Hidalguía: La Revista De Genealogía, Nobleza y Armas*, 49:295 (2002), 841–75.

[100] MC 1349.8.11. [101] Amelang, *Honored Citizens*, pp. 28–32. [102] See Chapter 5.

[103] These two families and their supporters were at loggerheads in 1371, and the fighting amongst their supporters caused consternation on the city council; see MC 1371.11.25. The source of the conflict lay in the fact that the city had been granted authority to collect a tax from all property holders, including knights, for use in constructing the city walls. For Francesc de Manresa's consent to pay, see MC 1371.1.31. For a tax refund for the Talamancas, granted four days after the strife was noted, see MC 1371.11.29. No other knights were taxed, strongly suggesting that no other knightly families held property within the city.

early 1370s would almost certainly have revealed other knights, if they held land or owned houses in town. While conflicts did erupt between the Manresan burghers and their castellan neighbours from time to time, particularly during the 1360s and 1370s, the struggles appear to have been largely external to civic politics. There is little evidence, in other words, of internal partisanship, and this may well be the result of the fact that some of the older families with knightly ties, such as the Casanovas, had seen their wealth and influence shrink by mid-century.[104] There seems to have been a distancing between knightly and burgher culture after the Black Death, which cut off so many long-standing alliances based on proximity, marriage alliance, and economic cooperation.[105] Together, this helped to foster a sense by the later fourteenth century that the castellans were actively foreign to Manresa, rather than natural or compelling faction leaders.

The contrast between the situation in the Catalan cities and the Valencian cities thus differed quite radically. Whereas in Manresa, there was no obvious Type C 'class struggle' between nobles and commoners over civic governance, authors such as Narbona Vizcaíno have presented a picture of late medieval Valencian civic politics in which such a struggle between knights and burghers was the paramount fact of urban political life.[106] The class divisions in Castilan urban government were even more marked: since Alfonso X in the mid-thirteenth century granted tax exemption to the nobility, there grew up in the towns a class of '*caballeros villanos*', or urban knights, who were not only tax exempt, but who also came to claim a monopoly of civic office.[107] The result was a radical division between nobles and commoners within the urban milieu, which went a long way towards stifling the formation of a bourgeois mentality in the late medieval Castilian cities.[108] The Manresan elites were therefore, along with other Catalan urban elites, some of the most free, in terms of freedom from aristocratic opposition and oppression, of any urban elites in the Iberian Peninsula. Fourteenth-century Catalan cities were thus particularly conducive to the formation of a non-noble, 'middle-class' ascendancy, in the Type C sense. A combination of an

104 See Table 3.1.

105 This story, pieced together from the Talamanca volumes mentioned above and in the bibliography, is told in a forthcoming chapter.

106 Rafael Narbona Vizcaino, *Valencia, municipio medieval: Poder politico y luchas ciudadanas, (1239–1418)* (Valencia, 1995).

107 Teofilo F. Ruiz, *Spain's Centuries of Crisis: 1300–1474* (Oxford, 2011), p. 25.

108 The 'revolt of the *communeros*' was a famous instance of Castilian burghers attempting to assert their collective rights; although only some of the sentiment expressed was commoner vs. noble. See Stephen Haliczer, *The Comuneros of Castile: The Forging of a Revolution, 1475–1521* (Madison, WI, 1981).

urban consulate, and an effective prohibition against noble interference in local government, were foundational to the 'bourgeois' directions taken by Manresan society during the fourteenth century.

After the conciliar regime was established in 1315, Manresa's four *consellers* made up the city's highest legislative and executive body, although their powers were shared with the larger body of the *jurats*. Thus, the Manresan government was modelled after the Barcelona government, which since the later thirteenth century also had an executive body of between four and six consuls, advised by a larger legislative body known as the *Consell de Cent*.[109] The precise interaction between these two groups at Manresa does not really come out in the council records, although there is some indication that the relative powers of the two bodies waxed and waned over the course of the century.[110] It has been noted that the Manresan council was kept under the watchful eye of the bailiff or his lieutenant, who had a duty to 'approve' all of the acts of the council, or object to them in the name of the king if they seemed prejudicial to royal interests. This policy was not reserved to Manresa, but has also been observed for Cervera, and therefore is likely to have been a deliberate facet of Jaume II's policy regarding his new municipal regimes.[111] The only leeway open to the councillors in this matter might have lain in the fact that the lieutenant bailiff was often a local man, and so in the event of a dispute with the bailiff, the lieutenant bailiff's signature could sometimes be sought instead.[112] Throughout the fourteenth century, *consellers* served one-year terms of office, beginning and ending with the municipal elections traditionally held on 1 April. There are occasional indications in the records that the *consellers* were not all equal in prestige: Barcelona is known to have had a *conseller en cap* (or 'head consul') and certain Manresan documents suggest that specific incoming councillors were replacing specific outgoing ones.[113] This might indicate a ranking system that is not explicitly alluded to in most Catalan civic constitutions.

Although, as it seems from their surviving records, one of the primary preoccupations of the *consellers* of Barcelona was to publish *banns*, which included decrees on the conduct of civic life, the *consellers* of Manresa very seldom imposed such moral or procedural decrees upon their fellow

109 Ferrer Mallol, 'Les corts de Catalunya i la creació de la Diputació del General o Generalitat en el marc de la guerra amb Castella (1359–1369)', p. 532.

110 This is discussed at length in Chapter 5.

111 Turull, *La configuració juridica*, pp. 133–4.

112 Pere Nadal was quite good at using the office of the *sotsbatlle* to further the interests of the councillors, while simultaneously remaining indispensable to the various royally-appointed bailiffs. E.g., MC 1375.4.4, MC 1375.4.28.

113 MC 1365.4.1.

citizens, even though they had the power to do so.[114] In a rare instance, which took place soon after the Black Death, the council decreed that a certain square located 'between the chapel of St Martin and the house of the canons of Santa Maria' would be walled off and gated.[115] This was done because the 'separate and enclosed' nature of the square had facilitated the dumping there of many 'vile and dirty substances' at night; further, according to rumour, many 'fornications and other sins' had occurred there; and finally, the square was very dangerous, and the safety of those crossing it could not easily be provided for. After such a description, it is difficult not to agree that enclosing this square was a wise step – although one might wonder how the town cesspit could also prove to be an alluring place for nocturnal trysts. The contrast with many contemporary urban governments is worth a moment's reflection: why did the Manresan councillors invoke their moral authority so seldom? Is their lack of pastoralism merely an expression of the size of the town? Was Manresa relatively free from difficult social problems? It is believed that the city had in excess of 5000 inhabitants prior to the Black Death, and perhaps half that number afterwards.[116] How does Manresa compare with other urban governments, ruling towns of a similar size, with regard to the frequency of social control statutes? Relatively little has been written for Catalonia, or for other medium-sized southern European towns, which can provide a direct comparison. The plague had virtually wiped out the Jewish community of Manresa, and thus a potential source of social tension and self-consciousness amongst the Manresan governors.[117] Also, the city was becoming more economically egalitarian, as wages shot up and land prices stagnated.[118] Was this

[114] A significant portion of the fourteenth-century Barcelona councillors' books are taken up with the publication of '*banns*' regulating various aspects of civic life.

[115] MC 1355.2.14. '*multe sordities et immunditie, puta, stercora et egestiones et alia sordida et fetida de nocte ponuntur. Et prout relacione plurimum se audivisse dixerunt fornicaciones et alia peccata propter loci occultacionem de nocte ibidem comititur, que iuxta ecclesiam fieri praesertim in loce ita sibi coniuncto est orrendum et etiam execrandum et ne deinceps fiat modis omnibus providendum. Attendens eciam ut dixerunt quod dictus locus propter sui separacionem et occultacionem est multum periculosus quia possent ibi perari insidie vicinis et eciam secus locum ipsum transeuntibus que commode et sine difficultate providere non possent.*' Mark Meyerson, in *Jews in an Iberian Frontier Kingdom*, p. 267, has noted that Valencian civic elites 'deemed it essential to distance Christians from all temptations and all sources of sin' after the Black Death and successive plagues, since, in part, they viewed the plagues as punishments from God. Note the conflation of spiritual sin and physical pollution.

[116] For Manresan demography in the fourteenth and fifteenth centuries, see Table 7.1, and relevant discussion.

[117] Manresa was thus not a locus of the sort of ritual violence described in David Nirenberg, *Communities of Violence: Persecution of Minorities in the Middle Ages* (Princeton, NJ, 1996), e.g., pp. 200–30.

[118] This theme is discussed at length in Chapter 7.

increasing homogeneity enough to mute social tension? Or was the lack of moral legislation simply the result of a relaxed attitude towards governance on the part of the Manresan patriciate? The benign nature of Manresan conciliar legislation suggests that, in general, the relationship between governors and governed at Manresa was more akin to what the 'consensual', rather than the 'confrontational', school of medieval English urban historiography would argue.[119]

Apart from their seldom-invoked moral authority, other powers of the councillors included naming procurators to conduct civic business with other authorities, naming syndics to represent the city at *Corts*, arranging the collection of taxes, and supervising the city's treasury. They also appointed various lesser civic officials. The councillors usually directed civic projects such as the building of the city walls, churches, and the *sèquia*. During emergencies, the councillors directed relief efforts such as the stockpiling of grain, and in 1337 they even ordered the entire city to partake in a pilgrimage to Montserrat in order to pray for rain. On that occasion, several leading citizens of the town donated between five and twenty *sous* each in order to help defray the costs of this day-long journey for the city's poor.[120] In extreme circumstances, the councillors proved capable of taking executive powers into their own hands, including that of incarceration, and they could also arrogate certain judicial functions to themselves.[121] Thus, while their powers in peacetime remained relatively circumscribed, they nonetheless were rapidly accepted as the natural leaders of the town as a *universitas* in times of crisis, and so their office could become a focal point for local executive power. On the other hand, during the White Company invasion scare of the 1360s and 1370s, Pere III proved willing to appoint a royal captain with a *plentitudinem potestatis*, who more or less rode roughshod over the powers of the councillors.[122] Thus, the powers of the councillors must be seen in terms of a larger continuum of royal, regional, and local power.

Between 1315 and 1323 the number of consuls remained at four, one for each quarter of the city. Perhaps as a measure to limit rivalries between the city's quarters, in 1323 Jaume II authorized an increase from four to six councillors, who were elected by profession rather

119 This trend is analysed in Peter Fleming, 'Telling Tales of Oligarchy in the Late Medieval Town', in Michael Hicks (ed.), *The Fifteenth Century*, vol. II: *Revolution and Consumption in Medieval England* (Woodbridge, Suffolk, 2001), pp. 177–93; Heather Swanson, *Medieval British Towns* (Basingstoke, 1999), pp. 89–96, and also in Shaw, 'Social Networks'.

120 MC 1337.3.22. Pere (II) Sarta, who was not especially wealthy, gave 5 *sous*. Berenguer Amargos gave 20 *sous*.

121 These functions of the council are detailed in Chapter 5.

122 For the appointment of the captain, see MC 1374.5.13.

than by quarter. They were to be aided by 30 *jurats*, on the model promulgated for Cervera in 1311.[123] Thus, in an early example of what would become standard in Catalonia during the fifteenth century, the 1323 system provided for two *consellers* to be elected from each of the city's three classes, or 'hands'.[124] The Catalan term '*mà*' means 'hand', or, figuratively 'faction'; the three hands were known as the *mà maior*, the *mà mitjana*, and the *mà menor* (greater, middling, and lesser). Ten of the thirty *jurats* were also supposed to be chosen from each hand. However, the hands system seems quickly to have fallen into disuse, and for most of the fourteenth century neither the 'hands' nor the professions of the consuls were recorded in the council manuals. It also cannot be concluded with certainty that these early 'hands' corresponded to the occupational groups of the *rentiers*, merchants, and *menestrals*, as they would do after 1393.[125] The question of how open or closed was the Manresan system, and who actually filled civic office, is an important one for any urban history and so will be addressed in detail in the next chapter. At that time it will be demonstrated that, for most of the century, the consuls' seats were reserved only to the city's wealthiest men, while jurats' chairs were tenable by men who were solidly upper middle class (in the Type B sense), or wealthier. In any event, the form, if not the spirit, of the 1323 system persisted until 1346, when election procedures were changed slightly.[126] Between 1348 and 1351 the Manresan town government records suffer an almost complete hiatus due to the upheavals of the Black Death. Formal record-keeping began again in 1351, and after 1355, the town council reverted to a four consul system.[127]

Also in 1351, the city of Manresa became part of the Duchy of Girona, an apanage created for King Pere's newly born son the crown prince, and one which he intended to become the traditional territory of the crown prince of Aragon.[128] In this Pere was attempting to emulate the creation of the principality of Wales in England; the most immediate precedent was the very recent creation of the Dauphiné in France in 1350. While the prince was still a youth the Duchy of Girona did not actively figure in the affairs of Manresan citizens, but between the late 1360s, when

[123] Manresa 1323: EPLV, 99–100. For the 1311 system of Cervera, see Turull, *El règim municipal de Paeria*, p. 19.

[124] Carme Batlle Gallart and Joan Josep Busqueta Riu, 'Las familias de la alta burguesía en el municipio de Barcelona (siglo XIII)', *Anuario de Estudios Medievales*, 16 (1986), 81–92; Sabaté, 'Ejes vertebradores de la oligarquía urbana en Cataluña', pp. 137–8.

[125] See below, pp. 55ff.

[126] EPLV, 414.

[127] From MC 1355.4.6 onward, no more than four councillors are named for any given year.

[128] A study of the duchy and its institutions during the fourteenth century is sorely needed. For a description of the foundation of the duchy and its effects on Manresan government, see EPLV, 206–19.

prince Joan began to exercise governmental authority in his own right, and his accession in 1387, the office became palpably significant to the government and society of Manresa. During these two decades, certain judicial appeals were made to the Duke of Girona rather than to the King, and the Duke would sometimes take an active role in the governance of the city.[129] King Pere, however, always kept a close eye on events, and so Manresa did not ever lose the semblance of being an integral part of the royal patrimony; the Duke's authority only ever supplemented that of the king, rather than challenging or eclipsing it in any serious way. Thus, the erection of the Duchy of Girona created one more layer of government and bureaucracy in a state which was rapidly maturing towards early modern levels of governance. In general, the existence of the Duchy had a positive effect on the lives of the Manresan elites, since it gave talented Manresan citizens access to a number of high-paying, high prestige jobs in the Duke's court, which were easier to obtain than royal offices, due to a smaller pool of competitors.[130]

Other more purely local changes occurred in the Manresan civic government in the wake of the Black Death. In 1352, the *consellers* successfully petitioned the king to declare that no butchers or bakers would be allowed to sit as *consellers* or *jurats*. This was ostensibly done in response to the demographic losses incurred during Black Death, under the principle that those who provided the city's sustenance should not be distracted from their work by civic duties.[131] In August 1362, as a second wave of plague was creating the city's first real demographic crisis, the *consellers* petitioned the king for two further limitations on municipal office.[132] In one document, it was decreed that no one could be *conseller* unless he had lived in the city for five years.[133] This decree, a clear response to the shifting demographics and increased mobility of these decades, is actually quite lenient when one peers beneath the surface. In fact *jurats* are not mentioned at all, and so a person of sufficient status (and wealth) could presumably hope to be a *jurat* almost immediately upon moving to the city. The stricture of a minimum five-year residence for *consellers* shows some concern that the holders of the city's highest office have

129 For an appeal to the duke, see FT2 1372.9.25; for the duke sending a letter to the councillors of Manresa regarding the city's walls, see MC 1367.6.18.

130 For the Manresan Berenguer Sarta's career in the Duke's scrivany, see e.g., MC 1372.12.14. For Jaume Sarta's son-in-law as a (financial) officer of the duke, see JS 1377.2.10.

131 Marc Torras makes this case in EPLV, 229–38. But butchers were often excluded from late medieval civic officeholding, due to the bloody and taboo nature of their work. For this in England see Gervase Rosser, 'Urban Culture and the Church 1300–1540', in David M. Palliser (ed.), *The Cambridge Urban History of Britain*, vol. I: *600–1540* (Cambridge, 2000), pp. 335–69, at pp. 340–1.

132 For the demographic crises see Chapter 7.

133 LV, 239.

a significant relationship with the city, but at the same time it shows a real willingness to welcome new families into the highest ranks of the patriciate. The statute also shows a certain optimism that wealthy men would be moving into the city with the aim of putting down roots there. How often this actually happened is hard to discern, though in the longer term, ongoing demographic losses meant that emigration was increasingly rare as the fifteenth century began. Some new families did make an appearance on the conciliar lists in the 1390s, and other immigrants are attested in the *Liber Manifesti*, so the law may have had some relevance to actual practice.[134] Regardless, the relatively light restrictions of this law do suggest that by 1362 the civic elite considered itself to be shrinking, and in need of augmentation by outside men of sufficient wealth and status.

A second document dating from the crisis of August 1362 stated that no scribe, whether he worked for the public scrivany, or for the scrivanies of the *veguer* or *batlle*, was to be *conseller* or *jurat* while he held such a post.[135] Also, no one holding fiscal office in the city was eligible to be a *jurat* or *conseller*. In addition to the implications that scribes were in short supply after this second wave of plague, the act can be seen as a response to the explosion of paperwork that had been created by the city's sale of record numbers of *censals* during the 1358–62 period, as the Castilian war intensified. The council manuals contain several references to an increased need for treasurers and auditors during these years, and just as the bakers and butchers had been essential in a time of epidemic and potential famine, accountants and treasurers now assumed greater importance in an era of unprecedented *censal* debt. Note that unlike butchers, the scribes and fiscal officers were allowed to be *consellers* and *jurats* once they left office. While the legislation against suggests that it was the men themselves who were being kept from office, the legislation regarding scribes and treasurers is definitely practical in nature. Apart from these strictures, the highest office in the city remained theoretically available to (non-Jewish) citizens of any profession, although it has been pointed out that in practice only the very wealthy became consuls.[136] In 1364–5, a further reorganization of the city's government appears to have taken place in conditions of some social tension within the council, and it is possible that the consuls were briefly forced to share power, on an equal basis, with the *jurats*.[137] If such a radical change did occur, the town

[134] See especially Table 3.1 for the conciliar lists.

[135] LV, 240–1.

[136] This theme is taken up in Chapter 3.

[137] MC 1365.4.1. For an example of the 'special council' mandating the consuls to act see MC 1365.5.2; for majority decision in the 'special council' see MC 1365.4.30. See Chapter 5, pp. 142–3.

government had returned to a more 'normal' configuration by 1369 at the latest.[138]

The final change to the conciliar regime of the fourteenth century came in 1393, when after a series of unrests Joan I promulgated a series of reforms in urban governments across Catalonia.[139] Joan's changes are often seen as having favoured more egalitarian elements in the cities, by allowing the *menestrals*, or 'artisans' to hold one-third of the seats on the *Consell de Cent* in Barcelona.[140] The *menestrals* were now definitively classified as members of the *mà menor*, however, while the *rentiers* and a few other elite citizens such as lawyers were classified as members of the *mà major*, and the city's merchants were, on the whole, classified as members of the *mà mitjana*. Each hand, in fact, was given a one-third representation on the council at Barcelona under Joan's system. The same system was likewise implemented at Manresa. Here, however, it is possible to combine an analysis of the 1408 *Liber Manifesti* with the town council manuals, in order to determine precisely who was serving on the Manresan council, and what were their occupations and relative wealth. The details of this analysis will be left to later chapters, but it can be said that the *menestrals* who held the consuls' office at Manresa were hardly working-class journeymen, or even small shopkeepers. Despite the fact that the *menestrals* were classified as belonging to a 'third hand' of Manresan society, those who held office were extremely wealthy wholesale capitalists, whose wealth often rivalled or exceeded the members who sat for the *mà major* and the *mà mitjana*. Therefore, the reforms of Joan I should not be taken as a concession to the working or middling classes of Catalan urban society, except perhaps insofar as an admission of the wealthiest 'craftsmen' may have mitigated a sense of exclusion previously felt by urban craftsmen. This assumes that craftsmen would have preferred wealthy members of their own number to hold office, rather than none at all, and it also assumes that, prior to 1393, even the wealthiest craftsmen had been habitually excluded from urban office due to the nature of their occupations. At Manresa, there is at present no evidence for either point.

Even if the new rules did appease some less wealthy citizens' desire to see members of their own profession represented on the town councils, there is also evidence that King Joan's rules were in line with a more general trend, occurring at this time in cities across Western Europe, towards

[138] MC 1369.4.1. [139] This has been discussed above; see n. 98.

[140] For a political analysis of the relations between the crown and the Barcelona government between 1386 and 1393, see Carmen Batlle, *La crisis social y económica de Barcelona a mediados del siglo XV*, vol. I (Barcelona, 1973), pp. 80–130.

an increasing 'closedness' amongst urban councils.[141] Whether this was primarily the result of concurrent political policy, or whether politics were merely responding to an economic downturn which decreased upward mobility, is one of the critical questions in European urban history of the later fourteenth century.[142] At Manresa, the 1393 system kept the number of *consellers* at four, and the 'hands' system based on *rentiers* ('citizens'), merchants, and *menestrals* was made much more explicit. As has been seen in England, an increasing rationalization of office, accompanied by a certain increase in civic pomp, can be seen at Manresa after the 1380s, and was therefore also part of a general European trend.[143] It will be demonstrated later that the legislation implemented by Joan I helped to create a sense of exclusivity amongst Catalan urban elites, and it therefore helped to create a sense of Type-D class exclusiveness, and a closing of the Catalan urban oligarchies over the course of the fifteenth century.[144]

THE *JURATS* AND LOWER URBAN OFFICIALS

While the preceding discussion has concentrated mostly on the consuls, who were the city's highest-ranking representatives, something should also be said of the second-highest ranking officials, the *jurats*. Although relatively little is known about the function of their office, it is clear that the *jurats* stood at some distance from the *consellers* in terms of prestige. Not only were they significantly less wealthy than the *consellers* on average, but they were not granted any formal title as the result of their office.[145] Because no constitution has survived from 1315, the exact number of *jurats* who served during the 1315–23 period is not known. There might conceivably been no *jurats* between 1315 and 1323, since Max Turull records that in Cervera there had been no *jurats* prior to 1311,

141 For this in Florence, see David Herlihy, 'The Rulers of Florence, 1282–1530', in A. Molho et al. (eds.), *City States in Classical Antiquity*, pp.197-221; and in Herlihy, *Women, Family and Society in Medieval Europe: Historical Essays, 1978–1991* (Providence, RI, 1995), pp. 353–80; and Kent, 'Power of Elites', p. 167.

142 This 'loss of nerve' idea forms the principal argument in Jaume Aurell i Cardona, *Els mercaders catalans al quatre-cents: Mutació de valors i procés d'artistocratització a Barcelona, 1370–1470* (Barcelona, 1996). Aurell was undoubtedly influenced by the older and still unchallenged argument to be found in Benjamin Z. Kedar, *Merchants in Crisis: Genoese and Venetian Men of Affairs and the Fourteenth Century Depression* (New Haven, CT, 1977).

143 Ruth H. Frost, 'The Urban Elite', in Carole Rawcliffe and Richard Wilson (eds.), *Medieval Norwich* (London, 2004), pp. 235–53, at 236–8.

144 This is noted by Guilleré, 'Les élites urbaines Catalanes à la fin du moyen age', p. 275.

145 For the wealth gap between *consellers* and *jurats* see Table 3.6 (a and b).

but only *consellers*.[146] Turull argues that the *jurats* had been introduced into Cervera in 1311 by Jaume II in order to break a narrow oligarchy that had developed around the office of the *consellers*. The councils of *jurats* were therefore created in order to ensure broader representation in civic politics. In Manresa, as has been mentioned, the *jurats* and *consellers* together made up a body known as the *consell special*. This was distinct from the *consell general*, a much larger body derived from earlier citizen assemblies which during the fourteenth century almost never gathered in a formal assembly. It is believed that the *jurats* of the smaller towns served a similar function to the *Consell de Cent* of Barcelona, which was to advise the *consellers*, and occasionally act as a check on their powers.[147] It is true that there are no meetings recorded in the fourteenth-century council manuals in which the *consellers* met without the *jurats*, meaning that a certain number of *jurats* were required in order to form a quorum.

Further scrutiny of the manuals will likely reveal periods in which the powers of the *jurats* vis-à-vis the *consellers* waxed and waned. Perhaps the most obvious instance, already hinted at, was the reform of 1365, which occurred almost immediately following the 1 April election. This reform appears to have strengthened the powers of the *jurats*, even though the same reform cut their number in half. In an act dated 5 April 1365, the *consell special*, which now included sixteen *jurats* and four *consellers*, mandated that no money could be dispensed by the town's *clavarius*, or treasurer, without their approval. Many acts in the months following April 1365 show the *consell special* ordering the *consellers* to perform various executive tasks, which would indicate that the *consell special*, rather than the *consellers*, now pretended to hold the ultimate authority in the city. This is important because it means that the vote of each *jurat* was now equal to the vote of a consul. The *consell special* even began to write as though they had power over the city's royal bailiff. One such entry runs: 'the *consellers* of the *consell special* require the *consellers* (i.e., the consuls) to require the bailiff to compel the people to pay the new weekly tax'. This significant and novel tax was being implemented in order to cover the city's *censal* debts and was not at all popular.[148] But it was not only the *consell special* whose powers were augmented in the spring of 1365. Another entry ascribes a similar authority to the entire *consell general*, an older, much larger body of citizens whose power now temporarily came back to the fore. In fact, this entry was written five days before

[146] Confusingly, Cervera's *consellers* were called *jurats* and their *jurats* were called *consellers*. Even more confusingly, the Cerveran *consellers* had been called *paers* prior to 1311. I have here described the Cerveran government utilizing Manresan terms, for the sake of simplicity. See Turull i Rubinat, *La configuració juridica*, pp. 130–1.

[147] See *ibid.*, p. 133.

[148] MC 1365.5.7.

the previously quoted entry, and constitutes an earlier draft of the same act. In it, the *consell general* mandated that the money from the 'weekly tax' would go to pay *censals and violaris*, and the *consell general* ordered the *consellers* (consuls) to talk to the bailiff about enforcing the collection of the tax.[149] This topsy-turvy situation was symptomatic of the somewhat 'revolutionary' mentality which was occurring in civic life during the Castilian war and its aftermath, roughly from 1359 to the 1370s. Although the general sense of upheaval lasted throughout this period, the clear ascendancy of the *jurats* was to prove much shorter lived. In the council manuals, the rhetorical ascendancy of the *jurats* already begins to peter out during the fall of 1365, and it disappears from the records altogether after the elections of 1367. The political events of these years, however, form the subject of a later chapter.

The electoral system implemented by Jaume II in 1323, with its body of *jurats* to augment the *consellers*, must generally be judged a success in terms of limiting political and factional rivalry within the city government. For most of the fourteenth century, there were very few occasions in which any one man was able to monopolize the office of *conseller* in the way that the *consellers* of Cervera had done prior to 1311.[150] The only period in which a particular *conseller* dominated civic politics was during the 1370s, when Francesc Nerell, a nominal *rentier* of merchant stock, was elected for an unprecedented three terms in a row between 1369 and 1371, followed by terms in 1373, 1376, 1378, and 1382.[151] Once more, the Manresan political situation, which discouraged particular individuals from dominating civic politics, is similar to what has been found in contemporary English cities, and is likely a function of the effectiveness of royal power, which generally sought to avoid such monopolization.[152] Like the ascendancy of the *jurats*, the dominance of Francesc Nerell also came during the particularly 'revolutionary' period of the 1370s, when urban regimes in Catalonia and throughout Western Europe were experiencing a high point of populism – one which, speaking generally, would never again be reached in the context of urban government.[153] After the

149 MC 1365.5.2.

150 Turull i Rubinat, *La configuració jurídica*, pp. 130–2.

151 Source MC. The rubrics for the elections are recorded on or near 1 April of each year. For more on Nerell's career, see Chapter 5, esp. pp. 143ff.

152 Shaw, 'Social Networks', and David R. Carr, 'The Problem of Urban Patriciates: Office Holders in Fifteenth Century Salisbury', *Wiltshire Archaeological and Natural History Magazine*, 83 (1990), 118–35.

153 For this in general see Samuel K. Cohn Jr, *Lust for Liberty: The Politics of Social Revolt in Medieval Europe, 1200–1425* (Harvard, MA, 2008), pp. 3 and *passim*. For this in Florence see John M. Najemy, *A History of Florence 1200–1575* (Oxford, 2006), pp. 156–87. For this 'urban revolutionary fervour' from an English perspective see Pamela Nightingale, 'Capitalists, Crafts

mid-1370s, however, most of the sense of urgency that attended urban government through the 1360s and early 1370s began to fall away, and the government began to settle into the more orderly, indeed relatively dull, routine that it would maintain for most of the early fifteenth century.

Below the prestigious and occasionally turbulent level of politics amongst the *consellers* and the *jurats*, the crown and the city officials gradually discovered that political and fiscal innovation necessitated an increasingly specialized set of urban officials with well-defined roles. The fourteenth century at Manresa was a period of marked innovation, proliferation, and specialization of urban office; indeed it was a great age of bureaucratic articulation in cities and royal courts across Europe.[154] In 1300, there were almost no regularized urban offices at Manresa, whereas in 1400, these offices were numerous, distinct, and for the most part continued in use until modern times.[155] During the first part of the century, these offices were largely held ad hoc; for example, certain individuals would be sold the right to 'farm' (i.e., to collect, with the expectation of personal profit) a given tax, and the tax farmer might therefore be named the *clavarius* (key-keeper, or treasurer) of that tax, as can be seen in the case of Pere (II) Sarta in 1339.[156] The individual in question would be expected to render an account to the council upon the completion of his delegated task. Later on in the century, particularly after the Castilian war of 1356–75 and the concomitant evolution of the *censal* system put enormous strains on the fiscal system of the city, full-time treasurers became normative.[157] The *maestre racional* who emerged during the war was a financial professional in charge of managing the city's

and Constitutional Change in Late Fourteenth-century London', *Past & Present*, 124 (1989), 3–35.

154 This is argued in Benjamin Z. Kedar, 'The Genoese Notaries of 1382: The Anatomy of an Urban Occupational Group', in Harry A. Miskimin, David Herlihy, and A. L. Udovitch (eds.), *The Medieval City: In Honor of Robert S. Lopez* (New Haven, CT, 1977), pp. 73–94. For an increasingly complex financial administration in Genoa in the fourteenth century see Steven A. Epstein, *Genoa and the Genoese, 958–1528* (Chapel Hill, NC, 2001), pp. 233–6; also Kedar, 'Genoese Notaries'; and for Pistoia see David Herlihy, *Medieval and Renaissance Pistoia: The Social History of an Italian Town, 1200–1430* (New Haven, CT, 1967), pp. 231–8. Such an expansion of the urban bureaucracy across Western Europe was probably inevitable given the increase in fiscal sophistication that occurred during the fourteenth and fifteenth centuries, as described in M. Boone, K. Davids, and P. Janssens, *Urban Public Debts, Urban Government and the Market for Annuities in Western Europe (14th–18th Centuries)* (Turnhout, 2003). For a parallel process in England see Barrie Dobson, 'General survey 1300–1540', in David M. Palliser (ed.), *The Cambridge Urban History of Britain*, vol. I: *600–1540* (Cambridge, 2000), pp. 273–90 at 278–81 and pp. 287–8.

155 These are detailed for Manresa in Marc Torras Serra, 'Els consellers i altres càrrecs municipals de Manresa del segle XV'.

156 SF 1339 1k10. 157 This process is detailed in Chapter 5.

all-important public debt, and received a healthy salary for his efforts.[158] In this, the Catalans were clearly copying Italian innovations. The Genoese, for example, had set up their own *maestre racional* in 1339.[159]

In addition to their increasingly professionalized financial officers, the town maintained scribes, *operarios infra* and *extra civitatem*, *mustaçafs*, town criers and porters.[160] Scribes had also been employed in the local scrivanies of the bailiff and the town council since the early fourteenth century. The *operarios* were officials appointed by the town council whose job was to oversee all existing and ongoing public construction both within and without the city; the sphere of the *operarios extra civitatem* soon came to be seen as coterminous with the *vegueria* of Manresa.[161] Their important function of overseeing the conditions of public roads gave the citizens of Manresa a considerable say in the functioning of the trade arteries of the Bages – this often flew in the face of centuries of decentralizing feudal tradition. The *mustaçafs* were another urban official, originally borrowed from Islamic urban regimes, whose function was to oversee the smooth functioning of the civic markets. In addition, the *sotsveguer* (lieutenant vicar) and the *sotsbatlle* were often local men, who served as valuable liaisons between urban government and the courts of the appointed royal officials who were resident in town.[162] Because the *batlles* and *veguers* were often brought in from other parts of Catalonia, the services of a local man as lieutenant was both invaluable for the incoming appointee, and also helped local elites to feel as though they maintained some measure of influence over local royal administration. In general, the proliferation and regularization of urban offices over the course of the fourteenth century helped to ensure a professionalization of the bureaucracy, by providing an increased and continual demand for those with the skills of a notary, administrator, or an account-keeper. This bureaucratic 'revolution' (and the term is in this case at least somewhat justifiable) went hand in hand with a revolution in education amongst the urban elites of the fourteenth century. Whereas there is very little evidence to indicate that any but a handful of Manresan elites were literate and numerate in the thirteenth century, by the fourteenth century these skills were in much higher demand, if for no other reason than that Manresan society had

158 For the salaries of Manresan urban officials, see Table 7.6.

159 Epstein, *Genoa and the Genoese, 958–1528*, p. 233.

160 For an overview of urban officials in contemporary Lleida, see Jordi Bolòs i Masclans, *Dins les muralles de la ciutat: Carrers i oficis a la Lleida dels segles XIV i XV* (Lleida, 2008).

161 For the *operarios extra civitatem*, see LV, 99–100. Daileader, 'Town and Countryside in Northeastern Catalonia, 1267–c.1450', mentions similar officials in Perpignan, called 'sobrepostas de la horta', who appeared at roughly the same time; they were first mentioned in 1339.

162 For Bertrand Casanova as *sotsbatlle*, see MC 1359.1.30. For Pere Nadal being *sotsbatlle* while he was also the treasurer for the city, see MC 1375.4.4, MC 1375.4.28, and MC 1375.9.11.

gone from an oral to a written culture. This was part of a more general trend in later medieval Europe, which must be assigned a prominent role in helping to transform the world from a 'traditional' to a 'modern' regimen.[163]

CONCLUSIONS

From the political, as opposed to the economic, perspective, the crucial period of institutional formation for the Catalan cities was the sixty-year period between 1276 and 1336. As will be explained in Chapter 6, this transformation laid the foundation for the 'financial revolution' which would come between about 1320 and 1380. The clear relationship between these two transformations, and their collective significance for Catalan-Aragonese history, has not yet become a major topic of historiographical analysis. With respect to the Bages, it was during the period between 1276 and 1336 that the kings of Catalonia brought the local nobility to heel through the creation of a new vicarial court. At the same time, the Crown reclaimed its ancient rights to the bailiwick of Manresa, promulgated a series of economic decrees designed to increase burghers' ability to extract surplus value from the city and its surrounding territory, and created a new urban consulate giving citizens a chance to meet local nobles and clerical hierarchs on something like an even footing. The government of Manresa, despite undergoing a number of minor changes throughout the fourteenth century, remained essentially the same in institutional particulars, although the number of civic offices was multiplied, and the functions of these offices were made more explicit. The fact that there were no nobles in the civic government was perhaps the primary reason why there was relatively little civic strife over the course of the fourteenth century. A lack of a Type D class distinction amongst *rentiers*, merchants, and *menestrals* for most of the century also contributed to a general feeling of social inclusivity amongst the urban elites. This lack of distinction also extended to the rules for attaining political office, and contributed further to the relative lack of factionalism in the government. Of course, the presence of strong, effective royal power would be another reason for relative calm in the city – and the effectiveness of

163 This theme has received more attention from early modernists; it forms the backbone of such studies as Charles Tilly, *Coercion, Capital and European States: AD 990–1992*, revised (Oxford, 1992). See also Tilly and Blockmans, *Cities and the Rise of States in Europe, AD 1000 to 1800*. For a medievalist's assessment of the power of the emergent bureaucracy, see e.g., Daniel Lord Smail, 'Notaries, Courts, and the Legal Culture of Late Medieval Marseille', in Kathryn Reyerson and John Drendel (eds.), *Urban and Rural Communities in Medieval France: Provence and Languedoc, 1000–1500* (Leiden, 1998), pp. 23–50.

this power will be one of the principal themes of later chapters. A final contributing factor to the stability of urban government seems to have lain in the easy-going nature of the town government itself. The Manresan councillors were for the most part unconcerned with promulgating edicts relating to civic morals, even though it was perfectly within their power to do so. All of these factors combine to give the impression that, overall, Manresan government was much more one of consensus than of conflict.

This is not at all to say that Manresan political institutions, or the exercise of political power, remained stagnant during the course of the fourteenth century. Indeed, much of Chapters 4 and 5 is dedicated to showing how dramatically the urban political situation changed, particularly in the decades after the Black Death. For the present, it should be remarked that, although major institutional changes were rare after 1315, the degree of change over the long fourteenth century in almost every aspect of Manresan governance is striking. This reflected the changes in the city's physical appearance and architectural fabric, introduced at the beginning of this chapter. During the early part of the century, the citizens invested heavily in symbols of civic pride and booming trade. During the later part of the century, the city scrambled to surround itself with walls, which ended up being symbolic of an increasing compartmentalization, not only between city and countryside, but between increasingly disparate groups of urban citizens, who were being artificially segregated into ranks by intellectual fashion. In the political sphere, the offices of *conseller* and *jurat* went from being non-existent in 1300 to being well established by 1400, having over that time waxed and waned considerably in their respective spheres of influence. As will be detailed in Chapter 5, Manresan civic government also went from providing a good deal of public services earlier in the fourteenth century, to providing very few by century's end. This was particularly the result of the introduction of the *violari* and *censal*-system of government debt during the Castilian war, which successfully appropriated the majority of the city's revenue, until the *consellers* felt that they had almost no room in the budget for any sort of project outside of funding the debt. This worked in the interests of the *consellers* and other patrician elites, who could generally afford to pay private fees for doctors and schooling, and whose income was increasingly derived from debt shareholding. The introduction of this system also helped to 'tame' the councillors, by limiting their spheres of influence, as did an increasingly efficient royal bureaucracy, which was in part funded by the new bond system. Whereas the councillors of the early fourteenth century were essentially collective actors on a regional feudal playing field, by the later fourteenth century, they were increasingly becoming part of a 'state', which had moved beyond them. That the fifteenth-century Trastámara kings decided that they preferred to support regional nobles rather than urban elites was a matter of taste and policy which stood in sharp distinction to the House of Barcelona, and helped to further hasten the demise of the Manresan consulate as a politically viable force. These themes, however, will be taken up at greater lengths in subsequent chapters.

Chapter 3

A PORTRAIT OF THE MANRESAN PATRICIATE

INTRODUCTION: THE MANRESAN PATRICIATE AND 'CITIZENSHIP' IN THE LATE MIDDLE AGES

The previous chapter presented an overview of the primary political structures at Manresa. The most important civic officers were the consuls and the *jurats*, although they were always overshadowed by the presence of the *veguer* and the royal bailiff. During the course of the fourteenth century, the number of consuls varied between four and six, while the number of *jurats* varied between sixteen and thirty. Taken together, Manresa's consuls and *jurats* made up the *consell special*, a deliberative body which handled the vast majority of the city's business. It was shown that a major change took place in the structure of the council from 1393, when Joan I tied occupation to political eligibility, thus unwittingly creating a sharp and, from a Manresan point of view, unaccustomed cleavage amongst burghers who in previous decades had tended to think of themselves as a more or less unified bourgeoisie.[1] In Joan's schema, modelled on the one he had created at Barcelona, the seats on the council were reserved proportionally to members of three occupation-based 'hands'. The *mà major* (literally the 'Big Hand') consisted primarily of nominal *rentiers* and lawyers, while the *mà mitjana* (Medium Hand) consisted primarily of nominal merchants, and the *mà menor* (Little Hand) consisted primarily of nominal *menestrals*, or artisans. This chapter will present an overview of the families who held civic office, together with an analysis of the wealth, occupations, and pedigree of both the consuls and the *jurats*. In this way, this chapter can address some of the perennial questions regarding medieval office-holding, including how oligarchical or how democratic the government may have been at various levels, and whether wealth, family status, or occupation was the primary determinant of political success.

[1] The strongest evidence for this is the lack of occupational titles given to *consellers* before 1393.

This chapter will therefore serve to define an important segment, indeed the leading segment, of what we are calling the Manresan 'bourgeoisie'. In general, this term is here applied to those citizens who gained significant rights and had access to economic freedoms and advantages, as outlined in the previous chapter, which set them apart from the surrounding feudal world. They are thus distinct from non-citizens who were generally either feudal tenants, or else part of a small minority of feudal lords or clergy. But those who were thought of by important men as 'burghers' tended to be also those burghers who held civic office: this more specific group we call the 'patriciate'.

As for the term 'elite', this can best be used to indicate the economically ascendant members of Manresan society without reference to office: they would thus constitute a Type B (wealth-based) class, rather than a Type D (office-based) class. Our concern, however, now lies with what we are calling Type D distinctions, and indeed, it will be shown that, since wealth was an important determinant of access to office, the two are interwoven. While those who held consulships were generally wealthier and of a higher social status than mere *jurats*, the term 'patriciate' will be applied to both groups. The term patriciate can also be extended to the households of these office-holders, and to a lesser extent the households of relatives who benefited from their kinsmen's status. In some instances, the benefits to related householders were obvious: Romeu Sarta, for example, became consul several years after his older brother Jaume (II) Sarta became a regular holder of that office.[2] More often, the benefits to kin-households were less plain but palpable nonetheless, as when Pere (II) Sarta won a series of tax-farming contracts through his contacts with the better-connected Morrer family.[3] When contemplating the patriciate, then, it is important to remember that the actual office-holders were supported and surrounded in their daily lives by families, including wives, children, uncles, parents, cousins; but also by business partners, neighbours, those on whom they relied for various goods and services and a host of other community members in their relatively small and isolated world. In this way, the patriciate should be seen an organic part – albeit one of the most active and powerful parts – of the bourgeoisie which is our general concern.

Before the definitive establishment in 1393 of 'hand' membership as prerequisite for election to the town council, the primary legal qualification for eligibility was that a man must be a Manresan 'citizen'. As elsewhere in Western Europe, both urban citizenship and urban political

[2] MC 1374.4.18. [3] E.g. FS 1324 3n10.

office were open only to males. But how exclusive was this concept of 'citizenship', and how did it affect the social, political, and economic life of the city during the fourteenth century? At Perpignan, a distinction between citizens and non-citizen inhabitants had been made as early as 1197.[4] At Manresa, no citizen lists have been discovered prior to the 1408 *Liber Manifesti*, and so little can be said about the early history of urban citizenship at Manresa. Although some statutes passed after the 1362 plague indicate that citizenship restrictions were lessened at Manresa during the last decades of the fourteenth century, it is clear from the *Liber Manifesti* that full citizenship at Manresa remained a carefully guarded privilege and was open only to the very wealthy.[5] By 1408, the majority of the city's householders were said merely to be 'of Manresa', rather than 'citizens of Manresa'. The exclusivity of citizenship is unexpected, since no entrance fees are mentioned in any of the later fourteenth-century immigration statutes. The finding does, however, correspond with some of the only other citizenship figures that we have, the entry figures for the 'freedom' of the city of Exeter found by Maryanne Kowaleski.[6] The similarity between the citizenship figures in Manresa and Exeter suggests a continuity of European practice on this score which begs further exploration. In Exeter, certain economic privileges were also accorded to freedom members, but if this was the case with Manresan citizens, they remain to be discovered. As a result of the restrictive citizenship policy at Manresa, only 88 of Manresa's 548 male householders, or about 16 per cent, were full citizens, while 20 out of 92 women householders, or 21 per cent, were widows of citizens. Citizenship was therefore a privilege accorded to relatively few Manresan inhabitants. Moreover, the average wealth of male citizens was a very high £761; the average wealth of citizens' widows was £320, and the average wealth of the non-citizen was about £150.[7]

Despite the status that it conferred, it is clear that citizenship at Manresa was not restricted to the sons of citizens, as was, for example, the case in contemporary Lille.[8] This is proven by certain entries in

[4] Philip Daileader, *True Citizens: Violence, Memory, and Identity in the Medieval Community of Perpignan, 1162–1397* (Leiden, 2000), p. 17.

[5] For the statutes, see Chapter 5, pp. 138–9.

[6] Maryanne Kowaleski, *Local Markets and Regional Trade in Medieval Exeter* (Cambridge, 2003), p. 96, finds that 21 per cent of householders, and 4 per cent of the total population (all males), were full citizens eligible for office. See also Ruth H. Frost, 'The Urban Elite.' In *Medieval Norwich*. Ed. Carole Rawcliffe and Richard Wilson (London, 2004), pp. 235–53, 394–400, at p. 236.

[7] LM.

[8] At Lille in the fifteenth century, sons of citizens had to pay 4s/2d to claim their father's citizenship, but outsiders had to pay 60s. If rates of pay were similar to those in Manresa, workers might expect

the *Liber Manifesti*. Pere ça Roca, for example, was a Manresan citizen who had originally hailed from the village of Sant Pedor.[9] In this case, ça Roca's significant wealth (£624) probably did not hurt his bid for Manresan citizenship. Furthermore, the fact that nearly 75 per cent of Manresa's fifty wealthiest householders were citizens shows that at Manresa, at least by the end of the fourteenth century, citizenship was not too jealously guarded by existing elites. This observation can be tempered by the fact that a noticeable minority of wealthy inhabitants did not hold citizenship; perhaps some of these had not yet met residency requirements.[10] These findings do indicate that the above-mentioned immigration statutes of the 1360s and 70s did not, as they at first seem, grant free citizenship to all immigrants who stayed for a period of five or ten years – they must therefore have been conferring residence status and tax breaks only, while reserving actual citizenship to a more exclusive group of immigrants. Otherwise, there would be more relatively poor, newly immigrant householders in the 1408 *Liber Manifesti* than there are in fact.

At its worst, however, the concept of citizenship at Manresa only excluded a maximum of one quarter of wealthy male citizens from holding civic office. Citizenship was thus a significant, but not an overwhelmingly potent, weapon in the political arena, and it did not allow a small minority of urban patricians to keep other elites out of office. If citizenship restrictions did contribute to oligarchization, its effects at Manresa were slight.[11] Wealth itself, or rather the lack of sufficient wealth, as will be shown, was a much more insurmountable barrier to high civic office than issues of citizenship. This relative lack of exclusiveness amongst the wealthy in the years around 1400 was probably encouraged by the shrinking size of Manresa's patriciate. The simple lack of men able to support themselves in 'a respectable manner' would have acted to smooth over certain social divisions which might have become more pronounced in a larger community.[12] In general, then, the fourteenth-century Manresan patriciate maintained a relatively egalitarian approach to the institution of citizenship.

to get about 2s/day. Note, however, that this would hardly have been an insurmountable barrier for even moderately prosperous immigrants. See David Nicholas, *The Later Medieval City: 1300–1500* (London, 1997), p. 59.

[9] LM 165r. [10] This can be discerned from LM.

[11] This is contrary to the observation on citizenship and oligarchy discussed in Nicholas, *Later Medieval City*, p. 58.

[12] This argument is made in Frost, 'Urban Elite'.

THE MANRESAN POLITICAL ELITE AND THE QUESTION OF OLIGARCHY

This chapter presents some fruits of an extensive databasing of the nearly complete and reasonably detailed series of Manresan town council manuals which cover the period 1315–1415. This data has been cross-referenced where possible with entries from the *Liber Manifesti.* Taken together, these two sources enable us to provide a much more nuanced quantitative picture of the Manresan patriciate than can usually be achieved by late medieval urban historians. Where many historians have to be content with mere impressions of various trends in a given patriciate, or at best with lists of the names of office-holders, our data enable us to measure such traits as the relative wealth, occupation, and family status of various office-holders. The relatively compact size of Manresa also makes it possible for an individual researcher to form a detailed impression of the doings of prominent families; for example, who was active in council sessions, who had business and marriage alliances with whom and similar information. As a result of this precision, much of the information presented in this chapter will be done with reference to tables. In any event, the succeeding two chapters provide a detailed 'thick description' of the practice of government in Manresa, and so this present chapter can be regarded as setting the stage for the narrative treatment provided hereafter.

Proceeding in this vein, Table 3.1 presents a portrait of Manresa's core patriciate in the fourteenth century, that is, those families who held the consulship. Those consular families which had served only once or twice by 1413 are excluded from the table. An exception to this is a group of six families who were very politically active in the 1403–13 period, whose careers are included for the sake of comparison with older and more prominent families. As reported at the bottom of Table 3.1, there were a total of thirty-one families who had held office only once during the century under scrutiny, and a total of nine families who had held the consular office twice (these figures include those listed on the table). All of the other consular families whose names are reported in the council manuals are listed. The table shows the number of family members who held office and the total known instances in which family members held office, and also gives a sense of the family's wealth ranking in 1408. In addition, one column shows the number of times that family members held the consulship and the juratship during the period 1403–13. This period is of special relevance because it encompasses the decade around 1408, when the *Liber Manifesti* was begun, but it is also remarkable because the names of the *jurats*, which were largely omitted during the fourteenth

Table 3.1 *Manresa's most prominent conciliar families, 1317–1413*[13]

Family name	Times served/ Number served	Conciliar span	Span type	Family gross wealth ranks, 1408–11	In Office 1403–13 (Con/Jur)	1st records in public scrivany
Amargos*	27 / 7	1332–1412	Full	3, 8, 29	7 / 10	1299
Nerell	15 / 3	1333–1398	Full	41, 73	0 / 1	1317*
Ferrer*	12 / 7	1329–1413	Full	11, 49, 60, 71	4 / 5	1292*
Sarta*	12 / 4	1367–1413	Late	17, 40, 64, 79	1 / 3	1313*
Andreu*	10 / 4	1324–1408	Full	6	2 / 2	1292*
Sallent	8 / 4	1329–59	Early	7	0 / 3	1314*
Palau	8 / 2	1356–84	Post BD	158	0 / 1(2)	1314
Boti	8 / 3	1325–80	Mid	96	0 / 0	1347
Vidal*	7 / 2	1368–1410	Late	24, 52, 104	3 / 2	–*
Vilella	7 / 3	1329–1413	Full	95, 127	1 / 4	1308
Prat, dez*	7 / 3	1325–1413	Full	56, 116	1 / 9	1316*
Orriols	6 / 1	1352–71	Post BD	extinct	–	1346*
Mas*	6 / 2	1392–1414	Recent	9, 14, 72	3 / 4	1363
Casanova	5 / 2	1345–82	Mid	43	0 / 3	1308*
Comb*	5 / 2	1365–1412	Late	2, 10	2 / 2	1370*
Exartell*	5 / 1	1388–1412	Recent	87	2 / 1(2)	–
Mir	5 / 2	1317–38	Early	extinct	–	1295
D'arters	4 / 3	1331–46	Early	166	0 / 1	1358
Colter	4 / 1	1352–85	Post BD	extinct	–	1291
Corb	4 / 2	1335–1410	Full	86	1 / 3	1356

(*cont.*)

13 Source: MC.

This table lists by name only the families who held a consulship more than twice prior to 1403. Those who held consular office only once or twice between 1315 and 1402 are summarized at the bottom of the table. (An exception is that six families, who held the consulship only once or twice, but who were politically active between 1403 and 1413, are listed by name, because the names of the *jurats* were known between 1403 and 1413, and thus the experience of these families gives an indication of the different ratios between consulships and *jurat*ships which might occur.)

The consulship was normally held for one year, from 1 April until 31 March. Consular lists are taken from MC. They are missing for the terms beginning 1318–23, 1326–8, 1330, 1338, 1341–2, 1344, 1347–8, 1350, 1359, 1361, 1367, 1385–7, 1389–91, 1399–1402. Lists are partial for 1339, 1343, 1346, 1351.

Explanation of column headings: 'Name' is Catalanized where possible. It is possible that D'arters and Exartello are the same name, as is St Joan and Joan. This would increase the rankings of these families. An asterisk (*) in this column indicates a family that was highly politically active in 1403–13; these families have also been included on Table 3.7. There is admittedly some arbitrariness in the selection of these families, but the final choice was derived from the general prominence of the family in the MC during the period 1403–13.

'Times served/Number served' indicates the total number of times that a family member has been a councilor, followed by the number of different family members who have been councillor. Dividing first number by the second will yield an average number of consulships held per family member.

'Span type' indicates the longevity of the family's conciliar career, and is provided as a convenience to the reader. These are necessarily somewhat subjective, and reflect the dates in which family members held consulships. 'Full' indicates a family which has held consulships throughout the period 1315–1413. 'Early' describes a family which held office prior to the Black Death.

Table 3.1 (*cont.*)

Family name	Times served/ Number served	Conciliar span	Span type	Family gross wealth ranks, 1408–11	In Office 1403–13 (Con/Jur)	1st records in public scrivany
Galçeran	4 / 3	1372–98	Late	46	0 / 2	1325*
Poall	4 / 2	1331–65	Early	306	0 / 2	1333
Boixo	3 / 1	1317–55	Early	70	0 / 3	1313
Canet	3 / 1	1333–1406	Full	65	1 / 3	1324*
Canyell	3 / 1	1325–1412	Full	12, 197	1 / 3	–
Eymeric	3 / 1	1358–75	Post BD	extinct	–	1314*
Far	3 / 2	1357–64	Post BD	124	0 / 0	1337
Gamiçans	3 / 3	1333–89	Mid	1, 54	0 / 0	1336
Joan	3 / 2	1324–33	Early	552	0 / 0	–
Morrer	3 / 2	1317–55	Early	88, 99, 169	0 / 3	1300*
Nadal	3 / 1	1376–84	Late	76	0 / 0	1350
Podio	3 / 3	1331–65	Early	53, 111, 128	0 / 0	1324*
St. Joan*	3 / 1	1407–14	Recent	13	3 / 2	–
Socarrats	3 / 3	1345–1406	Full	not manifested	1 / 3	1316
Solà	3 / 2	1317–36	Early	145	0 / 1	1291*
Torres	3 / 2	1324–56	Early	35, 55, 84	0 / 3	1345
Ubacho*	3 / 2	1362–1411	Post BD	15, 120	2 / 0	1396
Comanicosa*	2 / 1	1395–1405	Recent	44181	1 / 6	1329
Desglesies*	2 / 1	1332–38	Early	23, 34	0 / 4(5)	1375*
Muntcunill	2 / 2	1325–94	Full	not manifested	0 / 2	1312*
Cubach	1	1403	Recent	169	1 / 4	–
Miquel*	1	1393	Recent	16, 27, 78	0 / 8	1318*
Camp	1	1358	Post BD	32	0 / 2	1311

Total number of families who served 2 times: 9
Avg wealth rank, 1408: 94[14]
Total number of families who served 1 time: 29
Avg rank, 1408: 45

'Mid' indicates families which held consulships during the mid-century, on either side of the Black Death. 'Post BD' means Post Black Death, and indicates a family which held office in the generation after 1348. 'Late' indicates a family which began to hold the consulship after the 1360s, and 'recent' indicates a family which only came to hold the consulship from about the 1390s.

'Family gross wealth' is listed for primary and collateral branches ranked between 1 and 200 (of 640 Manresan households in the *Liber Manifesti* of 1408). The minimum fortune represented is £200.

'In office' indicates the consulships and *jurat*ships held by all family members between 1403 and 1413. These years are some of the few in which both *consellers*' and *jurats'* names have been preserved. Numbers in parentheses are projected from the fact that the list from 1410 is missing. Because many *jurats* served regularly every four years (because of the particulars of the system inaugurated in 1393), those who served in 1406 likely served in 1410 as well.

'1st records in public scrivany.' The significance of the records in the public scrivany is described in the text. Families with an asterisk (*) in this column had a member who signed the 1262 accord with the provost and canons of Santa Maria. (For which, see LV, 31–5.)

14 These figures include the six families with 1 or 2 consulships, who held *jurat*ships between 1315 and 1413, listed above.

Table 3.2 *Average consulships per family, 1324–1413*[15]

Date	Number of councillors	Number of families	Consulships per family	Percent increase from 1324–53
1324–53	92	50	1.84	–
1354–83	97	38	2.55	38.5
1384–1413	76	28	2.71	47.3

century, are recorded regularly. Other information in Table 3.1 pertains to the span of time during which family members were active on the town council, and also the first known mention of the family name in the civic archives. The implications of the information presented in this table with respect to wealth and pedigree are addressed throughout this chapter. The first question that will be addressed is the level of oligarchy in the civic government, and to that end some additional information on office-holding is presented in Tables 3.2 and 3.3.

It is no longer open to question whether later medieval patriciates in Western Europe became more 'closed' as the fourteenth and fifteenth centuries wore on, even if precise timing, and an analysis of the causes of this phenomenon, have proven more difficult to pin down from region to region, or from city to city.[16] A consensus is emerging that although official strictures on who could hold office became tighter, in practice towns in England, the Low Countries, Italy, and elsewhere in Catalonia continued to see a relative openness of oligarchy to new men in the early fifteenth century.[17] After that time, urban oligarchies in most of

[15] Source: MC.

[16] For the case of Zaragoza, see Enrique Mainé Burguete, *Ciudadanos honrados de Zaragoza: La oligarquía zaragozana en la baja edad media (1370–1410)* (Zaragoza, 2006). An interesting study of an urban elite confronting noble encroachment in Castile at the end of the fifteenth and early sixteenth centuries is Francisco Javier Goicolea Julián, *La oligarquía de Salvatierra en el tránsito de la Edad Media a la edad moderna: Una contribución al estudio de las elites dirigentes del mundo urbano alavés, 1400–1550* (Logroño, 2007).

[17] For the notion that English oligarchies were relatively open around 1400, and then became more restrictive later, see Jennifer Kermode, 'Obvious Observations on the Formations of Oligarchies in Late Medieval English Towns', in John A. F. Thomson (ed.), *Towns and Townspeople in the Fifteenth Century* (Gloucester, 1988), pp. 87–106, at 95; Charles Phythian-Adams, *Desolation of a City: Coventry and the Urban Crisis of the Late Middle Ages* (Cambridge, 2002), pp. 142–7; David Gary Shaw, *The Creation of a Community: The City of Wells in the Middle Ages* (Oxford, 1993), pp. 170–5; for entry to the freedom of Exeter becoming relatively more restricted by the later fourteenth century, however, see Kowaleski, *Exeter*, pp. 96–9; although Exeter likewise was not a 'permanently closed system of government', pp. 114–15.

Western Europe definitively settled into an 'early modern' pattern of relative closedness. The fact that this process was Europe-wide suggests that supra-national phenomena, such as increasing bureaucratization, the late medieval economic downturn and state formation, could be seen as probable causes, but this point remains debatable. At the level of the individual town, quantitative data which both illustrates the trend towards aristocratization and illuminates its possible causes has often been lacking, and Catalonia is no exception. A long-standing tradition in the Catalan and Italian urban literatures suggests that urban society across the north-west Mediterranean suffered a decline in mercantile acumen after about 1380, and an accompanying ossification of urban political culture.[18] The question of how these two trends was related is still in need of a more explicit treatment, for the question is an important one. Did, for example, the consolidation of late medieval urban elites have to do with the increasing power of national bureaucracies at the same time?

For relative openness in fourteenth-century councils in the Low Countries, see Jan Dumolyn, 'Dominante klassen en elites in verandering in het laatmiddeleeuwse vlaanderen', *Jaarboek voor Middeleeuwse Geschiedenis*, 5 (2002), 69–107; and Hans-Joachim Kann, 'Élite and Government in Medieval Leiden', *Journal of Medieval History*, 21:1 (1995), 51–75; also, for France and the Low Countries, see David Nicholas, *Urban Europe, 1100–1700* (Basingstoke, 2003), pp. 100–14.

For the idea that the Florentine oligarchy was relatively open at the same period, see D. Herlihy, 'The Rulers of Florence, 1282–1530', in Anthony Molho, Julia Emlen, and Kurt Raaflaub, *City-States in Classical Antiquity and Medieval Italy* (Ann Arbor, MI, 1992), pp. 197–221, 209–12; see also John M. Najemy, *A History of Florence 1200–1575* (London, 2008), pp. 182–4; and for elsewhere in Italy see Philippe Jansen, 'Élites urbaines, service de la commune et processus d'aristocratisation: Le cas de Macerata aux XIVe–XVe siècles', in *Les élites urbaines au moyen age: Actes du XXVIIe congrès de la société des historiens médiévistes de l'enseignement supérieur public (Rome, Mai 1996)* (Collection de l'Ecole Française de Rome, 238; Série Histoire Ancienne et Médiévale, 46) (Paris, 1997), pp. 201–26, at p. 223; and more generally in Benjamin Z. Kedar, *Merchants in Crisis: Genoese and Venetian Men of Affairs and the Fourteenth Century Depression* (New Haven, CT, 1977).

The same phenomenon is discussed in the Catalan literature in Flocel Sabaté Curull, 'Ejes vertebradores de la oligarquía urbana en Cataluña', *Revista d'Història Medieval*, 9 (1998), 127–53, 128; also Carme Batlle Gallart, 'La haute bourgeoisie Barcelonaise vers 1300', in *Les Sociétés urbaines en France méridionale et en péninsule Ibérique au moyen age. Actes du Colloque de Pau, 21–3 Septembre 1988* (Paris, 1991), pp. 229–40; Carme Batlle Gallart, 'La oligarquía de Barcelona a fines del siglo XV: El partido de Deztorrent', *Acta Historica et Archaeologica Mediaevalia*, 7–8 for 1986–7 (1986), 321–35; Josep Fernández Trabal, 'De prohoms a ciudadanos honrados: Aproximación al estudio de las élites urbanas de la sociedad catalana Bajomedieval (s. XIV–XV)', *Revista d'Història Medieval*, 10 (1999), 331–69, 338. This is also a major theme in Jaume Aurell i Cardona, *Els mercaders catalans al quatre-cents: Mutació de valors i procés d'artistocratització a Barcelona, 1370–1470* (Barcelona, 1996). At Girona, very few families were able to monopolize office over the course of the fourteenth and fifteenth centuries: Christian Guilleré, 'Les élites urbaines catalanes à la fin du Moyen Age: L'exemple géronais', in *Les élites urbaines au moyen age: Actes du XXVIIe Congrès de la Société des Historiens Médiévistes de l'Enseignement Supérieur Public (Rome, Mai 1996)* (Paris, 1997), pp. 269–85, 273–4.

18 This is a major argument in Carrère, *Barcelone*; Aurell, *Els Mercaders*; and Kedar, *Merchants in Crisis*, inter alia.

In many cases this seems plausible.[19] A related question is to what extent aristocratization was tied in with the 'financial revolution' that made widespread urban rents available to local elites from the later fifteenth century – the timing suggests that this is probably also a factor.[20]

The data presented in Table 3.2 adds to this debate by measuring the extent to which Manresan consular office was monopolized over the course of the century between 1315 and 1415. It presents data in thirty-year periods, commencing with the regular availability of consul data in 1323. These roughly correspond to the pre-plague period, the period between 1350 and 1380, and the period between 1380 and the redaction of the *Liber Manifesti.* The results of this analysis are not what might be expected. The figures do show a very definite jump in the 'monopolization' of office over the course of the fourteenth century, but the key date is 1348, rather than 1380, as some strains of the historiography would suggest. This indicates that the increasingly oligarchic tendencies of the Manresan office-holders over the course of the fourteenth century were due more to simple demographics than to any significant policy shift or discernible change in social patterns. If the observed oligarchic tendencies did increase somewhat after 1380, this likewise parallels a slightly downward trajectory in Manresan population over the same period.[21] Adjusted for population losses, therefore, the picture of monopolization that emerges is surprisingly static over the course of the century. This accords with the graphed findings of Philip Daileader for Barcelona and Perpignan, suggesting that the Manresan political experience was in this regard part of a discernible, yet not readily explainable, Catalan pattern.[22]

[19] See e.g. Stephen H. Rigby, 'Urban "Oligarchy" in Late Medieval England', in John A. F. Thomson (ed.), *Towns and Townspeople in the Fifteenth Century* (Gloucester, 1988), pp. 62–86, 81; Bernard Chevalier, 'Le pouvoir par le savoir: Le renouvellement des élites urbaines en France au début de L'âge moderne (1350–1550)', in *Construction, Reproduction et Représentation des Patriciats Urbains de l'Antiquité au XXe Siècle: Actes du Colloque des 7, 8 et 9 Septembre 1998 Tenu à Tours, Dans les Locaux du Conseil Général d'Indre-et-Loire.* Ed. Claude Petitfrère (Tours, 1999), pp. 73–81. One of the few who argue against this is Samuel K. Cohn, 'Popular Revolt and the Rise of Early Modern States', *Historian: The Magazine of the Historical Association*, 89 (2006): 26–33, who would like to see a 'stimulation from below' as a reason for a shift to an uneasy oligarchy in the early modern state.

[20] An interesting argument is put across by José Antonio Jara Fuente, 'Elites y grupos financieros en las ciudades castellanas de la baja edad media', *En la España Medieval*, 27 (2004), 105–30, who argues that increasing aristocratization in Castile had to do with the increasing ability of the state to extract wealth. This theme is found in some of the Valencian literature, e.g. Pau Viciano Navarro, 'Entre la comercio i el mercat: Els inversors en la gestió de la fiscalitat reial i municipal al país Valencia', in *Corona, municipis i fiscalitat a la baixa edat mitjana: Col.loqui* (Quaderns de l'Institut d'Estudis Ilerdencs, 13) (Lerida, 1997), pp. 603–22. For further discussion on the financial revolution in Catalonia, see Chapter 6.

[21] Manresan demographic trends for the later medieval period are found in Table 7.1

[22] Daileader, *True Citizens*, pp. 236–7 (Figures 5, 6, and 7).

Table 3.3 *Percentage of 265 known consulships held per family, 1317–1413*[23]

Number of consulships held	Number of families	Percentage of total known consulships (per family)
27	1	10.2
15	1	5.7
12	2	4.5
10	1	3.8
8	3	3.0
7	3	2.6
6	2	2.3
5	4	1.9
4	5	1.5
3	15	1.1

Percentage 'Monopolized' (by families holding office 10–27 times): 28.7
Percentage 'Somewhat monopolized' (by families holding office 4–8 times): 36.5
Percentage 'Not monopolized' (by families holding office 3 or less times): 34.8

It also accords with the findings of Stephen Bensch for Barcelona in the pre-1300 period.[24] During that time, Bensch argued that the lack of formal definition of the patriciate until the later thirteenth century, together with a lack of long-established pedigrees, contributed to a willingness of patricians to accept new families into their ranks. It will also be argued below that a relative lack of pedigree, and the relative newness of the consular office (even by 1400), contributed to a similar set of findings at Manresa. A probable economic factor for this finding lies in the continuing health of the leather and cloth sectors during the later fourteenth century, as has been chronicled in earlier chapters. Ideology is also likely to have factored into the observed pattern: one of the themes of this study is that an ideology of relative egalitarianism amongst urban elites

[23] Source: MC.
Notes: This table does not include the families which held office only once or twice, as listed at the end of Table 3.1. If these are added, the total number of known consuls comes to 265. Only the five families who had held the consulship 10 or more times are counted as having monopolized the office by 1413. Below these was a larger group who held office between 4 and 8 times over the course of the century. These families individually held 3 per cent or less of the total known consulships and thus none of them can be said to have maintained a monopoly on the consul's office. The lower boundary of this middling group of semi-monopolists was defined by the large gap between the number of families who held four consulships (five families) and those who held three consulships (fifteen families).

[24] Stephen P. Bensch, *Barcelona and its Rulers, 1096–1291* (Cambridge, 1995), pp. 347–93; esp. at 392.

was enforced by royal officials during the last century of the House of Barcelona, and also came naturally to wealthy urban citizens during the fourteenth century. This sense of fairness and relative openness in Catalan urban governments of both the satellite cities and the metropolis would dramatically erode during the fifteenth century.

Based on this simple measure of monopolization, it can be seen that during the first century of the consular office, roughly 5 per cent of Manresan households had access to the consulship. This is despite the many demographic, economic, and political changes that occurred during the same period. This pattern of 'moderate monopoly' of the Manresan consuls' office is further corroborated by Table 3.3. That table shows how, during the first century of the consulate, roughly one-third of the consuls' seats were reserved to men who might be called 'heavy monopolizers'. A further third was routinely granted to 'moderate monopolizers', and the final third was left open to men whose family would only grace the consul's chair between one and three times in a century. As will be shown in the following sections, however, a pattern of 'moderate monopoly' with respect to the populace as a whole did not necessarily mean that consulships would be distributed fairly amongst elites of differing occupation, let alone amongst men of differing wealth levels. There is also evidence that the level of monopolization of the consular office was increasing during the very end of our period, beyond what would be expected through shrinking population alone.

Table 3.4 provides a closer look at the men who made up the 'heavy monopolizers' of some of the consul seats. It should be pointed out that the pattern presented in Table 3.4 only holds in the years after 1393, when Joan I reorganized civic government. Before 1393, there is little evidence for a cyclic re-election of the same men to the consul's seat. After that time, the presence of 'permanent members' was much more in evidence, although it was still subject to a customary, unwritten restriction which prevented them from holding consular office more often than once in three years.[25] During the decade between 1404 and

[25] After 1393, the policy that no one should hold the consulship more frequently than every three years was strictly observed. This meant that an outgoing *conseller* had to sit out two years before he could be elected again. There were no breaches of this protocol between 1403 and 1413, but it did not keep these 'permanent members' of the council from returning with regularity every fourth year. We find, for example, that Bernat Amargos held the consulship in 1403, 1406, and 1409, as he had done in 1396, and possibly in 1399; his brother Pere was consul in 1404, in 1408 when he was late a year and in 1411 when he was not; Thomas Ferrer held it 1404, 1407, and 1410; and Joan Vidal held it in 1403, 1406, and 1409. The source for this is MC. Nicholas notes that this was common throughout contemporary continental Europe, and so Manresan practice should be seen as reflecting a larger European trend. Cf. Nicholas, *Later Medieval City*, pp. 143–9.

Table 3.4 *'Permanent members' of the Council of Four, 1403–13*[26]

Name	Years served as councillor	Years served as *jurat*	Rank	Wealth in £ Barc.
B. Amargos	1403, 1406, 1409	1404, 1408, 1412	3	3,576
P. Amargos	1404, 1408, 1411	1403, 1407	29	1,170
Th. Ferrer	1404, 1407, 1410	1406, (1410)	11	2,219
J. Vidal	1403, 1406, 1409	1404, 1408, 1412	24	1,216
J. St Joan	1407, 1410, 1413	1405, 1409	13	2,050
B. des Comb	1408, 1411	–	10	2,285
J. de Canyell	1408, 1411	1404, 1412	12	2,183
J. Corb	1405, 1409	1404, 1408, 1412	86	490

1413, then, one or two of the four consulships were effectively reserved for half a dozen politically and economically ascendant men. These were Bernat and Pere Amargos, Thomas Ferrer, Jaume St Joan, and Joan Vidal, who together formed a rotating *junta* of consuls. The remaining consulships were distributed amongst a broader group of ten to thirty families, each with a greater or lesser chance of obtaining a chair in a given year. The office-holding regularity observed in these cases is so very precise that there is virtually no chance of it having been due to fair and open elections. Thus, the pattern observed from Table 3.4 should be added to the longer-term findings presented in Tables 3.2 and 3.3. However, the increase in monopolization during the first years of the fifteenth century was not so great as to warrant calling it a watershed in the city's political history. This trend does reflect the general trends of shrinking population, decreasing social mobility and increasingly rigid social distinctions, and does point towards a general 'European' pattern of slowly increasing urban oligarchization.[27] It is also interesting to observe what this changed pattern of monopolization means in terms of royal control of civic office. While Jaume II was concerned in the beginning of the fourteenth century to limit monopolization by certain individuals of civic office, out of fear that such monopolization led to an increase in civic unrest and a corresponding loss of royal control, the situation had

[26] Source: MC and LM.
Notes: The period 1403–13 is covered not only because it happens to fall within five years on either side of 1408, when LM was begun, but also because this period is one of the first we have in which the names of all of the *jurats* are recorded, (normally only the consuls' names were recorded) with the exception of 1410. Since the *jurats* for 1410 are not listed, '(1410)' means that this term is conjectural. In this table, the label 'Rank' equals Gross wealth ranking, according to LM, for this head of household.

[27] This European pattern has been alluded to above in n. 20.

altered radically by the early fifteenth century. By that time, royal control was so well established that the Crown could afford to allow a few men to monopolize the consul's office.[28] The notion that a given individual, or faction, could seize power in the face of opposition by Crown or urban officials was by this time virtually unthinkable.

PROFESSION AND ACCESS TO URBAN OFFICE

If the Manresan evidence suggests that monopolization of urban office stayed relatively stagnant over the first century of the consulate, with a possible increase of monopolization occurring in the years around 1400, what then can be said about how a man's profession, or any type of status based on his profession, determined access to civic office? It should be remembered that, unlike in fifteenth-century Barcelona for example, there is very little evidence to suggest that there were longstanding Type D class divisions in fourteenth-century Manresa, or other divisions based on occupational type.[29] The distinctions between citizens, merchants, and *menestrals* which were periodically introduced into civic government by royal edicts, such as those in 1323 and 1364, were not routinely employed by the city's scribes until after 1393.[30] Furthermore, while the 'hands' regulations of 1393 did begin to create more formalized Type D class divisions, this had still made relatively little impact on the structure of society prior to 1410. For one thing, this system, imposed from above as it was, was not terribly logical or practical in the Manresan context. One obvious problem was that there were simply too few wealthy merchants, *menestrals*, or *rentiers* to constitute a stable and long-term quorum based on occupational status. For example, there were no more than twenty-five merchants and drapers in the city in 1408, many of whom were quite poor. In theory, according to the 1393 regulations, these twenty-five men were supposed to fill thirty-three seats on the city's newly instated *consell de cent* (which was comprised of twenty-five *jurats* and seventy-five members of the *consell general*). Obviously, substitutions had to be made, or else numbers had to be fudged. And while the 1393 election rules had made some effort to equalize the representation of citizens, merchants, and *menestrals* on the hundred-person *consell de cent*, no provision was

[28] This situation was analogous to that in England, where the monarchy was equally keen to prevent monopolization of office by a single individual or faction. See David R. Carr, 'The Problem of Urban Patriciates: Office Holders in Fifteenth Century Salisbury', *Wiltshire Archaeological and Natural History Magazine* 83 (1990): 118–35, at 122.

[29] For this observation, see Jeff Fynn-Paul, *Family, Work, and Household in Late Medieval Iberia: A Social History of Manresa in the Time of the Black Death* (forthcoming).

[30] This has been discussed in Chapter 2.

made to dictate the specific occupations of either the individual *jurats* or the *consellers*.

Nor was there in fourteenth-century Manresa any significant Type C struggle between nobles and non-nobles – since there were few if any nobles resident in the city, and these were barred from urban office – or between the partisans of nobles, or indeed any evidence for long-standing conflicts based on 'vertical' factional struggles.[31] It would therefore seem, in line with Stephen Bensch's findings for thirteenth-century Barcelona, and in line with several studies of later medieval English towns, that the strong presence of royal authorities in the city helped to keep both horizontal and vertical strife in Catalan cities to a level far below that encountered in many late medieval Castilian, Valencian, and Italian cities.[32]

The laws passed in 1393, which specify that the *consell general* should be divided equally amongst the three 'hands', seem to imply that the consuls' chairs should also be partitioned equally amongst these three groups. Indeed, it has been argued for Barcelona that the reforms of the late 1380s and 90s helped create equal representation on the town council.[33] The data in Table 3.5, however, suggests that this equality did not, at Manresa, extend to the consulate. A crucial phrase had been left out of the 1393 accords, namely a clear stipulation that the consulate itself

[31] While the Manresan city council was zealous to keep references to factional strife out of the records, one obscure passage from the Corts of Perpignan in 1350–1 shows that Manresa was experiencing serious factional strife in the aftermath of the Black Death. *Cortes*, I-ii, 440.

[32] The recent assertions to the contrary by Flocel Sabaté are not based on enough specific evidence to be convincing in this regard. See Sabaté, 'The Defection of the Medieval Catalonian Bourgeoisie: A Mutation of Values or a Bibliographic Myth?', in María Asenjo González (ed.), *Urban Elites and Aristocratic Behaviour in the Spanish Kingdoms at the End of the Middle Age* (Brepolis, 2013), pp. 111–32. See also Sabaté Curull, 'Oligarchies and Social Fractures in the Cities of Late Medieval Catalonia', in María Asenjo-González (ed.), *Oligarchy and Patronage in Late Medieval Spanish Urban Society* (Brepolis, 2009), pp. 1–27. For Stephen Bensch's reflections on the surprise he felt at finding so little social conflict in Barcelona sources, especially compared with Italian records, see Bensch, *Barcelona and its Rulers*, pp. xiii–xiv. For Valencia, see Rafael Narbona Viczaíno, 'La conflictividad social en las ciudades de la Corona de Aragón: siglos XIII–XV', in José Antonio Munita Loinaz (ed.), *Conflicto, violencia y criminalidad en Europa y América: IV Jornadas de Estudios Históricos del Departamento de Historia Medieval, Moderna y de América* (Vitoria-Gasteiz, 11 al 13 de Noviembre de 2002) (Bilbao, 2004), pp. 79–104; for Castile see e.g. Angus Mackay, 'Faction and Civil Strife in Late Medieval Castilian Towns', *Bulletin of the John Rylands University Library of Manchester*, 72:3 (1990), 120–31; Ágata Ortega Cera, 'Arrendar el dinero del rey: Fraude y estrategias financieras en el *Estrado de las Rentas* en la Castilla del siglo XV', *Anuario de Estudios Medievales*, 40:1 (16 June 2010), 223–49. José Hinojosa Montalvo, 'Bandos y bandositats en la gobernación de Orihuela en la Baja Edad Media', *Anuario De Estudios Medievales*, 36 :2 (2006), 713–50; Miguel Ángel Ladero Quesada, 'Lignages, *bandos* et partis dans la vie politique des villes castillanes (XIVe–XVe Siècles)', in *Les sociétés urbaines en France méridionale et en péninsule Ibérique au moyen age. Actes du Colloque de Pau, 21–23 Septembre 1988* (Paris, 1991), pp. 105–30.

[33] Carme Batlle, *Historia de Catalunya*. Vol. III, *L'Expansio Baixmedieval (segles XIII–XV)*, (Barcelona, 1998), pp. 242–3; 271–3.

Table 3.5 *Professions of twenty-one Manresan consuls, 1403–13*[34]

Profession	Number of consellers in profession	Terms served by men of profession	Average terms/ man	Percentage of total terms served by men of profession
Rentier	7	16	2.29	44.4
Lawyer	4	6	1.33	16.7
Coriaterius	3	6	2	16.7
Merchant	3	4	1.33	11.1
Notary/Scribe	2	2	1	5.6
King's Household	1	1	1	2.8
Yeoman Farmer	1	1	1	2.8
Total (of 44 terms)	21	36	1.62	100

should be divided equally amongst the three hands. In the absence of any direct regulation of the consulate, Table 3.5 shows that the *rentiers* and lawyers of the *mà major* managed to attain the lion's share of consulships between 1403 and 1413.[35] The question then becomes, did the *ciutadans* of the *mà maior*, most notably the *rentiers* and lawyers, attain ascendancy on the Council of Four because of their membership in an occupationally based 'hand' (a Type A class), or did their political success largely stem from their superior personal fortunes, or perhaps from family pedigree?[36]

Part of the answer lies in a more nuanced look at the occupations of the *consellers*. Table 3.5 confirms that the city's *rentiers* successfully monopolized political office to an extent out of proportion with their control of the city's resources. Based on the *Liber Manifesti*, it can be calculated that the city's twenty-six *rentiers* controlled 17.9 per cent of the wealth, while its twenty-five merchants controlled 10.2 per cent of the wealth. The city's five lawyers controlled a full 5 per cent of the wealth, and its twenty-five furriers controlled 8.2 per cent. To compare ratios, it can be calculated that merchants, who controlled 10.2 per cent

[34] Source: LM and MC.
Notes: The consul lists for the years 1403–13 are recorded regularly, at or soon after the first of April when the elections were held. The lists (except 1410) can be found at MC 1403.4.2, MC 1404.4.7, MC 1405.4.1, MC 1406.4.1, MC 1407.4.4, MC 1408.4.2, MC 1409.4.15, MC 1411.4.1, MC 1412.4.11, and MC 1413.4.1.

[35] Lawyers and *rentiers* were both considered to be of the '*mà maior*' or '*ciutadans*' in the 1393 regulations. See LV 322–47.

[36] It can be calculated from LM that in 1408 the average Manresan merchant was worth £639; the average 'craftsperson' £527; and the average notary £449. The average *rentier*, however, was worth £1,076, and the average lawyer was worth £1,546.

of the wealth and 11.1 per cent of the seats on the council, had a ratio of 1.1 seats per percentage point of wealth. By the same calculation, the *rentiers* had a ratio of 2.5 seats per point, the furriers had 2.0 seats, and the lawyers had by far the highest ratio with 3.3 seats per point. Lawyers also had the highest proportion of people within their profession represented on the council, with four of the city's five lawyers sitting at least once during the decade. This is not surprising, insofar as the lawyers' legal expertise was routinely required in many matters of government, so that their presence was probably considered as much a duty as a privilege of their profession. That the town's lawyers were all very wealthy did not make them any less desirable. And in fact this pattern of office-holding by those with legal training is now well established for urban regimes throughout late medieval and early modern Europe. Manresa around 1400 was thus no exception to this rule.[37]

The preponderance of lawyers and *rentiers* on the council between 1403 and 1413 might suggest that occupation (or, in the case of the *rentiers*, lack of a profession) was a primary determinant of access to office at Manresa. This evidence does not, however, preclude the theory that it was wealth, rather than occupation, which determined one's odds of attaining the consulship. The fact that the lawyers were by far the wealthiest occupational group per capita in the city, with the *rentiers* a strong second, is enough to require further investigation. The *rentiers* were worth £1,076 on average, which was nearly twice as wealthy as the average merchant (£639) or *coriaterius* (£511). Since in many cases, higher levels of respectability produced less income from the same patrimony (e.g., higher-risk merchanting would be expected to return more than lower-risk rent-holding), sons who inherited less might feel compelled to take on a less respectable profession in the hope of building their patrimonies more quickly.[38] With this as the case, it is natural to find that there would be a preponderance of *rentiers* at the highest wealth levels; again, this leaves the question of occupation vs wealth quite open.

Furthermore, the notion that the consulate was dominated by wealth, rather than any given occupation-based group, is backed up by the strong showing of the city's furriers, who were technically of the *mà menor*, or *menestrals*, on Table 3.5. Three furriers served six terms between 1403 and 1413, while during the same decade the three merchants who sat on the council served only four terms. The three furriers who sat on the council

37 For this phenomenon in general see Nicholas, *Urban Europe*, pp. 104–14.

38 This observation is based partly on the fact that rentierism based on *censal* ownership, which paid about 5.14 per cent in 1408, would have to pay less than entrepreneurialism, or else no one would have engaged in trade at all.

were worth £2,183, £2,050, and £724 in 1408, respectively, while the three merchants who sat were worth £1,581, £1,212, and £467.[39] The two wealthiest furriers accounted for five of the six terms, while the two wealthier merchants sat once, and the poorest of the three, Bernat Exarcell, sat twice. Yet it still cannot be definitely determined from these numbers that the furriers were a more powerful presence on the council than the merchants. Indeed, one of the city's two most powerful furriers, Joan Canyell, was first listed in the *Liber Manifesti* as a merchant.[40] This was then crossed out and replaced with the term *coriaterius*, indicating that there was some confusion over the matter. A look at Canyell's assets shows that he was indeed a practising *coriaterius*, insofar as he owned a workshop with a lime kiln and a 'garden' in the *coriateria*. But he also maintained £500 in the company of the merchant Francesc de Camp. Canyell as an economic agent was therefore a hybrid, both a *coriaterius* and a merchant, but in 1408 he chose to be officially named as a *coriaterius*. This choice clearly did not hinder him from becoming one of the most prominent men in Manresan politics during the first decade of the fifteenth century.

Finally, the professions of many of Manresa's most prominent consular families were showing a decided swing towards rentierism during the early fifteenth century.[41] While the Amargos, Ferrer, Nerell, and Vitalis families, in particular, had been content to call themselves merchants in 1365, by 1408 merchanting was decidedly in decline. This does, however, mean that the notion of being a 'gentleman' without an occupation was not by this point very strongly imbued in the ideology of the Manresan ruling elite. This fact makes it more likely that it was still simple wealth (Type B), rather than professed occupation (Type A), which was the prime criterion for holding the consular office, and thereby gaining a Type D class distinction, in the years after 1400.

WEALTH AND CIVIC OFFICE

In the general absence of definitive evidence for or against the influence of occupational status on civic office-holding, with the obvious exception of the city's lawyers, it makes sense to turn to an evaluation of the wealth levels of the city's consuls and *jurats*. Table 3.1 presents, amongst other things, the wealth rankings of prominent office-holders as they stood in the period 1408–11. The data presents a variegated picture. Of the forty-three consular families on the list, only nineteen had a primary branch in the top fifty households, with a fortune worth more than £704. A

[39] LM. [40] LM 94v. [41] See Table 3.1.

Table 3.6(a) *Wealth and office-holding at Manresa (consuls and* jurats*), 1403–13*[42]

Consuls				
Wealth ranking (H.hold)	Minimum fortune (in £ Barc.)	Gross wealth percentile (0 = Top)	No. councillors in bracket	Percent of councillors in bracket
1–17	1810	0.0–2.6	19/36	52.0
1–29	1170	2.7–4.5	7/36	20.0
1–95	435	4.5–15.0	10/36	28.0
Jurats				
Wealth ranking	Minimum fortune	Gross wealth percentile (0 = Top)	No. *jurats* in bracket	Percent of jurats in bracket
96–640	3	16.0–100.0	0/36	0.0
1–50	704	0.0–7.8	77/189	40.7
1–101	411	7.9–15.6	48/189	25.4
1–145	273	15.7–22.6	31/189	16.4
146–640	3	22.7–100.0	33/189	17.5

further ten families were ranked between fifty and one hundred, with a modest fortune of between £704 and £411. Five families had fallen, or perhaps had always been ranked, below one hundred, with fortunes that placed them squarely in the middle class. Only six of the consular families appear to have been extinct in the city by 1408. Based on this information, one might be forgiven for forming the opinion that wealth was not a terribly influential factor in attaining civic office by the early fifteenth century. In fact, as Tables 3.6(a) and (b) both show, nothing could be farther from the truth. If Table 3.1 seems to present a mixed

42 Source: LM and MC.
Notes: Table 3.6(a) shows the wealth rankings of consuls and *jurats* known to have served between 1403 and 1413. The sections on consuls and *jurats* are broken into 'wealth brackets' which correspond to the number of consuls and *jurats* in each bracket. It will be noted that no Manresan whose wealth ranked them below 95 out of 640 householders (i.e., below the top 15th percentile), served as a consul during these years. The *jurat*ship was much more open to men of smaller fortune. Names are taken from MC: See note to Table 3.5, above, for individual references. Wealth rankings are taken from LM, and are for individual heads of household, not families. 'Minimum fortune' means the smallest fortune found in that wealth bracket.
Table 3.6(b) presents a different view of the same information, by showing what percentage of all Manresan householders in each wealth bracket served as either consul or *jurat*.

Table 3.6(b) *Wealth and office-holding at Manresa (consuls and* jurats*), 1403–13*

Wealth ranking	Minimum fortune	Percent of household heads serving as councillor	Percent of household heads from conciliar family[43]	Percent of household heads serving as a *jurat*
1–50	704	37.2	66.0	79.0
51–101	411	8.8	50.0	48.8
102–152	254	0.0	28.0	37.7
153–203	195	2.7	24.0	17.4
204–254	160	0.0	22.0	11.1
255–305	128	0.0	20.0	9.3

picture regarding wealth and office-holding, this is only a measure of how difficult it was for families to maintain first-rate patrimonies during the upheavals of the later fourteenth century.

Tables 3.6(a) and 3.6(b) provide definite proof that it was in fact wealth, rather than occupation, which conferred membership in Manresa's political elite.[44] The Manresan political system, in other words, was relatively open to men of whatever profession, so long as they disposed of certain very high levels of wealth. The same holds true of the *jurats*, who also show pronounced economic homogeneity of a second-tier nature. In the decade between 1403 and 1413, more than half of the city's consuls came from the wealthiest seven households, that is, the top 2.5 per cent of households.[45] Nearly three quarters of *consellers* had personal fortunes in excess of £1,170 which was twenty times the annual salary of a *conseller* of Barcelona. Put another way, three out of four seats on the council were effectively reserved to the top twenty-nine householders, who constituted 4.5 per cent of the total number of households. The remaining 28 per cent of the consulships, roughly one out of four seats, were reserved to a wider constituency comprising the upper

43 Women householders are included for the 'conciliar family' category, but excluded from the 'serving' categories, since they were ineligible for office.

44 This corresponds with findings for other contemporary cities, although good data is relatively scarce. See Ruth H. Frost, 'The Urban Elite', in Carole Rawcliffe and Richard Wilson (eds.), *Medieval Norwich* (London, 2004), pp. 235–53, 394–400, at 244–5; and Kann, 'Élite and Government in Medieval Leiden', 65–7.

45 See Table 3.6 (a).

15 per cent of households. These observations can be compared with those presented in Table 3.3, which argued that about one-third of the consular offices had been 'less monopolized' during the first century of the office. The findings in Tables 3.6(a) and (b) suggest that, at the very end of this period, monopolization was increasing. This is also corroborated by the existence of 'permanent members' of the council, discussed below.

Further analysis shows that these seats were usually reserved to families of consular blood. Here is where, perhaps, a bit of pedigree came into the distribution of civic offices: if one were not one of the wealthiest citizens, being from a consular family would give one a certain advantage over those who were not. This can be seen, for instance, in the case of the Vilella and Canet families, who were no longer in the city's highest echelons in terms of wealth, but who did manage to attain a consulship between 1403 and 1413. Families such as the Palacio and the d'Arters had sunk even lower from their earlier heights of wealth and political participation, but were still able to maintain a presence on the council of twenty-four *jurats*. Below the top twenty or thirty households, consulship tenure fell precipitously, until it stopped entirely after the ninety-fifth household, that is, at the fifteenth percentile. It is therefore possible to say that the wealth of this household, some £432, represented about the minimum fortune required for eligibility to the consulship, except in extraordinary circumstances. Generally speaking, however, one had to have a fortune of £2,000 or above in order to secure a more or less continuous presence on the council, as will be seen below. Either way, middle class people had next to no hope of becoming a *conseller*, whatever their professed occupation might have been. The office of *jurat* was more open to middle-class people, although it remained virtually closed to those at the lower end of the economic spectrum.[46]

[46] It is interesting to put these alongside figures published by Carr for Salisbury, because they represent some of the only comparable data available at present. Carr's figures do, however, include a wider number of urban offices than are analysed here for Manresa. At Salisbury, a remarkable number of even the poorest householders seem to have participated in civic office in the early fifteenth century: over 50 per cent of the householders in every wealth bracket apparently held some form of urban office. This is a much larger group than would be found at Manresa even if other urban offices were included in our analysis. In this light, Manresan government would appear to have been more 'closed' than the findings indicated for Salisbury. David R. Carr, 'The Problem of Urban Patriciates: Office Holders in Fifteenth-century Salisbury', *Wiltshire Archaeological and Natural History Magazine*, 83 (1990), 118–35; 130–1. Without citing specific evidence, Kent notes that lower-status Italian municipal offices were available to a wide range of urban citizens, also more than we find at Manresa; Dale Kent, 'The Power of the Elites: Family, Patronage, and the State', in John M. Najemy (ed.), *Italy in the Age of the Renaissance, 1300–1550* (Oxford, 2004), 165–83, at 171.

FAMILY, PERSONAL MERIT, AND POLITICAL OFFICE

Having tested the influence of profession and wealth on access to civic office in Manresa, the issue of family status remains to be addressed. The age and wealth of the family are two factors which come into play. To what extent were there Type D class divisions at Manresa, between different groups of non-nobles, based on lineage? An indicator of family age, particularly of the length of time that the family has been resident in Manresa, is presented in the right-most column in Table 3.1. This shows the date of the earliest family notarial book that exists in the Manresan archive. While not foolproof, cross-referencing with the town council manuals suggests that the picture thus created of family longevity is reasonably accurate. In other words, families who appear in the council manuals almost invariably have family books in the scrivany, while those without family books generally do not appear in the council manuals.[47] Since only the wealthiest families, who redacted the most business, bore the expense of maintaining their own notarial books in Manresa's public scrivany, the date of the earliest records also provide some indication of the date by which the family had 'arrived' as an economic power player in the city. Since, like most of the sources in Manresa's archive, the notarial records begin only in the 1290s, little can be known of the city's family histories prior to that decade. But it is significant that those families whose books extend back before 1300 were, with the exception of the Colters, politically ascendant from a very early date.

Three of the top five conciliar families had books extending back to the 1290s, including those merchants-turned-*rentiers* the Amargos and the Ferrers, and the more strictly *rentier* Andreu family. The Sartas, who were the city's principal merchants in 1408, also had early books, as did the Nerell. Another two families whose first books date from the 1290s, the Mir and the Sola, dominated the council in the 1320s and 1330s but then suffered ill fortune: the Mir became extinct, and the Sola lost economic prominence. All eight families who held the consulship eight or more times by 1413 had, in fact, begun personal notarial books prior to 1315. This is an indication that the most successful families did in fact have some longevity attached to their names: they had been amongst the wealthiest families in Manresa prior to the establishment of the consulate. This elite group of eight families accounted for some 38 per cent of the consulships recorded in the town council manuals between 1317 and 1413. What does this indicate about the impact of

[47] M. Torras, B. Masats, R. Valdenebro, and L. Virós, *Catàleg dels Protocols Notarials de Manresa* (Barcelona, 1993); pp. 105–52 lists the *Llibres particulars* that were begun between 1291 and 1400.

pedigree on Manresan politics? While many studies of late medieval and early modern towns attempt to link pedigree and office-holding, the totality of our findings suggest a degree of caution. Once again, there is no evidence to show that pedigree per se, rather than simple wealth, was a primary determinant of civic office-holding during the fourteenth century.[48] The question of personal pedigree is likely to have become more significant during the fifteenth century, when Type D class distinctions became more pronounced in the Catalan cities. During the fourteenth century, however, Manresan wealth was to a large degree inherited, rather than made – with the notable exception of some of the furrier families who rose to prominence at the end of the century. In general, however, social mobility was never great, even during the 'boom time' of the early 1300s. Since wealth was a prime determinant of civic office, it makes sense to see a relatively small group of wealthy families maintain their position in the ranks of the patriciate during our period.

This is especially true because at Manresa, unlike in some English and French towns, the fourteenth century was generally quite kind to families' ability to maintain 'dynasties', even if these were usually limited to three or fewer households per generation.[49] Stephen Bensch has likewise found that Barcelona patrician families were generally able to maintain their civic prominence across several generations – at least prior to 1300.[50] The knightly Talamancas and the other castellan families of their acquaintance, and the bourgeois Sartas and the families of their kin and associates, were with a few exceptions able to maintain their lineages throughout the long fourteenth century.[51] Even though the Black Death had reduced the population of Manresa by an estimated 60 per cent between 1348 and 1408, Table 3.1 shows that only four of thirty-seven families who attained the consulship three or more times in the fourteenth century were extinct by 1408.[52] This strong continuity in the male line is very striking, since it might be assumed that family continuity in the fourteenth century would occur at a much lower rate

48 For evidence that the link between wealth and political power was not so fluid in later medieval England, see Heather Swanson, *Medieval Artisans: An Urban Class in Late Medieval England* (London, 1989), p. 150.

49 Jennifer Kermode, *Medieval Merchants: York, Beverley, and Hull in the Later Middle Ages* (Cambridge, 1998); Sylvia Thrupp, *The Merchant Class of Medieval London* (orig. pub. Chicago 1948) (Ann Arbor, MI, 1996), pp. 191–205; David Nicholas, *The Later Medieval City: 1300–1500* (London, 1997), p. 56.

50 See Bensch, *Barcelona and its Rulers*, pp. 174–83 on Barcelona's twelfth- and thirteenth-century patrician continuity. But see Kermode, *Medieval Merchants*, p. 4, for the synopsis of a contrary historiographical view.

51 Again, see Talamanca and Sarta papers cited in bibliography; this is the subject of forthcoming work.

52 This demographic data is presented in Table 7.1.

than that found for Bensch in the thirteenth century. The major hurdle faced by fourteenth-century Manresans was the plague year of 1348 itself. Families which survived that date were quite likely to have survived in the male line for the entire course of the century. Although a systematic study of family discontinuity in 1348 has not been attempted here, a glance at the inventory of Manresa's notarial books, the town council manuals and the information presented in Table 3.1 suggests that no more than about 20 per cent of the city's families failed in the male line in that year. At Manresa, there was almost always a son or two, or barring that, a nephew or cousin, who survived the various waves of plague in order to maintain continuity.

From this can be drawn a further observation, namely that at Manresa, patrician family continuity was not really a function of having enough male heirs. Instead, the principal limiting factor was the amount of wealth that a family could amass. In this, all of the Manresan sources clearly show that, after about 1360 at the latest, older Manresan families found it very difficult to amass further wealth, to the extent that they could increase the number of households carrying their family name whose wealth enabled them to live as patricians.[53] The new families of the 1390s, who were mostly *menestrals* of the *coriaterius* (leather wholesaler) profession, did not succeed in raising more than a household or two to patrician status.[54] Since inheritance was semi-partible, meaning that it favoured the first-born son while allowing for decreasing patrimonies for successively younger sons, families were generally able to maintain economic status over several generations, but still, especially after 1360, found it difficult to create entirely new households-worth of pre-eminent wealth.

Thus, Manresan patrician families in the long fourteenth century fared well in terms of physical continuity in the male line, and also in terms of their ability to maintain a household or two at patrician levels of wealth. This still did not guarantee that they would maintain householders who would be of sufficient age and experience to gain acceptance into the highest ranks of civic government – particularly since Manresan families probably became smaller after the Black Death.[55] Jaume (II) Sarta was not elected to the consul's seat until he was about fifty years of age; he

[53] See n. 36 above for the average wealth of merchants and *rentiers*.

[54] This is evident from counting the number of households at above-average wealth with a given last name that can be found in LM. In most cases, the wealthy *menestrals* of the 1390s and early 1400s are not mentioned in MC in previous decades, and in the LM, these families were overwhelmingly represented by a single patrician household.

[55] This is argued from the Manresan inheritance and kinship networks found in the Talamanca and Sarta papers; once more as described in forthcoming work.

Table 3.7 *Pedigree among fourteen politically ascendant families, 1403–13*[56]

Family served in consulship between		Number of families	1st mention in public scrivany
1317–1413	(Full span)	4	1299, 1292, 1313, 1292
1317–1350	(Early span)	1	1375
1351–1413	(Post Black Death span)	1	1396
1365–1413	(Late span)	3	1313, 1370, none
1385–1413	(Recent span)	5	1318, 1318, 1329, none, none

might have been closer to sixty.[57] This evident age requirement helps to explain further the long gaps which can be observed in the careers of even the most active consular families, such as the Amargos family and the Andreu. This also helps to explain why, of the thirty-seven conciliar houses listed in Table 3.1, only ten, and not necessarily the most powerful ones, had political careers which spanned the entire century – despite the high rate of family continuity. Likewise, of this group of thirty-seven families, another ten families had flourished only prior to the Black Death, while the remaining seventeen families rose to prominence sometime after 1350.

The data in Table 3.7 presents another view of the pedigree status of the most politically ascendant families at Manresa, this time concentrating on the decade 1403–13. These data suggest quite forcefully that, indeed, family pedigree mattered much less than personal wealth when it came to the highest echelons of political power. Fully eight of the fourteen most active political families (the fourteen family names marked with an asterisk in Table 3.1) had not held conciliar office until 1365. Five of these fourteen, that is, more than a third, had not held office until as recently as 1385 or later. Within each group, family backgrounds and political success were varied. The most successful of the five 'recent' families in terms of offices held was the de Mas. The two most prominent office-holders from that family were a father and son, both named Arnau, who were both trained lawyers. Of this family, nothing is heard prior to mid-century. The second most successful family was the Exartell. Their political fortunes

56 Source: MC.
Notes: This sample of families is the same as those marked with an asterisk on Table 3.1. 'Span type' is taken from Table 3.1, and is explained in the note to that table. '1st mention in public scrivany is also taken from Table 3.1, and indicates the year in which the family began to keep personal notarial records in the Manresan scrivany.

57 For J. Sarta as 'first' consul, see MC 1367.9.3.

were based almost entirely on the success of one member of the family, Bernat. As of 1413, Bernat Exartell was the only one bearing his name to have served as either *conseller* or *jurat*. Although Bernat was a merchant, he was not a particularly wealthy one, and his fortune was by far the smallest of all the recently ascendant families. Bernat's success may therefore be a relatively rare example of the exceptionally competent administrator, who was promoted to high government posts more for his outstanding natural ability than for his personal fortune or his pedigree. Another example of this pattern is Pere Nadal, the able notary, treasurer, lieutenant bailiff, and finally consul, whose career blossomed in the 1370s and 80s.[58] The remaining new families were uniformly headed by the above-mentioned nominal *menestrals*, including some of the capitalistic furriers who were amongst the wealthiest men in the city after 1400. In the case of these families, wealth broke down any Type D class barriers that might have worked against them as *menestrals*. It should be remembered that demographic conditions were working in favour of these new families. In the face of a long population decline, which had then lasted more than half a century, Manresa's patricians chose to welcome newly rich families into their ranks rather than exclude them and risk extinction altogether.

CONCLUSIONS

The aim of this chapter has been to provide a relatively static or 'Structuralist' portrait of the men and family groups who held civic office at Manresa over the first century of the consulate, roughly the period 1315–1415. It has measured monopolization of office, as well as the influence of occupation, wealth, and family status, on office-holding. The analysis shows that, like oligarchies in many contemporary Western European towns, the Manresan oligarchy remained relatively open to people of new wealth and new blood throughout this period.[59] The openness of Manresan oligarchy remained surprisingly constant in the long fourteenth century, particularly when one plots this against the city's demographic trends. Only at the very end of this period did monopolization begin to increase amongst a handful of men who arrogated a minority of the consul seats to themselves. This occurred in an atmosphere of increasingly rigid social taxonomy, which slowly affected citizens' identities. Attitudes towards work also changed over the course of the century, leading citizens to self-identify much more consciously with the notion of being either a '*ciutadan*', a merchant, or a *menestral*. The fact that access

58 Pere Nadal is mentioned in Chapter 5, esp. pp. 154–5.

59 On open oligarchies, see n. 17, above.

to political office was, by the end of the fourteenth century, allotted on the basis of these demonstrably slippery occupational labels did slowly begin to polarize Catalan urban society.[60] By that time, at least, the city's lawyers and *rentiers* did hold the majority of the town's high government office, but it remains true that these were also the lifestyles pursued by the majority of the city's wealthiest men. The fact that many wealthy *rentier* families of the early fifteenth century had been represented by merchants as late as 1365 further suggests that a strong Type D class ideology was not yet solidly established at Manresa. Although its influence was relatively slight, it is true that dynastic politics also played a part in determining the shape of Manresa's town council. An old and respected name did provide advantages in municipal elections, as such a name will almost always do. Despite the presence of some oligarchic tendencies, however, there is also evidence that councillors tended to be those men who were respected, connected, and also competent to carry out the duties of running their city.[61] And it is certainly true that rampant corruption, such as has been described in the Castilian urban milieu, was not a significant feature of Catalan urban governance.[62]

In all, then, Manresan public office during the fourteenth century was relatively open – if one was in possession of the requisite wealth. Public office was not reserved to a narrow class of 'citizens', or to men of a particular vertical faction, or to men of a particular Type D 'caste' or class. Significant wealth was required if a man wished to become a consul, and great wealth did much to ensure that he could be consul much more frequently, if he so desired. To be a *jurat*, a man had to be in the upper middle classes, at least, as well as a citizen. After 1393, the strictures on urban government became more regulated. A man had to belong to one of the three hands, and the wealthiest and most influential *consellers* were able to get themselves 're-elected' on a mathematically regular basis every fourth year. It will be noted that this pattern of increasing oligarchy mitigated by 'enforced rotation' mirrors trends found in many contemporary urban governments – further corroborating one of the general themes of this study, that purely local or national explanations are not sufficient to explain the development of several important social and political phenomena in late medieval urban history.[63] At Manresa, most of the men who monopolized office by the turn of the fifteenth century

60 This is also argued in Guilleré, 'Les élites urbaines catalanes à la fin du Moyen Age', p. 275.

61 This theme of both family continuity in office and increasing pomp around civic office is found in Frost, 'Urban Elite', pp. 236–8.

62 For a forthright view on the unbridled corruption in Castilian urban politics, see Mackay, 'Faction and Civil Strife in Late Medieval Castilian Towns'.

63 Nicholas, *The Later Medieval City*, pp. 143–50.

were also significant holders of the civic debt, and were thus increasingly less likely to embark on politically, socially, or fiscally disruptive courses of action, out of line with the wishes of the Crown. Despite all of these caveats, however, the Manresan system says much for the wisdom and effectiveness of the House of Barcelona over the last century of its reign in Catalonia. Because of the relative fairness and openness of the urban political system, there was much less social tension than in many contemporary cities in Castile, Italy, or even Valencia.

Chapter 4

PLAGUE, WAR, AND CALAMITY

The makings of the fourteenth-century crisis at Manresa and the historiography of the late medieval crisis

Previous chapters have introduced us to the institutional framework of the Manresan government and presented a quantitative overview of the city's political elite. Chapter 5 will chronicle the actual functioning of Manresa's government during the middle and later fourteenth century, with a focus on the particularly turbulent years between 1348 and 1381. These few decades witnessed a significant series of transformations in Manresa which give this time period a solid claim to be called a 'crisis'; it is arguable that the city and the capabilities of its bourgeoisie were more transformed during these decades than at any subsequent time in its history. The shocks endured by the populace between 1348 and 1381 included a dramatic and sustained drop in population levels in the city and the surrounding region; unprecedented and permanent macroeconomic shifts in wages, prices, and interest rates; a financial and fiscal revolution that permanently debilitated municipal discretionary spending; rapidly increasing bureaucratization and centralization under the pressure of a twenty-year war; and invasion threats, endemic disease, famine, constitutional turmoil, and class warfare between the cities and the nobles stemming from fiscal wrangling in parliament. The individual and cumulative effects of these remarkable strains, and the equally remarkable mettle and resourcefulness shown by the urban citizenry, the king, and the Crown officials in dealing with them, will form the narrative basis of Chapter 5.

In order to set the stage for the narrative that follows, however, it is necessary to introduce the reader to three key issues that form its backdrop. The first is the notion of the 'later medieval crisis'. This is addressed here in order to highlight the ways in which the Manresan 'crisis' narrative presented in Chapter 5 both confirms and challenges some of the major ideas in what has now become a relatively complex literature. Rather than ignore much of this literature, which is based on other regions (particularly England, the Low Countries, and Italy), it is particularly rewarding to attempt to get a handle on its main strands, since they pertain to institutional and other developments which were in some degree common to much of Western Europe during this period. In this way, the Manresa and Catalan experience provides a valuable addition to the still too-localized accounts of the urban crisis phenomenon. Second, this chapter will introduce some historical context, by presenting a brief narrative of the Black Death in relation to Manresa and Catalonia. Third, it will address the beginning of the Castilian war, which began as a war with Genoa in 1351 and eventually snowballed into the nearly twenty-year Castilian–Catalan conflict.

The so-called 'crisis' of the later Middle Ages is a trope well known to medievalists, which has already been touched upon in Chapter 1. Depending upon one's focus, this crisis can be addressed under a number of rubrics, such as the 'crisis of the fourteenth century', the 'crisis of the fifteenth century', the 'later medieval urban crisis', the 'crisis of the nobility' or the 'late medieval economic crisis'. The notion of a later medieval crisis gathered intellectual momentum from the observations of certain economic historians active in the mid-twentieth century, particularly M. M. Postan for England and R. S. Lopez for Italy, who noted that the Black Death and other disasters caused a severe population contraction, leading to a number of economic problems whose intricacies are beyond the scope of the present discussion. By the 1960s, English urban historians had noticed that many British towns shrank quite alarmingly in the fourteenth and fifteenth centuries, and the publication of a number of urban studies in the 1970s and early 1980s, particularly Charles Phythian-Adams' *Desolation of a City*, promoted the idea of an 'urban crisis' of the later Middle Ages.[1] For a while, urban historians across Europe sought to link this 'urban crisis' with a political crisis as well; a wave of revolutionary activity was reported by Mollat and Wolff, for instance, and in Italy the Ciompi Revolt of 1378 was seized upon as a potentially revolutionary moment.[2] Since the 1980s, however, urban historians have become much more cautious in their ascription of the label 'crisis', and the result has been a number of studies which temper both the economic and political aspects of this phenomenon. For one thing, urban historians have re-remembered that if there was a 'crisis of the fourteenth century', it was not purely urban, but affected the entire socio-economic system.[3] For another, not all economic and social aspects

1 Charles Phythian-Adams, *Desolation of a City: Coventry and the Urban Crisis of the Late Middle Ages* (Cambridge, 1979).

2 Michel Mollat and Philippe Wolff, *Ongles bleus, Jacques et Ciompi: Les révolutions populaires en Europe aux XIVe et XVe siècles* (Paris, 1970). This notion has been re-examined in Samuel K. Cohn Jr, *Lust for Liberty: The Politics of Social Revolt in Medieval Europe, 1200–1425* (Cambridge, MA, 2008).

3 This is emphasized by the editors in Christopher Dyer and Kate Giles, *Town and Country in the Middle Ages: Contrasts, Contacts and Interconnections, 1100–1500* (Leeds, 2005).

of urban life were gloomy in the aftermath of the Black Death: some towns are known to have fared better than others, some industries fared better than others, and it has been argued that both male and female wage labourers enjoyed higher living standards and greater personal freedom, at least through 1400.[4] Likewise, it has proven quite difficult to point to definitive urban political changes which occurred as a result of 'political crisis' in these decades.[5] At worst, many towns witnessed a slow ossification of their oligarchies, and this seems to be tied with the general economic downturn.

In Catalonia, the historiographical emphasis has traditionally focused on a 'crisis of the fifteenth century' rather than of the fourteenth.[6] This preoccupation stems from a number of issues. One is that the Catalan population, while hard hit during the Black Death, did not decline as steeply, prior to 1400, as the population of some other parts of Europe, notably northern Italy.[7] In the fifteenth century, however, Catalonia witnessed a period of prolonged demographic decline. Another factor which has focused Catalan attention on the fifteenth century is the extinction of the House of Barcelona in 1410 and the coming of the Castilian Trastámara family to the throne of Aragon.[8] The new royal family was never very comfortable with Catalonia as their seat of power, as the monarchs of the House of Barcelona had been during the fourteenth century. Thus, the relationship between the Trastámaras and the Catalans, whose province was still the most economically and demographically dominant in their realm, was strained at the best of times. The Busca–Biga conflict which developed in Barcelona during

[4] For wages see Gregory Clark, 'Work, Wages and Living Conditions: Building Workers in England from the Magna Carta to Tony Blair', in *L'Edilizia prima della rivoluzione industriale secc. XIII–XVIII: Atti della trentaseiesima settimana di studi, 26–30 Aprile 2004*. Ed. Simonetta Cavaciocchi (Florence, 2005), pp. 889–932. For an improvement of women's conditions see P. J. P. Goldberg, *Women, Work, and Life Cycle in a Medieval Economy: Women in York and Yorkshire c.1300–1520* (Oxford, 1992). For the mixed economic situation, by region and industrial sector, in later fourteenth-century England see e.g. Pamela Nightingale, 'The Rise and Decline of Medieval York: A Reassessment', *Past and Present: A Journal of Historical Studies*, 206 (2010), 3–42, and Barrie Dobson, 'General Survey 1300–1540', in David M. Palliser (ed.), *The Cambridge Urban History of Britain*, vol. I: *600–1540* (Cambridge, 2000), pp. 273–90.

[5] This is one of the principal arguments in Cohn, *Lust for Liberty*.

[6] This is argued in Carmen Batlle Gallart, *La crisis social y económica de Barcelona a mediados del siglo XV*, 2 vols. (Barcelona, 1973); Claude Carrère, *Barcelone: Centre économique à l'époque des difficultés 1380–1462* (Paris, 1967); Jaume Aurell i Cardona, *Els mercaders catalans al quatre-cents: Mutació de valors i procés d'artistocratització a Barcelona, 1370–1470* (Barcelona, 1996); Alan Ryder, *The Wreck of Catalonia: Civil War in the Fifteenth Century* (Oxford, 2007); and for Manresa in Marc Torras, *La crisi del segle XV a Manresa* (Manresa, 1996).

[7] This pattern is argued in Paul Freedman, *The Origins of Peasant Servitude in Medieval Catalonia* (Cambridge and New York, 1991), pp. 164–6.

[8] Cf. Jaime Vicens Vives, *Els trastàmares: El segle XV* (Barcelona: 1956, 1961).

the second quarter of the fifteenth century, the economic slowdown of Barcelona which occurred during the same period and of course the Catalan civil war have likewise led to a focus on this century, rather than the fourteenth.[9]

Some attention has naturally been paid to the problems besetting Catalonia during the fourteenth century. The half-century reign of Pere III (1336–87) is still seen by most historians in a negative light, due in no small part to the evaluation made decades ago by Ramon d'Abadal.[10] For decades, Pere III has been portrayed as a king who weakened the state by squandering the royal patrimony. A more recent appreciation of the importance of the public debt for state formation has, however, tempered some of this earlier negativity. This system was largely a product of Pere's reign, and it can be argued that Catalonia was a much stronger state at the end of Pere's reign than it had been at his accession. In general, however, the fourteenth century as a period of 'crisis' has remained relatively overlooked in comparison with the fifteenth. What decline may have occurred during this century is often seen as a mere prelude to the 'real' drama and crisis of the fifteenth century. Thus, following Vicens Vives, landmark studies such as those by Carrère, Batlle, and Aurell have all begun in 1380.[11] And most of those fundamental studies which spent some time assessing fourteenth-century decline, by the likes of Pierre Vilar and Jocelyn Hillgarth, are ageing and increasingly in need of revision.[12] More recent studies by the likes of Sánchez, Ferrer, and Kagay have tended to focus on pieces of this puzzle, particularly on financing and parliamentary debates, and can likewise benefit from a combination of temporal and prospographical contextualization.[13]

[9] For the Busca and Biga, see esp. Batlle, *La crisis social*, and Ryder, *The Wreck of Catalonia*, esp. ch. 5.

[10] Ramon d'Abadal i de Vinyals, *Pere el Cerimoniós i els inicis de la decadència política de Catalunya* (Barcelona, 1987).

[11] Vives' *Els trastàmares* was a synthesis of several earlier works; see also *An Economic History of Spain* (Princeton, NJ, 1969). See n. 6, above, for the other references.

[12] Pierre Vilar, *La Catalogne dans l'Espagne moderne: Recherches sur les fondements économiques des structures nationales* (Paris, 1977). For an analysis which highlights the ramshackle, ad hoc nature of Catalan naval power in the western Mediterranean, and thus of many Catalano-Aragonese institutions of the fourteenth and fifteenth centuries, see J. N. Hillgarth, *The Problem of a Catalan Mediterranean Empire 1229–1327* (London, 1975). The 'decline thesis' is also analysed, perhaps too inconclusively, in MCOA, 182–7.

[13] E.g., Manuel Sánchez Martínez, 'Corts, parlaments y fiscalidad en Cataluña: Las "profertes" para las guerras Mediterráneas (1350–1356)', in *XV Congreso de Historia de la Corona de Aragón, I: El poder real en la Corona de Aragón, siglos XIV–XVI. 5 vols. (Zaragoza,* 1996), 4, pp. 251–72; Maria Teresa Ferrer i Mallol, *Entre la paz y la guerra: La corona Catalano-aragonesa y Castilla en la baja edad media* (Barcelona, 2005); Donald J. Kagay, 'War Financing in the Late-medieval Crown of Aragon', *Journal of Medieval Military History*, 6 (2008), 119–48.

In this light, the 'thick description' presented in Chapter 5 can help to reshape the 'crisis' debate in terms of 'transition'. First, our narrative will address the notion, hailing most influentially from the work of Ramon d'Abadal, that Catalan royal power was gravely weakened during the later reign of Pere III.[14] For many decades the Crown was portrayed as being virtually powerless in the face of the Catalan parliament, or *Corts*, at the national level – with the implication that Catalan royal government was at this time ineffective at the local level as well. In the process, the role of the *Corts* can be reassessed. This assembly has been seen by historians as diverse as d'Abadal, Maria Teresa Ferrer, and Kagay as having usurped political initiative from the Crown, particularly after the formation of the *Diputació* in 1359.[15] The *Diputació* was a 'permanent arm' of the Catalan *Corts*, which was set up by the delegates to handle the now-permanent public debt. Until quite recently, the *Diputació* was seen in terms of its political function, rather than its economic function, and was therefore seen as a major challenge to the powers of the Crown. This has now been rectified, and the views of the challenges presented by the *Diputació* somewhat tempered, though the older views remain resilient.[16]

Our reading of the Manresan council manuals also helps to delineate further the relationship between the *Corts* and the local governments. It is revealed that apart from their choice of who to send, local governments really had very little say in what went on in the *braç reial*, which represented the cities.[17] And the notion that the Catalan Crown under Pere

14 d'Abadal, *Pere el Cerimoniós.* Pierre Vilar, in 'Le déclin catalan du bas Moyen Age: Hypothèses sur sa chronologie', *Estudios de Historia Moderna*, 6 (1956–9), 5–68, tends to place the blame more on economic events than inept government, but the impression he gives of Pere's abilities as a king are not positive.

15 The *locus classicus* is María Teresa Ferrer Mallol, 'El patrimoni reial i la recuperació dels senyorius jurisdiccionals en les estats Catalano-Aragonesos a la fi del segle XIV', *Anuario de Estudios Medievales*, 7 (1970–1), 351–491. For more recent assessments which keep to the same general theme see Maria Teresa Ferrer Mallol, 'Les corts de Catalunya i la creació de la Diputació del General o Generalitat en el marc de la guerra amb Castella (1359–1369)', *Anuario de Estudios Medievales*, 34:2 (2004), 875–938, and Manuel Sánchez Martínez, 'La diputació del General: Quan i per què es va crear?', *L'Avenç: Història del països Catalans*, 303 (2005), 24–8. This latest calls the traditional 1359 date into question, although it is clear that the formation was a product of the war years around that time. See also Manuel Sánchez Martínez, 'El naixement de la Generalitat de Catalunya', *Quaderns del Museu d'Història de Catalunya*, 6 (2003), 15–18; Kagay, 'War Financing in the Late-medieval Crown of Aragon'. For background see Donald J. Kagay, 'The Emergence of "Parliament" in the Thirteenth-century Crown of Aragon: A View from the Gallery', in Donald J. Kagay and Theresa M. Vann (eds.), *On the Social Origins of Medieval Institutions: Essays in Honor of Joseph F. O'Callaghan* (Leiden: 1998), pp. 223–41.

16 Ferrer Mallol, 'Les corts de Catalunya'.

17 As yet little has been done on the *braç reial* of the fourteenth century Catalan *Corts*. See Josep Maria Pons Guri, 'Aspectes judicials de la Cort General a l'època medieval', in *Les corts a Catalunya: Actes del congrés d'història institucional, 28, 29 i 30 d'abril de 1988* (Barcelona, 1991),

III (1336–87) was powerless in the face of either parliamentary or local intransigence is revealed in the following pages to be quite demonstrably false.[18] The following analysis also shows that the Catalan Crown itself, rather than any economic force, was the primary source of the serious crisis that rocked urban governments in Manresa and across Catalonia during this time period.[19] Rather than this being due to royal weakness, this appears to have been due to the Crown's all-too-effective ability to place fiscal and political pressure on both the *Corts* and town governments. Successive crises in wars with Genoa, Castile, and the French mercenary companies saw the Crown apply unprecedented pressure on its towns between the 1350s and 1370s. This pressure put severe strains on Catalonia's urban patricians. Serving as a *conseller* or *jurat* became increasingly unpleasant, as these officials were subjected to threats from Crown officials on the one hand, and from popular discontent on the other.

Another issue that arises is whether this pressure – from the Crown, from below and from the elevated physical threats of war, famine, and disease – took its toll on the previously buoyant entrepreneurial and civic spirit of Catalonia's merchant elite. In other words, how did the 'crisis' affect not only the economic behaviour, but also the ideological outlooks, of the Catalan urban elites? This question addresses not merely the issue of merchant mentality, but also points to the role of the towns in the currently rather muddled narrative of Catalan decline. The reigning authority on mercantile behaviour and outlook in this period is Jaume Aurell, whose *Els mercaders Catalans* deals with the subject at length.[20] Aurell holds that the demographic and economic shocks of the 1348–80

pp. 142–5. Once again, the fifteenth century is somewhat better covered: see Esther Martí Sentañes, 'El síndic municipal a Corts a la Corona d'Aragó, durant el regnat d'Alfons El Magnànim: El cas de Lleida', *Anuario de Estudios Medievales*, 34:2 (2004), 831–73, and Antoni M. Udina Abelló, 'El braç reial a les corts Catalanes durant el regnat del Magnànim', in Salvador Claramunt (ed.), *El món urbà a la Corona d'Aragó del 1137 als decrets de nova planta: XVII Congrés d'Història de la Corona d'Aragó / Congreso de Historia de la Corona de Aragón, Barcelona, Poblet, Lleida, 7 al 12 de Desembre de 2000* (Barcelona, 2003), pp. 1013–21.

[18] The notion that the Crown was not powerless in the face of civic elites has also been concluded for Valencia in Rafael Narbona Vizcaíno and Enrique Cruselles Gómez, 'Espacios económicos y sociedad política en la Valencia del siglo XV', *Revista d'Història Medieval*, 9 (1998), 193–214, 203. It is pointed out by Sabaté that Vives and Vilar had long ego noted the 'alliance between urban elites and the Crown' as an essentially unchanging feature of later medieval Catalan society. This thesis obviously requires further examination – i.e., the stages of a dynamic relationship need to be elucidated – in the light of the decline thesis. Flocel Sabaté Curull, 'Ejes vertebradores de la oligarquía urbana en Cataluña', *Revista d'Història Medieval*, 9 (1998), 127–53, 129.

[19] A similar conclusion is reached regarding the relationship between the English Crown and its cities in an important article by Christian D. Liddy, 'Urban Conflict in Late Fourteenth-century England: The Case of York in 1380–1', *English Historical Review*, 118:475 (2003), 3–32.

[20] Aurell, *Els mercaders Catalans*.

period caused Catalan merchants to go into a period of self-doubt, during which time they ceased to be entrepreneurially fearless, innovative, and active. Instead, they gradually succumbed to the tempting sedentary lifestyle of the *rentier*, while being co-opted into the increasingly aristocratic fashions and modes of thought that came to dominate urban life after 1400. Note that this is a facet of the wider historiographical issue of European psychological reactions to the plague.[21] Aurell's vision of post-1380 decadence contrasts with an earlier 'heroic era' of the Catalan merchant prior to 1348, and it seems likely that Aurell got his basic ideas from a similar interpretation of Italian merchant culture described by Benjamin Kedar.[22] In both Kedar and Aurell, the earlier, pre-plague 'merchant hero' is portrayed as eschewing aristocratic trappings, embracing egalitarian bourgeois values, and ready to physically participate in a far-flung network of long-distance trade. This resulted in high levels of capital accumulation which ultimately raised per capita income for many middling and working-class urban dwellers.

Study of the Sarta family papers reveals that the Amargos, Sarta, and des Valls business partnership began the 1350s optimistically, by opening up a number of trading offices in the major cities of the Crown of Aragon and southern France.[23] Already by the 1360s, however, this optimism began to wane, not only because the Castilian war was going badly, but also due to the lucrative *violaris* which were flooding the market during wartime. Jaume (II) Sarta's international interests were not, it would seem, carried on by his son Jaume (III) when the elder Jaume retired in the later 1370s. It can also be demonstrated that men such as the Amargos and the Sartas, who were Manresa's leading business interests in the later fourteenth century, simultaneously constituted the core of the Manresan political elite. A change in merchants' mentality, therefore, would necessarily be intimately connected with a change in the mentality of urban political elites. Did Catalan merchants begin to suffer from self-doubt after 1348, or after 1380? Did this contribute to a diminution of civic vitality, which sapped the vibrancy of Catalan culture

21 See e.g. David Herlihy and Samuel K. Cohn Jr, *The Black Death and the Transformation of the West* (Cambridge, MA, 1997), pp. 59–82; Samuel K. Cohn, 'The Black Death, Tragedy, and Transformation', in John Jeffries Martin (ed.), *The Renaissance World* (New York, 2007), pp. 69–83; John Aberth, *The Black Death: The Great Mortality of 1348–1350: A Brief History with Documents* (New York, 2005), pp. 117–68. For Genoa see Benjamin Z. Kedar, *Merchants in Crisis: Genoese and Venetian Men of Affairs and the Fourteenth Century Depression* (New Haven, CT, 1977), pp. 116–17.

22 Kedar, *Merchants in Crisis*.

23 This can be seen, for example, in the hiring of many new overseas agents, or 'factors', by the partnership during these years. E.g., JS 1351 3k3; JS 1352.9.9; JS 1353 9.9; JS 1354.7.5; JS 1367.7.8.

and possibly of the state itself? By asking these questions, it can be determined whether the medium-sized towns of Catalonia did indeed take part in something like a national or regional decline, and if so, whether the reasons for it were social, political, economic, psychological, or a combination of these. Our findings suggest that there was indeed a civic malaise which gripped Manresan politics from the 1360s and 70s – a sense of hopelessness in the face of unprecedented debt, the diminished scope for the independence of urban government in the face of royal interventionism and exhaustion from the use of so many civic resources to construct the enormously expensive city walls required by threats of imminent invasion. This, combined with the reduced purchasing power that will be described in Chapter 7, and the reduced clientage networks that resulted from straitened incomes, helped encourage elites to 'turn away' from a sense that their city was a major player on the regional and national stage. A sense of political and social hopelessness does not present the entire picture, however. If there was a 'turning away' from active entrepreneurialism on the part of Manresan merchants, this was due in part to the effects of the Catalan financial revolution, which as addressed more thoroughly in Chapter 6, introduced government annuities at rates which competed successfully with rates from international business.

As an additional element of the 'crisis' discussion, our thick description also addresses the issue of rebellion and revolt, which has long been a hallmark topic of later medieval urban studies.[24] The later fourteenth century in particular witnessed a great increase in the frequency of rebellions across Western Europe.[25] The period 1378–82 in particular has been noted as a 'flashpoint' during which an extraordinary number of rebellions were observed.[26] Although Samuel Cohn has been able to study urban rebellion in England, Flanders, France, and Italy, a dearth of secondary sources has thus far prevented historians from contextualizing Iberian instances with the broader European experience. Philippe

[24] This mode of analysis which privileges moments of 'revolution' and 'tumult' has been intelligently called into question in Patrick Lantschner, 'The "Ciompi Revolution" Constructed: Modern Historians and the Nineteenth-Century Paradigm of Revolution', *Annali di Storia di Firenze* 4:0 (2009), 277–97.

[25] The main overviews of this issue are found in Cohn, *Lust for Liberty*; an overview of Cohn's thesis, which is at times disappointingly vague with regards to the later fourteenth-century revolts, is presented in Samuel K. Cohn, 'Popular Revolt and the Rise of Early Modern States', *Historian: The Magazine of the Historical Association*, 89 (2006), 26–33; the original authority on the late medieval revolts is Michel Mollat and Philippe Wolff, *Les révolutions populaires en Europe aux XIVe et XVe siècles* (Paris, 1970).

[26] This is noted in Cohn Jr, *Lust for Liberty*, p. 3. See also David Nicholas, *The Later Medieval City: 1300–1500* (London, 1997), pp. 126–36.

Wolff described a riot in Barcelona in 1391, contemporaneous with the outbreak of anti-Semitic violence in that year, but generally speaking few urban disturbances from this period have come to light in the Catalan secondary literature.[27] It can be determined from the books of royal privileges kept by various Catalan towns that Girona and Manresa, at least, did experience an outbreak of civic disturbances between 1379 and 1381.[28] Further details about these disturbances are very difficult to obtain, however, since any references to them in the urban council records have been carefully excised. This timing places them during the 1378–81 'flashpoint' noted by Wolff and Cohn, when famous disturbances such as the English Peasants' Revolt and the Florentine Ciompi revolution occurred as part of a rash of lesser-known incidents. The timing of the Manresan and Gironese outbreaks suggests that the immediate cause was a simple copycat effect: because townspeople all over Europe were rebelling at this time, the Catalan townspeople were likewise caught up in a wave of 'rebellious fever'.[29] This copycat effect would be repeated ten years later in the 1391 pogrom in Castile and Aragon. The groundwork for both of these waves of disturbances, however, was laid by the longer-term series of economic, social, and political changes which characterize the later fourteenth-century crisis.[30]

The causes of urban revolt, particularly during the 'flashpoint' of 1378–82 identified by Wolff and Cohn, might be a simple matter of a torch touched to dry tinder. A pragmatic approach to this problem of urban revolution, increasingly visible in recent historiography, leads us to question whether these revolts were significant in any transcendent way. This new spirit is reflected in a recent article which seeks to summarize historians' changing takes on the 1378 Ciompi revolution in

27 Philippe Wolff, 'The 1391 Pogrom in Spain. Social Crisis or Not', *Past and Present: A Journal of Historical Studies*, 50 (1971), 4–18, 16. The old rumour of the 1381 Catalan financial crisis has been re-examined in Gaspar Feliu Montfort, 'Mercaders-banquers Barcelonins: L'endeutament de la monarquia i la fallida de la taula de canvi de Pere des Caus i Andreu d'Olivella el 1381', *Barcelona – Quaderns D'història*, 13 (2007), 197–210. Some work on this subject appears in A. P. Usher, *The Early History of Deposit Banking* (Cambridge, MA, 1943), pp. 258–68; and more specifically in Ramon Gubern, 'La crisis financeria de 1381 en la Corona de Aragon', *X Congres Internacional de Ciencies Historiques, Atti*, vol. VII (Barcelona, 1955), 413–14. A. P. Usher, *The Early History of Deposit Banking in Mediterranean Europe* (Cambridge, MA, 1943).

28 For Manresa, addressing disturbances in late 1381, LV, 277–9. For Girona, addressing disturbances in the summer and fall of 1379, see Christian Guilleré, *Llibre Verd de la ciutat de Girona, 1144–1533* (Paris, 2000), pp. 539–40.

29 This is argued in Cohn, *Lust for Liberty*; for a similar effect spreading the idea of pogrom from town to town, see Wolff, 'The 1391 pogrom in Spain'.

30 This is argued in J. Fynn-Paul, 'Civic Debt, Civic Taxes, and Urban Unrest: A Catalan Key to Interpreting the Late Fourteenth-century European Crisis', in Lawrin Armstrong, Martin M. Elbl, and Ivana Elbl (eds.), *Money, Markets, and Trade in Late Medieval Europe: Essays in Honour of John H. A. Munro* (Leiden, 2007), pp. 119–45.

Florence.[31] Such an attitude towards rebellion could not contrast more strongly with the views of several earlier generations of urban historians. A long line of thought running from Marx and Pirenne, and continuing through the 1980s, presumed that revolution was a principal engine of historical change. In this climate, the views of J. H. Elliott were ignored in many circles, but now strike us as particularly clear-sighted: in 1969, Elliott pointed out that no society prior to the eighteenth century was capable of conceptualizing a 'revolution' which would fundamentally alter the nature of society.[32] This, Elliott argued, would have to await the development of a public that had achieved a high degree of political sophistication. Only then, in Elliott's words, could 'liberties' become 'liberty'.[33] In line with this view, recent thought on medieval revolt holds that participants were almost invariably interested in the redress of specific wrongs (such as perceived misgovernment on the part of a specific official or group of officials), the defence of specific local liberties or, at their most idealistic, the desire to return to the political status quo of an idealized past.[34]

Modern discussions of medieval revolt therefore see disturbances less in terms of broad typologies, and often point to the shifting groups of participants who might from year to year or decade to decade be composed of different social groups. Cohn's vast database of rebellion has highlighted the fact that older (Type A) notions of 'class struggle' have been difficult to find in the late medieval urban context, and calls into question the few remaining typological theories such as those of Charles Tilly.[35] Instead, Cohn, Dumolyn, and other recent commentators have tended to see rebellion in terms of social networks, which usually conglomerated around some element of a disenfranchised or otherwise aggrieved urban elite. The present study acknowledges these local and personal causes of rebellion, without disregarding the fact that Type C (noble–commoner)

31 Lantschner, 'The "Ciompi Revolution" Constructed'.

32 J. H. Elliott, 'Revolution and Continuity in Early Modern Europe', *Past and Present*, 42 (1969), 35–56; at 56.

33 *Ibid.*, 56.

34 Jan Dumolyn and Jelle Haemers, 'Patterns of Urban Rebellion in Medieval Flanders', *Journal of Medieval History*, 31:4 (2005), 369–93.

35 For Cohn's questioning of Tilly's typology, see Cohn, 'Popular Revolt and the Rise of Early Modern States', p. 26. One of the few recent attempts to defend fourteenth-century revolts on the continent in largely Marxist terms is William Chester Jordan, 'Famine and popular resistance: Northern Europe, 1315–22', in Joseph Canning *et al.* (eds.), *Power, Violence and Mass Death in Pre-Modern and Modern Times* (Aldershot, 2004), pp. 13–24. Before Jordan, the last principal holdout was Rodney H. Hilton, 'Status and Class in the Medieval Town', in T. R. Slater and Gervase Rosser (eds.), *The Church in the Medieval Town* (Aldershot, 1998), pp. 9–19. While Dumolyn and Haemers, 'Patterns of Urban Rebellion in Medieval Flanders', 371, attempt to use some of Tilly's terminology, in fact their subsequent analysis largely overwrites these ideas.

and Type D (commoner–commoner, usually revolving around access to urban office, and sometimes involving guild membership) class struggles were clearly evident in many late medieval towns, while entrenched factional struggle could also cause cycles of political disturbance.

The trend which views medieval revolts as normative parts of the political cycle owes much of its intellectual foundation to the work of David Nirenberg. In his famous study *Communities of Violence*, Nirenberg posits a Foucaultian theory of violence between religious groups, arguing that interfaith violence was often ritualized and to a degree sanctioned by authorities.[36] Samuel Cohn also makes the interesting assertion that medieval rebellion was, contrary to prevailing scholarly opinion, generally far more successful, at least prior to 1425, than not – a finding which lends itself to the idea that revolution was not exceptional, but rather a normative facet of political life in many medieval urban settings.[37] The disturbances evident at Manresa during the 1360s, 70s, and 80s, which are touched on in the succeeding chapter, were ritualized insofar as the Crown's tolerance of the privileges of the nobility led to a certain degree of sanctioned and 'pardonable' violence. Thus, Type C class disturbances between noble tenants and urban citizens, at least, were a more or less natural outcome of the division of Bages society into blocs of noble tenants, ecclesiastical tenants, and royal subjects. Type D class struggles, as already noted, were not yet a feature of Manresan life in the fourteenth century. If there were any Type C class disturbances – and this might have been the issue behind the disturbances of the 1379–81 period – these were uniformly opposed by urban elites, nobles, and Crown officials, and, contrary to Cohn's findings, do not seem to have created any serious changes in Catalonia. The unrest of the later 1380s, though it remains poorly understood, appears to have had both Type A and Type D elements, insofar as merchants and *menestrals* might have been campaigning against a *rentier* monopoly of civic office.[38] This would be a single known fourteenth-century instance in which such a revolt led the Crown to broker a solution – a solution which appears to have been effective. In general, however, there is relatively little evidence for ritualized or recurring violence in the Catalan royal cities, or indeed for

[36] David Nirenberg, *Communities of Violence: Persecution of Minorities in the Middle Ages* (Princeton, NJ, 1996). See also Mark D. Meyerson, 'Victims and Players: The Attack of the Union of Valencia on the Jews of Morvedre', in Thomas E. Burman, Mark D. Meyerson and Leah Shopkow (eds.), *Religion, Text, and Society in Medieval Spain and Northern Europe: Essays in Honor of J.N. Hillgarth* (Toronto, 2002), pp. 70–102.

[37] Cohn, 'Popular Revolt and the Rise of Early Modern States', pp. 30–1.

[38] For this explanation see Carme Batlle, *Historia De Catalunya*, vol. III, *L'Expansio baixmedieval (segles XIII–XV)* (Barcelona, 1998), pp. 242–3; 271–3.

successful rebellion. Nor can it be stated, as a rule, that either purely local and personal causes, or purely typological causes, were the prime mover in any given dispute.

One of the more ambitious recent attempts to redefine a typology of medieval urban rebellion according to modern tastes is that of Jan Dumolyn.[39] Dumolyn suggests that such revolts in medieval Flanders went through three stages. These included a 'nascent phase' of urban development that lasted through about 1280; a communal phase occurring between about 1280 and 1400 in which craft guilds featured prominently in civic politics and in urban disturbances; and a third period lasting from 1400 onward, in which craft guilds played a decreasing part and rebellion occurred in a context of increasing state power. It will be noted that Dumolyn's typology of rebellion primarily depends upon institutional evolution over time, particularly the level of state centralization: if one takes the Western European urban literature as a whole, it seems as though such a typology would hold not only for the Low Countries, but also for England, France, Italy, Catalonia, and Castile as well – because all of these European regions tended to experience a similar, if slightly varying, chronology of nascent urban liberty, popular action revolving around guild power and increasing state control. In the case of Catalonia-Aragon, however, guilds played little role in urban life prior to about 1400, because during the thirteenth and fourteenth centuries they were de facto, if not necessarily de jure, banned by the Crown.[40]

In line with the narrative of Dumolyn, the Manresan picture of political disturbance takes place in a context of rapidly increasing royal power and interventionism in Catalonia after 1350. It will be seen that, although various groups in town were quite unhappy at various times during the Castilian war and its aftermath, the most serious disturbances were touched off by disputes between nobles and citizens. These began at the parliamentary level, with disputes between how much would be paid by the nobles of the *braç militar* and the royal subjects of the *braç real*, but were sometimes fought between tenants of royal and noble estates in the countryside. These disputes brought the citizens of Manresa armed into the countryside on more than one occasion; at least one brash knight and his adherents were bold enough to ride into town and assault some Manresan citizens right in the heart of the city.[41]

39 Dumolyn and Haemers, 'Patterns of Urban Rebellion in Medieval Flanders'.

40 María Isabel Falcòn Pérez, 'La manufactura del cuero en las principales ciudades de la Corona de Aragón (siglos XIII–XV),' *En la España Medieval*, 24 (2001), 9–46, at 13–14.

41 For these incidents, see below.

In general, however, the narrative which follows shows that the relationship between Manresa's political elite, its royal officials, and the humbler classes of citizens was, even in this era of extreme pressure, generally one of consensus, rather than of conflict.[42] The literature on rebellion during this period shows that almost all Western European states became more adept at 'regulating revolution', particularly after the 1380s.[43] The Catalan Crown was no exception. The reason for this is that by 1380, the techniques of statecraft shared by all Western European states as a result of their common institutional culture had been advancing quite rapidly for at least several decades, and governments could learn from, adapt to and respond effectively to new circumstances much more effectively than at any other time in the post-Roman era. The increased royal presence in Catalan cities meant that negotiation between royal and urban elements now took place more regularly than before, although the Manresan evidence does not show, as Liddy's findings did for York, that certain of the townspeople had become partisans of a royal party, while others remained outside the royal bloc.[44] In other words, despite the growth of royal influence at Manresa, it is difficult to find clear evidence of royal partisanship within the elite. As will be shown, conflict and negotiation involving royal power was much more likely to have pitted the patriciate, more or less as a whole, against the bailiff, the *veguer* or both. Another result of the strong royal presence was the lack of Castilian or Italian-style factionalism at Manresa in the fourteenth or fifteenth centuries, any more than Stephen Bensch found them at Barcelona in the high medieval period.[45]

42 Flocel Sabaté Curull, 'Oligarchies and Social Fractures in the Cities of Late Medieval Catalonia', in María Asenjo-González (ed.), *Oligarchy and Patronage in Late Medieval Spanish Urban Society*, (Turnhout, 2009), pp. 1–27, esp. pp. 4–9, argues that Catalan urban governments were routinely beset by as much factional strife as those of Castile.

43 This is argued for the Crown of Aragon in Rafael Narbona Vizcaíno, 'La conflictividad social en las ciudades de la Corona de Aragón: siglos XIII–XV', in José Antonio Munita Loinaz (ed.), *Conflicto, violencia y criminalidad en Europa y América: IV Jornadas de Estudios Históricos del Departamento de Historia Medieval, Moderna y de América (Vitoria-Gasteiz, 11 al 13 de Noviembre de 2002)* (Bilbao, 2004), pp. 79–104. Again, note the contrast with Castile, where urban conflict was often encouraged by the Crown.

44 Liddy, 'Urban Conflict in Late Fourteenth-century England', pp. 3ff.

45 Stephen P. Bensch, *Barcelona and its Rulers, 1096–1291* (Cambridge, 1995), pp. 10–11; Fleming, in 'Tales of Oligarchy', pp. 179–80, finds disputes between guilds with overlapping interests, e.g. drapers and tailors, and lower class opposition. Peter Fleming, 'Telling Tales of Oligarchy in the Late Medieval Town,' in Michael Hicks (ed.), *The Fifteenth Century, II: Revolution and Consumption in Medieval England* (Woodbridge, Suffolk, 2001), pp. 177–93. Note that in Castile, royal minorities could also be the cause of much conflict; but this was not to factor into Catalan politics for the entire late medieval period. Fernando Arias Guillén, 'Conflictividad en la ciudad de Murcia (1325–37). El influjo de Don Juan Manuel y la intervención de la corona', in Beatriz Arizaga Bolumburu and Jesús Ángel Solórzano Telechea (eds.), *La convivencia en las ciudades medievales: Nájera. Encuentros Internacionales del Medievo 2007* (Logroño, 2008), pp. 115–32.

At Manresa, the elite was emphatically not 'shaped by conflict', even though this claim has recently been made for elites throughout Iberia and Italy.[46]

How do the non-elites fit into this pattern of civic disturbance, revolution and increasing state control? At Manresa, the city's working and poor citizens hardly appear at all in the sources except as partisans of the urban elite. This is likely because, as Chapter 8 will demonstrate, there really was very little 'pauperization' of the sort which has been claimed for the cities of the later medieval Crown of Aragon, or of the sort which has been claimed for the Tuscan cities studied by David Herlihy.[47] The Manresan evidence shows quite clearly, and quite surprisingly, that the decades around 1400 were a time of unprecedented prosperity for the working and middle classes of Manresa. While Herlihy has estimated that perhaps 50 per cent of Florentines were propertyless paupers, at Manresa this figure was less than 10 per cent.[48] This lack of dire poverty undoubtedly contributes to the lack of disturbances by the 'lower orders' that can be observed during our period. Certainly, the Crown was either unwilling or unable to manipulate the wage market in the later fourteenth century in a way that would jeopardize the gains of working people during the 1348–85 period, and the House of Barcelona did not manipulate the currency so as to cause measurable inflation.[49] The post-Black Death wage shocks did cause social disturbances in the *remença* areas east of the Bages, however, since these tenants were subject to much harsher feudal laws than their non-*remença* fellows. In England, manipulation of the land and labour markets has long been characterized as a primary cause of the uprising of 1381.[50] In Catalonia, however, the *remença* struggle was played out in the longer term and did not really come to a head until the mid-fifteenth century.[51] Fortunately for the

[46] Sabaté Curull, 'Oligarchies and Social Fractures in the Cities of Llate Medieval Catalonia'.

[47] For a recent assertion of late medieval '*pauperismo*' in Aragon, see Narbona Vizcaíno, 'La conflictividad social en las ciudades de la Corona de Aragón', p. 81. Herlihy and Klapisch-Zuber assert this in *Tuscans and their Families*, p. 101.

[48] See for example Tables 8.3, 8.6 and 8.7.

[49] For an analysis of the English statutes see Samuel Cohn, 'After the Black Death: Labour Legislation and Attitudes Toward Labour in Late-medieval Western Europe', *Economic History Review*, 60 (2007), 457–85. For unsuccessful labour statutes in Aragon passed in the wake of the Black Death, which are similar to those in England, see Melanie Shirk, 'Royal Reaction to the Black Death in the Crown of Aragon, 1348–1351', unpublished Ph.D. dissertation, (University of Kansas, 1975), Appendix IV. For the currency, see Gregory B. Milton, *Market Power: Lordship, Society, and Economy in Medieval Catalonia (1276–1313)* (Basingstoke, 2012), p. 74 n. 11.

[50] Richard H. Britnell, 'Feudal Reaction after the Black Death: The Palatinate of Durham', *Past and Present: A Journal of Historical Studies*, 128 (1990), 28–47, 28.

[51] The *remença* struggle is described in Paul Freedman, *The Origins of Peasant Servitude in Medieval Catalonia* (Cambridge, 1991). See also Jaime Vicens Vives, *Historia de los remensas (en el siglo XV)* (Barcelona, 1978).

peasants of the Bages, this type of lordship was prevalent just east of their region, and so the Bages was spared the worst of the *remença* oppressions and disturbances.[52]

Another factor that might have been expected to cause social tension in the Bages and yet has left few marks in the records was inter-religious persecution. Although the city's Jewish community was quite vital in the early fourteenth century, it all but disappears from the Manresan records after the Black Death of 1348.[53] Though there were massacres of Jews in some Catalan towns, no such disturbance has been recorded for Manresa.[54] Although a small number of Jews continued to inhabit the city until the pogroms and mass conversions of 1391, it is probable that many of those Jews who survived the plague of 1348 at Manresa emigrated to Barcelona or Vic. Thus, the economic and social insignificance of the Manresan Jewish community after 1348 contributed to the fact that Manresa was spared much of the rising tension between Christians and Jews that was characteristic of other cities in post-Black Death Iberia.[55] As for the earlier fourteenth century, relations between Christians and Jews in Manresa appear to have been relatively peaceful and normative. Likewise, as has been mentioned, there were no Islamic or *mudejar* peasants in the countryside of the Bages, as there were in the more newly conquered regions of the Crown of Aragon. Because of this accidental homogeneity, Manresa provides an example of an Iberian city in which interfaith conflict played little part during the later medieval centuries.

FAMINE AND PLAGUE IN CATALONIA TO 1356

As mentioned in Chapter 2, Manresan civic government enjoyed a heyday of regional influence during the early fourteenth century. At that time, civic elites saw themselves primarily as regional actors who might occasionally butt heads with prelates such as the Bishop of Vic and with various noble houses, such as the Cardona, who were accustomed to social and political prominence in the Bages. The early fourteenth-century city government was also notable for the social good that it was

52 Britnell, 'Feudal Reaction', 40.

53 This is evident from the absence of records found in Marc Torras *et al.* (eds.), *Catàleg dels protocols notarials de Manresa*, vol. I (Barcelona, 1993), p. 197, as well as from the fact that Jews all but disappear from the Talamanca, Sarta, and MC records after 1348.

54 For a list of towns in which massacres occurred, see Nirenberg, *Communities of Violence*, p. 237.

55 For this see Nirenberg, *Communities of Violence*, pp. 231–50. For this in the Kingdom of Valencia, albeit with the caveat that the Black Death per se was not very important in causing a deterioration of Christian–Jewish relations, see Mark D. Meyerson, *Jews in an Iberian Frontier Kingdom: Society, Economy, and Politics in Morvedre, 1248–1391* (Leiden, 2004), ch. 5 (pp. 210–71).

able to do. This was the result of a high level of discretionary spending, and meant that the Manresan councillors could preside over a sophisticated system of public education and even a public medical system, amongst many other services.[56] Such a system enabled urban elites to participate in a culture of largesse, indeed of *noblesse oblige*, which enabled them to reinforce the sense that they were both social superiors to the majority of Manresan inhabitants, and their social benefactors as well. Patrician munificence thus helped to create a sense amongst the populace that civic government was run for their benefit, and this social esteem in turn increased the desire of elites to sit as members of the town council.

While William Jordan has emphasized the crisis of the early fourteenth century for northern Europe, with its notable famines, this crisis seems to have bypassed Iberia almost entirely.[57] It has been traditional for Catalan urban historians to discuss the droughts and famines of the 1330s as the beginning of an unrelenting crisis that was to last for most of the century, but the Manresan experience suggests that, although the city did experience famine at this time, the town council was more than ready to meet the challenge presented by these natural disasters.[58] In fact, the consuls 'hedged their bets' by ordering a procession to the nearby monastery of Montserrat in order to pray for rain, while simultaneously embarking on a thoroughly terrestrial, economically appealing plan to create an extensive irrigation system that spanned the plain (*pla*) of the Bages. Though this ambitious plan cut across the land of the Bishop of Vic, and caused him to excommunicate the councillors on more than one occasion, work on the sèquia continued apace until the wars and financial crises of the 1350s and 1360s put a twenty-year hiatus on construction.[59] In other words, there is every indication that the so-called *mal any premier* of 1333 was not a major turning point in the history of Manresa. Instead, the city's vitality remained almost entirely intact until the arrival of the Black Death itself.[60] Even in the face of this second, unprecedented catastrophe, it can be demonstrated that Jaume (II) Sarta and other members of the Manresan entrepreneurial

56 See further discussion of this, with regards to the salaries and wages of municipal workers, in Chapter 7.

57 William Chester Jordan, *The Great Famine* (Princeton, NJ, 1997); for the notion that this crisis also bypassed the Kingdom of Valencia, see Meyerson, *Jews in an Iberian Frontier Kingdom*, p. 210 n.1.

58 The most recent synopsis of this phenomenon in demographic terms is found in Batlle, *L'expansió baixmedieval*, pp. 251ff.

59 For more details on the *sèquia* see Chapter 5, esp. pp. 123–6.

60 For an overview of the impact of the plague in Iberia, see Saturnino Ruiz de Loizaga, *La peste en los reinos peninsulares: según documentación del Archivo Vaticano (1348–1460)* (Bilbao, 2009).

elite were ready to confront the 1350s by investing in a new network of long-distance business contacts. The men of the 1350s were more than ready, it seems, to use their newly inherited wealth to continue the self-bettering practices of their forefathers. They were helped by the fact that, for many decades after the epic French invasion of the 1280s had been beaten off, the scourge of war played almost no role in Catalan life. The largely pacific policies maintained by Jaume II for most of his long reign helped Catalonia and its royal cities to experience a period of massive growth, and the relatively weak fiscal system of the Catalan Crown during these decades ensured that fiscal pressure remained quite minimal. The fact that the bulk of the Catalans' martial energies during the 1320s through the early 1350s were dedicated to naval offensives meant that there was little or no unwanted impact on Catalan infrastructure or dire fiscal need.

As will be argued below, it was really the war with Castile which caused the turning point in Manresan civic vitality, a turning point from which the city and its patriciate never recovered. The so-called 'War of the Two Peters' began in 1356 and officially ended in 1366, but invasion threats and hostility between Castile and Aragon remained unabated during the Castilian civil war (1366–9) and afterwards, until 1375. It was this nearly twenty-year period which turned the 'fourteenth-century crisis' into a true crisis for the people of Manresa and Catalonia, but it was not merely warfare itself which made this period much more difficult to endure than it otherwise would have been. One exacerbating factor was the continuing virulence of the Black Death itself. The plague did not strike Catalonia only in 1348, but also in 1362, in 1374, and several times thereafter.[61] In addition, there were sometimes smaller, more localized outbreaks of plague between the larger, more generalized ones.[62] Each of these waves of plague continued to erode the size of the workforce, causing an increase in wages which, in each instance, added to the economic challenges faced by wealth-holders and entrepreneurs.[63] Even these changes would not have been so bad per se, had the Aragonese government not simultaneously worked out how to implement a very effective system of public debt, known as the *censal* system, which for

[61] The demographic crisis is detailed in Chapter 7.

[62] E.g. the plague of 1370–1, mentioned in MC 1371.11.10.

[63] Robert S. Lopez and Harry A. Miskimin, 'The Economic Depression of the Renaissance', *Economic History Review*, 14 (1962), 408–26; 525–9; Carlo Cipolla, 'Economic Depression of the Renaissance?', *Economic History Review*, 16 (1963), 519–24. For a more recent, more nuanced view, which stresses 'challenges' posed by the demographic crises to businessmen, see Edwin S. Hunt and James Murray, *A History of Business in Medieval Europe, 1200–1550* (Cambridge, 1999), pp. 142–50.

the first time in history forced the towns to make interest payments on a public debt of unprecedented size.[64] Because the debt system was so effective in extracting surplus wealth and revenue, its implementation had a negative impact on Catalan urban society during the later fourteenth century, and was perhaps the single most negative effect of increasing state power on the cities. Had the war and the plague not been interacting in concert with the bond system, the situation in Catalonia during the 1360s and 1370s would have been much less dire. As it was, the combination of all three factors led to an unforeseeable effect that, in the long run, had a very destructive impact on Manresa's urban vitality.

Before the war, however, came the plague. The Black Death of 1348 was undoubtedly the greatest demographic catastrophe to strike Europe since the period of the barbarian migrations. The details of how this affected Manresa and the surrounding region are recounted later in this volume, in Chapter 7. Still, it seems likely that the economic, social, and political impact of this first wave of plague per se has probably been exaggerated.[65] When historians attempt to measure the impact of the plague in the later fourteenth and fifteenth centuries, it is sometimes possible to overlook the fact that they are viewing the cumulative effects of recurrent outbreaks of a disease which was to remain endemic in Europe for several centuries. Our evidence suggests that conditions between each wave of plague may have been markedly different from one another. A close study of the decades in question can thus reveal to us something of the incremental nature of the effects of plague, in terms of economy, society, politics, and *mentalité*. The incremental nature of the effects of the plague should be taken as another of the themes developed in the narrative presented in this chapter and the next.

It became apparent in the winter of 1362–3 that the Black Death was not to be a single event, since at that time a second wave of plague began to peak in Catalonia.[66] Manresa experienced a third serious visitation in 1374–5, and many authors writing on other regions throughout Europe have noticed similar cycles of ten to fifteen years between major outbreaks of the disease.[67] At Manresa, at least, it seems clear that the town's economy and society would not have been so affected, had the

[64] As detailed in Chapters 5 and 6.

[65] This was posited for England long ago by A. R. Bridbury in 'The Black Death', *Economic History Review*, 2nd ser. 26 (1973), 557–92; and is now supported for Italy by the analysis in Shona Kelly Wray, *Communities and Crisis: Bologna During the Black Death* (Leiden, 2009).

[66] Batlle, *L'expansió baixmedieval*, p. 252; mentioned as having 'recently occurred' in MC 1363.5.3.

[67] Samuel K. Cohn Jr, 'Epidemiology of the Black Death and Successive Waves of Plague', *Medical History. Supplement*, 27 (2008), 74–100, 85–6; Freedman, *The Origins of Peasant Servitude*, pp. 154–66; also MCOA, pp. 165–6.

1348 plague remained an isolated event. The 1348 plague was certainly devastating; it caused the Manresan government to all but cease functioning for the better part of a year and caused endless legal snafus, many of which were not resolved for decades.[68] But evidence suggests that the 1348 plague did not decisively change the attitudes of the town fathers, nor did it change the functioning of the economy or society of Manresa in a discernible way. In addition to the Sarta evidence, it is true that both Pere III and the Manresan town councillors seemed as eager as ever to go to war with Genoa in 1351 and 1352. By contrast, the depressive, morbid innovations that have been emphasized by some historians as hallmarks of later fourteenth-century culture did not become evident in Manresan society until after the second wave of plague, at the earliest.[69] It was at this time that the town fathers began to perceive their town as being underpopulated, as wages and prices continued to climb and the pressures of the Castilian war did not abate. As will be shown below, by the third wave of plague in the mid-1370s, there is evidence of genuine despair in the town council records, which, amongst other things, would lead to avoidance of civic office by the later 1370s. Thus, although the second and third waves of plague were not nearly as severe as the first in terms of population loss, each plague event had a percussive impact on the attitude of the Manresan patriciate, which became increasingly despondent after each blow.

As for the 1348 plague itself, far from catching the Manresan population by surprise, it is probable that the Manresan councillors had an advanced report of the coming epidemic by April 1348, or even earlier.[70] Boccaccio suggests that the instinct of many wealthier people was to flee the towns on news of the coming epidemic, and hope that the isolation of country living might help them to survive. Although the plague was unprecedented in its virility, early fourteenth-century Europe was no stranger to epidemics of disease, and so it is important to remember that the Manresan populace would have had a model for what was happening to them, even if, as the death toll began to mount, it must have seemed to many as though the Last Judgement was indeed upon them. The plague reached Barcelona in May of 1348, and reached Manresa within a week

68 See n. 77, below. See also William M. Bowsky, 'The Impact of the Black Death upon Sienese Government and Society', *Speculum*, 38 (1964), 1–34, and M. W. Flinn, 'Plague in Europe and the Mediterranean Countries', *Journal of European Economic History*, 8:1 (1979), 131–48.

69 See P. Wallace Platt, *King Death* (Toronto, 1996); and Samuel K. Cohn Jr, *The Cult of Remembrance and the Black Death: Six Renaissance Cities in Central Italy* (Baltimore, MD, 1997).

70 See also Chapter 7, n. 24. For a balanced argument that, by the fifteenth century, the plague had been largely absorbed by English society as just another reminder of the possibility of sudden demise, see Rosemary Horrox, 'Introduction', in Rosemary Horrox (ed.), *Fifteenth-Century Attitudes: Perceptions of Society in Late Medieval England* (Cambridge, 1997), pp. 1–12.

or two of this.[71] Afterwards, the disease raged in the homes and streets of the city, and did not abate for perhaps twelve weeks. By the end of the summer over 50 per cent of the town's inhabitants had succumbed. In such circumstances, most institutions were simply overwhelmed. Across Catalonia, bailiffs whose job it was to do inquests *post mortem* either died, or their officials died, or else they were afraid to conduct business given the pandemic that was raging around them. During and shortly after the plague, earlier reserves of anti-Jewish feeling, which had been stirred by the invective of the Dominicans, had erupted in many Catalan cities into full-scale pogroms.[72] As noted earlier, there is no evidence for a pogrom at Manresa, but whether by plague, voluntary migration, or other means, the Jewish community of Manresa all but ceased to exist after 1348. The advent of the *censal* meant that the need for short-term loans, which had been one of the Jews' speciality, was never again as great as it had been before. This is perhaps one reason why the Manresan *call* was never repopulated.

In the wake of the plague, the first order of business for the Manresan political elite was to restore some sort of institutional order. There is fragmentary evidence that the town government was functioning by the summer of 1349, even though the regular keeping of council records did not officially recommence until 1352.[73] The second order of business was to sort out the unprecedented legal snafu that had been created by the plague.[74] For surviving and newly appointed government officers, the primary challenge was to find legal heirs for the deceased – a process which was still ongoing in December 1350, that is, fully two and a half years after the first onslaught.[75] Many Manresan houses still stood empty when the government records recommenced in 1352. At a meeting of the Catalan *Corts* in August of 1350, half of the attendant knights' seats remained vacant due to unsettled legal claims on their estates.[76] Other tasks, such as being able to declare a manse vacant when no heirs could be found, could only legally be done after two decades had elapsed,

[71] For Barcelona see Bisson, MCOA, 109. [72] See n. 53, above.

[73] Although there are some entries in the *Manuales Concilii* (and in the Sarta family books) for late 1348 and 1349, the entry MC 1349 3i8 contains the proclamation '*Hic inceperunt regiam scribaniam Petrus d Gostemps, Jacobus Granoya, Barnardus de Cumbis, et Arnau d Comella*'; all four of them appear to be new names in the scrivany. The names Petrus Rubei, Pontius de Voltraria, and Francesc de Franquedine, which were common prior to May 1348 no longer appear, leaving the impression that there was a complete turnover in scribal personnel as a result of the Black Death. The town council manuals do not begin again in earnest until August 1352 (AHCM/AM I-5).

[74] For demographic figures see Table 7.1 and relevant discussion.

[75] This is in evidence from AHCM/AM I-4, MC 1350 3i12 to the end, which is in fact a bailiff's inquest into the many homes standing vacant in the city.

[76] *Cortes*, I-2, 341–2.

and this custom undoubtedly added to the look of desertedness which characterized the countryside as the century progressed.[77] Even legal procedures altered with the plague, partly as the result of so many new scribes being drafted into the royal scrivanies: in late April or early May of 1351, an order was given that all scribes at Manresa should switch from the old Roman-style dates to the modern reckoning by days of the month.[78] And although this section is attempting in some ways to moderate some of the more dire claims for the after-effects of the 1348 plague, it is true that certain aspects of life changed forever.[79] One of the most important was that the wages of labourers shot up by perhaps 50 per cent within a matter of months, prompting Pere III to pass a statute of maximum wages in 1350. This was similar to the better-studied laws passed by Edward III and the English parliament in 1349 and 1351.[80]

THE ORIGINS OF THE CASTILIAN WAR

Moving from the topic of the plague to the Mediterranean political scene after 1348, an observer could be forgiven for surmising that the Black Death had made very little impression on the surviving statesmen of the main contending powers. In fact, the advent of the plague played very nicely into the hands of Pere III, when he used the confusion caused by the outbreak of the plague to extricate himself from the clutches of rebellious Unionists, who had been holding him a virtual prisoner in the city of Valencia.[81] Pere then spent the succeeding months wreaking his revenge and re-establishing his authority in his province-kingdoms of Valencia and Aragon. Genoa, for its part, began a war against the Byzantine emperor over the possession of some Greek islands in 1348, and in 1350, the Venetians joined in league against them. In 1351, Pere III made the fateful decision to ally Catalonia-Aragon with the Venetians and the Byzantines, as a step in the Catalans' continuing struggle against the Genoese over the islands of Sardinia and Corsica. Pere made clear that the purpose of this alliance was nothing less than the destruction of Genoese power, and the reason that he was so adamant was because the Genoese had been supporting the rulers ('judges') of Sardinia in their

77 For this procedure see FT2 1369.11.30; FT2 1371.4.27, both of which would have been standing vacant for twenty years in the aftermath of the plague.

78 In the council manuals, the switch occurs between MC 1351 16k5 and MC 1351 5.12; Jaume Sarta's book goes from 1351 3k3 to 6.27. The Talamanca family books likewise show 1351 3i4 and 1351 8.20.

79 For an optimistic assessment of the ability of communities to cope with the Black Death itself (as a single occurrence, rather than the aggregate effects of generations of plague that were at this point still in the future), see Wray, *Communities and Crisis*.

80 See n. 49, above.

81 Bisson, MCOA, 107–9.

simmering revolt against Catalan rule since 1347. These alliances resulted in the epic and destructive, yet seemingly indecisive, naval battle of the Bosphorus. This was fought in February 1352, and saw the combined Catalan, Venetian and Byzantine fleets fight the Genoese to a draw.[82] Despite having lost many of their ships in the east, the Catalans were able to rebuild their fleet in a very short period, in time to win a decisive naval battle against the Genoese off Sardinia in 1354. This resulted in the seizure of Genoa itself by the Duke of Milan, and enabled Pere to sail to Sardinia, whence he recaptured Alghero. With the Genoese in a state of disarray which would ultimately lead to their decline as a major naval power, the Catalans were henceforth able to keep Sardinia, although the island was not entirely pacified until well into the fifteenth century.

For several years after his fragile success in Sardinia, Pere continued to act with as much aggression as ever on several political fronts. But the Genoese threat to Sardinia continued to be foremost in his mind. To this end, he continued to press annual demands upon his cities, taxing them in 1353, 1354, and 1355 at the maximum rate for which there was any precedent – this despite the fact that these cities' populations had likely fallen by more than half only a few years previously.[83] But the king soon came to the conclusion that in order to secure his position against further Genoese interference, he would have to disrupt the trading alliances which existed between Genoa and Castile. Emboldened by the chaotic state of affairs in Castile, as well as in Genoa, Pere outfitted a fleet of ships whose orders were to attack Genoese and Genoese-allied shipping – including that of Castile. Because of an ongoing rebellion by his nobles, Pedro of Castile was unable to do anything while Pere's fleet seized shipping in his ports. In his own letter, quoted in Pere's chronicle, Pedro states that 'If we had not been in some difficulties at the time when most of these things happened, we would have been able to restrain [these attacks] in such a manner as befitted Our honor and Our service.'[84]

Regarding the course of the war, Jocelyn Hillgarth's narrative remains the most comprehensive, though the parliamentary politics of the period 1356–66 are usefully augmented by Kagay.[85] Regarding the outbreak of the war, Hillgarth informs us that '[Pere of Aragon's] projects soon included the large-scale acquisition of land from Castile. He told the

[82] Steven A. Epstein, *Genoa and the Genoese, 958–1528* (Chapel Hill, NC, 2001), pp. 219–21. MCOA, 109–11.

[83] One aspect of the political complexities of these years is described in Mario Lafuente Gómez, *Guerra en ultramar: La intervención aragonesa en el dominio de Cerdeña, 1354–1355* (Zaragoza, 2011). For the political situation in these years see Fynn-Paul, 'Civic Debt, Civic Taxes', 130–1.

[84] Mary and J. N. Hillgarth, trans. *Pere III, Chronicle*, vol. II, p. 498.

[85] Particularly in Kagay, 'War Financing in the Late-medieval Crown of Aragon'.

count of Foix that he would have 3000–4000 horse, against Pedro I's 2000.'[86] Pere also decided to use Pedro's bastard half-brother, Enrique de Trastámara, as a weapon against Pedro, calculating that by thus continuing the Castilian civil war, he would be able to ensure that Pedro's forces were never larger than what he himself could muster. In retrospect such a plan does not seem entirely reckless. But in the event, Pere was seriously mistaken, since within a year he and his subjects were fighting for their very independence, facing invasions on several fronts. Even at the time, Pere's statement that 'all those of the council were very unwilling to give counsel' shows that none of his top advisors took war with Castile lightly; it must always have appeared a great gamble, albeit one whose potential rewards were also great.

Although Pere attempted to hide the fact that he was the primary aggressor in this war, in a ruse which has largely succeeded over the past 650 years, a close reading of the sources reveals that the *Corts* of Perpignan, originally to be held on 24 June 1356, were not called in order to address the Sardinian question, as has been assumed, but were actually called to pursue an agenda of war with Castile.[87] The initial call went out some three months before war was actually declared on 4 September. Pere and his councillors therefore knew exactly what they were doing when they declared war on Castile, and Pere's rationale was no doubt a mixture of anger at the Castilians' Genoese alliance and the fact that the Castilians continued to have designs on Murcia, Alicante, and other Aragonese lands, particularly through the claims of Pere's stepmother. Clearly, the Catalans had prepared for the opening of hostilities when they did occur. Official notification of the war went out from the royal chancery in Barcelona on 4 October. A letter to this effect reached Manresa on 5 October, and on the following day, the Manresan *consellers* matter-of-factly recorded their debt of 24625s to the Barcelona money changer Jaume de Vilar, who had already advanced this sum to the king in Manresa's name 'for the war which he has with the King of Castile'.[88]

[86] J. N. Hillgarth, *The Spanish Kingdoms, 1250–1516: Precarious Balance, 1250–1410*, vol. I (Oxford, 1976), p. 378.

[87] *Cortes*, I-ii, 497–8.

[88] MC 1356.10.6; considering that Manresa had already paid extraordinary subsidies of 30,000s in 1353, another 30,000s in 1354 and 36,000s in 1355, to pay another 24,625s in 1356 was remarkable enough; but the question arises of when the city agreed to pay this subsidy, which appears to have been a fait accompli by the time Pere sent his letters of 4 October. Catalan custom was very firm on the point that all extraordinary subsidies had to be approved in the *Corts*, and they had to be approved for a stated purpose. The answer must be that the subsidy was voted during the *Corts* of Perpignan, held in June, July, and August of 1356, even though, to

Because this issue was to have such far-reaching implications for the well-being of Manresa and the other Catalan cities, it is important to ask why they might have agreed to support such a drastic move as war with Castile, even after Pedro's letter of 8 August, which left a wide berth for reconciliation between the two kingdoms, despite Rafael Tasis i Marca's assertion that the letter was *un veritable ultimàtum.*[89] Traditionally commentators have viewed Pere's actions as reckless, not least because his government is held to have been highly inefficient compared with those of the surrounding states, including Castile.[90] This, surely, is to give too little credit to the administrative abilities of the fourteenth-century House of Barcelona. The evidence from Manresa shows that the financial administration of the Crown of Aragon was not as rickety as Hillgarth's account would portray. In an assessment of Pere's finances and constitutional situation which still reflects the mainstream of historiographical opinion, Hillgarth writes:

> In 1356 when the war with Castile began, Pere III had no financial reserves. Pedro I had vast resources. He could mobilize troops rapidly and pay them regularly. Pere was dependent on grants from his Corts. These took time to summon, and, even during a foreign invasion insisted on the redress of grievances before voting money (for a specified purpose, sometimes restricted to defence of their local area). The grant took months to collect . . . Pere had to rely largely on loans from his cities . . . [91]

Yet it has here been demonstrated that Pere had managed to collect extraordinary sums in 1353, 1354, 1355, and now in 1356, through means which were by this point regular, speedy, and efficient, much more than older accounts give him credit for. This was based to a large degree upon the impression of haphazardness and protest that the

judge from the surviving printed records, these *Corts* were held merely to address the question of war with the Genoese, rather than with the Castilians. Cf. *Cortes*, I-ii, 497–8.

These *Corts* were initially to be held on 24 June 1356, but they were prorogued, first to 30 June, and then to 7 July. On this day the official deliberations began, and of them nothing was recorded until 6 August, when the *Corts* presented a small number of 'recommendations' and requests about the Genoese war. The published transcripts of this *Corts*, like several others during these decades, are obviously incomplete. Most notably, no concluding date or signatures exist in the surviving transcript, so the ending date of the *Corts* is not at present known. It was merely two days after the presentation of the petitions of 6 August that Pedro of Castile dated his letter to Pere from Seville, a letter which Pere claims not to have received until 4 September, the very day when he dated his own defiance to Pedro. Considering the import of this debate, which according to Pere himself bitterly divided his council, the king's statement that he received Pedro's letter and sent his own reply on the same day is probably a fiction. Cf. Mary and J. N. Hillgarth, trans., *Pere III, Chronicle*, vol. II, p. 499.

89 Rafael Tasis i Marca, *Pere el Cerimoniós el els seus fills* (Barcelona, 1994), p. 64.

90 Hillgarth, *The Problem of a Catalan Mediterranean Empire 1229–1327*. This is echoed by Bisson, MCOA, 118–19.

91 J. N. Hillgarth, *The Spanish Kingdoms*, vol. I, p. 383.

transcriptions of the *Corts* might present to readers. But politics has always been about behind-the-scenes tacit agreements, which can easily remain invisible to an outsider who merely witnesses the bluster and hyperbole of parliamentary debate. Attempting to understand the workings of British government from transcripts of debates in the House of Commons would, at nearly any point in history, produce a similar impression of chaos, often to the point of pandemonium. And yet even after the war with Castile began to go badly, Pere was still able to raise extraordinary levies with impressive rapidity. For example, the Manresan council recorded that within six weeks of receiving a summons to *Corts* at Girona, as reported on 12 April 1358, it was indebted once more to the Barcelona money changer Jaume de Vilar for the very large sum of 78,000s. This was three times the amount owed in 1356.[92] If there was any doubt as to the speed of this transaction, the Manresan *consellers* actually used the word *subito* to describe their sudden indebtedness to the king.[93]

Furthermore, Manresan records show that the Catalan *Corts* did not take very long to summon, either in peacetime or during a war. The above example shows that the *Corts* of Girona were over within six weeks of the dating of the summons; even under normal circumstances the letters of summons to *Corts* usually arrived at Manresa only two or three weeks before they were set to occur.[94] The subsidies of 1356 and 1358 were granted for no more specific purpose than to pursue the war with Castile, and they did not take months to collect. This is because the sums were advanced by Barcelona money changers almost immediately upon the grant of a subsidy. The king may often have had his money even before the *Corts* were concluded. It was the bankers and money changers who then had to collect over the succeeding months from the various cities, prelates, and nobles who were indebted to them. In the case of Manresa, Pere de Vilar collected his 78,000s in 7,000s instalments, paid over three years.[95] And the Manresan government took its financial obligations to these creditors seriously: the reason for this is that the law required them to pay very heavy fines if the city did not pay on schedule. Finally, the Manresan evidence shows that most of the money advanced to the Crown during the war was not made as a loan from his cities, but was taken by the king as an exaction. The towns themselves were put in debt, and the citizens of the towns

92 MC 1358.4.12 for summons; MC 1358.5.26 for debt of 78,000s. This was to be repaid over two years.

93 MC 1358.5.26.

94 For an example of a speedy wartime summons, MC 1361.9.17 records a royal letter, dated 13 September 1361, which summoned Manresan syndics to a *Corts* on 1 October.

95 For the 7,000s instalments, see MC 1358.5.18.

were left to repay their debts as best they could. In Manresa's case this was to cause hardships whose effects were felt for decades. The relatively recently 'discovered' fiscal revolution that will be discussed in Chapter 6 has not yet been brought to bear on the current historiographical assessment of Pere's reign. The implementation of a regular system of taxes in the 1320s helped to double royal revenue from the cities, as Table 6.3 makes clear. The ability to borrow enabled urban nominal revenue to increase to triple 1320s levels by the 1360s, when there was pressing need.[96] In the light of this dramatically increasing fiscal power on the part of the Crown, Hillgarth's stark picture of Pere's financial weakness, then, which was written in response to the sometimes too-confident writings of earlier Catalan historians, needs to be modified. This is not to say that Hillgarth was incorrect in the main: Pere's financial machinery was subject to much more interference than Pedro's, and it seems clear that the King of Aragon did receive many financial setbacks at the hands of his nobles and his parliament, as the war advanced. It is, however, important to see Pere III as something more than a paper tiger in the face of his parliament, at any stage of the war. In the face of the Catalan towns, at the very least, his power could not have been much more absolute, despite the appearances of freedom provided by the *Corts*. At no time during his reign did Pere lack the ability to put his royal towns into as much debt as they could realistically bear.

Besides being relatively confident of their own evolving financial network, the Catalan elite had other palpable reasons to feel that war with Castile would not be ruinous. At the outset of the war, the Catalan merchants probably saw, along with their king, that the Castilian action was a logical extension of the naval war with Genoa, since the two were clearly aiding one another; and the naval war had thus far been going in the Catalans' favour. Still, naval war was one thing, and something that the Catalans were generally quite good at. A land war with Castile was an entirely different kettle of fish, as events soon proved.[97] Which brings up the question of how much choice the Catalan urban elites actually had in the matter of the Castilian war. It would seem from the actions of the Manresan bailiff, as noted below, that the Manresan patriciate was not at all happy to be entering into a new phase of the war. It is hard to believe that delegates from Manresa for the *Corts* of 1356, with their city worn out as it was by large subsidy payments for the Genoese war in the

96 Fynn-Paul, 'Civic Debt, Civic Taxes', 119–35; for more on revenue see Chapter 7.

97 For a description of the opening moves of the war (albeit one which on its own admission does not pretend to be a comprehensive narrative of these events), see Maria Teresa Ferrer i Mallol, *Entre la paz y la guerra: La Corona Catalano-Aragonesa y Castilla en la baja edad media*, Anuario de Estudios Medievales. Anejo, 59 (Barcelona, 2005), pp. 349ff.

previous three years, would have acceded willingly to a fourth year of subsidies at only a slightly reduced rate – particularly when one views this in terms of the relatively light burden which the city had borne during the 1330s and 1340s.[98] The delegates must also have known that war with Castile was unlikely to be limited to a single campaigning season. Did the *Corts* willingly agree to go to war with Castile? Or were they forced into this decision? It is also possible that the *Corts* voted the subsidy of 1356 for the Genoese war, and the Crown then diverted it to the Castilian front in the name of self-defence – although in this case one would expect to hear some type of outcry from the delegates which is not recorded in the transcriptions that have come down to us. Whatever the case, it is clear that the power of the *braç reial*, that is, the cities represented in *Corts*, did not make an effective opposition to the king's wishes in 1356. As will become apparent from the narrative in Chapter 5, royal impositions on the cities would only increase during the next two decades of war.

[98] Fynn-Paul, 'Civic Debt, Civic Taxes', pp. 130–1.

Chapter 5

THE PRACTICE OF GOVERNMENT AT MANRESA DURING THE FOURTEENTH-CENTURY CRISIS

TOWN GOVERNMENT DURING THE EARLY YEARS OF THE CASTILIAN WAR, 1356–60

The previous chapter set the stage for the narrative that follows by introducing several strands of the late medieval 'crisis debate', and by introducing the Black Death and the origins of the Castilian war, which were two major components of the maelstrom which enveloped Manresa during these years. This chapter will now describe the practice of urban government at Manresa as it was experienced by the patriciate themselves. The primary source for this narrative is the town council manuals, which additionally preserve many royal letters and the *consellers*' responses to them. The *Llibre Verd* of Manresa, which also preserves a series of royal letters addressed to Manresa during this time, was likewise extremely useful in this regard.[1] The publication of several towns' *Llibres Verds* enables a comparison of royal letters sent to the various towns, and makes it possible to judge whether given royal directives were general or particular to a specific town.[2] The action in this chapter begins *in medias res*, continuing from the origins of the Castilian–Aragonese war addressed at the end of Chapter 4. This chapter then ends with a conclusion which summarizes some of the historiographical themes introduced in Chapter 4 and in the present chapter, as nuanced or revised in light of the Manresan experience.

It was argued at the end of the last chapter that the war with Genoa begun in 1351 flowed, with hardly a hiccup, into a war with Castile. This

[1] Josep M. Gasol and Marc Torras Serra (eds.), *El Llibre Verd de Manresa: 1218–1902* (Barcelona, 1996).

[2] An important initiative begun in the later 1980s saw the publication of a number of the *Llibres Verds*. In addition to the Manresan volume, see also Christian Guilleré (ed.), *Llibre Verd de la ciutat de Girona, 1144–1533* (Barcelona, 2000); Vicente García Edo (ed.), *El Llibre Verd Major de Perpinyà (segle XII–1395)* (Barcelona, 2010); Jaume Sobrequés i Callicó *et al.* (eds.), *Llibre verd de Barcelona* (Barcelona, 2004); Jordi Vallès i Cuevas (ed.), *El Llibre verd de Vilafranca* (Barcelona, 1992). For additional books, including others published under the alternate heading of 'Llibres de privilegis', see Bibliography.

interpretation is significant, since the usual accounts of this 'War of the Two Peters' put the conflict as lasting only between 1356 and 1366.[3] The traditional narrative obscures the fact that Catalonia-Aragon was at war every year between 1351 and 1375, in a series of conflicts which were to a large degree interrelated; recent work has, however, begun to address this issue.[4]

In the previous chapter it was described how the Crown announced, in the autumn of 1356, that the city of Manresa found itself suddenly indebted to a Barcelona money changer to the tune of nearly 25000 *solidi*. Since this represented perhaps half of the city's normal annual revenue, the first order of business for the Manresan *consellers* was to determine how the city should pay for it.[5] On 6 October, a long list of Manresan residents was drawn up, intended to represent the *consell general* of the *universitas* of the city; meetings of the *consell general* had in recent decades become a relatively rare occurrence and this was certainly unusual in itself.[6] But now, in an extraordinary move, the bailiff of the city forced all members of the *consell general* to swear to pay this subsidy, under the penalty of 2,000s payable to the *veguer*.[7] The bailiff at the time was Ferrer de Manresa, who may well be the same Ferrer de Manresa named in Pere's chronicle as a member of the royal council which took the decision to go to war.[8] Ferrer may have been acting under the notion that the royal interest lay in silencing anti-war dissent. Whether or not this was the case, the de Manresas were a knightly family who had claimed lordship of the city of Manresa in the twelfth and early thirteenth centuries, and it was probably by virtue of this long-standing sense of authority in Manresa that Ferrer felt empowered to bully the council with unusual bravado.[9] Not surprisingly, Ferrer's heavy-handedness made him unpopular with many leading citizens: in January 1357, immediately upon expiry of Ferrer's three-year term of office, the town council elected two legal procurators 'to prosecute certain officials who in the recent past held royal office

3 The 'War of the Two Pedros' has now received some historiographical treatment. The most detailed account is Maria Teresa Ferrer i Mallol, *Entre la paz y la guerra: La corona Catalano-aragonesa y Castilla en la baja edad media* (Barcelona, 2005); also Donald J. Kagay, 'The Defense of the Crown of Aragon during the War of the Two Pedros', *Journal of Military History*, 71:1 (2007), 11–33, esp. 22. Some mention of the conflict is given in Manuel Sánchez Martínez, 'The Invocation of *Princeps Namque* in 1368 and its Repercussions for the City of Barcelona', in L. J. Andrew Villalon and Donald J. Kagay (eds.), *The Hundred Years War: A Wider Focus*, History of Warfare, 25 (Leiden, 2005), 297–330. For a general account of the war, see MCOA, 111–17.

4 Kagay, 'The Defense of the Crown of Aragon during the War of the Two Pedros'.

5 The actual figures for the city's revenue are presented in the economics section of this volume, specifically in Chapter 6, Tables 6.1 to 6.4.

6 E.g. MC 1358.10.(?). (exact date not given).

7 MC 1356.10.6.

8 Mary and J. N. Hillgarth, trans., *Pere III, Chronicle*, vol. II (Toronto, 1980), p. 499.

9 For the de Manresas see Chapter 2, p. 34.

in the *vegueria* and bailiwick of Manresa, and caused certain damages to the *universitas* and individuals of the city'.[10] It is not clear how the city's lawsuit turned out, but it is true that no subsequent bailiff tried to enforce a similar measure on the townspeople.

While Ferrer's actions made the patricians' debt more legally binding, it did not solve the basic issue of how to pay it off. Thus, the council continued to deliberate on how to raise the 24,625s owed to Jaume de Vilar. Because their regular revenue was now stretched to the limit, the townsmen realized that raising funds through the new and relatively untried means of selling *censals* and *violaris* was the most realistic way of raising the money. Although they could not have known it at the time, the year 1356 would mark the beginning of Manresa's permanent funded debt, which would last until the end of the *ancien régime*. *Censals* and *violaris* were annuities paid to investors by the city in return for a lump-sum investment. *Censals* were payable in perpetuity, and at this time were earning a rate of about 7 per cent, while *violaris* were payable only for the lives of one or two holders, and thus paid at the much higher rate of 16 per cent.[11] These methods of raising cash had become popular in Catalonia only in the past decade or two; they had first appeared in Manresa during the Mallorcan conflicts of the 1340s, but the amounts raised were small enough that they were soon paid off.[12] The fact that the *consellers* considered the sale of *censals* to be a new and potentially dangerous departure, as indeed it turned out to be, is evidenced from the vigorous debate recorded on 27 November 1356. A very important consideration that arose was to whom the city would sell its *censals* and *violaris*. The idea of having a powerful lord or a Barcelona money changer as their long-term creditor was as unpalatable to the council as the idea of *censals* themselves. In the end it was decided to sell *censals* to the Manresan partnership of Bernat Amargos, Bernat de Valls, and Jaume Sarta.[13] This company was chosen because it had close ties to the conciliar regime, and also because it was one of the few Manresan bodies that could raise the required capital on such short notice. Indeed, theirs is the only company that appears in the fourteenth-century council records as *censal* owner.[14] In this way one can see in operation the movement of mercantile capital into the coffers of the state.

[10] MC 1357.1.28. [11] For explanations and rates of *censals* and *violaris*, see Table 6.5.

[12] EPLV, 191–9.

[13] The earliest attestation of this company in the Sarta papers is SF 1348 913. Note that the Florentines only sold to citizens of the city – not even of the *contado*; Herlihy, *Tuscans and their Families*, ch. 1.

[14] In fact, Jaume Amargos was *conseller* at the time of the debate, and his family members had held the consulate at least four times since 1325. The Sartas would hold their first consulship in 1367. See Table 2.1.

Because of this novel and increasing fiscal pressure, the city became embroiled in a number of lawsuits over the jurisdiction of the *vegueria* and *batllia* of Manresa, in which it appears very clearly that the city viewed the jurisdiction of the *veguer* and the bailiff as its own fiscal 'turf'. In March 1357 the city created procurators 'to defend the jurisdictions of the *vegueria* and the bailiwick from any diminution'.[15] In July they sent to the king to ask if the *sotsvegueria* of Moyà could be added to their own *vegueria*.[16] Later on in the same year the town became embroiled in a struggle with the Abbot of Sant Benet over the jurisdictions of four parishes, all of which lay very close to the Abbey of Sant Benet. From this proximity alone, it is nearly certain that the Abbey of Sant Benet had administered these parishes at some point in the past, even though, as the townsmen claimed, the bailiff of Manresa had recently been accustomed to dispense justice in them.[17] When the Bishop of Vic found in favour of the Abbot, the town protested in a lawsuit that continued through August 1358. At that time the *consellers* empowered a notary to go to the king to argue their case before him, but a week later they thought better of it and sent two of their own, namely Dominic Vidal and Jaume Sarta, to go and plead personally before the court.[18] Their suit was at least partly successful, as shall be seen presently.

This sudden interest in jurisdictions was not merely coincidental; rather it stemmed directly from the city's desperate need to increase its tax revenue. The lawyers hired in 1357 to defend the jurisdictions of the *vegueria* and bailiwick against any diminution reflect a similar scramble initiated by other Catalan legal entities to increase their own revenue at the same time. That so many latent border disputes were suddenly taken up at this time is a clear sign that revenues were becoming straitened, not only in the various royal cities, but in ecclesiastical and noble dominions as well. During this crisis of jurisdictions the patriciate had several conspicuous successes in its struggle to increase its direct economic exploitation of the *vegueria*. In January 1358 the city was allowed to appoint its first *operarios operis caminorum*, who were to oversee the work on all roads within the *vegueria*.[19] Two lesser members of the patriciate, from non-conciliar families, were chosen for this task.[20] Soon these

[15] MC 1357.3.23. [16] MC 1357.7.21.

[17] MC 1357.12.8. The four parishes were St Fructuos, St Benet de Bages, Sta Maria de Navarcles, and Torriçen.

[18] MC 1358.8.17 and 1358.8.28.

[19] For similar officials in Perpignan, see Philip Daileader, 'Town and Countryside in Northeastern Catalonia, 1267–c.1450: The "sobreposats de la horta" of Perpignan', *Journal of Medieval History*, 24:4 (1998), 347–66.

[20] MC 1358.1.2. These were Pere dez Far and Berenguer de Sobrebalç.

operarios, or overseers, were to become simply *operarios extra civitatem*, as opposed to the *operarios infra civitatem* who had been appointed since 1323.[21] The *operarios extra civitatem* had broad powers to direct public works and spend public money within the Bages, and the city's control of this office was thus a conspicuous symbol of its dominance over the region. At the same time, the city's great irrigation project, the *sèquia*, continued apace. A separate treasurer, the *clavarius peccuniae cequie*, had been created to direct the fiscal aspects of this project, which also asserted the townsmen's dominance over the surrounding countryside.[22] In 1362, faced with ever mounting expenses, the king granted permission for the city to levy tolls on major roads throughout the *vegueria*, providing an even more palpable link between the civic administration and the *veguer*'s territory. The tolls to be collected were very high: eight pence for a cart, four pence for a large animal, and one penny per *animal minut*. The consequence of this action, and others like it, was to fan the ire of the local castellans and landlords against the king and the citizenry of Manresa. Tensions would only rise further as the war dragged on and fiscal pressures became even more acute.[23]

Meanwhile, whatever optimism the Catalans may have felt at the outset of the war was shattered when the city of Tarazona in western Aragon was suddenly captured by Pedro of Castile in March of 1357. King Pere, who was in Saragossa at the time, was highly alarmed, and worked to have a truce imposed by a papal legate, which did have the palpable effect of preventing another major campaign from being fought in the summer of 1357. Thus the Catalan cities were spared from having to pay a royal subsidy that year. Even without having to pay a subsidy in 1357, the Manresan civic treasury was showing its first signs of severe strain – a condition which would remain endemic for the next two decades. In March of that year, the new bailiff sanctioned the council's motion to stop payments to the town's principal doctor, Magister Bernat de Figerola, who may have been receiving a salary as high as 800s per year.[24] In this time of budgetary crisis such a highly paid civil servant was an obvious target: on the same day that Figerola lost his salary, he was replaced 'for the good of the city' with a new doctor, Magister Johannes

21 LV, 99–100. 22 For an example of the *clavarius peccunie sequie*, see MC 1357.3.23.

23 MC 1362.3.14.

24 MC 1351.4.20 is the earliest mention of Bernat de Figerola as a *fisicus* in the town. The previous doctor, Pere d'Agostenchs, was receiving 800s per year in *violaris* from the town in 1332 (MC 1332.12.1), and in March of 1348 he received another 800s which was specifically called his annual salary. MC 1348.3.20. For some details on the Manresan civic medical system, such as it was, see Michael R. McVaugh, 'Le coût de la pratique et l'accès aux soins au XIVe siècle: L'exemple de la ville de Manresa', *Médiévales: Langue, Textes, Histoire (Paris)*, 46 (2004), 45–54.

de Scolla, who agreed to work as the city's *fisicus* for the almost token annuity of 100s.[25] In all likelihood, de Scolla made up for this paltry salary by charging his patients additional fees. Through this action, the city effectively switched from a public to a private health-care system, as it would soon do with the city's education system and even with the *sèquia*.[26] In such an atmosphere the city's traditional half-public, half-private charity network also began to break down. The government now had to authorize the use of force to compel people to make their usual donations for the upkeep of paupers.[27] For his part, the well-to-do Dr Figerola did not take the loss of his salary sitting down: he filed lawsuits against the city which ran on for many years. Four years after the case began, in March 1361, the doctor came to the council with a royal letter, dated 21 December 1360, which ordered the *veguer* and bailiff to secure all property owed to him; but the *veguer* appears to have argued that he had not received a copy of this letter, and the council voted the considerable sum of 200s to pay procurators to protest to the king against Figerola's suit.[28]

The city's traditional fiscal administration was another early casualty of the war. From the Manresan perspective, it is clear that the city was hardly 'taking matters into its own hands' in defiance of the king regarding fiscal matters, as has sometimes been alleged. It seems clear that the town councillors were, on the contrary, doing everything they could think of in order to create a system which could comply with increasing (and, it must be said, evidently necessary) royal demands.[29] The city's fiscal machinery had been overwhelmed by the first wave of *censal* sales in 1356. In response, in October 1357, the confused mass of ad hoc *clavarii* (treasurers), such as the *clavarius peccunie cequie* mentioned above, were amalgamated into a single office held by one individual. The city's first town treasurer was therefore instated, and he was given licence to use any of the city's 'impositions or other money' for the coming six months 'to pay off all money owed by the city'.[30] He was also told that he did not have to inform the council when making minor payments, a departure

25 MC 1357.3.23. For professional incomes, see Tables 7.5 to 7.7.

26 The first complaint about the expense of the *sèquia* comes in April 1358, just before the summons to *Corts* that would lead to the May 1358 subsidy. MC 1358.4.27.

27 MC 1361.3.19. 28 MC 1361.3.19.

29 This is asserted by Kagay for Perpignan in 1359; see Donald J. Kagay, 'War Financing in the Late-medieval Crown of Aragon', *Journal of Medieval Military History*, 6 (2008), 119–48, at 133; while it is possible that certain councils were feeling defiant here and there, the Manresan experience suggests that this 'view from above' be tempered with the realization that councillors knew that Pere's demands were by and large necessary, though they required an implementation of the very latest techniques in fiscal administration.

30 MC 1357.10.6.

from previous practice in which the *jurats* were to be notified in all instances. This small detail is not insignificant; it is indicative of a rapidly increasing pace of bureaucratization and professionalization of the city's fiscal administration. On 23 November 1357, presumably after the new *clavarius* had conducted a thorough audit of the city's accounts, the councillors empowered four procurators 'to seek out all debts owed to the city'.[31] But they soon realized that the creation of a single *clavarius* was not sufficient to cope with the new exigencies of wartime finance, since many other appointments continued which conflicted with the authority of the new office. In January 1358, the *consellers* admitted that 'the *universitas* has created too many economic procurators, syndics, and actors, and the said procurators have, it is said, spent much money for which they have not bothered to render an account'.[32] The council's simple but drastic solution to this problem was to revoke the commissions of all its procurators, except those handling the business about the boundaries of the *vegueria* and the bailiwick, and also those handling the case versus Dr Figerola.

The newly elected Manresan *consellers* for 1358–9 had been in office less than two weeks when they received a royal letter commanding them to appoint two syndics who would go to Girona to discuss a new subsidy for the Castilian war.[33] This renewal of the war would lead in 1359 to a dramatic naval assault on Barcelona led by King Pedro himself – an act which would drive home the desperate nature of the war to all Catalans. In the meantime, the Manresan council reported in May of 1358 that it was once more indebted to the Barcelona money changer Jaume de Vilar, the same man who had been the city's creditor in 1356.[34] This time, the city owed him 78,000 *solidi*, to be paid in 7,000s instalments, every four months. This subsidy is notable because it is one of the last times that the council did not immediately attempt to sell *censals* and *violaris* in order to raise the funds. They were still attempting to use the old system, whereby the city's tax revenue would go directly to a single money changer in a number of instalments that were arranged like a short-term loan. Eight days after this was recorded, the city noted that 'because of the 7,000s that the city suddenly has to give to the lord king' (which was actually owed to the money changer Jaume de Vilar), the council would have to sell *censals* in order to raise the funds.[35] In other words, the town realized that in order to pay Jaume de Vilar, they would have to sell bonds, which

[31] MC 1357.11.23. [32] ... *de quibus compotum reddere non curat.* MC 1358.1.2.
[33] MC 1358.4.12. [34] MC 1358.5.18.
[35] MC 1358.5.26; for the term of four months, see MC 1360.6.26. In this entry it is stipulated that 3,500s are owed for a two-month period.

would enable them to put their tax revenue towards the payment of interest on annuities, rather than the direct payments owed to Jaume de Vilar. It will be noted that even at 16.7 per cent interest (the highest known rate on *violaris*), this enabled the same tax revenue to support a payment nearly seven times what could be paid directly.[36] In this way, the town was beginning to substitute long-term for short-term credit; they were using long-term credit to fund payments on short-term loans advanced to the Crown by moneylenders.

Already, the first *censal* sale for the new subsidy of May 1358 necessitated a further reorganization of the office of the *clavarius* and, more importantly, a new reorganization of the city's taxes. From now on, as the council secretary informs us, all taxes except for the taxes on meat and wine were to go to pay annuities. This is another significant step in the ongoing financial revolution. The meat tax, meanwhile, was to pay for continuing work on the *sèquia*, and the wine tax was presumably to go to other expenses, though, in an ominous corollary, the *jurats* noted that 'if the regular taxes were not sufficient, the treasurer could also sell the meat and wine taxes in order to pay annuities'.[37] To mark the extreme importance which the *consellers* ascribed to the new office of treasurer, they provided it with a salary of 500s. In these times of financial complexity and uncertainty, with myriad new creditors hounding the city for *censal* payments, many of them powerful knights and wealthy Barcelona bankers, Manresa's treasurer was assigned a significant portion of what Dr Figerola had lost. By October 1358 the city's financial situation was deemed dire enough that the *clavarius* was granted an unprecedented emergency power to pay all expenses of the town for a period of four months.[38]

This emergency measure was further necessitated by the fact that the pressures of the war had caused violence to erupt in the city, and order was beginning to break down on all levels. An entry, probably datable to October 1358, paints a picture of encroaching anarchy. More significantly, it describes one of the few recorded instances in which the council took executive power into its own hands in the face of royal impotence. As usual the entry is all too terse: it states that certain people 'who do not fear royal power' have been wounding many citizens of the city, 'and what is worse, is that further woundings and deaths are occurring' as shock waves of revenge followed the initial attacks. The *consellers* noted that those who committed the crimes then fled the city. Because of the violence, they said, 'there is no one who can conduct the business

[36] Again, for these rates see Table 6.5. [37] MC 1358.5.26.
[38] MC 1358.10.(?) (exact date not given).

of this city'.[39] In response, the council named a committee who were given the extraordinary power of making 'denunciations "with effect" against those whom they see fit, both against the perpetrators of the said crimes, and against whatever royal officials of this city, if they do not punish the said crimes'.[40] The entry even indicates that those accused of violence could be held prisoner by the newly formed committee. Despite their obvious mistrust of their royal officials at this time, the council were careful to secure the permission of the lieutenant bailiff, although, significantly, he was the lowest-ranking royal official in the city with any claim to competence to endorse such a decision. As a further safeguard, the councillors granted themselves the power to appeal to the king in difficult cases.

Before speculating on the reasons behind this outbreak, the entry discussed above should be seen in light of a second entry dated three months later, in January 1359. It states the extent of the city's problems, though not their substance, in no uncertain terms:

> Know that rancours, contentions, discord and ill will are occurring at a terrible rate amongst the inhabitants of the city, between both knights and citizens, because of which, at the instigation of the enemy of the human race, many wounds and deaths have occurred amongst the inhabitants of this city, and know that every day rumours and great tumults continue to arise in the city, because of which all the people of the city come rushing armed into the streets . . .

In this instance, the town's principal response was to name procurators to fight all lawsuits that might be charged against the citizens of the city 'by persons of any status'.[41] This last phrase should be read to mean that some or all of the lawsuits in question had been filed by knights or other noblemen, or perhaps by prelates such as the Abbot of St Benet or the Bishop of Vic. The 'violence, rumours and tumults' of the autumn and winter of 1358–9 stemmed in part from two causes that have been a focus of this narrative, namely the social upheaval and alarm caused by military reverses, which would soon get worse, and also the city's aggressive pursuit of an expanded tax base in the Bages. The latter cause naturally put the city in conflict with the *seigneurs* of the countryside, whose tenants might be harassed in any number of ways by the civic tax collectors. Both entries discussed above contain indications that knights were involved in the strife, and it is very likely that they were a primary cause of the violence, as they would continue to be for the remainder of the war. In

39 *non esse qui negocia dicte civitate pro ut convenet procuret et tractet ad utilitatem ipsius civitatis.*

40 *denunciationes cum effectu quos eis visum fuerit, tam contra perpatratores dicta maleficia quam contra quosvis officiales regios dicte civitatis si dicta ciminia vel excessis non punitur . . .*

41 MC 1359.1.20.

October, the *consellers* mention that the perpetrators of the violence fled the city afterward, and in January, knights are singled out as perpetrators, victims and the potential filers of lawsuits. It should be noted that the filing of lawsuits was a natural corollary to, and even a continuation of, physical violence in the fourteenth-century Bages.[42] Because the royal authority was very effective at imposing and collecting fines, even from nobles, filing lawsuits had become an obvious way to achieve vengeance for the physical aggression of others. When the 'knights and citizens' are mentioned in the January entry, it must be considered unlikely that these knights were resident in the city, since only two families of knights, the de Manresa and the de Talamanca, appear to have owned property in the city.[43]

But in order to find the root cause of this violence, one has to turn to the national stage, where a major conflict was raging in the *Corts* between the cities of the *braç reial* and the knights and nobles of the *braç militar*. It seems that the royal cities paid a major subsidy in May of 1358 and agreed to a schedule of future payments stretching over the next three years.[44] The second estate, that of the knights and nobles, however, remained intransigent on the issue, possibly because the agreement to a three-year schedule of payments represented a fiscal novelty which they saw as a clear threat to their own liberties. This seems to indicate, amongst other things, that the estate of the nobles wielded a much more significant and practical opposition to the Crown than the *braç reial* at this point. The escalation of this episode is marked by a royal letter, which arrived in Manresa in July of 1358. In it the king, using rhetoric that was part shrewd affectation and part genuine outrage, lamented that even though 'the king of Castile has unjustly made war on us and wishes to take our territory' the nobles of Catalonia have refused to help him in his need.[45] By a letter dated 7 August, Pere summoned Manresa to appoint syndics for a parliament to be held in Barcelona on 25 August.[46] The published process of this *Corts*, which fills over 200 pages, is almost entirely composed of an attempt to

42 This phenomenon is quite evident in the town council records and elsewhere and deserves to be studied. The clearest example of this in the MC is 1372.5.23, in which a violent conflict between the knight Ramon de Ocina and the Manresan patrician Guillem Ferrer led to the filing of reciprocal lawsuits.

43 See n. 117, below.

44 See MC 1358.10.(?) for mention of the 84,000s that had been agreed to in May; also see MC 1359.6.22 for mention of another 6,887s/8d payment that was one of the instalments of this subsidy. This finding contradicts the opinion of the original editors of the *Cortes*, that the *Corts* of Girona in May had merely been a preliminary to the meeting at Barcelona in August–October 1358. See the opinion expressed in *Cortes*, II, p. 730, n. 1.

45 MC 1358.7.24(?). As stated in the introduction, the years 1357–9 are some of the very few in which council entries occasionally occur out of chronological order.

46 MC 1358.8.9.

reconcile the king with three of his most powerful barons, the Viscount of Cardona, the Count of Urgell and the Countess of Empuries.[47] The barons in question refused to appear at the *Corts*, citing a number of reasons for their reticence, the truth of which has yet to be explored.[48] By October 1358 not only the king, but also the *braç ecclesiastic* and the *braç reial*, were entirely fed up with the dissimulation of the barons, who by not appearing at the *Corts* were in essence refusing to pay any new subsidy towards the Castilian war. On 19 October, those two estates presented the king with a *consell*, or plan, in which they suggested that since the refractory barons had not contributed to the war effort during the previous two years, they should be made to pay retroactively at their customary rate, which for the Viscount of Cardona and the Count of Urgell was the upkeep for twenty-five horsemen.[49]

In the same month that the motion suggesting a retroactive payment by the barons was presented to the king by the *braços reial* and *ecclesiastic*, violence erupted in the Bages. The seat of the Viscount of Cardona bordered the Bages along most of its north-western frontier, and furthermore, Cardona's brother held a significant fief in the Bages, which in the *fogatge* of 1365 contained thirty-eight hearths.[50] Thus the Bages was a natural theatre for the animosity between the *braç reial* and the supporters of the Viscount of Cardona to boil over into open violence.[51] The constitutional crisis would continue, until in 1359, the *Diputació del General* of Catalonia was created as a permanent arm of the *Corts*, in order to manage the ongoing payments that had been pledged. Although this has been seen as a major victory for the *Corts* against the king, the Manresan evidence suggests that the victory was only made possible by the power of the nobles in the *braç militar*. Furthermore, it is also true that the formation of the *Diputació* came at precisely that moment when long-term payments, including substantial components of *censals* and *violaris*, began to be managed by the *Corts*. This was an eminently practical solution to the problem of how to manage long-term debt through an institution

47 *Cortes*, II, pp. 505–714 (p. 714 onward contains a *fogatge*).

48 See for example *Cortes*, II, pp. 621–31. Reason six (p. 625) mentions a private war between the Infans Ramon Berenguer on one side and the viscount of Ripoll, the count of Osona and Bernat de Cabrera.

49 *Cortes*, II, p. 689.

50 Josep Iglesies Fort, 'El fogaje de 1365–1370: contribución al conocimiento de la poblacíon de Cataluña en la segunda mitad del siglo XIV', *Memorias de la Real Academia de Ciencias y Artes de Barcelona*, 34:11 (1962), 249–356, at 106, lists a Berenguer de Cardona, *cavaller*, who held the Castle of Avinyó.

51 Christian D. Liddy, in 'Urban Conflict in Late Fourteenth-century England: The Case of York in 1380–1', *English Historical Review*, 118:475 (2003), 3–32, at 32, notes how in England urban citizens' interest in parliament grew stronger in the 1370s and 80s, when issues of taxation came to a head at the national level. The same process can be discerned in Catalonia.

which previously had no permanent presence. Rather, therefore, than seeing the formation of the *Diputació* as a pure capitulation on the part of the Crown, it is much more likely to have been a combination of practicality and compromise.

Although little is known about the immediate effects of the violence that accompanied the parliamentary dispute, it is probable that the procurators named by the city in January 1359 to defend Manresan citizens against all lawsuits brought by 'people of whatever status' were in fact created to defend the city against suits filed by the Viscount of Cardona and his followers. The viscount was personally named in a similar action noted on 24 November 1360, in which the procurators were to defend the city against 'all lawsuits' filed by the 'Viscount of Cardona or others of whatever status'. In 1361 we learn that the city had lost its appeal. Manresa was ordered by the king to pay 13,000s to Cardona for a reason that was specifically left unmentioned: *ratione in instrumentum contenta.*[52] A second reference to this payment was made in 1362 when the city paid 6,100s, presumably the second instalment of the original 13,000s, to Cardona on the order of the *veguer* of Barcelona. It is therefore probable that at some point during the disturbances of 1358 and 1359, the Manresans had done a significant amount of damage to the viscount's property. It is also very telling that the *veguer* of Barcelona awarded damages to Cardona despite the fact that Cardona had been in defiance of the king at the time. It is probable that the *veguer*'s sentence was meted out because by this time the *braç militar* and the Crown had worked out a compromise. In upholding the royal laws, the king's officials were therefore restoring order and maintaining their status as monopolizers of violence.

Another notable fact regarding the violence of 1358 and 1359, as in other outbreaks of violence in Manresa during the fourteenth century, is that it was not primarily caused by urban factionalism. This is not to say that urban factional struggles did not filter into the performance of violence once the violence had begun, but in this case it was touched off by the national rivalry between the various estates in parliament, which led to an intolerable regional situation. The citizens of the royal lands could argue that they had consented to pay subsidies at unprecedented levels in order to defend all the inhabitants of the principality, including the residents of seigneurial lands. Meanwhile the same seigneurial tenants, who often lived within a bowshot of the royal tenants, were seen as having paid nothing. One can certainly sympathize with the Manresans' resentment, even though the Viscount's tenants who suffered at the Manresans' hands had no control over the conditions that determined

[52] MC 1361.7.6.

their fiscal status. When we compare the 1358–9 violence and that which erupted in the early 1370s, it seems as though fiscal issues arising from the divisions between the nobility and the royal demesne were a more common cause of violence during the fourteenth century than factionalism. The 1371 case of a knight wounding the Manresan patrician Guillem de Ferrer because of a dispute between the city and the castellany over new royal taxation fits into the same pattern.[53] Most of the time, the bailiff and the *veguer* appear to have kept intra-urban violence relatively under control. But the old supra-legal pretensions of the castellan class, which enabled them to escape or at least emboldened them to eschew the full surveillance of royal justice, still simmered in the Bages throughout the fourteenth century, and these pretensions erupted into violence whenever conditions for the maintenance of royal order were less than ideal.

As though the situation in Manresa were not dire enough in January of 1359, between exorbitant taxes, the menaces of the King of Castile by land and by sea and 'terrible rancours' occurring in the city and countryside, the town soon learned, only ten days after the rancours were recorded, that their king had determined to sell the jurisdictions of a number of the royal castellanies within the *vegueria* of the Bages in order to support the war effort.[54] It might be imagined that the king's decision made him quite unpopular. The *consellers* were disturbed at the sales because these jurisdictions were likely to be sold into the hands of the very feudal lords whom the Manresans had been fighting. Yet the *consellers*' main concern was not this, so much as the fact that a number of Manresan citizens held certain *franquitates*, which included feudal dues, rents, or lands held in allod, within the disputed castellanies. Because of these concerns for their property, the Manresan government vastly preferred that the castellanies remain under the jurisdiction of the *veguer* rather than fall into the hands of a private lord. Their concerns were so strong that despite their already heavy tax burden, they eventually agreed to pay for the redemption of the castellanies, albeit only after much contentious debate.[55] It is important to note, since some historians have seen this sale of jurisdictions as a sign of Pere III's particular weakness, that by offering the jurisdictions of these castellanies for sale, the Crown was not resorting to novelty. The practice of selling royal jurisdictions can be found even during the pacific years of Jaume II's early reign.[56] And more to the point, it was not a sign of royal weakness at all, insofar

[53] MC 1371.9.12 and MC 1372.5.23. [54] MC 1359.1.30. [55] MC 1360.10.4.

[56] For Jaume II promising in 1293 not to separate the castle of Mura from the royal patrimony and then receiving the hefty sum of 6,700s in exchange for not selling it, LV, 72–3.

as the inhabitants of the cities found that they had little choice but to buy back the jurisdictions, just as the royal financiers knew they would. Of course, many of these alienated domains did end up in the hands of local nobles, and the buy-back of the royal demesne occupied much of the 1380s and 1390s. By 1400, however, most of the land had been recovered.[57] In any event, it should now be considered that the 'financial revolution' represented by the *censal* system made the castles of the royal demesne much less important to the royal fisc than the towns themselves, since town revenues were the anchor of the *censal* system, and towns were where the great majority of *censal* investors lived and worked.[58] Thus, earlier historians' preoccupation with the sale of rural demesne properties should now be seen as missing the main point – a point that was perfectly understood by contemporary Crown officials: with the erection of the *censal* system, the royal fisc was becoming far stronger during the 1360s and 70s than it ever had been; the sales of rural royal properties were thus, relatively speaking, a mere sideshow.

Not that the Manresans didn't try everything in their power to oppose this obviously underhanded fiscal technique. They discovered that while Jaume II had indulged in this practice, he had then promised that he would not do so again. In 1300, the king had granted a privilege to Manresa promising that the royal castellanies of the Bages would remain tied to the county of Barcelona in perpetuity.[59] This privilege of 1300 was mentioned by the *consellers* in 1359 when they sent procurators to the king for the purpose of preventing the sales. The *consellers*' protest directly challenged the royal tactic, and armed with their royal privilege the *consellers* felt they had a very strong legal case in their favour. Yet, even in this situation, the Crown's interests once more prevailed over those of the city. When the Crown lawyers were presented with Manresa's royal privilege, they cynically argued that, since these jurisdictions could not legally be sold, and yet had been, it was incumbent upon the Manresans to redeem the illegal sales for the royal fisc. Wrangling over this issue continued for over a year and a half, until October 1360. In that month, the *consellers* began a three-day debate over the issue of 'buying or redeeming' the castles that had been sold by the Crown. In the end, the sale of the jurisdictions therefore amounted to a further tax on Crown subjects.

These entries which record the three-day debate over the repurchasing of royal jurisdictions in October of 1360 are some of the very few that

57 Again, this is chronicled in María Teresa Ferrer Mallol, 'El patrimoni reial i la recuperació dels senyorius jurisdiccionals en les estats Catalano-Aragonesos a la fi del segle XIV', *Anuario de Estudios Medievales*, 7 (1970–1), 351–491.

58 For the financial revolution, again, see the following chapter.

59 LV, 84–5.

provide a glimpse of the political process of the Manresan town government in terms of individual speeches. Unlike in many Italian towns, the Catalan records contain few detailed minutes of town council meetings. But in this case, we know that thirteen of the *jurats* argued that the city should not buy the jurisdictions back, on the principle that the king had no right to sell them in the first place. Only one person is recorded as saying that they should be bought, although we know that his side would eventually carry the debate. The solitary speaker argued that these jurisdictions should be redeemed both *ad commodum civitatis* and *pro honore domini regis*. This reads like the argument of a man with economic interests in the castellanies, employing a rhetoric of loyalty to the Crown in order to safeguard his own purse. This speaker painted the repurchase of royal jurisdictions as an act of fidelity to the king, whose financial need threatened to tarnish his royal honour. This plays on the notion that the honour of the king was synonymous with the honour of the royal city of Manresa, especially in the face of the knights and castellans of the Bages who stood to gain at the king's expense. In the end, the pro-redemption party did win the debate, since on 7 October the city agreed to repurchase all of the jurisdictions for an unspecified amount.[60] It is possible that the town retained the rights to these castles after the repurchase – the Crown may have allowed the revenues from these castles to go towards paying the towns' escalating burdens. This is suggested by the action of the town council in 1367, which wrote a letter to the king asking permission to alienate their rights to several of these castles for one year, in order to raise more ready cash.[61]

In addition to the struggle over the royal jurisdictions, 1359 had brought further financial crisis, as large and ongoing subsidy payments threatened to overwhelm the city's ability to pay them. As the crisis deepened, the *consellers* sent envoys to the king requesting an expansion of the bailiff's powers of coercion over those who owed outstanding taxes. This was significant, because it marks the first time that such an act is recorded in the council manuals. Under normal circumstances, the city's tax system functioned well without the intervention of the bailiff. But the council's request suggests both that resistance to tax collection was mounting and that the council now found it expedient to increase the efficiency of its collection process.[62] Also, the newly reorganized accounting and auditing systems very likely made the

[60] MC 1360.10.7. [61] MC 1367.11.19.

[62] Mark Meyerson has also found that 1358 and 1359 were pivotal years in the relationship between the Crown and the urban Jewish community of Morvedre in the Kingdom of Valencia. In February of 1359 King Pere admitted that his excessive tax demands had caused a depopulation of the Jewish quarter. In order to lure settlers back, Crown officials offered tax breaks of a type

detection of defaulting and recalcitrant debtors more effective. The envoy to the Crown was also instructed to ask the king to impound all those goods 'which had been detained' for the payment of taxes, and also to ask that the king would make a new proclamation ordering everyone to pay their taxes.[63] This note incidentally reveals that the councillors had been exercising executive authority by impounding the goods of debtors. It also reveals the precarious nature of their use of executive power, since they were asking the king to authorize their use of force. The bailiff, presumably, felt it beyond his jurisdiction to make such an authorization, which is itself an interesting indicator of the degree of royal control that was being exercised over local royal officials. The record of the envoy to the king is the second time since the outbreak of the war that the councillors are revealed to have been using force on their own initiative. Not surprisingly, the king acceded to the councillors' request, since it kept executive power firmly in his own hands while it facilitated the tax collection that oiled his war machine. By October of 1359 the bailiff had been empowered to compel taxpayers to show their goods to a panel of tax estimators. Specifically, he was to note all those who claimed that they could not 'pay their *terçs*' because of poverty, and presumably to verify whether this was actually the case.[64] The mention of *terçs*, which was a type of judicial fine, shows that a number of people had fallen into arrears with their tax payments and had been assessed fines as a result. The stiff nature of these fines, along with the fact that *terçs* were not usually imposed on otherwise law-abiding citizens, would naturally cause resentment and increase the need for coercion.

The resort to force, therefore, generated a good deal of resentment against the royal officials and municipal appointees who were enforcing this unusually strict collection of taxes; and the *consellers* themselves could not escape this increasing resentment for very long. A rift between the municipal and the royal government came in November 1360, only one month after the council had agreed to repurchase jurisdictions over the royal castles. At this time, the king ordered the *veguer* and bailiff of Manresa, together with a royal porter, to compel the Manresans to pay part of the 12,000 florins (132,000s) that the king had agreed to pay to the Genoese in order to secure the release of some Catalan prisoners. This, incidentally, suggests that in fact the Genoese were continuing to actively engage the Catalans at sea after 1356, as allies of Castile – an important aspect of the 'War of the Two Peters', that has escaped the notice of

very similar to those employed in Manresa after 1362. See Mark D. Meyerson, *Jews in an Iberian Frontier Kingdom: Society, Economy, and Politics in Morvedre, 1248–1391* (Leiden, 2004), pp. 231–7.

[63] MC 1359.1.30. [64] MC 1359.10.28.

most commentators. The townsmen protested that they had not agreed in *Corts* to pay this sum, and it was therefore an illegal imposition.[65] Ten weeks later the city named procurators to prosecute Pere Truny, a royal porter who had possibly come to collect the city's share of the Genoese ransom money, but who had ended by dealing 'a number of blows' to unnamed Manresan citizens.[66] It is not unlikely that Truny was attacked by a Manresan mob and had to flee. And yet it would be overhasty to conclude that the relationship between royal and town government had entirely broken down at this point. A few weeks after the Truny case was recorded the city paid the bailiff £7 (140s) for unspecified 'labours', presumably for his hand in compelling taxpayers to pay their dues. This is a good illustration of how the citizens and the civic government could turn against the royal porter, whom they perceived as an outsider, even while the people tolerated the bailiff's use of force against them at the instigation of their own civic government. The bailiff was a much more intimate part of Manresan life and was therefore less of a target for popular discontent than were the itinerant porters.

WAR, DEBT, AND PLAGUE: 1361–6

The year 1361 brought the peace of Deça in May, and with it a hope that the war with Castile might finally be winding down. Unfortunately, the Catalans' respite was to be very brief indeed. September brought the news of an equally menacing threat from another front entirely. In the first indication of a mercenary threat that was not to abate for a decade and a half, the king warned the Manresan councillors that some 'foreign men' had invaded Roussillon, and that others were gathering to invade 'Roussillon and other parts of Catalonia'.[67] These were the 'Great' or 'White' mercenary companies, which had been freed from their engagements to the Dauphin of France by the treaty of Brétigny in 1360. In an outbreak of post-war violence which would remain endemic in France until the seventeenth century, the out-of-work soldiers ravaged much of the French countryside in 1360 and 1361, and had now reached Roussillon. Since the Catalan Crown held that Roussillon was an integral part of Catalonia, Pere responded to this emergency by invoking the statute *Princeps Namque*, which required all Catalans to come to the aid of the king for the repulsion of an attack on Catalan soil. This was the first of an unprecedented number of convocations of this regalian right that Pere would exercise during the 1360s, and Sánchez has seen

[65] MC 1360.11.13. [66] *quibusdam iecibus.* MC 1361.1.3.
[67] MC 1361.9.17. The letter was dated 1361.9.13.

this as a deliberate policy on Pere's part, which allowed him to overcome much of the opposition he had recently been facing from the *braç militar*. Still, custom dictated that the measure had to be approved in *Corts*, and thus the Manresans were summoned to Monzón on 1 October 1361. Unfortunately the town records are disorganized and scanty for this year and so nothing is recorded of the city's response to this summons.

The stand-off with the mercenaries continued into 1362, while both Iberian kings attempted to enlist their aid against the other. Pedro for his part worked to neutralize Pere's ally the sultan of Granada. Pedro sensed the palpable military inferiority of the Aragonese on land, and was confident that he would be able to annex significant parcels of Aragonese territory if he continued to press the fight. Therefore, in June of the same year, Pedro once more invaded Aragon and laid siege to the city of Calatayud. On 7 July, the Manresan council recorded that the king had summoned them to a *Corts* at Barcelona on 10 July. On 1 September 1362 the town dutifully recorded that it now owed another 7390s payment 'in order to resist the king of Castile'.[68] For the salary and expenses of the two syndics who had gone to the recent *Corts* of Barcelona, the city had to pay a total of 813s, more than the annual salary of the city's doctor that had been suspended for lack of funds. At this time the city also paid out 600s (£30) to the syndics to the earlier *Corts* of Monzón. One of these syndics was Francesc Nerell, the same man who would go on to become one of Manresa's most autocratic *consellers* (though his platform was populist) during the crisis of the early 1370s. One of the Barcelona syndics was Guillem d'Orriols, who was to become Nerell's most trusted accomplice.[69]

This latest invasion by Pedro caused real alarm in the city, beyond any previous event of the war. The Manresan council records that the King of Castile had besieged Calatayud 'with great power and horses'. But what alarmed them much more was the fact that their own king had enlisted a number of White Companies *adversus regem Castille*.[70] The council rightly feared that despite their nominal allegiance to the King of Aragon, these foreign mercenaries might damage or even sack the city 'because of their great numbers and especially because the city is not enclosed'.[71] This revealing statement suggests that whatever fortifications the city possessed in 1362 were either old, or incomplete, or both. In response

68 MC 1362.9.1. This parliament is discussed in Donald J. Kagay, 'The Government Besieged by Conflict: The Parliament of Monzón (1362–1363) as Military Financier', in L. J. Andrew Villalon and Donald J. Kagay (eds.), *The Hundred Years War: A Wider Focus*, (Leiden, 2005), pp. 117–50.

69 MC 1362.11.9. 70 MC 1362.8.1. 71 *Non est clausa*. MC 1362.8.1.

to the threat posed by the White Companies to their vulnerable city, the king and the *consellers* decided that the citizens must immediately begin the work of constructing proper fortifications. The councillors therefore authorized a committee of three men from each quarter as 'economic syndics', who were to plan and construct new defences as they saw fit. These men were given power to make whatever ordinances were necessary to their task, and they were also charged to organize the city's available labourers into groups of ten, fifty and one hundred, as was the custom with the town militia.[72] Each group of three men was to oversee one quarter of the city. This committee soon proved too unwieldy to function properly, and in a later undated entry, two men were named as *operarios muri*, or masters of the wall works, and given authority to oversee the fortification of the entire city.[73] In the event, the White Companies passed through Catalonia without harming Manresa. Since the city was not on any of the major routes through the principality, even taking the Pyrenean passes into account, it is unlikely that any significant bodies of troops passed through the Bages. With the passing of the companies, the city was spared from the effort of having to construct defences, but, as it turned out, only for the short term. In 1368, when the companies would again menace Catalonia, this time as adversaries of the King of Aragon, Pere ordered Manresa to be fully fortified within a short space of time.[74]

At the same time that the White Company drama was unfolding, much of Catalonia found itself to be in the grip of a severe drought – one which threatened to create the worst famine since the 1330s. Poor harvests in 1361 led to grain shortages in the winter of 1361–2, which only got worse as spring arrived and no rains came. In April 1362 the Manresan government therefore dedicated £60 (1,200s) toward the purchase of grain.[75] In July 1363, just before harvest time, the councillors reported a continuing dearth of wine, indicating that the previous years' *vendimia* had also been poor.[76] But in an era of endemic bubonic plague, prolonged famine could lead to even worse scourges. With the population thus weakened by hunger, the Catalan populace began to succumb to a fresh wave of the plague. This visitation began in the summer of 1362. The new plague lasted through the fall of 1362 and into the winter, adding the threat of sudden death by contagion to the miseries of the Castilian invasion, the menace of the White

[72] MC 1362.8.1. [73] MC 1362. 8(?).

[74] The wall-building was also occurring at Barcelona; see Sánchez Martínez, 'The Invocation of *Princeps Namque*'. For the council's new efforts respecting the walls, see MC 1368.10.3 and 1368.10.6.

[75] *Ad opus emendi frumentum*. MC 1362.4.30. [76] MC 1363.7.9.

Companies, oppressive taxes, and the citizens' desperate efforts to encircle themselves with defensible fortifications. The famine would continue for more than a year, and the city was still organizing grain imports by October 1363.[77]

Typically, the *consellers'* laconic record of this plague outbreak says nothing about its duration or severity. Yet this record is one of the most significant council entries of the fourteenth century. It may be summarized:

> Because of the pestilence which recently ravaged the city, and because of the many payments which we must make to the king, this city stands in need of people who practise the mechanical arts; likewise it is our duty to attempt to populate the city by whatever means possible. Therefore we proclaim that all those who are not natural to the city and who wish to stay in it for more than ten days must write their name in the book of the city. These shall be free from all *fogatges, questias reyals*, and other occasional taxes; likewise they shall be free from all regular civic taxes (*imposicions*) for a period of five years.[78]

The first thing to be gleaned from this entry is that the plague of 1362–3 hit the city with some severity. Catalan historiography has made much of a reference which calls this plague the *mortaldat dels infants,* but it is clear that the Manresans also experienced it as a *mortaldat dels menestrals.*[79] Beginning with the plague of 1362, the town councillors continuously felt their city to be underpopulated, and for several decades after that date they attempted to legislate in ways which would increase the number of householders in the city. The year 1362 thus marks a very important psychological turning point in the mentality of Manresa's citizens and government in terms of demographics. The city had been crowded, and even overpopulated from the vantage point of the lower classes, during the first half of the fourteenth century. Between 1348 and 1362, despite the ravages of the Black Death, the Manresan councillors gave no indication that they felt the city's population to be inadequate. From 1363, however, their attitude changed dramatically. The immigration policy they inaugurated in May of that year (quoted above) would continue to attract a trickle of new householders for the next thirty years, but never enough to offset losses.[80] In neighbouring Cervera, the town councillors felt the city to be so underpopulated by 1382 that they petitioned the

77 MC 1363.10.17. 78 MC 1363.5.3.

79 See for example Carme Batlle Gallart, *Historia de Catalunya.* Vol. III, *L'Expansio baixmedieval (segles XIII–XV)* (Barcelona, 1998), p. 252.

80 A similar finding, that the plagues of the 1360s created more of an acute labour shortage than earlier visitations of plague, was described for Flanders in David Nicholas, *Medieval Flanders* (London, 1992), p. 221, and for England in A. R. Bridbury, 'The Black Death', *Economic History Review*, 26:4 (1973), 577–92. See also Chapter 7.

king to allow criminals fleeing from seigneurial lands to settle in their city.[81] The petition was duly granted. An unsettling sense of dwelling in a world of increasing entropy, similar to the one that informed some currents of later medieval art and literature, now became part of the mentality of the Catalan urban dweller.[82]

The councillors soon felt the need to amend their new immigration policy. While their first law had provided a considerable incentive for people to move into the city, they had done nothing to ensure that their own citizens would not be tempted by the incentives of other cities, especially of Barcelona, where wages were up to 50 per cent higher and life was much more varied.[83] On 9 May, therefore, the *consellers* enacted a truly draconian measure against emigration: all those who sold their house, land, or other goods with the intent of moving elsewhere would have to pay a prohibitive 5 *sous* per *livre*, or 25 per cent, tax on their entire estate to the town government. This was to go directly in support of the various taxes by which the city was bound.[84] In addition, the need for tax revenue led them to pare down their initial promise of ten years' tax exemption for new immigrants down to five. Still, within a few weeks immigrants began to inscribe their names in the city's book. The immigrants were almost entirely from rural hamlets in the Bages, although the first man entered on the rolls was one Jaume, a shopkeeper from Barcelona.[85]

In addition to the shortage of labour caused by the second plague, the *consellers* were clearly concerned about the shortage of taxpayers it created: while the city's debt burden continued to grow, the plague of 1362 had wiped out a significant portion of the taxpaying households.[86] As the population continued to shrink, the debt burden remained to be shared amongst fewer survivors. This fact of life in later fourteenth-century Mediterranean Europe has not been adequately discussed as a factor behind the contraction of the European economy. Certainly this phenomenon was having an adverse effect on the Manresan economy. On the same day that the *consellers* inaugurated their new immigration policy, they recorded that the treasurer had examined his books and determined that the city's regular impositions were no longer sufficient

81 *Llibre De Privilegis De Cervera, 1182–1456)*, 1st edn (Fundacio Noguera, 1991), pp. 317–18.

82 This theme is elaborated upon in P. Wallace Platt, *King Death* (Toronto, 1996); and Samuel K. Cohn Jr, *The Cult of Remembrance and the Black Death: Six Renaissance Cities in Central Italy* (Baltimore, MD, 1997).

83 For the difference between wage rates in Manresa and Barcelona, see Table 7.3 and relevant discussion.

84 MC 1363.5.9. 85 MC 1363.5.19.

86 This is argued in Fynn-Paul, 'Civic Debt, Civic Taxes', 35–42.

to pay its *censal* annuities. As a short-term expedient, all of the city's impositions were sold for the upcoming four months.

Meanwhile, a *fogatge*, or hearth tax, had been declared, presumably at the *Corts* of Monzón in February 1363, and the city was now forced to sell 21000s worth of new *censals* to make a payment on the *fogatge*.[87] As though this were not burden enough, one month earlier the king had required the city to pay for the upkeep of a contingent of twenty-five *clients*, or mercenaries, who were probably mounted men-at-arms.[88] Eight Manresan men, two from each quarter, were appointed to collect a new *tallia* for the maintenance of this company. Not surprisingly, on 6 April the *consellers* reported that the eight men were having some difficulty in collecting the money.[89] In an effort to speed up the tax collection, the *veguer* and *batlle* imposed a deadline upon the tax collectors, after which date they would be personally responsible for paying a penalty of 500 gold *morabatins*.[90] In this difficult situation, the eight members of the committee, all of whom were well-to-do and well connected to city government, claimed that they had not consented to this penalty and were therefore not bound to it.[91] Unfortunately, the entry breaks off at this point and nothing more was written on the matter. It is very interesting to learn that the town patricians claimed to have the right to consent to fines imposed upon them by the bailiff and *veguer*. This was clearly a challenge to the authority of the royal officials and it is unfortunate that it cannot be known how this challenge played out. Yet the incident highlights an important change taking place in the civic government. Years of high taxation had created a situation in which it was becoming increasingly unpleasant to be a *conseller* or *jurat*. A civic official was now inescapably sandwiched between the ire of their neighbours and the impatience of the powerful agents of the Crown. In this dispute may be seen one of the early foreshadowings of the situation described in the royal privilege of 1380, in which the councillors had complained that the city's best men were avoiding public service.[92]

It was also on 3 May that the *consellers* clarified the principle that all those who lived within the *batllia* of Manresa were to contribute to royal *questias*. By this time the city had successfully petitioned to have the *batllia* enlarged, and a letter of 8 October 1358 from the bailiff general of Catalonia gave them permission to place new marker stones in an effort

[87] MC 1363.5.3. For the *fogatge* at Monzón, see *Cortes*, II, pp. 149–50. This is mentioned at the *Corts* of Barcelona, beginning 10 March 1364.

[88] MC 1363.3.26. Note this is the same number as required of the viscount of Cardona.

[89] MC 1363.4.6.

[90] For the equivalency in *sous* (1 morabatí = 9s), see MC 1372.5.21.

[91] MC 1363.4.6.

[92] For two documents dealing with this issue in 1380, see LV, 269–72.

to mute controversy. This entry, incidentally, suggests that the town had been making collections, called *questias*, in addition to the regular impositions and those levied for *fogatges*. Several of the otherwise unnamed *tallias* such as the one collected by Jaume Sarta and Bernat de Valls that begin to appear regularly in the council manuals from 1363 were presumably levied in order to service the bourgeoning *censal* burden.[93] There are also indications that the town was now using these extraordinary *tallias* simply in order to meet its diurnal expenses, a situation that would worsen as the decade progressed. In the summer of 1363 the city gave *plenum posse* to another treasurer, Bernat de Area, who received authority to hear accounts from whomever he saw fit, in addition to the authority to collect what was due to the city. Bernat was to receive the very high rate of 3 *sous* per *livre*, or 15 per cent, of the money that he extracted from the citizens. It is probable that some of this commission was destined to go to the guards who were to help Bernat in his efforts.[94]

Few records survive from the Manresan council manuals for 1364, a year which began with the Castilians laying siege to Valencia itself. This dire danger seems finally to have shaken Pere III out of his lethargy, and brought him to lead a relief force to his capital. The funds for this were provided by a *Corts* held at Tortosa. Manresa's share of this subsidy included the provision of 100 mules.[95] It is clear that there was considerable local resistance to this latest subsidy, coming as it did after years of bad news from the front. Less than a week after the order to requisition the mules was received, the council was forced to make a motion asking the royal officials, including the bailiff and the *sotsveguer*, and also the deacon of Manresa, to 'respect the rights that pertain to the citizens and inhabitants of this city', and to redress the 'oppressions and molestations' done by these officials.[96] Although the forces that Pere managed to assemble proved to be much smaller than the Castilian army, Pedro of Castile chose to withdraw in the face of Pere's determination – an action which brought a badly needed morale boost to the Aragonese side, and perhaps the first truly good news of the war. Building on that momentum, Pere was able to relieve the Castilian siege of Morvedre (in Valencia) in the spring of 1365.[97] With this, the direct threat from the Castilians proved to be over, although the threat from the White

93 MC 1363.5.15. For details of extraordinary payments, see Table 6.4 and accompanying discussion.
94 MC 1363.7.15.
95 For the summons to Tortosa see MC 1364.1.22; for the mules see MC 1364.2.29.
96 MC 1364.3.6.
97 To support this invasion, the town councillors noted that they were bound to make payments by the first and last day of March 1365, 'as agreed in the *Corts* of Monzón and Barcelona'. MC 1365.3.5.

Companies and even Pere's own Trastámara allies would continue to menace the Catalans for another decade.

By the summer of 1365, the Manresans were still being compelled to organize the relief of Morvedre, since it was feared that the Castilians might counter-attack at any moment. At the end of July, the special council sent a letter to the king asking that the *sotsveguer* and bailiff would not force the city's inhabitants to serve in the army. This suggests that until this point, town levies were still being employed, rather than mercenaries.[98] This was at the same time that a contingent of twenty-five crossbowmen was being raised for the Valencian front. Throughout the summer, the government collected a new and obviously onerous 'weekly tax' and the councillors made nearly continuous injunctions to the bailiffs to use force to compel the payment of taxes; for the first time, the use of armed guards is explicitly mentioned.[99] The impression is that the city government was under heavy pressure from the Crown, and that the people felt themselves to be under heavy pressure from the town government and the royal officials; the special council may well have been meeting in private homes in order to avoid the wrath of the mob. That the citizens were especially restive can be seen from the decree made by the bailiff that the townspeople not carry weapons; this decree was resisted by the council, who argued blandly that it was 'against the good of the city'. Whether they were afraid of castellans or of intramural factions, it is clear that the atmosphere in the city was not pacific.[100]

The records for 1364 and early 1365 may well have been garbled because there was ongoing strife in the city council during these years. The election that was held on 1 April 1365 marked a brief yet fairly radical turning point in the functioning of city government, which remained in an unusual state of flux until 1369, when Duke Joan stepped in and set new electoral procedures.[101] (This was the crown prince, the future King Joan I, who would interfere so decisively in the governments of Barcelona and Manresa in the later 1380s and early 1390s. Joan seems to have acquired a taste for rearranging urban constitutions early in his career.) In April 1365, the entire special council, which included both *jurats* and councillors, was for the first time expressly empowered to make

98 MC 1365.7.31.

99 MC 1365.9.5. For a similar 'weekly penny' being instituted at York some fifteen years later, see Liddy, 'Urban Conflict', 24. The point is that the Catalan ministers were following an expedient which was apparently current in other Western European finance councils at the time.

100 MC 1365.10.28.

101 MC 1365.4.1. For an example of the 'special council' mandating the *consuls* to act see MC 1365.5.2; for majority decision in the 'special council' see MC 1365.4.30.

executive decisions for the town. These were to be decided by a simple majority in which the *jurats* and *consellers* voted together – an arrangement which obviously gave the upper hand to the *jurats* who, as shown in a previous chapter, were significantly lower on the socio-economic scale than the *consellers*. The sense that the special council was acting in a less than fully legal manner is reinforced by the fact that they began to hold their meetings in private homes, rather than the church of Sant Miquel where they were accustomed to meet; also, it is recorded that Dominic Vidal was opposed to the form of the election that had been made on 1 April and that he would appeal to the king.[102]

This election also marked the rise of the populist leader Francesc Nerell, who was not elected *conseller* this year, but was the first-named of the *jurats*. Between 1367 and 1382, Nerell would be elected consul many times, and he would come to dominate the Manresan council in a way that few men had done or would do in the future. This election also marked the first time that the 'hand' (i.e. occupation-based party) of any of the councillors or *jurats* was made explicit in the council manuals. The three named 'hands' were the 'citizens', who were represented by five *jurats*; the 'merchants', also represented by five *jurats*; and the '*menestrals*', who were represented by six *jurats*. The 'hands' of the consuls were not recorded. Interestingly, Nerell was listed as a 'merchant' in 1365 in another source, and so he may have been holding office as a member of the *mà mitjana*.[103] This suggests that the occupational labels used by many of the town representatives were not set in stone at this time, but could be manipulated for political ends by the councillors themselves. By 1367, the 'hands' had been dropped once more from the conciliar lists. And by 1369, the system had once again been changed, this time under the auspices of Duke Joan. In this year thirty *jurats* were elected, with the injunction that merely fifteen of them could constitute a quorum. Joan may have been genuinely interested in securing a broader base of representation on the town government, in order to defuse tensions over what was now the greatest recorded tax burden in the city's recorded history. With an eye towards a more democratic representation, it was decided that a father and son could not serve at the same time, nor even could two brothers. No mention of 'hands' was made in this or any successive election until after Joan's 1393 reform: this does not appear to have been a very popular concept with the Manresan councillors. Some of the antipathy may have been due to the fact that, in a small (and shrinking) town, there were not enough 'respectable' men to make such distinctions useful. Some of it was also a reflection of the egalitarian streak

[102] MC 1365.4.4; MC 1365.4.1. [103] See Table 6.1.

which, as has been discussed previously, was characteristic of Catalan urban patricians, particularly during the fourteenth century.

FORTIFICATION, DESPERATION, AND POLITICAL INNOVATION, 1367–75

By the autumn of 1367, the town council was once more meeting inside the church of Sant Miquel. A glimpse into the nature of the council's meetings can be gained from a statute which required that all consuls and *jurats* must stand inside the doors of the church, since during meetings many of them had taken to standing outside, 'because of which, the business of the city cannot be done effectively'. Infractions were to be punished with a penalty of five *sous*.[104] Later that autumn, the city was scandalized when a number of hosts were stolen from one of the city's churches; this incident may be what precipitated a rare visit from the Bishop of Vic, who arrived in November.[105] Unfortunately, the citizens soon received yet another summons to *Corts*, this one to be held at Vilafranca. Jaume (II) Sarta, serving his first term as a Manresan *conseller*, was one of the two syndics chosen to attend.[106]

In April of 1367, King Pere's ally and pretender to the Castilian throne, Enrique de Trastámara, had been defeated by an English–Castilian army at the Battle of Nájera.[107] In mortal fear that Pedro of Castile would once again invade his lands in order to avenge himself, Pere began negotiations with the English and pledged that he would now act to oppose Enrique's plans. This series of events in effect reopened the Castilian war, which would continue in its new phase through the mid-1370s.[108] Pere's policies had the unfortunate effect of driving Enrique into the arms of the French, and with their help, Enrique re-equipped his forces and marched through northern Catalonia in September of 1367. Pere invoked *Princeps Namque* in a hasty attempt to defend his realms, but the best that he could do was defend the city of Cervera, and watch as Enrique marched unopposed through his lands. The summons to *Corts* in November of 1367 was a response to this situation. By August of 1368, Pere had summoned another *Corts* at Barcelona, this time on the rumour that Bertrand du

104 MC 1367.9.10.

105 For the hosts, see MC 1367.10.15; for the bishop's visit see MC 1367.11.3.

106 MC 1367.11.3.

107 The following is summarized in Sánchez Martínez, 'The Invocation of *Princeps Namque*'.

108 The next phase of the Castilian war was to prove, for Manresans at least, even more difficult and exhausting than the first; though once again, the ability of the city and its citizens to finance a new wall and large numbers of urban militia during this second phase of the war period speak to the fact that the talk of 'exhaustion' was due to a combination of perception, posturing, and reality that is difficult to measure precisely.

Guescuelin was also preparing to march through Catalonia at the head of a mercenary force, nominally allied with the king. Despite the ostensible alliance, the Catalans' fear of du Guescuelin was justifiably intense. Part of the goal of the *Corts* of August 1368 was to commute the response to *Princeps Namque* to a money payment, with the aim of providing the king with the chance to keep more mercenaries in his pay. It was also decided that the principality of Catalonia was woefully under-fortified, and that as many fortifications as possible had to be brought up to date with the latest defensive designs.

The impetus for the new fortification programme came as much from fear of the king's hired mercenaries as from the Castilians under Pedro. The French mercenary companies, some of whom would maintain an uneasy alliance with Pere III until the end of the war in 1375, were generally looked upon throughout Catalonia as foreign invaders for the duration of the war. Already in June 1367, the Duke of Girona sent a letter to the city instructing them to appoint a new minister for the overseeing of the wall works of Manresa; the experience of many cities in southern France had shown that only well-fortified locales were safe from the mercenaries, should they decide to rebel. Efforts were now resumed on the circuit begun in 1362, and would continue apace. By 1383 the majority of the work was complete, although certain aspects of the job were not completed until 1400.[109] In 1367, as works were resumed, a *clavarius murii* (treasurer of the walls) was appointed, and the collection of the weekly tax continued apace. Despite these measures, in July the wall work once more came to a temporary halt due to lack of funds.[110] Also in July, yet another military contingent was being raised at Manresa. These men were called *clients* ('mercenaries'), which suggests that the Crown had been dissatisfied with the earlier citizen levies and was now using more professional soldiers. The mercenaries were, however, led by the city's own consul Francesc Ferrer, and, very interestingly, this force was supposed to meet up with the duke's army in Sardinia.[111] This passage

109 MC 1367.6.18. For the state of the work in 1383, see EPLV, 333–5; for the completion of the wall works by 1400, see Raquel Valdenebro i Manrique, 'L'evolutió urbana de Manresa i les seves muralles', in Enric Castells i Rufas and Joan Badia i Guitart (eds.), *Manresa medieval: Historia, art, i cultura a la edat mitjana* (Manresa, 2001), pp. 169–89, at 172, which is justly suspicious about Sarret i Arbós' eleventh- and thirteenth-century circuits.

110 MC 1367.7.1.

111 MC 1367.7.24; for passage to the duke see MC 1367.7.28; for Francesc Ferrer as consul see MC 1367.8.16. For the passage to Sardinia see MC 1367.8.27. Note that this mitigates somewhat against Kagay's assertion ('The Defense of the Crown of Aragon', 13–15) that Aragonese forces at this time were led largely by nobles or by captains who recruited in the style of later military entrepreneurs. While these elements were undoubtedly important if not dominant, civic militias were clearly playing a significant part in Aragonese armies through the fourteenth century. See J. Fynn-Paul, 'The Role of Local Entrepreneurs in Military Finance and Supply during the

provides rare proof that urban militias were indeed being led by town consuls (in addition, presumably, to the *veguer*), and that this duty might even lead consuls to serve overseas. By 1369, the city was paying for the maintenance of yet another force of mercenaries, this time sent to the city of Cervera in fulfilment of yet another invocation of *Princeps Namque*. This is a further suggestion that mercenaries had begun to replace urban levies, and corresponds with Sánchez's assertion that *Princeps Namque* had been turned into a more flexible 'modern' instrument during the 1368 negotiations.[112]

Thus, from 1367 until the threat of invasion finally subsided in 1375, the Crown pursued an intensive programme of wall-building at Manresa, which was to have both immediate and long-term effects on the city and its institutions. In the process of creating more efficient institutions for the rapid completion of such an exorbitantly expensive project, the government of Manresa (with the consent and aid of the Crown) was to reach high points of power over the church, the nobility and the people of the Bages which, as it was, would never again be equalled until the modern era. For its part, the Crown likewise showed in this period of crisis an ability to dominate urban government that might not otherwise have been suspected. The Crown officials forced the citizens to maximize their contributions for the wall, even as the townsmen continued to support a civic militia on overseas garrison duty in Sardinia, maintained interest payments on outstanding bonds and contributed to further extraordinary levies.[113] In September of 1368, new orders to proceed with fortification were received, but the project was still in a rudimentary stage and was being conducted entirely by the urban government, as it had been in 1362.[114] One of the first things the government did upon receiving this new order was to reduce the wages of the wall workers to 8d per day and 4d per half day, under the pretext that they were a lazy lot who performed very little work. The reality, of course, was that the town could ill afford to pay wages that were competitive with other types of menial labour, especially given the fact that since the last plague the going rate was three or more times higher than they were now paying. One might wonder how efficient the wall workforce could be at this rate of pay, and how many of the labourers were boys and women. Two days after the wage reduction, the *clavarius* was given new powers to enforce the collection

Aragonese-Castilian War (1356–75)', in J. Fynn-Paul (ed.), *War, Entrepreneurs and the State in Europe and the Mediterranean, 1300–1800* (Leiden, 2014), pp. 32–60.

112 MC 1369.4.13; Sánchez Martínez, 'The Invocation of *Princeps Namque*'.

113 For the passage to Sardinia, see MC 1367.8.27.

114 MC 1368.9.26; for the weekly tax and the *clavarius*, MC 1368.9.28; again, for Manresan wage rates, see Tables 7.2 to 7.5.

of the 'weekly tax', which was once again dedicated to the construction of the wall.

By the following year, with the continuing threat of invasion, it had become apparent to the Crown that the Manresan citizens alone could not supply the money needed to construct the city walls in such a brief time. The Manresan wall works were, after all, part of a Catalan-wide programme. This included desperate construction efforts at Barcelona which taxed the social and financial fabric of the capital to the utmost.[115] As part of its general scramble for emergency revenue, the Crown tacitly authorized (in acts that were not written into the council manuals) the collection of taxes from 'men outside the city' (known as the *tallia hominum forensium racione muri*) and even, in an unprecedented move, from knights who owned land inside the city.[116] For example, the knight Berenguer de Manresa was assessed the substantial sum of 50s for a tract of land that he owned inside the city walls in a space called 'La Parada'. Such a large sum suggests that this assessment was intended as a tax to be applied retroactively. Other local castellans were also made to pay similar assessments over the next few years.[117] Further indication that this was done as part of a stepped-up royal program is provided by the king's augmentation of the powers of the *veguer* – in particular when he named the serving *veguer*, the squire Ramon de Merlesio, as the 'commissar of the wall works' in addition to his duties as *veguer*.[118] The money for these taxes was given to the commissar by the 'collector of the money for the principal wall'. This novel form of taxation was more than enough to cause significant alarm within the ranks of the castellanate, who had never submitted to taxation at the hands of the royal officials who worked for the city, or the *veguer*. The rationale for this extraordinary tax, of course, was that the city of Manresa served as a strong point for the entire Bages, perhaps the only place which, when properly fortified, could withstand a siege by a large mercenary company or Castilian force.

At this crucial juncture, it might have appeared to contemporaries as though the royal officials and the townsmen were about to complete a historic coup over the nobles, making them liable for property taxes both inside the town walls and within the *vegueria* of the Bages. It is

115 Josefina Mutge Vives, 'Preocupacions del govern municipal barceloní en el 1371 a través dels testaments dels consellers', *Acta Historica et Archaeologica Mediaevalia*, 23–4 (2003), 331–51.

116 See MC 1370.1.22 for the name of the tax.

117 For Blanche de Talamanca paying, MC 1372.4.13. For Francesc de Manresa, see MC 1371.1.31. For Joan de Rau, see MC 1373.3.29.

118 Merlesio was *veguer* since MC 1367.6.18, and is mentioned again as *veguer* in MC 1368.10.11. He is first mentioned as commissar in MC 1369.12.22; by January another royal agent, Bernat de Ladornosa, is mentioned as supervisor of the '*menium inferioris*' (MC 1370.1.19). By September 1370, Merlesio is styled '*commisarius electus per dominum regem*'.

possible that the *braç militar* had acceded to these taxes in the *Corts* at some point, but the castellanate of the Bages was clearly furious about them, particularly when they were renewed again in 1371. The result was a full-scale constitutional crisis which saw the local castellanate in a state of semi-rebellion which would last until the end of the war. In April of 1371, Ramon de Talamanca filed a lawsuit against the town of Manresa stating that this form of taxation violated his right to pay taxes only with the consent of the *braç militar* in parliament. The absence of subsequent taxes on noble property in the Manresan council manuals suggests that de Talamanca and his fellow castellans did not have to submit to this form of exaction for long.[119] Why then did the Crown pursue this avenue? It is likely to have been a very deliberate step. The royal administrators were fully aware of the probable unconstitutionality of their actions, and that they were unlikely to withstand legal challenges in the long run; but they nonetheless realized that before the new taxes could be challenged, they would result in significant and badly needed revenue. And they did pay – knights, peasants, and perhaps even the Abbot of St Benet, who in 1370 was busily fortifying his own abbey, perhaps using his efforts as an excuse not to pay the wall tax. The town certainly did not appreciate his efforts, and actually sued him over the matter of his fortification activities.[120] At one point, the town council noted with disgust that the Bishop of Urgell had neglected to pay the *imposicion* on meat while he had been staying in the city, and voted the sum of 6s/8d to make up for his intransigence.[121] The fact that the town took official notice of the bishop's action at this time is indicative of their mood, which was eager to see prelates and nobles 'pay their fair share' of the present national tax burden.

Not unexpectedly, the knights of the Bages did not restrict their protests to lawsuits; as had been the case with the earlier constitutional struggles of the 1350s, they soon began to take violent action as a means of registering their displeasure. A number of skirmishes between the knightly factions of the Talamancas, the de Manresas, the Ocinas and various Manresan citizens are mentioned in the council manuals for 1370 and 1371, likely as a direct result of this attempt to tax knightly property through urban channels, and the 'anti-privilege' mentality which was prevalent at that moment. Not all of the fighting was restricted to Type C class conflicts between nobles and non-nobles. At one point, the de Talamanca and de Manresa factions began fighting with one another inside the city walls, and the councillors had to elect a commission to

[119] For Ramon's protest, see RT 1371.4.15.

[120] For a disgruntled peasant see MC 1371.12.18; for the tussle with the abbot, see MC 1370.7.26.

[121] MC 1372.1.21.

attempt a reconciliation between the factions.[122] In the following year, Ramon de Ocina and his supporters entered the city and drew their weapons on Guillem and Berenguer Ferrer, members of the consular family whose scion Francesc had led the city's mercenary contingent in 1367.[123] After 1371, however, such skirmishes are mentioned less frequently, and despite the unrest, the knights continued to pay at least through 1373.[124] Nor was the issue entirely one-sided; that is, a case of the Crown against recalcitrant knights. The knights were simultaneously being relied upon by the Crown to lead the Catalan armies, and they were also frequent investors in the government bonds that were being paid by the city of Manresa.[125] Knightly violence, like much contemporary violence, therefore took place in a more multi-directional context than is usually realized.[126]

How did the town government fare during this period of extraordinary royal pressure?[127] The royal interest in rapid fortification certainly helped the Manresan council to expand its powers over the people of the Bages, as when the *operarios extra civitatem* were given *plenum posse* to enforce their will regarding the upkeep of roads and bridges throughout the Bages.[128] At the same time, the town councillors were put under tremendous pressure to bring in an exorbitant amount of taxation. The weekly tax, for example, continued right through 1374. In one instance the citizenry as a whole is known to have been contributing 500s (£25) per week, which amounts to just less than 1 *sou* per household per week, at a time when wages for a full-time worker were about 2s per day.[129] While the ability to collect taxes gave the Manresan patricians additional power, it also exposed them to dangers from both Crown officials and from the mob, and led to civic office becoming less popular through at least the end of the 1370s.[130] As we have seen, the arrival of a royal porter

122 MC 1370.11.25. 123 For the Ocina incident see MC 1371.9.12.

124 The last payment for these property taxes from a specific knight is noted in MC 1373.3.29; Joan de Rau, militis; but note that another mandate to tax the estates of 'knights and certain *generosii*' was given to the bailiff in MC 1374.2.28.

125 E.g. for some payments to knights in 1371 alone, see MC 1371.11.27; MC 1371.6.6; MC 1371.7.30; MC 1371.8.11.

126 This theme has been developed in the medieval Spanish historiography largely in the context of a multi-religious setting. See David Nirenberg, *Communities of Violence: Persecution of Minorities in the Middle Ages* (Princeton, NJ, 1996); and Mark D. Meyerson, 'Victims and Players: The Attack of the Union of Valencia on the Jews of Morvedre', in Thomas E. Burman, Mark D. Meyerson, and Leah Shopkow (eds.), *Religion, Text, and Society in Medieval Spain and Northern Europe: Essays in Honor of J. N. Hillgarth* (Toronto, 2002), 70–102.

127 MC 1374.2.10. 128 MC 1373.4.8. 129 MC 1374.2.1. For wages see Table 7.2.

130 Attendance became a highly contentious issue during the 1370s. Banns urging attendance on councillors and threatening them with fines for non-attendance or improper attendance (such as standing in the porch of St Miquel rather than in the building itself) can be found in MC

provided the instigation for an outburst of violence. The town council records unsurprisingly blame the porters themselves for these outbursts, which were very likely not so one-sided. In addition to the Truny case noted above, in October of 1368 a porter came to collect money for the king's mercenaries, and is recorded as having begun shouting at unnamed persons 'with a horribleness of words' (*cum horribilitatem verborum*). As a result, the Manresan council made denouncements to the *veguer*, the bailiff, as well as to the king and the Duke of Girona.[131]

Increased royal pressure also caused a good deal of debate and friction within the ranks of the patriciate itself. One of the most divisive issues was that of whether to tax by 'manifest' or by a simple head tax. In one example of a head tax, Jaume Sarta was authorized to collect 600 florins, one per household (a florin was worth 11s). This was to be collected on top of the weekly tax and all of the other exactions. He was told that he could collect 'a little more from the *maiores* and a little less from the *menores* as he saw fit'.[132] The overall idea, however, was that this was to be a relatively equal contribution by each householder. Clearly, this was a very unpopular measure in a town where the wealthy few held assets that were twenty or thirty times those of the average citizen.[133] Another way to assess taxes, of course, was to base them on a person's ability to pay. This was the purpose of taxing 'by manifest'; the technique was widespread in the later medieval Mediterranean and was probably borrowed from Italy. Taxation by manifest sought to evaluate the wealth of each householder, and to assign a tax based on this assessment. The 1408 *Liber Manifesti* would later be drawn up in the same spirit. At the beginning of the fortification crisis, the idea of taxation by manifest was suggested by the government of Francesc Nerell. This motion was made soon after he came into power in the elections of 1 April 1369. By 28 April, Nerell had won the point: it was declared that all taxes for that year, except those for the wall, were to be done 'by way of a manifest'.[134] This was to be the case 'unless the special council's decree was revoked by the general council'. Nerell rightly figured that such a populist measure was unlikely to be struck down in the city's most democratic deliberative body. There is insufficient evidence, however, to state for sure whether Nerell's democratic fiscal methods were actually carried out in 1369.

1370.4.19; MC 1371.10.30; MC 1372.4.21; MC 1377.5.12. Even the *conseller*'s chair became difficult to fill, e.g. LV, 269: '. . . *acciditque multociens quod aliqui de habitatoribus dicte civitatis qui apti sunt ad ipsum consiliarie officium, ipsum recipere recusant seu dubitant* . . . .'

131 MC 1368.10.3. 132 MC 1374.12.20.

133 Compare for example Table 8.4 on the largest Manresan patrician fortunes, with Tables 8.2 and 8–3.

134 MC 1369.4.28 and MC 1374.5.1.

After the 1370 election, Nerell again declared his intention of collecting taxes by means of a manifest.[135] This time, there is proof that his intentions were put into motion. Four syndics were appointed to hear accounts from all of the city's citizens, under penalty of 100s. They could either come before the commission or, if the commission willed, they would come to the house of the declarant. A few months later, a separate panel of four judges was elected in order to settle disputes arising over the nature of the declarations.[136] The actual process of creating a manifest, however, was vehemently opposed by many of the city's richest men, and by 24 July, the populist party could no longer maintain enough votes in the special council to maintain Nerell's resolution.[137] The manifest was scrapped, and the standard method of collecting taxes by household was reinstated. This policy was obviously detrimental to the vast majority of the citizens, and must have created a great deal of tension. Throughout the summer and autumn, the aisles of Sant Miquel frequently rang with the rhetoric of heated political debate, but no major policy changes were enacted regarding the distribution of the tax burden for the remainder of the war. It is interesting, in the longer term, to note that what the Manresan popular party could not push through during the 1360s and 70s – a period held by most urban historians to be a high point of later medieval 'populism' – the town government managed to accomplish on numerous occasions during the fifteenth century. This is one factor counting against an interpretation of town governments becoming more autocratic in the fifteenth century.

If the town government chafed under the hands of the commissar of the walls, who as will be recalled was appointed by royal fiat in 1369, the council records do not show it until January 1374, when the councillors began to complain that a 'certain commissar' had been making proclamations which were against the constitutions of Catalonia and the privileges of the city of Manresa. They therefore elected a commission to go before the king and decry the actions of the commissar. If the citizens hoped that their audience with the king would result in the abolition of the commissar's office, they did get what they asked for – with an ironic twist that is typical of Pere III. In place of the commissar, the king appointed the *donzell* Hug de Rosanes as 'Captain General' of Manresa and the Bages, who beginning in May wielded broad military powers throughout the region. To the captain's office were added all of the powers of the *veguer*.[138] This novel creation was appointed at the time

[135] MC 1370.5.3 and 1370.5.8. [136] MC 1370.7.8. [137] MC 1370.7.24.

[138] Hug replaced the regular *veguer*. The first mention is MC 1374.5.13. For him simultaneously wielding the powers of the vicariate and the captainship, cf. MC 1374.7.26. For an in-depth

of yet another rapidly escalating threat: in this instance, the Mallorcan pretender Jaume IV was amassing troops for an invasion of Roussillon and Catalonia. The new captain's first action was to go on a tour of the Bages, with the purpose of inspecting all of the region's fortifications. Jaume (II) Sarta was appointed to accompany him as the representative for the city.[139] By July, the captain was requisitioning wheat to ensure that the fortifications were well stocked – and the citizens were undoubtedly chafing at his heavy-handedness.

The councilmen were also unhappy about having to pay the captain's salary, since the *veguer*'s salary had customarily been paid from the royal treasury.[140] By renaming the *veguer* as the captain, the king was, amongst other things, attempting to shift the burden of his salary directly onto the municipality, contrary to custom. Thus, the councillors now attempted in turn to foist the responsibility for the captain's salary onto the *Diputació*, under the pretence that the captain's office was a part of the war effort, and should thus be payable by the extraordinary taxation that was managed by the *Corts*.[141] The *Diputació*, it will be remembered, was a permanent core council of the *Corts*, consisting of members from all three branches, whose formation has been seen as a major blow to Aragonese royal authority in Catalonia.[142] Although the *Diputació* had been in control of the collection of taxes for the *Corts* since 1358, their powers did not directly manifest themselves at Manresa until 1369, when the first porters from the *Diputació* arrived in order to collect funds.[143] The fact that these porters disappear from the records almost as suddenly as they appear indicates that the Crown may have temporarily lost the right to have the usual royal porters transfer the money to and from the offices of the *diputats*, but quickly regained the prerogative. While the existence of the *Diputació* probably caused some constitutional difficulties for the Crown, it seems clear from the Manresan records that in the short term, the king's powers remained both broad and effective: the powers of the royal commissar and the captain to collect taxes from the castellanate and to effectively override the Manresan town government at will are a clear manifestation of continued royal authority.

In further evidence of the city government's relative impotence, their attempts to protest the actions of the captain, on the grounds that he

study of the longer-term evolution of the captaincy as a dialectic between royal and local power during the later fourteenth and early fifteenth centuries in the cities of Sicily, see Fabrizio Titone, 'Aragonese Sicily as a Model of Late Medieval State Building', *Viator* 44:1 (2013), 217–49.

139 MC 1374.5.13.

140 For the salary of the *veguer* see ACA *Batllia* 1161, 45v and 46v.

141 MC 1374.7.28.

142 For recent literature on the fourteenth-century *Diputació* see n. 00, above.

143 MC 1369.12.22.

acted beyond the normal powers of the *veguer*, also came to nothing.[144] By August, the captain was once more organizing the workforce of the Manresan walls into hundreds, fifties, and tens – the same organization traditionally used for the city militia. He may well have been using the city militia as a labour force, given that the fear of invasion was now reaching a fever pitch.[145] By September, with invasion fears still running high, the captain noted with dismay that there had been a bad harvest, and that the price of wheat was increasing on a daily basis. Hoarding would no doubt have added to the sudden price increase, as was normal during invasion threats. On 14 October, the captain once more toured the Bages, and the next day he mandated the evacuation of the nearby town of Santpedor, a few kilometres north of Manresa, having found it to be indefensible. Several hundred people were ordered to pack up their food and movable goods, and relocate to the haven of Manresa until further notice.[146] On 31 October, the captain delegated a commission of men to determine which houses had to be destroyed in order to provide for the defence of the city, and to maintain a constant vigil on the walls throughout November.[147] As Jaume of Mallorca's invasion materialized, Pere once more invoked *Princeps Namque* and called up one man for every ten households, which in Manresa would have provided a contingent of sixty men.[148]

Fortunately for the citizens of the Bages, by January of 1375 the invasion scare was rapidly dissipating. Unfortunately for them, the previous years' bad harvests – which might have been exacerbated by severe flooding in 1373 – meant that the price of grain was now approaching famine levels. The city's response to this famine was very well organized; in fact it was far better co-ordinated than the efforts of the 1330s had been. This provides tangible proof of the advances in bureaucratic organization that had occurred over the previous forty years. Pere Nadal, the scribe and notary who was the city's indispensable secretary in these years, was given authority to run a *botige*, or subsidized grain market, in the city, which was an increasingly common and sophisticated response to famine in Catalan cities in the fourteenth century.[149] He was to arrange for the buying of grain, and the city's bakers were ordered to buy all of their

144 MC 1374.7.28.

145 MC 1374.8.9 for the organization of the workforce by hundreds, fifties, and tens; and MC 1374.9.10 for the captain's expression of invasion fears.

146 MC 1374.10.15.

147 MC 1374.10.31 for the destruction of houses; MC 1374.11.21 for the wall watch.

148 MC 1374.11.23.

149 For the *botige* see MC 1375.1.19. The city's response to the famine is chronicled in Marc Torras Serra, 'La carestia de Blat de 1374–1376 a Manresa', *Miscel.lània d'Estudis Bagencs*, 9 (1994), 99–138. Contrast this with less efficient earlier fourteenth-century systems as found in Josefina

wheat from that market, at the prices that were stipulated there. An independent commission was also set up to make and enforce laws regarding the operation of the city's market. Fines collected by the inspectors were to go to the poor, *pro amore dei*. In February, the invasion fears had lessened to the extent that the recent Sunday (weekly) taxes were being refunded to the citizens – no doubt to help them purchase the grain that was at that time so dear. The famine would continue into the summer of 1375, but that year's harvest was good, and so the citizens were spared further difficulties. Meanwhile, what was to prove a lasting settlement to the Castilian conflict was finally concluded in the spring of 1375. As soon as this was known, the town government immediately began to question the usefulness of the captain's office. In May, they petitioned the Crown through their representative at court that the captain's office be abrogated, or barring that, that his salary at least not be paid by the city.[150] Once more, their petition was not immediately heeded, since there was still a captain operating at Manresa through at least February of 1376.[151] In July of 1375, there was a great disturbance involving the *veguer*, the army of Manresa and the Count of Pallars, which necessitated the arrival of the king in the city.[152] The king's visit seems to have put the situation to rights, and after that summer, tensions in the Bages finally began to defuse. Although the captain continued to exercise his authority for some months, by February Pere Nadal had managed to get himself appointed as lieutenant captain – a move that would have appeased many in the city.[153] During the trying times of the 1360s and 70s, Nadal had often been the lieutenant bailiff, and had sometimes acted as something of a fifth column for the town's interest during disputes with the royal officials.[154] Despite this, the bailiffs clearly found that Nadal was as indispensable to them as he was for the town government, and so they continued to appoint him, despite any misgivings they might have had. In this way, the town government subtly worked to lessen the contrast between the Crown officials' wishes and their own. As lieutenant bailiff, Nadal had the right to authorize any action pertaining to the bailiff's office in his absence. He also served as the town's treasurer on a regular basis, even as he continued to ply his primary trade as a

Mutgé Vives, 'L'Abastament de Blat a la ciutat de Barcelona en Temps d'Alfons el Benigne (1327–1336)', *Anuario De Estudios Medievales*, 31:2 (2001), 649–91.

150 MC 1377.5.8. 151 MC 1376.2.22.

152 MC 1374.7.4 and 7.6 for the disturbance; MC 1379.7.29 and 7.31 for the royal visit.

153 MC 1376.2.22.

154 Pere Nadal appears as a *scriptor curie balie* in MC 1361.3.19; he was sworn in as lieutenant *veguer* in MC 1362.4.9 and is listed as both lieutenant bailiff and lieutenant *veguer* in MC 1362.8.1. He was a regular holder of these and other municipal offices through the 1370s.

scribe.[155] Finally, after February of 1376, Nadal's services as lieutenant captain were no longer required, since the Captain's office was now allowed to lapse.

Pere Nadal was not the only Manresan citizen upon whom the Manresan government could rely to help bridge the gap between royal and local government. Jaume dez Far hailed from a family first recorded in Manresa in 1337. By the 1350s, Jaume had been named as a royal councillor, and in 1357 he served as *consul* for Manresa.[156] In 1358, his relative Berenguer also served as *consul.*[157] This arrangement was beneficial both for the dez Far family, whose prestige was thereby increased, and also for the Manresan government, since Jaume dez Far continued to maintain his position as a royal councillor until the mid-1370s. It is interesting to discover that Jaume dez Far continued to hold important offices at Manresa, even while he remained a royal councillor. For example, in 1369 dez Far is listed as the treasurer for Manresa, which brought in an impressive salary of 700s.[158] By 1371, Jaume dez Far had been knighted, an achievement which immediately brought him into the social circle of the Talamancas and the other knights of the Bages.[159] Dez Far was able to decisively intervene in the inheritance struggle between the Talamancas and the Ocinas in 1372, an event which brought the Duke of Girona into the conflict, on the side of the Ocinas.[160] By 1375, Jaume's son Jacmino was styling himself a *donzell.*[161] Throughout the crises of the early 1370s, Jaume dez Far was appealed to on numerous difficult occasions: in one instance the city wrote both to the Duke of Girona and to Jaume dez Far, indicating that dez Far was indeed the Manresans council's 'go-to man' at the royal court.[162] The career of Jaume dez Far shows another way in which talented Manresans could climb the social ladder during the mid-fourteenth century: by becoming useful to the royal court as a man knowledgeable about the Bages, he and his family were enriched, and eventually ennobled. Along the way, dez Far provided numerous invaluable services to the city of Manresa, and for a brief period he was even able to intervene as a social equal in the conflicts of the local castellanate. However, no further references to dez Far are found in the council manuals after 1376, so it is possible that Jaume was deceased after this date.[163] From this time onwards, however, the dez Far

[155] For Nadal functioning as a scribe see MC 1361.3.19 and MC 1369.5.8; for him acting as a treasurer see MC 1370.3.9; for him as the town's market official or *Mustaçaf* see MC 1372.3.23; for him selling *censals* to raise money for the wall works see MC 1374.5.26.

[156] MC 1357.12.19. [157] MC 1358.5.18.

[158] MC 1369.5.5. He receives a *violari* of 700s, which probably represents his annual salary. For comparable salaries earlier in the 1360s, see Table 7.6.

[159] MC 1371.6.6. [160] RT 1373.9.1. [161] MC 1375.3.25.

[162] MC 1372.11.19. [163] MC 1376.8.4.

family became firm members of the castellanate of the Bages, and after the death of Jaume, the family's links to the Manresan patriciate were severed. Thus, while joining the royal court could provide a fast track to personal wealth and honour, it served, in the case of the dez Far, to elevate the entire family to a position from which they felt they were superior to the goings-on of the urban patriciate.

THE AFTERMATH OF WAR, 1375–87

In 1375, after more than twenty years of continuous, often desperate and financially ruinous warfare, the inhabitants of Manresa felt themselves to be fiscally exhausted. Throughout this period, the plague had continued to eat away at the population of the town, and the prices of manufactured goods continued to increase. Wages also increased, an effect that was detrimental to the city's rich, but this worked in the short and medium term, at least, to the benefit of the city's lower and middle classes. Although no evidence has come to light regarding mortality in the city due to the plague that hit Catalonia during the famine of 1374–5, there are mentions in the records of an otherwise unrecorded plague that struck during 1370–1.[164] One of the few images of the plagues that appears in the town council manuals is a payment to a blacksmith, who made the iron pieces for the coffins of the *albats* who had died in the recent mortality. '*Albats*' is a poignant Catalan word that means 'children who died before the age of discretion'; literally 'the white ones', with implications of innocence. In some respects, this image of a loss of innocents/innocence is very well suited to the mood in the city after 1375. A generation of invasion fears, coupled with endemic plague and frequent famine and unaccustomed outbursts of violence, had done its share to sap the optimism of previous decades. The fact that the city was now saddled with a significant debt burden also weighed heavily in the minds of many town administrators. In 1373, however, they had successfully petitioned the Crown to buy back many of the *violaris* that had had been sold during the 1360s. By that time, it had become clear to all of Catalonia's fiscal elite that the mechanism of the *violari*, which depended upon a personal knowledge of whether the two named people were alive or dead, was entirely unworkable given the vastly increased scale of bond issues that had become normative during the war. From now on, the Catalans would cease to sell *violaris*, and deal only in the much lower-interest *censals*. This had the positive effect of bringing down Manresa's interest payments considerably.

[164] MC 1371.11.10.

Also in 1375, the councillors realized that the most cost-effective way to complete the *sèquia*, which had been begun in the 1330s as a response to famine-causing drought, was to privatize it. This was especially true since nearly all of the revenues of the town government went to servicing the public debt. The townspeople's recent experience with famine had driven home the point that the *sèquia* had to be completed as soon as possible. By November of that year, the project had been sold to a consortium of Manresan citizens 'and their associates' for the price of 42,800s.[165] The town then authorized a periodic sale of *censals* in order to meet the regular payments that were due to the consortium. In this way, new, more sophisticated fiscal techniques provided some relief to the city's woes, even as they had helped the city to raise the revenue necessary to fend off the Castilians and the French companies.

Although Catalonia was to enjoy a long spell of freedom from foreign invasion after the truce of 1375, the new debt system meant that Manresa continued to be burdened with very high payments for many years thereafter.[166] This situation was not unique to Manresa, and was present in Catalonia generally.[167] This indebtedness probably contributed to a migration away from royal lands into seigneurial lands, where the *censal* burden, and thus the tax burden, may well have been lighter. By 1377, the town councillors were complaining that many people were leaving Manresa altogether, with the result that there were too few people to pay the *censals* with which the town was burdened.[168] In spite of this continuing debt burden, Pere III was still concerned to retrieve the royal patrimony that had been sold off during the war, so that he spent much of the late 1370s and 1380s attempting to force his cities to pay for its recovery.[169] There are some indications that the Crown went bankrupt in 1381, causing the ruin of several important Barcelona bankers.[170]

165 MC 1375.11.8.

166 For the debt payments see Marc Torras Serra, 'El deute públic a la ciutata de Manresa a la Baixa Edat Mitjana', in Manuel Sánchez Martínez (ed.), *Fiscalidad real y finanzas urbanas en la Cataluña medieval* (Barcelona, 1999), pp. 155–83.

167 Flocel Sabaté Curull, 'La insolvència municipal a la segona meitat del segle XIV', in Manuel Sánchez Martínez (ed.), *Fiscalidad real y finanzas urbanas en la Cataluña medieval* (Barcelona, 1999), pp. 255–80.

168 MC 1377.1.10; see Fynn-Paul, 'Civic Debt, Civic Taxes', 142.

169 This story is told in María Teresa Ferrer i Mallol, 'El Patrimoni reial i la recuperació dels senyorius jurisdiccionals en les estats Catalano-Aragonesos a la fi del segle XIV', *Anuario de Estudios Medievales*, 7 (1970–1), 351–491. Fynn-Paul, 'Civic Debt, Civic Taxes'. See also MC 1381.2.18.

170 Gaspar Feliu Montfort, 'Mercaders-banquers barcelonins: l'endeutament de la monarquia i la fallida de la taula de canvi de Pere des Caus i Andreu d'Olivella el 1381', *Barcelona. Quaderns d'història*, 13 (2007), pp. 197–210. Note that the Venetian fiscal system was also under severe strain under the same period: the two crises are very likely related. Reinhold C. Mueller and

The long decades of war and the fiscal pressure brought to bear by the bond system also helped to shepherd Manresa from a model of civic largesse towards a privatization of services previously maintained at the public expense. During the war years not only the teachers, but also the doctors, had been moved off the civic budget, and the fees were made the responsibility of individual taxpayers.[171] It was the urban poor, of course, who lost in the bargain. As will be argued in Chapter 8, however, the poor and working classes were also experiencing a dramatic increase in living standards, so it is true that they were at this time less likely to object to privatization of urban services. It was as part of this general trend towards privatization that the *sèquia* was brought into the hands of a consortium of investors, with the resultant loss of public oversight. Likewise, the new austerity also brought a stagnation or diminution in the salaries of many urban officials, meaning that there was less incentive for the non-rich to hold public office of any sort.

After decades of royal threats and pressure, public opprobrium brought by years of high taxes and the fact that town government now provided very few tangible benefits to the urban populace, it is perhaps not to be wondered that, by the late 1370s, prominent citizens had become unwilling to stand for municipal office. It might also have been the case, then, that the general atmosphere of rebelliousness that was spreading across Europe in the 1370s was also making it increasingly uncomfortable for wealthy citizens to stand for office. Given the frequency of revolts against urban leaders that occurred between 1378 and 1382, in particular, it seems clear that there was a strong anti-establishment ethos running through contemporary popular culture throughout those years.[172] This would translate into a good deal of discomfort for those who would otherwise stand for urban office, though such popular malcontent might be nearly invisible in our sources. Thus, in this increasingly charged atmosphere, we find several more instances of the civic elite refusing to stand for office. In March of 1380, the king had to write to the town council, admonishing them to do their civic duty. Pere explained to the councillors that it had been brought to his attention that some inhabitants of the town who were suited to office (i.e. were wealthy enough) in fact refused to stand, with the result that the civic government was finding it difficult to attain a quorum. Some men had claimed that if they stood for

Frederic C. Lane, *The Venetian Money Market: Banks, Panics, and the Public Debt, 1200–1500* (Baltimore, MD, 1997), pp. 461–3.

171 This is discussed with regards to municipal wages and salaries in Chapter 7.

172 For a close-up view of the social and political complexities that this could engender in the urban milieu, see Pamela Nightingale, *A Medieval Mercantile Community: The Grocers' Company and the Politics and Trade of London, 1000–1485* (New Haven, CT, 1995), pp. 228–317.

civic office, they would not be able to pursue personal business outside the city, as their finances required. The king's solution to this was that the councillors could appoint surrogates to act on their behalf while they were absent, and his majesty hoped that this would decrease their apprehension. Assuming that this excuse was based in genuine concerns, it does not speak well of the government's ability to maintain a full council of *jurats* and consuls, at a time when there was a general reluctance to stand for office. It would seem as though there were so few *jurats* at this point that the absence of one or two of them from the city might seriously hinder the ability of the government to function. In any event, this royal letter is doubtless indicative of a deeper problem.[173] Just two months later, the town's bailiff had to decree that any *consellers* who did not make it to the town meetings were now liable to a fine.[174]

It was not until the end of 1381, however – a tumultuous year in European history which had already seen the famous English uprising, and which closer to home saw Aragonese royal insolvency precipitate a crisis in the Catalan financial system – that the simmering discontent at Manresa boiled over into open violence. Unfortunately, our records of this event, as of so many others, are all too laconic. The most immediate evidence for serious unrest comes from a royal letter of 15 January 1382, in which Pere III writes from Valencia ordering the people of Manresa to submit to the 'peace and truce' of the *veguer* and the bailiff of the town, and to put aside their feuds, which had been causing various types of destruction. The king ends by noting that he will not change his mind on this issue, or extend the six-day limit that he has imposed for the signing of the truce, for any reason.[175] An examination of the town council records reveals two possible causes for this disturbance: one controversy came to a head in late October 1381 between the royal bailiff and the shearer Jaume de Soler Ferran, over Jaume's ability to hold one of the towers in the city wall as a private home without restriction. Another controversy, however, was much more likely to have caused serious disturbances. This was an eruption of the long-standing battle between townspeople and the knights (*persons generoses*) who owned property in the town (including the Talamancas and the de Manresas) over whether or not the knights would contribute towards the debt incurred by the city in the construction of the city walls.[176] As with the 1359 unrest, and the unrest of the early 1370s, it is probable that this third wave of disturbances was largely a case of the citizens against the knights, and thus an extension of the ongoing feud between the *braços reial* and *militar* over the distribution of national

[173] LV, 269. [174] MC 1380.5.14. [175] LV, 277–8.
[176] MC 1381.10.28 and 1380.11.29.

fiscal burdens, played out at the local and regional levels. It has already been shown that the knights in question were not resident in the town at the time. It is possible that this issue caused the outbreak of some factional strife amongst groups of patricians in town, since some families may have come out in favour of certain of the knights' parties. Whatever was the case, there are no further references to disturbances in the royal letters or our local sources. In this way, the revolutionary 'flashpoint' of 1378–81 passed through Manresa without any incident of transcendent importance. But one event stemming from this period of revolution did eventually have a transformative, and largely negative, effect on Catalan urban society as a whole. In 1386, simmering discontent over the public debt, which had been accumulated through 1375, finally boiled over into a series of confrontations in Barcelona.[177] While Pere III was inclined to solve the problem by perpetuating the social status quo or even by giving more urban representation to the lower classes, he died in January of 1387 after a fifty-year reign. His son and successor Joan I drew up a series of constitutional solutions in various Catalan cities, including Manresa, which have already been mentioned. Joan's urban constitutions ostensibly created a more egalitarian system by allowing more merchants and *menestrals* to sit on the councils. In the long term, however, they helped to strengthen Type D class divisions between the three 'hands', which would cause turmoil and dramatically sap Catalan urban vitality in the fifteenth century.'

CONCLUSIONS

This chapter has examined the evolution of urban government at Manresa during the fourteenth century, and the story is one in which the Crown, its regional and local representatives, and the Manresan patriciate played the dominant roles. Regional nobles, the higher clergy, and other elements of the Manresan and regional population also feature as occasional actors in this dialogue. The fourteenth century was undoubtedly a momentous time for urban government in Catalonia, and it certainly witnessed the high point of urban power at Manresa. When, precisely, was the apogee of urban power? One could argue that this occurred during the 1320s and 1330s. This was after the creation of the consulate had given the Manresan patricians a clear political voice, but prior to the chaos of the Black Death, before the public debt system began to sap the resources of the civic treasury, and before the high taxation of

[177] This is described in Batlle, *Historia De Catalunya*, vol. III: *L'Expansio baixmedieval (segles XIII–XV)* (Barcelona, 1998), pp. 242–3; 271–3.

the Castilian war era of 1351–75 began to sap the resources of individual elites. It was also a fresh time in the civic psyche, since the consulate was newly created and its powers had yet to be circumscribed by practice or memory. The royal interventions of the later 1360s and early 1370s, notably the installation by royal fiat of the Captain of the Wall Works, certainly contributed to a feeling amongst urban elites that their consulate was not at all possessed of a plenitude of power; patricians and non-patricians alike now experienced at first hand how easily the royal will could impose upon their cherished local freedoms. Indeed, these freedoms now could not but seem more imaginary than real. The distaste with which Manresans viewed civic office in the later 1370s and early 1380s attests to this feeling that the earlier promise held out by the consulate now seemed significantly reduced – at least until the 1393 reforms of Joan I sparked a new interest in civic government amongst the urban patriciate.

One could also make a case for the later 1360s and early 1370s as a high point of civic power. Certainly this was the period when Manresan citizens held the most sway over the local nobility, and were most able to exercise power over the whole of the Bages through the office of the *operarios extra civitatem*. Civic and royal officials now jointly chose to deal with the local nobility, and sometimes even the higher clergy, in a high-handed manner, one which in the previous century would had been unheard of. They even had a recently knighted former *consul* who could serve as a bulwark against the local castellany and a sympathetic agent at court. And it is also true that while civic power in the 1320s and 1330s seemed relatively limitless, the city did not during this period engage in many high-profile actions as a regional actor – apart from the decision to build the *sèquia*. So while civic power seemed greater in the 1320s and 1330s than it did later in the century, in fact the city and its officials engaged in less projection of their powers outside the parish boundaries than they did during certain later decades. Still, the fact that the city's actions during the 1360s and 70s were done in conditions of extreme duress, and almost always with direct royal backing, reveals the beginning of a trend in which the royal centralizing power became so potent that the governments of individual cities found themselves circumscribed, more limited in what they could do without being seemingly at the beck and call of the king's representatives. When civic elites did have room to manoeuvre, this was done in relatively narrow formats, such as ensuring that a lieutenant bailiff or lieutenant to the Captain of the Wall works was a local man. Civic elites might play the officials of the *Diputació* against royal officials in an attempt to lessen their increasing tax burdens. But these examples also serve to illustrate how the city's projections of its political power in the 1360s and 1370s, while still impressive, were already indicative of a creeping loss of autonomy.

Another major theme of this chapter has been the so-called 'crisis', or more specifically the 'urban crisis', of the fourteenth century. The preceding analysis has suggested that the natural aspects of this crisis did not have such direct social and political repercussions as might be imagined. Some disasters which are known to have struck other parts of Europe simply passed Manresa by; others were of relatively limited impact. There appears not to have been a famine in the 1310s in Catalonia, as was experienced in much of France, for example. The drought of the 1330s seems merely to have increased civic resolve to create a man-made solution to insure against future famines. Even the Black Death, while it is likely to have struck down half or more of the civic populace over a few-month period, did not greatly sap the will or resolve of the civic elites who survived the crisis. The second major wave of plague in 1362–3, however, did begin to cause consternation amongst civic elites, and caused them to adopt favourable immigration policies to counteract a perceived labour shortage. By the mid-1370s, further plagues had brought civic elites to despair; they particularly lamented that they could not find enough householders to pay the consumption taxes which were required to maintain the public debt. This economic duress and psychological malaise undoubtedly began to take a toll on the entrepreneurial spirit of the civic elites, who found government bonds to be a very lucrative alternative to the physical and mental discomfort of active trading.

But the despair of the Manresan elites was not simply brought about by natural disasters and demographic decline. The economic consequences of depopulation were certainly a problem for urban elites: they caused wages to increase, and the prices of manufactured goods to increase along with them. These themes will be taken up in the next section, but are addressed here because they make up a significant component of the fourteenth-century crisis. In addition to this rather 'natural' movement of prices and wages as a response to decreasing population, two man-made factors played heavily into the despair displayed by civic elites in the 1370s, and thereby exacerbated the sense of 'crisis' felt by many urban inhabitants of the time. One was the Castilian war itself, which dragged on in various forms for nineteen years; another was the creation of the public debt system. If it were not for these two elements, and the dangers they caused, the mood of the Manresan civic elites might have been quite different, despite the recurring waves of plague. And it should be noted that war and the public debt were mutually reinforcing hazards. Even desperate war brought invasion threats relatively infrequently. The economic pressure brought to bear upon Catalonia due to the introduction of the public debt system during a time of military duress, however, was continually felt throughout the war period and long afterwards. It was therefore a combination of sometimes desperate war, continually high civic debt, depopulation, declining purchasing power amongst elites and price increases which combined to make the 1360s, 1370s, and 1380s seem like a time of crisis. If Manresa and the other Catalan royal cities experienced a time of 'crisis' during the fourteenth century, it peaked during the 1370s and early 1380s, and it contained a blend of elements both Europe-wide and uniquely Catalan.

It should be emphasized that the military aspect of this Catalan crisis was more or less entirely the result of Crown policy. Pere III did not, it seems clear, have to become involved in a war with Pedro of Castile, nor did he have to anger Enrique of Trastámara in 1367. Both times, he quickly found himself to be sorely pressed by Castilian manpower and resources, and it was only through the introduction and perfection of the debt system, which had been in its experimental stages during the 1340s, that the Crown of Aragon was saved from significant loss of territory in the end. This chapter has shown that, far from being a rickety underpowered state, which was shedding valuable royal patrimony, the Crown of Aragon was able to marshal a good deal of financial muscle relative to its size, on a scale which might have matched even the most vaunted Italian city-republics. Rather than being effectively obstructionist, as decades of commentary have portrayed them, the *Corts* with the partial exception of the *braç militar* served largely as a rubber stamp for royal exactions during the war period. The Crown knew very well how much it could expect from each of its cities, and these amounts were duly requested with as much regularity as could possibly be borne. The increasing bureaucratic sophistication of government at the local and national levels also served to strengthen the efficiency of royal government throughout this period. By the 1370s, governmental procedures were not too much less articulate than they would be at the beginning of the sixteenth century.

Finally, this chapter has also touched upon the nature of revolution and revolt, versus what has been described as 'consensus government', in fourteenth-century Manresa. It has been pointed out that by the time that the 'crisis' became most severe, that is, during the period from about 1348 to 1381, Manresa was a very homogenous society by medieval standards. There were almost no resident nobles; there were no Type D class divisions to speak of between *rentiers* and merchants, or *ciutadans* and non-*ciutadans*, and even Type B class divisions based on wealth did not have a marked impact on the nature of social unrest in the city's history. As will be discussed in the next section, living standards amongst rich and poor were by the later fourteenth century rapidly converging, rather than diverging. After 1348, there were few Jews living in Manresa, and the introduction of the *censal* further served to displace Jews from their traditional roles as local financiers. Manresa had no known *mudejars* living in the vicinity, nor were there even *remença* peasants whose extreme oppression might have exacerbated social tensions. The greatest social disturbances seem to have been caused by waves of anti-noble sentiment which swept through Manresa during the war years, particularly when the nobility were perceived to be dragging their feet and had not agreed to support a 'fair share' of the taxation at the national level. Some anticlericalism is even evident as this trend reached a crescendo during the 1370s. At the high point of the crisis, during the later 1360s and early 1370s, fiscal pressure began to drive wedges between the civic populace and the urban office-holders, as the latter were held accountable by royal officials for collecting a number of novel taxes which were sustained for years on end at a very high level. This situation was, however, far from normative, and many patricians were evidently very uncomfortable with the role of being in power, if it came at the cost of public opprobrium. For most of the century, elites held civic office accompanied by the sense that their government was generally 'for the city', and they could naturally expect that the majority of urban citizens would look up to them as embodiments of the civic will.

On top of this relative homogeneity on many fronts, there was also a broad sense of shared destiny between the House of Barcelona, at this point represented by Pere III and his son Duke Joan, and the Catalan urban elites. For at least two centuries prior to 1410, the rulers of Catalonia-Aragon had shown themselves willing to embark on policies which were more or less favourable to the interests of Barcelona merchants, and thus of Catalan urban elites more broadly. Even the Castilian war, which began as a naval dispute resulting from the Catalans' desire to take Sardinia from the Genoese, was not at first contrary to the perceived interests of many urban elites. Compared with the suspicion and hostility shown between elements of the Catalan urban elite and the Trastámara kings, Manresa during the reign of Pere III was experiencing something of a golden age of harmony between royal and civic interests. That the king could rule with a personal touch is evident in the royal visit of 1375. This was likely brought about by a regional disturbance between royal officials and urban elements, but it resulted in a mutually satisfactory plan for reconciliation. On more than one occasion during the peak of the crisis period, Pere showed himself willing to let bygones be bygones, as long as his restive subjects would agree to submit to the royal peace and continue to pay their taxes more or less on time.

The principal themes of this and the preceding chapter can be tied together by asking what longer-term effects, if any, the 'crisis' of the later fourteenth century may have had on Manresan civic vitality, on the civic elites, and on other groups of the Manresan populace. The best answer is probably that the crisis, in its various aspects, did sap civic vitality, and it did mark the beginning of a long, slow but ultimately definitive circumscription of the power of the civic government. Ultimately, it also led to a relative disempowerment of the non-elite inhabitants of Manresa as well. A comparison between Manresa in the fourteenth century with Manresa in the thirteenth and later fifteenth centuries, for example, provides ample reason to give us pause. During the long fourteenth century, taken as a whole, the Manresan patriciate was a strong regional power player. During the earlier and later periods, it was disorganized and lacking in both political power and effective economic clout. In both the earlier and the later periods, the lack of a politically and economically significant civic patriciate left the urban populace prey to the whims of ecclesiastical and seigneurial elites, who in the earlier period imposed hated feudal dues upon them, and who in both periods exercised arbitrary violence upon the populace with little fear of retribution to keep them in check.[178]

In short, when there was no civic elite to speak of, the entire citizenry lost a good deal of economic and political freedom, which made their odds of living fulfilling lives that much lower. Whether one defines a bourgeoisie as a non-noble civic elite, or the civic populace at large (and this book tends to emphasize the former, while at the same time including elements of the latter in its definition), it is clear that the Manresan bourgeoisie was enjoying a heyday of power and prestige between about 1300 and 1450. This power and prestige was, however, lost during the course of the fifteenth century. In the process, the Manresan citizenry also lost a good deal of dignity, a dignity in which all townsmen had to some extent been able to participate during the civic heyday. Dignity is difficult to measure, but it is surely one of the most important measures of personal agency and fulfilment. This makes it very difficult to argue, as the power of the Manresan patriciate continued to decline in the years after 1400, that the city's non-elite inhabitants were better off without them. It should by this point be apparent that it is not possible to describe the developmental trajectories of Manresa itself, or of the various groups

[178] For a relatively detailed discussion of this issue with regard to the Crown of Aragon and Catalonia, which shows between the lines how a lack of urban power enabled local nobles to act with impunity in the aftermath of the Catalan civil war, see James Casey, *Early Modern Spain: A Social History* (London, 1999), pp. 165–91. See an older discussion and notes by J. H. Elliott, *The Revolt of the Catalans* (Cambridge, 1984), pp. 51–3.

who made up its citizenry, without an understanding of the fiscal and economic developments that played so prominent a role in the 'crisis' of the later Middle Ages. It is the purpose of the next section of this book to describe these economic developments, with an eye to gauging their political causes and their social and political effects.

PART II

Economy

Chapter 6

THE ARAGONESE FINANCIAL REVOLUTION

A nexus of state formation and personal investment

INTRODUCTION

In the previous chapter it was argued that during the crises of the later fourteenth century, an increase of royal control over urban government was evident in almost every sphere in which there was interaction between royal and urban agents. It was suggested that a significant factor in this process was the evolution of the government annuity system known as the *censal* system.[1] This system, whose evolution and

[1] The subject of municipal public finance, which during the fourteenth century in Catalonia created a system akin to a modern government annuity system, with public sales of perpetual annuities known as *censals*, and (until about 1370) sales of dual-life instruments known as *violaris*, has been the subject of a veritable explosion of literature in recent decades. The leader of this historiographical revolution is Manuel Sánchez Martínez, whose *El naixement de la fiscalitat d'estat a Catalunya: Segles XII–XIV* (Vic, 1995) remains fundamental. Sánchez has edited several volumes dealing with this topic. A more recent and very influential volume is Manuel Sánchez Martínez, *La deuda pública en la Cataluña bajomedieval* (Madrid, 2009); for the closest statement to the effect that the debt system of the fourteenth-century Crown of Aragon was a 'financial revolution', see especially the Introduction, pp. 7–20.

Other important edited volumes which deal primarily with regions across Iberia are Manuel Sánchez Martínez, *Estudios sobre renta, fiscalidad y finanzas en la Cataluna bajomedieval* (Madrid, 1993); Manuel Sánchez Martínez, Antoni Furió and Prim Bertran i Roigé, *Actes colloqui corona, municipis i fiscalitat a la Baixa Edat Mitjana*, Quaderns De l'Institut (Lleida, 1996); Manuel Sánchez Martínez (ed.), *Fiscalidad real y finanzas urbanas en la Cataluña medieval* (Barcelona, 1999); Manuel Sánchez Martínez, *Pagar al rey en la Corona de Aragon durante el siglo XIV* (Barcelona, 2003). Perhaps the most incisive discussion of the socio-economic effects of the *censal* system to date is Flocel Sabaté Curull, 'Ejes vertebradores de la oligarquía urbana en Cataluña', *Revista d'Història Medieval*, 9 (1998), 127–53. On the ability of Pere III to milk his cities to the point of insolvency, see Flocel Sabaté Curull, 'La insolvència municipal a la segona meitat del segle XIV', in Manuel Sánchez Martínez (ed.), *Fiscalidad real y finanzas urbanas en la Cataluña medieval* (Barcelona, 1999), pp. 255–80.

On the *Corts* and fiscality see Manuel Sánchez Martínez and Pere Orti Gost, *Corts, parlaments i fiscalitat a Catalunya: Els capitols del donatiu (1288–1384)* (Barcelona, 1997).

For Valencia, a very solid exposition of the development of the *censal* system has been published in Juan Vicente García Marsilla, *Vivir a crédito en la Valencia medieval: De los orígenes del sistema censal al endeudamiento del municipio* (Valencia, 2002). The social effects of the system were often quite different than in Catalonia, however, owing to the much stronger presence of nobles in the towns and in municipal government; see Rafael Narbona Vizcaíno and Enrique Cruselles Gómez, 'Espacios económicos y sociedad política en la Valencia del siglo XV', *Revista d'Història Medieval*, 9 (1998), 193–214; Remedios Ferrero Micó, 'Los beneficiarios del municipio: Arrendatarios y

significance forms the primary narrative of the present chapter, had a hugely transformative effect on the nature of state power in Catalonia. As is now increasingly understood, the *censal* system became a cornerstone upon which the later medieval Aragonese and early modern Spanish state would come to be founded.[2] Indeed, the Catalan developments should be seen as part of a general trend in fourteenth-century Europe, which saw a great increase in bureaucratic sophistication, including financial sophistication, in the governmental centres of Western Europe at all levels from the local to the national. Perhaps the most palpable element of this change was a massive increase in revenue that was experienced by

censualistas de la ciudad de Valencia', in *Corona, municipis i fiscalitat a la Baixa Edat Mitjana: col.loqui* (Lleida, 1997), pp. 643–74.

For cities in the Kingdom of Aragon proper, which remain relatively under-studied, see Juan Abella Samitier, 'La deuda pública de los municipios aragoneses en los siglos XIV y XV', *Anuario de estudios medievales*, 39:1 (2009), 47–64.

For Mallorca there are various works of Pau Cateura Bennàsser, e.g. *El crèdit i el sistema financer del regne de Mallorca (segles XIV–XV)* (Palma, 2009); Pau Cateura Bennàsser, *L'administració atrapada crèdit, finances i adaptacions fiscals en el regne de Mallorca (segle XV)* (Palma, 2008).

In sharp contrast with the cutting-edge fiscal system that was developed in the fourteenth-century Crown of Aragon, the Castilian fiscal system remained poorly conceived and in general more ad hoc throughout the medieval period and the early modern era. See Antonio Collantes de Terán Sánchez and Denis Menjot, 'Hacienda y fiscalidad concejiles en la Corona de Castilla en la Edad Media', *Historia. Instituciones. Documentos*, 23 (1996), 213–54; Antonio Collantes de Teran Sánchez, 'La élite financiera en la Sevilla bajomedieval: Los mayordomos del concejo', *Revista d'Història Medieval*, 11 (2000), 13–39; Antonio Collantes de Terán Sánchez, 'Les impôts municipaux indirects ordinaires et extraordinaires de Séville', in Denis Menjot and Manuel Sánchez Martínez (eds.), *La fiscalité des villes au moyen age (Occident Méditerranéen). Les systèmes fiscaux* (Toulouse, 1999), pp. 463–83; María Asenjo González, 'Ciudades y deuda pública en Castilla: La adaptación fiscal del impuesto de la "alcabala real" a las nuevas exigencias de la sociedad política (1450–1520)', in Simonetta Cavaciocchi (ed.), *La fiscalità nell'economia Europea secc. XIII–XVIII/Fiscal Systems in the European Economy from the 13th to the 18th Centuries. Atti della Trenatanovesima Settimana di Studi, 22–26 Aprile 2007* (Florence, 2008), pp. 531–44.

For a broader scope of coverage that shows similar public debt systems evolving in many cities throughout contemporary continental Western Europe, see Manuel Sánchez Martínez and Denis Menjot (eds.), *La fiscalité des villes au moyen age (France méridionale, Catalogne et Castille)*, vols. I–III (Toulouse, 1996–2002); Denis Menjot, Albert Rigaudiére, and Manuel Sánchez Martínez, *L'Impôt dans les villes de l'Occident méditerranéen: XIIIe–XVe siècle: Colloque tenu à Bercy les 3, 4 et 5 octobre 2001* (Paris: 2005). On this topic see also the important collection by M. Boone, K. Davids, and P. Janssens, *Urban Public Debts, Urban Government and the Market for Annuities in Western Europe (14th–18th Centuries)* (Turnhout, 2003).

2 The social and political implications of emergent public debt systems in the later fourteenth and fifteenth centuries are now increasingly understood. See Antoni Furió Diego, 'Deuda pública e intereses privados. Finanzas y fiscalidad municipales en la Corona de Aragón', *Edad Media: Revista De Historia*, 2 (1999), 35–79. For an argument that these debt systems created some economic integration, and a hegemony of towns over countryside, in Valencian cities, but also helped to co-opt 'burghers' into the 'aristocracy' to increasingly dominate the cities, see Pau Viciano Navarro, 'Entre la comercio i el mercat: Els inversors en la gestió de la fiscalitat reial i municipal al país Valencia', in *Corona, Municipis i Fiscalitat a La Baixa Edat Mitjana: Col.loqui.* (Lleida, 1997), pp. 603–22.

many monarchies and local governments, to which the term 'state' may be applied with increasing justification as the century progresses.[3]

This chapter will attempt to detail not only the economic and political impact of this new financial system, but also its broad-ranging social effects. Although the epicenter of this transformation was in the field of finance, its nature was such that it had a major transformative effect on relations between nobles and commoners, amongst urban patricians, employers and employees, family members and kin, townspeople and their towns. Jan Dumolyn has argued that the two principal themes of late medieval urban history are the 'fourteenth-century crisis' and the process of state formation.[4] The powerful role of the individual as an investor should not be lost in these broad themes. In the previous chapter we saw that the fourteenth-century 'crisis' was experienced in Catalonia as a series of shocks, both man-made and natural. The chief natural, that is, not man-made, component to this crisis was the Black Death itself, which instigated a series of economic shocks to wages, prices and incomes; the story of these demographic and macroeconomic shocks will form the basis of the next chapter. The man-made shocks have traditionally been identified as warfare and repression – but we will argue here that the *censal* system worked hand in hand with warfare to produce entirely unforeseen developments which acted as shocks upon Manresan society – even if the effects of these shocks were varied, and not uniformly baleful. The combination of the new financial system,

3 The prime mover of the debate over the effects of late medieval and early modern fiscal systems on state formation is Charles Tilly, *Coercion, Capital and European States: AD 990–1992* (London, 1992). See an interesting addition on 'composite states' (which is clearly relevant to the later medieval Crown of Aragon) in Harald Gustafsson, 'The Conglomerate State: A Perspective on State Formation in Early Modern Europe', *Scandinavian Journal of History*, 23:3–4 (September 1998), 189–213. For a discussion of this phenomenon in general see Hanno Brand, 'Urban Elites and Central Government; Co-operation or Antagonism? The Case of Leiden at the End of the Middle Ages', *Publications du Centre Européen d'Etudes Bourguignonnes (XIVe–XVIe S.)*, 33 (1993), 49–60. For the link between annuities and state formation in the fourteenth century see Marc Boone, Karel Davids and Paul Janssens, 'Urban Public Debts from the 14th to the 18th Century: A New Approach', in *Urban Public Debts: Urban Government and the Market for Annuities in Western Europe (14th–18th Centuries)*, Studies in European Urban History (1100–1800), 3 (Turnhout, 2003), pp. 3–11. For this process in Latin Europe in general, see Thomas Ertman, *Birth of the Leviathan: Building States and Regimes in Medieval and Early Modern Europe* (Cambridge, 1997), ch. 2. For this with relation to Florence, from which the Catalans took many fiscal cues, see Anthony Molho, 'The State and Public Finance: A Hypothesis Based on the History of Late Medieval Florence', *Journal of Modern History*, 67, Suppl. (1995), 97–135, and David Herlihy, 'The Rulers of Florence, 1282–1530', in Anthony Molho, Kurt Raaflaub, and Julia Emlen (eds.), *City States in Classical Antiquity and Medieval Italy: Athens and Rome, Florence and Venice* (Stuttgart, 1991), pp. 197–221, at 214–15. For this in Castile, see José Antonio Jara Fuente, 'Elites y grupos financieros en las ciudades castellanas de la baja edad Media', *En La España Medieval*, 27 (2004), 105–30.

4 Jan Dumolyn, 'Dominante klassen en elites in verandering in het laatmiddeleeuwse vlaanderen', *Jaarboek voor Middeleeuwse Geschiedenis*, 5 (2002), 69–107.

the plague, increasing bureaucracy, and warfare thus worked to create a series of unique changes that are only now becoming fully apparent. In contrast to the long-standing view of the later medieval 'crisis', then, as being first and foremost a naturally induced crisis stemming from the plague, it can now be suggested that the man-made components of fourteenth-century change, rather than the plague or even the labour crisis it created, contributed most decisively to the transformation of later medieval Manresan, and indeed Catalan, society.

Because the adoption and evolution of a government annuity system in Catalonia was so like what early modernists call a 'financial revolution', and, given the national scale of this system, there seems no reason not to employ the term here.[5] It is arguably every bit as appropriate to describe financial developments in later fourteenth-century Catalonia as for the sixteenth-century Habsburg Netherlands.[6] This movement was revolutionary, because it created a system of government annuities which was entirely non-existent in 1330, but which was fully evolved by 1380. After 1380, the system had developed to a point that it would remain virtually unchanged until the end of the *ancien régime*.[7] When speaking of government annuities, we are in actuality referring to two distinct instruments known as *violaris* and *censals*, which were at first

[5] This use is suggested by Sánchez Martínez in his 'Introducción' to *La deuda pública en la Cataluña bajomedieval* (Madrid, 2009), pp. 7–20. It is also implied by Boone in his introduction to *Urban Public Debts*. For a summary of the literature on the early modern 'financial revolutions', of which the switch from short- to long-term finance is considered to be a major component, see W. Fritschy, 'A Financial Revolution Reconsidered: Public Finance in Holland during the Dutch Revolt, 1568–1648', *Economic History Review*, 56:1 (2003), 57–89. The *locus classicus* for the idea of a 'financial revolution' is P. G. M. Dickson, *The Financial Revolution in England: A Study of the Development of Public Credit, 1688–1756* (New York), but more influential for late medieval studies of public finance has been James Tracy, *A Financial Revolution in the Habsburg Netherlands: Renten and Renteniers in the County of Holland, 1515–1565* (Berkeley, CA, 1985). A seminal article on how the Dutch financial system was transferred to England is Douglas North and Barry Weingast, 'Constitutions and Commitment: The Evolution of Institutions Governing Public Choice in Seventeenth Century England', *Journal of Economic History*, 49:4 (1989), 803–32. On the medieval origins in France and Italy of the public credit instruments which would eventually foster the early modern financial revolutions, see James Tracy, 'On the Dual Origins of Long-term Urban Debt in Medieval Europe', in Marc Boone, Karel Davids, and Paul Janssens (eds.), *Urban Public Debts: Urban Government and the Market for Annuities in Western Europe (14th–18th Centuries)* (Turnhout, 2003), pp. 13–24. See also John Munro, 'The Medieval Origins of the Financial Revolution: Usury, Rentes, and Negotiability', *International History Review*, 25:3 (2003), 505–62. These articles sum up the older Italian literature on the subject. For the beginnings of public debt in the Medieval Crown of Aragon, see Manuel Sánchez Martínez, *Fiscalidad real y finanzas urbanas en la Cataluña medieval* (Barcelona, 2000). See also the synopsis by Pere Ortí Gost, Manuel Sánchez Martínez, and Max Turull Rubinat, 'La genesis de la fiscalidad municipal en Cataluña', *Revista d'història medieval*, 7 (1996), 115–34.

[6] Tracy, *Financial Revolution*.

[7] P. Toboso Sánchez, *La deuda pública castellana durante el Antiguo Régimen (juros) y su liquidación en el siglo XIX* (Madrid, 1987), p. 645.

employed in tandem; by the 1370s, the *violari* was phased out in favour of the *censal*. By the end of the fourteenth century, *censals* had come into the investment portfolios of almost every Catalan of economic significance, whether they were a man or a woman, a knight, ecclesiastic, or burgher.[8] The significance of the annuity was that it was a new form of economic asset, one which was easy, secure, and widely available and which therefore came to take up a significant share of Catalan investment capital.[9] These newly created financial assets made it possible, for the first time in history, to become a *rentier* without holding any real estate, and without having to collect payments from individual borrowers through the threat of lawsuit or violence. Instead, these assets were guaranteed by the state, paid in regular annual or semi-annual instalments and were secured by a regularized stream of consumption taxes. In contrast to states such as Florence, where only residents of the capital could invest in government annuities, in Catalonia investment was open to everyone.[10] Likewise, whereas in Florence annuities were only issued by the city of Florence itself, in Catalonia annuities were issued by all of the royal jurisdictions, including very small villages.[11] The Manresan evidence shows that the annuity system was even employed in regional seigneurial villages.[12] Their widespread availability and use meant, amongst other things, that many investors in the small cities found that to the extent that they placed money in *violaris* and *censals*, they were no longer bound to their local countryside in order to produce returns on their income. These investors discovered that, by holding *violaris* and *censals*, they could move anywhere in the country – in the long run, this probably encouraged migration to the capital, away from the smaller cities.[13]

It was long ago argued by Pierre Vilar that this system turned the relatively independent-minded townspeople of the early fourteenth

[8] J. Fynn-Paul, 'Occupation, Family, and Inheritance in Fourteenth-Century Barcelona: A Socio-Economic Profile of One of Europe's Earliest Investing Publics', *European History Quarterly*, 45:3 (2015).

[9] As demonstrated in Table 6.6, by 1408 the *censal* had attracted over two-thirds of the lending income at Manresa; this amounts to about 14 per cent of all Manresan wealth.

[10] David Herlihy and Christiane Klapisch-Zuber. *Tuscans and their Families: A Study of the Florentine Catasto of 1427* (Yale, 1985), ch. 1.

[11] This is shown by several studies printed in Manuel Sánchez Martínez (ed.), *La deuda pública en la Cataluña bajomedieval* (Madrid, 2009).

[12] For a *censal* over the village of Falchs, see LM 13r. For one over the village of Castellfollit, see LM 90r; for one over the town of Tarrega, LM 144r.

[13] While the population of Manresa fell precipitously during the fifteenth century and stayed low (for which see Table 7.1), the population of Barcelona also fell during the fifteenth century, and reached a nadir of nearly half its 1340 levels by 1477, but it rebounded strongly in the subsequent decades. From about 35,000 inhabitants in 1340, the city had perhaps 28,500 in 1500. See Carme Batlle, *Historia De Catalunya*. Vol. III, *L'Expansio baixmedieval (segles XIII–XV)*, Historia de Catalunya, 3 (Barcelona, 1998), p. 254.

century into a class of royal stakeholders.[14] In this view, urban elites were more likely to become integrated in the evolving state, because they invested significant portions of their patrimony in the state, and received similarly large proportions of their income from the state. Indeed by the late fifteenth and sixteenth centuries it is now conceded that Catalan-Aragonese urban elites had been successfully transformed into an oligarchic, royal-stakeholding class.[15] Recently it has been argued that the urban treasuries themselves were slowly co-opted by the state apparatus, becoming less and less independent over the same period.[16] It should be noted, however, that the Catalan-Aragonese government's successful co-option of urban elites into the emerging state apparatus was not a unique achievement: rather, this was typical for Western Europe over the same period. Therefore, we must be careful not to place too much emphasis on the *censal* system itself for this development: for example, a very similar process of royal co-option of urban elites occurred in later fourteenth-century England, despite the lack of a developed municipal annuity system there.[17]

Given these transformative effects, perhaps the most important question that can be asked, when attempting to grapple with the nature of the financial revolution, is: 'Why did it happen?' Was it the product of an organic, seemingly ineluctable process, or of deliberate royal policy? What were the political and economic repercussions of this system, and why should this be considered a significant step in Catalan-Aragonese state building? The Catalan financial revolution was a multi-step process, in which the Crown was almost always a primary and deliberate actor. Over the course of several decades, the Crown built upon previous institutional innovations in order to perfect the system which was more or less fully in place by 1380. The process began with the reassertion of royal sovereignty over the cities, especially by Pere el Gran and Jaume II, as discussed in Chapter 2. Furthermore, it can be stated that the Catalan financial revolution was a process which took place as a

14 Pierre Vilar, *La Catalogne dans l'espagne moderne: Recherches sur les fondements économiques des structures nationales* (Paris, 1977).

15 Sabaté Curull, 'Ejes vertebradores de la oligarquía urbana en Cataluña'. See also José Ángel Sesma Muñoz, 'Fiscalidad y poder: La fiscalidad centralizada como instrumento de poder en la Corona de Aragón (siglo XIV)', *Espacio, Tiempo y Forma*, 3:1 (1988), 447–63.

16 Narbona Vizcaíno and Cruselles Gómez, 'Espacios económicos y sociedad política en la Valencia del siglo XV', 209. This has also been found in later fourteenth-century Flanders, see e.g. James M. Murray, *Bruges, Cradle of Capitalism* (Cambridge, 1994), pp. 17–18.

17 For a description of distinct arrangements made by the English Crown during this period, which were undoubtedly influenced by continental developments, see Christian D. Liddy, 'Urban conflict in late fourteenth-century England: The case of York in 1380–1', *English Historical Review*, 118:475 (2003), 3–32, 3. A similar co-option of urban elites by the Crown has been found in contemporary Flanders. See e.g. Murray, *Bruges, Cradle of Capitalism*, pp. 17–18.

negotiation between the Crown and the royal cities of Catalonia, begun on the initiative of royal financiers, who were quick to realize the potential of the increasingly regular tax revenues that were being extracted from their cities. However, once *violaris* and *censals* came into widespread use by the Crown, particularly during the Castilian war (1356–75), the fact that they were sold on the open market meant that many aristocrats and churchmen began to purchase these instruments as well.[18] Familiarity through ownership taught a wide circle of Catalan wealth-holders about the value, ease, and convenience of these instruments, with the result that by the 1370s, noble families throughout the Bages were not only buying but issuing these instruments of their own accord.[19] Of course, these issues had the full legal backing of the Crown's judicial system, which was understandably crucial to their continuing circulation.[20]

The process will be explained in greater detail below; for the present a brief overview of its principal stages is in order. For cities such as Manresa, which had fallen into feudal hands between the eleventh and thirteenth centuries, the first step in this process came when the Crown reclaimed the towns themselves, together with their judicial and fiscal jurisdictions, as was done at Manresa by 1315. As has been shown in Chapter 2, the creation of *veguerias* helped to ensure that burghers could routinely and safely trade with the countryside, which encouraged the growth of regional commerce. This was further bolstered by a the promulgation of a series of fairs and local monopolies which were intentionally implemented by the Crown, in Manresa's case by Jaume II (1291–1327), and which further helped to increase the wealth of the townspeople.[21] Then, in preparation for the invasion of Sardinia in the 1320s, Jaume II began to sheer the sheep whose fleece he had so carefully been tending. At the royal behest, a system of subsistence taxes on bread, meat, fish, wine and the like was implemented, taxes which came to be known as *imposicions*. These *imposicion* systems were simultaneously set up in Manresa and Barcelona, and were in effect in Cervera by the late 1330s.[22] It must therefore be

[18] This can be seen from purchaser lists in AHCB Consell de Cent, *Clavaria*, XI-1-XI-12–14.

[19] Sánchez, 'Dette publique, auctités princières et villes dans les Pays de la Couronne d'Aragon, (14e–15e siècles)', in Boone *et al.*, *Urban Public Debts*, pp. 27–50; 39–41; Christian Guilleré, 'Les élites urbaines catalanes à la fin du moyen age: L'exemple géronais', in various, *Les élites urbaines catalanes à la fin du moyen age* (Paris, 1997), pp. 269–85.

[20] On the regulation of public credit markets by Italian communes see Maristella Botticini, 'A Tale of "Benevolent" Governments: Private Credit Markets, Public Finance, and the Role of Jewish Lenders in Medieval and Renaissance Italy', *Journal of Economic History*, 60:1 (2000), 164–89.

[21] As discussed in Chapter 2.

[22] For Iberia see generally the essays in Sánchez Martínez, Furió and Bertran i Roigé, *Actes colloqui corona, municipis i fiscalitat a la baixa edat mitjana*; Sánchez Martínez, *Pagar al rey en la Corona de Aragon durante el siglo XIV (estudios Sobre Fiscalidad y Finanzas Reales y Urbanas)*; for the details of the Cerveran situation in the transitional period of the late 1330s, see Pere Verdés Pijuan,

presumed that this was done by Catalan royal fiat. The *imposicions* were collected by means of a tax farm, which was sold to local individuals or, more commonly, to groups of investors who thereby spread the risk of loss. These consortia paid ready cash to local governments, in return for the right to oversee the collection of tax dues for periods of three or four months. So far, this system was relatively unremarkable – it did not differ substantially from the ancient feudal tax system which had preceded it, except that the number and value of the taxes collected through the farms was, as will be shown below, significantly increased.

What made this system truly remarkable was when the Catalan Crown began to insist that its localities could sell *violaris* or *censals* which were worth many times the cities' annual tax revenue, and whose interest payments would be covered by the *imposicions*. This was done sparingly in the 1340s, but was forced upon the cities from the late 1350s to the extent that, from this point onward, they now began to carry permanent debt burdens, in the same way that modern states now do. It should be noted that Florence was implementing a similar system at almost precisely the same time, and it should therefore be assumed that the Catalan financiers were copying this innovation directly from Italian models.[23] This meant that the Crown could now, in very short order, demand from its cities sums which were worth many times the towns' annual tax revenues. This gave the Catalan kings the equivalent of a credit card – and therefore represented a historic and massive increase in the spending power of the Crown. For example, if the revenue from Manresa was £2,000 in pounds of Barcelona per year, the most that the king in 1330 could expect to get from Manresa for a given campaign season would be less than £2,000. By 1360, however, with effective interest rates at about 12 per cent, the king could conceivably demand up to

'Les finances municipales à Cervera (1338–1339)', in *Funcionament de les Finances Locals al Llarg de la Història: Actes del III Congrès Internacional d'Història Local de Catalunya, Barcelona, 17–18 de Novembre de 1995*, Actes, 3 (Barcelona, 1996), pp. 205–14; Juan Vicente García Marsilla and Jorge Sáiz Serrano, 'De la peita al censal: Finanzas municipales y clases dirigentes en la Valencia de los siglos XIV y XV', in *Corona, municipis i fiscalitat a la baixa edat mitjana: Col.loqui.* (Lleida, 1997), pp. 307–34; Antoni Furiò Diego, 'Deuda pública e intereses privados: Finanzas y fiscalidad municipales en la Corona de Aragón.' *Edad Media: Revista de Historia* 2 (1999), 35–79; Boone, Davids and Janssens, *Urban Public Debts*; Manuel Sánchez Martínez, *Fiscalidad real y finanzas urbanas en la Cataluña medieval* (Barcelona, 2000); Sabaté, 'La insolvència municipal a la segona meitat del segle XIV'. For the impact of these taxes on commodity prices during the fifteenth century in Barcelona, see Ramon Agustí Banegas Lopez, 'Comer carne y pagar impuestos: El impacto de las imposiciones municipales en el comercio barcelonés de carne durante el siglo XV', *Anuario de Estudios Medievales*, 39:1 (2009), 329–55.

23 The Florentine system is classically explained in A. Molho, *Florentine Public Finances in the Early Renaissance, 1400–33* (Cambridge, MA, 1974). The Venetian system is likewise masterfully articulated in Reinhold C. Mueller and Frederic Chapin Lane, *The Venetian Money Market: Banks, Panics, and the Public Debt, 1200–1500* (Baltimore, 1997).

£16,000 in a single lump sum for a given campaign season, secured on the £2000 revenue produced annually by the Manresan *imposicions*. Like a modern consumer who uses their paycheck to pay only the interest on their credit card bills, Pere III was now able to use the taxes from his royal cities merely to pay interest on the loans that had been given to him. And it was lucky that he was able to successfully implement such a system, since, even with this new financial weapon, he was barely able to hold his own against the kings of Castile and fortify his cities against the French Companies during the 1360s and 70s. The historiographical 'discovery' of the financial revolution in Catalonia is primarily the work of Manuel Sánchez Martinez and his pupils.[24] Sánchez's work, in turn, builds on the fact that urban finance has in the past decade become one of the greatest growth industries in continental late medieval urban historiography. The evidence presented throughout this chapter and this book for the socially, politically, and economically transformative nature of the Catalan financial revolution contributes to this emerging narrative. The consideration of this material on public debt, it should be noted, is grounds per se for a significant revision of older narratives of fourteenth-century Catalan history by the likes of Vives, Soldevila, Vilar, Batlle, Hillgarth and Bisson.[25]

THE EVOLUTION OF THE CATALAN FINANCIAL REVOLUTION: DEVELOPMENT OF THE *IMPOSICION* SYSTEM

The following sections will discuss the Catalan financial revolution in terms of fiscal relations between the town and the Crown; later sections of this chapter will show the impact of this system on the personal finances of Manresan households, and on the city's investing elite as a whole. From 1276, when Manresa was once again joined to the royal patrimony, the city owed a certain amount of revenue to the Crown each year. From 1329, at the latest, we know that this was collected in the form of regular indirect taxes, known as *imposicions*, which were levied on such staples as wheat, wine, meat and fish. The work of Jean Broussolle, who in 1955 published a detailed study of Barcelona's *imposicions* system, is the starting point for understanding the development of Catalan urban

[24] Sánchez Martínez, *La deuda pública en la Cataluña bajomedieval*, esp. 'Introducción', pp. 7–20.

[25] The narratives cited can be found in Jaime Vicens Vives, *An Economic History of Spain* (Princeton, NJ, 1969); Feran Soldevila and Ferran Valls i Taberner, *Historia di Catalunya* (Montserrat, 2002); Vilar, *La Catalogne dans l'espagne moderne*; Carme Batlle Gallart, *Barcelona a mediados del siglo XV: Historia de una crisis urbana* (Barcelona, 1976); J. N. Hillgarth, *The Spanish Kingdoms, 1250–1516: Precarious Balance, 1250–1410*, vol. I (Oxford, 1976); MCOA.

taxes in the fourteenth century.[26] Broussolle discerned that as late as the 1320s the city's tax system was not regularized. Even there in the capital, the control over municipal tax levies had passed firmly into the control of Barcelona's *consellers* only in 1283. Between 1283 and 1330, according to Broussolle, the tax system entered an evolutionary phase, in which the sales of these indirect taxes on staples were made only irregularly; no pattern can be discerned, so that it is not known for certain whether these early *imposicions* were used for regular or extraordinary tax levies.[27] In the face of such irregularity, Broussolle believes that between 1283 and 1330 most of the ordinary revenue paid by Barcelona to the Crown 'came from other sources' (*consistant en d'autres impôts*), by which he presumably meant older feudal dues about which almost nothing is known.[28] In 1330, when a new royal campaign was launched against Genoa, Barcelona's tax system was reorganized into the form that would obtain in the city until the outbreak of civil war in 1462. The difference between the number and value of *imposicions* sold in 1328 and in 1330 is striking, and clearly marks a watershed in the municipal finances. Whereas in 1328, only four taxes were sold, in 1330 twenty-four were sold, and the number would remain close to this level thereafter. The city collected £6,332 in taxes in 1328, while it collected £39,892 in 1330.

Manuel Sánchez has now further subdivided this evolutionary period. He notes that prior to 1321, extraordinary expenses were generally raised from the Catalan cities by means of ad hoc tax collections known as *tallias*. From 1321, however, most Catalan cities began to raise sums for extraordinary taxes by selling *imposicions*. Late as it may seem, the earnest development of this type of urban tax system dates only from this year.[29] The first known references to *imposicions* date from only a few years before: they are referenced in 1314 in Barcelona and in 1316 in Tortosa.[30] By combining the narratives of Broussolle and Sánchez, the years between 1321 and 1329 can be seen as a further experimental period, in which the *imposicions* were not yet accepted as annual and permanent, while after 1330 they were ensconced as a cornerstone of urban finance.

When considering the portrait of Catalan urban finances outlined above, it is interesting to note that the revenue from Manresan *imposicions* shows a large increase between 1329, when the first figures become available, and 1339, when the next figures are available. As summarized in Tables 6.1 and 6.2, the Manresan figures did not increase nearly as

[26] Jean Broussolle, 'Les impositions municipales de Barcelona de 1328 à 1462', *Estudios de Historia Moderna*, 5 (1955), 1–164.

[27] Broussolle, 'Les impositions municipales', 14–16.

[28] Stephen P. Bensch, *Barcelona and its Rulers, 1096–1291* (Cambridge, 1995), pp. 319–21.

[29] Manuel Sánchez, *El naixement de la fiscalitat d'estat a Catalunya*, pp. 91–2.

[30] EPLV, 152.

Table 6.1 *Manresan annual tax revenues*[31]

Date (y.m.d)	Amount (£)	Description
1254.9.30	450	Estimated from donation of Jaume I to the viscount of Cardona of Vilafranca del Penedes, Manresa, and several rural locales; total revenue from the fief guaranteed to be worth £1,000 per annum
1329–30	1,136	Estimated by quadrupling 3 months' taxes
1339–40	2,205	Estimated from 12 month sum of £1,763.38, missing meat tax; £442 estimated for meat tax by doubling meat tax in 1329
1358–9	2,014	Estimated from 4 months' taxes, adding £450 for meat tax
1359–60	2,315	Estimated from 4 months' taxes, adding £450 for meat tax
1364	2,000	From Torras; 12 months' regular taxes; unknown whether this contains meat tax revenue
1365	3,043	From Torras; total for annual *censal* payments, represents minimum tax revenue generated by the city this year, including regular and extraordinary taxes
1373–4	3,311	12 month sum of Pere Nadal's expenditures as '*clavarius peccunie imposicionum pro solvendo annualium*', i.e., this figure equals the total annual *censal* payments, and is the minimum amount raised this year from regular and extraordinary taxes
1415	2,202	From Torras; 12 months' *censal* payments; minimum taxes raised from Manresa
1417	1,651	From Torras; 12 months' *censal* payments
1418	1,523	From Torras; 12 months' *censal* payments

much as the Barcelona figures over the same period, but there was an increase of nearly 100 per cent when a missing meat tax is added to the total, and of 50 per cent when this is left out. In 1329, Manresan revenue from *imposicions* stood close to £1,000 while from 1339 onward it stood closer to £2,000. The most likely explanation for this increase is that, in 1330 or shortly thereafter, Manresa's taxes were organized according to Barcelona's new system, and were therefore reorganized at the behest of the Crown.

The earliest known Manresan tax evidence supports the theory that the Catalan royal bureaucracy collected taxes with increasing efficiency

[31] Sources: 1254: Ambrosio Huici Miranda, *Documentos de Jaime I de Aragon*, III, 154–5. 1329: MC 1328.12.31–1329.1.16. 1339: AHCM Tr. a. 4054 (Familia Sarta) 1340.9.18 (14k10). 1358: MC 1358.10(?) (AHCM/AM I-6 last folio). 1359: MC 1359.9.3. 1364–65, 1415–18: Marc Torras, *La crisi del segle XV a Manresa*, 62. 1373: MC 1374.9.1.

Table 6.2 *Revenue from some specific taxes in Manresa (in pounds of Barcelona)*[32]

Tax name	1329, April–June[33] (orig. 3 months, est. for 4 months)	1358 May–August (4 months)	1359 Sept.–Dec. (4 months)
Wheat	75.81	126.3	227[34]
Wine	36.24	–	180
Meat	73.48	–	–
Shoemakers	20.28	25.5	–
Drapers	14.63	40	82.5
Furriers	28.26	40	41.3
Public lands	–	13	11.1
Animals	20.61	28.4	13.9
Wool	4.32	9.2	13.5
Shopkeepers	–	6.3	4.7

between 1250 and 1350.[35] Although it is not known precisely how, or in what proportions, the Crown raised revenue from Manresa prior to 1321, a document of 1254 confirms that a moderate sum was being raised from the city each year, in addition to the payment made by the city's Jewish *call*.[36] In this document, King Jaume I granted the city of Manresa,

[32] Sources: See Table 6.1.
Notes: Catalan-Latin names for these taxes are, in order: *bladi, vi, carn, sabaterie, draperie, coriaterie, honorum, animalium, lini, merçerie*.

[33] Originally the figures in this column were for given 3 months, but I have added 33 per cent to this total in order to make them more easily comparable to the 1358 and 1359 figures.

[34] High autumn figures for wheat taxes are presumably indicative of elevated revenue brought in at harvest season.

[35] Thus building on a solid earlier foundation. On the late twelfth-century fiscal innovations of the Catalan count-kings, see Thomas N. Bisson, *Fiscal Accounts of Catalonia Under the Early Count-kings (1151–1213)* (Berkeley, CA, 1984); esp. pp. 151–8.

[36] A hint at the levels of revenue received by the Crown from Manresa's *aljama* is found in a royal letter recorded in MC 1345.11.17 (15k12), in which an annuity of £200 was assigned from the royal revenues to the viscount of Cardona as the result of a lawsuit. £100 of this was to come from the revenues from a royal castle, and another £100 from the *alhama* of Manresa. It is possible that the *aljama*'s revenues would not cover the entire £200. Compare this with £600 received annually by the Crown from the *aljama* of Valencia at the end of the fourteenth century, mentioned in Hillgarth, *Spanish Kingdoms*, vol. II, 147, and the figure seems reasonable. Compare also with the figures reported by Mark Meyerson, in *Jews in an Iberian Frontier Kingdom: Society, Economy, and Politics in Morvedre, 1248–1391* (Leiden, 2004), who found, p. 17, that the *aljama* of Morvedre paid a regular tribute of £50 from 1274. This amount was still being paid in the 1360s, but after 1372 the tribute was raised to £100 (p. 252). It is therefore probable that, after the reorganization of Manresa's tax system in 1330, the regular city taxes became far more important to the king, in relative terms, than the payment from the *aljama*. Conversely, revenue from the *aljama* was much more important to the Crown prior to 1330. Thus, fiscal reform in the Crown of Aragon is probably a major underlying cause in the decline of the Jewish communities as sources of royal revenue during the fourteenth century.

together with Vilafranca del Penedes and three smaller locales, as a fief to his vassal Ramon Folc IV, Viscount of Cardona. In return Ramon Folc owed Jaume the feudal service of thirty knights.[37] The grant was made for the duration of the viscount's life. He died in 1276, in the same year as his king. In the original transfer of 1254, Jaume I promised Ramon Folc that Manresa, together with the similarly sized Vilafranca del Penedes and three minor locales, would bring him £1,000 per year. Although we have no population figures for the thirteenth century, we can get a rough estimate of the relative size of these burghs form the *fogatge* of 1365.[38] Assuming from this source that the two larger cities were roughly equal in size, and that they made up the vast bulk of this revenue, which based on population levels in 1365 would come to 90 per cent, Manresa's share comes to about £450 per year. From this figure, it appears as though royal revenue had more than doubled between 1254 and 1329. Some of this was due to increasing population and industrial capacity, but the Barcelona evidence strongly suggests that the tax reform of 1330 was a significant factor in increasing royal revenue.

Evidence from 1339 until 1364 shows that Manresa's annual revenue from regular impositions now stood at just over £2,000. Since the Black Death cut the population of the city by as much as half in 1348, it is very curious to see that revenue from *imposicions* did not change dramatically between 1339 and 1358–64, when the next figures are available. The best explanation seems to be that the wage and price increases catalogued in the next chapter offset the expected drop in nominal revenues. Some of this stability might also have been due to increased wealth on the part of survivors. Judging from the discussion of our demographic sources presented in the next chapter, there were probably less than half as many people in Manresa in the 1350s as there had been in 1348, but judging from these imposition figures, the survivors appear to have been spending as much on food and other basics as the pre-1348 population.

So far so good, from the point of view of the Catalan royal treasury officials: it appears on the surface as though its new revenue system survived the Black Death without any serious loss. Unfortunately, simply maintaining the same levels of revenue in the 1350s which the state had

37 Miranda, *Documentos*, III, pp. 154–5.

38 That Manresa and Vilafranca del Penedes were roughly equal in size, at least by the later fourteenth century, can be ascertained from the *fogatges* of 1365, 1378, and 1381. In 1381 Manresa was assigned 463 *focs*, and Vilafranca was assigned 453 *focs*. Josep Iglesies Fort, 'El fogaje de 1365–1370: Contribución al conocimiento de la población de Cataluña en la segunda mitad del siglo XIV', Memorias de la Real Academia de Ciencias y Artes de Barcelona, 34:11 (1962), 249–356. (For the suggestion, however, that these numbers are far too low, see Table 7.1 and relevant discussion.)

Table 6.3 *Nominal and real royal income from Manresa, 1254–1380*[39]

Date	1254	1329	1339	1358–9	1364	1365	1374	1380
Nominal income	£450	£1,135	£2,200	£2,164	£2,000	£3,043	£3,311	£2,000 (est.)
Wage index	n.a.	100	100	148	157	157	186	211
Est. real income	n.a.	£1,135	£2,200	£1,351	£1,274	£1,938	£1,780	£948

obtained in the 1340s actually translated into a serious loss of revenue for the Crown, since increasing wage and price levels meant that its real income, that is, the amount of goods and services that the state could purchase with its revenue, actually fell quite dramatically over this same period. Table 6.3 places known royal income against the wage multipliers that we present in the next chapter.[40] Since, according to the venerable but still valuable researches of Earl Hamilton, commodity price levels mirrored wage levels after the Black Death, this comparison may provide a useful estimate of the king's real income.[41] This was highest during the brief period between the 1330s and the Black Death. By the late 1350s, increasing wages and prices had decreased the Crown's real income from Manresa by at least a third. During the war years of 1356–75, real royal income was increased to its pre-plague levels. But after the mid-1370s, interest rates fell, and the *censals* sold during the war were redeemed, and nominal income fell back towards prewar levels. By the mid-1380s, assuming that, as we must suspect from the available evidence, nominal tax levels did not increase after 1374, increasing price levels would have eaten even more deeply into the king's real income, reducing it to its lowest level in fifty years.

THE FISCAL SYSTEM CONTINUED: 'EXTRAORDINARY' TAXES

Given this genuine crisis in royal finances that was apparent to fiscal officials soon after the Black Death, it is not to be wondered that the

39 Sources: The nominal income data is taken from Table 6.2, above.
Notes: The estimate for 1358–9 is taken by averaging the two estimates for those years from Table 6.2; estimates for 1365 and 1374 are the amount actually raised to pay *censals*, and represent the minimum amount raised from the city that year. Real income estimates are rounded to the nearest pound.

40 See Table 7.2.

41 Although interest rates can be found (though usually not in tabular form) in the work of Sánchez and his pupils, prices remain under-studied. For these, one still must turn to Earl Hamilton, *Money, Prices, and Wages in Valencia, Aragon, and Navarre, 1351–1500* (Cambridge, MA, 1936). This trend is evident for all three regions studied by Hamilton.

Crown began a desperate scramble for alternative means of increasing revenue when it decided to wage war during the 1350s. One of these means was the increased use of traditional extraordinary levies. Another of these was a push by the Crown to have its cities and towns sell *violaris* and *censals* to a much greater extent than had been tried in the early 1340s. These will be dealt with here in turn. The system of extraordinary taxes was already well developed by the time Pere III began to hyper-exploit it in the 1350s. Although extraordinary royal levies had been a part of Catalan fiscality for centuries, the principal prelude to Pere's own use of the system began late in the reign of his grandfather Jaume II, who in the 1320s used this means to help finance his acquisition of Sardinia. It has already been shown how Jaume carefully built up his financial infrastructure so that it would yield a greatly increased regular revenue from the cities. At Manresa, this included the series of economic and political reforms which at first might seem to have little to do with revenue extraction, although when one sees them in their entirety, one can see that they were all calculated to raise Manresa to the status of a significant regional economy. Taken in its entirety, Jaume's new fiscal regime has been called 'a new page in the history of royal and municipal finance' by Manuel Sánchez.[42] Thus, it must be concluded that Jaume II was a truly exceptional economic planner, who lived to benefit from his own planning, but who also set the stage for future attempts at expansion. Thus, when Pere III came to the throne in 1336, he inherited a fiscal system which was greatly improved over what it had been a few decades previously. As can be seen from Table 6.4, the series of extraordinary payments begun by Jaume II in the 1320s were only increased in number and frequency until the end of the 1370s, by which time the city was financially exhausted. This list is not complete, since several subsidies levied after known sessions of the *Corts* remain unaccounted for, but the known figures provide a sense of the high level and frequency of extraordinary taxes that were being raised from the Catalan cities during the middle decades of the fourteenth century.

In fact, one can say that between 1353 and 1380, extraordinary taxation became so regular that it became merely another means of regular taxation. The only check on the royal will regarding these taxes was that permission be granted by the *Corts*, and although much has been made of the *Corts*' intransigence, there were few, if any, sessions that did not

[42] For this phenomenon, see J. Fynn-Paul, 'Civic Debt, Civic Taxes, and Urban Unrest: A Catalan Key to Interpreting the Late Fourteenth-century European Crisis', in Lawrin Armstrong *et al.* (eds.), *Money, Markets and Trade in Late Medieval Europe: Essays in Honour of John H. A. Munro* (Leiden, 2007), pp. 119–45, at 129.

Table 6.4 *Known extraordinary payments levied at Manresa, 1325–78*[43]

Date (y.m.d)	Amount (in s.Barc)	Collection method	Reason
1325.1.28	20,000	*tallia*	Sardinia
1329.12.31	10,000	*imposicions*	Granada
1332.3.3	20,000	not stated	'Various reasons'
1335.7.12	20,000	*tallia*	Genoa and Saracens
1336	20,000	*tallia*	Genoa and Saracens
1337.10.20	20,000	*tallia*	Genoa and Saracens
1343.3.3	28,000	*violari*	Mallorca[44]
1344	16,000	*violari*	Mallorca[45]
1353.7.17	30,000	*violari/censal*?	Genoa[46]
1354	30,000	*violari/censal*?	Genoa, Sardinia
1355.4.14	38,000	*violari/censal*?	Sardinia
1356.10.6	24,625	*violari/censal*	Castile
1358.5.18	39,000	*violari/censal*	Castile
1359	39,000	*violari/censal*	Castile
1361.3.11	2,315	debt collection	paid to Genoa, prisoners
1362.9.1	7,390	not stated	Castile
1362.4.8	6,100	not stated	to Viscount of Cardona
1363.4.6	11,000	*violari/censal*	*fogatge* Corts of Monzón
1363.10.17	16,490	*violari/censal*	for unnamed expenses
1365.4.19	28,000	*tallia*, 'weekly'	Castile
1369.12.22	12,000	*tallia*	to build city walls
1370.4.6	12,000	*fogatge*	not stated
1370.8.16	16,000	*tallia*	not stated (city walls?)
1371.4.24	6,000	not stated	marriage of Duke of Girona
1372.8.14	10,000	not stated	to pay civic debts
1373.3.28	10,000	*tallia*, 'weekly'	to build city walls
1373.8.27	4,000	not stated	to pay civic debts
1373.9.16	12,000	*tallia*	(might be duplicate)
1374.1.18	6,000	*tallia*	to build city walls
1374.1.2	2,000	*tallia*, on foreigners	levied on '*homines forenses*'

(*cont.*)

[43] Sources: MC unless stated in additional note.
Notes: Dates are taken from the date of the MC entry or other document recording the payment; the dates of the MC reference or document usually antedate the dates of a given payment, since most large payments were made in installments, often on a quarterly basis. A '*tallia*' often meant a levy specifically collected from each Manresan householder for the purpose of raising the stated sum. 1 Pound (£) = 20 *sous* (s).

[44] Reference: LV, 123. [45] Reference: EPLV, 197.

[46] In the arrangement for this payment, the city was indebted to the Barcelona moneylender Jaume Villela. In order to secure this debt, 'ten or twelve *probi homines*' of the city were to be held hostage in Santpedor until the loan was paid off. 10 *sous* per day were allotted to them from the goods of the city for their pains.

Table 6.4 (*cont.*)

1374.10.12	4,000	loan, 'with usury'	various
1374.12.2	7,000	*censal*	not stated
1374.7.8	3,402	*tallia*	to build wall '*inferioris*'
1375.1.3	2,540	loan 'with usury'	famine relief: for '*clibaniis*'
1375.1.30	20,000	*censal*	for relief (buying grain?)
1375–1377	51,400	*censal*	for *cequia*[47] (1377.12.4)
1377.10.20	6,710	*censal*	to redeem *censals*
1377.12.18	13,000	*tallia*	not stated (originally 12ks)

Average over 53 years: 11,758s (£588) per year.
Annual increase over regular revenue, estimated at £2,000 per year: 29.4 per cent.

eventually produce a substantial levy.[48] Another point to be noted is that Manresa's portions of the extraordinary levies were quite similar. Most of the annual payments demanded by the king, and, in effect, assigned by the *Corts*, were between 20,000s and 40,000s. This suggests that each city's portion was formulaically assigned according to its number of habitants, or its annual revenue, or some such generally understood custom. Thus, we see once again that the acrimony of political debate in the *Corts* had very little influence on the actual amounts of money that were eventually levied from the inhabitants of the royal cities. When it came to the size of the levies voted by the *Corts*, there were no surprises: everyone at the royal court, in the *Corts*, and in the city itself seems to have known exactly what was expected of the Manresan treasury. This is confirmed by the *censal* sales made by the city for its own benefit between 1375 and 1378, sold in order to speed the construction of the *sèquia*. The project was begun in the late 1330s after the terrible famines of 1333–4 and 1336–7. Work on the *sèquia* was allowed to flag after the Black Death and during the Castilian war, but the threat of starvation caused by the famine of 1374–5 prompted the Manresans to complete their monumental engineering project in the hopes of averting future dangers. After the financial drains suffered by the city between 1350 and 1375, it is quite surprising to discover that the *consellers* could in fact raise large sums in order to complete the *sèquia*. Yet they found it possible to sell over 51,000s in *censals* over a three-year period. That the city could raise 17,000s per year for three years at this time of financial exhaustion suggests that the royal subsidies of 20,000 to 40,000s per year had in fact been realistic figures. Another factor that bespeaks moderation and

47 Reference: MC 1377.12.4.

48 On this see the arguments in Chapter 5, and also Sabaté Curull, 'La insolvència municipal a la segona meitat del segle XIV'.

balance on all sides is that, according to the known figures, extraordinary royal demands amounted to only one third of the city's normal annual revenue. If the missing subsidies are accounted for, this level may well amount to about 50 per cent of normal revenue. Thus, we can say that while the Manresan fisc had been exploited close to maximum capacity for many years, and that the town was fiscally exhausted by the late 1370s, the *imposicion* and *censal* systems still ensured that money could be forthcoming. Another factor which saved the urban fisc was the fact that interest rates on annuities fell by at least several per cent during the course of the 1370s. While this helped the king, it would also have had the effect of deflating the investment returns of the town's leading citizens, who as we know from the *Liber Manifesti* and the town council records were the city's primary creditors. Thus, even if the pressure on urban finances would have been relieved somewhat by 1380, the individual citizens would have felt themselves to be much poorer, and therefore less capable of bearing any given tax burden. The result was similar: a feeling of financial exhaustion on the part of the citizens, which led to a general sense of civic impotency.

THE CENSAL SYSTEM OF GOVERNMENT ANNUITIES IN CATALONIA AND THE MARKET 'CRASH' OF THE 1370S

The establishment of a regular revenue stream through *imposicions*, and the augmentation of this through what quickly became an on-demand, predetermined wartime revenue through the *Corts*, actually encompasses only a small portion of what the Crown of Aragon was able to raise from its Catalan dominions during the Castilian war. The real 'secret weapon' to come out of this war was the creation of what would become a regular and permanent system of government annuities in Catalonia. The regular revenue from the *imposicions*, and the calculable levels of extraordinary revenue available through wartime 'donations', provided the essential basis upon which this annuity system could now be enacted. By raising loans on these regular revenue streams, the Crown could now raise a sum which was between seven and twenty times its annual revenue, depending on the interest rates that it could command through annuity sales.[49] This idea was in some ways revolutionary, as will be shown, but in some ways it built naturally upon long-standing traditions in Mediterranean urban finance. In Venice and Genoa, urban governments had been compelling citizens to buy 'annuities' of a similar nature since the twelfth century, except that the annuities yielded rates which were far below the returns

[49] See Fynn-Paul, 'Civic Debt, Civic Taxes'.

that could be had from competing investment types.[50] (Other towns in Northern France had begun to sell long-term annuity instruments by the thirteenth century, but the Venetian and Genoese systems were by far the largest, most consistently implemented, and most sophisticated in Europe until the fourteenth century.)[51] These so-called 'forced loans' existed as a compromise solution, which balanced two competing considerations. First, the elites who controlled the government were very loath to give up potentially lucrative capital to the government at a total loss. Thus, they reasoned that getting some return on their taxes by issuing them as low-yielding 'loans' was better than nothing. Secondly, below-market interest rates saved the government money – particularly through the early fourteenth century, when many investment types yielded upwards of 15 per cent.[52] The result was this 'forced loan' system, which although it sounds alien at first is really quite ingenious and logical. The perennial problem with this scheme, of course, was that these low-yielding annuities had to be 'forced' upon citizens, since no one would willingly purchase annuities that provided a lower return than one could get from other similar-risk investments. Purchasers would often sell these low-yielding annuities on a secondary market, for the purposes of recovering as much of their principal as they could, to investors who expected to realize a more competitive rate.[53]

Naturally, there was a limit to how much money that business-savvy urban elites were willing to cough up at well below market rates. Thus, even forced loans came up against a ceiling, beyond which raising further revenue was like attempting to squeeze blood from a stone. Therefore, various Italian governments began experimenting with public sales of annuities or annuities which offered much more competitive rates (rates which were competitive, that is, with overseas investment, agricultural

[50] For this 'financial revolution' of twelfth-century Italy, see Philip Jones, *The Italian City-State: From Commune to Signoria* (Oxford, 1997); Munro, 'The Medieval Origins of the Financial Revolution'.

[51] For northern French towns selling long-term debt by 1218, see Tracy, 'Dual Origins', p. 16. It must be said, however, that Tracy's conclusions about 'dual origins' of long-term debt in Europe are not always clear; his apparent criticism of the Barcelona system is, it seems, mostly based on incorrect assumptions drawn from the scarce secondary sources in English. His argument that towns 'both north and south of the Alps' 'regularly failed to meet their annual interest obligations' (p. 24) is likewise, based on the Venetian evidence presented in Mueller, and the Florentine evidence presented in Molho, and the Catalan evidence, simply wrong. All of these polities were exceptionally good at meeting their obligations, all things considered. Opinions derived from this paper must therefore be taken with caution. Sánchez now says as much in *La deuda pública en la Cataluña bajomedieval*, pp. 8–10.

[52] See e.g. Table 6.7.

[53] For the secondary market on Venetian annuities see Mueller and Lane, *The Venetian Money Market*, p. 458.

investment, moneylending, and other schemes that were competing for investor capital). By the mid-1340s, when Florence was reeling from the collapse of much of its banking sector due to English royal defaults, the Florentines began to institute regular 'forced loans' on liquid property, in the process consolidating all of their urban public debt into a fund known as the *monte*. In order to raise additional revenue, and to prevent excessive opposition, the Florentine assembly sometimes voted to have their 'forced loans' pay at double or triple the normal rate, that is, 10 or even 15 per cent – thus making them far more palatable to wary elites. When even this failed, the government got into the practice of offering *monte* shares at public auction, meaning that they were available for purchase to all Florentine citizens, at rates that made them attractive vis-à-vis competing investment opportunities.[54] There were also secondary markets for forced loan shares in Florence, as in Venice and Genoa, at which a purchaser would buy shares at less than face value, thus increasing their yields in accordance with what the market would support.

In virtual lockstep with the Florentine annuity system, the Catalans quickly implemented a parallel system, which as stated took advantage of the revenue streams available on the royal patrimony. James Tracy has argued that the Catalan annuity types may have come from northern France, which seems plausible based on their names and yield; but his criticism of the Catalans as not holding public auctions is unjustified.[55] In fact, in all known instances the Catalans sold their annuities at public auctions.[56] If they preferred holders to be local or regional, this did not preclude 'foreigners' (from other Catalan regions) to hold annuities.[57] In the historiography of the early modern Low Countries, James Tracy has become famous for elucidating the method through which the Habsburg territories created a system of revenue which would later become the basis of the Dutch annuity system. This phenomenon has been widely regarded as the world's first 'financial revolution'.[58] In fact, the Florentines and the Catalans, at least, had undergone precisely the same sort of financial revolution during the fourteenth century. According to Tracy,

[54] For the Florentine instruments, see Molho, *Florentine Public Finances in the Early Renaissance, 1400–33*.

[55] Tracy, 'Dual Origins', p. 22.

[56] For the Manresans holding public auctions of annuities, often in Barcelona, see e.g. MC 1370.3.23, which authorizes Bartholomeu Amargos to sell 1,000s of *censals* 'for whatever price'; and MC 1375.1.31 for Berenguer de Tresseres receiving authority from the municipal government to sell *violaris* if he cannot find enough buyers to buy *censals* at the (historically high) rate of 10:1.

[57] For sales to foreigners evidenced in the *Liber Manifesti*, see note 18, above.

[58] For a revision of this idea see Munro, 'The Medieval Origins of the Financial Revolution'. Marc Boone, in 'A New Approach', is more cautious.

the principal steps required to have a financial revolution are (a) to establish a regular stream of tax revenue, which (b) can be used to support a permanent long-term debt based on public sales of shares.[59] This is precisely what happened in fourteenth-century Catalonia. Sánchez has described how the tool of the *imposicion* was conceived during the 1310s and applied towards the payment of extraordinary subsidies during the 1320s.[60] From 1330, according to Broussolle, a large number of annual *imposicions* became normalized at Barcelona.[61] This was also the case at Manresa. As also chronicled by Sánchez, at Barcelona the *imposicion* system was quickly superseded by the system of *violaris* and *censals*.[62] The first evidence for Manresan sales of *violaris*, indeed the first evidence of a nascent public debt, comes from 1343, as Florence was consolidating its *monte*.[63]

The Catalan annuity system thus emerged as the result of a series of deliberate royal policy implementations designed to increase revenue from the royal patrimony, which were mostly undertaken during the reigns of Jaume II and Pere III. Let us take a moment to look at this system in more detail. The types of annuity offered by the Catalan government at first consisted of two types, namely *censals* and *violaris*.[64] A *censal* can be described as a perpetual annuity, received in cash by an investor at fixed intervals during the year, in return for his or her investment of an (invariably substantial) cash sum.[65] The return on a *censal* is held by most commentators to have been 7.14 per cent. These figures have found their way into the general summaries of Thomas Bisson and Carmen Batlle.[66] As shown in Table 6.5, rates for both the *censal* and *violari* varied in response to the flux of the credit market, as would only make sense with an instrument which was being sold to the public on the open market.[67] The *censal* was also perpetual, meaning that it could be transmitted to an heir upon the death of the owner/recipient. The *Liber Manifesti* makes clear that royal municipalities of all sizes, from large towns to hamlets, issued their own *censals*, and the Manresan council manuals

59 Tracy, *Financial Revolution*, p. 221. See synopsis in Fritschy, 'Financial Revolution Reconsidered', 57–8.

60 Sánchez Martínez, *El naixement de la fiscalitat d'estat a Catalunya*, pp. 91–2.

61 Broussoulle, 'Les impositions municipales', 14–16.

62 Sánchez Martínez, *El naixement de la fiscalitat d'estat a Catalunya*, ch. 7.

63 EPLV, 191–9.

64 For the idea that these may have come from northern French exemplars, see Tracy, 'Dual Origins', p. 22.

65 On these issues see Munro, 'The Medieval Origins of the Financial Revolution' and Tracy, 'Dual Origins'.

66 MCOA, 171, gives a rate of 7 per cent for *censals* and 15 per cent for *violaris*; Batlle, in *L'expansio baixmedieval*, p. 319, mentions 7 per cent for *censals*.

67 Munro, 'The Medieval Origins of the Financial Revolution', 535.

Table 6.5 *Rates of return on investments in Catalan* censals *and* violaris[68]

Date (y.m.d.)	Rate Type	(per cent)	Details
1346.1.28	Viol.	14.8	For lives of B. de Talamanca, *militis*, and his son
1358.6.4	Viol.	14.3	Ratio of 7:1; sold by city of Manresa
1365.5.3	Viol.	16.7	Ratio of 6:1; estimated; sold by city of Manresa to Jaume Sarta (for duration of a single life)
1373.4.29	Viol.	16.7	Ratio of 6:1; Manresa ordains redemption of *violaris* previously sold at this rate
1408–11	Viol.	14.3	Single instance of *violari* in *Liber Manifesti*, with '*violari*' actually crossed out for '*censal*'
1359.1.9	Cens.	7.1	Ratio of 14:1; annual *censal* of 500s sold for 7,000s
1369	Cens.	8.3	Ratio of 12:1; sold at Barcelona
1373.4.29	Cens.	8.3	Manresa ordains redemption of *censals* previously sold at this rate
1373.4.29	Cens.	7.1	Manresa ordains new *censals* to be sold at this rate
1374.12.2	Cens.	7.1	Annual *censal* of 500s sold for 7,000s
1375.1.31	Cens.	10.0	Manresa ordains sale of *censals* at this rate
1376	Cens.	8.4	Sold by Barcelona, quoted by Usher
1376	Cens.	9.1	Sold by Barcelona, quoted by Usher
1385	Cens.	6.9	Paid at Barcelona, quoted by Usher
1386	Cens.	7.1	Paid at Barcelona, prevailing rate
1386	Cens.	7.0	Paid at Barcelona
1389	Cens.	6.3	Ratio of 16:1; paid at Barcelona
1389	Cens.	5.9	Ratio of 17:1; paid at Barcelona, prevailing rate
1393	Cens.	7.1	Paid at Barcelona, prevailing rate
1394	Cens.	6.3	Paid at Barcelona, quoted by Usher
1394	Cens.	5.9	Paid at Barcelona, quoted by Usher
1408–11	Cens.	5.4	Average of 39 rates quoted in *Liber Manifesti*

[68] Sources: I. *Violari* Rates. 1346: AHCM Tr. 175 (B. Talamanca); 1358, 1365, 1373: MC; 1408: *Liber Manifesti*, 1408. II. *Censal* Rates. 1359: MC; 1369: AHCB *Consell de Cent, Clavaria*, XI-8, 1368–9, 15v; 1374 and 1375: MC; 1376, 1385, 1394: A. P. Usher, *Early History of Deposit Banking*, 351, 357; 1386: AHCB *Consell de Cent, Clavaria* XI-12–13–14 (1383–86), vol. XIV (volumes not clearly distinguishable), fols. 7r, 3v; 1389: AHCB, *Consell de Cent, Clavaria*, XI-15 (1389–90), fol. 15r (*censal* sales go on from folio 15r to 109v); 1393: AHCB, *Consell de Cent, Clavaria*, XI-17 (1393) fols. 11v forward (From this point in the tome most *censal* sales are at 14:1. The *censal* section starts on fol. 10r); 1408: *Liber Manifesti*, 1408.

suggest that this practice probably became widespread in the 1360s.[69] The extent of the implementation of this system in the royal patrimony is therefore much more widespread than is generally realized. In Catalonia, the Crown ensured that the *censal* could always be redeemed by the issuing municipality, since it was to the king's advantage for his cities to be less, rather than more, in debt.[70] In royal municipalities such as Manresa, the town authorities were always careful to receive royal permission before selling or redeeming *censals* and *violaris*.[71] Furthermore, the Crown always maintained the right to buy back higher-interest annuities and replace them with lower-interest annuities during bear markets, enabling it to drive down interest rates on its own outstanding issues, to the extent that the market would allow for this.[72]

The *violari* was a variant of the life annuity, a legal concept which has been traced back to Carolingian times, but which gained new life as the primary instrument in the annuity system which mushroomed in Catalonia during the 1350s and 1360s.[73] By the early fourteenth century, Catalan *violaris* were usually payable for the duration of the lives of two named recipients; to this we can add the observation that in Manresa at least, the second of these was usually a member of a younger generation than the purchaser. For example, a mother and daughter or father and son would typically be named as recipients. The major distinction between the *violari* and *censal* was that upon the death of both recipients, the *violari* agreement came to an end: the annuity payment would cease, and, most importantly, the principal, that is, the sum originally invested, would *not* be repaid.[74] Investment in a *violari* was therefore, on the face of it, a fairly serious gamble, based on the buyer's estimation of his and his co-recipients' projected lifespan. The interest rate normally hovered

69 Sánchez, in *El naixement de la fiscalitat*, pp. 129–34, speaks of the use of *censals* as a Catalan financial 'system' from the 1360s. A. Furió, in 'Crédito y endeudamiento', pp. 515–16, indicated that *censals* were first sold in Girona from 1359, but Guilleré, in *Girona Medieval*, pp. 50–1, says that from 1350 'there was no year in which *censals* and *violaris* were not sold' ('A partir de 1350, ho hi ha cap any sense emissions de *censals* i *violaris*'). It is likely that the smaller Catalan municipal entities began to sell their first *censals* at the same time as the larger ones, since all were equally indebted to the Crown by the acts of the *Corts*.

70 Munro, 'The Medieval Origins of the Financial Revolution', 535.

71 Yvan Roustit, 'La consolidation de la dette publique à Barcelone au milieu du XIVe siècle, *Estudios de Historia Moderna*, 4 (1954), 13–156, at 50–5, discusses the matter of royal permission and the Barcelona government. For certain aspects of the royal correspondence between the Crown and the city of Manresa during the first period of *censal* sales, and a sense of how involved such negotiations could become, see LV, 119–23, 148–54, 203–4.

72 For examples of this at Manresa, see MC 1370.3.9; and MC 1377.7.16.

73 A. P. Usher. *The Early History of Deposit Banking in Mediterranean Europe*, vol. I (Cambridge, MA, 1943), pp. 143–9.

74 Usher, *Early History of Deposit Banking*, p. 150, states that the principal on life annuities such as the *violari* were 'not ordinarily repayable'.

around 14 per cent, however, meaning that it only took seven years in order for the investment to begin turning a serious profit. Of course, if the recipients died before this time, the investment would incur a net loss, but our evidence shows that even after the Black Death, many Catalan investors felt this to be well worth the gamble it entailed.[75] As was the case with *censals*, towns retained the right to redeem *violaris* at any time.[76] And as with various *censal* buy-backs, we can witness that as early as the *Corts* of Monzón in 1363, and again including 1370 and 1377 at Manresa, the king authorized municipal authorities to redeem higher-interest *violaris* by selling lower-interest *censals*.[77]

From our sources it is clear that, in the period before 1360, Catalan financial authorities genuinely believed that *censals* and *violaris* posed an equal risk to the royal finances.[78] The authorities began to prefer *censals* over *violaris* only after the Catalan municipalities became heavily indebted from 1362. Even so, the evolution of financial opinion on this matter took a full decade to mature. The Manresan council sold *censals* and *violaris* indiscriminately until 1373, and they finally issued a definitive statement against the sale of further *violaris* only in 1374.[79] From this date, *violaris* quickly disappear from Manresan and Catalan financial markets.[80] By 1408, only a handful of *violaris*, most of them of an interpersonal nature, were still being paid out at Manresa.[81] In this way, the Manresan records enable us to locate a previously unknown, and very important, 'phasing out of the *violari*', which we can pinpoint precisely to the year 1374. The shift occurred rather abruptly, just as wages and prices reached an all-time high. In light of this, we can read the very high interest rates on *censals*, which peaked in the mid-1370s at an all-time high of 10 per cent, as a

75 J. Fynn-Paul, 'Occupation, Family, and Inheritance in Fourteenth-Century Barcelona: A Socio-Economic Profile of One of Europe's Earliest Investing Publics', *European History Quarterly*, 45:3 (2015).

76 Roustit, 'La consolidation de la dette publique', 67–8.

77 For Monzón, see Roustit, 'La consolidation', 67. For Manresa, see MC 1370.3.9; and MC 1377.7.16.

78 This attitude is apparent in MC 1356.11.27.

79 For the 1373 redemption of *violaris* by the sale of *censals*, see MC 1373.4.29; for the statement against *violaris*, see MC 1374.1.10. For an example of the town council's, and the Crown's, earlier lack of discrimination between the two forms, see LV, 148–54. Another example of apparent indifference between the two forms can be found in one of the city's first recorded debates on the sale of *censals* and/or *violaris*, in MC 1356.11.27. In many entries it appears as though the term '*censal*' was used to cover both *censals* and *violaris*. See MC 1363.5.3, which also specifically indicates that the Manresans sold *violaris* in order to raise the sum voted at Monzón in February 1363, despite the king's prohibition against doing so, quoted by Roustit, 'La consolidation', 67.

80 Josep Fernández Trabal, *Una família catalana medieval: Els Bell-lloc de Girona, 1267–1533*. (Montserrat, 1995), p. 106, also notes that after 1380 the *violari* virtually disappears from the Bell-lloc family portfolio. It was replaced by the *censal*.

81 Source: LM.

reaction by the market to the fact that the higher-interest *violaris* were no longer available on the market.[82] However, the Crown's financiers had calculated properly, and after a very few years, the spike settled back to the accustomed range of 7 per cent. From 1380, rates slowly declined even further, and for reasons not fully understood they reached a new low level of 5.4 per cent by 1408.

For the exact same reason why the Catalan financiers grew to dislike the *violari*, these rapidly became one of the most popular investment options in Catalonia during the Castilian war period. The reason for the popularity of the *violari* is not difficult to deduce: experience had proven that it was much more profitable than the *censal*, despite the risks attached to it. Both the Manresa and the Barcelona evidence shows a clear investor preference for *violaris* over *censals*, and Josep Fernández Trabal's experience with the Bell-lloc family of Girona points to the same conclusion.[83] Fernández notes that investment in *violaris* was of primary importance to the Bell-lloc family of Girona between 1346 and 1380. An audit at the death of Guillem I de Bell-lloc in 1371 found that he was receiving annual payments of £348.5 in *violaris*, along with a mere £33.5 in *censals*. Although, pound for pound, *censals* required twice the capital investment of *violaris*, the 1371 audit reveals Guillem's preference for *violaris* over *censals* at a ratio of more than 5:1. The fact that Guillem's successor Pere continued to purchase *violaris* until these became unavailable during the late 1370s indicates that the family felt no change of heart after the death of one of the previous *violari* beneficiaries. In Manresa, the *violari* was also very popular with investors. As in Girona, the heyday of *violari* investment stretched from the 1350s through the 1370s. The Castilian war (1356–75) did more than anything else to ensure that *violaris* were available in large quantities. In 1365 the Manresan merchant Jaume (II) Sarta received a sum of £33/6s/8d on a *violari* payable for the duration of his life only.[84] The payment works out to 666.66s, which at a ratio of 6:1 suggests an investment of 3999.96s, that is, 4000s.[85] Although Sarta began a new company with two other partners from 1351, and had been very active in overseas trade through the 1350s, he obviously found it hard to resist investing in *violaris* at such a lucrative rate.[86] This was in spite of the fact that, in order to secure the very high rate of 6:1, or nearly 17 per cent return per annum, Jaume had to agree to a *violari* for the duration of his own life only.[87] The principal invested by Jaume in

[82] For the interest rates, see Table 6.5. [83] Fernández i Trabal, *Els Bell-lloc de Girona*, pp. 106–7.
[84] MC 1365.5.3. [85] This example has been tabulated in Table 6.5.
[86] For evidence of the Sarta/Amargos/de Valls company, see AHCM Tr. 224 (Jaume Sarta) 1351 3k3, in which Jaume receives homage from a *factor* (company employee) in Valencia.
[87] Although MC 1373.4.29 for evidence that other *violaris* had been sold at this rate.

1365 amounted to nearly 20 per cent of his son's total investment capital, which stood at 20,610s in 1408.

Such an investment significantly reduced the elder Jaume's ability to invest in trade. Not only the Sartas, but their business partners also, invested heavily in *violaris* during this period. As part of their *compania*, the partners Jaume Sarta and Berenguer des Vall received equal payments of £45/16s/8d in a mixture of *censals* and *violaris* every January.[88] In this case the minimum investment for each partner, at 6:1, would have been 5,500s. The real total was higher, since lower-paying *censals* made up part of the annuities. Usher, who studied these instruments back in the 1930s, also concluded that *violaris* were popular because they made investing sense. He estimated that even given the shortness of medieval life expectancies, the purchase of a *violari* by anyone under thirty-five should have, statistically, turned a profit.[89] He concludes that the addition of a second life, especially of one in a younger generation, would increase the value of *violaris* 'considerably'. After noting that, even during the tumultuous plague years of the fourteenth century, the suppliers of capital funds for *violaris* 'seem to have had much the best of the bargain unless they were along in years', Usher concludes that governments would only offer life annuities (*violaris*) as the 'last resort of a hard pressed borrower whose credit was not good enough to attract funds on a less onerous basis'.[90]

This history of *censals* and *violaris* raises two issues which are of paramount importance for understanding the development of Catalan society in the later fourteenth and fifteenth centuries, namely, why the *violari*, which was so popular, could suddenly be phased out in the mid-1370s, and secondly, what social and economic effects might have stemmed from the Catalans' sudden love affair with the government annuity, which began rather suddenly in the 1350s, and never abated thereafter? Let us tackle the issue of the *violari* phase-out first. The first thing to note is that this was not a simple changing of one financial instrument for another. Prior to 1374, the *violari* routinely bore interest rates of upwards of 15 per cent, whereas the *censal* bore rates which averaged about 7 per cent. Thus, it should be noted that this 'phasing out of the *violari*' could not have worked, had interest rates not plummeted during the 1370s. And this is precisely the story that evidence from other investment types in the regions tells us. In Manresa, we know that interest rates on personal loans fell from about 14 per cent to 7 per cent. We cannot pinpoint this to the 1370s, but this fall is not inconsistent with such

88 MC 1371.1.8; MC 1371.1.9.

89 Usher, *Early History of Deposit Banking*, p. 151.

90 *Ibid.*, p. 151.

a decline. When we look to rates on government annuities in Florence, Genoa, and Venice, we can see that government annuities in those cities likewise underwent a precipitous drop, beginning in the same year as the Catalan annuities: 1374.[91] This suggests that the phenomenon we are witnessing was not local to Catalonia, but was part of some wider, as yet unremarked 'Mediterranean Market Crash'. And since annuities were by their nature always in competition with entrepreneurial investments in the Mediterranean, this strongly suggests that the Market Crash was not limited to the annuity market, but extended to other investment types as well. After all, if returns on entrepreneurial activity, that is, on investment in overseas trade through *commendas* or the like, were significantly higher than the 5–7 per cent range that was available for *censals* after the mid-1370s, the burden of proof must surely lie with that person who could demonstrate that investors would choose to earn significantly less per year rather than actively or passively invest in overseas trade, as they had been doing for centuries. Since there was a dramatic decline in interest rates in the 1370s, and since our evidence strongly suggests that this decline was market-wide, we are next left with the question of what could be the reason for such a market crash. And as it turns out, a reason is not difficult to find: the plague of 1374, which in much of the Mediterranean region was experienced as the third major wave of plague, had just struck, driving wages and prices further towards a peak which would crest in the 1380s.[92] With expenses rising to 200 or even 300 per cent of pre-plague levels, it is not to be wondered that the extremely high interest rates seen in Mediterranean annuity markets prior to 1374, which after all mirrored extremely high returns on entrepreneurial activity, would have to start coming down, to reflect greatly reduced profit margins across the board.

The steep decline in interest rates on annuities, and the implication that there was a serious decline in entrepreneurial profits after this period, suggests an answer to a question which had been dogging Mediterranean urban historians for upwards of half a century: why did investment in *commendas*, and other indicators of a bullish investment market in overseas trade, suddenly dry up after about 1380? Historians such as Jaume Aurell have sought to create a link between the adoption of the *censal* system and the decline of Catalan commerce. This would seem to make sense on the surface, since, after all, the *censals* had to compete successfully with other available investment opportunities, including that of entrepreneurial investment, in order to claim a share of the investment

91 Fynn-Paul, 'Civic Debt, Civic Taxes', 142–5.

92 For Manresan prices and wages, see Chapter 7.

Table 6.6 *Number, value, and types of financial investments held by Manresans in 1408*[93]

Type of loan or investment	No. loans	%	Value (£)	% total value	Average value (£)
Censal (Manresa)	39	15.7	14,775	53.0	379
Censal (Other jurisdictions)	11	4.4	1,562	5.6	142
Censal (Personal or Unknown)	15	6.0	658	2.4	44
Violari (none from Manresa)	8	3.2	556	2.0	70
Personal loan (not to relative)	125	50.2	7,840	28.2	63
Personal loan (to relative)	12	4.8	695	2.5	58
Emphyteusis	33	13.3	1,672	6.0	51
To religious institutions	4	1.6	83	0.3	21
For rental of a field	1	0.4	2	0.0	2
Total known loans	248	68.7	27,843	94.6	112
Total unknown loans	113	31.2	1,595	5.4	14

market.[94] According to Aurell, the sons of Catalan merchants began to eschew the active and precarious mercantile trade, opting instead for the easier lifestyle of the *rentier*. In the *censal* they found a ready source of low-risk, long-term income. It is certainly true that prior to the 1350s investment options were less professionalized, more ad hoc and therefore arguably more productive to the private sector. And it is true that after 1360, much of the capital that had previously been free to channel into myriad personal and small business ventures was inexorably drawn into the coffers of the state, like so many iron filings to a giant magnet. Crown financiers had finally learned how to fully tap into the gold mine of personal investment capital. This development marks a major step in the process of fiscal centralization that led from the feudal states of the

93 Source: LM.
Notes: This table reports Manresan citizens' 'financial' investments, meaning investments which were not made in real estate or movable goods. The term 'loan' is used on the table as shorthand for all types of financial investment listed. The column heading 'No. loans' includes all loans and investments whose type can be determined from the *Liber Manifesti*; the total of these was 248. '%' means the percentage of 248 known loans. 'Value' is the total value of all loans of a given type, and '% of total value' means the percentage of Manresan investment wealth, which totalled £27,843, which was invested in the given loan type. The average value of each loan is then computed in the final column.
The category 'Unknown Loans' recorded at the bottom of the table are those whose value is recorded in the *Liber Manifesti* but whose type is unspecified. It will be noted that the type for the great majority (95 per cent) of all loaned capital is known. Most of the loans whose type was not specified were very small.

94 This theme is developed at length in Jaume Aurell i Cardona, *Els mercaders catalans al quatre-cents: Mutació de valors i procés d'artistocratització a Barcelona, 1370–1470* (Barcelona, 1996).

thirteenth century to the absolutist states of the sixteenth century. It also, inevitably, spelt the end of the unstructured boom time of the thirteenth- and early fourteenth-century investment cultures.

Should most of the blame for the perceived 'failure of nerve' of the Catalan merchant classes be laid at the door of the *censal* system? It can be seen from Table 6.6 that, by 1408, *censals* and *violaris* took up nearly two-thirds of Manresan non-land investment capital, capital that would otherwise have gone into mercantile enterprises, real estate, or agricultural speculation.[95] But our evidence suggests that another significant factor must also have been the precipitous fall in business returns and interest rates during the 1370s. While one can imagine risking one's capital in overseas investments that promised a return of 20 per cent or more, as was the case through the 1330s and 40s, it is difficult to imagine doing so for profits of less than 10 per cent. And yet such low profit margins must have been the norm after 1380, or else *censal* rates, which directly competed with rates on mercantile enterprise, could not have dipped as low as they did. Whatever were the prevailing cultural trends amongst the Barcelona bourgeoisie, it cannot be supposed that the Sartas, the Amargos and their fellow Catalan entrepreneurs would suddenly become so lethargic as to invest in 5.4 per cent-yielding *censals* if they could earn 15 per cent in trade. In short, the marked deceleration of Catalan trade towards 1400 should not be blamed primarily on social attitudes, or even the advent of the *censal* system alone, but rather on a combination of very low returns from trade and land on the one hand, combined with the ready availability of standardized, low-risk *censals*, whose safety and desirability had now been proven after two generations of trial, error, improvement and acclimation.

THE INVESTMENT UNIVERSE OF CATALAN URBAN ELITES IN THE LONG FOURTEENTH CENTURY IN A SOUTHERN EUROPEAN CONTEXT

It will be noted that our discussion of the Catalan *censal* system has moved from an analysis of its function as a tool of royal finance, to its social and economic role as an investment opportunity at the local level. It has been suggested that the *censal* system contributed in no small degree to a lessening of 'entrepreneurial spirit' amongst the Catalan urban classes after about 1380, although it is true that steadily increasing prices and

[95] Table 6.6. The comparison comes from the only similar work that has been done on medieval urban patrimonies, in David Herlihy and Christiane Klapisch-Zuber, *Tuscans and their Families* (New Haven, CT, 1985), Graphs 99–103 and related discussion.

wages, bringing with them decreasing returns on mercantile activity, would certainly have slowed this activity in any event. This is important from the perspective of an urban historian, because after 1380 there is so little evidence of urban building, urban renewal, and so little initiative on the part of Catalan urban governments.[96] Why did they suddenly stop acting with the boldness that they had earlier in the century? It was argued in the previous chapter that urban elites now felt themselves to be sapped of power, both as individual economic actors and also as a group, as members of an urban elite which in the earlier part of the century had been wont to challenge the local nobles and bishops as though they were their equals.

While the previous chapter addressed these issues in political and social terms, an economic dimension can now be added to help explain this marked diminution of civic vitality. Because urban elites were most crucial for expressing and embodying this vitality, it is necessary to understand how these elites were making and sustaining their fortunes, that is, how they were investing their funds. When one thinks of an 'investor', modern readers tend to think of business-savvy, wealthy entrepreneurs. One imagines, therefore, that a discussion of Catalan investors deals only with a wealthy male elite. This, however, is not at all a proper picture of the Manresan investing classes. In fact, most Manresan householders had some capital to dispose of, and every urban citizen had to make a decision about where to invest their (often meagre) savings: would they buy a cider press? A candle mould? Would they invest in a share of the local flour mill? Would they make loans to farmers in return for a share of next years' harvest? Even poor widows had to decide how they would attempt to make their living: would they buy raw wool that could be spun? Would they set up a boarding home? Would they set up as bakers? Or brewers? Or would they purchase a field from a relative at a good price and rent it out? All of these represent investment choices, and it should therefore be stressed that a discussion of investors does not limit us to the choices of a few wealthy male 'investors'. Even at the highest rungs on the economic ladder, there were wealthy widows at Manresa, and newly wealthy householders of both sexes, who had amassed their fortunes in disparate ways. All of these people, however, were greatly affected by the economic conditions which surrounded them, and the

[96] One exception to this are the guildhalls begun in Barcelona from the 1390s. Margarita Tintó Sala, 'Les cases gremials de Barcelona i el seu entorn urbà', in Salvador Claramunt (ed.), *El món urbà a la Corona d'Aragó del 1137 als decrets de nova planta: XVII Congrés d'Història de la Corona d'Aragó / Congreso de Historia de la Corona de Aragón, Barcelona, Poblet, Lleida, 7 al 12 de Desembre de 2000* (Barcelona, 2003), vol. II, pp. 895–910. At Manresa, however, there was almost no urban building between about 1350 and 1450.

most general pattern that can be discerned in the later fourteenth century is that wealthy investors had it quite good until the later 1360s and 1370s, after which returns fell dramatically during what we have called the 'Market Crash', and from this point most people found it much more difficult to maintain a well-to-do lifestyle.

Before discussing the Catalan data on individual investment returns, it will be expedient to review the well-established Tuscan chronology. Studying Pistoiese returns for investment in wheat, David Herlihy found that prior to 1280, these hovered around 9 per cent, after which they began a steady rise.[97] They attained a remarkable 15 per cent by the 1330s. Regarding this Herlihy memorably observes:

> This handsome return indicates a strong demand for capital in Pistoia's countryside. Peasants, crowded on the land, many of them seeking to survive on farms of inadequate size, desperately needed credit to aid them in their labours and to tide them over years of scarcity.[98]

Indeed, during this period, which is known as an age of prosperity because it was favourable for the accumulation of capital by the moneyed classes, a 15 per cent profit was conservative, reflecting the relatively low risk of an investment in wheat. In riskier markets such as overseas luxury trade or personal loans, returns were even higher. Thus, Herlihy found Pistoiese notaries who redacted 'thinly disguised' usurious contracts at interest rates of 20 or even 50 per cent.[99] Indeed, high returns on agricultural investments were partly determined by the fact that agricultural capital had to compete with the often spectacular returns on overseas trade, which in the thirteenth and early fourteenth centuries yielded profits of 20 per cent or more.[100] The brisk trade in rural *commendas* in the early fourteenth-century Bages is an indication of how Christian investors were able to use this instrument to lend to one another – and the high interest rates and agricultural returns of the period provided a strong incentive to do so.[101] This boom time, however, came to an abrupt end in the 1370s in Italy: the demographic and other disasters of the mid-fourteenth century caused rates of return on these investment types to fall, within a few decades, to below half their previous level, and

97 David Herlihy, *Medieval and Renaissance Pistoia: The Social History of an Italian Town, 1200–1430* (New Haven, CT, 1967), p. 140.

98 *Ibid.* 99 *Ibid.*

100 For a comparison of overseas trading profits to profits from interpersonal loans, see Benjamin Z. Kedar, *Merchants in Crisis: Genoese and Venetian Men of Affairs and the Fourteenth Century Depression* (New Haven, CT, 1977), pp. 62–5.

101 For a discussion of this in Valencia see Juan Vicente García Marsilla, *Vivir a crédito en la Valencia medieval: De los orígenes del sistema censal al endeudamiento del municipio* (Valencia, 2002), esp. pp. 55–70.

they would never recover their former levels.[102] By 1427, the redactors of the Florentine Catasto assumed that capital invested in any of the principal channels would not earn more than a modest 7 per cent.[103] In Manresa in 1408, likewise, most investors had to be content with a return of just over 5 per cent on their capital, a rate which according to J. H. Elliott was still prevailing in the sixteenth and seventeenth centuries.[104]

Table 6.6 shows a breakdown of the different investment choices that were made by Manresan householders at the start of the fifteenth century. This provides invaluable insight into the intersection of individual households with the economy at large. Every householder was faced with a certain limited range of investment types, which tended to fall into four main categories. These were investment in land, real estate, business capital and, fourthly, in money loans of various types. For the present, we will concern ourselves with the principal types of financial investment that could be made. These are distinct because they represent purely capital-based investments, that is, they do not represent investment in any real good, but rather represent a loan of pure money to another person, which earns interest because of the work that the money is doing. Granted, these borrowers are expected to put the money to work in some other way, whether in the form of additional loans or as some form of investment in agriculture, manufacture or entrepreneurial activity. But the fact that the financial sector of a town such as Manresa was so advanced as to have several different types of financial investment in common use by a large number of wealthy householders provides us with a reminder of the ubiquity and depth of development of the Catalan money economy by this point.

To return to Table 6.6, it can be seen that of the known loans recorded in the *Liber Manifesti*, interpersonal loans accounted for over 50 per cent of the total number of loans but only 28.2 per cent of the total lent capital. (Mortgages, a form of loan in wide use in late medieval north-west Europe, were unknown in fourteenth-century Catalonia.)[105] *Censals*, on the other hand, accounted for 26.1 per cent of the number of loans, and amounted to over 60 per cent of the value of all lent capital. Considering that *censals* were not commonly available until 1360, it can be expected that the entire lending economy of Manresa greatly shifted after this time period. Indeed it could be argued that this accounts for the decline of the *commenda* which is seen over the same time period.[106] The Catalan

[102] See Chapter 8; Herlihy, *Pistoia*, p. 155, holds a similar opinion.

[103] Herlihy, *Pistoia*, p. 140.

[104] J. H. Elliott, *Revolt of the Catalans* (Cambridge, 1984), p. 139.

[105] On these northern mortgages see Murray, *Bruges, Cradle of Capitalism*, p. 134.

[106] This decline is an impression gained from the Talamanca and Sarta papers.

commenda was a financial device that linked people of all social standing in a very broad and thick web of interpersonal connections. Also, in the early fourteenth century the *commenda* was commonly redacted for small amounts, meaning that even the humblest peasants were wont to take advantage of this investment opportunity, and could expect to do so frequently. But wealthier people also took advantage of the *commenda* and used it to invest capital in one another's businesses, real estate, and other enterprises. After about 1360, the *censal* certainly sucked up a lot of this investment money, and siphoned it into the government's coffers. At the same time, one would expect that the wealthy would have continued to accept *commendas* from poorer people, so that they could invest in more *censals*, thus perpetuating the cycle of *commenda*-giving by petty investors. The fact that *commendas* became less common across the social spectrum after the 1370s, whether lent by the rich or the poor, suggests that it was not the advent of the government annuity per se which caused the demise of the *commenda*, but rather the collapse of interest rates mentioned above. Because *commendas* required the receiving partner to share the interest gained with the investor (in Catalonia, the passive investor usually received one third of the profits), this arrangement only made sense when interest rates were very high, say, in the neighbourhood of 15 per cent. If interest rates fell down to 7 or even 5 per cent, receiving one third of this paltry amount suggests a profit margin so small that it would not be worth anyone's time. Thus, it seems likely that the era of the *commenda* drew to a close with the end of the era of double-digit investment returns.

The very high average value of *censal* investments versus personal loans also suggests that the newly emergent option to invest in *censals* was reserved to wealthy Manresans. Therefore, when the interpersonal *commenda* became unprofitable after the interest rate decline of the 1370s, the poor were then left out of the financial economy, unless they were going to make very small interpersonal loans. Further, when the Manresan elite turned towards *censal* investment, they strongly preferred those issued by their own local government. This stems from a number of causes. First, as local elites, they could expect to have a strong influence over local government, and could thus feel reassured that this body would continue to meet its *censal* obligations. In addition, there was the very real sense that the limits of a burgher's political power more or less ended with the boundaries of their *vegueria*. As soon as one invested in funds from another *vegueria*, the odds that one could run into legal snafus with the details and timing of repayment increased significantly, which translated into a net loss of value for the investment. Thus, if one could invest in a *censal* earning 7 per cent in one's own *vegueria*, versus a *censal* earning

7 per cent in a neighbouring *vegueria*, the added risk of investing in the alien *vegueria* meant that one's actual profit margin might be 6 or 5 per cent – thus the strong prevalence for local annuities that we see in the Manresan evidence.

Not only is *commenda* evidence almost entirely lacking from Manresan sources from the age of the 1408 *Liber Manifesti*, but the personal loan sector was also not terribly active at this time. One reason for this is that, in comparison with the *censal*, the personal loan represented a riskier, shorter-term and inherently less convenient means of investment. By the 1380s, experience had proven that there was a much higher risk that any given individual would default on their investment than that the town government would do. A demand-side explanation for the paucity of the small-loan sector will be examined in Chapters 7 and 8: in a nutshell, it appears as though all but the most destitute Manresan householders were, in the years around 1400, doing quite well in an atmosphere of high wages, low land prices and high per capita wealth. There was therefore little need for them to borrow funds in order to make ends meet.

Although the loan sector was relatively small, and interpersonal loans were often smaller than the sums invested in *censals*, the loan sector remained one of the primary competitors for funds which might otherwise go into government annuities. A knowledge of how these forms evolved and were employed by Manresan householders serves to give us a better sense of the economic milieu into which the government annuity intruded. It further gives us a sense of how annuity rates stood in relation to interpersonal loan rates over the longer term, and finally, the study of interpersonal loans gives us one of our primary means for witnessing the web of interpersonal relationships which were built on economic ties during our time period. Table 6.7 provides the known interest rates for interpersonal loans at Manresa. By 1408, the personal loan was earning an average annual interest of about 7 per cent, which put them about 2 points above the *censal*. Despite this profit advantage, it is clear that the disadvantages associated with interpersonal loans, including their short-term durations and relative unreliability, meant that Manresa's elite were less inclined to make these loans than they might otherwise have been in the absence of a developed *censal* system. What is also noticeable from the 1408 data set is the fact that there were no Jews involved in the Manresan lending sector. It is unlikely that Jews' property would have been recorded in a *Liber Manfesti*, in any event, because of their special status as wards of the king, and the fact that they could not become Manresan citizens, but it is also true that the Jewish quarter of Manresa stood abandoned, or nearly so, after 1348, so that the great majority of lending that

Table 6.7 *Interest rates for interpersonal loans*[107]

Date (y.m.d)	Rate (%)	Description
1235	12	Maximum rate for loans made by Christians (royal decree)
1235	20	Maximum rate for loans made by Jews (royal decree)
1325.11.5	20	Charged by Manresan Jew to two couples from Talamanca
1326.1.30	15	Charged by a Jew of Vic
1334.1.13	12	Charged by a Jew of Vic to a donzel (noble squire)
1339.1.22	11	Charged by a Jew of Vic to two rural couples
1339.11.27	12	Charged by a Jew of Vic to a donzel
1340.3.27	15	Charged by B. de Talamanca (knight) for grain loan
1340.11.28	9	Charged by a Jew of Vic
1345.11.28	9	Charged by a Jew of Vic to a knight
1348.1.31	20	Charged by 2 Jewish brothers to B. de Talamanca
1325–45	20	Standard Rate Charged by Jews of Vic on overdue loans[108]
1330–40	15	Average charge on grain loans at Pistoia
pre-1348	20–50	Charged in 'thinly disguised' usurious contracts redacted by some Pistoiese notaries
1380	5	Interest limit payable to Florentine state creditors from this date
Averages:		
1325–48	13.66	Average rate of 9 interpersonal loans recorded above
1408–11	7.00	Average rate of 24 interpersonal loans (some composite) recorded in the *Liber Manifesti*

went on after this time was done by Christians. Prior to 1348, there had been a vibrant Jewish moneylending sector of the Manresan economy;

[107] Sources: 1235: *Cortes* I-1, 131. 1325: AHCM Tr. 175 (Familia Talamanca); 1340, 1348: AHCM Tr. 175 (B. Talamanca: Included in the same volume as Familia Talamanca); 1330–40: Herlihy, *Pistoia*, 140; 1408: *Liber Manifesti* 1408. The loans made by the Jews of Vic are recorded in Arcadio Garcia Sanz, '*Los intereses en los préstamos de los judíos de Vic*', 251, 254–5.

Notes: For further discussion of high rates on investment returns before 1348, see B. Z. Kedar, *Merchants in Crisis*, esp. pp. 62–5. In 1380, Florence enacted a law limiting payments to state creditors at 5 per cent, which Anthony Molho, in *Florentine Public Finances in the Early Renaissance 1400–1433*, p. 22, calls 'substantially below that which could be obtained in the commercial or banking enterprises of those times'. From the information in the *Liber Manifesti*, presented above, and especially from the *censal* data presented in Table 6.5, this interest rate was only 2 per cent less than the rate paid by other 'safe' investments after the mid-1370s. Prior to the mid-1370s, however, Molho's analysis would have been correct. The Florentine law of 1380 was thus a swift and shrewd reaction to a steep fall in western Mediterranean interest rates.

[108] Most of the contracts published by García Sanz end with a clause stating that, if the loan goes overdue, a rate of 4d per pound per month will be charged (this is the monthly ceiling, amounting to 20 percent *per annum*, set by Jaume I in the *Corts* of 1235). Cf *Corts*, I-1, 131.

many of these families originally hailed from Vic, but some of them, particularly the Vitalis family, maintained connections in Manresa, from which they anchored their investment network in the Bages.[109]

The first data in Table 6.7 come from a series of royal decrees made in 1235 by Jaume I, which established the legal limits of interest rates. At that time, Jaume decreed that Christians could charge up to 12 per cent on loans of any type, and Jews could charge 20 per cent in any credit transaction. The limit of 20 per cent was reiterated in 1241, when it was restated as a monthly rate.[110] King Jaume's decrees of 1235 represent his attempt to reconcile the needs of the booming Catalan economy, and especially the needs of the Crown's financiers, with the Church's ban on usury. The king decided that, below a certain rate, the charging of interest was indeed permissible. Benjamin Kedar notes a similar phenomenon in Genoa and in Venice, where legal interest rates chargeable by Christians of 15 per cent and 12 per cent respectively were set by similar decrees.[111] That Jaume was fed up with church interference on this issue is humorously revealed in the closing sentence of his 1235 interest decree: 'And if perchance any debtors should make a complaint to the church (about the fact that they had been charged interest), the debtors are to be whipped through the streets and their petition will be dismissed entirely.'[112]

Despite the king's pragmatism, the church's long-term opposition to usury did create a social stigma against usury that prevailed in Catalonia into the fourteenth century, making it difficult to find explicit statements of interest rates in Manresan documents, except in the case of Jews, which were explicitly recorded, following a common medieval double standard.[113] The advent of the government annuities in mid-century went very far towards normalizing the concept of inter-Christian lending, and so by the early fifteenth century the redactors of the *Liber Manifesti*

[109] In the sources utilized for this study, the Vitalis family appears most frequently in the Talamanca papers, e.g. FT1 1320 pi11 and FT1 1325 pk11.

[110] *Cortes*, I-1, p. 134. By openly allowing interest to be charged by Christians, the king's regulation certainly flies in the face of the Church's campaign against usury, which was increasingly virulent during this period. We have seen that the House of Barcelona, however, did adopt many business-friendly policies during the thirteenth and fourteenth centuries. For a process against usury in 1297 which in general serves to uphold the fact that the Crown of Aragon remained relatively lenient in enforcing Church strictures during the thirteenth and fourteenth centuries, see Claude Denjean, *La loi du lucre: L'usure en procès dans la Couronne d'Aragon à la fin du moyen age* (Madrid, 2011). On medieval usury in general see again Munro, 'The Medieval Origins of the Financial Revolution'.

[111] Kedar, *Merchants in Crisis*.

[112] '*Et si forte debitores querminoiam ecclesie fecerint, currant eos per villam flagellando et amittant penitus peticionem.*' *Cortes*, I-1, p. 131.

[113] The notarial fiction has worked to a considerable extent: as recently as the 1960s, García Sanz could write an entire article on the interest charged by medieval Jews at Vic without mentioning the existence of Christian creditors.

felt fewer qualms on the issue. As a result, the rates for twenty-four interpersonal loans, including some composites of multiple loans, can be gleaned from that source.

When we corroborate known interest rates on interpersonal loans with those found on government annuities, the evidence is not inconsistent with a precipitous drop on both sets of interest rates during the 1370s. Although the personal loan data is missing for the period 1348–1408, our 'before' and 'after' picture shows that, at some point over the intervening sixty years, rates had fallen to roughly half of what they had previously been. It has been argued above that these rates would have fallen in tandem, because they represent investment options that were all in competition with one another for investors' limited funds. There is enough evidence to state that between 1348 and 1400, at the least, all the interest rates on financial transactions fell by roughly half. This happened during precisely those decades when prices, including the price of labour (i.e. wages) increased by a similar ratio.[114]

CONCLUSIONS

The present chapter has attempted to highlight some of the social, political, and economic effects of the evolving government annuity system, to assess the impact of the precipitous fall in interest rates that occurred during the 1370s and to relate this financial and economic story to the narratives of state formation that were introduced in the last chapter. Let us begin our summary with an assessment of the impact of the Catalan 'financial revolution' – a revolution whose importance was only dimly understood a generation ago. During the economic boom time of the early fourteenth century, when the Crown had succeeded in building and protecting a regionally powerful urban elite without yet being able to effectively tax it, and while economic returns remained at the same time very high, the Manresan patriciate enjoyed a heyday of economic, political, and social influence within their own region, together with a good deal of independence from the Crown. While this independence was never truly tested during these decades, the citizens, and especially the body of consuls, could and did act as though they were one of their region's plenipotentiaries, similar in stature to bishops or barons, who had themselves always acted with a good deal of independence and initiative. As the annuity system created by the financial revolution evolved, however, more and more elites voluntarily entered into economic relations with the local government, at the same time that the Crown began to

[114] See Tables 7.3 and 7.4.

tighten its grip on the local political situation, particularly during the Castilian war and its aftermath. While the local citizens might have felt during the 1360s as though they were taking the government for a ride, since they were often earning upwards of 15 per cent on their *violaris*, during the 1370s the Crown took advantage of falling interest rates and phased out the *violari* for the *censal*, whose rates by 1390 were approaching 5 per cent. This redounded to the advantage of the Crown, which was able to keep the local elites in its financial pocket, while having to pay very low interest rates in order to secure their continued complacency and loyalty. In fact, it was now in the economic interest of the local elites to maintain the Crown's system of annuities in the most smoothly running order as possible. While the Crown reaped the benefits of low annuity rates, the local elites found themselves to be financially sapped by the same decreasing interest rates, which greatly reduced their sense of independence. More efficient tax collection, which local elites supported because this ensured the timely payment of *censal* dues, only furthered this sense of civic belt-tightening. Decreased social mobility further helped to ensure that the upper echelons of Manresan society became more and more effectively 'closed' to new members, although it has been shown that there were exceptions. Thus, while the economic boom of the early part of the century lent itself to independent action on the part of the Manresan patriciate, by the end of the fourteenth century, we are witness to an urban government whose character had become considerably more docile, even though it had undergone very few overt changes in form. Thanks to the Catalan financial revolution, the civic elite of 1400 was much more closely tied to national and local fiscal structures than it had ever been. And due to a combination of increased fiscal efficiency, falling investment returns and increasing social ossification, the elites of the medium-sized Catalan cities, at least, were in much less of a position to assert themselves as regional and national players than they had been on the eve of the Black Death.

Falling interest rates on government annuities in the 1370s also had distinct impacts on each of Manresa's economic strata. As the *censal* began to replace the earlier *commenda* as a principal investment medium for wealthy people, the poor people of the Bages were increasingly excluded from the investment market, meaning that they would have had fewer two-way economic ties with their economic superiors. The Talamanca and Sarta papers show us that prior to 1348, many rustics and poor urban dwellers were seeking people all over their region with whom they could place money *commendas*, in return for a share of the profits which were readily had in the booming economy of the day. During the post-Black Death era, poor people now found it much more profitable to engage themselves as day labourers, since this brought increased remuneration, as will be discussed in the following chapter. Falling investment returns, plus the advent of the *censal*, thus helped contribute to the increasing social rigidity after about 1380 that has been noticed by Jaume Aurell. The fact that this ossification has been noticed across Europe at the same time suggests that falling investment returns – which were Europe-wide at this time – were having a similar impact elsewhere.

The Type B (wealth-based) middle classes at Manresa were largely excluded from annuity investment by their high prices and low investment returns. This meant that the increasing prevalence of annuities helped to create a heightened sense of class division in Catalan society. When interest rates on annuities fell to the low rate of 5 per cent, middle-class people who wished to increase their fortunes despite some risk and bother continued to use older methods of investment, such as trading and interpersonal loans, which might bring 7 rather than 5 per cent. In the pre-annuity era, class divisions based on investment type would not have been nearly as cut and dried as they were to become by the later fifteenth century.[115] By that time, *rentiers* were easily distinguished by their annuity-holding tendencies, while merchants continued to rely on alternative investment strategies.[116] Prior to about 1370, even a confirmed *rentier* would have been investing in a combination of real estate and agricultural loans and would, in general, have had a portfolio which overlapped considerably with that of many middle-class people and self-professed 'merchants'. The annuity, with its lack of connection to any local production process (except for the fiscal revenues of the local government), would also have divided the *rentiers* more sharply from the local interests and industries that in previous decades would have helped to integrate them into the local economy. Over time, this gave them a feeling of being more strongly connected with the royal administration than with local economic interests.

For wealthy people, the sudden and dramatic decrease in investment returns experienced during the 1370s would have been nothing short of devastating. Whereas prior to the 1370s double-digit investment returns were virtually guaranteed via a number of channels, after this decade, such profit opportunities were entirely a thing of the past. Real estate prices were stagnant, entrepreneurial activities were almost certainly less profitable and the government annuity brought rates less than half of

115 For late fifteenth- and sixteenth-century *rentiers* at Barcelona, see James S. Amelang, *Honored Citizens of Barcelona: Patrician Culture and Class Relations, 1490–1714* (Princeton, NJ, 1986), pp. 26–7.

116 LM. These figures will be published in subsequent work.

what prevailed prior to 1375.[117] In a bearish economic climate, there is always a tendency towards social stagnation. There will be fewer social climbers in times when money is relatively hard to come by. With the price of labour and manufactured items also increasing, the civic elite felt straitened across the board, and would have had to employ far fewer servants than they had prior to the Black Death era.[118] In fact, the price of labour was deemed to be so high that authorities across Spain and Italy began to allow for the regular importation of slaves beginning in the 1350s and 60s, after a hiatus of nearly three centuries.[119] This creation of a whole new social underclass of slaves, which simultaneously created a class of Catalan slave-owners, only heightened the sense of hierarchy which crept into Catalan society after 1380.[120] This rigidity, and the diminution of civic spirit seen in the years after 1380, therefore have very much to do with the fact that, from the point of view of the investor, the economy had collapsed. Whereas in the last chapter we emphasized the political reasons for this loss of civic vitality, we can now add to this story the fact that the economy was in most cases providing little encouragement.[121]

In sum, then, it can be observed that the financial revolution in Catalonia served to increase the tax burdens on towns, thus decreasing their political independence and their discretionary spending. It also served, in the medium-sized towns at least, to dislocate the citizenry from its local and regional moorings, making emigration more likely in an age of shrinking populations. On the national level, it built up a centralized fiscal state, meaning that it created a larger and more unified financial bureaucracy, which is certainly another hallmark of state formation. Furthermore, the new system created a citizenry which tended to see the state as a benefactor. Did the *censal* system provide the state with more power to act against the towns and civic interests? This is not a straightforward question. It undoubtedly contributed to the strength of the state in the long run, and it also co-opted local elites into the royal administration. But the most significant effects of the annuity system on town–Crown relations were probably those described in the previous chapter, which showed how it enabled the Crown to greatly increase its returns on relatively limited civic revenues. The unintentional effect of this was to cause the urban regimes to lose their earlier powers of

117 For real estate prices, see Table 7.11. 118 See Tables 7.4, 7.5 and relevant discussion.

119 J. Fynn-Paul, 'Empire, Monotheism, and Slavery in the Greater Mediterranean Region from Antiquity to the Early Modern Era', *Past and Present*, 205 (2009), 31–4.

120 Aurell, *Els mercaders catalans*, pp. 322–6.

121 LM and MC suggest that the leather industry was an exception, based on the wealth of several politically prominent leather wholesalers.

discretionary spending, while it co-opted nearly all available urban revenue to debt payments. Still, the effects of the financial revolution on town–Crown politics were hardly absolute. Longer-term history showed that the financial revolution did not stop Barcelona from very effectively rising up against the Crown in the later fifteenth century. It undoubtedly provided the citizens of Barcelona with the tools to sustain their revolt for as long as they did.[122] But this is not due to any inherent advantage in the financial system created by the financial revolution, but rather the fact that it created a tool which could prove to be a double-edged sword when the monarchy proved inept. What is certain, however, is that the financial revolution radically transformed the nature of Catalan society at almost every level: its impact was so great that one might argue that it was an even greater agent of late medieval change than the demographic shocks engendered by the plague.

Despite what an earlier generation of analysts may have alleged, and despite the vicissitudes of the Castilian war and the negative effects of the late medieval crisis, it must be concluded that over the longer term the Catalan-Aragonese state did quite well for itself in the fourteenth and fifteenth centuries.[123] The financial revolution of the fourteenth century was an integral part of this success story.[124] The success of Catalonia-Aragon is especially evident when it is judged against the standard of Genoa, which was a great rival to Catalonia for the century prior to 1354, but which ever afterward began a slow decline, as marked for example by the lordship of the Duke of Milan in the 1390s.[125] The fifteenth century was most notable for the Catalan conquest of Naples, which was begun by Alfonso V (1416–58) in 1436, and cemented in the 1440s – all this despite fierce but increasingly impotent Genoese opposition. Naples proved no ephemeral addition to the Crown, but remained united to it for several centuries, until the War of the Spanish Succession. It is notable that this conquest was carried out entirely on the resources of the Crown of Aragon proper, and it can therefore be argued that, at least in relation to its neighbouring competitors, the Catalan-Aragonese financial system was sufficient to pursue a significant expansionist policy. The real problems for Aragon came when, partly because the new house of the

[122] This concentration of capital remains largely implicit in Alan Ryder's mostly political narrative, *The Wreck of Catalonia: Civil War in the Fifteenth Century* (Oxford, 2007).

[123] The steady pushing back of Genoa, rendering it territorially impotent in the Mediterranean by the 1450s, has for example not been picked up by a major commentator. The older narratives have been listed in n. 25, above.

[124] This contrasts with the still influential conclusions reached in Ramon d'Abadal Vinyals, *Pere el Cerimoniós i els inicis de la decadència politica de Catalunya* (Barcelona, 1987).

[125] Steven A. Epstein, *Genoa and the Genoese 958–1528* (Chapel Hill, NC, 2000), pp. 248–51.

Trastàmaras felt little loyalty to Barcelona, Alfonso moved his capital to Naples. This inaugurated a period of absentee monarchism which helped to spark the Catalan civil war of 1462–72. Not only did this prove devastating to Barcelona and Catalonia, but the trend of absentee monarchism only got worse with the union of Castile and Aragon in 1479, and especially after Charles V became Holy Roman Emperor in 1519. Thereafter Catalonia, like so many sixteenth-century European provinces with long traditions of self-rule, had to be content with being merely one part of a conglomerate state. It is not to be doubted, however, that the significant steps towards fiscal centralization and state building that were taken by the House of Barcelona in the long fourteenth century helped Catalonia-Aragon to become a dominant, expansionist power in the western Mediterranean during the fifteenth century. In turn, the Aragonese Mediterranean empire was one of the principal forces behind the sudden rise of the Spanish monarchy in the sixteenth century – one which Castilianist narratives focusing on the American expansion tend to overlook. The naval power of the Spanish Crown in the Mediterranean, which turned the tide of Turkish expansion at Lepanto, was likewise founded upon the fourteenth-century fiscal reforms of the House of Barcelona, whose effects at Manresa have formed the principal subject of this chapter.

Chapter 7

DEMOGRAPHY, WAGES, AND PRICES IN THE AGE OF THE BLACK DEATH

INTRODUCTION

Previous chapters have alluded to the demographic and macroeconomic (as opposed to fiscal) aspects of the 'crisis of the fourteenth century'; the present chapter now seeks to present some of these trends as they can be constructed from Manresan, Barcelonese, and other Catalan sources. In the process, a number of related social, political, and fiscal trends can be understood more clearly. The prime mover in the story told in this chapter is the Black Death itself, a great pestilence which killed perhaps half of the people in Catalonia in a few-month period beginning in about May 1348. The sudden massive population decline led to a great shortage of labourers compared to the pre-plague economy. This resulted in a tremendous increase in nominal wage rates. Labourers, in other words, quickly felt their new power, and almost immediately demanded rates that were significantly higher than what they had received prior to the plague. Polities across Europe reacted by enacting statutes of labourers, but these were generally ineffective at combating the massive market forces they were gauged to tame: employers were forced on an ad hoc basis to pay higher wages, or see their workshops go untended, and lords were forced to grant easier terms to tenants and labourers, or else see their fields go untended.[1] While pioneering studies in England once emphasized the greed of the workers, more recent scholarship has tended to see the situation from the perspective of the working classes.[2] Indeed,

[1] The first systematic study of the statutes is Samuel K. Cohn, 'The Black Death, Tragedy, and Transformation', in John Jeffries Martin (ed.), *The Renaissance World*, The Routledge Worlds (New York, 2007), pp. 69–83. For the ability of labourers to demand better conditions by 'voting with their feet', see John Hatcher, 'England in the Aftermath of the Black Death', *Past and Present: A Journal of Historical Studies*, 144 (1994), 3–35. See also Richard H. Britnell, 'Feudal Reaction after the Black Death: The Palatinate of Durham', *Past and Present: A Journal of Historical Studies*, 128 (1990), 28–47; Wim P. Blockmans, 'The Social and Economic Effects of Plague in the Low Countries: 1349–1500', *Revue Belge de Philologie et d'Histoire: / Belgisch Tijdschrift voor Filologie en Geschiedenis*, 58:4 (1980), 833–63.

[2] See Hatcher, 'England in the Aftermath of the Black Death', pp. 3–6.

from a purely mechanical point of view, one can point out that workers in any one locality had little choice but to demand higher wages, since the aggregate effect of increased labour costs quickly drove up the prices of commodities. The aged but still valuable researches of Earl Hamilton for Iberia, and of several historians for England and the Low Countries, prove that commodity prices rose almost in lockstep with wage rates, generally reaching levels of about two to three times the 1347 rate by the 1380s.[3]

One aim of this chapter is to emphasize the fact that the plague was not a unique occurrence, and that the economic effects of the epidemic were augmented by each wave of plague. In fact the plague became endemic in Europe after 1348, generally striking in about fifteen-year intervals, which became more irregular over time as populations became more resistant and as local conditions varied. For example, in Catalonia the plague struck in 1362 and 1371–4, in each case causing a new surge in wages and prices.[4] The second and third waves of plague certainly caused a great deal of hardship in Catalonia, and significantly increased the sense of doom and depression that contemporaries felt regarding the nature of life itself. One finds clear evidence that individual entrepreneurs felt quite exuberant through the mid-1350s, perhaps relishing their luck at surviving the plague, and enjoying newly inherited wealth. The second wave of plague seems to have impacted Catalan attitudes in a much more negative way. Chapter 5 has shown how the same pattern holds for civic vitality in Manresa: whereas the 1350s were a relatively buoyant and optimistic period, the second and third waves of plague seem to have exacerbated, together with the Castilian war and the advent of the *censal* system, a sense that the cities of Catalonia were becoming less independent, less meaningful, and less powerful than they had been in the first half of the fourteenth century. The present chapter seeks to add to this notion, by showing how the second and third plagues presented

[3] For Iberia see Earl Jefferson Hamilton, *Money, Prices, and Wages in Valencia, Aragon, and Navarre, 1351–1500* (Cambridge, MA, 1936). For English prices see Robert C. Allen, 'The Great Divergence in European Wages and Prices from the Middle Ages to the First World War', *Explorations in Economic History*, 38:4 (2001), 411–47. And also John H. Munro, 'Builders' Wages in Southern England and the Southern Low Countries, 1346–1500: A Comparative Study of Trends in and Levels of Real Incomes', in Simonetta Cavaciocchi (ed.), *L'Edilizia prima della rivoluzione industriale secc. XIII–XVIII: Atti della trentaseiesima settimana di studi, 26–30 Aprile 2004* (Florence, 2005), pp. 1013–76; David L. Farmer, 'Prices and Wages, 1350–1500', in Edward Miller (ed.), *The Agrarian History of England and Wales,* vol. III: *1348–1500* (Cambridge, 1991), pp. 431–525.

[4] Carme Batlle Gallart, *Historia de Catalunya,*vol. III, *L'Expansio baixmedieval* Barcelona, 1998, p. 252. For 1362–3, see MC 1363.5.3. For a similar catalogue in Valencia, see Agustín Rubio Vela, *Peste negra, crisis y comportamientos sociales en la España del siglo XIV: La ciudad de Valencia (1348–1401)* (Granada, 1979).

significant economic and demographic difficulties, which had already begun after 1348.

Much of the debate around the effects of the Black Death has centred on the question of how 'well off' the lower orders were as a result of the labour shortage. This issue will be the main subject of Chapter 8, but its basic outlines can be traced here as a means of introducing the importance of the economic indices presented below. There is a good deal of literature which argues that increasing prices meant that the gains felt by the average person were quite modest: according to this theory, what they made up for in nominal wages was largely eaten up by the high prices they had to pay for food and clothing.[5] Thus, according to this interpretation, the 'real wages' of the labouring classes remained mostly unchanged. The present study seeks to address a relatively neglected aspect of this equation, which is the price of land. The massively shifting land–labour ratio meant that even if commodities were dearer, land in Catalonia and in its cities by no means kept pace with commodity prices.[6] It is quite clear from the data presented below that the price of a Catalan manse remained more or less constant over the long fourteenth century, while wages increased nearly threefold. The high incidence of home ownership in Manresa, as presented in the next chapter, likewise confirms that the average Manresan was quite well-to-do in terms of land. This would contradict some spotty evidence presented by Herlihy and by certain English studies which suggest that land prices either rose or that few benefited from their decline.[7] The livestock prices presented

[5] The data most cited is found in Hatcher, 'England in the Aftermath of the Black Death'. David L. Farmer, 'Crop Yields, Prices and Wages in Medieval England', *Studies in Medieval and Renaissance History*, n.s.6 (1983), 115–55. See also Munro, 'Builders' Wages in Southern England and the Southern Low Countries, 1346–1500'. The most recent synopses of builders' wages in England suggests that real wages grew from the Black Death until about 1450, reaching a peak which they would not again equal until the mid-nineteenth century. My Catalan findings seem to agree with this interpretation in the main, although perhaps Catalan real wages fell before 1450. See Gregory Clark, 'Work, Wages and Living Conditions: Building Workers in England from the Magna Carta to Tony Blair', in Simonetta Cavaciocchi (ed.), *L'Edilizia prima della rivoluzione industriale secc. XIII–XVIII*, pp. 889–932, esp. Figure 8 on p. 919. For a recent synthesis that stresses regional variability in Europe, see Samuel Kline Cohn, 'After the Black Death: Labour Legislation and Attitudes towards Labour in Late-medieval Western Europe', *Economic History Review*, 60:3 (2007), 457–85.

[6] For an overview of this phenomenon for Western Europe in general, see Jan Luiten Van Zanden, *The Long Road to the Industrial Revolution: The European Economy in a Global Perspective, 1000–1800* (Leiden, 2009), pp. 29–31.

[7] On Italian land and livestock prices, see David Herlihy, *Medieval and Renaissance Pistoia: The Social History of an Italian Town, 1200–1430* (New Haven, CT, 1967), pp. 130–3. For studies indicating that wealthier villagers tended to make the most gains, at the expense of the majority, as a result of cheaper land after the Black Death, see Zvi Razi, *Life, Marriage and Death in a Medieval Parish* (Cambridge, 1980), pp. 147–50, and L. R. Poos, *A Rural Society after the Black Death: Essex 1350–1525* (Cambridge, 1991), pp. 16–20. For the idea that demand for land generally decreased

below, taken together with the evidence of large food stores held in Manresan cellars as presented in the next chapter, suggest that some key means of production (i.e. land and livestock) became much cheaper for the average person after 1348, resulting in higher living standards for the average person in terms of food available for consumption. Finally, the falling interest rates that are in evidence from the 1370s mean that the price of capital fell. The low rates of indebtedness presented in Chapter 8 show that Manresans largely managed to free themselves from debt during the later fourteenth century. Yet, if they needed it, money was roughly half as expensive after 1370 as it had been previously. Rising wage rates also meant that people could pay back loans much faster – especially if they had been contracted in times of lower wages. Each wave of plague and wage increase made it easier for individuals to pay back outstanding loans; but even in the absence of such a mechanism, lower interest rates naturally favour the borrower. Taken as a whole, then, the economic indices presented here are essential to paint a clear picture of how both average people and elites experienced life in the aftermath of the later fourteenth-century plagues. The final chapter will then take up some of the social and political implications raised by these indices: most particularly, the question of how they relate to the notion of a 'crisis' of the fourteenth century, and the related issue of 'urban decline'.

THE POPULATION OF LATE MEDIEVAL CATALONIA

Demography has not been a priority for later medieval historians during recent decades, and the result is that the demographic trends for later medieval Catalonia and the Crown of Aragon remain somewhat tentative. There is definite need of further study, both in interpreting existing sources and in researching new ones.[8] It is unlikely, however, that much will ever be able to be said with certainty about the dynamics of Catalan urban or rural populations prior to 1348, since no significant sources for this period have been discovered.[9] From indirect evidence such as archaeology and topography it has therefore been assumed that Catalonia more or less followed general European population movements during the high Middle Ages. From a very modest level around the year 1000, the population grew significantly during the eleventh and twelfth centuries. This growth accelerated and reached a crescendo during the thirteenth

in Devon after the Black Death, see Maryanne Kowaleski, *Local Markets and Regional Trade in Medieval Exeter* (Cambridge, 2003), pp. 15–16.

8 The standard reference is Agustín Rubio Vela, *Peste negra, crisis y comportamientos sociales en la España del siglo XVI: La ciudad de Valencia (1348–1401)* (Granada, 1979), pp. 154–78.

9 J. N. Hillgarth. *The Spanish Kingdoms*, vol. I (Oxford, 1976), p. 29.

century, so that towards 1300 the land could no longer sustain those who attempted to live from it. At that point, so-called 'Malthusian' pressures began to check the population increase, possibly reversing it.[10] Although there was a great famine between 1315–17 in England, France, and Northern Europe, Catalan demographers have found no evidence to suggest that these years were especially dire.[11] Catalonia's first and probably its worst famine of the fourteenth century occurred in 1333–4.[12] This was certainly exacerbated by overpopulation, though the extent of the losses has not yet been determined. Jordi Nadal, who remains a principal authority on medieval Catalan demography, places the decline in Catalan population between 1300 and 1347 at 5 per cent, and this would have included losses from 1333–4.[13] Manresan sources mention no deaths from starvation in 1333–4. Instead, the records of the town council state only that there was danger of this occurring in the city and its *vegueria*.[14] A bad harvest in 1336 precipitated a second famine during the winter and spring of 1336–7. On this occasion the council was better prepared to meet the crisis: in March of 1337 they ordered every able-bodied inhabitant of Manresa to join in a pilgrimage to the abbey at Montserrat, a journey of over fifteen kilometres, where they would join in a communal prayer for rain. Able-bodied people found in their homes during the pilgrimage were to be fined.[15] Since the second famine turned out to be less severe than the previous one, the pilgrims could feel that their supplications had not been in vain.[16] All in all, however, the 'crisis of the early fourteenth century' was not nearly as dramatic as it was in France, or as politically or demographically significant as it appears to have been in England.[17]

[10] For a summary of the debate between Postan, Harvey, Brenner and others on the principal movements of European (mainly English) demography between 1300 and 1348, see R. M. Smith, 'Demographic Developments in Rural England, 1300–1348: A Survey', in Bruce M. S. Campbell, *Before the Black Death: Studies in the 'Crisis' of the Early Fourteenth Century* (Manchester, 1992), pp. 25–78.

[11] Batlle, *L'Expansió baixmedieval*, p. 87. John Edwards, in *Christian Córdoba: The City and Its Region in the Late Middle Ages* (New York, 1982), p. 11, notes that Castile was 'not particularly affected' by the famine of 1315–17. The story of this famine is most comprehensively chronicled in William Chester Jordan, *The Great Famine* (Princeton, NJ, 1997).

[12] This is discussed in Chapter 4.

[13] Nadal, Jordi. *La población española (siglos XVI a XX)* (Barcelona, 1971), p. 66.

[14] MC 1334.2.19 (11k3). The phrase they use is *est dubium*.

[15] MC 1337.3.22 (11k4).

[16] The council also pursued a more practical course in response to the two droughts: they conceived of and constructed the great irrigation system known as the *sèquia*. This has been addressed in Chapter 2. For details on the *sèquia*, see Joaquim Sarret i Arbos, *La Cequia de Manresa* (Manresa, 1906).

[17] The standard work on this crisis in England is Bruce Campbell, *Before the Black Death: Studies in the 'Crisis' of the Early Fourteenth Century* (Manchester, 1992). For France see Jordan, *The Great Famine*.

The famines of the 1330s were soon overshadowed by the Black Death of 1348. The plague first reached Mallorca in December 1347, having been spread by ships out of Marseilles. The plague had spread to Roussillon by January 1348, and reached Manresa and most of the rest of Catalonia by May of that same year.[18] The current consensus is that the plague carried off between a quarter and a third of the Catalan population. This view has been endorsed by Thomas Bisson, though Jordi Nadal has estimated a total loss of only 20 per cent.[19] Christian Guilleré, who estimated a 15 per cent loss at Girona, used testamentary evidence which requires multiplication by two variables before it can be used to estimate a citywide figure. His estimate is therefore one of the more tentative, as well as being one of the lowest.[20] Other than these figures, we have little to guide us on Catalan losses in the first wave of plague. Turning to the surrounding regions, few reliable estimates of plague mortality exist in the historiography of Castile. In northern France, Guy Bois has estimated a 30 per cent loss from the Black Death in certain regions of eastern Normandy.[21]

In contrast to the general estimates for plague mortality, which tend to be in the 20 to 35 per cent range, many local studies have yielded more chilling figures, in the range of 50 per cent or even higher. The most comprehensive Catalan study, by Pladevall, has estimated that 66 per cent of the inhabitants of the plain of Vic perished in 1348.[22] The study of Perpignan published by Richard Emery has received less notice from recent Catalan demographers, but it remains important: Emery calculated that of 125 scribes and legists working in Perpignan, between 54 and 58 per cent had perished in the plague.[23] From southern France, Christian Guilleré has published a letter in which the vicar of Narbonne, writing to the *jurats* of Girona in April 1348, warned them against the

18 Ole J. Benedictow, *The Black Death 1346–1353: The Complete History* (Martlesham, UK, 2006), pp. 77–81. (Note, however, that 'January 1349' on page 77 should read 'January 1348'.)

19 MCOA, 165; Jordi Nadal, 'La vraie richesse: Les hommes', in Joaquim Nadal and P. Wolff (eds.), *Histoire de Catalogne* (Toulouse, 1982), pp. 61–90, esp. p. 62; Paul Freedman, *The Origins of Peasant Servitude in Medieval Catalonia* (Cambridge, 1991), p. 162; Carmen Batlle, in *L'Expansió baixmedieval*, avoids committing to an overall estimate, citing a lack of comprehensive studies.

20 Christian Guilleré, 'La peste noire à Gérone (1348)', *Annals de l'Institut d'Estudis Gironins*, 27 (1984), 87–161.

21 Guy Bois. *The Crisis of Feudalism: Economy and Society in Eastern Normandy, ca. 1300–1550* (Cambridge, 1984), p. 57.

22 Antoni Pladevall i Font, 'La disminució de poblament a la Plana de Vic a mitjans del segle XIV', 361–73. This study is quoted by Elisenda Gràcia i Mont, *Estructura agrària de la Plana de Vic al segle XIV* (Barcelona, 1989), p. 25, and via this route has worked its way into the standard accounts of Bisson, Freedman, and Batlle.

23 Richard W. Emery, 'The Black Death of 1348 in Perpignan', *Speculum*, 42 (1967), 611–23, at 614–15.

coming plague.[24] He estimated that one quarter of his city's inhabitants had already perished during the plague, but his estimate was written at a time when the epidemic was still raging, and so the final estimate of the dead would presumably have been much higher. Incidentally, the vicar believed that the plague had been started by a group of men disguised as mendicant friars. These, he reports, had been hired by 'the enemies of France' to place noxious aromatic potions in churches, homes, wells, and food supplies. From Manresa, we have a bailiff's inquest that yields a very high mortality figure: in a random sample of eighty-eight homeowners taken in 1350, forty-three of them, or 49 per cent, were listed as 'recently deceased'.[25]

As it happened, the epidemic of 1348–50 was not to be a one-time occurrence. The plague bacillus remained quite active in Europe for the next three and a half centuries, and the last well-known epidemic occurred in Marseilles as late as 1720. In Barcelona, one of the last major outbreaks occurred during the siege of 1651–2, and an earlier outbreak in 1589–90 may have wiped out one quarter of the city's population.[26] For the late medieval period, Carmen Batlle, following Pierre Vilar, notes recurrences of the plague in 1362, 1371, 1374, 1381, 1396, 1410, 1429, 1439, and 1448.[27] She notes that another outbreak in 1457 was especially grave, an allegation supported by the Manresan evidence.[28] Though the epidemic in 1362–3 was called 'the children's plague' by some chroniclers, the actions of the Manresan councillors suggest that this outbreak inaugurated the acute labour shortage that would vex Catalan elites for a century and a half.[29]

Unfortunately, the demographic sources for Catalonia and Manresa commence only from 1365, after the labour shortage had become acute. In addition to several fragmentary surveys, three complete but still problematic lists drawn up for the hearth taxes known as *fogatges* exist for the

[24] Guilleré, 'La peste noire à Gérone (1348)', 55: 'vobis . . . notificamus quod in Narbona . . . est et fuit per totam quadrigesimam et adhuc non desivit, tanta gentium mortalitas ex qua quarta pars habitantium secundum comunem opinionem extiterit interfecta.' (I inform you that in Narbonne, throughout Lent and continuing to this day, there has been such a mortality amongst the people that according to general opinion a fourth part of the inhabitants have been killed.) The letter is also cited in David Nirenberg, *Communities of Violence: Persecution of Minorities in the Middle Ages* (Princeton, NJ, 1996), p. 233.

[25] See below, n. 5.

[26] James S. Amelang, *Honored Citizens of Barcelona: Patrician Culture and Class Relations, 1490–1714* (Princeton, NJ, 1986), 8.

[27] See Pierre Vilar, 'Le declin catalan du bas Moyen Age: Hypothèses sur sa chronologie', *Estudios de Historia Moderna*, 6 (1956–9): 1–68, at p. 6.

[28] For the '*mortaldat dels infants*' see Batlle, *L'Expansio baixmedieval*, p. 252, and Vilar, 'Le declin Catalane', 6. For the Manresan evidence see Table 7.1.

[29] This is discussed in Chapter 5, pp. 138–9.

latter fourteenth century. The dates usually assigned to these are 1365, 1378, and 1381, though these are contestable, as will be discussed below. Although some demographers have treated the 1378 and 1381 surveys as significantly different data sets, in fact the numbers they report are so similar, and the three plague-free years that separate them represent so insignificant a time span, that they may be taken as a single demographic source. After these, the next complete survey does not occur until 1497. Taken together, these surveys suggest that in contrast to Italy, where population levels began to recover by the 1450s, Catalonia continued to lose population throughout the entire fifteenth century.[30] The destructive civil war of 1462–72, which seems to have been devastating to the population of Manresa, probably had much to do with this.[31] The protracted conflict also caused a mass exodus from Catalonia to Valencia, adding to the prosperity of the latter kingdom even as it drained the vitality of the *principat*. Indeed, Hillgarth saw the civil war as the event that finally wrecked Catalonia's medieval prosperity, and this impression has been confirmed by the work of Alan Ryder.[32]

In her summary of the demographic evidence, Carmen Batlle endorses the now-traditional view that Catalan population had peaked at half a million in the early fourteenth century. The number is based on Jaume Vicens Vives' estimate of a peak population of 900,000 for the entire Crown of Aragon. For her estimate of the population at the time of the 1365 *fogatge*, however, Batlle follows an unnamed study for an estimate of 468,000. From the 1378 and 1381 *fogatges*, which she treats as a single source, she estimates 374,000; and in 1497, she suggests that there were only 268,000 souls inhabiting the *principat*.[33] An obvious problem with this set of figures is that they yield a scarcely credible 6.4 per cent decrease between the pre-plague peak of circa 1300–30 and the era of acute labour shortage in 1365. Given that the Black Death killed at least 20 per cent of the populace in 1348, it is clear that either the 1300–30 figure is too low or the 1365 figure is too high. Bisson suggests that it is in fact the first number, based on Vicens Vives' estimate of 900,000 for the entire Crown of Aragon, that is probably too low, although he seems reluctant to put the pre-plague peak at much more than 500,000 despite his belief that

30 For fifteenth-century Italy, see Brian S. Pullan, *A History of Early Renaissance Italy: From Mid-thirteenth to the Mid-fifteenth Century* (London, 1973), pp. 208–12. David Herlihy and Christiane Klapisch-Zuber, in *Tuscans and their Families*, p. 64, contended that Tuscan population stabilized after 1410; Cohn suggests the same in Samuel K. Cohn Jr, *Creating the Florentine State: Peasants and Rebellion, 1348–1434* (Cambridge, 2000), p. 214.

31 See Table 7.1 and sources for the effects of the civil war on Manresan population.

32 J. N. Hillgarth, *The Spanish Kingdoms*, vol. II, pp. 296–7; Alan Ryder, *The Wreck of Catalonia: Civil War in the Fifteenth Century* (Oxford and New York, 2007).

33 Batlle, *L'Expansio baixmedieval*, pp. 89, 255.

the Black Death carried off between 25 and 35 per cent of the Catalan population.[34]

Nadal's figures are even lower than Batlle's: he estimates 477,000 for 1347, 381,000 for 1359 and 340,000 for 1365. His estimate for 1347 is based upon the hypothesis, arrived at by conjecture, that the Black Death killed 20 per cent of the populace.[35] Nadal's estimate for the latest medieval survey, in 1497, is a scant 224,356. This figure is in

[34] MCOA, 169–5.

[35] This is a particularly confused issue in the historiography, and so justifies a longer footnote. The 20 per cent figure is found in Jordi Nadal, 'La vraie richesse', p. 62. Nadal then added this to his estimate for 1359–60. He tells us that he derived his figure for 1365–6 by subtracting 12.13 per cent from his 1359–60 figure, which he says was the rate of attrition observed in the number of royal hearths between 1359 and 1365. Precisely which surveys were used by Nadal to determine this rate of attrition is not addressed. More importantly, Nadal's series of calculations indicates that he and Vilar are not in agreement over the dating of the *fogatges*, a situation not commented upon in Freedman's synopsis of late medieval Catalan demography. For Vilar's chronology, see Pierre Vilar, 'Quelques problèmes de démographie historique en Catalogne et en Espagne' ['Communication faite à l'assemblée de la Société en juin 1964']. *Annales de Démographie Historique* (1965), 2–31, at 17.

Freedman follows Vilar's chronology of the fourteenth-century *fogtages*, which places them at 1365, 1378, and 1381, while Nadal appears to place them at 1359, 1378, and 1381. Freedman's account of the dating of the *fogatges* is now standard and should be quoted in full: 'The manuscripts claim to have been drawn up in 1359, 1376, and 1378. Iglésies, and later Vilar, rectified the order of the surveys. It now appears that the '1359' census was the latest, from 1381; that the '1376' census dates from 1365, and that the 1378 census is accurately dated. For the chronology and sources of the *fogatges*, see Freedman, *Origins of Peasant Servitude*, p. 163.

But there is still some disagreement. According to Iglésies, Vilar, and Freedman, the '1359' *fogatge* dates from 1381, whereas Nadal treats the '1359' *fogatge* as though it truly dates from 1359, even though he also mentions a *fogatge* from 1381, which should be impossible. Likewise, Nadal makes no mention of the '1376' *fogatge* that is now believed to date from 1365, unless this is the survey that he used to calculate the attrition rate for royal hearths between 1359 and 1365. In this case, it still appears as though Nadal has conjured four *fogatges* from three. Though Nadal's figures are at present the most authoritative, these confusions reveal that the later fourteenth-century *fogatge* data stands in need of further examination. Because the '1359' *fogatge* and the 1378 *fotatge* report almost an identical number of hearths for many localities, including Manresa, and because these figures are significantly different form the '1365' figures, we will side with the majority opinion and assume for the rest of this discussion that the '1359' *fogatge* is indeed from 1381.

Only slightly less uncertain than the gap between pre-plague peak and the 1365 *fogatge*, if we assume along with Iglésies, Vilar, and Freedman that there is no 1359 *fogatge*, is the true extent of the loss that occurred between the 1365 *fogatge* and the nearly identical surveys of 1378 and 1381. The figures quoted by Hillgarth, of 530,000 and 400,000 for 1365 and 1378 respectively, were revised by Jordi Nadal, whose calculations lowered them to 340,184 and 293,352. Nadal's figures make a pre-plague peak of 500,000, followed by a 30 per cent loss between 1333 and 1365, seem more credible. See Nadal, 'La vraie richesse', 62.

The entry dated 1374.12.20 from the Manresan council manuals, quoted in Table 7.1, suggests that the councillors had approved the re-use of the number of hearths from the 1365 *fogatge* for a new survey: hence it is probable that the '1376' *fogatge* is not 'misdated', but rather a re-use of the earlier *fogatge* numbers. This would have been done for convenience, and possibly because it was felt that the population of the principality had not declined by a significant number between these dates; in any event, if population had declined during this time, the re-use of the 1365 *fogatge* numbers was to the Crown's advantage.

Table 7.1 *The population of Manresa, 1300–1500*[36]

Date	Hearths	Estimated population	% Decline (base 1365)	Source
1300	1,000–1,550	4,500–7,000		Estimate only; see text
1365–70	691	3,110	0.0	Fogatge of 1365
1374	691	3,110	0.0	MC 1374.12.20
(1378	*463*	*2,084*	*33.3*	*Fogatge of 1378)*
(1381	*463*	*2,084*	*33.3*	*Fogatge of 1381)*
1408–11	602[37]	2,709	12.9	AHCM I-165
1453	425	1,913	38.5	AHCM I-168
1480–82	263	1,184	61.9	AHCM I-169
1490–93	263	1,184	61.9	AHCM I-171
1497	272	1,224	60.6	Fogatge of 1497

Population has been estimated using a multiplier of 4.5 inhabitants per household.[38]

accord with the consensus that by 1500 Catalonia had suffered a total population decrease of over 50 per cent from the pre-plague peak.[39] While this loss sounds staggering, it should be kept in mind that in the Pistoiese countryside Herlihy noted a 25 per cent population decrease between 1244 and the eve of the Black Death, and another 40 per cent decline between 1348 and 1383. These were followed by a further loss between 1383 and 1404, for a total loss of over 70 per cent off the thirteenth-century medieval peak.[40] It therefore appears as though the

[36] Sources: The figures from *llibres de manifests* (AHCM volumes) are from Marc Torras Serra, *La crisi del segle XV a Manresa*, 37–8. On the somewhat convoluted dating and citations of the *fogatges* see Paul Freedman, *Origins of Peasant Servitude*, 163, n. 32.
Notes: Number of hearths in the base year of 1365 = 691.

[37] This figure represents the number of households whose heads were alive and resident at Manresa in 1408–11. This has been chosen, rather than the total number of households and estates recorded (640), because it represents a minimum figure. It could be argued, however, that the figure of 640 is more accurate, since this represented the total number of households which the Manresan redactors considered to be active in their city at any one time, barring the accidents of householder death or relocation, and the accession of Manresan heirs.

[38] Urban household multipliers have not received much attention in recent decades. David Herlihy remains the best source for estimating the size of a southern European urban household in the later middle ages. To my knowledge, no attempt has yet been made for an Iberian city. In *Tuscans and their Families*, 69, Herlihy reports that the mean household size in Florence in 1380 is known to have been 4.19. I have chosen 4.5, partly because of the arguments of J. Krause, who in 'The Medieval Household: Large or Small?' argued convincingly against J. C. Russell's earlier attempts to argue that English household multipliers were smaller than 4.5 or 5.

[39] Nadal, 'La vraie richesse', 62.

[40] Herlihy, *Medieval and Renaissance Pistoia*, pp. 68–71. For English and French sources citing between a 33 and 50 per cent loss between 1348 and 1500, see n. 17, above.

current estimate of late medieval Catalan depopulation is, if anything, too modest. The caution evident in the latest figures is a prudent one stemming from the lack of a reliable pre-plague source. Current estimates of the medieval peak are probably too low, especially as they rest on Nadal's undoubtedly too conservative estimate of a 20 per cent loss in 1348.

Fortunately, Manresa's archives contain a number of sources that can complement and even challenge some of the figures provided by the *fogatges*. They therefore represent an important contribution to Catalan demography as a whole. Most valuable are the Manresan *llibres de manifests* which give exact counts of heads of household, including richest and poorest, but excluding clergy and perhaps a few of the lower nobility, for the years 1408–11, 1453, 1480–2, and 1490–3. Table 7.1 combines these with the other verifiable sources for the city's population.[41] Taken together, the story they tell is one of dramatic decline. In 1300, Manresa was a bourgeoning regional centre. It had recently been made the capital of a *vegueria*, an ambitious ecclesiastical building programme was proceeding apace, and its citizens felt confident enough to assert their right to the title of *civitas*, perhaps even to an episcopal chair. How chimerical these visions seemed by 1497. By that time, Manresa was scarcely more than a large village. Little of its former importance remained, except for its (now complete) churches, a circuit of turreted walls and its now somewhat ill-fitting title of *civitas*.

When the available demographic figures for Manresa are examined, an anomaly stands out in the number of hearths reported by the *fogatges* of 1378 and 1381. The 1365 figure, confirmed by the Manresan councillors in December 1374, was 691 households. Meanwhile, the *Liber Manifesti* of 1408–11 counted 602 households headed by living and resident householders, suggesting a simple decrease of 12.5 per cent over thirty-four years. If we incorporate the 1378 and 1381 figures of 463 households into this data, however, we are left with a curious zigzag pattern, whereby Manresa's population fell precipitously to 67 per cent of its former level in the four years between 1374 and 1378, and then climbed back up to 87 per cent of the 1365–74 total by 1408. Only then, according to this model, did the city finally begin its fifteenth-century decline. The supposed decline between 1365–74 and 1378 is rendered all the more startling by the fact that the city registered at least fifty-six

[41] For evidence that the de Talamancas and the de Manresas were two of a handful of knightly families owning property within the bailiwick of Manresa (perhaps the only such), see MC 1381.10.28 and 1380.11.29.

new householders during the same period.[42] It is therefore likely that the 1378 and 1381 figures are not correct, and the obvious conclusion is that the *fogatges* of 1378 and 1381 have for some reason under-reported the true number of households. Even if the 1374 confirmation is ignored, there are no grounds for supposing that the city lost 33 per cent of its population between 1365 and 1378. And yet the details of the December 1374 confirmation suggest that the number of 691 hearths was still an apt census figure at that time. On 20 December, the town councillors agreed to pay a royal subsidy of one florin per household. If the councillors felt that the 1365–70 *fogatge* was grossly exaggerating the number of households in their city, especially since this was only three years from the 1378 figure of 463 *focs*, they would have made some protest to the king, which so far as can be told they did not do. Instead it must be assumed that the councillors thought 691 to be a reasonable estimate of the city's number of households: they would have had a very good idea of the true figure, since they had drawn up a *Liber Manifesti* as recently as 1369.[43] Unfortunately this manifest was sabotaged just before it was completed, and no known copies have survived.

If it is indeed the case that the 1378 and 1381 *fogatges* under-reported the true number of households for Manresa, what is left is a much more believable pattern of slow but continuous decline in the later fourteenth century. This presents another dilemma, which is that Manresan population losses thereby become less severe than might be expected. Between 1365 and 1408, many European populations tended to contract more severely than Manresa's 12.5 per cent. The best direct southern European comparison remains Pistoia, in which Herlihy found a 37 per cent decline during the twenty-one years between 1383 and 1404.[44] In England, the population of perhaps 5 million on the eve of the Black Death is held to have dropped to less than 3 million by the mid-fifteenth century, and France is held to have lost more than one third of its population during the same period.[45] Paul Freedman has also noted this pattern

42 This figure is taken from data compiled from MC 1365–78.

43 MC 1369.5.1. The drawing up of this manifest is discussed in Chapter 5, pp. 150–1. It is likely that the manifest was destroyed after the next year's council voted against using this method of taxation. Using a manifest was a highly politicized issue since it caused taxes to be assessed based on wealth and thus ensured that all people bore a proportional share of the communal tax burden. The usual method of consumption taxation ensured that the poor (and politically under-represented) bore a disproportionate share of the tax burden. Tax assessment by manifest was also potentially dangerous insofar as royal officials could use such a manifest for future assessments. For the rejection of the manifest by the *jurats*, see MC 1370.8.20.

44 Herlihy, *Medieval and Renaissance Pistoia*, p. 70.

45 The English and French figures are found in Josiah C. Russell, 'Population in Europe', in Carlo M. Cipolla (ed.), *The Fontana Economic History of Europe*, vol. I: The Middle Ages (Glasgow,

of a seemingly 'delayed' demographic decline experienced by Catalonia, relative to other population centres.[46] Two Catalan historians have studied a 1393 survey from the county of Pallars that showed a population level close to the 1365–70 *fogatge* figure, while the 1378 and 1381 surveys would have registered a 60 per cent decline.[47] Regarding this anomaly Freedman suggests that the surveys of 1378 and 1381 undercounted hearths in mountainous regions such as Erill.[48] The 1408 *Liber Manifesti* provides evidence that these two surveys underestimated the number of hearths in cities as well as in mountainous regions, albeit at a less exaggerated rate of 33 versus 60 per cent.[49]

A final, highly significant pattern to emerge from the Manresan evidence is the very marked decline in Manresa's population between 1453 and 1480 – some 38 per cent in twenty-seven years, as compared with a 30 per cent decline in the forty-five years between 1408 and 1453. The probable causes of the post-1453 fall are the combined effects of the plague of 1457, which was called 'especially severe' by Batlle, and the civil war of 1462–72. The manifests enable us to pinpoint, for the first time, the period 1455–80 as the true nadir of the city's demographic fortunes, the time period which saw Manresa's population plummet until it could hardly be counted as more than a small market town.

So much for the population trends in Manresa after 1365. Can anything be said of the period prior to this? Nadal estimated about a 12 per cent mortality in the plague of 1362–3, and there seems little reason to argue with him on this score. If some Manresan historians have posited a higher figure, this seems impossible to prove; and in any event this plague did not cause nearly the amount of political or social disruption experienced by the city after the Black Death.[50] As noted above, one piece of evidence helps us to estimate mortality rates in the city during the Black Death itself. A tome whose cover identifies it as the Manresan council manual for December 1350 through January 1352 is not, as it turns out, a council

1972), pp. 25–71. See also John Hatcher, *Plague, Population, and the English Economy, 1348–1530* (Basingstoke, 1977). For a more recent confirmation of Hatcher's figures see Richard Britnell, 'The economy of British towns 1300–1540', in David M. Palliser (ed.), *The Cambridge Urban History of Britain*, vol. I: *600–1540* (Cambridge, 2000), pp. 313–33.

46 Freedman, *Origins*, pp. 164–6. Although for an argument that Holland was not as strongly affected by demographic decline as other Western European regions see Bas J. P. van Bavel and Jan Luiten van Zanden, 'The jump-start of the Holland economy during the Late Medieval Crisis, c.1350–c.1500', *Economic History Review*, 57:3 (2004), 503–32.

47 See Ignasi Puig and Montserrat Duran, 'La crisi demogràfica de la baixa edat mitjana i el règim senyorial en el Pireneu català: La Baronia d'Erill el 1393', *Urgellia*, 6 (1983), 387–400.

48 Freedman, *Origins of Peasant Servitude*, p. 163.

49 *Ibid.*, pp. 169–74.

50 See Benet i Clara, 'La població de la ciutat de Manresa als segles XVI–XVII', in *Primer Congrés d'Història Moderna de Catalunya. Actas*, vol. I (Barcelona, 1984), pp. 85–9.

manual at all.[51] Rather, it is a record of the Manresan bailiff's inquest into the homes of forty-one Manresan heads of household who had recently died. Since record keeping in the city had virtually ceased between May 1348 and December of 1350, it can be inferred that most of the victims being tallied in this list are likely to have been victims of the Black Death. By itself, this sample can tell us little about the number of those who died in the plague, except to give us a bare minimum number of householders who perished. This would be 41 of 742, or 5.6 per cent, with the latter figure being derived by adding 41 to the 1365 figure of 691 households. In the course of describing the houses of the deceased, however, the bailiff's assessor followed the usual practice of situating these houses by referring to the names of the owners of the adjacent homes and properties. Because the houses described were townhouses, they normally shared walls with between two and four other dwellings. To a reader of this list it soon becomes apparent that a high proportion of the homeowners and landowners adjacent to these homes had also died. Legally, a home or piece of land whose owner has died is described as belonging to the 'heirs of' such and such a person. When one tallies the adjacent houses and properties that belonged to a named individual, versus those belonging to the 'heirs of' the previous owner, one finds that forty-three owners out of eighty-eight, or 49 per cent, had recently died. It should be noted that by tallying only the adjacent properties, and not the homes that were actually under inquest, one arrives at an entirely random sample of Manresan homeowners. To include the houses under investigation would undermine the randomness of the sample, since these properties were under inquest because the owners had died.

It is also true that not all of the mortality in this sample was necessarily caused by the Black Death, since even during plague years, people continued to die of natural causes. Emery found that during the course of a normal two-year period, 6.35 per cent of the scribes of Perpignan perished from regularly occurring causes.[52] If this rate is applied to Manresan homeowners and property owners, it can be concluded that between May 1348 and December of 1351, when the Manresan bailiff's inquest was half over, one arrives at a figure of 9.53 per cent for normal attrition between plague and inquest. This suggests that just under 40 per cent of the homeowners had actually died in the plague. The Manresan bailiff's inquest therefore suggests that between 40 and 50 per cent of the city's homeowners died in the plague of 1348. This is very much in keeping with the findings of Emery and Pladavall. Some English

51 In AHCM/AM I-4 1348.2.8–1352.7.31.

52 Emery, 'The Black Death of 1348 in Perpignan', 615.

demographers have concluded that rates of mortality were higher in the towns than in the countryside, giving figures of something like 50 per cent for towns and 30 per cent for the countryside.[53] Given the Catalan evidence for high mortality in town and country, it is possible that such generalizations cannot be applied from region to region.

As a final piece of evidence regarding mortality rates in the Black Death, we can turn to the records of the *Corts*. In a list of Catalan knights who were invited to attend the *Corts* of Perpignan in August 1350, seventeen out of thirty-five letters, exactly 49 per cent, were sent to the 'heirs of' a recently deceased knight.[54] Since these knights were relatively prosperous members of the castellany, it should be expected that, if anything, mortality amongst this group was lower than amongst the castellany at large. In contrast to this bleak figure, only seven out of forty-two barons, or 17 per cent, had perished in the plague and not had their estates settled. Extreme wealth might therefore have been an effective ward against the Black Death, although it is possible that the baronies were so important that their inheritance issues were more speedily set forth than was the case with the castellanies. In any event, the possession of a rural estate and a significant fortune seems to have been of little avail to many members of the castellanate.[55]

WAGES AND SALARIES

The effects of these demographic shocks on the Catalan economy, as indeed on the European economy, were experienced over a period of about three decades as a dramatic rise in nominal wages and prices. This effect increased as subsequent waves of the plague struck. After the first wave of bubonic plague in 1348, Catalan nominal wages jumped by about 50 per cent.[56] With continuing depopulation, wages by the 1380s and 90s had reached a plateau of about 200 per cent of pre-plague levels. Gregory Clark has found that in England during these same years, real wages peaked at a level that they would not again reach until the 1870s.[57]

53 A. F. Butcher, 'English Urban Society and the Revolt of 1381', in R. H. Hilton and T. H. Aston (eds.), *The English Rising of 1381* (Cambridge, 1984), pp. 84–111, at p. 87.

54 *Cortes*, I-2, 341–2.

55 *Cortes*, I-2, 340–1. This figure could underestimate noble mortality, since the question of succession among the nobility might have been resolved more quickly than amongst the heirs of knights and townsmen.

56 This is taken from Table 7.2.

57 Clark, 'Work, Wages and Living Conditions', p. 919. The same conclusion is stated in Allen, 'The Great Divergence in European Wages and Prices from the Middle Ages to the First World War', 435.

The effects of the plague on the social order should therefore not be underestimated. It should be emphasized that our Catalan figures cannot be used with quite as much confidence, since they are 'nominal wage' figures rather than 'real wage' figures. That means our figures represent the actual amount of money, in *diners de tern* of Barcelona, which a person received per day. These figures must be adjusted for the price of goods in order to arrive at an estimate of 'real wages'. The normal way for economic historians to do this is to divide their nominal wage figures by the value of an agreed-upon 'basket of goods' which, it is hoped, represents the things that an average person would both need and wish to purchase in the process of normal household life. In this way, economists attempt to measure whether or not the nominal figures represented a genuine increase in purchasing power. While some Catalan prices have come to light during the course of our research, as yet there are not enough figures, either published or unpublished, to create a 'basket of goods' for the purpose of measuring real wages in a definitive sense. In the meantime, nominal wages will have to serve – though some price data presented below can provide some suggestions as to the course taken by real wages as well. Although wage rates for later medieval Europe are usually computed from surviving workmen's wages, the Manresan documentation also enables us to say something about the earning power of salaried employees who hailed from the middle and upper classes. These salary rates for professional work will be presented below, after the section on wages.

Both wages and salaries were paid in the *diner de tern* of Barcelona, about which something further should be said at this point.[58] This system of money is based upon the Carolingian system of pounds, shillings, and pence, where one shilling, called a *sou* (plural *sous*) in Catalan, equalled twelve pence, called a *diner* (plural *diners*). Twenty shillings, or 240 pence, equalled a pound, known in Catalan as a *lliura*.[59] In 1346, Pere III introduced an Aragonese gold florin into the currency system of his realms, in imitation of the Genoese, Venetian, and Florentine gold coinage which were all highly admired and used by merchants and financiers throughout the Mediterranean world.[60] The value of this coin was fixed by an edict of 1365 at eleven *sous* of Barcelona and remained at that level for the rest

58 A brief overview of the coinage system is also available above on pp. xix–xx.

59 The abbreviation for pound was 'll'; for *sou* 's'; and for *diner* 'd'.

60 Batlle, in *L'Expansio baixmedieval*, p. 308, notes that the florin was introduced soon after the conquest of Mallorca as a prestige coinage. The inauguration of this coin also took advantage of a favourable gold/silver ratio. See Carlo Cipolla, *The Monetary Policy of Fourteenth Century Florence* (Berkeley, 1982), pp. 16–17.

of the century.[61] Because this tended to overvalue the Aragonese florin vis-à-vis the silver currency, this new gold coin never gained wide acceptance at Manresa, nor was it generally used to quote salaries for Catalan municipal officials. Throughout the later medieval period, wages, salaries, and the prices of most commodities were generally quoted in *sous* or *lliures*, based on the silver *diners de tern*.[62]

More than half a century ago, in 1962, José María Doñate described the historiography of wages and prices in the Crown of Aragon as *escasisima* (quite sparse), and, with a handful of exceptions, this remains an apt description.[63] In Doñate's day, as in ours, knowledge of wage levels prior to 1380 rests primarily on the researches of Earl Hamilton for Navarre, whose study was published in 1933.[64] Hamilton has wage series for Aragon (after 1380) and Valencia (after 1395), but as yet no series of wages has been published for Catalonia. There is enough Catalan evidence, both published and in the Manresan records, to suggest that Catalan nominal wages did not do much more than double their pre-Black Death level between 1347 and 1400. This is a significant scaling back of the current estimates which have them quadrupling or quintupling over the same period.[65] The most important, though poorly organized, set of published data for this period remains Doñate's 1962 series from the Valencian town of Vilarreal, covering the years between 1348 and 1400.[66]

61 Pierre Vilar, *Catalunya dins l'Espanya moderna*, vol. II (Barcelona, 1979), p. 177. See also Carme Batlle Gallart, *La crisis social y economica de Barcelona a mediados del siglo XV*, 2 vols. (Barcelona, 1973), p. 84. Peter Spufford, *Handbook of Medieval Exchange* (London, 1986) has very little data on the *diner de tern* of Barcelona, reflecting the state of publication on the subject. My own investigation into the ACA Royal Treasury registers confirms that this rate held between 1366.6.1 (reg. no. 347) and 1408.4.4 (reg. no. 407). Between 1350.4.3 (reg. no. 323) and 1364.5.12 (reg. no. 345) the Aragonese florin fluctuated between 12s 3d and 11s 6d Barcelona. I have not investigated the registers beyond 1408.

62 See Hamilton, *Money, Prices, and Wages*, pp. 270–2, for Valencian salaries; for Barcelona salaries see Y van Roustit, 'La consolidation de la dette publique à Barcelone au milieu du XIVe siècle,' *Estudios de Historia Moderna*, 4 (1954), 13–156. For Manresan salaries, see tables in this chapter.

63 José M. Doñate, 'Salarios y precios durante la segunda mitad del siglo XIV', *VII Congrés d'Història de la Corona d'Aragó*, 2 (1962), 417–506; 417 n. 1. See also Fernando Zulaica Palacios, 'Fluctuaciones económicas en un período de crisis: Precios y salarios en Aragón en la baja edad media (1300–1430)', Zaragoza, Doctoral Thesis, 1993. Fernando Zulaica Palacios, 'Evolución de los precios y salarios aragoneses entre 1300 y 1430', *Aragón en la edad media*, 12 (1995), pp. 123–52; and Caterina Argilés i Aluja, 'Preus i salaris a la Lleida dels segles XIV i XV segons els llibres d'obra de la seu', Doctoral Thesis, Universitat de Lleida, 1994.

64 What work has been done, e.g. by Doñate, Zulaica, and Argilés, remains virtually unknown except to a handful of specialists. But there is probably a lesson to be learned here, which is that a good economic series is one of the more enduring contributions that a historical researcher can make.

65 These estimates, quoted in Batlle, *L'Expansió baixmedieval*, pp. 296–300, are likely based on Hamilton's unadjusted wage data, which shows Navarrese nominal wages quintupling over the period in question.

66 See n. 63, above.

The published records of the Catalan *Corts* have yielded a number of rates from the labour statutes of 1350 and a single pre-Black Death reference from 1321, which was 1s/day for a draper's assistant.[67] With respect to unpublished sources, the Manresan council manuals have yielded a number of references, especially between 1370 and 1375 when the city hired many workers in a desperate scramble to upgrade its defences. In Barcelona the records of the *Consell de Cent* yield an occasional reference, but the *Obreria de la Seu* series in the Cathedral archive, deliberately ignored by Hamilton because it is not consistent over the long term, yields hundreds of references for the years between 1375 and 1395. The data that has been analysed thus far is summarized in Table 7.2. According to our findings, between 1360 and 1400, Catalan wage levels hovered between 1.57 and 2.11 times their pre-plague level.[68] They therefore followed what has now come to be accepted as a standard European pattern for wage increases during this period.[69] During the 1350s, they rose to 150 per cent of their previous levels, then climbed quite slowly during the 1360s. During the late 1370s they began to climb again, reaching a peak of just over 200 per cent of their pre-plague levels during the 1380s. After the ascension of Joan I in 1387 wages dipped slightly, recovering

[67] For the 1321 references, see *Cortes*, II, 264. The labour statutes appear as Appendix IV in an unpublished dissertation by Melanie Shirk, 'Royal Reaction to the Black Death in the Crown of Aragon, 1348–1351', University of Kansas, 1975.

[68] These findings are not dissonant with Zulaica's findings for Zaragoza and environs, or for Argilés' findings for Lleida, both of which calculate real wages based primarily on the price of wheat. Zulaica's findings are particularly interesting because they date back to 1297; he sees a rise of perhaps 50 per cent in the price of wheat between 1300 and 1348, and then a modest rise of perhaps 50 per cent further between 1348 and 1420. At the same time, wages rose by about 80 per cent between 1300 and 1348, and continued to rise by another 120 per cent of 1300 levels by 1400. In short, while the price of wheat rose to 200 per cent of 1300 levels by 1420, salaries had risen to about 300 per cent of 1300 levels by 1420. In general the purchasing power of labourers thus increased about 50 per cent between 1300 and 1420, with the majority of this gain coming after 1348.

[69] For an exposition of this pattern in nominal wages, see Henry Phelps Brown and Sheila V. Hopkins, *Seven Centuries of the Prices of Consumables, Compared with Builders' Wage-rates* (London, 1956), p. 11. The authors found a steep climb in wage rates between 1350 and 1370, amounting to a 66 per cent increase for craftsmen and a 100 per cent increase for labourers. Both series levelled off at their new high rates between 1370 and 1402, and were followed by another gain of between 12 and 20 per cent between 1402 and 1412. Wages for craftsmen and labourers stayed at the 1412 rate until the 1530s and 40s respectively. Phelps Brown and Hopkins' real wage indices have been recalculated by John Munro in 'Wage-stickiness, Monetary Changes, and Real Incomes in Late-medieval England and the Low Countries, 1300–1500: Did Money Matter?', *Research in Economic History*, 21:1 (2003), 185–297, esp. 243–4. These indices show an increase between 1346–50 and 1401–5 from an index number of 36.5 to 68.7; over the longer term, then, nominal and real wage trends were in broad agreement during the period under question. However it is now accepted that real wages actually fell between 1350 and 1370–80 in England and the Low Countries. For an explanation of this trend, see Munro, 'Builders' Wages', pp. 1036–41, and accompanying tables.

Table 7.2 *Nominal wage trends in Catalonia, 1321–1400*[70]

Period	Average wage (*sous*/day)	Number of references	Index (1321–50 = 100)
(1321–50)	1.35	14	100
1350–9	2.00	1	148
1360–9	2.12	12	157
1370–9	2.52	70	186
1380–9	2.82	46	208
1390–9	2.76	40	204

some of this loss during the mid-1390s. In accordance with Hamilton's graphs for Valencia, Aragon and Navarre, Catalan wages stayed close to their mid-1390s level for the entire first half of the fifteenth century.[71]

An interesting and important distinction is also revealed when the Manresa and Vilarreal data is separated from the Barcelona data: it appears as if wages in the capital were significantly higher than in the smaller towns, as can be seen in Table 7.3. This data suggests that workmen in the metropolis earned on average a full shilling more per day than their provincial brethren. Barcelona workers earned nearly 250 per cent of the

70 Sources: One reference from 1321 has been taken from the *Cortes*, I-1, 264. Other references for 1350 and before have come from Doñate, '*Precios y salarios durante la segunda mitad del siglo XIV*' and Shirk, *Royal Reaction to the Black Death*, Appendix IV, 161–8. A single reference for 1357 has come from MC 1357.12.19. References for the 1360s have come from Doñate, and AHCB, *Consell de Cent, Obreria* XIV-3, 87r, and AHCB *Consell de Cent, Clavaria*, XI-8, 1368–9. References for the 1370s, 80s, and 90s have come from Doñate, MC, and the Arxiu de la Catedral de Barcelona (ACB), *Obra de la Seu* series. In addition, four references for the 1390s have come from AHCB, *Consell de Cent, Clavaria*, XI-17, 170v, 172v, 174v, and 188r.
Notes: The figures from the statutes of labourers promulgated in *Corts* in May 1350, have been included in the 'pre-Black Death' category, since they correspond almost exactly with other pre-plague data, and also because they were the *Corts*' attempt to keep wages at pre-plague rates. For all categories, only working-class labour for adult males has been included, and the most common figures are for masons and stonecutters (Catalan *piquers*). In the Manresan council manuals, as well as in the *Obreria de la Seu* series, there is no appreciable difference in wage rates between these two principal work types.

The figures given in the 'Number of references' column, with the exception of those from 1350–9, should be given more weight than if they were references to an individual workman being paid, for two reasons. First, many of the references used, including those promulgated by the *Corts*, were statutory. They were therefore intended to apply to many workers. Secondly, for the period after 1375, data from the Barcelona *Seu* have been used only in representative quantities so as to avoid overshadowing references from Manresa, Vilarreal, and the Barcelona *Consell de Cent*.

71 Hamilton, *Money, Prices, and Wages*, p. 73 (Valencia), p. 113 (Aragon), and p. 181 (Navarre).

Table 7.3 *Wages in Barcelona vs. wages in smaller towns (Manresa and Vilarreal)*[72]

	{Barcelona}		{Smaller cities}	
Period	Daily wage	Wage index	Daily wage	Wage index
1370–9	3.36s	248	2.13s	158
1380–9	3.27s	242	2.34s	173
1390–9	3.09s	229	2.37s	176

pre-plague peak during the late 1370s and early 1380s, while workmen in Manresa and Vilarreal earned closer to 170 per cent of pre-1348 levels. This would provide a strong incentive for workers to flock to Barcelona during the later fourteenth and fifteenth centuries, as the *fogatges* suggest that they did in fact do. Note, too, that wages declined in the capital from the 1380s, while they continued to rise, albeit at a relatively slow rate, in the two smaller cities during the 1380s and 90s. This finding is also consistent with a flight from the smaller cities and the countryside to the capital: it suggests that, from the 1380s, the labour crisis in Barcelona was beginning to abate as the result of immigration from across the principality, while in the smaller cities, demographic problems slowly worsened. In all of these work sites, it would appear as though wage differentials between employees and supervisors were not very high at all during the Black Death era, a finding which suggests that the labour market was firmly on the side of any male who could lift a shovel.[73]

At these high wage rates, Table 7.4 suggests that there was little supervision premium at either Manresa or Barcelona, a finding which could be read as a 'democratization of the workforce'. Recently, some early

[72] Sources: See Table 7.2.
Notes: As in Table 7.2, base wage index is for the period 1321–50.

[73] This goes against the findings of certain historians working in England and the Low Countries. See D. Knoop and G. P. Jones, 'Masons' Wages in Medieval England', *Economic History*, 2:8 (1933), 473–99, esp. 474–6. Munro, in 'Builders' Wages', now suggests a much more nuanced reading of English and Flemish real wage trends. Although he stresses (on pp. 1036–41) that real wages in England did not equal pre-plague peaks until the 1380s, his Table 2 (p. 1052), would indicate that they increased almost continually, following a minor drop after the 1348 plague, until the 1470s. This would be in line with Hatcher's arguments in 'Aftermath of the Black Death', cited above. Flanders wages generally follow the same trend (Table 4, p. 1054), though monetary policy seems to have caused inflation that ate into gains during certain periods of the later fourteenth century. Ronald Findlay and Kevin H. O'Rourke, in *Power and Plenty* (Princeton, NJ, 2007), pp. 112–17 also read Munro's data in a positive light, i.e., supporting the idea of a 'Golden Age'.

Table 7.4 *Wages for day laborers and their supervisors*[74]

Date	Location	Title	Daily wage
1374.1.18	Manresa	Master of the wall works	3s
1374.1.18	Manresa	Piquer, (labourer), wall works	2s/6d
1374.1.18	Manresa	Manobras (labourer), wall works	2s/6d
1375.5.5	Barcelona	Master of the works	3s/4d
1375.5.5	Barcelona	Piquer	3s/6d
1382–3	Vilarreal	Master of the wall works	3s
1382–3	Vilarreal	Manobra, wall works	2s
1387.7.29	Barcelona	Master of the works	4s
1387.7.29	Barcelona	Manobra	4s
1387.7.29	Barcelona	Piquer	4s
1387.7.29	Barcelona	Piquer	3s/6d

modern economic historians have also become curious about the 'skill premium' between skilled and unskilled workers, taking as a starting point the modern economic theory that in developed economies, the skill premium is less, while in undeveloped economies, the skill premium is more.[75] In this literature, it has been suggested that e.g., masons might be counted as 'skilled workers' while porters and the like would be considered unskilled. It has been suggested by van Zanden that north-west Europe in the late medieval and early modern period exhibited a lower skill premium than the rest of Europe, possibly contributing to the 'Little' and Great Divergences. Neither the Manresa data or the more extensive Barcelona *Obra* series however shows little consistent difference in wages between skilled and unskilled groups. One might be tempted to read this as evidence of an 'advanced' economy in which skill premiums (the costs of human capital) were relatively low. While this would be consistent with our argument that the Catalan economy was 'advanced' for its day, the safest conclusion to be drawn from this particular data is that in the post-Black Death context, what we are witnessing with the *Obra* wage series and other contemporary figures is a demand shock, where skill premiums flattened because the need for labourers of all kinds, both skilled and unskilled, was suddenly exaggerated.

To conclude this discussion of wage rates, some prices for skilled labour can be added, mostly relating to governmental and/or legal functions.

74 Sources: See note to Table 7.2.

75 Jan Luiten van Zanden, 'The Skill Premium and the "Great Divergence"', in *European Review of Economic History*, 13 (2009), 120–30.

Table 7.5 *Daily wages for professional work*[76]

Date	Location	Description	Daily wage (s/d)
1363.10.14	Manresa	*Sindics* to *Corts* (two individuals)	10s
1365.4.5	Manresa	Judicial arbitration with Bishop at Artes	8s
1365.8.22	Manresa	Royal porter	5s
1367.11.3	Manresa	*Sindics* to *Corts* (two individuals)	5s
1369.12.15	Manresa	Royal porter	6s
1370.1.16	Manresa	Council business, travelling	3s
1370.4.19	Manresa	Judicial arbitration	6s
1370.6.27	Manresa	Judicial arbitration w/travel expenses	11s
1370.9.28	Manresa	Errand to Duke w/travel expenses	7s
1370.11.3	Manresa	Messenger	2s/6d
1373.11.23	Manresa	Travel to Barcelona to discuss Town Wall	7s
1374.11.29	Manresa	Travel to Cervera re: '*Princeps Namque*'	4s
1375.9.7	Manresa	Town Councillor, voyage to Barcelona	8s/6d
1375.9.28	Manresa	Travel to Barcelona	4s/6d
1376.11.29	Manresa	Defending city in Lawsuit	4s
1377.7.18	Manresa	Judicial arbitration	10s
1393	Barcelona	Royal porter	3s
1393	Barcelona	Scribe, city council	5s
Average of these 18 figures:			6s/day

These are interesting because they provide strong empirical evidence for a relatively narrow earning gap between workmen and professionals during the later fourteenth century, showing the high premium that was being commanded by labour at this time. It is certainly contrary to common notions of Type A class divisions in medieval Europe that the scribe for the city council of Barcelona, or even a lawyer involved in judicial arbitration, could earn less than twice the wage of the ditch digger working outside his window. These figures certainly suggest that the urban elites had cause to fear a 'collapse' of class distinctions during the second half of the fourteenth century.

Turning from wages to salaries, that is, from diurnal to annual remuneration, it becomes apparent that salaries did not at all keep pace with nominal wages during the dynamic period between 1348 and 1380. In fact, municipal salaries appear to have stagnated almost entirely during this period, meaning that they lagged behind labourers' wages by a factor

[76] Sources: Manresa: MC as noted. Barcelona: see note to Table 7.2.

of 100 per cent. This pattern of stagnation is clearly seen in the cases of the city councillors, the schoolmasters, the council's scribe, the trumpeter and the messenger for the council. The city lawyer's salary was increased from 100s to 200s on the eve of the Black Death, and it stayed at this rate until the liquidity crisis of the 1370s, when it was reduced to its earlier level of 100s. The only high salary introduced during this period was paid to the civic treasurer. This is unsurprising since he was seen as vital to the management of the city's mushrooming civic debt, which was crucial to the economic interests of both the Crown and the Manresan civic elite. Significantly, even the treasurer's salary did not remain substantial for very long: it too was slashed to almost nothing during the crisis of the 1370s. At the same time, the wage evidence presented above suggests a second factor in the stagnation of salaries, and this was that the demand for manual labour had simply increased by a factor which was out of all proportion with the demand for middle class tasks.

Thus it is relatively easy to establish that municipal salaries were stagnating, and that the culprits were a combination of urban fiscal crisis and a vastly increased demand for manual labour as opposed to other forms of work. It is also relatively easy, though not unproblematic, to establish an annual income for labourers, since one can simply multiply a daily wage by a medieval work-year of about 210 workdays, and arrive at a figure of about 250s per year prior to the Black Death, and about 500 to 600s per year by the 1370s and 80s.[77] When this is compared with the salaries presented to Manresan officials, however, including those of doctors, lawyers, and scribes, it is immediately apparent that the salary figures are often lower than the expected earnings of a labourer. Nor is the Manresan data anomalous on this point: other scholars working in regions across Europe have reported professional salaries that, if compared, would amount to less than 200 times the daily wage that they

[77] There remains little data that can establish the length of a medieval work-year. In a recent summary, Gregory Clark shied away from anything more specific than noting that a work-year would probably have been 'well below' the 312 days that the standard six-day workweek would imply. See Clark, 'Work, Wages and Living Conditions'. For a more detailed attempt to establish a medieval work-year, see Herman van der Wee, *The Growth of the Antwerp Market and the European Economy, 14th–16th Centuries*, 3 vols., (The Hague, 1963) Appendix 48, pp. 540–4. Van der Wee's calculations are addressed in Munro, 'Wage-stickiness, Monetary Changes, and Real Incomes in late-medieval England and the Low Countries, 1300–1500: Did Money Matter?', 201. For Italy, Stuard uses a longer work-year of 260 days, based on de la Roncière's calculations. This would mean that the earnings of labourers would have been that much closer to those of salaried workers, traders and *rentiers*. Susan Mosher Stuard, *Gilding the Market: Luxury and Fashion in Fourteenth-Century Italy* (Philadelphia, PA, 2006), pp. 132–3; Charles-M. de la Roncière, *Prix et salaires à Florence au XIVe siècle (1280–1380) (Collection de l'Ecole Française de Rome)* (Rome, 1982).

have reported for a manual labourer.[78] This suggests two possibilities: either doctors and lawyers were earning less than wage labourers by the 1370s, or else the salaries represented above were not the only income of the professionals in question. Logic dictates that the latter assumption is more likely to be true.[79] Most posts in the Manresan government did not require, on average, more than ten or fifteen hours of work per week.[80] Also, the presence of many *ad hoc* payments for lawyers and scribes in our documentation, including individual payments from the city which amounted to more than an official annual stipend, shows that the annual stipends listed in Table 7.6 were, by the later fourteenth century at least, intended as little more than *honoraria*. There is also evidence of the same official holding more than one stipend; which makes sense given that few, if any, of the city's offices were conceived of as being full-time positions. For example, between 1378 and 1381, Pere Çalmella was *veguer* and bailiff of Manresa at the same time. His trumpeters and messengers for the *vegueria* held similar offices from the municipality of Manresa. Each office brought its own stipend.[81] There is also some evidence that lesser officials like trumpeters and criers were paid ad hoc in addition to their salaries.[82] This prevalence of ad hoc payments for many positions, and the fact that professionals often attempted to collect several stipends at one time, renders it difficult to determine precisely how much the average Manresan professional expected to make. One way to shed light on the situation is to compare Manresan stipends to those paid by the capital cities of Barcelona and Valencia, and by the Crown.

78 J. H. Elliott, *The Revolt of the Catalans* (Cambridge, 1984) concluded that seventeenth-century salaries reported for *veguers*, bailiffs, and judges ranged from 'very moderate' to 'ridiculously low', pp. 84–8. For a rare study of late medieval salaries in Castile, which however provides many figures and less analysis than might be desired, see José Damián González Arce, 'Trabajar para el príncipe: Los salarios de los servidores en la casa del príncipe de sturias y Gerona (Juan de Aragón y Castilla, 1478–1497)', *Anuario de Estudios Medievales*, 39:2 (17 November 2009), 777–842.

79 Elliott did not come to this conclusion, but he did suggest that (a) it was difficult to find good men to fill low-paid government posts and (b) some lawyers may have volunteered for low-paying judgeships in the hope of future political advancement. On the second point it could be suggested that, in most cases, salaried officials accepted these low stipends both because their posts did not require 'full time' labour (many may have been virtual sinecures) and also because even 'low' stipends amounted to between 10 and 20 per cent of a full annual income (see Tables 7.6 and 7.7). Therefore, some lawyers may have counted 100–200s per annum stipends as a valuable addition to their annual earnings.

80 Max Turull Rubinat, *La configuració jurídica del municipi Baix medieval: régim municipal i fiscalitat a Cervera entre 1182–1430* (Barcelona, Fundacio Noguera, 1990), p. 225, has shown that the town council of Cervera met an average of 34.6 times per year, or just under once every ten days, during nine sample years between 1332 and 1393. Then, as now, much council business was conducted outside of the formal meetings, but it is clear that official requirements were only a few hours per week.

81 ACA, *Batllia* 1161, 46r–46v.

82 For example, ACA, *Batllia* 1161, 39v.

Table 7.6 *Manresan municipal salaries, including some payments ad hoc*[83]

Date	Occupation	Annual stipend	Notes
1336–1410	Town councillor	40s	
1375.2.27	Town councillor	50s	unique instance of this rate
1329.5.20	Lawyer, ad hoc	100s	
1332.9.18	Lawyer, for the council	100s	
1333.6.22	Lawyer, for the council	400s	includes ad hoc payments
1336.3.27	Lawyer, for the council	100s	
1348.3.28	Lawyer, for the council	200s	
1360.6.26	Lawyer, for the council	200s	
1373.4.8	Lawyer, for the council	100s	
1332.2.28	Surgeon, municipal	100s	
1336.3.26	Doctor, municipal	100s	also earned 800s[84]
1357.3.23	Doctor, municipal	100s	
1358.5.26	City treasurer	500s	
1360.4.24	City treasurer	700s	
1363.4.28	City treasurer	800s	
1372.3.20	City treasurer	50s	
1331.3.16	Schoolmaster, municipal	250s	also MC1332.3.14
1332.9.15	Schoolmaster, municipal	100s	two masters hired this year
1332.9.15	Schoolmaster, municipal	60s	two masters hired this year
1334.9.20	Schoolmaster, municipal	100s	
1357.1.28	Schoolmaster, municipal	200s	
1372.8.23	Schoolmaster, municipal	100s	plus students' fees (1st mention of such fees)
1353.7.6	Scribe, for the council	120s	
1370.3.12	Scribe, for the council	100s	
1371.2.19	Scribe, ad hoc, for council	200s	
1372.5.11	Scribe, ad hoc, for council	500s	
1329.4.3	Guard, for council	110s	
1333.5.11	Guard and crier	110s	
1335.8.11	Crossbowman, for council	100s	to be paid annually
1372.6.9	Guard, for council	20s	
1374.4.18	Guard, ad hoc, for council	20s	
1376.7.3	Guard, for council	20s	
1329.5.16	Groundskeeper	80s	manages civic property
1357.11.3	Groundskeeper	100s	
1358.4.12	Groundskeeper	200s	
1362.8.5	Groundskeeper	200s	

(*cont.*)

83 Source: MC.

84 This additional income was called a *violari* in MC 1332.12.1 and a salary in MC 1348.3.20. In MC 1332.4.5 it was called a *pensione seu violari*.

Table 7.6 *(cont.)*

Date	Occupation	Annual stipend	Notes
1374.7.26	Groundskeeper	260s	
1376.6.6	Groundskeeper	50s	
1357.7.28	Trumpeter, for the council	100s	
1358.8.4	Trumpeter, for the council	100s	
1374.3.10	Trumpeter, for the council	100s	
1336.7.2	Messenger for the council	110s	
1374.4.18	Messenger for the council	100s	
1375.9.28	Messenger for the council	100s	
1336.10.4	Tax collector, ad hoc	100s	for *tallia* of 35,000s
1345.4.22	Supervisor of the *cequia*	263s/3d	total annual wages
1373.8.27	Accountant, for council	120s	new office
1373.12.28	Director of the wall works	55s	engineer for the council
1373.2.1	Superintendent, wall works	500s	king's appointee, also bailiff

Nothing confirms the sense that Manresan annual stipends were largely honorary more than a comparison of the consuls' salaries at Manresa, which was 40s, with the post-plague salaries of the Barcelona and Valencian councillors, which stood at 1,200s and 1,000s respectively. This can be seen from the figures presented in Table 7.7. It is very interesting that even the salaries paid by the metropoles, which would have been quite comfortable prior to the Black Death, did not keep pace with wages. Instead they stagnated, just like the Manresan stipends. It is striking, for example, that the lawyer for the castellan Talamanca family was paid an annual salary of 500s in 1319, while sixty years later the lawyer for the *veguer* of Manresa drew the same salary. These findings are in accord with Earl Hamilton's Valencian data. In Valencia, as in Manresa, salaries were generally stagnant in the latter fourteenth century. They rose a mere 13 per cent between 1351 and 1400.[85]

Just because salaries stagnated, however, does not mean that the recipients were content with what, in the face of rising prices, translated into a significant loss of real income. In 1379, Barcelona's city councillors proposed to augment their salary by an incredible 66 per cent – an increase that still would not have compensated for the recent jumps in nominal wages. The proposal was, however, rejected, presumably due to a public

[85] Hamilton, *Money, Prices, and Wages*, p. 68. His Valencian wage data commences only in 1380, and so it can tell us little about the tremendous inflation which had taken place during the previous three decades.

Table 7.7 *Professional salaries and stipends (paid by authorities other than the Manresan City Government)*[86]

Annual Date	Location	Description	Salary/ stipend
1319.1.20	Talamanca	Personal lawyer for castellan family	500s
1356–93	Valencia	City lawyer	1,000s
1395–1400	Valencia	City lawyer	800s
1379–81	Manresa	Lawyer for the *batlle* and *veguer*	500s
1379–81	Manresa	Assessor of the *batlle*	300s
1379–81	Manresa	Royal *batlle* of Manresa	500s
1379–81	Manresa	Royal *veguer* of Manresa and Bages	2,000s
1379	Barcelona	City councillor	1,200s
1379	Barcelona	City councillor (proposed)	2,000s
1351–1400	Valencia	City councillor (*jurat*)	1,000s
1373.1.7	Manresa	Scribe for the *batlle*	180s
1351–8	Valencia	Trumpeter	120s
1367–1400	Valencia	Trumpeter	180s
1379–81	Manresa	Messenger/Crier (for *veguer* and *batlle*)	45s
1379–81	Manresa	Trumpeter (for *veguer* and *batlle*)	20s

outcry, a lack of funds or both.[87] To the extent that professionals relied on municipal stipends for their income, they were therefore much worse off than wage earners after the Black Death. In order to maintain their standard of living, officials and professionals had to seek *ad hoc* payments, or else turn away from the previously more lucrative civic offices and pursue private ends. This latter trend corresponds with the decrease of public spending and increase of private consumption in Catalonia during the latter fourteenth century, which is one of the larger themes of this study.

A glance at the salaries of Catalonia's major office-holders, such as the *veguers* and the councillors of the principal cities, provides further evidence that a later fourteenth-century Catalan professional expected to earn closer to 1,000s per year than the 100s suggested by the Manresan stipends. Barcelona's councillors felt in 1379 that they required 2,000s per year in order to live in a style befitting their office. Perhaps they chose that figure in order to achieve parity with the royal *veguers*. The

86 Sources: AHCM Tr. 175 (Familia Talamanca); Hamilton, *Money, Prices, and Wages*, 270–1; Carmen Batlle, *La crisis social de Barcelona del siglo XV*, vol. I, 87; ACA *Batllia* 1161, 45v and 46v.

87 Batlle, *La crisis social de Barcelona del siglo XV*, vol. I, p. 87.

veguer of Manresa took a salary of 2000s in 1379–81. In marked contrast to the *veguer*, whose jurisdiction covered the entire Bages region and who commanded its contingents of the royal army, the bailiff of Manresa took a still significant but much humbler 500s per annum. This can be compared with Earl Hamilton's figures for the councillors, notaries, and lawyers for the city of Valencia. City lawyers received 1,000s per year between 1351 and 1393, as did councillors between 1351 and 1400 and the city treasurer between 1371 and 1400. In a few instances, the Manresan documents suggest that Manresan officials expected to earn figures in this range. For example, in 1358 the newly reorganized office of town treasurer was assigned a salary of 600s per year. In 1360 this was raised to 700s, and in 1363 it was raised again to 800s. It seems clear that the treasurer's salary was intended to provide him with an adequate annual income in itself, so that he could devote all of his time to managing the civic finances as these became vastly more complicated during the first years of the Castilian war. In the event, Manresa's treasury did not have the funds to pay its officials in the style of the metropoles, especially in an era of skyrocketing municipal debt. As previously noted, the treasurer's salary was slashed to a token 50s by the early 1370s.

Returning to the figures for Manresa, it becomes apparent that even though most salaries were token honoraria, the general trend shows salaries stagnating during the 1350s and 60s, and being slashed across the board during the 1370s. This inability to pay even token stipends would undoubtedly have contributed to the lack of enthusiasm for civic office which has been noted in previous chapters during the later 1370s and early 1380s.[88] One result of these civic cutbacks was that the city's schoolmasters were, for the first time, officially encouraged to accept fees from their students in addition to their newly reduced stipends. This move represents a decisive and permanent shift from a public to a largely private funding scheme for the city's educational system. Another indication that the city could no longer afford to pay its servants by the 1370s is reflected in the salaries of the bailiff's guards. These fell precipitously from a decent 110s in the 1330s, which included 80s cash plus 30s clothing allowance, to a token 20s per year in the 1370s. If it is to be presumed that the town guards of the 1370s earned a living wage from some quarter, then clearly the burden of paying the guards' salaries had been shifted from the city onto those unfortunates who were the objects of their attentions. And civic salaries were not the only municipal responsibility to be privatized in Manresa after the Castilian–Aragonese

[88] LV, 269. See also Chapter 5, n. 132.

War. It has been shown in Chapter 5 how the great irrigation project known as the *sèquia*, begun in the late 1330s, was originally funded by the city, but it was farmed out to the highest bidder in 1375.[89]

ANNUAL INCOMES OF THE MANRESAN UPPER CLASSES, INCLUDING *RENTIERS*

From the data presented in the last section, it can be estimated that a Catalan professional in the 1370s and 80s expected to earn between 800 and 1,400s per year from their labour, with the high-status *veguers* commanding 2,000s. The wages for professional work listed in Table 7.5, which average 6s per day, also give us an annual salary in this range, since multiplying 6s by 200 days would provide an annual income of 1,200s. By themselves, these figures might remain open to some doubt and scepticism as to how closely they corresponded to the actual incomes of Catalan urban elites. One way to relate these salary findings with elite income levels is to estimate the income of the Manresan upper classes, based on their assets as declared in the *Liber Manifesti*. This method has the additional benefit of simultaneously corroborating the *Liber Manifesti* figures, should they happen to correspond with estimated elite labour earnings, which, fortunately, they do quite well. The total assets declared by Manresan elites in the *Liber Manifesti* make it possible to suggest a realistic upper limit to what a *rentier* could earn, given that the prevailing rate of investment returns was about 5 to 7 per cent in 1408.[90] To calculate possible earnings, as presented in Table 7.8, a measure of 'investment wealth' was constructed. This means that the value of each citizen's primary house, household furnishings, and debts have been subtracted from their gross wealth. The remaining investment wealth includes the value of all land, secondary houses, loans and investments, and business capital. Maximum income has been estimated using a return of 5 per cent on total investment wealth, a calculation that assumes full employment of all of these resources at the interest rate prevailing in Catalonia towards 1400. Even though investment rates were somewhat higher in the 1350s,

89 MC 1375.7.23.

90 Interest rates for *censals* are reported in Table 6.5. R. S. Lopez, in 'The Trade of Medieval Europe: The South', in M. M. Postan and H. J. Habbakuk, eds., *The Cambridge Economic History of Europe*, Vol. II, *Trade and Industry in the Middle Ages* (Cambridge, 1952), p. 334, notes that profit margins fell steadily as commerce matured during the thirteenth and early fourteenth centuries. Herlihy, in *Medieval and Renaissance Pistoia*, p. 155, writes that in Italy, a famine and plague in 1339–40 'brought an abrupt end to th[e] era of favorable profit expectations'. The falling Catalan interest rates presented in the previous chapter suggest that merchants' profit margins continued to fall during the latter fourteenth century as well.

Table 7.8 *Estimated maximum income (exclusive of any salaries) of Manresa's twenty wealthiest citizens in 1408*[91]

Name	Listed profession	Investment wealth (£ Barc.)	Maximum annual earnings (*sous*) @ 5 per cent
Gamicans, Bernat	Tailor	3,698	3,698
Combs, Ramon des	Royal councillor	979	979
Amargos, Bernat de	none (*rentier*)	3,130	3,130
Grevalosa, Pere de (heirs)	none (*rentier*)	2,450	2,450
Santa Conte, Guillem de	none (*rentier*)	2,678	2,678
Andreu, Francesc	none (*rentier*)	2,130	2,130
Sallent, Eymeric de	Merchant	1,792	1,792
Amargos, Jaume	none (*rentier*)	1,973	1,973
Mas, Arnau de	Lawyer	2,058	2,058
Combs, Berenguer des	Lawyer	1,777	1,777
Ferrer, Tomas	none (*rentier*)	1,898	1,898
Canyell, Joan de	Furrier	1,818	1,818
Sant Joan, Bernat	Furrier	1,566	1,566
Ubaco, Pere de	none (*rentier*)	1,275	1,275
Miquel, Bernat	Leatherworker	1,421	1,421
Sarta, Jaume	Merchant	1,031	1,031
Draper, Arnau	Merchant	1,243	1,243
Valls, Asbert des, (heirs)	none (*rentier*)	1,050	1,050
Dalçamora, Francesc	Royal scribe	963	963
Figerola, Bernat de	Doctor	881	881

60s, and 70s than after 1380, the improbability of any *rentier* achieving a full employment of their resources renders 5 per cent a generous estimate of a householder's true earnings. By 1408, actual incomes are therefore likely to have been closer to half of what is estimated in Table 7.8.

Table 7.8 indicates that the salaries received by Catalonia's top civic officials were comparable to what a wealthy provincial *rentier* could earn annually on rents, investments, and business earnings. From this, it can be seen that only the very wealthiest Manresan citizens lived from their annuities at a level comparable to the *veguer* of Manresa, and few elite Manresans earned as much as a councillor of Barcelona or Valencia. This table also reveals the importance of professional salaries – it is tempting

91 Source: LM.
Notes: 'Investment wealth' is estimated by subtracting personal assets, such as homes and moveable goods, and debts, from gross wealth. Names are listed in order of gross wealth.

to dismiss these as inconsequential, but to do so would obviously be a mistake. Even stipends of 200 *sous* per year, which might by this point strike us as modest sums for a professional, must have been important additions to the income of upper-class families. This fact also provides a clue as to why even the very wealthiest Manresans continued to train as lawyers, doctors, and notaries. Even for Manresa's wealthiest men, practising a profession, and pulling in, say, 800s per year in stipends and ad hoc payments, was quite literally equivalent to inheriting a second fortune. To take specific examples, Manresan lawyers such as Arnau de Mas and Berenguer des Comes earned money from their very significant fortunes, and they easily could have lived as *rentiers*, but still they chose to collect professional salaries. This in fact made a good deal of economic sense. If these men earned between 500 and 1000s annually in lawyers' fees, this would represent an increase of between 25 and 50 per cent over their *rentier* income. Practising a profession, therefore, must have been one of the few ways that a man could build a fortune, rather than simply maintain it, as investment returns continued to slip during the latter fourteenth century. This incidentally helps to explain the very high average wealth of Manresa's lawyers, as demonstrated in Chapter 3.

One final and very telling point to be noted about the relationship between the incomes of the wealthiest Manresans and those of the labouring classes is the serious closure of the gap between these two figures that occurred in the decades after the Black Death. This gap was not only narrowing in terms of salaries versus wages, but in terms of patrician rental income versus wages. The next chapter will show how the gap between the rich and poor was surprisingly narrow in Manresa in 1408, when measured in terms of assets. The salary data suggests that upper-class Catalan burghers hoped to earn in the neighbourhood of about 1000s per annum prior to the Black Death, and yet it seems clear that after the Black Death, particularly after interest rates fell in the 1370s, this figure did not really increase. The contrast with labourers' wages, which more than doubled over the same period, is therefore great, and represents a very significant narrowing of the gap between rich and poor. By 1408, there is clear evidence to indicate that the wealthiest Manresan citizen was unable to earn more than 3,000s per year at a time when a workman could earn more than 450s from his labour, irrespective of any farming he did on the side. For most wealthy Manresans, annual earnings were more in the neighbourhood of 1,500–2,000s, which is perhaps three or four times what a workman could bring home. Although the difference between these income levels was enough to generate very different standards of living, this level of disparity cannot be considered extreme.

Not only was the income gap between rich and poor quite narrow in 1408, but it had been closing in a dramatic fashion over the past half-century. Still, bare figures seldom impress: let us therefore try to express this fundamental shift in the relationship between rich and poor by giving it a human face. This can be done by calculating the number of servants that a wealthy person could afford to keep in the face of economic change. As the English historiography has noted, a significant proportion of late medieval households were 'servant producing', meaning that the women and men in that household would go out and work for other people during the day, while a smaller proportion were 'servant employing'.[92] Our data shows that this long-standing social equation underwent a fundamental shift over the later fourteenth century. If, based on the above, 1,800s and 450s are taken to represent the rich/poor income gap in 1400, how did these figures stand in the spring of 1348? If workers' wages equalled 450s in 1400, then dividing by two as our figures suggest reduces them to 225s on the eve of the plague.[93] At the same time that workers' nominal wages were doubling, it has been shown that between 1350 and 1400, investment returns on *rentier* capital shrank from about 15 per cent in 1350 to around 5 per cent in 1400. These figures are based on the actual interest rates prevailing on government bonds and interpersonal loans over the course of this time, as reported in the previous chapter. Thus, a *rentier* who earned 1,800s in 1400 at 5 per cent could have been earning literally three times that level, or 5,400s, in 1350. Reducing these figures to a ratio reveals a deeply impressive trend: in early 1348, the ratio of *rentier* to workers' incomes stood at a very pronounced 24:1. By 1400, this ratio had fallen to a mere 4:1. This represents a narrowing of the income gap between rich and poor by a factor of six. Taken in terms of the number of servants that could be employed by the wealthy, we can say that for every six servants that a wealthy Manresan could hire prior to the Black Death, they could hire only a single servant in 1400. Even if this is off by half, poor people in 1400 were still earning vastly more money relative to wealthy people than they had been in the half-century prior to the plague. It is therefore not to be doubted that the socio-economic milieu of the later fourteenth century was profoundly different than that of the earlier fourteenth century, and that the relatively sudden shift in

[92] E.g. Charles Phythian-Adams, *Desolation of a City: Coventry and the Urban Crisis of the Late Middle Ages* (Cambridge, 1979), pp. 205–7; Poos, *A Rural Society after the Black Death*, p. 188; P. J. P. Goldberg, *Women, Work, and Life Cycle in a Medieval Economy: Women in York and Yorkshire c.1300–1520* (Oxford, 1992), pp. 305–18.

[93] For this calculation see Table 7.2. Nominal wages were almost exactly double their 1347 levels in 1400. This doubling is almost precisely mirrored in Clark's real wages table, cf. Clark, 'Work, Wages and Living Conditions', p. 919.

this relationship represented one of the most fundamental and dramatic developments of the later Middle Ages.

The work of Christopher Dyer on English incomes enables us to make further use of our income and estate valuation figures, by comparing the estates of Manresan castellans and patricians to their English equivalents. It will be noted that Dyer's sources estimate income at 20 per cent of the value of an estate, which is surely too high, and was done for tax purposes in an atmosphere of assumed evasion.[94] This monetary comparison assumes a rate of £4.5 pounds Barcelona per English pound, as was the prevailing rate in the years around 1408.[95] The results of this comparison are quite surprising, since they reveal that English and Catalan social classes were operating to a remarkable degree of parity, in terms of their disposable wealth. This finding therefore helps to offset a lingering northern European bias, which might assume that Catalonia, as part of an Iberian European 'fringe', would have been significantly poorer than England. Instead, these figures robustly suggest that Catalan knights and burghers were generally on an economic par with their English equivalents in the years around 1400 – although there were far fewer Catalans than there were English people, by a factor of about four.[96] Given that, as demonstrated in the next chapter, Manresan and Italian patrician fortunes were likewise roughly equivalent, these figures indicate that English, Italian, and Catalan incomes were, in the main, similar in scale by the early fifteenth century.[97] The degree of economic integration that this suggests might once have been surprising, although recent studies would predict that findings such as this should in fact be expected.[98] An undoubted value of making such a comparison is that

94 Christopher Dyer, *Standards of Living in the Later Middle Ages: Social Change in England c. 1200–1520* (Cambridge, 1994), pp. 29–34. It is here estimated that Manresan incomes after 1400 were closer to 5 per cent of the total value of an estate; see Table 7.8 and relevant discussion.

95 From Spufford, *Handbook of Medieval Exchange*.

96 For the population of England, which was about 2,000,000 in 1400, see Dyer, *Standards of Living*, p. 4. For population figures that place the Catalan population around 400,000 in 1400, see Batlle, *L'expansió baixmedieval*, p. 255, and discussion above.

97 For the comparison between Manresan and Pistoiese fortunes, see Tables 8.2 through 8.4.

98 There is still caution on this point, especially prior to the fifteenth century. It seems increasingly likely, however, that just as there was more integration along coastal routes in the North Sea and Baltic, so there was high integration amongst the coastal regions of the north-west Mediterranean, from Rome to Valencia. Southern market integration has not to my knowledge been studied; on the northern region see Richard W. Unger, 'Thresholds for Market Integration in the Low Countries and England in the Fifteenth Century', in L. Armstrong, M. Elbl, and I. Elbl (eds.), *Money, Markets and Trade in Late Medieval Europe: Essays in Honour of John H. A. Munro* (Brill, 2007), pp. 349–82. See also Stephan R. Epstein, 'Regional Fairs, Institutional Innovation, and Economic Growth in Late Medieval Europe', *Economic History Review*, 47:3 (1994), 459–82, and Oliver Volckart and Nikolaus Wolf, 'Estimating Financial Integration in the Middle Ages: What can we Learn from a TAR Model?', *Journal of Economic History*, 66:1 (2006),

Table 7.9 *A comparison of Manresan castellan and patrician fortunes with contemporary English equivalents*[99]

English baron	£1,000–£2,500
Wealthy London merchant (top 14%)	£1,000+
Minimum fortune for an English Knight	£200
Minimum fortune for English Gentry	£50
Bages castellan (average per castle)	£350
Manresan patrician (top 3%)	£222–£889

it serves to heighten our sense of the value of compiling data sets on medieval patrimonies and incomes in general. In this spirit it can be noted that Table 7.9 confirms contemporary observations to the effect that knights and wealthy merchants' incomes were approaching parity in the years around 1400.[100] Likewise, the fact that London merchants could amass fortunes significantly – but not astronomically – larger than those found amongst Manresan patricians is entirely what would be expected when comparing a great trading metropolis with a medium-sized city. Unfortunately, no work has yet been done for mercantile fortunes in Barcelona, but the Manresan figures suggest that future work will find a rough equivalence between merchant patrimonies in Barcelona, London, and other European metropoles.

PRICES

To this point, the present chapter has discussed wages, salaries, and incomes in terms of the actual numbers of coins or credits received in *diners de tern*, that is, what economists call 'nominal wages'. By adding

122–39. For England see Christopher Dyer, 'Trade, Urban Hinterlands and Market Integration, 1300–1600: A Summing Up', in James A. Galloway (ed.), *Trade, Urban Hinterlands and Market Integration c.1300–1600: A Collection of Working Papers Given at a Conference Organised by the Centre for Metropolitan History and Supported by the Economic and Social Research Council, 7 July 1999* (London, 2000), pp. 103–9.

99 All figures are in English pounds. Sources: For English aristocracy, Christopher Dyer, *Standards of Living in the Later Middle Ages*, pp. 29–34; for London merchants, *ibid.*, p. 193. Dyer notes that only 14 per cent of London merchants between 1350 and 1497 had estates worth £1,000 or more at time of death. The Talamanca castellany was worth at least £1,560 in 1332 but could have been worth much more; FTI 1332 n 8.

Notes: The conversion rate between pounds Barcelona and pounds stirling is taken to be 4.5 £/Barcelona per £/English. This can be ascertained from Peter Spufford, *A Handbook of Medieval Exchange*.

100 Dyer, *Standards of Living*, p. 193; see also Josep Fernández Trabal, 'De "prohoms" a ciudadanos honrados: Aproximación al estudio de las elites urbanas de la sociedad Catalana bajomedieval (s. XIV–XV),' *Revista d'Història Medieval*, 10 (1999), 331–69, 344.

some information on prices, it is possible to get a sense of 'real wage' rates, that is, a sense of whether or not the purchasing power of these nominal wages remained the same, or was subject to inflation. The data presented below suggests that prices of manufactured goods almost certainly increased on a par with wages, meaning that, in the aggregate, labourers found these items no easier to purchase. However, our findings also indicate that prices on land and livestock remained at broadly similar levels throughout the fourteenth century, even as wages increased. Thus, some of the most costly means of production were significantly easier to purchase in 1400 than they had been in 1347. Furthermore, since labourers had more money in an absolute sense due to increased wages, and since after the plague they had to pay less of their income on rent, livestock, and other significant expenditures, this means that, *ceteris paribus*, individual manufactured goods would have been easier for them to purchase in 1400 than before the plague. Thus, it is impossible to avoid the conclusion that life was, in general, significantly easier for those working-class people who survived the plagues.

How, more precisely, does one go about measuring 'real wages' by accumulating price data? The usual method, as introduced above, is for historians to create a 'basket of goods' or commodities, a list of consumables intended to represent an average family's budget. The creation of such a basket obviously requires price data for a number of commodities, data that are often lacking from sparse medieval sources, and so relatively few calculations of real wages exist in medieval European historiography. Two of the best studies that deal with the fourteenth century are Phelps Brown and Hopkins, *Seven Centuries of the Prices of Consumables Compared with Builders' Wage-Rates*, dealing with Southern England; for the Mediterranean world there is Roncière, *Prix et salaries à Florence au XIVe siècle.*[101] Others, such as Hamilton (*Money, Prices, and Wages in Valencia, Aragon, and Navarre, 1351–1500*) and Herlihy (*Medieval and Renaissance Pistoia*, and *Tuscans and their Families*), have listed nominal wages and commodity prices separately.[102] In such cases the authors have made some explicit judgements, while leaving readers to make further inferences from their price series.

As with nominal wages and salaries, the only authoritative source for reconstructing the behaviour of Catalan prices remains Hamilton's

[101] Henry Phelps Brown and Sheila V. Hopkins, *Seven Centuries of the Prices of Consumables, Compared with Builders' Wage-rates* (London, 1956); Roncière, *Prix et salaires à Florence au XIVe siècle.*

[102] Hamilton, *Money, Prices, and Wages*; Herlihy, *Medieval and Renaissance Pistoia*; David Herlihy and Christiane Klapisch-Zuber, *Tuscans and their Families: A Study of the Florentine Catasto of 1427* (New Haven, CT, 1985).

work from the surrounding regions of Valencia, Aragon, and Navarre. Summarizing the current state of our knowledge, Thomas Bisson writes: 'From about 1340 to 1380 prices and wages rose sharply, led by wages. Only after 1380 did the effects of depopulation and financial disorder combine to bring on a period of instability lasting until the 1420s.'[103] It is not surprising to learn that between 1340 and 1380 commodity prices quickly rose to claim most of the wage earner's increased income. Since an increase in wages is equal to an increase in the cost of production, an increase in prices should naturally follow. Another way of saying this is to note that in all economies, the cost of the necessities of life – what is considered sufficient for food, shelter and clothing – will rise to engulf most of the average income. In order to have luxuries, one must earn substantially more than the average income. Since most people are, by definition, close to the economic average, most people after the Black Death found that their windfall of inheritances and higher wages was soon absorbed by the increasing cost of motivating one of their fellow subjects to produce something for them.

With this in mind, the price data which has come to light from the Manresan sources can be examined in a bit more detail. One useful and oft-quoted commodity is *calç*, that is, the lime that was used for making cement. This had to be manufactured in an expensive lime kiln, and since its use was ubiquitous in construction projects, references to its price are relatively common. The standard Catalan unit for *calç* was a *quarter*. Those references which have turned up in the Manresan sources are summarized in Table 7.10. Even though the data are relatively sparse, there is enough to show us that, just as Hamilton found in the neighbouring regions, the price pattern for calç mirrors the trend that has been reported above for nominal wages. Thus, six quotes for sizeable orders of *calç* in 1340 averaged 6.3d per *quarter*, while five quotes between 1367 and 1374 averaged 14d, an increase of 222 per cent. Wages, according to Table 7.2, increased just over 200 per cent during the same time period. The correlation is therefore very close to what would be expected.

While little can be said about the prices of other staples or manufactured goods in Manresa, some prices for land and livestock have come to light. Unlike commodity prices, it should be expected that the price of these two items would not increase in a time of decreasing population, unless, in the case of livestock, it proved to be the case that the cattle population was also subject to plague. Otherwise, it is to be expected that in a time of decreasing population, there would be more land and more livestock per capita. Fortunately for the Catalans, it would appear

[103] MCOA, 172.

Table 7.10 *The price of* calç *in Manresa and Barcelona, pre- and post-1348.*[104]

{Pre-1348}		{Post-1348}	
Date	Price/Quarter (diners Barc.)	Date	Price/Quarter (diners Barc.)
1340.4.1k	5.0	1367	14.0
1340.5.8k	4.0	1371	17.0
1340.5.8k	9.0	1373.1.3	12.0
1340.6.2k	8.4	1373.8.16	12.0
1340.9.1k	8.5	1374.7.26	15.0
1340.8.5i	3.0	1414.2.9	18.0
		1414.2.17	18.5
Pre-1348 Average:	6.3	Post-1348 Average:	15.2
		Price increase: 241%	

Table 7.11 *Price of a manse in the Bages and the Plain of Vic, 1300–1410*[105]

Time period	Number sold	Average price per manse (*sous*)
1300–30	18.5	1,200
1330–80	11.3	1,009
1380–1415	39.8	980

from the Manresan price data as though their cattle population was in fact not affected by the plague bacillus, nor did it succumb to any serious shortage of food or other difficulty which would significantly reduce herd numbers.

104 Sources: 1340 quotes: AHCM a. 4054 (Familia Sarta); 1367 and 1371: ACB *Obreria de la Seu*; 1373–74: MC; 1414: AHCB, *Consell de Cent, Obreria*, XIV-4, 31r–31v.

105 Sources: AHCM Tr. 117 (Familia Talamanca); AHCM a. 4054 (Familia Sarta); AHCM Tr. 224 (Jaume Sarta); *Liber Manifesti*, 1408. In addition, four manse sales for the 1300–30 period and five for the 1330–80 period have been published for the area of Vic in Eliscenda Gràcia i Mont, *Estructura Agrària de la plana de Vic al segle XIV*, 152, 155, and 172–73.

Table 7.12 *Some prices of livestock in Manresa, 1298–1410*[106]

Animal type (and time period)	Number sold	Avg price (sous)
Mule:		
1298–1348	5.0	172
1408–1411	17.0	177
Ass:		
1298–1348	5.0	75
1408–1411	3.5	68
Cow:		
1298–1348	5.0	64
1408–1411	n.a.	n.a.

In order to measure the price of land, a unit known as a 'manse' has been chosen; this formed a significant part of the patrimony of many Manresan patricians throughout the fourteenth century.[107] A manse is not a precise unit of measure, but it was nonetheless fairly standardized, and Paul Freedman has aptly characterized it as 'the average holding of a moderately well-established peasant'.[108] A typical manse contained a house, some outbuildings, and the various types of cultivated and uncultivated land that are traditionally found on a self-sufficient Mediterranean farm. Occasionally a manse would contain a mill, a parish church, or similar rural structure. The manse was also the smallest unit of feudal obligation in the countryside. Those who lived and worked on a manse usually did not own or hold them outright, but instead held the land through homage to a lord. This was performed *ore et manibus* (with mouth and hands), usually in the presence of the owners themselves.[109] Tenants did, however, have very strong rights of tenancy, including the right to bequeath their manse to their heirs, upon the payment of a customary fee.

The data presented above reveals a strong tendency for Manresans to value manses at or around 1,000 *sous* throughout the fourteenth century.

106 Sources: 1 ass: AHCM V-4 1298.8.17k; 1 cow and 1 mule: AHCM Tr. 175a (*Familia Talamanca*), 1319.3.i; 1345.11.17k. The rest of the quotes are from AHCM Tr. 113 (Pere Sarta). Pere Sarta had at least one business partnership with a butcher, hence his frequent purchases of animals. 1408–11: *Liber Manifesti* 1408.

107 For early Sarta manse purchases, see e.g. SF 1313 11k1; SF 1318 15k2; SF 17k10; SF 1321 5k2; the pattern continues throughout the century.

108 Freedman, *The Origins of Peasant Servitude*, p. 37.

109 For Jaume Sarta and his wife both personally receiving the homage of a manse owner, see JS 1373.2.10. For an early, extensively written out act of homage to Pere Sarta, see FS 1318 15k2.

It is possible that, because the manse was not a definite measure, it was easier for prices to remain at this level by tradition. And it is clear that land prices by no means mirrored the jump in nominal wages between 1347 and 1400. Because of this, wage earners in Manresa could afford nearly twice as much land in 1400 as they could afford in 1347. Therefore, the standard of living can only have increased for the average person in this respect. For landlords, however, the stagnant price of land was not good news: while land prices stagnated, landlords' incomes fell by a factor of three, rendering land three times more expensive for them in 1400 than in 1350. It is also likely that, despite the doubling of agricultural commodity prices, landlords did not see much of a profit increase, since the rates of return on all investments fell significantly after the 1360s. It would, however, be too soon to suggest that stagnant land values meant that large numbers of manses were going uncultivated by 1400.[110] Land values had remained stagnant, but they had not yet collapsed. Of forty manses listed in the *Liber Manifesti* of 1408, only one was listed as being worth nothing, and two more were described as partially depopulated. This finding corresponds with the demographic evidence presented above, which indicated a relatively modest population decrease in Catalonia between 1365 and 1408. While in relative terms the demographic situation in the Bages may have seemed dire to those living in the later fourteenth century, the real depopulation of the Bages, and with it a total collapse of the rural land market, was still to come. Note that in his study on Pistoia, Herlihy, who remains one of very few historians to study land values for southern Europe after the Black Death, suggests that Pistoiese land actually rose to 150 per cent of pre-plague levels in the last quarter of the fourteenth century – though it did fall quite far, to just below pre-plague levels, in the period 1400–25.[111] It is possible that this represents, in part, a demand for security in a war-torn country which did not offer public debt shares to local elites – Manresa's stagnant land market might, in other words, have been partly a result of the introduction of *censals*.[112] Herlihy himself notes that inflation resulting from an increased ratio of money to people (i.e. an increase in the money supply per capita) may have

110 Cf. Batlle, *L'Expansió baixmedieval*, pp. 263–6.

111 One cannot but wish that Herlihy had presented his copious data in decennials or quinquennials, rather than quarter-centuries: but then again, the technology available to him was much more cumbersome than what is now taken for granted. For Pistoiese land prices, based on many sales of a 'stioro' of land, see Herlihy, *Medieval and Renaissance Pistoia*, p. 130.

112 Note that Florence did not allow non-Florentine elites, even those in the Florentine *contado*-cities, to invest in Florentine debt shares. This meant that elites had much more limited investment opportunities compared with their contemporary Catalan counterparts, and the expected result would be an increase in land prices. On Florence's debt-share policy, see Herlihy and Klapisch-Zuber, *Tuscans and their Families*, pp. 1–14.

accounted for some of the observed post-Black Death price increases.[113] However, even at their point of greatest inflation, Pistoiese land prices did not keep up with the known wage trends in Iberia or England, suggesting that land values probably did not keep up with nominal wage trends in Italy either.[114]

So much for rural land values in the vicinity of Manresa; what can be said about the price of urban properties? Unfortunately, these are much more difficult to trace, since there is no standardized unit such as the manse which can be tracked over the course of the century. Because there was a wide variance in the price of urban houses between roughly £10 and £300, several hundred house prices would be required from a brief space of time in order to establish an average price. The 1408 *Liber Manifesti* provides one such sample, but it would be much more difficult to duplicate this result for an earlier period. It can be said that the average Manresan house in 1408 cost a respectable £56.3, or 1,126s, which is interestingly comparable to the price of a manse. Since, as the discussion in the next chapter shows, urban real estate was not really a profitable investment opportunity for Manresans in 1408, it is unlikely that housing prices had been buoyant in the preceding decades.[115] It is therefore probable that urban housing prices roughly mirrored rural land prices, unless it could be proven that population loss in the countryside was occurring at a faster rate than population loss in provincial centres such as Manresa.[116]

Turning to livestock, just enough evidence has come to light in the Manresan sources to indicate that, like land, this 'commodity' was also characterized by stable prices during the later fourteenth-century era of rapid wage increases. As with land, it can be said that by about 1380, livestock was *ceteris paribus* twice as affordable to a labouring person as it had been in 1347. Once again, this contrasts with the available data from Italy, which contrary to expectations shows that Tuscan livestock became significantly more expensive during the later fourteenth century.[117] From the Bages data, it seems that neither mules nor donkeys were more expensive in 1408 than they had been prior to 1348.

The doctoral researches of two scholars, working in Zaragoza and Lleida, have unearthed a series of wheat prices, which, taken together, indicate that food prices remained below wage increases in both of these regions, further suggesting that labouring people in the Crown of Aragon

[113] Herlihy, *Medieval and Renaissance Pistoia*, p. 125.

[114] For these wage trends, see n. 3, above. [115] See Table 8.7.

[116] Unfortunately this would be difficult for the later fourteenth century since the *fogatges*, as described above, occur at inconvenient times for such an assessment.

[117] Herlihy, *Medieval and Renaissance Pistoia*, Table 15, p. 132.

found it easier to purchase the necessities of life in the decades after 1400 than was the case in 1300.[118] Those of Fernando Zulaica Palacios are particularly interesting because they date back to 1297; he sees a rise of perhaps 50 per cent in the price of wheat between 1300 and 1348, and then a modest rise of perhaps 50 per cent further between 1348 and 1420.[119] At the same time, wages rose by about 80 per cent between 1300 and 1348, and continued to rise by another 120 per cent of 1300 levels by 1400. In short, while the price of wheat rose to 200 per cent of 1300 levels by 1420, salaries had risen to about 300 per cent of 1300 levels by 1420. In general the purchasing power of labourers in terms of grain thus increased about 50 per cent between 1300 and 1420, with the majority of this gain coming after 1348.

CONCLUSIONS

The present chapter has presented new data on the demography, wages, salaries, patrimonial incomes, and prices obtaining at Manresa and Catalonia during the long fourteenth century. This section will recap the primary findings suggested by these series, and relate these economic trends to the more general themes of our study. First, it has been shown that the mortality rates at Manresa and in Catalonia in the Black Death were closer to 50 per cent than to 30 per cent, as has often been estimated. A number of different sources provide us with mortality rates of at least 50 per cent, while sources yielding lower numbers are entirely lacking. Despite this high initial mortality, it has further been shown that the Catalan pattern of population loss was somewhat arrested during the later fourteenth century, when contrasted with regions such as Italy. True depopulation was to become a factor in Catalonia further into the fifteenth century than had been the case elsewhere; and the civil war of 1462–72 left Manresa with a population scarcely greater than that of a large village. Thus, we can agree with David Palliser's observation on the English 'urban crisis' and state that whatever else one might say, Manresa experienced a very definite demographic decline during the later Middle Ages.[120] This demographic decline was undoubtedly a contributing factor in Manresa's decreasing importance as an urban centre, although it has been shown that the financial revolution and bureaucratization also

118 See n. 59, above.

119 Fernando Zulaica Palacios, 'Evolución de los precios y salarios aragoneses entre 1300 y 1430', *Aragón en la Edad Media*, 12 (1995), 123–52; graph 128.

120 David M. Palliser, 'Urban Decay Revisited', in David M. Palliser, *Towns and Local Communities in Medieval and Early Modern England*, Variorum Collected Studies Series, 830 (Aldershot, 2006), vol. XIII, pp. 1–21, at p. 9.

played significant roles in this. Still, when a city is reduced to the size of a village, it is difficult for it to play the same sort of role in national development as could a larger town. Thus, while there are some who would emphasize non-demographic effects on later medieval urban decline, size does still matter.

Regarding wages, it has been shown that nominal rates for builders' wages increased in the order of 200 per cent between 1347 and the 1380s, which scales back some estimates that have reached 400 or even 500 per cent. In this increasingly monetized economy, workers were able to demand payments in cash, rather than in kind. During the post-Black Death demand shock, supervision and skill premiums seem to have flattened out to near zero. All workers, skilled, unskilled, and supervisory, are likely to have witnessed a large jump in remuneration between 1348 and the 1380s. At the same time, salaries for more prestigious work were stagnating, and even declining; the falling interest rates described in Chapter 6 also ate into upper-class incomes, meaning that in general there was a very strong closure in the gap between working-class and upper-class earnings during the late fourteenth century – in the order of something like sixfold. The fact that upper-class people in 1380 could hire only a fraction of the number of servants that they could engage prior to 1348 represents an indisputable shift in the relations between the classes. The Manresan price data, when compared with wage and income information, furthermore suggests that land and livestock, at least, were much cheaper for the majority of people than they had been prior to 1348. Taken together with researches in Zaragoza and Lleida suggesting that the price of wheat did not keep pace with the increasing wages, this amounts to a significant gain in purchasing power regarding food and capital. These increases are, however, to be tempered with our findings, which suggest that the prices for manufactured goods rose at levels which kept pace with wages. Overall, however, it must be concluded that labouring Manresan inhabitants enjoyed a significant increase in their standards of living during the later fourteenth century. The next chapter will suggest by means other than price and wage measures that living standards for working and middling ranks of Manresans did indeed increase during the later fourteenth and early fifteenth centuries. But a 'golden age' for workers did not translate into a golden age for the Manresan elite. This was true both in economic and in political terms. Salaries for them stagnated and fell, and this took place during a shift towards privatization that was discussed in Chapter 5. When they were paid at all, salaries were increasingly doled out on an ad hoc basis. As interest rates fell, the *censal* investments of the elites generated less income, and investment in land provided them with no refuge, since stagnating land prices did not provide the prospect of greater returns. In such a climate, professional salaries, when they could be had, brought incomes that greatly complemented *rentier* earnings, meaning that professional men became increasingly prominent members of the elite. In this economically weakened state, the elites of Manresa found themselves much less able to resist the increasing reach of the royal bureaucracy. The secure, competitive incomes offered by the government bonds encouraged them to become part of the *censal*-overseeing regime that had become the primary *raison d'etre* of the local government by the 1380s.

Thus, the demographic decline inaugurated by the Black Death had economic repercussions which, over the course of the later fourteenth and early fifteenth centuries, were good for Manresa's lower and middle orders, but generally bad for the urban elites. These negative effects would be somewhat less pronounced in the case of elites who produced manufactured items for sale, such as the furriers and drapers. Such elites would not, however, be immune from the costs of increasing wages or from falling investment rates. As a result of these sustained economic hardships, the Manresan patriciate began to seem less and less important to the Aragonese monarchy, especially after 1400. Ironically, this was the case even as the government co-opted urban elites into its new *censal* system, and through other moves towards centralization. All of these trends, however, did not become painfully obvious until nearly a century after 1348. In the medium term, the prosperity of a good number of Manresan citizens in the decades around 1400, including the new wealth of many upper-class leather entrepreneurs, coupled with the revitalized patrician regime that took hold from the 1390s, gave no sense that Manresa had suffered 'decline', in a severe and absolute sense. Crisis there certainly was, in the economic, political, and social spheres; but decline is probably too strong a term to employ at any time before 1410; until that time there remained a good deal of resilience in both Manresa's economy and its political regime. In the final chapter of this study on Manresa, the living standards of the Manresan citizenry at the turn of the fifteenth century are measured and put into context, enabling us to engage more closely with the notion of a late fourteenth-century 'golden age'. Indeed, in the decades around 1400, it must have seemed to many average Manresans as though they and their city were enjoying a prosperity that they had never before known.

Chapter 8

FRUITS OF THE URBAN SYSTEM

Equality, inequality, and quality of life

INTRODUCTION

Having discussed the development of the Manresan urban system in terms of political institutions, political practice, the financial revolution, and demographic and macroeconomic upheavals, we are now in a position to evaluate the overall well-being of the city's inhabitants at the close of the fourteenth century. Ideally, one would like to be able to assess the performance of the urban system in creating opportunity, providing for the material needs of its citizens, and even to measure these citizens' sense of fulfilment and happiness. All of these goals and achievements would then be measured against the less varied, more restricted, and more traditional lifestyle which was available to the rural inhabitants of feudal estates, such as the nearby castellany of Talamanca. Current economic history is once more reasserting the notion that later medieval and early modern European city systems were unique in world history, insofar as they were cradles of a distinctive European bourgeoisie, or 'middle class', in nineteenth-century British parlance.[1] A bourgeoisie is created when societal forces combine to lift a substantial number of households out of their accustomed poverty, providing a sense of economic security and social mobility for men, women, and children who belong to or can aspire to join this group. Being bourgeois also provides something of the leisure and luxury which in many social systems is the unique

[1] On this now see Fynn-Paul, 'Let's Talk about Class: Towards an Institutionalist Typology of Class Relations in the Cities of Pre-modern Europe (c. 1200–c. 1800)', *Urban History*, 41:4 (2014), 582–605. See also David Nicholas, *Urban Europe, 1100–1700* (London, 2003); while Peter Clark is generally opposed to this idea that urban institutions 'mattered' in such a fundamental way, see the piece by Bas van Bavel, Maarten Bosker, Eltjo Buringh, and Jan Luiten van Zanden, 'Economy', in Peter Clark (ed.), *The Oxford Handbook of Cities in World History* (Oxford, 2013), pp. 385–402, where these former colleagues of mine argue contra Clark's usual line. On medieval urban living standards rising in much of Europe in the wake of the Black Death see more specifically Ronald Findlay and Kevin H. O'Rourke, *Power and Plenty: Trade, War, and the World Economy in the Second Millennium* (Princeton, NJ, 2009), pp. 113–14. A comprehensive argument on this phenomenon for post-Black Death England is found in John Hatcher, 'England in the Aftermath of the Black Death', *Past and Present: A Journal of Historical Studies*, 144 (1994), 3–35.

preserve of the upper classes. Economic historians, in particular, continue to see some characteristics of the late medieval European urban middle classes as crucial to the transformation of the world from traditional to modern during the period from roughly 1300 to 1800; most particularly, these classes are seen as playing a crucial role in jump-starting European capitalism.[2] Positive characteristics of the urban European bourgeoisie include incentives for (Type B) lower and middle classes to better themselves through education, training, saving, and other forms of discipline, and also by providing a desire to consume, spend, and materially compete against one's social peers. While this latter notion of a 'consumer revolution' was once the preserve of early modern historians, this paradigm has recently been applied to post-Black Death England and to Renaissance Italy.[3]

The easiest parts of this evaluation to assess are, naturally, those which can be quantified. Per capita wealth and the distribution of wealth are helpful in this regard, and so the bulk of this chapter will be dedicated to asking questions such as: how well off were Manresans? To what degree did urban inhabitants share in the city's wealth? Which professional groups benefited most from the city's economic and political system? How much poverty was present in the city? The last section of this chapter will then attempt to answer some of the more qualitative aspects of the 'quality of life' equation, by referring to some of the observations which have been made earlier in the volume. Were the Manresan citizens of 1400 happier than their companions in the countryside? Were they more secure than their own ancestors had been in 1300, or than their descendents would be in 1500, or more self-confident? Did they lead richer, more varied, and more fulfilling lives? Did they have more social opportunities?

The principal source for our evaluation of the material well-being of Manresans will be the *Liber Manifesti* of 1408, since this provides an almost unequalled snapshot of urban occupational and property distributions for any later medieval town. Because standards of living are relative, it is desirable to make a comparison between the *Liber Manifesti* data and that provided by other sources. Fortunately, a fruitful comparison is suggested

[2] See Nicholas, *Urban Europe, 1100–1700*, Jan Luiten van Zanden, *The Long Road to the Industrial Revolution: The European Economy in a Global Perspective, 1000–1800* (Leiden, 2009) and Jan de Vries, *The Industrious Revolution: Consumer Behavior and the Household Economy, 1650 to the Present*, (Cambridge, 2008), which has now been extended to the late medieval period by some analysts, as listed in n. 3.

[3] See e.g. Maryanne Kowaleski, 'A Consumer Economy', in Rosemary Horrox and W. Mark Ormrod (eds.), *A Social History of England 1200–1500* (Cambridge, 2006), pp. 238–59, 493–4; and Susan Mosher Stuard, *Gilding the Market: Luxury and Fashion in Fourteenth-Century Italy* (Philadelphia, PA, 2006), esp. ch. 7.

by David Herlihy's work on the Florentine Catasto of 1427. The Manresan and the Florentine cadastral surveys were redacted less than twenty years apart, and many points of comparison between Catalonia and Northern Italy are well established in the urban literature. Besides, in point of fact, Herlihy's work on the Catasto is perhaps the only other data set published to date that can provide meaningful comparisons with the majority of our *Liber Manifesti* measures.[4]

As the data presented below will show, a comparison of Tuscan and Manresan living standards reveals, perhaps surprisingly, that the Manresans enjoyed a more equitable distribution of wealth, higher per capita wealth and lower debt levels than their Italian counterparts, even those who lived in medium-sized cities. Likewise, there were fewer paupers in Manresa than in Italy. The Manresan evidence makes plain that the majority of Manresans were enjoying a prosperity corresponding with the so-called 'golden age' of labourers (including women workers) that remains a fixture of the English historiography of the later fourteenth century.[5] This historiography also most readily backs up our finding, as argued in the last chapter, that Manresan elites suffered in the post-Black Death era due to falling rents and high wages – the same movements which brought about the golden age that will be presented here. In the

4 The comparison between the city-states of Northern Italy and Barcelona underlies much of the argument in Stephen P. Bensch, *Barcelona and its Rulers, 1096–1291* (Cambridge, 1995). For a recent assessment of the 'unevenness' of recent developments in southern European urban historiography (which implies that Herlihy remains one of the most important sources for comparison on many topics), see Kevin Mummey and Kathryn Reyerson, 'Whose City is This? Hucksters, Domestic Servants, Wet Nurses, Prostitutes, and Slaves in Late Medieval Western Mediterranean Urban Society', *History Compass*, 9:2 (December 2011), 910–22.

5 This 'Golden Age of the labourer' or wage-earner, which was posited by Thorold Rogers more than a century ago, is confirmed with some caveats by Christopher Dyer, *Standards of Living in the Later Middle Ages: Social Change in England c. 1200–1520* (Cambridge, 1994), see esp. pp. 207–33. See a similar conclusion, with more technical nuance, in John H. Munro, 'Builders' Wages in Southern England and the Southern Low Countries, 1346–1500: A Comparative Study of Trends in and Levels of Real Incomes', in Simonetta Cavaciocchi (ed.), *L'Edilizia prima della rivoluzione industriale secc. XIII–XVIII: Atti della trentaseiesima settimana di studi, 26–30 Aprile 2004* (Florence, 2005), pp. 1013–76, who argues that conditions improved markedly only in the last quarter of the fourteenth century, i.e., more than two decades after the Black Death. The original observation is found in J. E. T. Rogers, *Six Centuries of Work and Wages: The History of English Labour* (London, 1884). This 'Golden Age' is also confirmed for early fifteenth-century Italy in Richard A. Goldthwaite, *The Building of Renaissance Florence: An Economic and Social History* (Baltimore, MD, 1982), esp. p. 66. Goldthwaite's argument is that this increased aggregate demand created a broader and deeper marketplace for non-essentials. David Herlihy, *Medieval and Renaissance Pistoia: The Social History of an Italian Town, 1200–1430* (New Haven, CT, 1967), pp. 151–5. Herlihy focuses more on the negative impact for businessmen and employers, than on the potential benefits of high wages for labourers. For a similar phenomenon in the later fourteenth-century Ghent despite an economic contraction due to the collapse of the wool trade, see e.g. David Nicholas, *The Metamorphosis of a Medieval City: Ghent in the Age of the Arteveldes, 1302–1390* (Leiden, 1987), pp. 130–4.

medieval urban historiography of England, it is acknowledged that certain industries, such as cloth-making, did benefit from continuing migration to towns and from expanding consumer markets in luxury items, which were the result of increasing disposable income on the part of the working and middle classes during the later fourteenth century.[6] In Manresa, it can be suggested that the leather sector, at least, was doing relatively well in the later fourteenth and early fifteenth centuries, with the result that some families were making money and working their way into the town's political elite, while many men were able to maintain themselves as shoemakers and other leatherworkers, with an average worth at least 50 per cent higher than that of a farm labourer.[7] This margin is equivalent to the post-1300 skill premium (i.e. the amount that skilled workers earned relative to the wage for unskilled labourers) that Gregory Clark has found for English workers.[8] It would seem as though Manresa in the years around 1400, like many English towns, did manage to maintain an air of resilience and vitality, even as they headed towards a depression in the mid- to late fifteenth centuries.[9] But whereas the English cities later recovered from the civil wars of that era, Manresa, at least, did not. The concluding section of this chapter will attempt to assess some reasons why Manresans, like some English town dwellers, were doing relatively well in the years around 1400, and will likewise suggest reasons why urban dwellers in Castile and Northern Italy were not doing as well.

THE DISTRIBUTION OF WEALTH IN MANRESA AND TUSCANY COMPARED

As noted above, the data which forms the basis of our comparison of Manresan and Tuscan living standards in this chapter is based on two cadastral surveys, the 1408 *Liber Manifesti* and the 1427 Florentine Catasto, which were drawn up according to a shared set of fiscal and

6 See Richard Britnell, 'The Economy of British towns 1300–1540', in David M. Palliser (ed.), *The Cambridge Urban History of Britain*, vol. I: *600–1540* (Cambridge, 2000), pp. 313–33, at pp. 320–1. Also Heather Swanson, *Medieval Artisans* (London, 1989), pp. 174–5.

7 For the *coriaterii* (leather wholesalers) as political elites, see Chapter 3. For workers' patrimonies, LM. The latter figures are detailed in a forthcoming work.

8 Gregory Clark, 'Work, Wages and Living Conditions: Building Workers in England from the Magna Carta to Tony Blair', in Simonetta Cavaciocchi (ed.), *L'Edilizia prima della rivoluzione industriale secc. XIII–XVIII: Atti della trentaseiesima settimana di studi, 26–30 Aprile 2004*, Atti delle settimane di studi e altri convegni, 36 (Florence, 2005), pp. 889–932, at pp. 894–6.

9 For this see John Hatcher, 'The Great Slump of the Mid-fifteenth Century', in Richard Britnell and John Hatcher (eds.), *Progress and Problems in Medieval England: Essays in Honour of Edward Miller* (Cambridge, 1996), pp. 237–72.

political aims. They are both products of a similar set of cultural trends and fiscal techniques, which was shared by this point in time between Catalonia and Italy. The background to this evolution may be briefly summarized as follows. By the middle of the fourteenth century, many cities in Italy, the Crown of Aragon and elsewhere in continental Europe had created regularized systems of taxation based on consumption taxes. These consumption taxes were very popular with the urban elites who controlled civic governments, because they helped to ensure that the burden of civic taxation fell disproportionately on the poorer citizens. Soon after these revenue streams were regularized, many governments began to finance long-term government loans based on the expectations of future receipts. What these governments could not have foreseen was that the Black Death and subsequent waves of plague would begin to reduce civic population at recurring intervals. Thus, while debt burdens continued to increase, population continued to decrease, resulting in an increased debt burden per capita. This put pressure on urban governments to increase consumption tax rates in an effort to keep up with falling revenue – and the predictable result was that the lower classes in many cities began to feel this pressure keenly.[10] These taxes, which struck at the very ability of the poor to keep themselves from starvation, caused unrest in cities across southern Europe – although actual rioting was much more common in Italy than in Aragon.[11] Even where riots were not overt, the unfairness of the consumption tax regime sometimes led 'populist' factions to push for a more equitable distribution of the tax burden – and the obvious alternative was to institute a property or income tax.

In Manresa, the pressures of war and indebtedness fuelled the rise of Francesc Nerell, who as we have seen in 1369 and 1370 attempted to push an income-based tax through the council. Although the town government did begin to collect data on the wealth of individual citizens, this 'manifest' was soon destroyed due to objections by the elitist party. But it is remarkable that town government was democratic enough that such a move could even be made at all. Such information could not only be used by local and royal officials as the basis for future exactions, but, despite any assurances of confidentiality, it was a clear violation of personal privacy which struck at the basis of many individuals' sense

10 This process is described in J. Fynn-Paul, 'Civic Debt, Civic Taxes, and Urban Unrest: A Catalan Key to Interpreting the Late Fourteenth-Century European Crisis', in L. Armstrong, M. Elbl, and I. Elbl, eds., *Money, Markets, and Trade in Late Medieval Europe: Essays in Honour of John H. A. Munro* (Leiden, 2007), pp. 119–45.

11 For the Italian rioting see Samuel K. Cohn Jr, *Lust for Liberty: The Politics of Social Revolt in Medieval Europe, 1200–1425* (Cambridge, MA, 2008), pp. 76–7.

of pride, honour, and self-worth. Despite these objections, the notion of a property tax did continue to gain ground in the fifteenth century and did come into common practice. The fact that the Manresan survey has so much in common with a Venetian survey described in 1411, and with the Florentine Catasto of 1427, which was based on this Venetian survey, clearly indicates that the Catalans were once more dialoguing with Italy as an exemplar of best fiscal practice, as they had earlier done with their public debt system and their gold coinage.[12] In Florence, thirteenth-century taxation of both the city and the *contado* was based on the '*estimo*', which was originally a tax on landed property. Since the overwhelming majority of property was in fact held in land, this was deemed to be the most sensible and efficient means to tax the total wealth of society. However, as commerce continued to expand, it became increasingly apparent that large reserves of liquid wealth were being entirely neglected. The government of Florence in 1345 began to make 'forced loans' on this wealth, but only in the city of Florence itself. In 1427, disaffection with this system coupled with extreme pressure from the expansionist Milanese state caused the Florentines to expand the old notion of the *estimo* to include an estimate of all wealth, landed and otherwise, for all citizens of the Florentine state.

The fact that the Manresan and Florentine cadastral surveys were modelled on a similar pattern therefore makes it relatively easy and logical to compare the data provided by the two documents. Unlike with certain well-known English cadastral surveys, both the Florentine and the Manresan surveys attempted to register the wealth of every household head; at Florence this was done even if these were servants living in the home of their master.[13] Accordingly at Manresa, we find valuations that range from over £4,000, a sum which could purchase at least two castle-lordships, to the meagre belongings of Guillmonetta, widow of Romeu Redon, whose total worth was £8.[14] Both the Tuscan and the Manresan surveys omit clergy, nobles, and foreigners, a fault which cannot be helped but which at least aids in the comparison of the two. At Manresa, it has already been established that there were relatively few nobles living in the city in the early fifteenth century. Likewise, it might be expected that the dean and chapter would include fewer than two dozen

[12] For the Venetian example see Herlihy and Klapisch-Zuber, *Tuscans and their Families*, pp. 9–10.

[13] For servants in the Catasto, see Herlihy and Klapisch-Zuber, *Tuscans and their Families*, pp. 11–13. For the *Liber Manifesti* of Manresa this point is unclear. For concerns with the completeness of the English lay subsidies of the late thirteenth and early fourteenth centuries, see Pamela Nightingale, 'The Lay Subsidies and the Distribution of Wealth in Medieval England, 1275–1334', *Economic History Review*, 57:1 (2004), 1–32, at 2–9.

[14] For Marta, LM 43r; for Guillmonetta, LM 144r.

householders, officially unmarried and childless.[15] A hearth survey of Manresa from 1497 suggests that the numbers of noble and clerical households were quite low. In that year, the remaining 272 commoners' households at Manresa were complemented by the households of eight *persons generoses*, fifteen canons, and ten other ecclesiastics.[16] The biggest difference between the Florentine and the Manresan surveys is that the Florentine redactors were instructed to omit the value of the householder's primary home; however, Herlihy and Klapisch-Zuber report that outside of Florence, primary dwellings were usually counted. In order to account for this difference, Manresan data has in the relevant instances been computed with or without the value of primary homes.[17] A second, more regrettable difference is that the Manresan survey does not contain the ages of the householders, or the number or ages of their dependants. Thus, many of the life-cycle and sex-ratio calculations that could be done with the Florentine data are simply not possible at Manresa.

Otherwise, the Florentine Catasto of 1427, the Venetian survey of 1411 mentioned by Herlihy and the Manresan *Liber Manifesti* all list similar variables for each household head. These include name, occupation, and valuations of immovable and movable goods, including land, homes, workshops, animals deemed 'worthy of value', money and precious metals, mercantile stocks, loans made, shares in the public debt, and debts incurred. At Manresa, property listings included how much rent was paid on these per year, and often the interest rates of loans were included. Herlihy and Klapisch-Zuber have explained the pitfalls and details of Catasto-style assessment at great length, therefore there is little need to rehearse them here.[18] Suffice to say that with any such document, there will be some confusion over special cases such as wardship and widows' and children's property rights, amongst others. There was always the possibility that some foreign property could be hidden from the redactors, but it should be pointed out that the city's wealthiest citizens had a vested interest in ensuring that their fellows came clean and did not seriously under-report their wealth. The Sarta papers reveal how intimately connected a Manresan patricians' business affairs could often

[15] Though much has been written of late on Catalan clerical concubinage. See e.g. Michelle Armstrong-Partida, 'Priestly Marriage: The Tradition of Clerical Concubinage in the Spanish Church', *Viator: Medieval and Renaissance Studies*, 40:2 (2009), 221–53; and M. A. Kelleher, '"Like Man and Wife": Clerics' Concubines in the Diocese of Barcelona', *Journal of Medieval History*, 28:4 (2002), 349–60.

[16] Josep Iglésies, *El fogatge de 1497: Estudi i transcripció*, vol. I (Barcelona, 1991), p. 18.

[17] See note to Table 8.1.

[18] David Herlihy and Christiane Klapisch-Zuber, *Tuscans and their Families: A Study of the Florentine Catasto of 1427* (New Haven, CT, 1985), ch. 1, pp. 1–27.

be with those of other elite families. There were probably relatively few 'big secrets' which could therefore be kept from the Manresan redactors. Furthermore, the Manresan historian Marc Torras has thoroughly researched the methods and means used to redact the various Manresan manifests; his conclusions also provide no reason for us to suspect any hidden differences between the Manresan and the Tuscan data.[19] The *Liber Manifesti* which we refer to for convenience as dating from 1408 was in fact redacted between 1408 and 1411. From the details provided in the initial entries, including that of Jaume Sarta, it can be discovered that the redactors sometimes entered the homes of the testators in order to inspect the moveable goods, although at other times it would seem that householders gave sworn testimony at the redactor's office.[20] Another factor which renders the Tuscan work especially suitable for comparison with Manresa is the fact that Herlihy and Klapisch-Zuber studied several medium-sized Tuscan cities in addition to Florence. These cities, whose size and role within Tuscany was comparable to Manresa's role within Catalonia, included Pisa, Prato, Pistoia, Cortona, Arezzo, and Volterra.[21] All six of these cities, which served as regional centres of production and distribution, and which housed substantial bourgeois elements in their own right, were analysed in *Tuscans and their Families*. Pistoia has been treated in the greatest detail by Herlihy, since it was also the subject of an earlier study entitled *Medieval and Renaissance Pistoia*.[22]

Having established the viability of comparing the Manresan and the Tuscan surveys, we can turn to the question of what these surveys can tell us about the nature of urban society in late medieval southern Europe. Although the more recent English and Low Countries literature has tended to emphasize a 'golden age' of workers, this must be understood alongside an older tradition which describes very high levels of desperately poor inhabitants in cities across later medieval Europe.[23] Michel Mollatt argued that poverty after the plague moved from the countryside to the city, and there have been few dissenting voices on this general

[19] These findings are summarized in Marc Torras Serra, *La crisi del segle XV a Manresa: Una aproximació a partir dels llibres de manifests* (Manresa, 1996).

[20] For evidence of the redactors entering the homes of the declarants (based on the level of detail shown by the number of vessels and boxes, etc.) see LM 1r–9r. For references to later declarants manifesting '*coram dictis electis*' see e.g. LM 86v.

[21] These secondary cities were often grouped together or otherwise singled out by Herlihy and Klapisch-Zuber for analysis; see especially *Tuscans and their Families*, ch. 4, 'Wealth and Enterprise', pp. 93–130.

[22] David Herlihy, *Medieval and Renaissance Pistoia: The Social History of an Italian Town, 1200–1430* (New Haven, CT, 1967).

[23] See n. 5@, above.

plane of argument.[24] Grim estimates of urban poverty can be found for places as disparate as London, northern France, and Florence.[25] It might be expected that the metropoles would contain larger numbers of poor householders, just as they would contain relatively large concentrations of extremely wealthy citizens. This might lead one to the conclusion that medium-sized towns would show fewer extremes of wealth and poverty. Strangely enough, there have been few studies of wealth distribution in medium-sized medieval towns, so that no pattern, tentative or definite, has really been established. Again, the Catasto data presents an exception. Here, historians of fifteenth-century Tuscany have concluded that, even at this relatively underpopulated age, the cities were populated by an underclass of wretched families.[26] In a passage reminiscent of Engels' description of Manchester, Herlihy describes the miserable lot of the Tuscan urban poor as the victims of a system which extracted far too much wealth and left them with virtually nothing to live on: 'everywhere, the deprived workers, eking out a living on the margins of subsistence, had little incentive to better their plight; strenuous efforts might win them greater income, but this would largely benefit others . . . '[27]

It is natural to expect to find a similar underclass in Catalan cities, due to a long-standing assumption of very low per capita wealth in pre-industrial Europe. In fact, as noted in the previous chapter, recent surveys by Robert Allen and Gregory Clark have reiterated the fact that per capita income in England in the decades after the Black Death was not equalled again until the 1870s in Britain.[28] These findings probably shed light on the surprisingly high living standards found at Manresa: the 1408 survey probably shows a city which was enjoying a high point of pre-industrial prosperity. Still, Allen's work has also emphasized that there was a 'little divergence' in European wages between north-west Europe, which after 1500 managed to maintain its fifteenth-century living standards, and the rest of Europe, in which living standards actually fell.[29] Our data fits into this

24 Michel Mollat, *The Poor in the Middle Ages: An Essay in Social History* (New Haven, CT, 1986), pp. 233–5.

25 Barbara A. Hanawalt, 'Reading the Lives of the Illiterate: London's Poor', *Speculum*, 80:4 (2005), 1067–1086, at 1070; Herlihy and Klapisch-Zuber, *Tuscans and their Families*, pp. 95–108; Mollatt, *The Poor in the Middle Ages*, p. 233.

26 A. Molho, *Florentine Public Finances in the Early Renaissance, 1400–33* (Cambridge, MA, 1974), p. 45.

27 Herlihy and Klapisch-Zuber, *Tuscans and their Families*, p. 107.

28 Robert C. Allen, 'The Great Divergence in European Wages and Prices from the Middle Ages to the First World War', *Explorations in Economic History*, 38:4 (2001), 411–47; 435; Clark, 'Work, Wages and Living Conditions', p. 919.

29 This wage divergence within Europe has now been christened the 'Little Divergence' to distinguish it from Pomeranz' notion of a world-scale 'Great Divergence'. See on this J. L. van Zanden, *The Long Road to the Industrial Revolution* (Leiden, 2009), pp. 95–100.

Table 8.1 *The distribution of wealth in Manresa, Pistoia, and the Pistoiese suburb of Piuvica (after Herlihy)*[30]

Population percentiles ranked by wealth	Manresa, 1408 (640 h.holds) % of wealth held (cumulative):		Pistoia, 1427 (1247 h.holds) % of wealth held	Piuvica, 1243 (238 h.holds) % wealth held	Piuvica, 1427 (96 h.holds) % wealth held
(0 = Poorest)	Net	'Patrimony'	(Cumulative)	(Cumulative)	(Cumulative)
0–10	0.6	0.1	0.0	1.7	0.0
0–20	2.0	0.8	0.0	4.4	0.0
0–30	4.2	2.0	0.5	7.7	0.0
0–40	6.9	3.8	1.8	12.4	0.7
0–50	10.6	6.4	4.1	18.3	2.9
0–60	15.5	10.1	7.9	25.5	7.1
0–70	22.1	15.5	14.3	36.0	12.9
0–80	31.5	24.2	23.9	50.0	26.1
0–90	48.4	41.2	41.0	67.9	45.0
0–95	63.3	57.8	n.a.	n.a.	n.a.
0–97	73.1		n.a.	n.a.	n.a.
0–98	79.1		n.a.	n.a.	n.a.
0–99	87.5		n.a.	n.a.	n.a.
0–100	100.0		100.0	100.0	100.0

picture by suggesting that in the case of Manresa, at least, the fall in living standards which occurred during the fifteenth century was steep indeed.

[30] Source: Manresa: LM. Pistoia and Piuvica: Herlihy, *Medieval and Renaissance Pistoia*, p. 188 (Pistoia); p. 183 (Piuvica).
Notes: This graph was constructed with cumulative deciles, so that the Manresan data could be more easily compared with the data presented by Herlihy. This does indeed show that the top 10 per cent of the population owned over 50 per cent of the wealth, except in Piuvica in 1243.
This distribution is based on the Catasto definition of 'taxable wealth' per householder. Herlihy explains that the Catasto did not record certain properties considered 'necessities of life', and therefore it under-represents Tuscan gross wealth. However, in the medium-sized cities, individual homes were usually counted as assets, and landed wealth was estimated, albeit below its market value; *Medieval and Renaissance Pistoia*, p. 17 (for homes), and p. 93 (for land). The extent of the omissions might be significant, especially for the bottom 30 to 50 per cent of Tuscan population. Therefore, two calculations of Manresan wealth have been devised, in order to present a range, between which probably lies the true mean of comparison.
Manresan 'net wealth' equals gross wealth minus debts. Since Manresan debt levels were low, this probably represents a figure somewhat higher than that recorded by the Catasto redactors. It is not possible to compensate for this except by comparing it with Manresan net wealth.
Manresan 'patrimony', as also explained in the text, is a figure which equals gross wealth, minus a householder's primary house, minus half of the value of their land. Since Herlihy reports that the exemption of a family's primary house from their Catasto estimate was largely ignored outside Florence, it is likely that the 'patrimony' calculation for Manresa is overcompensating for the Catasto omissions.

Table 8.2 *Average net wealth per household at Manresa, Pistoia, and Piuvica*[31]

Manresa, 1408	343 fl/household (640 households)
Pistoia, 1427	211 fl/household (1,247 households)
Piuvica, 1427	61 fl/household (96 households)

Manresan fortunes in Florentine florins, 1408 exchange rate.

Our first table (8.1) reveals that the distribution of wealth at Manresa was substantially more equitable at the beginning of the fifteenth century than it was in contemporary Tuscan cities. The distribution stood roughly midway between the similar distributions at Pistoia and Piuvica in 1427 and the much more equitable distribution obtaining in Piuvica in 1243. While it might be argued from the distribution of wealth as a whole that the different figures resulted from the presence of a very wealthy upper class at Pistoia, in fact the breakdown of each town by wealth brackets shows a striking difference in the percentage of wealth held by the Manresan and Pistoiese lower and middle classes. Whereas the lowest 40 per cent of Manresa's inhabitants controlled 7 per cent of the city's net wealth, the same proportion of Pistoiese citizens controlled scarcely one quarter of this amount. This becomes especially apparent in the middle wealth brackets: at that point the fiftieth and sixtieth Manresan percentiles controlled fully double the proportion of their Pistoiese counterparts, even though Pistoia was roughly double the size of Manresa and was situated in one of the wealthiest areas of Europe. The next two tables (8.2 and 8.3) complement the first, revealing that Manresan net wealth per capita was substantially higher than at Pistoia, and that this held true for the lower and middle classes. Even though the redactors of the Catasto deducted certain assets from their tallies in order to make allowance for 'the necessities of life', and this would have under-represented their wealth to a degree, the contrast between Tuscan and Manresan lower and middle class standards of living remains significant. Table 8.4 reveals that the gap between Manresan and Pistoiese households continued to close as one moves up the wealth brackets, meaning that the fortunes of the wealthiest patricians in both Manresa and Pistoia were strikingly equivalent.

[31] Source: LM.
Notes: This table is based on Manresans' net wealth, since Herlihy says that debts were subtracted from the Tuscan tallies. For the exchange rate between pounds of Barcelona and Florentine Florins in 1408, see Peter Spufford, *A Handbook of Medieval Exchange*.

Table 8.3 *Average wealth per household in Manresa and Tuscany*[32]

Household percentile	Manresa, 1408 (net wealth)	Medium-sized cities, 1427 (Catasto estimate)
10	42 fl.	1 fl.
20	70 fl.	13 fl.
30	97 fl.	25 fl.
40	128 fl.	50 fl.
50	164 fl.	80 fl.
60	223 fl.	125 fl.
70	296 fl.	200 fl.
80	449 fl.	400 fl.

Taken together, these wealth tables lead to a number of arresting conclusions about Manresan and Pistoiese society. The first, already discussed, is that the lower and middle classes of Manresa disposed of significantly more wealth than their counterparts at Pistoia.[33] The second finding, also very surprising, is that the wealthy classes of Pistoia were no wealthier than the Manresan elite. Also remarkable is the fact that there were roughly the same number of wealthy households at Manresa and Pistoia, even though Pistoia had roughly twice as many households than Manresa. Thus, while the two cities' elites were comparable in size and fortune, Manresa's patriciate was roughly twice as numerous and wealthy per capita as the Pistoiese patriciate. Not only that, but the substantial

[32] Sources: Manresa: LM. Tuscan Cities: Herlihy and Klapisch-Zuber, *Tuscans and their Families*, p. 103.

Notes: Manresan fortunes in Florentine florins, 1408 exchange rate. As in Table 8.1, households are ranked from poorest (=0) to wealthiest (=100). Florentine estimates are as per the Catasto, see note to Table 8.1. Manresan estimates are for net wealth.

The Florentine estimates are taken from the 'secondary city' data, which is third from the left of the graph on p. 103. Unfortunately, the authors did not label the cities in this graph and so it is not possible to know for certain which city this data represents. This graph was chosen both because it was a good average of the six secondary cities, and because, from the hint given in note 13 on p. 104, it is very likely that this graph represents Pistoia. The exact numbers for the secondary cities are not given, and so must be estimated from Herlihy's graph.

[33] It could be objected that, since there is no so-called 'basket of goods' for medieval Catalonia from which a price level can be calculated, the cost of living in Catalonia might have been significantly higher than in the Tuscan cities. If so, this could largely cancel out the apparent advantage of Manresa's lower and middle classes. However, it can be argued that our housing and food storage measures, discussed below, show that Manresans were much better off than their Italian counterparts when measured in terms of concrete assets. Thus, whatever gap there may have been in the costs of living between Catalonia and Tuscany, it was not large enough to cancel out the 100 to 400 per cent advantage enjoyed by the Manresan middle and lower classes.

Table 8.4 *The fifteen largest patrician fortunes at Manresa and Pistoia*[34]

Patrician Rank	{Manresa 1408, in:} £ Barcelona	Fl. Florins	Pistoia 1427: Fl. Florins
1	4,098	5,772	5,452
2	3,525	4,965	4,909
3	2,868	4,039	4,718
4	2,600	3,662	3,400
5	2,580	3,634	3,104
6	2,498	3,519	3,077 (estimate for four brothers)
7	2,408	3,391	2,587
8	2,218	3,124	2,553
9	2,093	2,948	2,531
10	2,072	2,918	2,521
11	1,879	2,646	2,441
12	1,867	2,630	2,439
13	1,810	2,549	2,420
14	1,796	2,530	2,400
15	1,651	2,325	2,142

wealth of the Manresan middle and lower classes was so much higher than at Pistoia, that Manresans in general disposed of much more wealth per capita than the Pistoiese, who come off looking very poor by comparison. Who would have guessed that the inhabitants of this out-of-the-way medium-sized Catalan town, with its sub-Pyrenean leather industry and modest regional market functions, would prove to be a wealthier place than Pistoia, whose medieval mansions still impress us with the wealth of its principal citizens? Samuel Cohn has argued that the urban fabric of Tuscany gave little outward sign of 'decay' during the Renaissance period.[35] But underneath the veneer, as it seems, there were a great many more Pistoiese families living in squalor and filth, whereas the Manresan citizenry of all classes was indeed enjoying something of a golden age. This is true despite the fact that the Manresan patriciate of the fourteenth century succeeded in building only a few houses which today strive to impress us with their grandeur or artistic merit. This lack of

34 Sources: Manresa: LM. Tuscany: Herlihy, *Medieval and Renaissance Pistoia*, p. 192.
Notes. Manresan fortunes are based on net wealth, in order to create further parity with the Catasto.

35 Samuel K. Cohn, 'The Political Economy of Urban Decline in the Renaissance', in Terry R. Slater (ed.), *Towns in Decline, AD 100–1600* (Aldershot, 2000), pp. 289–305.

Table 8.5 *Daily cost of food for an adult male in Catalonia, 1380*[36]

Bread	4.5d
Wine	4.6d
Meat	3.9d
Eggs	0.2d
Fish	0.2d
Extras (olive oil, figs, beans)	0.7d
Bread and wine diet	9.1d
Meat, bread, and wine diet	13.4d
Full diet, including extras	14.1d

remarkable houses in the Catalan cities was noted by a Florentine visitor to Barcelona in 1512, who emerged impressed with what the Catalans themselves described as an egalitarian architecture, or as they themselves were wont to describe it, 'a city for everyone'.[37]

FOOD STORES

An unusual document, now in the Archive of the Crown of Aragon in Barcelona, preserves for us the exact amount of money spent by the *veguer* of Manresa to feed his retinue while he was on campaign in the years between 1379 and 1381. The *veguer* was usually accompanied by his *assessor*, who was both a legal counsel and an assistant judge, along with a scribe, and several lesser men such as guards, messengers, and even a jongleur. All of these were provided with mules for the duration of a campaign for the purposes of increasing their speed and mobility.[38] From the *veguer*'s itemized accounts, which specify the amount spent on bread, wine, meat, and other dietary supplements per day and sometimes per meal, the amount of money required to feed a person for a day in Catalonia circa 1380 may be deduced. The results, based on food purchased for 435 daily rations over a twenty-eight-day period, are summarized in Table 8.5. The average cost for a bread and wine diet came to 9.1d per day. The average for a diet that included daily meat

36 Source: ACA *Batllia* 1161, 36r–45r.
Notes: As stated in the text, the sample provided by this document is for 435 individual daily rations. These were provided for between five and twenty-three men per day; the men dined at the *veguer*'s expense over the course of twenty-eight days on campaign.

37 Francesco Guicciardini, quoted in James Amelang, *Honored Citizens of Barcelona: Patrician Culture and Class Relations, 1490–1714* (Princeton, NJ, 1986), p. 3.

38 This information is taken from ACA *Batllia* 1161, 36r–45r.

portions, including eggs and fish which were sometimes substituted for meat, came to 13.4d per day. A fully varied diet including such occasional extras as cheese, olive oil, and figs came to 14.1d per day. Given his high social status, it is likely that the *veguer* fed himself and his men relatively well. Many poorer people probably did not eat meat every single day as did the *veguer*'s men.[39] On the other hand, most of the men fed by the *veguer*, such as his guards, his messengers, and his minstrel, were not of a high social status, and so it can be assumed that the *veguer* did not go out of his way to spend an inordinate amount on their meals. In fact, many of the more unusual items listed in Table 8.5 were purchased on the two major feast days during which the *veguer* found himself on campaign. These feast days were 29 September, the feast of Michaelmas, and 1 May, officially known as the feast of St Joseph the Tradesman, Husband of the Virgin. It can therefore be presumed that the rations calculated below were not unlike a normal Catalan diet, which was richer on feast days – when this could be afforded – and more standardized on other days.[40] If there is any difference between the prices paid by the *veguer* and those paid by people eating at home, it is likely that the *veguer* paid more, simply because he and his men were travelling. The rations were purchased in towns such as Manresa, Berga, and Igualda, as well as in small villages and during the siege of Querol Castle, so they do not reflect the particularities of buying in a larger or smaller population centre.

While the *veguer*'s record is of interest as a military historical document, and also as a measure of the sorts of food which medieval Catalans ate, for our present purposes this document is extremely valuable because it enables us to take the amounts of money quoted in the *Liber Manifesti* for household food stores, and convert them into an indicator of the number of daily rations that individuals of differing wealth brackets tended to keep stored in their homes. It thus enables us to make a reasonable estimate of whether or not the Manresan poor and middle classes were living hand to mouth at the start of the fifteenth century. Taken together, these sources also enable us to pinpoint that wealth bracket at which householders

[39] However, for a study of German miners in Pamplona in 1392, who ate a relatively varied series of foods including cheese, oil, herbs, vegetables, fruits, and spices, and which was remarkably similar to the diet enjoyed by the *veguer* and his men, see Fernando Serrano Larráyoz, '*Item perrexil, mostarda, lechugas et rauanosâ*. Notas sobre la alimentación de mineros alemanes en Pamplona a finales del siglo XIV (1392)', *Anuario de Estudios Medievales*, 38:1 (June 2008), 235–69, esp. 249–50.

[40] Many studies of medieval food and diet, e.g. Melitta Weiss Adamson, *Food in Medieval Times* (Greenwood, CT, 2008) and Bridget Ann Henisch, *Fast and Feast: Food in Medieval Society* (State College, PA, 1986), assume that people ate more on feast days and restricted diets on fast days, but quantitative data on how much more was eaten by various groups is difficult to come by.

Table 8.6 *Daily rations stored in Manresan cellars, 1408*[41]

Householders ranked by wealth (0 = poorest)	Percent of wealth in food	Average value of food stores (*sous* Barc.)	Number of daily rations (no meat) per: Person	Household	Number of daily rations (with meat) per: Person	Household
0–9	1.2	4	5	1	4	1
10–19	6.1	49	65	14	44	10
20–29	9.9	117	154	34	105	23
30–39	10.5	168	222	49	150	33
40–49	10.9	218	288	64	195	43
50–59	9.0	248	327	73	222	49
60–69	9.8	353	466	104	316	70
70–79	8.7	440	580	129	394	88
80–89	6.3	551	727	162	493	110
90–94	5.2	794	1,047	233	771	171
95–99	3.4	1,410	1,859	413	1,263	281

began to dispose of an appreciable stockpile of foodstuffs.[42] The results of this comparison are reproduced in Table 8.6. From the data, we learn that the very poorest Manresans were indeed living hand to mouth, like Herlihy's Tuscan underclass. But our analysis also shows that it cannot at all be presumed that all of the Manresan poor were destitute and on the brink of starvation.

Our analysis can proceed by first determining the percentage of their total wealth that middle- class Manresans of roughly the fortieth through the eightieth percentiles preferred to keep in the form of provisions, and the number that stands out is about 10 per cent. This did not decrease significantly until the eightieth percentile wealth bracket, which suggests that people did not feel as though they genuinely had enough food in their larders until they had about one hundred days' worth of provisions

41 Source: LM.
Notes: Householders are here ranked by gross wealth, since there is no comparison being made with the Catasto. Deciles are not cumulative. 'Percent of wealth in food,' means the average percentage of gross wealth held in food for each household in that decile. 'Average value of food stores' is also based on the average per household per decile. The rationale for choosing a household multiplier of 4.5 is explained in the note to Table 7.1. Daily rations rounded to nearest whole figure.

42 The movement of prices and wages between 1380 and 1408 are discussed in Chapter 7; there it was concluded that price levels were relatively unchanged between these dates, even though they had risen dramatically between 1350 and 1380.

(with meat) for a household of five people. This suggests that it was considered ideal if one had a stockpile of food in one's larder roughly equivalent to a single season's rations. It will be noted that the percentage of wealth held in food goes down at both ends of the spectrum. From this, it can be deduced that wealthy people in the eightieth percentiles and upwards felt secure enough in their food stores that they felt it possible to spend the differential on other things. The poorest 20 per cent, on the other hand, were too poor to keep a well-stocked larder, and so they spent less of their wealth on food than middle-class people, because they had other pressing needs which did not allow them the luxury of keeping an appreciable quantity of food in their cellars. Still, the tenth through the nineteenth percentiles of Manresan householders (ranked by gross wealth) managed to maintain two full weeks' worth of food in their larders, and it was only the very poorest 10 per cent of Manresan householders who were literally living hand to mouth; this group maintained only a day or two's worth of food in their homes. This suggests a regimen of buying one's daily bread on a day-to-day basis, occasionally supplemented by charity or begging. By the twentieth percentile of householders, we find food storage averaging about a month's rations. From this it is apparent that at least 80 per cent of Manresan householders were able, at this moment in history, to provide the necessities of personal sustenance for themselves. This, by most pre-modern standards, constitutes a high standard of nutrition.[43]

HOUSING: OWNERSHIP AND QUALITY

Not only were Manresan householders relatively well provisioned, they were well housed, as well. Table 8.7 shows that a truly remarkable number of Manresans owned their own homes, and three- quarters of the households owned homes more substantial than a hovel. It must therefore be concluded that very few Manresans rented their lodgings at the turn of the fifteenth century, and indeed, the almost total absence of rental properties in the portfolios of the town's wealthier householders not only confirms our high home ownership figures, but also suggests that no one considered rental real estate to be a viable investment option at this time.

Also worthy of notice is the fact that 36 per cent of Manresan householders owned a substantial, middle-class home, while another

43 For an argument that many urban poor in England owned no kitchen utensils, let alone maintained stockpiles of food, see Martha Carlin, 'Fast food and urban living standards in medieval England', in Martha Carlin and Joel T. Rosenthal (eds.), *Food and Eating in Medieval Europe* (London, 1998), pp. 27–51, esp. pp. 44–6.

Table 8.7 *Home ownership in Manresa, 1408*[44]

Type of home	Value in £ Barc.	Percentage of households owning (not cumulative)
Mansion	90+	15.8
Substantial home	30–90	35.7
Labourer's house	15–29	22.0
Hovel	1–14	11.1
Total households Owning own house	15+	73.5
Total households Owning own shelter (including hovels)	1+	84.5

16 per cent owned a home that could only be categorized as upper class. The Manresan prices on this table, and the quality assigned to houses of each price, are corroborated by a recent study of the real estate market in the town of Alzira in Valencia, in which labourers' houses were commonly valued at between £15 and £30, while substantial homes were

[44] Source: LM.
Notes: For the notion that artisans' houses in a smaller Valencian town during the years 1380 to 1420 cost between £15 and £30, but could be worth more than £50 in the case of entrepreneurs who lived on the high street, see Ivan Martínez Araque, 'Transmissió del patrimoni i mercat immobiliari Urbà. L'habitatge de les famílies artesanes en la vila d'Alzira durant els segles XIV–XV', *Anuario de Estudios Medievales*, 40:1 (16 June 2010), 201–21, at 215. However, the categories on this table are based primarily on the experience of entering several hundred house prices into a database. From brief descriptions located in the *Liber Manifesti*, one can acquire a feel for the redactors' sense of house pricing. An '*alberch*', the Catalan-Latin term used for a home, was very seldom worth less than £15. The prejudices of the redactors are evident in the record of this low-end house: 'an *alberch* located in *les berrenis*, for which they have paid merely (*solament*) £11.' (LM, 22r). The term '*casa*' was reserved for outbuildings, sheds, and the like. These were seldom valued above £15. Most often they were priced at £5–£10. One of the more enlightening listings is a tower in the city walls, which judging from the surviving tower on c. sobrerocha would have consisted of two rooms, one above the other, of perhaps 3x4m. This substantial space was valued at merely £5, and was probably used as a *casa*. (LM, 143r). That *cases* were buildings of small consequence is indicated by the commonly occurring phrase '*unes cases*' which are often indiscriminately estimated in a group. Stalls and workshops (*taulas* and *obredors*) were almost always valued between £3 and £8 for the former and between £5 and £15 for the latter. Some places of business, such as the large and well-equipped tanneries owned by the wealthiest men in the city, were worth up to £80. I have taken £90 as the lowest estimate for the value of a 'mansion' partly based on the fact that a house worth £90 was definitely more valuable than the most elaborate tannery or mill. Indeed, a house of £150, belonging to the old family of Grevalosa which had sent representatives to *corts* in the 1280s and 1290s, was described in LM as a 'palace' (*palau*) (LM, 165v). The average price of homes owned by men working in various professions has also provided good guidelines for the housing price ranges described here.

valued at £50 or more.[45] In this light, it must be asserted that more than half of all Manresans were quite comfortably housed by the standards of the day. This concrete indication of social status, which would have been one of the principal means through which contemporaries judged one another, might be taken to mean that roughly 50 per cent of Manresans belonged to the *maiores* and *mediocres*, while the other 50 per cent belonged to the *minores*. This estimate is hardly incredible, however, since in Herlihy's estimate, about 60 per cent of Florentines made up the city's *popolo minuto*.[46] At the highest end of the social spectrum, 16 per cent of Manresans owned homes worth equal to or more than some houses described in the *Liber Manifesti* as a 'palace' (Catalan *palau*).[47] This term is likely to have been reserved for the Catalan villa-style town home, some specimens of which survive in Manresa today. These homes, modelled on Barcelona exemplars, were three or four storeys high, had a central courtyard which was open to the sky, and often had very impressively large and ornamented front doors and internal staircases. The ground floor was used for storage and for stabling, while the upper floors contained the domestic apartments. Such homes were indeed impressive by any medieval urban standards, and remind us that there was still a very substantial and obviously wealthy patriciate resident at Manresa in the early fifteenth century. And the *Liber Manifesti* figures bear this out. In 1408, the city contained thirty-eight householders whose net worth was in excess of £1,000, twenty times the annual salary earned by Barcelona's very well-paid *consellers* and Valencia's city lawyers.[48] The city also contained a total of eighty-six householders, or 13.4 per cent, who were worth over £500. This income level was roughly the cut-off point for mansion ownership. Although by 1400 the city's early fourteenth-century prosperity was beginning to ebb, the continued presence of so many wealthy homeowners in their large mansions reminds us that Manresa remained in many respects the greatest economic dynamo, showcase and storehouse of wealth for the Bages, easily eclipsing the scattered estates of the local castellanate and the few religious establishments such as St Benet de Bages.

[45] Ivan Martínez Araque, 'Transmissió del patrimoni i mercat immobiliari urbà. L'Habitatge de les famílies artesanes en la vila d'Alzira durant els segles XIV–XV', *Anuario de Estudios Medievales*, 40: 1 (2010), 201–21, at 215.

[46] Herlihy and Klapisch-Zuber, *Tuscans and their Families*, p. 101. For an estimate that roughly 50 per cent of late medieval urban dwellers were poor, see David Nicholas, *The Later Medieval City: 1300–1500* (London, 1997), p. 248; and for an impression that 'most citizens' of Ghent could probably not afford houses prior to the 1370s, at any rate, see David Nicholas, *The Metamorphosis of a Medieval City: Ghent in the Age of the Arteveldes, 1302–1390* (Leiden, 1987), p. 100.

[47] See Table 8.7. [48] See Table 7.7.

DEBT

Unlike with food stores and housing, which are normally difficult for historians to measure, there exists a more substantial literature on the debt levels held by various citizens of late medieval and early modern towns. For north-west Europe, and particularly for England, many detailed studies have been made.[49] For southern Europe, the literature is once again much more meagre, and generally older, than it is for the north. Once more, it is David Herlihy who has provided us with the best, indeed virtually the only, set of debt figures which provide a satisfying comparison for the Manresan data.[50] A comparison of debt levels in Manresa and Tuscany once more presents a surprise, insofar as the Manresan householders fare significantly better than their Italian counterparts.[51] Table 8.8 provides a comparison of the debt levels at Manresa, Florence and the six Tuscan cities mentioned above. The graph attempts to compensate for certain exclusions in the Catasto by calculating a 'gross patrimony' for Manresan citizens.[52] This gross patrimony equals their gross wealth, minus their primary house, minus half of the value of their land. Since as mentioned above Herlihy tells us that exemption of a family's primary house from their Catasto estimate was largely ignored outside of Florence, it is likely that if anything the 'gross patrimony' calculation for Manresa actually overcompensates for the Catasto omissions. This has been done on purpose, to underscore the fact that Manresan debt levels were far

[49] E.g. Phillip R. Schofield, 'Credit and Debt in Medieval England: Introduction', in Phillip R. Schofield and N. J. Mayhew (eds.), *Credit and Debit in Medieval England, c.1180–c.1350* (Oxford, 2002), pp. 1–18; Derek Keene, 'Changes in London's Economic Hinterland as Indicated by Debt Cases in the Court of Common Pleas', in James A. Galloway (ed.), *Trade, Urban Hinterlands and Market Integration c.1300–1600: A Collection of Working Papers Given at a Conference Organised by the Centre for Metropolitan History and Supported by the Economic and Social Research Council, 7 July 1999* (London, 2000), pp. 59–81; Jennifer Kermode, 'Medieval Indebtedness: The Regions Versus London', in Nicholas Rogers (ed.), *England in the Fifteenth Century: Proceedings of the 1992 Harlaxton Symposium* (Stamford, CT, 1994), pp. 72–88. For the Low Countries see Tine de Moor, Jan Luiten van Zanden and Jaco Zuijderduijn, 'Micro-credit in Late Medieval Waterland: Households and the Efficiency of Capital Markets in Edam en de Zeevang', in Simonetta Cavaciocchi (ed.), *La famiglia nell'economia Europea secc. XIII–XVIII: The Economic Role of the Family in the European Economy from the 13th to the 18th Centuries. Atti Della 'Quarantesima Settimana Di Studi', 6–10 Aprile 2008* (Florence, 2009), pp. 651–68.

[50] Another older discussion can be found in Charles M. de La Roncière, 'Pauvres et pauvreté à Florence au XIVe siècle', in Michel Mollat (ed.), *Etudes sur l'histoire de la pauvreté (Moyen Age–XVIe Siècle) (Publications de la Sorbonne, Série 'Études', 8)*, 2 vols. (Paris, 1974), pp. 661–745.

[51] Although one could argue that indebtedness actually increased spending power, since it enabled householders to 'leverage' their goods, we can note that, in the context of late medieval poverty, indebtedness is usually taken to be a sign of inability to make ends meet, rather than expansion. Still, the modest debt levels seen at Manresa suggest that some householders were indeed using credit to 'leverage' their own optimistic economic strategies. See discussion relevant to Table 8.8, below.

[52] The omissions in the Catasto are described in Herlihy, *Tuscans and their Families*, pp. 11–17.

Table 8.8 *Debt levels in Manresa, six medium-sized Tuscan cities, and Florence (after Herlihy)*[53]

	Percentage of households at debt level (figures are cumulative):			
Debt level (percent of taxable wealth)	Manresa (Patrimony)	MSTCs (Catasto)	Florence (Catasto)	Manresa (Gross wealth)
100+	3.8	8.0	30.0	0.2
90	5.5			0.4
80	6.4			0.6
70	8.3			1.4
60	10.5			2.2
50	12.8			3.9
40	15.8	38.0	50.0	5.8
30	20.3		70.0	10.5
20	27.0		100.0	17.7
10	37.2			31.2
0–10	46.3			46.3
Debt free	53.7	n.a.	0.0[54]	53.7

less onerous than those prevailing in Tuscany, even with the omission of certain goods from the Tuscan survey. In Pistoia and the other Tuscan cities, an average of 38 per cent of the populace was burdened with very high debts, totalling at least 40 per cent of their taxable assets. In Florence, fully 50 per cent of the populace was so burdened. But at Manresa, only 16 per cent of the households were burdened by a 40 per cent debt level, making the Manresan debt level less than half, on average, than that in the Tuscan cities. If we abandon the attempt to compensate for Catasto omissions, and calculate debt levels instead on Manresan gross wealth, it

53 Sources: Manresa: LM. Tuscany: Herlihy and Klapisch-Zuber, *Tuscans and their Families*, 104–5. (Debt levels are not graphed, but explained in text.)
Notes: This table is constructed in this fashion so that the data can be directly comparable with that provided by Herlihy. For a clearer representation of the same data, see Table 8.9. 'MSTCs' stands for Medium-Sized Tuscan Cities, which were aggregated by Herlihy. These were Corona, Arezzo, Volterra, Pistoia, Pisa, and Prato. Debt levels have been calculated both on Manresan gross wealth (which would underestimate Manresan debt levels in relation to the Catasto, since the Catasto redactors made certain omissions from their record, as explained in the note to Table 8.1), and also on 'patrimony' (which would probably overestimate Manresan debt levels in relation to the Catasto). For a definition of 'patrimony' see text, and note to Table 8.1. The last column reveals a truer picture of Manresan debt levels, while a 'true' comparison with the Catasto probably lies between the figures reported in the 'patrimony' and 'gross wealth' columns.

54 Herlihy, in *Tuscans and their Families*, 105, claims that the wealthiest 30 per cent of Florentine households still held, on average, a debt burden of 25 per cent.

is revealed that true debt levels in the city were slight indeed. By this reckoning, nearly 70 per cent of Manresa's households carried a debt worth less than 10 per cent of their total assets. More than 50 per cent of Manresan households were entirely free of debt.

Table 8.8 was constructed for the express purpose of comparison with Herlihy's debt figures, by arranging the Manresan data in a form which attempts to parallel the way in which Herlihy structured the presentation of his own debt statistics. His methodology is by no means transparent. It would seem as though he lumped together all of the debtors who were in debt for a given percentage of their total assets, regardless of whether they were rich, middle class or poor. This is actually somewhat misleading, since it leaves the impression that the poorest segments of the population were uniformly indebted for over 100 per cent of their assets, the middle classes were uniformly indebted for 40 per cent of their assets and so forth. A brief reflection reveals that this would not have been the case in either Italy or Iberia. High debt burdens are not the exclusive prerogative of the lower classes; in reality one should expect to find frugal paupers, ambitious rising merchants and extravagant courtiers in Tuscan civic society, all of whom go against the simple picture of debt suggested in Table 8.8. It has also been true at all times that similar debt levels meant different things to different people, which to a high degree was dependent upon their level of wealth. While a patrician in debt for 40 per cent of his worth might consider his debt to be 'leverage', which enabled him to expand his business enterprises, a poor hunter living under such a burden might find it impossible to purchase fuel to last the winter.

With this in mind, Table 8.9 attempts to correct this misleading picture of urban dwellers' debts by providing a more accurate breakdown of how debt was distributed amongst the various classes of Manresan society. In this table, all Manresan households have been ranked by gross wealth and their debt level averaged for every ten percentiles of gross wealth. The pattern of Manresan debt revealed in this table is quite unexpected, and raises significant objections to certain long-standing attitudes towards indebtedness in late medieval Europe – attitudes which have been fuelled by Herlihy's own misleading figures. The Manresan data clearly shows that household indebtedness did not increase as a function of decreasing household wealth. In fact, a graph of our data would create a flattened bell curve, in which the debt levels of the richest and poorest households mirror each other. Roughly speaking, debt levels average 6 per cent in the highest and lowest twenty percentiles. Debt levels double in the twentieth to fortieth percentiles and the sixtieth to eightieth percentiles, reaching 12 per cent, and in the middle twenty percentiles they dip slightly to 10 per cent.

Table 8.9 *Debt levels in Manresa by gross wealth*[55]

Percentile by gross wealth (0 = poorest)	Average debt level (% of gross wealth)
90–100	7.3
80–89	5.4
70–79	13.1
60–69	13.9
50–59	11.3
40–49	7.9
30–39	14.6
20–29	10.2
10–19	6.5
0–9	4.8

Though unexpected, this pattern is easy enough to understand. The wealthiest Manresans maintained some debt, though the low levels suggest that this was done merely for convenience, for example, to maintain accounts with suppliers of goods and services, or to make small loans to relatives. Because returns on investments were so low circa 1400, there was little incentive for wealthy Manresans to borrow on the expectation of large profits. The economic climate thus encouraged the very wealthy to pursue a conservative fiscal policy, which was all the more feasible for the richest householders because social climbing was not the priority that it was for those in the sixtieth to eightieth percentiles. There were one or two exceptions, such as the royal councillor and Protonotary of Catalonia the Ramon des Comes, who was in terms of gross wealth the second-wealthiest man in the city. Ramon's lifestyle had caused him to incur great debts of 4,000 florins (£2,200), but even here, a close examination of the *Liber Manifesti* reveals that these were mostly owed to his own brother.[56] On his brother's credit, Ramon spent lavishly on properties which gave him feudal rights and titles, such as the Castle of Mora 'with its captaincies, which he has bought' (*que ha comprat*), for the very substantial sum of £1,000. Ramon had also purchased a significant share in the revenues of the bailiff of Manresa, for which he paid another

[55] Sources: Manresa: LM. Tuscany: Herlihy and Klapisch-Zuber, *Tuscans and their Families*, 104–5. Notes: Percentiles represent Manresan householders ranked by gross wealth. The top 10 per cent of householders are in the bracket 90–100, the second 10 per cent are in the bracket 80–89, etc.

[56] *LM*, 1408, 177r.

£500. It would be interesting to learn more of this family's strategy: did Ramon buy the Castle of Mora merely in order to appear to better advantage at court? Presumably Ramon's brother believed that furthering his brother's already successful court career would ultimately benefit the family; at the very least, he was probably convinced that the courtier's access to wealth more than made up for the credit risks he posed.

The second quintile (that is, the sixtieth to eightieth percentiles of householders ranked by gross wealth) maintained the highest debt levels of anyone in the city. This suggests a group of people who were interested in and capable of social climbing, both in terms of conspicuous consumption and in terms of leveraging goods in order to raise capital for entrepreneurial activity. People in this bracket had a substantial patrimony, and thus they could secure credit while resting assured that they had the ability to pay it off on a timely basis. At the same time, their patrimony was not so large that they could be entirely comfortable or lead a *rentier* lifestyle. Thus, as happens today, some of the greatest credit risks were undertaken by members of the upper middle class, in the hopes that with luck and hard work they might join the ranks of the truly well-to-do. The debts of these people tended to be concentrated in considerable sums of £25 to £100 or more, and they were contracted from private individuals within the city. Although little direct information is available, the pattern is consistent with the business partnerships that are evident in the Sarta papers.

People in the fortieth to sixtieth percentiles carried less of a debt burden than their immediate economic superiors, but more than the very rich or the very poor. In this bracket patrimonies were substantial enough to support some debt, but the opportunities to invest and to climb the social ladder would have been considerably fewer in number. In a happy confluence of circumstances, people in this bracket were also generally free from basic subsistence needs, so that they did not need to borrow for this reason, either. They tended to borrow sums valued between £5 and £20, and the money often went towards an essential item, such as the purchase of a house or a mule. This pattern stands in contrast with the debt levels of those householders who were directly below them on the economic ladder. The thirtieth percentiles, who were worth between £69 and £91, were the lowest stratum of Manresan society in possession of any money to spare. Even here, we have to look hard to find indebtedness due to poverty and want, and evidence of a rapacious or oppressive credit system. In fact, a closer look reveals that much of this debt was held by the farmers and farmers' widows who make up 25 per cent of this bracket, and the probable reason for this was that they were borrowing seed in advance of the next year's crop, as was standard practice for many small farmers in pre-modern Europe, including those found in the Talamanca papers. Thus, the debts found here do not correspond to economic oppression, so much as an affirmation of the creditors' sense that these borrowers were productive and worthy, and would generally be able to repay their debts each year at harvest time. Apart from the farmers, the debtors in this bracket represented a wide range of professions, including the town's lieutenant vicar, or *sotsveguer*, Berenguer de Cubines. With assets totalling merely £89 and debts of £13.5, Berenguer was barely able to maintain a semblance of respectability. The threadbare lifestyle of the city's *sotsveguer* in 1408 contrasts strongly with the situation obtaining between 1300 and 1380, when respected men, such as the notary and *conseller* Pere Nadal, and even the local knight Guillem de Talamanca, had held the same office.[57] In this fourth quintile, the small sizes of individual debts reflects the meagre means of the debtors. One tailor named Bernat Serra had accumulated a debt of twenty-five Aragonese florins to various individuals. One farmer who lived in a shack on the *Puig Cardoner* had borrowed five florins from the town's most prominent doctor, Bernat Figerola, a descendent of the doctor who had been embroiled in a decades-long lawsuit with the city during the 1350s, 60s and 70s.[58]

Contrary to most expectations, the lowest quintile of Manresan households were the least indebted bracket in the city. It must follow that these people were simply too poor to secure credit. Yet this goes against the analysis done by the likes of Mollatt, De la Roncière, and Herlihy on medieval indebtedness, which in an earlier, more Marxist age was ready to conclude both that poor householders were deeply and perpetually in debt, and that this invariably represented a form of servitude to cruel capitalist masters. In line with a more current 'credit as leverage' idea, other authors such as Richard Marshall have shown that in Italy, minor debts incurred at shops and places of business were the very foundation of late medieval urban life, and that in such a local network of credit and trust even the poorest householders could buy on credit.[59] It is to be assumed that such a system also obtained at Manresa. Other explanations must therefore be sought in order to explain why the Manresan poor were almost entirely debt free as a group. First of all, it has been shown that at this time, returns on personal loans were at the lowest level that they had been for centuries.[60] It is therefore certain that creditors would

57 AHCM V-20, 1v for Guillem de Talamanca, 74v for Pere Nadal.

58 For Figerola see Chapter 5, pp. 123ff.

59 See Richard K. Marshall, *The Local Merchants of Prato: Small Entrepreneurs in the Late Medieval Economy* (Baltimore, MD, 1999), p. 73.

60 See Table 6.7.

Table 8.10 *Price and frequency of obituary masses in Manresa, 1408*[61]

Percentile by gross wealth	Percentage of households in debt for obit.	Avg. expenditure per household (£ Barcelona)	Average no. of masses per household
80–100	29.7	27.6	2.3
60–80	9.4	17.0	1.4
40–60	12.5	27.4	2.3
20–40	9.4	13.3	1.1
0–20	0.0	0.0	0.0

Average price to endow an annual obituary mass, of 26 known prices: £11.9 per mass.

not have been terribly anxious to make loans to poverty-stricken individuals, who had a high chance of defaulting. But the demand side of the equation must also be addressed. The Manresan underclass must have felt little real need for credit, or somehow, they would have been in debt. In fact, this observation holds true for all Manresans, from the richest to the poorest, all of whom show remarkably low levels of indebtedness. It is very interesting that in an era of escalating public debt, private indebtedness was, for all practical purposes, remarkably low. It was not only the poorest, but indeed almost every Manresan householder in 1408, who found it both possible and desirable to avoid high levels of debt.

On the topic of the debt burdens of Manresan householders, obituary debt stands out because it was a very important source of indebtedness for the city's poorer working-class households (i.e., those in the fourth quintile, or the twentieth through the thirty-ninth percentiles, ranked by gross wealth). Although citywide only 40 of 640 households, or 6.2 per cent, were under an obligation of this kind, and debts for the masses accounted for only 6.0 per cent of the city's total debts, or £919 of £15,374 obituaries rank as the most common specified reason for borrowing in the *Liber Manifesti*. As Table 8.10 reveals, the obituary mass was a service deemed very important by all classes of Manresan citizens, because it set aside a lump of capital in perpetuity, which would produce enough annual revenue to pay a priest to say a set number of masses for the soul of a deceased person. In later medieval Europe, such masses were seen by many as highly efficacious means to speed a person's soul through purgatory and up to its final reward in heaven.[62] The practice,

[61] Source: LM.
Notes: Percentiles represent Manresan householders ranked by gross wealth.

[62] This has been examined in Paul S. Barnwell, "Four Hundred Masses on the four Fridays next after my Decease". The Care of Souls in Fifteenth-century All Saints', North Street, York', in

however, must have created a good deal of anxiety for poor people, who found it difficult to raise the required capital. This would create a situation in which the souls of the poor were perceived to be languishing in purgatory for more years than the souls of rich people, which were wafted that much more speedily towards the pearly gates by the prayers of chantry priests. How much the saintliness of poverty might have offset this would naturally have remained a matter of debate. At an average of £12 per mass, these spiritual safeguards would represent a substantial portion of the earthly goods of the poorer Manresan households. In fact, the wealthiest households were three times more likely to endow a mass as those in other wealth brackets. However, a strong core of piety ran through the Manresan households of every class, meaning that the demand for obituary masses was highly inelastic. This situation gave rise to the practice of taking out loans in order to pay for these masses, as a means of assuaging the anxiety of the pious poor. In fact, it seems as though the Church itself got into the habit of making 'loans' for obituary masses, since in six out of eight cases where the creditor is known, the creditor was an ecclesiastical institution. The city's Carmelite monastery figures three times, the Seu twice, and the Nunnery of Santa Clara figures once. It is possible that no money changed hands until the time of the endower's decease, when the Church would claim the money due from the endower's estate. If this was impossible, it is likely that the Church would have accepted interest payments each year, in return for the continuation of the contracts. Each year, the capital sum in question would generate a relatively small amount of interest, 9s/9d on average, at a rate of about 4.17 per cent on the average capital investment for a single 'mass'. Especially zealous individuals would endow multiple masses for a single person, or presumably for multiple family members. It is also possible that a 'mass' in fact consisted of several distinct celebrations of the Eucharist. Whatever was the current practice, the cleverness of this custom, from the point of view of the Church, was that it obligated individual households *in perpetuum*, so that when a number of these were owed by the community the Church was provided with a significant source of annual rent. If a householder were to default on the loan

Paul S. Barnwell, Claire Cross, and Ann Rycraft (eds.), *Mass and Parish in Late Medieval England: The Use of York* (Reading, 2005), pp. 57–87, 187–97. The theme of obituary masses touches upon the larger notion of memorialization and identity, which has attracted such authors as Philip Daileader, *True Citizens: Violence, Memory, and Identity in the Medieval Community of Perpignan, 1162–1397* (Leiden, 2000), and underpins the various studies in Michel García, Jon Andoni Fernández de Larrea, and José Ramón Díaz de Durana, *Memoria e historia: Utilización política en la Corona de Castilla al final de la edad media* (Madrid, 2010); but the implications of the Manresan custom lie beyond the scope of the present chapter.

payments for too many years, the Church could, in theory, initiate litigation to recover the 'principal' from the estate or the heirs of the obligated person.

Despite the high cost of £12 per mass, there is evidence that the third quintile of the fortieth through the sixtieth percentiles borrowed more than those in the second-wealthiest quintile. Moving into the fourth quintile, it can be seen that six out of the sixty-four householders in this group were under an obligation for an anniversary mass at the time that the *Liber Manifesti* was redacted. Although they spent less on average than those in the second or third quintiles for masses, their individual expenditure still averaged £13.3. In this economic stratum, where people's total wealth was merely £50 to £91, a debt of £13.3 was not to be undertaken lightly. In the lowest quintile, however, there is no evidence for obituary mass debts. The poorest fifth of the Manresan population was not disposed of enough collateral to secure loans for the souls of their loved ones, and, as the *Liber Manifesti* reveals, the Church was not in the habit of lending to those who had no means to repay.

CONCLUSIONS: A THEORY OF MANRESAN PROSPERITY

In this chapter, a remarkable prosperity has been established for the (Type B) lower and middle classes of Manresa at the beginning of the fifteenth century. This included widespread access to adequate food, housing, and other material assets and a relatively light debt burden which obtained across the economic spectrum. It has even been shown that upper-class fortunes, equivalent to 2,000 Florentine florins or more, were twice as common per capita in Manresa as at Pistoia, meaning that Manresans across the board enjoyed higher per capita wealth than their Pistoiese counterparts. The measured prosperity of Manresa's *coriaterii*, leather-trade wholesalers who were able to break into Manresa's political elite from the 1390s, was a significant social and political factor in urban life about this time. Thus, even though the upper classes in general were hit hard by the increasing wages and moribund rents of this age, some of them, at least, were able to capitalize on the prevailing trends. The discussion in this chapter has thus far concentrated on an exposition, rather than an explanation, of this unexpected prosperity. It has been suggested that the quiet prosperity found at Manresa shortly after 1400 corresponds well with what might be discovered in a contemporary English town. Maryanne Kowaleski has called the period between 1380 and 1430 one of 'golden mediocrity' at Exeter, for example.[63] Since Manresan lower

[63] Maryanne Kowaleski, *Local Markets and Regional Trade in Medieval Exeter* (Cambridge, 2003), p. 228.

and middle classes were enjoying a golden age, while the fortunes of its upper classes were decidedly mixed, this phrase is appropriate to describe Manresa as well. Once more, the comparison between Tuscany and Catalonia reveals more differences than a comparison between the English and Catalan towns – to the extent that the existing literature enables us to make such comparisons. If we find differences in the standard of living in Florence and Manresa, this is to be expected, since Florence was a regional metropolis, like Barcelona, and therefore would have attracted many more poor immigrants than a town such as Manresa. But the differences between Manresa and the smaller *contado* cities should not, one would expect, have been as great as what has been presented above.

The differences in urban living standards between Catalonia and Tuscany, it would seem, are primarily due to the differing goals of the political regimes in question. It has long been alleged that the Florentines exploited their *contado* to the hilt, with the result that the economic prosperity of the countryside was wrecked, in an effort to maintain Florentine independence.[64] Even within Florence, the pressing needs of the Florentine state in their dire wars against Milan and other aggressors ensured that the need for emergency financing was frequently great. For many decades after 1375, however, the Catalans were only infrequently involved in war, and faced no major invasion of their own soil. It must therefore be hypothesized that the Tuscans were paying higher taxes than the Manresans, and furthermore, that the Tuscan urban patriciates saw to it that their middle and lower classes bore the brunt of the burden. One does not need to look very far in order to discover why this state of affairs might have been in effect; the answer has very much to do with the fiscal systems of the two states. In Catalonia, the state had implemented its system of government bonds in such a way that the citizens of almost every royal jurisdiction, of whatever size, were allowed to organize the sale of *censals*, which were available to be purchased by anyone, of any social status or class, who saw fit to purchase such an obligation. This was, moreover, the primary means though which the state extracted money from its citizens, and local taxes, mostly consumption taxes, were used to pay interest on the bonds. In such a large system the state found that it could not apply too much direct pressure, or else, as nearly happened in the 1360s and 70s, the edifice would begin to fall apart. The Catalan kings were by no means paper tigers in the face of their parliament, but they did preside over a national fiscal machinery which was both effective

[64] A monograph which deals with this theme of exploitation of the *contado* is Samuel K. Cohn Jr, *Creating the Florentine State: Peasants and Rebellion, 1348–1434* (Cambridge, 2000).

enough and cumbersome enough that, generally speaking, it was best left alone.

In Tuscany, by contrast, the Florentines had passed a law restricting the ownership of Florentine bonds to citizens of Florence itself, that is, excluding the elites of the *contado* cities from bond ownership altogether. Not only would this have had the effect of encouraging a flight of capital to the metropolis, but it meant that the *contado* citizens were not part of the bond edifice at all. They therefore could not capitalize their wealth to the degree that the Florentine citizens could, since they had fewer investment options.[65] The sense of fiscal equilibrium that a bond system created between local elites and the state was therefore lacking in the *contado* cities, and the Florentine state would have had more incentive to squeeze every available penny from the *contado* inhabitants, as in fact they did attempt to do. Anthony Molho provides a bleak description of the state of the Florentine *contado* in the early fifteenth century, noting that it was underpopulated and that it had been despoiled of its wealth by the aggressive fiscal policies of the Florentine government. He states that although those who remained in the countryside laboured under a crushing burden of debt, the government did little to alleviate their condition.[66] When the Florentines attempted to assess the entire *contado* during the compilation of the Catasto of 1427, this attempt at further revenue extraction drove the citizens of several *contado* cities to revolt.

It was probably not the direct effects of taxation, however, that created such a gulf between the middle and labouring classes in the medium-sized Tuscan cities and those at Manresa, so much as the long-term disincentive to productivity that an onerous tax system would have generated. We have seen that Manresa's economy was prosperous enough to maintain eighty-nine shoemakers at an average wealth of £149, that is, fully 50 per cent more than the wealth of the average farm worker. Had Manresan taxes been oppressively high, the material rewards that attracted large numbers of men to set up as craftsmen would have been lessened, and a self-perpetuating cycle of depression, unemployment, and poverty should have resulted. A flight of upper-class capital also would have worked against the middle classes, since the import/export networks that gave local craftsmen access to regional markets were often maintained by the efforts of a few local capitalists. This capitalist function within each sector of the cloth and leather trades is clearly demonstrated by the example of the merchant tailors, drapers, and furriers of Manresa, which can be discovered in the *Liber Manifesti*. These are distinguished by high

65 For the flight of capital to Florence, see Molho, *Florentine Public Finances*, p. 30.
66 *Ibid.*, p. 45.

levels of wealth and ample trading capital, despite their 'working class' occupational title. The negative cycle that emerges from the Florentine pattern of oppressive taxation therefore goes far to explain Herlihy's rather grim Tuscan figures. In Florence itself, the result of years of aggressive fiscal policies and disincentives to production would further contribute to the stark picture of extravagantly wealthy elites and teeming destitute underclasses which emerges from the Catasto figures, because Tuscany's largest city proved an irresistible draw for those who had no reason to stay in the countryside.[67]

By contrast, the Manresan fiscal system seems to have left its individual citizens relatively unscathed – despite the fact that royal taxation in 1408 was undoubtedly more onerous than it had been in the early fourteenth century.[68] The later medieval Catalans have, after all, long maintained a reputation for their skills at evading royal taxation. Ramon d'Abadal cites a celebrated discourse of King Martí from 1406, in which the king declared that 'one glory of the Catalans is that, while the rest of the world is subject to the exactions of their lords, and are downtrodden by forced contributions to their lords' treasuries, the Catalans are raised above other people because they are exempt from such taxation'.[69] In a similar vein, despite our emphasis of royal power in previous chapters, we should not entirely dismiss the ability of the *Corts* to frustrate royal attempts at taxation.[70] Based on Manresan wealth distributions, it would seem that a combination of the *Corts*, together with the pro-urban policy of the later House of Barcelona that is evident in King Martí's statement, both combined to ensure that Catalan urban dwellers did not suffer from overly harsh exactions. An effective royal administration did not at all have to go hand in hand with destructive levels of taxation – rather, this speaks of a judicious and mutually beneficial balance in operation during these decades.

As long as the House of Barcelona and the Catalan *Corts* were working more or less on the same page, the Catalan cities retained a certain degree

67 For the depopulation of the *contado*, see Cohn, *Creating the Florentine State*; for immigration to the cities at the expense of the countryside in later medieval Europe in general, see Katherine A. Lynch, *Individuals, Families, and Communities in Europe, 1200–1800: The Urban Foundations of Western Society* (Cambridge, 2003).

68 This is argued in Chapter 6; see Table 6.3.

69 Ramon d'Abadal i de Vinyals, *Pere el cerimoniós i els inicis de la decadència política de Catalunya* (Barcelona, 1987), p. 287: '*Respecte a la manca del dret d'imposició, recordem que precisament en el célebre discurs apologetic del rei Martí—1406—deia com una glòria mes de Catalunya que tots els pobles del món o la més gran part estan subjectes a les taxacions de llurs senyors i als donatius que a aquests els plague, llevat dels Catalans, que estan exempts de tals taxacions.*'

70 Maria Teresa Ferrer Mallol, 'El patrimoni reial i la recuperació dels senyorius jurisdiccionals en els estats catalano-aragonesos a la fi del segle XIV', *Anuario de Estudios Medievales*, 7 (1970–1), 351–491, at 352–3.

of prosperity, despite the demographic and economic upheavals of the later fourteenth century. However, with the accession of the Castilian Trastámara dynasty in 1412, the conflict between the Catalan *Corts* and the king became more pronounced and intractable. The increasing Type D class conflicts between the honoured citizens created by Joan I in the 1390s and other would-be urban elites served to heighten these tensions, which went on to become one of the driving forces of the reigns of the Trastámara kings Fernando I (1412–16) and Alfonso V (1416–58). Fernando is supposed to have remarked that 'Catalonia, compared with Castile, was not a monarchy but a bureaucracy [*procuratio*]'.[71] Thomas Bisson describes the relations between Catalonia and the first two Trastámara kings as a relationship that could have been healed had the elder king lived. Under the long, largely absentee reign of Alfonso V, however, the situation deteriorated into a long-term constitutional conflict which eventually led to the civil war.[72] Sadly, the stand-off between the Catalan *Corts* and the national monarchy was to become an enduring feature of the united Spain in the early modern period. J. H. Elliott reminds us that the desire of the Catalan *Corts* to wrangle with Philip IV of Spain (1621–65) was one of the primary causes of the disastrous Catalan revolt of 1640, which eventually resulted in the loss of the counties of Cerdanya and Roussillon, the latter including its capital of Perpignan, to France.[73]

Finally, if Manresa was enjoying an era of political and material comfort in the years around 1400, what can we say about its cultural achievements? Did the creation of a bourgeois or middle-class space result in the creation of a unique bourgeois culture? First of all, it seems true that government participation in many Italian cities, particularly during the communal phase which peaked around 1300, did not have a parallel in Catalonia.[74] Whereas lesser citizens could feel as though they participated through their guild representatives in a more or less direct way in the rule of their cities, this situation had no analogue in Catalonia, where the guilds were actively excluded from participation in government by the Crown. Moreover, the participants in the Italian communal governments of the thirteenth and early fourteenth centuries could feel as though they were engaging at the highest level of politics, since in many instances their

71 MCOA, 39.

72 MCOA, 139–40. The story of the civil war is chronicled at large in Alan Ryder, *The Wreck of Catalonia: Civil War in the Fifteenth Century* (Oxford, 2007).

73 J. H. Elliott, *The Revolt of the Catalans* (Cambridge, 1984), pp. 215–47.

74 As argued in John M. Najemy, *Corporatism and Consensus in Florentine Electoral Politics, 1280–1400* (Durham, NC, 1982); for parallels in the Low Countries see P. Stabel, 'Guilds in Late Medieval Flanders: Myths and Realities of Guild Life in an Export-oriented Environment', *Journal of Medieval History*, 30:2 (2004), 190–1.

communes were de facto independent states. In Florence, popular participation in government waned after 1381, but many people continued to participate in civic office. It has been estimated that a larger percentage of Florentines held some sort of civic office under the early Medici rule than had been the case in previous decades, even if real power lay with an increasingly small elite.[75] In the Catalan cities, representative government came relatively late, with consulates becoming permanent and widespread only from the later thirteenth and early fourteenth centuries. Furthermore, the omnipresence of the royal authority created the sense that the cities were always local players, even when town governments were at their most confident and independent in the decades before the Black Death.

In Italy, republicanism developed over several centuries, and it existed in a large number of towns. It began during the communal movement of the later eleventh century, and many communes retained their independence until the fourteenth century. Given this amount of time and this many exemplars, the relatively widespread participation in communal government that the guilds allowed during the course of several generations and the scope for action and the imagination provided by political independence, the citizens of the Italian cities created a culture whose most obvious manifestations are known as the Renaissance. At the personal level, however, these citizens created and participated in a culture of widespread literacy and numeracy, which led many Italians to keep daily journals alongside their household accounts, for instance. Schools were set up as training grounds for future political leaders and public servants. This in turn encouraged citizens to become more reflective, and to entertain increasingly sophisticated opinions about the affairs of the day.[76] A similar effect has been well described for eighteenth-century England and Holland, under the rubric of 'coffee-house society'; but a version of the same process had occurred much earlier in Renaissance Italy. In Catalonia, by the middle of the fourteenth century, bourgeois men such as Jaume Sarta had become numerate, literate, rational, and

[75] Anthony Molho, 'Politics and the Ruling Class in Early Renaissance Florence', *Nuova Rivista Storica*, 52 (1968), 401–20. See also Nicolai Rubinstein, 'Oligarchy and Democracy in Fifteenth-century Florence', in Sergio Bertelli, Nicolai Rubinstein, and Craig Hugh Smyth (eds.), *Florence and Venice: Comparisons and Relations. Acts of Two Conferences at Villa I Tatti in 1976–1977*, 2 vols. (Florence, 1979), vol. I, pp. 99–112.

[76] See J. K. Hyde, *Literacy and its Uses: Studies on Late Medieval Italy*, 1st edn (Manchester, 1993); and Paul F. Grendler, *Schooling in Renaissance Italy: Literacy and Learning, 1300–1600* (Baltimore, MD, 1989); Irene Ceccherini, 'La genesi della scrittura mercantesca', in Otto Kresten and Franz Lackner (eds.), *Régionalisme et internationalisme: Problèmes de paléographie et de Codicologie du Moyen Âge. Actes du X^{ve} Colloque du Comité International de Paléographie Latine (Vienne, 13–17 Septembre 2005)* (Vienna, 2009), pp. 123–37.

worldly to a degree that would have been very rare for anyone of their ilk just a century before. The Catalan bourgeoisie even created an architecture which concretized a very particular Catalan urban egalitarianism, and which was perhaps unequalled in later medieval southern Europe.

Despite these very promising developments, the Catalan burghers were destined to have less of a chance to develop their uniquely urban culture than the Italians, for two main reasons. For one, the towns received their consulates quite late, meaning that the burghers had had a much weaker platform for expressing their political opinions, practising debate, and encouraging literacy during most of the thirteenth century. For another, the presence of the royal governors meant that deference was always the order of the day in public debate, and that individual opinions and ideas had always to be subordinated to the known or suspected will of the monarchy. In both Italy and Catalonia, the previous vitality of the urban cultures began to wane as the power of the state increased in the fifteenth and sixteenth centuries. In Catalonia, the relative youth of this culture and its deference to the Crown meant that it existed in a thinner veneer than it had done in Italy, that fewer people participated and they participated less fully. Although the late fourteenth century witnessed the advent of a 'Catalan humanism' whose extent and significance has yet to be explored, it would seem that the death of Martí 'the Humane' in 1410 also ended a royal regime which might have fostered this native Catalan movement. During the fourteenth century, then, the Catalan cities undoubtedly created a class of burghers who were worthy participants in the 'rise' of the European middle class. The fifteenth century, however, was to prove unkind to this nascent urban culture, as to Catalan civic vitality in general.

We therefore return to the theme of good government as the best explanation of Manresan prosperity at the dawn of the fifteenth century. Our definition of good government must also include a notion of good local government – that is, one which is set up in the interests of all urban dwellers, rather than one particular family, faction, or noble group. In this way, the much more egalitarian and homogenous urban culture of Manresa, despite the obvious class differences, made for a much more pacific and consensual government than could be found in Castile, for example, or even in Valencia. The inevitable effect of allowing one group to rule at the expense of the others, as in the Castilian system, was that urban wealth was squandered at the source on feuding, bribery and wasteful display, extorted or stolen. It was in the long run, of course, in which exploitative, exclusionist, and conflict-driven urban systems would prove to have the greatest detrimental effects, insofar as they separated potential entrepreneurs from political power and acted as a brake on potential economic growth. The reason why late medieval and early modern republics did much better than monarchies on a per capita basis, economically speaking, is precisely because they allowed entrepreneurs to make the laws, which in the aggregate ensured a maximization of profit.[77] Barring this, it stands to reason that a monarchy with a pro-urban policy would reap more economic benefits than one which allowed for the despoilment of its entrepreneurial classes in the cities. A microcosm of this process, and the result of pro-urban royal policy, is what we observe in early fifteenth-century Manresa.

[77] This has been convincingly argued in David Stasavage, *States of Credit: Size, Power, and the Development of European Polities* (Princeton, NJ, 2011). This despite the (somewhat opaque) attempt made by Epstein to refute such an easy correlation, e.g. in S. R. Epstein, 'Introduction: Town and Country in Europe, 1300–1800', in S. R. Epstein (ed.), *Town and Country in Europe, 1300–1800* (Cambridge, 2001), pp. 1–29.

Chapter 9

CONCLUSION

The rise and decline of Manresan civic vitality as a function of the city's 'bourgeois system', 1250–1500

RISE

The slow rise of the Manresan patriciate during the thirteenth century has been chronicled in the opening chapters of this volume; a critical turning point was the reign of Jaume II, which saw a number of institutional and legal reforms that catapulted the patriciates of the medium-sized Catalan towns into a new phase of regional and national importance. Probably the most important of Jaume's reforms at Manresa was the creation of a consulate in 1315. The effect of this institution on the political balance in the Bages was like the building of a great lighthouse at a busy but previously undistinguished harbour. This unmistakably important institution became the focus of a newly heightened political, legal, economic, and social authority in which many leading families could hope to share; beyond the consuls and their households, a much wider circle of Manresan householders could also take pride in this institution, and derive from it a sense of identity which made them virtually independent of any authority save the king himself. This institution infused the city with a greatly strengthened sense of shared lordship, of voting, debate, and participation; in short, of what Philip Jones called '*civilitas*'; and the cultural shift which occurred in the space of a few years was pronounced. While the city had possessed a council of citizens and *prohoms* for a century or more, this older system, due to its legal vagueness and relative impotence, had been much more subject both internally and externally to the influences of *dominatus* than the consular system would prove to be during the first century of its existence. King Jaume's reforms were part of a Catalonia-wide programme which had similar effects in cities such as Cervera and Girona. Under Jaume's programme of urban institutional reform, Manresa became the capital of its region, its markets gained monopolies on trade, and its leading citizens were elevated to a status rivalling the regional lower nobility. Jaume's actions should not be seen as part of some inexorable or inevitable process: only forty years prior to the creation of the consulate in 1315, Jaume's grandfather had been content to see Manresa operating as a feudal market town, firmly under the thumb of one of his barons, with its wealth-generating potential grossly under-actualized.

Another group of people who should be singled out for their extraordinary energies and vision is that generation of men and women who participated in Manresan civic life during the opening decades of the consular period. The names of many early fourteenth-century Manresans are known, but it is difficult to measure the individual contributions of each towards the civic embellishments which they collectively envisaged and implemented. Their vision, and the energies they expended towards attaining it, are worthy of special notice. Religious building on this scale, in such a short period of time, is virtually unique in medieval Catalonia, and therefore suggests that while the institutional framework was now in place for bold new things to happen at Manresa, it was the burghers themselves who acted to turn their city into a thriving example of urban vitality and opportunity. Amongst many energetic individuals who emerge from the pages of the Manresan records, one can single out the lawyer Ramon d'Esglesies, who during the 1320s, 1330s, and 1340s worked tirelessly on many of the city's most important projects. The records provide a sense that Ramon had won the trust and respect of nearly all of his fellow citizens, and that they counted on him to rise above partisan concerns for the greater good of his native city. Ramon d'Esglesies' example represents a type of civic maturity, and a model of citizenship, of the sort that would come to be admired by Italian civic humanists in subsequent decades.

Until the 1330s, therefore, an ongoing process of royal centralization worked in the city's favour, encouraging leading citizens to act with energy and even selflessness in a civic-minded fashion. To be sure, many citizens, such as the Pere Nadal who was active in the 1360s and 1370s, and his contemporary Jaume (II) Sarta, continued to act in such a fashion, even after conditions began to fall from this peak. There was an age of personal civic energy – one might almost call it a sort of civic heroism – which lasted from roughly 1315 through 1375, but which had already begun to fade from the mid-1350s, and which continued to fade over subsequent decades. Unfortunately, the process of royal centralization and reform did not freeze in the 1320s, as would have been best for Manresan civic vitality, but it continued to evolve quite rapidly. A momentous change came in 1330, which saw a reorganization of the civic tax system and the system of *imposicions*. From 1330 onwards, the central government was able to extract the recently engorged surplus revenue streams of the Manresan citizens with increasing efficiency. The introduction of the *censal* system from the 1340s put further upward pressure on tax rates, since *censals* were sold to such an extent that interest payments absorbed an increasing proportion of normal civic revenue. In the long term, the emergence of *censals* as an investment option drew a far greater proportion of the city's wealth into the royal coffers than simple taxation had ever done. If the period 1290–1330 can be seen as a time when royal policy was geared towards the generation of civic wealth, 1330–80 witnessed the perfection of a royal system for tapping into that wealth, with the *censals* operating as a voluntary tax on the citizens' private fortunes. One of the effects of this new arrangement, however, was the withering of wealthy burghers' ties to the local economy. Urban elites after 1380 did not need to maintain extensive local business ties in order to maintain their fortunes and status, as had been normative through the middle years of the fourteenth century.

In an unfortunate confluence of processes, it happened that as the government was perfecting its system of wealth extraction, the city was struck with a series of disasters which quite suddenly reversed the booming economic trends of the 1310s and 20s. Famine struck first, in 1333–4 and 1336–7. The immediate economic damage does not appear to have been very great, and the Manresan elites responded to these first calamities with the same characteristic energy they had shown during the previous decades. They devised a bold plan: the construction of a massive irrigation system which could water a large portion of the plain of the Bages. Work proceeded apace, and with royal help the Manresans overcame the opposition of the Bishop of Vic, one of the region's principal landholders. This project has been rightly praised by local historians, but it does represent, at one level, a great diversion of civic funds: although the Manresans did not know it, the time had passed when their surplus wealth would be dedicated to monumental civic architecture, or even to social programmes such as education and medicine. The new irrigation project was essentially utilitarian, though it brought a side benefit of boosting real estate values in the Bages.

While the townspeople maintained most of their earlier confidence after the famines of the 1330s, they faced an unforeseen and truly catastrophic challenge in the advent of the Black Death, which swept across the region in the summer of 1348, probably killing half of Manresa's population in a matter of weeks. For three years after this disaster, urban government functioned only intermittently. Factional fighting broke out in the aftermath of the plague, and amidst the turmoil a local knight got himself elected to the consulate, contrary to all precedent. Yet, despite even the Black Death, the survivors began to resume their lives by at least 1351, when regular records begin afresh. It is a testament to the residual optimism of the early 1350s that several of the wealthiest

Manresan householders employed their capital in new international business ventures, which in some capacity or another came to involve a significant proportion of Manresa's elite households in some capacity or other.

Unfortunately, further disasters continued to strike the city in rapid succession. It was from the 1360s that the situation grew truly dire, at least from the point of view of the patriciate. A second wave of plague in 1362 carried off a significant portion of the populace, enough so that, from this point forward, the town council declared a labour shortage. Wages rose sharply, followed closely by the costs of commodities. As this happened, investors found it increasingly difficult to get good rates of return on many forms of investment. Landlords found it difficult to hire workmen, and by the 1380s, wealthy townspeople could hire only one-sixth as many servants as they had been able to afford in the 1340s. One exception to this rule was the leather and cloth trades, which given the high prices of manufactured goods, were able to maintain a number of householders at comfortable, even affluent, standards of living.

The best investment returns to be had during the 1360s were on government *violaris*. This was because, in the midst of the series of demographic and economic disasters, Pere III (1336–87) initiated a different sort of disaster by involving his state in a war on Castile. This war soon proved to be beyond the government's means to conclude successfully, and the Castilian monarchs, scenting blood, proved dogged in their attempts to annex portions of Aragonese land. The Castilian war brought an increasing sense of menace and danger to the Manresans' *mentalité*, as threats of invasion occurred with regularity, and in economic terms the war quickly bankrupted the city treasury. Like the other royal lands in Catalonia, Manresa teetered on the brink of insolvency in every year between 1358 and 1375. The new *censal* system added to the city's hardships during these years, insofar as debt levels remained the same even as the city population fell dramatically, leaving the survivors with a proportionately increasing debt burden. This scissor effect certainly exacerbated Manresan insolvency through the 1370s.

One result of the Castilian war was that the city severely reduced its public services. It no longer paid the full salary of the city doctor, the teachers' salaries were cut and replaced by a system of fees, public almsgiving was reduced and the *sèquia* was privatized. Remuneration for urban office was paltry. In short, the city government's once considerable powers of patronage were now reduced to a trickle. The town government began to be seen as an enemy rather than a friend by the majority of Manresans, and able men began to shun civic office, although there would be some resurgence of interest in the consulship between 1393 and 1420. The Castilian war also necessitated a further, massive diversion of civic resources, in the form of a new circuit of city walls. In 1368 Pere III ordered several of his cities to commence construction on a complete ring of modern walls, to be paid for by the respective civic treasuries; those at Montblanc seem, judging from surviving work at Manresa, to represent the style of the Manresan works. Building continued at a rapid pace through the mid-1370s, at an enormous cost.

Partly because of and partly despite these disasters, the Manresan lower and middle classes (in the Type B, wealth-holding sense of the term) paradoxically began to experience an unprecedented prosperity. By 1408, some 80 per cent of the city's householders owned their own homes, most of which were substantial by the standards of the day. All but the poorest householders were able to stockpile considerable amounts of food in their cellars, and their daily wages now purchased double the quantities of land and livestock as their ancestors had been able to purchase before 1348. Nor was it inevitable that this situation should obtain in an era of sudden population decline: in Tuscany, where wages also rose relative to land prices, the poor and middle classes of the medium-sized cities were far worse off than their Manresan counterparts. One explanation for this very likely lies in the strictness of Catalan constitutional protections, which kept tax rates at a low level relative to rates in the surrounding countries.

Another explanation for this unexpected Manresan prosperity amongst the lower and middling groups, one that is more difficult to measure, is a spirit of egalitarianism which runs throughout the fourteenth-century records, and is especially evident in the council manuals. Indeed, this Catalan urban egalitarianism was still evident in early sixteenth-century Barcelona, despite decades of erosion. This phenomenon, which is more marked in Catalan cities than in any city in contemporary southern Europe, is striking, and it probably reached a high point during the fourteenth century. It is easiest to measure in the political sphere. Even though Manresa's high offices were generally distributed according to wealth, a spirit of moderation was maintained throughout the system. Civic office could have been monopolized much more closely than it in fact was. Likewise, a sense of simmering factionalism is all but absent from the records, belying any comparisons that might be made between Catalan royal cities and the cities of Castile. Factional discord did erupt at times, but it seems to have been a relatively small determinant of the council's decisions. Factionalism was based more on exogenous factors, involving the alien knightly class who did not live in the city, rather than on hardened feud lines centred on rival burgher houses, or based upon any class or occupational divisions. Likewise, prior to 1393 at least, people were not excluded from office based on their occupation. For most of the fourteenth century, there were no class divisions, either of Type C or Type D, which served to create divisions and rivalries amongst civic elites. Even after 1393, civic office continued to be open to everyone with a certain amount of money, regardless of their profession. Individual opportunism was likewise remarkably absent in the political sphere. As rare as it might once have been for a medieval urban historian to report, it does seem as though a spirit of order, fairness, and even good humour was at work in Manresan civic politics. The relative strength of royal institutions undoubtedly furthered this, but some of it was due to burgher mentality. This lack of political rapaciousness appears also to have translated into the social and economic spheres. In this way it would have contributed to the unexpected equality of wealth found in the pages of the *Liber Manifesti*.

If the lower and middling groups of Manresan householders were enjoying a golden age of prosperity in the decades around 1400, and the upper economic strata were as a whole still intact, it is true that things were not so rosy for the long-term prospects of the Manresan economic elite. In their private lives, urban elites found that they were rapidly losing income, while the security and competitive rates of *censal* investment discouraged bold business initiatives. Returns on land were abysmal, and the wealthy could no longer afford to hold dominion over rural feudal estates teeming with serfs, as men such as the Sartas had done in the 1310s. Bereft of their dominion over the countryside and their city, urban elites began to turn inward, retreating into their homes. Even their home life was now stripped of the sort of local ties which had become traditional amongst the burgher elite. Since elites could no longer afford to hire local people as servants, they began to purchase slaves, who were increasingly available in the Barcelona market after 1360.[1] Manresan elites were increasingly the masters and mistresses of one or two foreign slaves, rather than half a dozen local youths. The old ties with the land and the old trading networks withered, and elite income became increasingly tied to the orderly collection of taxes for a rapidly centralizing state. These shifting economic relationships

[1] For the economic advantages of slave ownership after the 1360s, see Jeffrey Fynn-Paul, 'Tartars in Spain: Renaissance Slavery in the Catalan city of Manresa, c. 1408', *Journal of Medieval History*, 34:4 (2008), 347–59.

combined with the effects of massive mortality during the Black Death to reduce the number of social contacts maintained by Manresan elite householders.

The sudden decrease in elite social network sizes also encouraged the hardening of class boundaries. The earlier practice of intermarriage between the castellanate and the urban patriciate became uncommon after the Black Death, while a new legal division between 'knights' and simple '*donzels*' in force from the 1350s increased the stratification amongst the Catalan aristocracy, and encouraged castellans to remove themselves further from the circles of the urban elites. In this increasingly 'aristocratic' atmosphere, Joan I's reforms of 1393 introduced an ineluctable distinction between 'citizens', merchants, and artisans, which slowly ate away at the sense of solidarity which had prevailed amongst fourteenth-century urban elites. An earlier sense of shared destiny had led to a pooling of collective civic energy, which could be focused on dominating the ecclesiastical and feudal interests that had long treated urban dwellers as little more than serfs. As the notion of the '*ciutadan*' wormed its way into the civic consciousness of the Catalan cities, however, the ambition to join on the one hand, and the desire to exclude on the other, turned one wealthy citizen against another in an artificial and ultimately self-destructive (Type D) struggle for status, at a time when the economy, the investment opportunities provided by *censals* and the advancing powers of the state were turning against the maintenance of earlier civic vitality. The new Type D elite were attempting to exclude their peers from the exercise of *civilitas*, and the result was a diminished return for all involved. Credit must, however, be given to Pere III (1336–87) for continuing the largely bourgeois-friendly policies of Jaume II. Even Joan I and his brother Martí (1396–1410) continued these to a degree that would change with the accession of the Trastámaras in 1412. It was perhaps inevitable that a Castilian monarch would expect to see more of the Castilian ideology of urban nobility in his cities; and over time the aristocratization of the urban social milieu which had begun under Joan I came more and more to foster the futile posturing, inefficiency, and violence characteristic of Castilian urban life. Without the guidance of the monarch, in other words, the Catalan bourgeoisie could not survive in a form that continued to favour the agency and productivity of potential urban entrepreneurs.

The effects of dwindling productivity amongst urban elites did not immediately make themselves felt on the Manresan middle and lower classes, but it was inevitable that patrician debility would negatively impact on the well-being of the entire city over the long run. The trades practised by the middle and lower classes could not function smoothly without the capital and business networks provided by the upper classes. As wealthy tradesmen became increasingly relegated to a third-class status in the urban hierarchy, men who achieved fortunes through trade were much more apt to adopt the *rentier* lifestyle which would win them the status of '*ciutadan*', and thus membership in the Type D urban nobility which was coalescing in the first decades of the fifteenth century. Likewise, the urban patriciate had for most of the fourteenth century provided protection against encroaching seigneurial interests, in large part by maintaining the royal favour which was only bestowed on subjects whose pockets were deep. As the patriciate became culturally assimilated into the nobility, and as its economic power and distinctiveness lessened, it began to lose its political identity and powers, with the inevitable result that, particularly after the civil war of 1462–72, the strong and resurgent nobility began to crowd in on the urban space and on urban culture from every angle. *Dominatus* crept back into the city, and *civilitas* was submerged. The lives of the lower- and middle-class householders were thereby circumscribed, and subject to limits and interruptions similar to those faced by their twelfth- and thirteenth-century ancestors.

Despite this evidence for decline, it must be added that between 1380 and 1420 the city was still a functioning regional capital, and urban life was, for those remaining, far more sophisticated, organized, convenient, and potentially fulfilling than it had been a century before. The cloth trade, the mercantile sector and the service industry were all twice as large as the agricultural sector during this period, and each of these sectors accounted for about 10 per cent of the total civic wealth.[2] The leather trade was twice as big as these industries, involving nearly a quarter of the populace and 20 per cent of the total civic wealth. Wealth generated in this sector by enterprising entrepreneurs enabled leading tradesmen to enter the ranks of the civic elite at the highest levels of wealth and political power. There was a substantial *rentier* sector, who were only partly coalesced into an auto-reproducing 'class' and who still invested a greater proportion of their money in land and feudal rights than in *censals*. Approximately a third of their money capital was lent to local borrowers, and this continued to build ties of patronage and serve regional banking functions. So if the *rentiers* were less tied to the community than their grandfathers had been, they were not yet entirely severed and aloof. Many urban women became the heads of substantial households, a position which gave them considerable independence of action and a greater set

[2] Source: LM.

of economic and lifestyle choices than was available to rural women. Female economic agency for both castellan and urban women increased during the later fourteenth century, particularly with regard to the types of business transactions managed by women which appear in our records after the 1350s. Husbands in these decades show ample signs of trusting wives with substantial matters of business, and it was commonplace for them to grant their wives power of attorney, in the understanding that they could act as legal proxies for them, in their absence, for all of the household's business affairs. There also seems little reason to doubt that in Catalonia, as in England, the work opportunities of lower and lower-middle-class women were likewise increased during the labour shortage that became acute from the 1370s.

The fourteenth century had also witnessed revolutions in material and mental culture. The 'material revolution' is almost universally underappreciated, but it brought substantial quantities of furniture, utensils, tools, and other household furnishings to the middling and wealthy citizens of Manresa, and represented a sea change from material conditions only a century before. This new level of household comfort and articulation would not be equalled in Catalan cities until the later nineteenth century. Meanwhile, a 'mental revolution' provided confidence, interest, and occupation to the minds of many. In 1280, Catalan urban society had been virtually illiterate: the clerical classes still had a near-monopoly on reading and letters. By 1380, it was commonplace for burghers to write and read, to be familiar with law and sophisticated business practices and to discuss their problems with a logic and understanding far superior to what their great-grandfathers could have attained. The effects of a relatively broadly based polyarchal government, based in law and compromise rather than domination and violence, were thus far-reaching. Following the better-studied Italian model, and given the examples that appear in our Manresan records, it is probable that the wives and daughters of burghers did not fail to be positively influenced by these developments, despite many mitigating male prejudices.[3] Taking together the tremendous improvements in legal culture, in the security of property, in individual rights, and the prevalence of discussion rather than violence and of increasing educational sophistication, it must be concluded that Catalan society underwent a 'mini-Enlightenment' during the later

[3] See e.g. Margaret L. King, 'Thwarted Ambition: Six Learned Women of the Italian Renaissance', in Margaret L. King, *Humanism, Venice and Women: Essays on the Italian Renaissance*, Variorum Collected Studies Series, 802 (Aldershot, 2005), Essay VIII, pp. 280–304; Holt N. Parker, 'Women and Humanism: Nine Factors for the Woman Learning', *Viator: Medieval and Renaissance Studies*, 35 (2004), 581–616; Lisa Jardine, 'Women Humanists: Education for What?', in Lorna Hutson (ed.), *Feminism and Renaissance Studies* (Oxford, 1999), pp. 48–81.

fourteenth century, which persisted despite the many shocks and buffets brought by war, plague, and financial evolution.

DECLINE

Manresa may have retained more of this residual economic, political, social, and intellectual vitality, had the city not continued to lose population throughout the middle of the fifteenth century. Some of this was due to plague, some was due to the lessening of ties to the local economy wrought by the *censal* system, some was due to the economic slowdown and some was due to the increasingly common desire of wealthy elites to live a life of comfort and status as a *ciutadan* in Barcelona, and some was due to the stifling nature of the novel Type D 'citizen' distinction which in a small town such as Manresa was a daily source of envy and distraction. Emigration was also encouraged by the decreasing effectiveness of the *veguer*, who by the fifteenth century followed the royal lead by refusing to rein in the excesses of local nobles.

In this atmosphere of declining population, declining civic vitality, lessening economic opportunity, and waning royal favour, civic embellishment all but ceased, and civic government became less important across the board. The civil war of 1462–72, which saw Manresa besieged or threatened several times, dealt a death blow to the cultural, economic, and political vitality of the Manresan bourgeoisie.[4] Manresa's already shrunken population was probably cut in half during the war, and what is more, the city's elite families were either ruined or fled *en masse*. They may have emigrated to Barcelona, or perhaps to Valencia, a city that is known to have received many Catalan refugees. In 1453 there had been some Manresan citizens worth more than £3,000. In 1480, the city's wealthiest citizen was worth a mere £800.[5] From 1480 there was, in effect, no longer a Manresan patriciate, at least of the sort which could meet the local nobility on equal terms. The knights of the countryside, who had been at least somewhat cowed by the alliance of *veguer* and consulate for over a century and a half, now emerged ready to plunge the Bages into a new incarnation of the old feudal violence. This rise of noble brigandage happened as soon as the economic interests of the

4 Alan Ryder, *The Wreck of Catalonia: Civil War in the Fifteenth Century* (Oxford, 2007), p. 148; pp. 162–75; p. 217.

5 Marc Torras Serra, *La crisi del segle XV a Manresa: Una aproximació a partir dels Llibres de Manifests* (Manresa, 1996), p. 129.

urban elites were no longer seen to be of vital importance to the monarchy. It is inevitable that the growth of the *censal* system would eliminate some of the *raison d'être* of the regional urban elites.

But the creation of a Type D caste of 'urban nobles' from the time of Joan I, coupled with the indifferent or even hostile attitude of the House of Trastámara towards these elites, who allowed the local nobility to regain the upper hand in the regional balance of power, proved to be a fateful blow. These changes were more significant than demographic decline, economic decline or the effects of war in causing Catalan civic decline, and they entirely changed the tenor of Catalan urban life and the fundamental nature of the urban system. These two factors undeniably hastened the decline of the Manresan elites, fostering their assimilation into a decidedly less 'bourgeois', less 'modern' urban culture than had existed in the fourteenth century. It is very likely that, with continued royal support, and in an atmosphere of continuing Type D equality amongst urban elites, the Manresan bourgeoisie would have survived the trials of the fifteenth century, in a way similar to English and Dutch urban elites. As it was, by the sixteenth century, the ambit of urban life at Manresa had virtually disappeared, and noble *bandolerismo* once again became the dominant way of life in the Bages.[6]

REGIONAL AND INTRA-EUROPEAN SIGNIFICANCE: THE 'LITTLE DIVERGENCE'

Such is the tale of the rise and fall of the Manresan bourgeoisie, who included the office-holding urban patriciate, their wealthy peers, and those lesser urban families who, wittingly or unwittingly, supported, bolstered, and in myriad ways partook in patrician success. What can be said about the larger importance of the remarkable lifestyle which, over the course of some two centuries, these people had created in Manresa and in its hinterland the Bages? One answer has to do with larger questions of regionalism. A vibrant network of urban-generated culture emerged in Catalonia after the establishment of regional capitals by Jaume II. This regionalism allowed a greater number of people, in many corners of Catalonia, to practise occupations distinct from the mechanistic functions of life. Indeed, it granted many non-noble people a much greater capacity to engage in economic activity unconstrained

[6] One of the most comprehensive studies of this in the region remains Julián de Chía, *Bandos y bandoleros en Gerona: Apuntes históricos desde el siglo XIV hasta mediados del XVII*, 3 vols. (Girona, 1888–90).

by feudal violence, feudal exactions, or the ties of personal subservience. The loss of this regional vitality was one of the primary blows suffered by Catalonia when its regional capitals were allowed to wither after 1380. And after the Catalan civil war, many of the specialized 'bourgeois' functions and talents which had developed in cities such as Manresa during the fourteenth century virtually ceased to exist in any Catalan city outside of Barcelona.

This debility, or, in Manresa's case, near destruction of the regional capitals, may have had far-reaching effects which are difficult to measure. It is possible that a greater vitality and resilience on the part of the smaller Catalan royal cities might have been sufficient to help Barcelona defeat the monarchy during the Catalan civil war. Stronger regional capitals, supported by a favourable royal policy, might also have helped to spread Catalan 'bourgeois values' to the rest of Spain after the union with Castile, and might have staved off some of the underlying causes of the seventeenth-century revolts. Had the fourteenth-century Catalan urban model become predominant in Castilian cities, it is not to be doubted that early modern Spain would have become a much more formidable economic power, endowed with far greater industrial and financial resources, than it proved to be. Had the Castilians imitated the fiscal and social models that were prevalent in the fourteenth-century Catalan cities, the early modern Spanish government would not have had to rely on Genoese or Flemish bankers for the majority of their credit operations. As it was, the particularly 'bourgeois' flavour of fourteenth-century Catalan urbanism was destined, through a combination of its own increasing debility and a lack of royal sympathy, to have very little impact on the nation state of early modern Spain.

The Catalan cities' lack of Type C or Type D class divisions, the lack of tax exemptions for a given ruling class and the consonant openness of urban political institutions to anyone with given levels of wealth, thus seem to have been critical to the fostering of long-term economic well-being, and were generally more characteristic of the cities of early modern north-west Europe, and of fourteenth-century Florence, than of early modern Italian or Spanish cities. These factors, it may be concluded, account for much of the so-called 'Little Divergence' in wages and living standards between north-west Europe and the rest of Europe during the fifteenth and subsequent centuries. Cultural vitality in the arts, philosophy, and the sciences, arguably stemming from greater levels of rationalization, seems also to have flowed from towns which had a greater level of intra-urban political equality in cities throughout the European polyarchal zone of the later medieval and early modern periods. This suggests that economic prosperity and cultural prosperity – two facets of civic vitality – went hand in hand, as a function of an optimalized polyarchal system. But the Catalan urban system was destined not to remain so egalitarian, so free from the encroachments of the Type C nobility, and thus 'optimalized', as it had been during the fourteenth century. As it was, this Catalan urban culture, which had produced promising signs of an emergent intellectual florescence, did not last long enough to have a significant impact on European culture at large. And at Manresa, it was not until the nineteenth century that the old institutional foundations could once again blossom into levels of well-being and cultural expressions which could rival or exceed those of the city's medieval Golden Age.

GLOBAL-SCALE SIGNIFICANCE: THE 'GREAT DIVERGENCE'

In these days of globalizing history, it also behoves us to say something about the larger, longer-term significance of this study of civic institutions and the bourgeoisie in late medieval Catalonia.[7] Of what relevance can such a study be to current concerns about long-term and broad geographical, historical, and economic developments? An obvious point regards the relevance of this study to the so-called 'Great Divergence' debate. One of the most influential urban historians of recent years is the British scholar Peter Clark. He has endeavoured to make precisely the broad temporal and geographical study of urbanism which epitomizes current trends in 'global' history, and in so doing has succeeded in setting the standard narrative for this process.[8] One striking thing about Clark's focus, however, is his deliberate disregard and evident dislike of the notion that urban institutions created a significant difference in economic growth. Instead, Clark's focus, and that of most of his followers and contributors, lies upon geography, topography, urban planning, size, economic interrelationships, urban–hinterland relations and the like. This starkly 'structural' point of view provides the ideological advantage of smoothing over differences between Western Europe and the rest of the world – because it is here that the major institutional difference lies. To wit, many of the most significant Western European cities have had regularly elected public officials with real legal power, for the better part of a millennium beginning in the eleventh century. Nothing comparable to this system, particularly when the strength and longevity of European

[7] The significance of this study to the 'transition from feudalism to capitalism' debate per se is best understood with reference to my forthcoming publications on family, work, and household, and will be addressed in more detail there.

[8] For this and what follows, see Chapter 8, n. 1.

urban regimes are taken into account, can be found outside of the Latin European system and its offshoots until the twentieth century.

This study strongly suggests that urban institutions are an elephant in Clark's drawing room, as it were, and that they can no longer be ignored in the major narratives of global urbanism. That is to say, the power of the urban consulate for creating agency amongst non-noble burghers seems unequalled in pre-modern political systems. What is unique about this urban institutional system is that it created a powerful 'class' whose range of lifestyles and allegiances was more varied than that of elites in most global monarchies and empires. Those who were empowered by the consular system did not always engage in trade; indeed many were *rentiers*, and some were outright noblemen, but taken as a whole, more of them engaged in trade as a primary means of making a living than any similarly politically empowered class in any other type of polity over the past millennium. The fact that the urban consulates were so widely adopted in the high middle ages, throughout Latin Christendom as it were, and that they remained intact for the most part until the present day meant that they evolved into a wide variety of particular systems, which share certain recognizable characteristics, but which had the effect of sometimes empowering a 'bourgeoisie' of the sort that we are here attempting to revivify. In brief, the urban consulates sometimes led to the empowering of a mercantile elite of the sort that we see in Genoa in the twelfth and thirteenth centuries, in Bruges beginning in the twelfth centuries, in Ghent a century later, in Florence in the fourteenth century, in London and Paris from the fourteenth century, in Antwerp beginning in the fifteenth, in many German and Hanse cities from the fourteenth and fifteenth centuries and in Catalonia beginning in the later thirteenth and fourteenth centuries, to name but a few of the most prominent groups.

Our Catalan study clearly illustrates that it was the raising of an urban consulate per se, more than any other political, social, cultural, geographical, topographical, or economic condition, which led to the creation of a mercantile-minded and powerful urban elite, which was in the Catalan case decidedly non-noble, and therefore open to any commoner who could make a modest fortune in trading, wholesaling, or property speculation. The elected nature of these offices, and the need they created for a '*res publica*', that is, for public laws and public rules, also provides a critical point of difference from the standard global monarchical and feudal systems, in which rulers are tempted to vest power primarily in their own persons. In a republican system, even a highly oligarchical one, the simple fact that officials are constantly acceding to and leaving office necessitates the creation of an abstract 'system' of governance in which 'offices' and 'officials', rather than individuals, are key concepts. It is also fundamental to creating a distinction between 'public' and 'private', and the creation of a system of accounting and accountability which to some extent acts as a natural brake on corruption. The bookkeeping, literacy, financial innovations, and other Weberian 'rationalizations' that developed in the hands of this class would have been employed very differently by European monarchies and states in the early modern period had these urban consulates not been so strongly defined. Chinese bureaucratic systems, while showing some points of similarity in this regard, appear to have remained more closely tied to imperial power, and less continually innovative, than the more independent urban consulates of Europe proved to be, at least in their most interesting manifestations. In addition, the European consular systems showed a tendency to adopt innovations created in other consular regimes, if these proved advantageous.

In short, it can be argued that without the spread and staying power of the urban consulate, the Great Divergence between Europe and the rest of the world would likely not have happened. It was the urban consulate which gave power to the merchants of Italy, of Catalonia, of Germany, the Low Countries, Great Britain, and even France; the Dutch Republic would never have been created in the absence of local 'oligarchy-republics', and the English parliament was greatly influenced by the urban governments as well. Indeed, the influence of urban republicanism on parliamentary formation in Europe in the later middle ages is a topic that stands strongly in need of revisitation. In the meanwhile, one can agree with the likes of North, McCloskey, Mokyr, van Bavel, and others who argue or strongly imply that specifically republican institutions (and the knowledge and culture they create) are key to understanding the economic growth that occurred in Europe during the late medieval and early modern centuries, and which gave rise to the Great Divergence.[9] Thus: to modify Acemoglu and Robinson's thesis, it is the (urban) institutions which matter most in global economic history during the five centuries between about 1200 and 1700; after this point, the

[9] Representative works in this vein include Douglass C. North and Barry R. Weingast, 'Constitutions and Commitment: The Evolution of Institutions Governing Public Choice in Seventeenth-Century England', *The Journal of Economic History* 49:4 (1989), 803–832; Joel Mokyr, *The Lever of Riches: Technological Creativity and Economic Progress* (Oxford, 1992); Joel Mokyr, *The Gifts of Athena: Historical Origins of the Knowledge Economy* (Princeton, NJ, 2004); Deirdre McCloskey, *The Bourgeois Virtues: Ethics for an Age of Commerce* (Chicago, IL, 2007); Deirdre McCloskey, *Bourgeois Dignity: Why Economics Can't Explain the Modern World* (Chicago, IL, 2011); Bas van Bavel, *Manors and Markets: Economy and Society in the Low Countries 500–1600* (Oxford, 2010); David Stasavage, *States of Credit: Size, Power, and the Development of European Polities* (Princeton, NJ, 2011); and Peer Vries, State, Economy, and the Great Divergence: Great Britain and China, 1650s to 1850s (Bloomsbury, 2015).

nationalized republican system of England begins to outshine the Dutch hybrid urban–national republic – but in both cases, centuries of consular urban government played arguably the key role in creating the conditions for the rise of the modern global 'bourgeoisie'.[10]

REINTERPRETING CLASS: MATERIAL AND INSTITUTIONAL PERCEPTIONS

Our discussion of the Great Divergence leads us to one final discussion on the historical and continuing role of 'class' divisions in perpetuating and creating inequalities between individuals and groups. In the introduction to this book, a new model of class was introduced which suggested that historians of the cities of medieval and early modern Europe, in particular, might benefit from the observation that certain of their notions of 'class' have been tied to what can be called 'material' considerations, and others were derived from a handful of 'institutional' factors. The latter idea suggests that there are a few class-determining institutions which, when both present and active, can create stark divisions between those who are accorded a higher or lesser status according to that particular institution's metrics. Thus, most commonly, the nobility and the town government could create divisions between people who possessed various gradations of nobility on the one hand, and various levels of access to urban office on the other. Slavery, of course, also figures into this picture at certain times and places; guild structures play into this; and outside Western Europe other institutions had similar class-determining properties.

This study of Manresa has served to highlight certain ideas on the relevance of class which can be of use not only to historians, but to students of class in modern society as well. In particular, it behoves us to remember that when looking at the role played by class in determining social inequalities, in some societies institutional factors will play a much stronger role, while in other societies, they will play less. Likewise, the presence of certain class-determining institutions, such as 'nobility' or a 'town council', will not necessarily mean that the class divisions created by these are strong. Thus, a given class-determining institution has to be both present and active (versus passive) in order to create strong class divisions. In the absence of strong class-determining institutions, material considerations – namely, wealth levels and occupation – will then act as primary determinants of class differences. But here again, different societies can place widely varying degrees of emphasis on social

[10] Daron Acemoglu and James Robinson, *Why Nations Fail: The Origins of Power, Prosperity, and Poverty* (New York, 2012).

gradations created by differences in material wealth. Likewise, different societies run the full spectrum in terms of how occupation creates or does not create 'class' distinctions. Thus, societies lacking in strong institutional differentiators might be strongly or weakly demarcated based on the construction and perception of material differences.

This might be all well and good, says the historian, but how is the aforementioned sociological model of practical use? Precisely because it would seem that in Western Europe prior to 1800, institutional determinants of class were both present and more strongly active than they have been since. Town governments, in the years after 1800, ceased to have the class-determining properties that they had previously held, and with the French Revolution, the diminution of the powers of the nobility began in earnest, in a way which led to its virtual disappearance in most places by the 1920s. Slavery, it will be noted, disappeared over pretty much the same time period as did the nobility. The emergence of 'modern' democratic society has thus managed, not always consciously, to dismantle most of the class-determining institutions which had been part and parcel of European life since the high middle ages.

This makes it all the more noteworthy, then, that what we are left with in modern democratic society are for the most part not the institutional, but the material elements of class. The latter have proven much more resilient, despite a persistent attack on them by more than a century and a half of Marxism and related movements. A reform of our wealth system would require a thorough reform of the economy which it is simply not within the purview of our current scientific knowledge to achieve; and in any event it seems probable that some gradations of wealth are actually desirable, in comparison with possible alternatives. On the other hand, one sometimes hears it said that modern society is developing into an 'education-based' class system, in which the highly educated from across the world connect with one another more readily than they do with their immediate neighbours, despite possibly large gradations in wealth. In this way, human capital formation can be seen as an extension of time-honoured differentiations in occupation. What is important to observe here, however, is that different societies can construct these material differences differently; in some European countries, differences in education create a more rigid class system, in the US, for example, this effect is less. The same can be said about gradations in wealth. The nobler goal, of course, is to help ensure that material considerations are less active determiners of class, rather than more active ones.

At different times in Manresa's late medieval history, class differences could be exacerbated by the increasing activeness of institutional and/or material considerations. Its society was most healthy, most creative, and most optimistic at times when these class differences were least active. The same can probably be said of Florence during its Renaissance golden age. Armed with a clearer vision of how these class differences waxed and waned over time in response to particular legislative initiatives, ideological fashions, social movements, and economic developments, we as social scientists can help to guard against the resurgence of institutional class determiners, while helping in various ways to minimize the damage done by material class distinctions in both the present and the future.

BIBLIOGRAPHY

UNPUBLISHED SOURCES

Most of the unpublished sources used in this study are housed in the Arxiu Comarcal del Bages (ACBG; Regional Archive of the Bages), until recently known as the Arxiu Històric de la Ciutat de Manresa (AHCM; Archive of the City of Manresa). Some additional material on royal government is located in the Arxiu de la Corona d'Aragó (ACA; Archive of the Crown of Aragon in Barcelona). Much of the economic data in Chapters 6 and 7 comes from manuscripts housed in the Arxiu Històric de la Ciutat de Barcelona (AHCB; Archive of the City of Barcelona) and in the Arxiu Capitular de Barcelona (ACB; Archive of Barcelona Cathedral).

ARXIU COMARCAL DEL BAGES (ACBG), FORMERLY ARXIU HISTÒRIC DE LA CIUTAT DE MANRESA (AHCM)

Manuals of the Manresan City Council

These are the official record of the proceedings of the town government. The meetings usually took place in the parish church of St Miquel, now destroyed, or in the refrectory of the monastery of the Carmelite friars. The manuals I-2 through I-11 were used most extensively in this study. Cited volumes coming before and after these were consulted but their contents were not recorded in minute detail. Registers are followed by their opening and closing dates.

AHCM/AM I-1	1291.5.1	1321.5.31
AHCM/AM I-2	1322.2.17	1338.5.13
AHCM/AM I-3	1344.2.11	1348.1.12
AHCM/AM I-4	1348.2.8	1352.7.31
AHCM/AM I-5	1352.8.14	1356.7.29
AHCM/AM I-6	1356.9.2	1358.11.12
AHCM/AM I-7	1358.10.28	1364.3.6
AHCM/AM I-8	1365.3.18	1373.5.18
AHCM/AM I-9	1373.6.1	1375.3.22
AHCM/AM I-10	1375.3.25	1381.10.3
AHCM/AM I-11	1381.10.14	1385.4.10
AHCM/AM I-12	1388.4.8	1390.4.9
AHCM/AM I-13	1390.4.12	1393.8.22
AHCM/AM I-14	1393.5.3	1398.8.16
AHCM/AM I-15	1398.10.19	1402.12.18
AHCM/AM I-16	1402.12.20	1408.12.18
AHCM/AM I-17	1408.12.19	1416.7.20

Liber Manifesti, 1408
AHCM/AM I-165

Personal notarial volumes of the Sarta family

AHPM a. 4054	(Familia Sarta)	1313–75
AHCM Tr. 113	(Arnau de Casaldoliver, Pere Ricolf, Pere Boixons, i Pere Sarta)	1324–56
AHCM Tr. 224	(Jaume Sarta)	1351–81 (actually 1389)
AHCM Tr. 323	(Ramon i Pere. Sarta)	1351–93

Personal notarial volumes of the Talamanca family

(No Reg. No.)	(Familia Talamanca I)	1317–69
AHCM Tr. 120	(Ramon Talamanca)	1328–81
AHCM Tr. 175	(Jaume d'Olzinelles i Berenguer de Talamanca)	1335–70
AHCM Tr. 343	(Familia Talamanca II)	1369–1433

Records of the Court of the Bailiff
These commence only from after the Black Death. The volumes used most extensively were:

AHPM Tr. 475 (Inventariorum, sentenciarum, compromissorum I)	1353–8
AHPM Tr. 476 (Inventariorum, sentenciarum, compromissorum II)	1358–65
AHPM Tr. 481 (Inventariorum, sentenciarum, compromissorum VIII)	1376–81
AHPM Tr. 148 (Inventariorum, sentenciarum, compromissorum X)	1384–93
AHPM Tr. 688 (Compromissorum et sentenciarum XIV)	1400–9

Records of the Court of the Veguer
These begin in 1276, but many registers are fragmentary. The volumes consulted most extensively were:

AHCM V-4 (Liber Curie Vicarii)	1296–9
AHCM V-19 (Liber Literarum et Preconitzacionum)	1366–73
AHCM V-20 (Literarum)	1384–94

ARXIU CAPITULAR DE BARCELONA (ACB)

Obreria de la Seu Series (1367–1448)
These record expenses and other information regarding work on the Cathedral, and have been used here for wage data, and for a few instances of the price of calç (lime). They were eschewed by Hamilton because they did not provide an unbroken series of commodity prices. The registers are labelled only by year. Those used most extensively were the volumes covering the period 1367–1400.

ARXIU HISTÒRIC DE LA CIUTAT DE BARCELONA (AHCB)

Consell de Cent, Clavaria
The records of the city treasurer.

Consell de Cent, Obreria
The expense accounts of the *Obrers,* who oversaw civic engineering projects.

Llibre del Consell
The records of the Barcelona city council, known as the *Consell de Cent.* These were consulted in order to inform some of the readings of the Manresan council manuals that are presented above.

ARXIU DE LA CORONA D'ARAGÓ (ACA)

Patrimoni Reial, Batllia, reg. 1161
This was one of the very few registers in the ACA dedicated to the fourteenth-century royal administration of Manresa and the Bages, excepting the royal letters of the *Cancelleria Reial,* which were not utilized for this study. However, much important correspondence between the king and the city has been preserved in the *Llibre Verd de Manresa,* which has been edited and published by Marc Torras Serra.

PUBLISHED SOURCES

Balanyà, Ismael, ed. *Llibre verd de Montblanc.* Montblanc, 1992.

Bisson, Thomas N., and American Council of Learned Societies. *Fiscal Accounts of Catalonia Under the Early Count-kings (1151–1213).* Berkeley, CA, 1984.

Bofarull de Brocá, Antonio, ed. *Crónica del rey de Aragón D. Pedro IV, el ceremonioso, ó, el punyalet.* Barcelona, 1850.

Bofarull Masacaró, Próspero, *et al. Colección de documentos inéditos del Archivo de la Corona de Aragón,* Vol. XIII. Barcelona, 1856.

Bosom, Sebastià, and Susanna Vila, eds. *Llibre de privilegis de la vila de Puigcerdà,* Barcelona, 2007.

Candela Oliver, Bibiana. *Cortes valencianas de finales del reinado de Pedro IV: Actas de 1369, 1371 y 1375.* Alicante, 2006.

Cingolani, Stefano M., ed. *Diplomatari de Pere el Gran. 1. Cartes i Pergamins (1258–1285).* Barcelona, 2011.

Cortes de los Antiguos Reinos de Aragón y de Valencia y Principado de Cataluña, 26 vols. Madrid, 1896–1922. (See new edition of some volumes.)

Danés Torras, Josep, ed. *Materials per a l'estudi de la masia.* Girona, 2010.

Falcón Pérez, María Isabel, ed. *Ordinaciones reales otorgadas a la ciudad de Zaragoza en el siglo XV: De Fernando I a Fernando II.* Zaragoza, 2010.

Furió, Antoni, and Ferran Garcia-Oliver, eds. *Llibre d'establiments i ordenacions de la ciutat de València (1296–1345),* vol. I. Valencia, 2007.

Ganss, George E., ed. *Ignatius of Loyola: The Spiritual Exercises and Selected Works.* Mahwah, NJ, 1991.

García Edo, Vicente, ed. *El Llibre Verd Major de Perpinyà (segle XII–1395).* Barcelona, 2010.

Gasol, Josep M. and Marc Torras Serra, eds. *El Llibre Verd de Manresa: 1218–1902*. Barcelona, 1996.

Gil Vincent, Vincent, ed. *Ordenances municipals de Vila-real (segles XIV–XVIII)*. Valencia, 2002.

Gimeno, Francisco M., Daniel Gozalbo, and Daniel Josep Trenchs, eds. *Ordinacions de la Casa i Cort de Pere el Cerimoniós*. Valencia, 2009.

Gonzalvo Bou, Gener, ed. *Les constitucions de Pau i Treva de Catalunya (segles XI–XIII)*. Barcelona, 1994.

Els Llibres De Privilegis De Tàrrega, 1058–1473. Barcelona, 1997.

Gubern, Ramon, ed. *Epistolari de Pere III*. Barcelona, 1955.

Guilleré, Christian, ed. *Llibre Verd de la Ciutat de Girona, 1144–1533*. Barcelona, 2000.

Hillgarth, Mary, and J. N. Hillgarth, trans. *Pere III, Chronicle*. Toronto, 1980.

Huici Miranda, Antonio, and María Desamparados Cabanes Pecourt. *Documentos de Jaime I de Aragón (1251–1257)*, 4 vols. Valencia and Zaragoza, 1976–82.

Iglesies Fort, José. 'El fogaje de 1365–1370: Contribución al conocimiento de la población de Cataluña en la segunda mitad del siglo XIV', *Memorias de la Real Academia de Ciencias y Artes de Barcelona* 34:11 (1962), 249–356.

Mañe Mas, Maria Cinta, ed. *Catàleg dels pergamins municipals de Barcelona, anys 1336–1396*, vol. II. Barcelona, 2007.

Miguel Rosell, Francisco, ed. *Liber feudorum maior: Cartulario real que se conserve en el Archivo de la Corona de Aragon*, 2 vols. Barcelona, 1945–7.

Puhl, Louis J. ed. *The Spiritual Exercises of St. Ignatius: A New Translation based on Studies in the Language of the Autograph*. South Bend, IN, 1951.

Sastre Moll, Jaume, ed. *Els Llibres d'Obra del Palau Reial de l'Almudaina (1309–1314)*. Palma, 2001.

Sesma Muñoz, J. Angel *et al.*, eds. *Acta Curiarum Regni Aragonum*, multiple volumes. Zaragoza, 2006 – present.

Sobrequés Callicó, Jaume *et al.*, eds. *Llibre verd de Barcelona*. Barcelona, 2004.

Soldevila, Ferran, ed. *Les quatre grans cròniques: Jaume I, Bernat Desclot, Ramon Muntaner, Pere III*. Barcelona, 1971.

Soldevila, Ferran, Jordi Bruguera, and M. Teresa Ferrer, eds. *Les quatre grans Cròniques, II. Crònica de Bernat Desclot*. Barcelona, 2008.

Soldevila, Ferran, *et al.*, eds. *Les quatre grans Cròniques. III. Crònica de Ramon Muntaner*. Barcelona, 2011.

Torras Serra, Marc, ed. *El Llibre Verd de Manresa*. Barcelona, 1996.

Torras Serra, Marc, B. Masats, R. Valdenebro, and L. Virós. *Catàleg dels protocols notarials de Manresa*. Barcelona, 1993.

Turull Rubinat, Max, Ignasi Baiges i Jardí, and Albert Turull. *Llibre de privilegis de Cervera, 1182–1456*. Barcelona, 1991.

Vallès Cuevas, Jordi, ed. *El Llibre verd de Vilafranca*. Barcelona, 1992.

Villar Torrent, Joan, ed. *Llibre de privilegis de Palafrugell (1250–1724)*. Barcelona, 2007.

SECONDARY SOURCES

Abella Samiter, Juan. 'La deuda pública de los municipios Aragoneses en los siglos XIV y XV.' *Anuario de Estudios Medievales* 39:1 (2009), 47–64.

Aberth, John. *The Black Death: The Great Mortality of 1348–1350: A Brief History with Documents*. Boston and New York, 2005.

Bibliography: published sources

Abulafia, David. *A Mediterranean Emporium: The Catalan Kingdom of Majorca*. Cambridge, 1994.

Acemoglu, Daron, and James Robinson. *Why Nations Fail: The Origins of Power, Prosperity, and Poverty*. New York, 2012.

Alberch Fugueras, Ramon. *La població de Girona: segles XIV–XX*. Girona, 1985.

Allen, Robert C. 'The Great Divergence in European Wages and Prices from the Middle Ages to the First World War.' *Explorations in Economic History* 38:4 (2001), 411–47.

Alonso Garcia, David. *El erario del reino: Fiscalidad en Castilla a principios de la edad moderna (1504–1525)*. Valladolid, 2007.

Amelang, James S. *Honored Citizens of Barcelona: Patrician Culture and Class Relations, 1490–1714*. Princeton, NJ, 1986.

Angelos, Mark. 'Urban Women, Investment, and the Commercial Revolution of the Middle Ages.' In *Women in Medieval Western European Culture*. Ed. Linda E. Mitchell. New York, 1999, 257–72.

Archer, Rowena E. '"How Ladies . . . Who Live on their Manors Ought to Manage their Households and Estates": Women as Landholders and Administrators in the Later Middle Ages.' *Woman is a Worthy Wight: Women in English Society c. 1200–1500*. Ed. P. J. P. Goldberg. Paris, 1992, 149–81.

Argilés Aluja, Caterina. 'Preus i salaris a la Lleida dels segles XIV i XV segons els llibres d'obra de la seu.' Unpub. PhD. Thesis, Universitat de Lleida, 1994.

Arias Guillén, Fernando. 'Conflictividad en la Ciudad de Murcia (1325–1337). El influjo de Don Juan Manuel y la Intervención de la Corona.' In *La Convivencia en las Ciudades Medievales: Nájera. Encuentros Internacionales del Medievo 2007*. Ed. Beatriz Arizaga Bolumburu and Jesús Ángel Solórzano Telechea. Logroño, 2008, 115–32.

Ariès, Phillippe, Georges Duby, and Arthur Goldhammer. *History of Private Life, Volume II: Revelations of the Medieval World*. Cambridge, MA, 1993.

Armstrong, Lawrin. *Usury and Public Debt in Early Renaissance Florence*. Toronto, 2003.

Asenjo González, María. 'Ciudades y deuda pública en Castilla. La adaptación fiscal del impuesto de la "alcabala Real" a las nuevas exigencias de la sociedad política (1450–1520).' In *La fiscalità nell'economia Europea secc. XIII–XVIII/ Fiscal Systems in the European Economy from the 13th to the 18th Centuries: Atti della Trenatanovesima Settimana di Studi, 22–26 Aprile 2007*. Ed. Simonetta Cavaciocchi. Florence, 2008, 531–44.

'El obraje de paño en Segovia tras las ordenanzas de los Reyes Católicos.' In *La manufactura urbana i els menestrals (ss. XIII–XVI): IX Jornades d'Estudis Històrics Locals Celebrades a Palma, 21–23 de Novembre de 1990*. Ed. Maria Barceló Crespí. Palma, 1991, 13–29.

'Las mujeres y el trabajo en las ciudades de la Corona de Castilla (siglos XIII–XV). Integración marginación.' In *La Donna Nell'economia Secc. XIII–XVIII: Atti della ventunesima settimana di Studi, 10–15 Aprile 1989*. Ed. Simonetta Cavaciocchi. Florence, 1990, 553–62.

Astarita, Carlos. *Del feudalismo al capitalismo: Cambio social y político en Castilla y Europa occidental, 1250–1520*. Valencia, 2005.

Aston, T. H., and C. H. E. Philpin. *The Brenner Debate: Agrarian Class Structure and Economic Development in Pre-industrial Europe*. Cambridge, 1987.

Aurell Cardona, Jaume. *Els mercaders Catalans al quatre-cents: Mutacio de valors i proces d'artistocratitzacio a Barcelona, 1370–1470*. Barcelona, 1996.

Aventin, Mercé. 'Els Masos a la baixa edat mitjana: Família Pagesa, petita explotació i mercat.' *Quaderns – Centre d'Estudis Comarcals de Banyoles* 19 (1998), 65–84.

Aventin, Mercé, and Josep Maria Salrach Marés. 'Mercat i comunitat: Dinamisme econòmic a la vila de Terrassa i la seva area d'influència (segle XIII).' *Acta Historica et Archaeologica Mediaevalia* 25 (2004), 105–30.

Banegas Lopez, Ramon Agustí. 'Comer carne y pagar impuestos. El impacto de las imposiciones municipales en el comercio Barcelonés de carne durante el siglo XV', *Anuario de Estudios Medievales* 39:1 (2009), 329–55.

Barel, Yves. *La ville médiévale: Système social, système urbain*. Grenoble, 1977.

Barnwell, Paul S. '"Four Hundred Masses on the Four Fridays Next After My Decease". The Care of Souls in Fifteenth-century All Saints', North Street, York.' In *Mass and Parish in Late Medieval England: The Use of York*. Ed. Paul S. Barnwell, Claire Cross and Ann Rycraft. Reading, 2005, 57–87.

Barraqué, Jean Pierre. *Saragosse à la fin du Moyen Age: Une ville sous influence*. Paris, 1999.

Batlle Gallart, Carme. *Barcelona a mediados del siglo XV: Historia de una crisis urbana*. Barcelona, 1976.

La crisis social y económica de Barcelona a mediados del siglo XV, 2 vols. Barcelona, 1973.

'Una família de Tàrrega a la ciutat de Barcelona: Els Oromir (1214–1329).' In *Estudis Històrics i Documents dels Arxius de Protocols*, 26 (2008), 61–98.

'La haute bourgeoisie Barcelonaise vers 1300.' In *Les sociétés urbaines en France Méridionale et en péninsule Ibérique au moyen age. Actes du Colloque de Pau, 21–23 Septembre 1988*. Paris, 1991, 229–40.

Historia de Catalunya. Vol. III, *L'Expansió baixmedieval (segles XIII–XV)*. Barcelona, 1998.

'La oligarquía de Barcelona a fines del siglo XV: El partido de deztorrent.' *Acta Historica et Archaeologica Mediaevalia*, 7–8 (1986), 321–35.

Batlle Gallart, Carme, and Joan Josep Busqueta Riu. 'Las familias de la alta Burguesía en el municipio de Barcelona (siglo XIII).' *Anuario de Estudios Medievales* 16 (1986), 81–92.

Batlle Gallart, Carme, María Teresa Ferrer, *et al. El "Llibre del Consell" de la ciutat de Barcelona. Segle XIV: Les eleccions muncipals*. Barcelona, 2007.

Baucells, Josep, *Vivir en la edad media: Barcelona y su entorno en los s. XIII/XIV (1200–1344)*, vol. IV. Barcelona, 2004.

Bavel, Bas van. *Manors and Markets: Economy and Society in the Low Countries 500–1600*. Oxford, 2010.

Bavel, Bas J. P. van, and Jan Luiten van Zanden. 'The Jump-start of the Holland Economy During the Late Medieval Crisis, c.1350–c.1500.' *Economic History Review* 57:3 (2004), 503–32.

Beghin, Cécile. 'Entre ombre et lumière: Quelques aspects du travail des femmes à Montpellier (1293–1408).' *Médiévales: Langue, Textes, Histoire (Paris)* 30 (1996), 45–54.

Benedictow, Ole J. *The Black Death 1346–1353: The Complete History*. Woodbridge, Suffolk, 2006.

Bennett, Judith M. 'Women and Men in the Brewers' Gild of London, ca. 1420.' In *The Salt of Common Life: Individuality and Choice in the Medieval Town, Countryside and Church. Essays Presented to J. Ambrose Raftis*. Ed. Edwin Brezette DeWindt. Kalamazoo, 1995, 181–232.

Benet Clarà, Albert. *L'Expansió del comtat de Manresa*. Barcelona, 1982.

Història de Manresa: Dels origins al segle XI. Manresa, 1985.

Bensch, Stephen P. 'Apprenticeship, Wages and Guilds at Puigcerdà (1260–1300).' In *El món urbà a la Corona d'Aragó del 1137 als decrets de nova planta: XVII Congrés d'Història de la Corona d'Aragó / Congreso de Historia de la Corona de Aragón, Barcelona, Poblet, Lleida, 7 al 12 de Desembre de 2000*. Ed. Salvador Claramunt, Barcelona, 2003, vol. I, 209–22.

Barcelona and its Rulers, 1096–1291. Cambridge, 1995.

Bergés, Carme, and Manuel Sánchez Martinez, eds. *El naixement de la Generalitat de Catalunya*. Cervera, 2003.

Bernardo Ares, José Manuel de. 'El régimen municipal en la Corona de Castilla.' *Studia Historica* 15 (1996), 23–61.

Bisson, Thomas N. *The Crisis of the Twelfth Century: Power, Lordship and the Origins of European Government*. Princeton, 2009.

'The "Feudal Revolution".' *Past and Present: A Journal of Historical Studies* 142 (1994), 6–42.

The Medieval Crown of Aragon: A Short History. Oxford, 1991.

Blanshei, Sarah Rubin. *Politics and Justice in Late Medieval Bologna*. Leiden, 2010.

Blockmans, Wim P. 'The Social and Economic Effects of Plague in the Low Countries: 1349–1500.' *Revue Belge de Philologie et d'histoire: / Belgisch Tijdschrift voor Filologie en Geschiedenis* 58:4 (1980), 833–63.

Blondé, B., P. Stabel, I. Van Damme, and E. Welch. *Buyers and Sellers: Retail Circuits and Practices in Medieval and Early Modern Europe*. Turnhout, 2006.

Blumenthal, Debra. *Enemies and Familiars: Slavery and Mastery in Fifteenth-Century Valencia*. Ithaca, NY, 2009.

Bois, Guy. *The Crisis of Feudalism: Economy and Society in Eastern Normandy, ca. 1300–1550*. Cambridge, 1984.

'On the Crisis of the Late Middle Ages.' *Medieval History Journal* 1:2 (1998), 311–21.

Bolòs, Jordi. *Diccionari de la Catalunya medieval (ss. VI–XV)*. Barcelona, 2000.

Dins les muralles de la ciutat: Carrers i oficis a la Lleida del ss. XIV i XV. Lleida, 2008.

Bolòs, Jordi, Antonieta Jarne, and Enric Vicedo, eds. *Família pagesa i economia rural, VII Congrés sobre sistemes agraris, organització social i poder local*. Lerida, 2010.

Bolòs, Jordi and Enric Vicedo, eds. *Poblament, territori i història rural, VI Congrés sobre sistemes agraris, organització social i podel local*. Lleida, 2009.

Bonnassie, Pierre. *La organización del trabajo en Barcelona a fines del siglo XV*. Barcelona, 1975.

'Sur la genèse de la féodalité Catalane: Nouvelles approches.' In *Il feudalesimo nell'alto medioevo*. Spoleto, 2000, 569–609.

Boone, Marc. 'Gestion urbaine, gestion d'entreprises: L'élite urbaine entre pouvoir d'état, solidarité communale et intérêts privés dans les Pays-Bas Méridionaux à l'époque Bourguignonne (XIVe–XVe siècle).' In *L'Impresa. Industria, commercio, banca secc. XIII–XVIII: Atti della ventiduesima settimana di studi, 30 Aprile–4 Maggio 1990*. Ed. Simonetta Cavaciocchi. Florence, 1991, 839–62.

'Social Conflicts in the Cloth Industry of Ypres (late 13th–early 14th centuries): The {Cockerulle} Reconsidered.' In *Ypres and the Medieval Cloth Industry in Flanders: Archaeological and Historical Contributions / Ieper en de middeleeuwse lakennijverheid in Vlaanderen: Archeologische en historische bijdragen*. Ed. Marc Dewilde, Anton Ervynck, and Alexis Wielemans (Archeologie in Vlaanderen, Monografie 2). Asse-Zellik, 1998, 147–53.

Boone, Marc. 'Some Comparative Perspectives: Oligarchy and Patronage in the Late Medieval Iberian Peninsula.' In *Oligarchy and Patronage in Late Medieval Spanish Urban Society*. Ed. María Asenjo-González, Turnhout, 2009, 153–9.

Boone, Marc. 'Stratégies fiscales et financières des elites urbaines et de l'etat Bourguignon naissant dans l'ancien Comté de Flandre (XIVe–XVIe siècle).' *Actes des Congrès de la Société des historiens médiévistes de l'enseignement supérieur public* 28:1 (1997), 235–53.

Boone, Marc, and Hanno Brand. 'Volksoproeren en collectieve actie in Gent en Leiden in de 14de en 15de eeuw.' *Tijdschrift voor Sociale Geschiedenis* 19:2 (1993), 168–92.

Boone, Marc, Karel Davids, and Paul Janssens, eds. *Urban Public Debts, Urban Government and the Market for Annuities in Western Europe (14th–18th Centuries)*. Turnhout, 2003.

'Urban Public Debts from the 14th to the 18th Century: A New Approach.' In *Urban Public Debts: Urban Government and the Market for Annuities in Western Europe (14th–18th Centuries)*. Ed. Marc Boone, Karel Davids and Paul Janssens. Turnhout, 2003, 3–11.

Botticini, Maristella. 'A Loveless Economy? Intergenerational Altruism and the Marriage Market in a Tuscan Town, 1415–1436.' *Journal of Economic History* 59:1 (1999), 104–21.

Bowsky, William M. *The Medieval Italian Commune: Siena under the Nine 1287–1355*. Berkeley, CA, 1981.

Brand, Hanno. 'Urban Elites and Central Government: Co-operation or Antagonism? The Case of Leiden at the End of the Middle Ages.' *Publications du Centre Européen d'Etudes Bourguignonnes (XIVe–XVIe S.)* 33 (1993), 49–60.

Brenat Donato, María. *Aproximació a la societat i economia de Tarragona a la plena Edat Mitjana*. Tarragona, 1996.

Bridbury, A. R. 'The Black Death', *Economic History Review* 26:4 (1973), 577–92.

Britnell, Richard. 'The Economy of British Towns 1300–1540.' In *The Cambridge Urban History of Britain*, vol. I, *600–1540*. Ed. David M. Palliser. Cambridge, 2000, 313–33.

'Feudal Reaction after the Black Death: The Palatinate of Durham.' *Past and Present: A Journal of Historical Studies* 128 (1990), 28–47.

Pragmatic Literacy, East and West, 1200–1330. Woodbridge, Suffolk, 1997.

Broadberry, Stephen, and Bishnupriya Gupta. 'The Early Modern Great Divergence: Wages, Prices and Economic Development in Europe and Asia, 1500–1800.' *The Economic History Review* 59:1 (2006), 2–31.

Broussolle, Jean. 'Les impositions municipales de Barcelona de 1328 a 1462.' *Estudios de Historia Moderna*, 5 (1955), 1–164.

Brown, Alison. 'Florence, Renaissance and Early Modern State: Reappraisals.' *Journal of Modern History* 56:2 (1984), 285–300.

Brown, Henry Phelps, and Sheila V. Hopkins. *Seven Centuries of the Prices of Consumables, Compared with Builders' Wage-rates*. London, 1956.

Brucker, Gene A. *The Civic World of Early Renaissance Florence*. Princeton, NJ, 1977.

Burns, Robert. *The Crusader Kingdom of Valencia: Reconstruction on a Thirteenth-century Frontier*. Cambridge, MA, 1967.

Caferro, William. *John Hawkwood: An English Mercenary in Fourteenth-century Italy*. Baltimore, MD, 2006.

Caille, Jacqueline. *Medieval Narbonne: A City at the Heart of the Troubadour World*. Ed. Kathryn L. Reyerson. Aldershot, 2005.

Camille, Michael. 'Signs of the City: Place, Power, and Public Fantasy in Medieval Paris.' In *Medieval Practices of Space*. Ed. Barbara A. Hanawalt and Michal Koblalka. Minneapolis, MN, 2000, 1–36.

Campbell, Bruce M. S. *Before the Black Death: Studies in the 'Crisis' of the Early Fourteenth Century*. Manchester, 1992.

English Seigniorial Agriculture: 1250–1450. Cambridge, 2000.

Campbell, Bruce M. S. and R. H. Britnell. *A Commercializing Economy: England 1086 to c.1300*. New York, 1995.

Carceller Cerviño, Maria del Pilar. 'Los bandos nobiliarios y la carrera política: Ascenso y privanza de Beltrán de la Cueva.' *Anuario de Estudios Medievales* 36:2 (2007), 783–801.

Carlin, Martha. 'Fast Food and Urban Living Standards in Medieval England.' In *Food and Eating in Medieval Europe*. Ed. Martha Carlin and Joel T. Rosenthal. London, 1998, 27–51.

Carmichael, Ann G. *Plague and the Poor in Renaissance Florence*. Cambridge and New York, 1986.

Carr, David R. 'The Problem of Urban Patriciates: Office Holders in Fifteenth Century Salisbury.' *Wiltshire Archaeological and Natural History Magazine* 83 (1990), 118–35.

Carrère, Claude. *Barcelone: Centre économique à l'époque des difficultés 1380–1462*, Vol. I. Paris, 1967.

Casado Alonso, Hilario. 'Oligarquía urbana, comercio internacional y poder real: Burgos a fines de la edad media.' In *Realidad e imagenes del poder. España a fines de la edad media*. Ed. Adeline Rucquoi. Valladolid, 1988, 325–47.

Casey, James. *Early Modern Spain: A Social History*. London, 1999.

Castells Rufas, Enric, and Joan Badia i Guitart, eds. *Manresa medieval: Història, art i cultura a l'edat mitjana*. Manresa, 2001.

Castillo Sainz, Jaime. 'Asistencia, matrimonio e inserción social: "La loable confraria e almoina de les orfenes a Maridar."' *Saitabi: Revista de Historia, Arte y Arqueología* 43 (1993), 135–45.

Català Roca, Pere, ed. *Els castells catalans*. 6 vols. Barcelona, 1967–1979.

Cateura Bennàsser, Pau. *L'Administració atrapada: Crèdit, finances i adaptacions fiscals al regne de Mallorca (s.XV)*. Palma, 2008.

Cateura Bennàsser, Pau, ed. *El crèdit i el sistema financer del Regne de Mallorca (segles XIV–XV)*. Palma, 2009.

Catlos, Brian. *The Victors and the Vanquished: Christians and Muslims of Catalonia and Aragon, 1050–1300*. Cambridge, 2004.

Cavaciocchi, Simonetta, ed. *La famiglia nell'economia europea, secc. XIII–XVIII (Atti della quarantesima settimana di studi, 6–10 Aprile 2008)*. Florence, 2009.

Ceccherini, Irene. 'La genesi della scrittura mercantesca.' In *Régionalisme et Internationalisme: Problèmes de Paléographie et de codicologie du moyen age. Actes du Xve Colloque du Comité International de Paléographie Latine (Vienne, 13–17 Septembre 2005)*. Ed. Otto Kresten and Franz Lackner. Vienna, 2009, 123–37.

Cercos Valles, María Luisa, and Javier Medrano Adán. 'La crisis bajomedieval en las Sierras Turolenses: Un modelo de análisis local (Puertomingalvo, 1400–1500).' *Anuario de Estudios Medievales* 34:1 (2004), 217–48.

Chevalier, Bernard. 'Les boucheries, les bouchers et le commerce de la viande à Tours au XVe siècle.' In *Commerce, finances et société (XIe–XVIe siècles). Recueil de travaux d'histoire médiévale offert à M. le Professeur Henri Dubois*. Ed. Philippe Contamine, Thierry Dutour, and Bertrand Schnerb. Paris, 1993, 157–69.

'Le pouvoir par le savoir: Le renouvellement des élites urbaines en France au début de l'âge moderne (1350–1550).' In *Construction, reproduction et représentation des patriciats urbains de l'antiquité au XXe siècle: Actes du Colloque des 7, 8, et 9 Septembre 1998 tenu à Tours, dans les locaux du Conseil Général d'Indre-et-Loire*. Ed. Claude Petitfrère. Tours, 1999, 73–81.

Chía, Julián de. *Bandos y bandoleros en Gerona: Apuntes históricos desde el siglo XIV hasta mediados del XVII*, 3 vols. Girona, 1888–90.

Chojnacki, Stanley. 'Dowries and Kinsmen in Early Renaissance Venice.' In *Women in Medieval Society*. Ed. Susan Mosher Stuard. Philadelphia, PA, 1977, 173–98.

'Getting Back the Dowry: Venice c. 1360–1530.' In *Time, Space, and Women's Lives in Early Modern Europe*. Ed. Anne Jackson Schutte, Thomas Kuehn, and Silvana Seidel Manchi. Kirksville, MO, 2001, 77–96.

Cipolla, Carlo. *The Monetary Policy of Fourteenth Century Florence*. Berkeley, CA, 1982.

Claramunt, Salvador. 'Pobre, iglesia e instituciones de caridad en la Barcelona del siglo XV.' In *Città e vita cittadina nei paesi dell'area Mediterranea: Secoli XI–XV. Atti del Convegno Internazionale in onore di Salvatore Tramontana (Adrano-Bronte-Catania-Palermo, 18–22 Novembre 2003)*. Ed. Biagio Saitta. Rome, 2006, 568–73.

Clark, Glenn, Judith Owens, and Greg T. Smith, eds. *City Limits: Perspectives on the Historical European City*. Montreal, 2010.

Clark, Gregory. 'Work, Wages and Living Conditions: Building Workers in England from the Magna Carta to Tony Blair.' In *L'Edilizia prima della rivoluzione industriale secc. XIII–XVIII: Atti della trentaseiesima settimana di studi, 26–30 Aprile 2004*. Ed. Simonetta Cavaciocchi. Florence, 2005, 889–932.

Clark, Peter. *European Cities and Towns: 400–2000*. Oxford, 2009.

Clemente Ramos, Julián. 'La explotación económica del campo Arañuelo y la economía rural de la tierra de Plasencia a mediados del siglo XV.' *Anuario de Estudios Medievales* 39:1 (2009), 245–74.

Cohn, Samuel K. 'After the Black Death: Labour Legislation and Attitudes Towards Labour in Late-medieval Western Europe.' *Economic History Review* 60:3 (2007), 457–85.

'The Black Death, Tragedy, and Transformation.' In *The Renaissance World*. Ed. John Jeffries Martin. New York, 2007, 69–83.

Creating the Florentine State: Peasants and Rebellion, 1348–1434. Cambridge, 2000.

The Cult of Remembrance and the Black Death: Six Renaissance Cities in Central Italy. Baltimore, MD, 1997.

'Epidemiology of the Black Death and Successive Waves of Plague.' *Medical History. Supplement* 27 (2008), 74–100.

Lust for Liberty: The Politics of Social Revolt in Medieval Europe, 1200–1425. Cambridge, MA, 2008.

'The Political Economy of Urban Decline in the Renaissance.' In *Towns in Decline, AD 100–1600*. Ed. Terry R. Slater. Aldershot, 2000, 289–305.

Popular Protest in Late Medieval English Towns. Cambridge, 2012.

'Popular Revolt and the Rise of Early Modern States.' *Historian: The Magazine of the Historical Association* 89 (2006), 26–33.

Cohn, Samuel K., and Steven A. Epstein, eds. *Portraits of Medieval and Renaissance Living: Essays in Memory of David Herlihy*. Ann Arbor, MI, 1996.

Coll Julià, Núria. 'Una compañía Barcelonesa para el comercio de Paños (1400–1484).' *Anuario de Estudios Medievales* 5 (1968), 339–408.

Collantes de Terán Sánchez, Antonio. 'La elite financiera en la Sevilla bajomedieval: Los mayordomos del concejo.' *Revista d'Història Medieval* 11 (2000), 13–39.

'Les impôts municipaux indirects ordinaires et extraordinaires de Séville.' In *La fiscalité des villes au moyen age (Occident Méditerranéen). Les systèmes fiscaux*. Ed. Denis Menjot and Manuel Sánchez Martínez. Toulouse, 1999, 463–83.

Collantes de Terán Sánchez, Antonio, and Denis Menjot. 'Hacienda y fiscalidad concejiles en la Corona de Castilla en la edad media.' *Historia. Instituciones. Documentos* 23 (1996), 213–54.

Connell, W. J. *La città dei crucci: Fazioni e clientele in uno stato repubblicano del '400*. Florence, 2000.

Constable, Giles. 'Was There a Medieval Middle Class? Mediocres (mediani, medii) in the Middle Ages.' In *Portraits of Medieval and Renaissance Living: Essays in Memory of David Herlihy*. Ed. Samuel K. Cohn, Jr and Steven A. Epstein. Ann Arbor, MI, 1996, 301–23.

Cracco, Giorgio. 'Social Structure and Conflict in the Medieval City.' In *City States in Classical Antiquity and Medieval Italy: Athens and Rome, Florence and Venice*. Ed. Anthony Molho, Kurt Raaflaub and Julia Emlen. Stuttgart, 1991, 309–29.

Cruselles, Enrique. *Los mercaderes de Valencia en la edad media, 1380–1450*. Lerida, 2001.

d'Abadal i de Vinyals, Ramon. *La Corona de Aragon en el siglo XIV*. Valencia, 1969–70.

Pere el cerimoniós i els inicis de la decadència politica de Catalunya. Barcelona, 1987.

Dacosta Martínez, Arsenio. 'Historiografía y bandos: Reflexiones acerca de la crítica y justificatión de la violencia banderiza en su contexto.' In *La lucha de bandos en el país vasco: De los parientes mayores a la hidalguía universal*. Ed. José Ramón Dìaz de Durana Ortiz de Urbina, Bilbao, 1998, 121–48.

Daileader, Philip. 'Catalonia and the Midi: Sixty Years of Medieval Urban History.' *Imago Temporis: Medium Aevum* 1 (2007), 31–58.

'Town and Countryside in Northeastern Catalonia, 1267–c.1450: The "Sobreposats de la Horta" of Perpignan.' *Journal of Medieval History* 24:4 (1998), 347–66.

True Citizens: Violence, Memory, and Identity in the Medieval Community of Perpignan, 1162–1397. Leiden, 2000.

'The Vanishing Consulates of Catalonia.' *Speculum: A Journal of Medieval Studies* 74:1 (1999), 65–94.

Davis, Robert C. *Shipbuilders of the Venetian Arsenal: Workers and Workplace in the Preindustrial City.* Baltimore and London, 1991.

Day, John. *The Medieval Market Economy.* Oxford, 1987.

Dean, Trevor. *Land and Power in Late Medieval Ferrara: The Rule of the Este, 1350–1450.* Cambridge, 1988.

Dejean, Claude. *La loi du lucre: L'Usure en procès dans la Couronne d'Aragon à la fin du Moyen* Âge. Madrid, 2011.

Denton, Jeffrey. *Orders and Hierarchies in Late Medieval and Renaissance Europe.* Toronto, 1999.

Diago Hernando, Máximo. 'Las corporaciones de caballeros hidalgos en las ciudades castellanas a fines de la edad media: Su participación en el ejercicio del poder local.' *Anuario de Estudios Medievales* 36:2 (2006), 803–38.

'La incidencia de los conflictos banderizos en la vida política de las ciudades castellanas a fines de la edad media: El caso de Cuenca.' *Hispania: Revista Española de Historia* 69:3:233 (2009), 683–714.

'El problema del aprovisionamiento de lanas para la manufactura pañera castellana a fines de la edad media.' *Anuario de Estudios Medievales* 38:2 (2008), 639–71.

Dillard, Heath. *Daughters of the Reconquest: Women in Castilian Town Society, 1100–1300.* Cambridge, 1984.

Dimmock, Spencer. 'English Small Towns and the Emergence of Capitalist Relations, c.1450–1550.' *Urban History* 28:1 (2001), 5–24.

Dobson, Barrie. 'General Survey 1300–1540.' In *The Cambridge Urban History of Britain*, Vol. I, *600–1540*. Ed. David M. Palliser. Cambridge, 2000, 273–90.

Dobson, R. B. 'Urban Decline in Late-Medieval England.' *Transactions of the Royal Historical Society* 5th ser. 27 (1977), 1–22.

Doñate, José M. 'Salarios y precios durante la segunda mitad del siglo XIV.' *VII Congrés d'Història de la Corona d'Aragó* 2 (1962), 417–506.

Dubled, Henri. 'L'organisation de la boucherie et a consommation de viande à Carpentras au XVe siècle.' *Bulletin Philologique et Historique du Comité des Travaux Historiques et Scientifiques* 1 (1969), 151–70.

Dufourcq, Charles E. 'Honrats, mercaders et autres dans le Conseil des Cent au XIVe siècle.' In *La ciudad hispanica durante los siglos XIII al XVI*, vol. II. Madrid, 1985, 1361–95.

Dufourcq, Charles E., and J. Gautier-Dalche. *Histoire économique et sociale de l'Espagne chrétienne au moyen age.* Paris, 1976.

Dumolyn, Jan. 'Dominante klassen en elites in verandering in het laatmiddeleeuwse vlaanderen.' *Jaarboek voor middeleeuwse geschiedenis* 5 (2002), 69–107.

Dumolyn, Jan, and Jelle Haemers. 'Patterns of Urban Rebellion in Medieval Flanders.' *Journal of Medieval History* 31:4 (2005), 369–93.

Dyer, Christopher. *An Age of Transition? Economy and Society in England in the Later Middle Ages*. Oxford, 2005.

'Social and Economic Background to the Rural Revolt of 1381.' In *The English Rising of 1381*. Ed. R. H. Hilton and T. H. Aston. Cambridge, 1984, 9–42.

Standards of Living in the Later Middle Ages: Social Change in England c. 1200–1520. Cambridge, 1994.

'Trade, Urban Hinterlands and Market Integration, 1300–1600: A Summing Up.' In *Trade, Urban Hinterlands and Market Integration c.1300–1600: A Collection of Working Papers Given at a Conference Organised by the Centre for Metropolitan History and Supported by the Economic and Social Research Council, 7 July 1999*. Ed. James A. Galloway. London, 2000, 103–9.

Dyer, Christopher, and Kate Giles. *Town and Country in the Middle Ages: Contrasts, Contacts and Interconnections, 1100–1500*. Leeds, 2005.

Eckstein, Nicholas A. 'Addressing Wealth in Renaissance Florence.' *Journal of Urban History* 32:5 (2006), 711–28.

Edwards, John. *Christian Córdoba: The City and its Region in the Late Middle Ages*. New York, 1982.

Elias de Tejada, Francisco. *Historia del pensamiento politico catalán, tomo i: La Cataluña clasica (987–1479)*. Seville, 1963.

Elliott, J. H. *The Revolt of the Catalans*. Cambridge, 1984.

Emery, Richard W. 'The Black Death of 1348 in Perpignan.' *Speculum* 42 (1967), 611–23.

English, Edward D. 'Emancipation, Succession, and Honor: Family Strategies in Medieval Siena.' In *A Distinct Voice: Medieval Studies in Honor of Leonard E. Boyle, O.P.* Ed. Jacqueline Brown and William P. Stoneman. South Bend, IN, 1997, 437–51.

Enterprise and Liability in Sienese Banking, 1230–1350. Cambridge, MA, 1988.

Epstein, Stephan R. 'Cities, Regions, and the Late Medieval Crisis: Sicily and Tuscany Compared.' *Past and Present* 130 (February 1991), 3–50.

Freedom and Growth: The Rise of States and Markets in Europe, 1300–1750. London, 2000.

'Introduction. Town and Country in Europe, 1300–1800.' In *Town and Country in Europe, 1300–1800*. Ed. S. R. Epstein. Cambridge, 2001, 1–29.

'Regional Fairs, Institutional Innovation, and Economic Growth in Late Medieval Europe.' *Economic History Review* 47:3 (1994), 459–82.

'Town and Country: Economy and Institutions in Late Medieval Italy.' *Economic History Review* 46:3 (1993), 453–77.

Epstein, Stephan. R., and Maarten Prak. *Guilds, Innovation and the European Economy, 1400–1800*. Cambridge, 2010.

Epstein, Steven A. *Genoa and the Genoese, 958–1528*. Chapel Hill, NC, 2001.

Wage Labor and Guilds in Medieval Europe. Chapel Hill, NC, 1991.

Ertman, Thomas. *Birth of the Leviathan: Building States and Regimes in Medieval and Early Modern Europe*. Cambridge, 1997.

Estaban Recio, María. *Palencia a fines de la edad media: Una ciudad de señorio episcopal*. Valladolid, 1989.

Falcón Pérez, María Isabel. *Los infanzones de Aragón en la edad media*, Zaragoza, 2008.

'La manufactura del cuero en las principales ciudades de la Corona de Aragón (siglos XIII–XV).' *En la España Medieval* 24 (2001), 9–46.

'Sobre la industria del vestido en Zaragoza en el siglo XV: Las ordenanzas de la cofradía de sastres, calceteros y juboneros.' In *Aragón en la edad media* 12 (1995), 241–65.

Zaragoza en el siglo XV: Morfología urbana, huertas y término municipal. Zaragoza, 1981.

Farmer, David L. 'Crop Yields, Prices and Wages in Medieval England.' *Studies in Medieval and Renaissance History* 6 (1983), 115–55.

Feliu Montfort, Gaspar. 'Els antecedents de la remença i els mals usos.' *Quaderns de la Selva* 13 (2001), 209–28.

'Mercaders-banquers barcelonins: L'Endeutament de la monarquia i la fallida de la taula de canvi de Pere des Caus i Andreu d'Olivella el 1381.' *Barcelona. Quaderns d'història* 13 (2007), 197–210.

Fernández Trabal, Josep. 'El conflicte remença a la Catalunya del segle XV (1388–1486).' *Afers: Fulls de Recerca i Pensament* 17:42–3 (2002), 587–624.

Una família Catalana medieval: Els Bell-lloc de Girona, 1267–1533. Barcelona, 1995.

'De mercaders a terratinents. Formació del patrimoni rural de la Família Bell-lloc de Girona, 1302–1398.' *L'Avenç: Història del Països Catalans* 94 (1986), 42–7.

Fernández Trabal, Josep. 'De "prohoms" a ciudadanos honrados: Aproximación al estudio de las elites urbanas de la sociedad Catalana bajomedieval (s. XIV–XV).' *Revista d'Història Medieval* 10 (1999), 331–69.

'De "prohoms" a "honrats". Orígenes y justificación de la nobleza de los ciudadanos honrados de Catalunya.' *Hidalguía: La Revista de Genealogía, Nobleza y Armas* 49:295 (2002), 841–75.

Fernández Trabal, Josep, ed. *Història dels Llupià (1088–1771) i dels seus llinatges: Icard, Roger i Vilaseca.* Canet, 2006.

Ferrer Mallol, Maria Teresa. 'Les Corts de Catalunya i la Creació de la Diputació del General o Generalitat en el Marc de la Guerra Amb Castella (1359–1369).' *Anuario de Estudios Medievales* 34:2 (2004), 875–938.

Entre la Paz y la Guerra: La Corona Catalano-Aragonesa y Castilla en la baja edad media. Barcelona, 2005.

'El patrimoni reial i la recuperació dels senyorius jurisdiccionals en els estats Catalano-Aragonesos a la fi del segle XIV.' *Anuario de Estudios Medievales* 7 (1970–1), 351–491.

Ferrero Micó, Remedios. 'Los beneficiarios del Municipio: Arrendatarios y censualistas de la ciudad de Valencia.' In *Corona, Municipis i Fiscalitat a la baixa edat mitjana: Col.loqui (Quaderns de l'Institut d'Estudis Ilerdencs 13).* Lerida, 1997, 643–74.

Ferro, Víctor. *El dret públic Català: Les institucions a Catalunya fins al decret de nova planta.* Vic, 1987.

Findlay, Ronald, and Kevin H. O'Rourke. *Power and Plenty: Trade, War, and the World Economy in the Second Millennium.* Princeton, NJ, 2009.

Fleming, Peter. 'Telling Tales of Oligarchy in the Late Medieval Town.' In *The Fifteenth Century*, Vol. II, *Revolution and Consumption in Medieval England.* Ed. Michael Hicks. Woodbridge, Suffolk, 2001, 177–93.

Flinn, M. W. 'Plague in Europe and the Mediterranean Countries.' *Journal of European Economic History* 8:1 (1979), 131–48.

Font Rius, José María. *Estudis sobre els drets i institucions locals en la Catalunya medieval.* Barcelona, 1985.

'The Institutions of the Crown of Aragon in the First Half of the Fifteenth Century.' In *Spain in the Fifteenth Century, 1369–1516.* Ed. J. R. Highfield, London, 1972, 171–92.

Freedman, Paul. *The Diocese of Vic: Tradition and Regeneration in Medieval Catalonia.* New Brunswick, NJ, 1983.

The Origins of Peasant Servitude in Medieval Catalonia. Cambridge, 1991.

'Senyors i pagesos al camp feudal.' In *Els grans espais baronials a l'edat mitjana: Desenvolupament socioeconòmic. Reunió científica – I curs d'estiu comtat d'Urgell, Balaguer, 10,11 i 12 de Juliol de 1996.* Ed. Flocel Sabaté and Joan Farré, Lerida, 2002, 11–21.

'An Unsuccessful Attempt at Urban Organization in Twelfth-century Catalonia.' *Speculum: A Journal of Medieval Studies* 54:3 (1979), 479–91.

Frost, Ruth H. 'The Urban Elite.' In *Medieval Norwich.* Ed. Carole Rawcliffe and Richard Wilson. London, 2004, 235–53.

Fuente, María Jesús. 'Mujer, trabajo y familia en las ciudades castellanas de la baja edad media.' *En la España Medieval* 20 (1997), 179–94.

Furió Diego, Antoni. 'Crédito y endudamiento: El censal en la sociedad rural valenciana (siglos XIV–XV).' In *Señorío y feudalismo en la peninsula Ibérica (ss. XII–XIX).* 4 vols., vol. I. Ed. Esteban Sarasa Sánchez and Eliseo Serrano Martín. Zaragoza, 1993, 501–34.

'Deuda pública e intereses privados. Finanzas y fiscalidad municipales en la Corona de Aragón.' *Edad Media: Revista de Historia* 2 (1999), 35–79.

Fynn-Paul, Jeff. 'Civic Debt, Civic Taxes, and Urban Unrest: A Catalan Key to Interpreting the Late Fourteenth-Century European Crisis.' In *Money, Markets, and Trade in Late Medieval Europe: Essays in Honour of John H. A. Munro*, Ed. L. Armstrong, M. Elbl, and I. Elbl. Leiden, 2007, 119–45.

'Empire, Monotheism and Slavery in the Greater Mediterranean Region from Antiquity to the Early Modern Era.' *Past and Present: A Journal of Historical Studies* 205 (2009), 3–40.

'Let's Talk About Class: Towards an Institutionalist Typology of Class Relations in the Cities of Pre-modern Europe (c. 1200–c. 1800).' *Urban History* 41:4 (2014), 582–605.

'Occupation, Family, and Inheritance in Fourteenth-Century Barcelona: A Socio-Economic Profile of One of Europe's Earliest Investing Publics.' *European History Quarterly* 45:3 (2015), 417–45.

'Reasons for the Limited Scope and Duration of "Renaissance Slavery" in Southern Europe (ca. 1348–ca. 1750): A New Structuralist Analysis.' In *Schiavitù e servaggio nell'economia europea, secc. XI–XVII: Serfdom and Slavery in the European Economy, 11th–18th Centuries. Atti delle 'Quarantunesima settimana di studi', 14–18 aprile 2013.* Ed. Simonetta Cavaciocchi. (Atti delle 'Settimane di Studi' e altri Convegni, 45; Fondazione Istituto Internazionale di Storia Economica 'F. Datini'). Florence, 2014.

'The Role of Local Entrepreneurs in Military Finance and Supply during the Aragonese-Castilian War (1356–75).' In *War, Entrepreneurs and the State*. Ed. J. Fynn-Paul. Leiden, 2014, 32–60.
'Tartars in Spain: Renaissance Slavery in the Catalan City of Manresa, c. 1408.' *Journal of Medieval History* 34:4 (2008), 347–59.
García Fernández, Ernesto. *Gobernar la ciudad en la edad media: Oligarquías y elites urbanas en el País Vasco*. Vitoria-Gasteiz, 2004.
García Herrero, María del Carmen. 'La contribución de las mujeres a la economía de las familias dedicadas a activitates no agrarias en la baja edad media Española.' In *La famiglia nell'economia Europea secc. XIII–XVIII: The Economic Role of the Family in the European Economy from the 13th to the 18th Centuries. Atti della 'quarantesima settimana di studi', 6–10 Aprile 2008*. Ed. Simonetta Cavaciocchi. Florence, 2009, 569–98.
García Marsilla, Juan Vicente. 'Crédito y banca en el Mediterráneo medieval: La quiebra del cambista valenciano Francesc de Pals.' *Anuario de Estudios Medievales* 25 (1995), 127–50.
Vivir a credito en la Valencia medieval: De los origenes del sistema censal al endeudamiento del municipio. Valencia, 2002.
García Marsilla, Juan Vicente, and Jorge Sàiz Serrano. 'De la peita al censal: Finanzas municipales y clases dirigentes en la Valencia de los siglos XIV y XV.' In *Corona, Municipis i fiscalitat a la baixa edat mitjana: Col.loqui*, Lerida, 1997, 307–34.
García Sanz de Baranda, Julián. *La ciudad de Burgos y su concejo en la edad media*. 2 vols. Burgos, 1967.
Giuliodori, Serena. '"De Rebus Uxoris". Dote e Successione Negli Statuti Bolognesi (1250–1454).' *Archivio Storico Italiano* 163:606 (2005), 651–85.
Glete, Jan. 'Cities, State Formation and the Protection of Trade in Northern Europe, 1200–1700.' In *The Dynamics of Economic Culture in the North Sea and Baltic Region in the Late Middle Ages and Early Modern Period*. Ed. Hanno Brand and Leos Müller, Hilversum, 2007, 13–23.
Goicolea Julián, Francisco Javier. 'La expansión territorial de los núcleos urbanos y la articulación de las relaciones con sus aldeas en la Rioja alta medieval.' *Anuario de Estudios Medievales* 32:1 (2002), 293–331.
La oligarquía de Salvatierra en el tránsito de la edad media a la edad moderna. Una contribución al estudio de las elites dirigentes del mundo urbano alavés (1400–1550). Logroño, 2007.
Goldberg, P. J. P. *Women, Work, and Life Cycle in a Medieval Economy: Women in York and Yorkshire c.1300–1520*. Oxford, 1992.
'Women in Fifteenth-century Town Life.' In *Towns and Townspeople in the Fifteenth Century*. Ed. John A. F. Thomson. Gloucester, 1988, 107–28.
Goldthwaite, Richard A. *Banks, Palaces, and Entrepreneurs in Renaissance Florence*. Ashgate, 1995.
The Building of Renaissance Florence: An Economic and Social History. Baltimore, MD, 1980.
The Economy of Renaissance Florence. Baltimore, MD, 2009.
Private Wealth in Renaissance Florence: A Study of Four Families. Princeton, NJ, 1968.
Gonzáles Antón, Luis. *Las Cortes de Aragón*. Zaragoza, 1978.

González Arce, José Damián. 'La cofradía laboral como precedente del gremio: Los mercaderes de Toledo durante el reinado de los reyes Católicos.' *En la España Medieval* 31 (2008), 177–216.

Gremios y cofradías en los reinos medievales de León y Castilla (s. XII–XV). Palencia, 2009.

'Sobre el origen de los gremios Sevillanos.' *En la España Medieval* 14 (1991), 163–82.

'Trabajar para el príncipe. Los salarios de los servidores en la casa del príncipe de Asturias y Gerona (Juan De Aragón y Castilla, 1478–1497).' *Anuario de Estudios Medievales* 39:2 (2009), 777–842.

González Calle, Jesús Antonio. 'Luchas de bandos en Asturias en la Época de los reyes Católicos.' In *Isabel la Católica y su Época: Actas del Congreso Internacional Valladolid-Barcelona-Granada, 15 a 20 de Noviembre de 2004*. Ed. Luis Ribot, Julio Valdeón, and Elena Maza, Valladolid, 2007, 519–44.

González de Lara, Yadira. 'Enforceability and Risk-sharing in Financial Contracts: From the Sea Loan to the Commenda in Late Medieval Venice.' *Journal of Economic History* 61:2 (2001), 500–4.

Gonzalvo Bou, Gener. *La Pau i Treva a Catalunya: Origin de les corts Catalanes.* Barcelona, 1986.

Gràcia Mont, Elisenda. *Estructura agrària de la Plana de Vic al segle XIV*. Barcelona, 1989.

Graus, F. 'The Late Medieval Poor in Town and Countryside,' in Sylvia Thrupp, ed. *Change in Medieval Society: Europe North of the Alps, 1050–1500*, 237–47. New York, 1964.

Grendler, Paul F. *Schooling in Renaissance Italy: Literacy and Learning, 1300–1600.* Baltimore, MD, 1989.

Gubern, Ramon. 'La crisis financeria de 1381 en la Corona de Aragon.' *X Congres Internacional de Ciencies Historiques, Atti.* 7 (1955), 413–14.

Guerrero Navarrete, Yolanda. 'Burgos y Enrique IV. La importancia del sector ciudadano en la crisis Castellana de la segunda mitad del siglo XV.' *Hispania* 47:166 (1987), 437–84.

Guiance, Ariel, ed. *Entre el cielo y la tierra: Escatología y sociedad en el mundo medieval.* Buenos Aires, 2009.

Guilleré, Christian. *Diner, poder i societat a la Girona del segle XIV*. Girona, 1984.

'Les élites urbaines Catalanes à la fin du moyen Age: L'Exemple Géronais.' In *Les élites urbaines au moyen age: Actes du XXVIIe Congrès de la Société des Historiens Médiévistes de l'Enseignement Supérieur Public (Rome, Mai 1996)*. Paris, 1997, 269–85.

Girona medieval: L'Etapa d'apogeu, 1285–1360. Girona, 1991.

'La peste Noire à Gérone (1348).' *Annals de l'Institut d'Estudis Gironins*, 27 (1984), 87–161.

Günzberg Moll, Jordi. *Los notarios y su organización en Barcelona (siglos XIII–XVI).* Madrid, 2004.

Gustafsson, Harald. 'The Conglomerate State: A Perspective on State Formation in Early Modern Europe.' *Scandinavian Journal of History* 23:3–4 (1998), 189–213.

Guzzetti, Linda. 'Dowries in Fourteenth-century Venice.' *Renaissance Studies: Journal of the Society for Renaissance Studies* 16:4 (2002), 430–73.

Hajnal, John. 'European Marriage Patterns in Perspective.' In *Population in History: Essays in Historical Demography*. London, 1965, 101–46.

Haliczer, Stephen. *The Comuneros of Castile: The Forging of a Revolution, 1475–1521*. Madison, WI, 1981.

Hambly, Gavin R. G. *Women in the Medieval Islamic World*. London, 1999.

Hamilton, Earl Jefferson. *Money, Prices, and Wages in Valencia, Aragon, and Navarre, 1351–1500*. Cambridge, MA, 1936.

Hanawalt, Barbara A. 'Reading the Lives of the Illiterate: London's Poor.' *Speculum* 80:4 (2005), 1067–86.

The Wealth of Wives: Women, Law, and Economy in Late Medieval London. Oxford, 2007.

Hartman, Mary S. *The Household and the Making of History: A Subversive View of the Western Past*. Cambridge, 2004.

Harvey, Barbara. 'Introduction: the "Crisis" of the Early Fourteenth Century.' In *Before the Black Death: Studies in the 'Crisis' of the Early Fourteenth Century*. Ed. Bruce M. S. Campbell. Manchester, 1991, 1–24.

Hatcher, John. 'England in the Aftermath of the Black Death.' *Past and Present: A Journal of Historical Studies* 144 (1994), 3–35.

'The Great Slump of the Mid-fifteenth Century.' In *Progress and Problems in Medieval England: Essays in Honour of Edward Miller*. Ed. Richard Britnell and John Hatcher. Cambridge, 1996, 237–72.

Plague, Population, and the English Economy, 1348–1530. Basingstoke, 1977.

Heers, Jacques. *Le clan familial au moyen age. Étude sur les structures politiques et sociales des milieux urbains*. Paris, 1974.

Herlihy, David. 'The Distribution of Wealth in a Renaissance Community: Florence, 1427.' In *Towns and Societies*. Ed. Philip Abrams and E. A. Wrigley. London, 1978, 131–58.

Medieval and Renaissance Pistoia: The Social History of an Italian Town, 1200–1430. New Haven, 1967.

Opera Muliebria: Women and Work in Medieval Europe. New York, 1989.

Pisa in the Early Renaissance: A Study of Urban Growth. New Haven, CT, 1958.

'The Rulers of Florence, 1282–1530.' In *City States in Classical Antiquity and Medieval Italy: Athens and Rome, Florence and Venice*. Ed. Anthony Molho, Kurt Raaflaub and Julia Emlen. Stuttgart, 1991, 197–221.

'Women's Work in the Towns of Traditional Europe.' In *La donna nell'economia secc. XIII–XVIII: Atti della ventunesima settimana di studi, 10–15 Aprile 1989*. Ed. Simonetta Cavaciocchi. Florence, 1990, 103–30.

Herlihy, David, and Samuel K. Cohn Jr. *The Black Death and the Transformation of the West*. Cambridge, MA, 1997.

Herlihy, David, and Christiane Klapisch-Zuber. *Les Toscans et leurs familles: Une étude du 'catasto' florentin de 1427*. Paris, 1978.

Tuscans and their Families: A Study of the Florentine Catasto of 1427. New Haven, CT, 1985.

Hibbert, A. B. 'The Origins of the Medieval Town Patriciate.' *Past and Present* 3 (1953), 15–27. Reprinted in *Towns and Societies: Essays in Economic History and Historical Sociology* Ed. P. Abrams and E. A. Wrigley. Cambridge, 1978, 91–104.

Hillgarth, J. N. *The Problem of a Catalan Mediterranean Empire 1229–1327*. London, 1975.
The Spanish Kingdoms, 1250–1516, Vol. I, *Precarious Balance, 1250–1410*. Oxford, 1976.
Hilton, R. H. *Class Conflict and the Crisis of Feudalism: Essays in Medieval Social History*. London, 1985.
English and French Towns in Feudal Society: A Comparative Study. Cambridge, 1995.
'Status and Class in the Medieval Town.' In *The Church in the Medieval Town*. Ed. T.R. Slater and Gervase Rosser. Aldershot, 1998, 9–19.
Hinojosa Montalvo, José. 'Bandos y bandositats en la gobernación de Orihuela en la baja edad media.' *Anuario de Estudios Medievales* 36:2 (2006), 713–50.
Holt, Richard. *The English Medieval Town: A Reader in English Urban History, 1200–1540*. London and New York, 1990.
'Gloucester in the Century After the Black Death.' *Transactions of the Bristol and Gloucestershire Archaeological Society* 103 (1985), 149–61.
Homer, Sidney, and Richard Sylla. *A History of Interest Rates*, 3rd rev. edn. New Brunswick, NJ, 1991.
Horrox, Rosemary. 'The Urban Gentry in the Fifteenth Century.' In *Towns and Townspeople in the Fifteenth Century*. Ed. John A. F. Thomson. Gloucester, 1988, 22–44.
Horrox, Rosemary, ed. *Fifteenth Century Attitudes: Perceptions of Society in Late Medieval England*. Cambridge and New York, 1994.
Howell, Martha C. *Commerce Before Capitalism in Europe, 1300–1600*. Cambridge, 2010.
The Marriage Exchange: Property, Social Place, and Gender in Cities of the Low Countries, 1300–1550. Chicago, IL, 1998.
Women, Production, and Patriarchy in Late Medieval Cities. Chicago, IL, 1990.
Hughes, Diane Owen. 'Urban Growth and Family Structure in Medieval Genoa.' *Past and Present: A Journal of Historical Studies* 66 (1975), 3–30.
Hunt, Edwin S. *The Medieval Super-Companies: A Study of the Peruzzi Company of Florence*. Cambridge, 1994.
Hunt, Edwin S. and James Murray. *A History of Business in Medieval Europe, 1200–1550*. Cambridge, 1999.
Hutton, Shennan. '"On Herself and All Her Property": Women's Economic Activities in Late-medieval Ghent.' *Continuity and Change* 20:3 (2005), 325–49.
Women and Economic Activities in Late Medieval Ghent. Basingstoke, 2011.
Hyde, J. K. 'Contemporary Views on Factional and Civil Strife in Thirteenth and Fourteenth Century Italy.' In *Violence and Civil Disorder in Italian Cities, 1200–1500*. Ed. L. Martines. Berkeley, CA, 1972, 273–307.
Literacy and Its Uses: Studies on Late Medieval Italy. Manchester, 1993.
Society and Politics in Medieval Italy: The Evolution of the Civil Life, 1000–1350. London, 1973.
Iglesies Fort, Josep. 'El fogaje de 1365–1370: Contribución al conocimiento de la poblacíon de Cataluña en la segunda mitad del siglo XIV.' *Memorias de la Real Academia de Ciencias y Artes de Barcelona* 34:11 (1962), 249–356.
Izquierdo Benito, Ricardo. *Un espacio desordenado: Toledo a fines de la Edad Media*. Toledo, 1996.

Jansen, Philippe. 'Élites urbaines, service de la commune et processus d'aristocratisation: Le cas de Macerata aux XIVe–XVe siècles.' In *Les élites urbaines au moyen age: Actes du XXVIIe congrès de la société des historiens médiévistes de l'enseignement supérieur public (Rome, Mai 1996)*. Paris, 1997, 201–26. Rome, 1997.

Jara Fuente, José Antonio. 'Elites y grupos financieros en las ciudades castellanas de la baja edad media.' *En la España Medieval* 27 (2004), 105–30.

Jardine, Lisa. 'Women Humanists: Education for What?' In *Feminism and Renaissance Studies*. Ed. Lorna Hutson. Oxford, 1999, 48–81.

Jarrett, Jonathan A. *Rulers and Ruled in Frontier Catalonia, 880–1010: Pathways of Power*. Woodbridge, Suffolk and Rochester, NY, 2010.

Jewell, Helen M. *Women in Medieval England*. Manchester, 1996.

Jones, Philip. *The Italian City-State: From Commune to Signoria*. Oxford, 1997.

Jordan, William Chester. 'Famine and Popular Resistance: Northern Europe, 1315–22.' In *Power, Violence and Mass Death in Pre-Modern and Modern Times*. Ed. Joseph Canning, Hartmut Lehmann and Jay Winter. Aldershot, 2004, 13–24.

The Great Famine. Princeton, NJ, 1997.

Women and Credit in Pre-Industrial and Developing Societies. Philadelphia, PA, 1993.

Junyent, Eduardo. *La ciutat de Vic i la seva historia*. Barcelona, 1976.

Kagay, Donald J. 'The Defense of the Crown of Aragon during the War of the Two Pedros.' *Journal of Military History* 71:1 (2007), 11–33.

Kagay, Donald J. 'The Emergence of "Parliament" in the Thirteenth-century Crown of Aragon: a View from the Gallery.' In *On the Social Origins of Medieval Institutions: Essays in Honor of Joseph F. O'Callaghan*. Ed. Donald J. Kagay and Theresa M. Vann. Leiden, 1998, 223–41.

'The Government Besieged by Conflict: The Parliament of Monzón (1362–1363) as Military Financier.' In *The Hundred Years War: A Wider Focus*. Ed. L.J. Andrew Villalon and Donald J. Kagay. Leiden, 2005, 117–50.

The Usatges of Barcelona: The Fundamental Law of Catalonia. Philadelphia, PA, 1995.

'War Financing in the Late-medieval Crown of Aragon.' *Journal of Medieval Military History* 6 (2008), 119–48.

Kann, Hans-Joachim. 'Élite and Government in Medieval Leiden.' *Journal of Medieval History* 21:1 (1995), 51–75.

Kaplan, Marion. *The Marriage Bargain: Women and Dowries in European History*. London, 1985.

Kedar, Benjamin Z. 'The Genoese Notaries of 1382: The Anatomy of an Urban Occupational Group.' In *The Medieval City. In Honor of Robert S. Lopez*. Ed. Harry A. Miskimin, David Herlihy and A.L. Udovitch, New Haven, CT, 1977, 73–94.

Merchants in Crisis: Genoese and Venetian Men of Affairs and the Fourteenth Century Depression. New Haven, CT, 1977.

Keene, Derek. 'Changes in London's Economic Hinterland as Indicated by Debt Cases in the Court of Common Pleas.' In *Trade, Urban Hinterlands and Market Integration c.1300–1600: A Collection of Working Papers Given at a Conference*

Organised by the Centre for Metropolitan History and Supported by the Economic and Social Research Council, 7 July 1999. Ed. James A. Galloway. London, 2000, 59–81.

Survey of Medieval Winchester, 2 vols. Oxford, 1985.

'Towns and the Growth of Trade.' In *The New Cambridge Medieval History*, vol. IV, *c.1024–c.1198*, Part I. Ed. David Luscombe and Jonathan Riley-Smith, Cambridge, 2004, 47–85.

Kelleher, Marie A. *The Measure of Woman: Law and Female Identity in the Crown of Aragon*. Philadelphia, PA, 2010.

Kent, Dale. 'The Power of the Elites: Family, Patronage, and the State.' In *Italy in the Age of the Renaissance, 1300–1550*. Ed. John M. Najemy. Oxford, 2004, 165–83, 282–4.

Kermode, Jennifer. 'Medieval Indebtedness: The Regions Versus London.' In *England in the Fifteenth Century: Proceedings of the 1992 Harlaxton Symposium*. Ed. Nicholas Rogers. Stamford, CT, 1994, 72–88.

Medieval Merchants: York, Beverley, and Hull in the Later Middle Ages. Cambridge, 1998.

'Obvious Observations on the Formations of Oligarchies in Late Medieval English Towns.' In *Towns and Townspeople in the Fifteenth Century*. Ed. John A. F. Thompson Gloucester, 1988, 87–106.

'Urban Decline? The Flight from Office in Late Medieval York.' *Economic History Review*, 2nd ser. 35 (1982), 179–98.

King, Margaret L. 'Thwarted Ambition: Six Learned Women of the Italian Renaissance.' In *Humanism, Venice and Women: Essays on the Italian Renaissance*. Aldershot, 2005, 280–304.

Kirshner, Julius. 'Materials for a Gilded Cage: Non-dotal Assets in Florence, 1300–1500.' In *The Family in Italy from Antiquity to the Present*. Ed. David I. Kertzer and Richard P. Saller. New Haven, CT, 1991, 184–207.

Klapisch-Zuber, Christiane. 'The "Cruel Mother": Maternity, Widowhood, and Dowry in Florence in the Fourteenth and Fifteenth Centuries.' In *Feminism and Renaissance Studies*. Ed. Lorna Hutson. Oxford, 1999, 186–202.

A History of Women in the West, Vol. II, *Silences of the Middle Ages*. London and Cambridge, 1992.

'"Kin, Friends, and Neighbors"': The Urban Territory of a Merchant Family in 1400.' In *The Italian Renaissance: The Essential Readings*. Ed. Paula Findlen. Malden, MA, 2002, 97–123.

Kowaleski, Maryanne. 'The Commercial Dominance of a Medieval Provincial Oligarchy: Exeter in the Late Fourteenth Century.' *Mediaeval Studies* 46 (1984), 355–84.

'A Consumer Economy.' In *A Social History of England 1200–1500*. Ed. Rosemary Horrox and W. Mark Ormrod. Cambridge, 2006, 238–59, 493–4.

'The History of Urban Families in Medieval England.' *Journal of Medieval History* 14:1 (1988), 47–63.

Local Markets and Regional Trade in Medieval Exeter. Cambridge, 2003.

'Town and Country in Late Medieval England: The Hide and Leather Trade.' In *Work in Towns 850–1850*. Ed. Penelope J. Corfield and Derek Keene, Leicester, 1990, 57–73.

Krause, J. 'The Medieval Household: Large or Small.' *Economic History Review*, 2nd ser. 9 (1956–7), 420–32.

Ladero Quesada, Miguel Ángel. *Ciudades de la España medieval*. Madrid, 2010.

La hacienda real de Castilla (1369–1504): Estudios y documentos. Madrid, 2009.

'Lignages, bandos et partis dans la vie politique des villes castillanes (XIVe–XVe siècles).' In *Les sociétés urbaines en France méridionale et en péninsule Ibérique au moyen age. Actes du Colloque de Pau, 21–23 Septembre 1988*. Paris, 1991, 105–30.

Lafuente Gómez, Mario. *Guerra en ultramar: La intervención aragonesa en el dominio de Cerdeña (1354–1355)*. Zaragoza, 2011.

Lalinde Abadía, Jesús. *La jurisdicción real inferior en Cataluña*. Barcelona, 1966.

Lansing, Carol. *The Florentine Magnates: Lineage and Faction in a Medieval Commune*. Princeton, NJ, 1991.

Lantschner, Patrick. 'The "Ciompi Revolution" Constructed: Modern Historians and the Nineteenth-Century Paradigm of Revolution.' *Annali di Storia di Firenze* 4:0 (2009), 277–97.

Le Goff, Jacques. *Medieval Civilization 400–1500*. Hoboken, NJ, 1990.

Lerner, Robert E. 'The Black Death and Western European Eschatological Mentalities.' *American Historical Review* 86 (1981), 533–52.

Liddy, Christian D. 'Urban Conflict in Late Fourteenth-century England: The Case of York in 1380–1.' *English Historical Review* 118:475 (2003), 3–32.

Lightfoot, Dana Wessell. 'The Projects of Marriage: Spousal Choice, Dowries, and Domestic Service in Early Fifteenth-century Valencia.' *Viator: Medieval and Renaissance Studies* 40:1 (2009), 333–53.

Llorens Solé. *Solsona i el solsonès in la història de Catalunya*, 2 vols. Lerida, 1987.

Lopez, Robert S. 'Hard Times and Investment in Culture.' In *Social and Economic Foundations of the Italian Renaissance*. Ed. Anthony Molho. London and New York, 1969, 95–116.

'The Trade of Medieval Europe: The South.' In *The Cambridge Economic History of Europe*, Vol. II, *Trade and Industry in the Middle Ages*. Ed. M. M. Postan and H. J. Habbakuk. Cambridge, 1952, 306–401.

Lynch, Katherine A. *Individuals, Families, and Communities in Europe, 1200–1800: The Urban Foundations of Western Society*. Cambridge, 2003.

MacKay, Angus. 'Faction and Civil Strife in Late Medieval Castilian Towns.' *Bulletin of the John Rylands University Library of Manchester* 72:3 (1990), 120–31.

Spain in the Middle Ages: From Frontier to Empire, 1000–1500. London, 1977.

MacKenney, Richard. *Tradesmen and Traders: The World of the Guilds in Venice and Europe c.1250–c.1650*. Basking Ridge, NJ, 1987.

Mainè Burguette, Enrique. *Ciudadanos honrados de Zaragoza. La oligarquía zaragozana en la baja edad media (1370–1410)*. Zaragoza, 2006.

'Infanzones contra ciudadanos: Luchas por el poder en la parroquia de la Magdalena (Zaragoza).' In *Homenaje a la Professora Carmen Orcástegui Gros (Aragón en la edad media, 14–15)*. 2 vols. Zaragoza, 1999, 941–53.

Maire Vigueur, Jean-Claude. *Cavaliers et citoyens: Guerre, conflits et société dans l'Italie communale, XIIe–XIIIe siècles*. Paris, 2003.

Mandingorra Llavata, María Luz. 'La configuración de la identidad privada: Diarios y libros de memorias en la baja edad media.' *Historia. Instituciones. Documentos* 29 (2002), 217–35.

Marín García, María Angeles. 'Las carnicerías y el abastecimiento de carne en Murcia (1450–1500).' *Miscelánea Medieval Murciana* 14 (1987–8), 49–99.

Marshall, Richard K. *The Local Merchants of Prato: Small Entrepreneurs in the Late Medieval Economy*. Baltimore, MD, 1999.

Martí Arau, Albert. 'Governar el deute en temps de crisi: Castelló d'Empúries (1386–1421).' *Anuario de Estudios Medievales* 40:1 (2010), 129–79.

Martí Setañes, Esther. 'El síndic municipal a corts a la Corona d'Aragó, durant el regnat d'Alfons el Magnànim: El cas de Lleida.' *Anuario de Estudios Medievales* 34:2 (2004), 831–73.

Martin, John Jeffries, and Dennis Romano. *Venice Reconsidered: The History and Civilization of an Italian City-state, 1297–1797*. Baltimore, MD, 2002.

Martín, José Luis. 'Les corts catalanes del 1358.' *Estudis d'Història Medieval* 4, 1971, 69–86.

Martines, Lauro, ed. *Violence and Civil Disorder in Italian Cities, 1200–1500*. Berkeley, CA, 1972.

Martínez Martínez, María. *Las mujeres en la organización de una sociedad de frontera: La etapa colonizadora-repobladora de Murcia, 1266–1272*. Murcia, 2000.

Marzal Palacios, Francisco Javier. 'La esclavitud en Valencia durante la baja Edad Media (1375–1425).' Unpub. Ph.D. Dissertation, Universitat de Valencia, 2006.

Mas Casas, Jose María. *Ensayos históricios sobre Manresa*. Manresa, 1882.

Masschaele, James. 'The Renaissance Depression in Debate: The View from England.' *The History Teacher* 27:4 (August 1994), 405–15.

McCloskey, Deirdre. *Bourgeois Dignity: Why Economics Can't Explain the Modern World*. Chicago, IL, 2011.

The Bourgeois Virtues: Ethics for an Age of Commerce. Chicago, IL, 2007.

McGee, Timothy J. 'Dinner Music for the Florentine Signoria, 1350–1450.' *Speculum: A Journal of Medieval Studies* 74:1 (1999), 95–114.

McGough, Laura. 'Women, Private Property, and the Limitations of State Authority in Early Modern Venice.' *Journal of Women's History* 14:3 (2002), 32–52.

McIntosh, Marjorie K. 'Women, Credit, and Family Relationships in England, 1300–1620.' *Journal of Family History: Studies in Family, Kinship and Demography* 30:2 (2005), 143–63.

McKee, Sally. 'Households in Fourteenth-century Venetian Crete.' *Speculum: A Journal of Medieval Studies* 70:1 (1995), 27–67.

McVaugh, Michael R. 'Le coût de la pratique et l'accès aux soins au XIVe siècle: L'exemple de la ville de Manresa.' *Médiévales: Langue, Textes, Histoire (Paris)* 46 (2004), 45–54.

Meek, Christine E. 'Women, Dowries and the Family in Late Medieval Italian Cities.' In *The Fragility of Her Sex? Medieval Irish Women in the European Context*. Ed. Christine Meek and Katharine Simms. Dublin, 1996, 136–52.

Menjot, Denis. 'Hidalguía et caballería à Murcie: Contours sociaux d'une aristocratie urbaine du XIIIe au XVe siècle.' In *Les sociétés urbaines en France méridionale et en péninsule Ibérique au moyen age. Actes du Colloque de Pau, 21–23 Septembre 1988*. Paris, 1991, 219–27.

'La ville et ses territoires dans l'Occident médiéval: Un système spatial. État de la question.' In *La ciudad medieval y su influencia territorial: Nájera. Encuentros Internacionales del Medievo 3, 2006*. Ed. Beatriz Arízaga Bolumburu and Jesús A. Solórzano Telechea. Logroño, 2007, 451–92.

Menjot, Denis, and Manuel Sánchez Martínez. *La fiscalité des villes au moyen age.* Toulouse, 1996.

La fiscalité des villes au moyen age (Occident Méditerranéen). Vol. II, *Les systèmes fiscaux.* Toulouse, 1999.

Menocal, Maria. *The Ornament of the World: How Muslims, Jews, and Christians Created a Culture of Tolerance in Medieval Spain.* Boston, MA, 2002.

Meyerson, Mark D. *Jews in an Iberian Frontier Kingdom: Society, Economy, and Politics in Morvedre, 1248–1391.* Leiden, 2004.

The Muslims of Valencia in the Age of Fernando and Isabel: Between Coexistence and Crusade. Berkeley, CA, 1991.

'Victims and Players: The Attack of the Union of Valencia on the Jews of Morvedre.' In *Religion, Text, and Society in Medieval Spain and Northern Europe: Essays in Honor of J. N. Hillgarth.* Ed. Thomas E. Burman, Mark D. Meyerson, and Leah Shopkow. Toronto, 2002, 70–102.

Michaud, Francine. 'The Peasant Citizens of Marseille at the Turn of the Fourteenth Century.' In *Urban and Rural Communities in Medieval France: Provence and Languedoc, 1000–1500.* Ed. Kathryn Reyerson and John Drendel. Leiden, 1998, 275–89.

Un signe des temps: Accroissement des crises familiales autour du patrimoine à Marseille à la fin du XIIIe siècle. Toronto, 1994.

Milani, Giuliano. *L'Esclusione dal comune. Conflitti e bandi politici a Bologna e in altre città Italiane tra XII e XIV Secolo.* Rome, 2003.

Miller, Edward. *The Agrarian History of England and Wales:* Vol. III, *1348–1500.* Cambridge, 1991.

'English Town Patricians, c. 1200–1350.' In *Gerarchie economiche e gerarchie sociali secoli XII–XVIII: Atti della 'dodicesima settimana di studi', 18–23 Aprile 1980.* Ed. Annalisa Guarducci. Florence, 1990, 217–40.

Milton, Gregory B. *Market Power: Lordship, Society, and Economy in Medieval Catalonia (1276–1313).* Basingstoke, 2012.

'The Transition from Ecclesiastical Scribania to Professional Notariate in Santa Coloma de Queralt.' *Journal of Medieval History* 39:1 (2013), 1–19.

Mokyr, Joel. *The Gifts of Athena: Historical Origins of the Knowledge Economy.* Princeton, NJ, 2004.

The Lever of Riches: Technological Creativity and Economic Progress. Oxford, 1992.

Molho, Anthony. *Florentine Public Finances in the Early Renaissance, 1400–33.* Cambridge, MA, 1974.

Marriage Alliance in Late Medieval Florence. Cambridge, MA, 1994.

'The State and Public Finance: A Hypothesis Based on the History of Late Medieval Florence.' *Journal of Modern History* 67 (1995), 97–135.

Molho, Anthony, Julia Emlen, and Kurt Raaflaub, eds. *City-States in Classical Antiquity and Medieval Italy.* Ann Arbor, MI, 1992.

Mollat, Michel. *The Poor in the Middle Ages: An Essay in Social History.* New Haven, CT, 1986.

Mollat, Michel, and Philippe Wolff. *Ongles Bleus, Jacques et Ciompi: Les révolutions populaires en Europe aux XIVe et XVe siècles.* Paris, 1970.

Les révolutions populaires en Europe aux XIVe et XVe siècles. Paris, 1993.

Montagut Estragués, Tomàs de. 'Els functionaries i l'administració real a Catalunya (segles XIII–XIV).' *Annexos d'Acta Medievalia, Sèrie d'História Medieval* 1 (1983), 137–50.

Moor, Tine de, Jan Luiten van Zanden, and Jaco Zuijderduijn. 'Micro-credit in Late Medieval Waterland: Households and the Efficiency of Capital Markets in Edam en De Zeevang.' In *La famiglia nell'economia Europea secc. XIII–XVIII: The Economic Role of the Family in the European Economy from the 13th to the 18th Centuries. Atti della 'Quarantesima settimana di studi', 6–10 Aprile 2008*. Ed. Simonetta Cavaciocchi. Florence, 2009, 651–68.

Moore, R. I. *The First European Revolution 900–1215*. Oxford, 2000.

Morelló Baget, Jordi. *Municipis sota la senyoria dels creditors de censals: La gestió del deute públic a la baronia de la Llacuna (s.XV)*. Barcelona, 2008.

Mueller, Reinhold C., and Frederic C. Lane. *The Venetian Money Market: Banks, Panics, and the Public Debt, 1200–1500*. Baltimore, MD, 1997.

Mugueta, Iñigo. *El dinero de los Evreux: Hacienda y fiscalidad en el reinode Navarra (1328–1349)*. Pamplona, 2008.

Muir, E. *Civic Ritual in Renaissance Venice*. Princeton, NJ, 1981.

Mummey, Kevin, and Kathryn Reyerson. 'Whose City Is This? Hucksters, Domestic Servants, Wet Nurses, Prostitutes, and Slaves in Late Medieval Western Mediterranean Urban Society.' *History Compass* 9:12 (2011), 910–22.

Muñoz, María Rosa, and Regina Pinilla. *Les municipalites et leur participation dans les cortes Valenciennes de l'époque forale. Parliaments, Estates and Representation* 13:1 (1993), 1–15.

Muñoz Gómez, Víctor. 'La participación política de las elites locales en el gobierno de las ciudades castellanas en la baja edad media: Bandos y conflictos de intereses (Paredes de Nava, final del s. XIV – inicio del s. XV).' *Anuario de Estudios Medievales* 39:1 (2009), 275–305.

Munro, John H. 'Builders' Wages in Southern England and the Southern Low Countries, 1346–1500: A Comparative Study of Trends in and Levels of Real Incomes.' In *L'Edilizia prima della rivoluzione industriale secc. XIII–XVIII: Atti della trentaseiesima settimana di studi, 26–30 Aprile 2004*. Ed. Simonetta Cavaciocchi. Florence, 2005, 1013–76.

'The Medieval Origins of the Financial Revolution: Usury, Rentes, and Negotiability.' *International History Review* 25:3 (2003), 505–62.

'The Usury Doctrine and Urban Public Finances in Late-medieval Flanders (1220–1550): Rentes (annuities), Excise Taxes, and Income Transfers from the Poor to the Rich.' In *La fiscalità nell'economia Europea secc. XIII–XVIII/ Fiscal Systems in the European Economy from the 13th to the 18th Centuries. Atti della trenatanovesima settimana di studi, 22–26 Aprile 2007*. Ed. Simonetta Cavaciocchi. Florence, 2008, 973–1026.

'Wage-stickiness, Monetary Changes, and Real Incomes in Late-medieval England and the Low Countries, 1300–1500: Did Money Matter?', *Research in Economic History* 21:1 (2003), 185–297.

Mutge Vives, Josefa. 'L'Abastament de peix i carn a Barcelona, en el primer terç del segle XIV.' In *Alimentació i societat a la Catalunya medieval*. Barcelona, 1988, 109–36.

La ciudad de Barcelona durante el reinado de Alfonso el Benigno (1327–1336). Barcelona, 1987.

La jurisdicción real inferior en Barcelona durante el reinado de Alfonso el Benigno (1327–1336), in *Castilla y el mundo feudal: Homenaje al professor Julio Valdeón*. Valladolid, 2009, 369–80.

'Preocupacions del govern municipal Barceloní en el 1371 a través dels testaments dels consellers.' *Acta Historica et Archaeologica Mediaevalia* 23–4 (2003), 331–51.

Mutgé Vives, Josefina. 'L'Abastament de blat a la ciutat de Barcelona en temps d'Alfons el Benigne (1327–1336).' *Anuario de Estudios Medievales* 31:2 (2001), 649–91.

Nadal Farreras, J., and P. Wolff, eds., *Histoire de Catalogne*. Toulouse, 1982.

Nadal Oller, Jordi. *La población española (siglos XVI a XX)*. Barcelona, 1971.

Najemy, John M. *Corporatism and Consensus in Florentine Electoral Politics, 1280–1400*. Chapel Hill, NC, 1982.

'The Dialogue of Power in Florentine Politics.' In *City States in Classical Antiquity and Medieval Italy: Athens and Rome, Florence and Venice*. Ed. Anthony Molho, Kurt Raaflaub, and Julia Emlen. Stuttgart, 1991, 269–88.

'Governments and Governance.' In *Italy in the Age of the Renaissance, 1300–1550*. Ed. John Najemy. Oxford, 2004, 184–207.

'Guild Republicanism in Trecento Florence: The Successes and Ultimate Failure of Corporate Politics.' *American Historical Review* 84:1 (1979), 53–71.

A History of Florence 1200–1575. Hoboken, 2008.

Narbona Vizcaíno, Rafael. 'La conflictividad social en las ciudades de la Corona de Aragón: Siglos XIII–XV.' In *Conflicto, violencia y criminalidad en Europa y América: IV Jornadas de estudios históricos del departamento de historia medieval, moderna y de América (Vitoria-Gasteiz, 11 al 13 de Noviembre de 2002)*. Ed. José Antonio Munita Loinaz. Bilbao, 2004, 79–104.

Memorias de la ciudad. Ceremonias, creencias y costumbres en la historia de Valencia. Valencia, 2003.

'Oligarquías políticas y elites económicas en las ciudades bajomedievales (siglos XIV–XVI).' *Revista d'Història Medieval* 9 (1998), 9–15.

Valencia, municipio medieval: Poder político y luchas ciudadanas, (1239–1418). Valencia, 1995.

Narbona Vizcaíno, Rafael, and Enrique Cruselles Gòmez. 'Espacios económicos y sociedad política en la Valencia del siglo XV.' *Revista d'Història Medieval* 9 (1998), 193–214.

Navarro Espinach, Germán. 'Los negocios de la Burguesía en la industria precapitalista Valenciana de los siglos XIV–XVI.' *Revista d'Història Medieval* 11 (2000), 67–103.

Navarro Espinach, Germán, and Joaquín Aparici Martí. 'La producción textil en Teruel medieval.' *Teruel* 88–9 (2002), 73–100.

Nicholas, David. *The Domestic Life of a Medieval City: Women, Children, and the Family in Fourteenth-Century Ghent*. Lincoln, NE, 1985.

The Growth of the Medieval City: From Late Antiquity to the Early Fourteenth Century. London and New York, 1997.

The Later Medieval City: 1300–1500. London, 1997.

The Metamorphosis of a Medieval City: Ghent in the Age of the Arteveldes, 1302–1390. Leiden, 1987.

'Town and Countryside: Social and Economic Tensions in Fourteenth-century Flanders.' *Comparative Studies in Society and History* 10 (1968), 458–85.

Urban Europe, 1100–1700. London, 2003.

Nightingale, Pamela. 'Capitalists, Crafts and Constitutional Change in Late Fourteenth-Century London.' *Past and Present*, 124 (1989), 3–35.

'The Lay Subsidies and the Distribution of Wealth in Medieval England, 1275–1334.' *Economic History Review* 57:1 (2004), 1–32.

A Medieval Mercantile Community: The Grocers' Company and the Politics and Trade of London, 1000–1485. New Haven, CT, 1995.

'The Rise and Decline of Medieval York: A Reassessment.' *Past and Present: A Journal of Historical Studies* 206 (2010), 3–42.

Nirenberg, David. *Communities of Violence. Persecution of Minorities in the Middle Ages.* Princeton, NJ, 1996.

'Muslims in Christian Iberia, 1000–1526: Varieties of Mudejar.' In *The Medieval World.* Ed. Peter Linehan and Janet L. Nelson. London, 2001, 60–76.

North, Douglass C., and Barry R. Weingast, 'Constitutions and Commitment: The Evolution of Institutions Governing Public Choice in Seventeenth-Century England.' *The Journal of Economic History* 49:4 (1989), 803–32.

O'Connor, Isabel A. *A Forgotten Community: The Mudejar Aljama of Xàtiva, 1240–1327.* Leiden, 2003.

Oliva Herrer, Hipólito Rafael, and Pere Benito Monclús, eds. *Crisis de subsistencia y crisis agrarias en la edad media.* Seville, 2007.

Olmos Herguedas, Emilio. 'El poder urbano y sus estrategias para influir sobre el territorio. Aproximación metodológica desde las ordenanzas concejiles castellanas.' In *La ciudad medieval y su influencia territorial: Nájera. Encuentros internacionales del medievo 3, 2006.* Ed. Beatriz Arízaga Bolumburu and Jesús A. Solórzano Telechea. Logroño, 2007, 493–519.

Ortega Cera, Ágata. 'Arrendar el dinero del rey: Fraude y estrategias financieras en el estrado de las rentas en la Castilla del siglo XV.' *Anuario de Estudios Medievales* 40:1 (2010), 223–49.

Ortega Villoslada, Antonio. 'El trabajo femenino en Mallorca: La labor de la mujer en la actividad marítima de la primera mitad del siglo XIV.' *Espacio, Tiempo y Forma* 3:17 (2004), 461–9.

Ortí Gost, Pere. 'El consell de Cent durant l'edat mitjana.' *Barcelona: Quaderns d'Història* 4 (2001), 21–48.

'Les "imposicions" municipales Catalanes au XIVe siècle.' In *La fiscalité des villes au moyen age (Occident méditerranéen)*, vol. II, *Les systèmes fiscaux.* Ed. Manuel Sánchez Martínez and Denis Menjot. Toulouse, 1999, 399–422.

'El municipi de Barcelona i les parròquies del seu entorn al segle XIV.' *Anuario de Estudios Medievales* 31:1 (2001), 33–48.

'La primera articulación del estado feudal en Cataluña a través de un impuesto: El bovaje (ss. XII–XIII).' *Hispania: Revista Española de Historia* 61:3:209 (2001), 967–98.

Renda i fiscalitat en una ciutat medieval: Barcelona, segles XII–XIV. Barcelona, 2000.

Palliser, David M. 'Introduction.' In *The Cambridge Urban History of Britain*, vol. I, *600–1540*. Ed. David M. Palliser. Cambridge, 2000, 3–15.

'Urban Decay Revisited.' In *Towns and Local Communities in Medieval and Early Modern England*, vol. XIII. Aldershot, 2006, 1–21.

'Urban Society.' In *Towns and Local Communities in Medieval and Early Modern England*, vol. IX. Aldershot, 2006, 132–49.

Parker, Holt N. 'Women and Humanism: Nine Factors for the Woman Learning.' *Viator: Medieval and Renaissance Studies* 35 (2004), 581–616.

Parkin, Frank. *Max Weber*. London, 2002.

Persson, Karl Gunnar. *An Economic History of Europe: Knowledge, Institutions and Growth: 600 to the Present*. Cambridge, 2010.

Phelps Brown, E. H., and S. V. Hopkins. 'Seven Centuries of the Prices of Consumables Compared with Builders' Wage-Rates.' *Economica* 23 (Nov. 1956), reprinted in E. H. Phelps Brown and Sheila V. Hopkins. *A Perspective of Wages and Prices*. London, 1981.

Phythian-Adams, Charles. *Desolation of a City: Coventry and the Urban Crisis of the Late Middle Ages*. Cambridge, 1979.

'Urban Decay in Late Medieval England.' In *Towns in Societies: Essays in Economic History and Historical Sociology*. Ed. Philip Abrams and E. A. Wrigley. London, 1978, 159–86.

Pinto, Giuliano. '"Honour" and "Profit": Landed Property and Trade in Medieval Siena.' In *City and Countryside in Late Medieval and Renaissance Italy: Essays Presented to Philip Jones*. Ed. Trevor Dean and Chris Wickham. London, 1990, 81–91.

Pirenne, Henri. *Les anciennes démocraties des Pays-Bas*. Paris, 1910.

Economic and Social History of Medieval Europe. New York, 1937.

'The Stages in the Social History of Capitalism.' *American Historical Review* 19 (1914), 494–514.

Les villes du moyen age. Brussels, 1927.

Les villes et les institutions urbaines. Paris, 1939.

Pladevall Font, Antoni. 'La disminució de poblament a la Plana de Vich a mitjans del segle XIV.' *Ausa* 4:44 (1963), 361–73.

Plana Borràs, Josep. 'Els Benet, una família de mercaders barcelonins (primera meitat del segle XIV).' *La Societat Barcelona a la Baixa Edat Mitjana, Annexos d'Acta Medievalia, Sèrie Història Medieva* 1 (1983), 53–65.

Planas Marcé, Sílvia. *La Girona Jueva, el call*. Girona, 2001.

Platelle, Henri. *Histoire de Valenciennes*. Lille, 1982.

Platt, Colin. *King Death*. Toronto, 1996.

Pons Guri, Josep Maria. 'Aspectes judicials de la cort general a l'època medieval.' In *Les Corts a Catalunya: Actes del Congrés d'Història Institucional, 28, 29 i 30 d'abril de 1988*. Barcelona, 1991, 142–5.

'Relació jurídica de la remença i els mals usos a les terres Gironines.' *Revista de Girona: Literatura – Ciencias – Artes. Asociación Literaria de Gerona: (later Revista de Girona)* 32:118 (1986), 36–43.

Poos, L. R. *A Rural Society after the Black Death: Essex 1350–1525*. Cambridge, 1991.

Postan, M. M. 'Feudalism and its Decline: A Semantic Exercise.' In T. H. Aston, *et al.*, eds., *Social Relations and Ideas: Essays in Honour of R. H. Hilton*. Cambridge, 1983, 73–87.

Prak, Maarten Roy, Catharina Lis, Jan Lucassen, and Hugo Soly. *Craft Guilds in the Early Modern Low Countries: Work, Power and Representation.* Aldershot, 2006.

Prosser, Gareth. 'The Later Medieval French Noblesse.' In *France in the Later Middle Ages, 1200–1500.* Ed. David Potter. Oxford, 2002, 182–209.

Pryor, John H. 'Commenda: The Operation of the Contract in Long Distance Commerce at Marseilles During the Thirteenth Century.' *Journal of European Economic History* 13:2 (1984), 397–440.

Puig, Ignasi, and Montserrat Duran. 'La crisi demogràfica de la baixa edat mitjana i el règim senyorial en el Pireneu català: La Baronia d'Erill el 1393.' *Urgellia* 6 (1983), 387–400.

Pullan, Brian S. *A History of Early Renaissance Italy: From Mid-thirteenth to the Mid-fifteenth Century.* London, 1973.

Rafat Selga, Francesc. 'Manresa en l'exportació de safrà durant el segle XIV.' *Miscellania d'Estudis Bagencs* 9 (1994), 9–25.

Razi, Zvi. *Life, Marriage and Death in a Medieval Parish.* Cambridge, 1980.

Reyerson, Kathryn L. *The Art of the Deal: Intermediaries of Trade in Medieval Montpellier.* Leiden, 2002.

Reyerson, Kathryn, and John Victor Drendel, eds. *Urban and Rural Communities in Medieval France: Provence and Languedoc, 1000–1500.* Leiden, 1998.

Reynolds, Susan. *An Introduction to the History of English Medieval Towns.* Oxford, 1977.

Kingdoms and Communities in Western Europe, 900–1300. Oxford, 1984.

Ribalta, Jaume and Max Turull Rubinat. 'Ciutat i poder en el feudalisme declinant a la Catalunya baixmedieval: Diferencació social i distribució social de l'espai urbà a Cervera, 1340–1382.' *Anuario de Estudios Medievales* 22 (1992), 79–144.

Rich Abad, Anna. *La comunitat Jueva de Barcelona entre 1348 i 1391 a través de la documentació notarial.* Barcelona, 1999.

'Família, patrimoni i individualitat: Les dones Jueves a Barcelona entre 1349 i 1391.' In *Actes del II Congrés per a L'estudi dels Jueus en els territoris de Llengua Catalana: Barcelona-Cervera, del 25 al 27 d'octubre del 2004.* Barcelona, 2005, 375–93.

Riddy, Felicity. '"Burgeis" Domesticity in Late Medieval England.' In *Medieval Domesticity: Home, Housing and Household in Medieval England.* Ed. Maryanne Kowaleski and P. J. P. Goldberg. Cambridge, 2008, 14–36.

Rigby, Stephen H. 'Urban "Oligarchy" in Late Medieval England.' In *Towns and Townspeople in the Fifteenth Century.* Ed. John A.F. Thomson. Gloucester, 1988, 62–86.

Rigby, Stephen H., and Eleanor Ewan. 'Government, Power and Authority 1300–1540.' In *The Cambridge Urban History of Britain*, Vol. I, *600–1540.* Ed. David M. Pallisser. Cambridge, 2000, 291–312.

Riu de Martin, Maria del Carme. 'La producción y enta de cal en la baja edad media Catalana: Su utilización en la muralla de Barcelona.' In *Os reinos Ibéricos na idade média: Livro de homenagem ao Professor Doutor Humberto Carlos Baquero Moreno.* Ed. Luís Adão da Fonseca, Luís Carlos Amaral, and Maria Fernanda Ferreira Santos, Vol. II. Porto, 2003, 963–9.

Riu Riu, Manuel. 'La financion de la vivienda, propiedad horizontal y pisos de alquiler en la Barceloa del siglo XIV.' *La ciudad hispanica durante los siglos XIII al XVI*, 1397–1405. Barcelona, 1985.

La vila de Berga i els Berguedans a la dareria del segle XIV. Barcelona, 1989.

'The Woollen Industry in Catalonia in the Later Middle Ages.' In *Cloth and Clothing in Medieval Europe: Essays in Memory of Professor E.M. Carus-Wilson*. Ed. N. B. Harte and K. G. Ponting (Pasold Studies in Textile History, 2). London, 1983, 205–29.

Rivera Sentís, F. Xavier. 'Ramon Serra el vell: Poder, condició i caritat d'un mercader cerverí a les acaballes del segle XIV.' *Miscel.lània Cerverina* 10 (1996), 37–70.

Romano, David. 'La ordinación de 1281 de las veguerías catalanas.' In *Homenaje al Dr. D. Juan Reglà Compostol*. Valencia, 1975, 111–23.

Romano, Dennis. *Patricians and Popolani: The Social Foundations of the Venetian Renaissance State*. Baltimore, MD, 1987.

Roncière, Charles M. de la. 'Pauvres et pauvreté à Florence au XIVe siècle.' In *Études sur l'histoire de la pauvreté (moyen age – XVIe siècle)*. Ed. Michel Mollat. Paris, 1974, 661–745.

Prix et salaires a Florence au XIVe siècle (1280–1380). Rome, 1982.

Rosser, Gervase. 'Big Brotherhood: Guilds in Urban Politics in Late Medieval England.' In *Guilds and Association in Europe, 900–1900*. Ed. Ian A. Gadd and Patrick Wallis. London, 2006, 27–42.

'Urban Culture and the Church 1300–1540.' In *The Cambridge Urban History of Britain*, Vol. I, *600–1540*. Ed. David M. Palliser. Cambridge, 2000, 335–69.

Roustit, Yvan. 'La consolidation de la dette publique à Barcelone au milieu du XIVe siècle.' *Estudios de Historia Moderna* 4 (1954), 13–156.

Rubinstein, Nicolai. 'Oligarchy and Democracy in Fifteenth-century Florence.' In *Florence and Venice: Comparisons and Relations. Acts of Two Conferences at Villa I Tatti in 1976–1977*. Vol. I, Ed. Sergio Bertelli, Nicolai Rubinstein, and Craig Hugh Smyth. Florence, 1979, 99–112.

Rubio Vela, Agustín. *Peste negra, crisis y comportamientos sociales en la España del siglo XIV: La ciudad de Valencia (1348–1401)*. Granada, 1979.

Ruggiero, Guido. *Violence in Early Renaissance Venice*. New Brunswick, NJ, 1980.

Ruiz De Loizaga, Saturnino. *La peste en los reinos peninsulares: Según documentación del archivo Vaticano (1348–1460)*. Bilbao, 2009.

Ruiz Domènec, José Enrique. 'La crisis económica de la Corona de Aragón: Realidad o ficción historiograáfica?' *Cuadernos de historia* 8 (1977), 71–117.

'El origen del capital comercial en Barcelona.' *Miscellanea Barcinonensia* 31 (1972), 55–88.

'Sistema de parentesco y teoría de la alianza en la sociedad Catalana (c.1000–c.1240).' In *Amore, Familia, Sexualidad. (Reunidos y Presentados Por Arturo R. Firpo)*. Ed. Paul Veyne. Barcelona, 1984, 113–40.

'The Urban Origins of Barcelona: Agricultural Revolution or Commercial Development?' *Speculum: A Journal of Medieval Studies* 52:2 (1977), 265–86.

Ruiz, Teófilo F. *The City and The Realm: Burgos and Castile, 1080–1492*. Aldershot, 1975.

Crisis and Continuity: Land and Town in Late Medieval Castile. Philadelphia, PA, 1994.

Spain's Centuries of Crisis: 1300–1474. Oxford, 2011.

'The Transformation of the Castilian Municipalities: The Case of Burgos 1248–1350.' *Past and Present* 77 (1977), 3–32.

'Women, Work, and Daily Life in Late Medieval Castile.' In *Women at Work in Spain: From the Middle Ages to Early Modern Times*. Ed. Marilyn Stone and Carmen Benito-Vessels. New York, 1998, 101–20.

Russell, Josiah. *Medieval Regions and their Cities*. Bloomington, IN, 1972.

Rycroft, Peter. 'The Role of the Catalan "Corts" in the Late Middle Ages.' *English Historical Review* 89 (1974), 421–69.

Ryder, Alan. *Alfonso the Magnanimous: King of Aragon, Naples, and Sicily, 1396–1458*. Oxford, 1990.

The Wreck of Catalonia: Civil War in the Fifteenth Century. Oxford, 2007.

Sabaté Curull, Flocel. 'The Defection of the Medieval Catalonian Bourgeoisie: A Mutation of Values or a Bibliographic Myth?' In *Urban Elites and Aristocratic Behaviour in the Spanish Kingdoms at the End of the Middle Age*. Ed. María Asenjo González. Turnhout, 2013, 111–32.

'Ejes vertebradores de la oligarquía urbana en Cataluña.' *Revista d'Història Medieval* 9 (1998), 127–53.

'La feudalització de la societat Catalana.' In *El temps i l'espai del feudalisme: Reunió científica. VI curs d'estiu Comtat d'Urgell (Balaguer, 11, 12 i 13 de Juliol de 2001)*. Ed. Flocel Sabaté and Joan Farré. Lerida, 2004, 221–76.

La feudalización de la sociedad Catalana. Granada, 2007.

Fiscalitat i feudalisme: Tàrrega, 1329, recompte i reestructuració. Barcelona, 1991.

Història de Lleida. Vol. II, Alta edat mitjana, Lerida, 2003.

'La insolvència municipal a la segona meitat del segle XIV.' In *Fiscalidad real y finanzas urbanas en la Cataluña medieval*. Ed. Manuel Sánchez Martínez (Anuario de Estudios Medievales, Anejo 35). Barcelona, 1999, 255–80.

'Oligarchies and Social Fractures in the Cities of Late Medieval Catalonia.' In *Oligarchy and Patronage in Late Medieval Spanish Urban Society*. Ed. María Asenjo-González. Turnhout, 2009, 1–27.

La tenencia de castillos en la Cataluña medieval. In *Alcaídias y fortalezas en la España medieval*. Alicante, 2007, 69–136.

'El veguer a Catalunya: Anàlisi del funcionament de la jurisdicció reial al segle XIV.' *Butlletí de la Societat Catalana d'Estudis Històrics* 6 (1995), 147–59.

Salicrú Lluch, Roser. *Esclaus i propietaris d'esclaus a la Catalunya del Segle XV: L'assegurança contra fugues*. Anuario de Estudios Medievales, 34. Madrid and Barcelona, 1998.

'Slaves in the Professional and Family Life of Craftsmen in the Late Middle Ages.' In *La famiglia nell'economia Europea secc. XIII–XVIII: The Economic Role of the Family in the European Economy from the 13th to the 18th Centuries. Atti della 'Quarantesima settimana di studi', 6–10 Aprile 2008*. Ed. Simonetta Cavaciocchi. Florence, 2009, 325–42.

Salrach Marés, Josep M. *La fam al món: Passat i present*. Vic, 2009.

'La pesta negra i els orígens del problema remença.' In *Pere el Ceremoniós i la seva epoca (Anuario de Estudios Medievales, Anex 24)*. Barcelona, 1989, 13–34.

Sánchez Martínez, Manuel. *La deuda pública en la Cataluña bajomedieval*. Madrid, 2009.

'La diputació del General: Quan i per què es va crear?' *L'Avenç: Història del Països Catalans* 303 (2005), 24–8.

Estudios sobre renta, fiscalidad y finanzas en la Cataluna bajomedieval. Madrid, 1993.

Fiscalidad real y finanzas urbanas en la Cataluña medieval. Barcelona, 2000.
'The Invocation of Princeps Namque in 1368 and Its Repercussions for the City of Barcelona.' In *The Hundred Years War: A Wider Focus.* Ed. L. J. Andrew Villalon and Donald J. Kagay. Leiden, 2005, 297–330.
El naixement de la fiscalitat d'Estat a Catalunya: Segles XII–XIV. Vic, 1995.
'El naixement de la Generalitat de Catalunya.' *Quaderns del Museu d'Història de Catalunya* 6 (2003), 15–18.
Pagar al rey en la Corona de Aragon durante el siglo XIV. Anuario de Estudios Medievales, 50. Barcelona, 2003.
'La presión fiscal en un año dificil: Cataluña, a mediados de 1374 – mediados de 1375.' *Mayurqa* 27 (2001), 25–45.
'Questie y subsidios en Cataluña durante el primer tercio del siglo XIV: El subsidio para la cruzada granadaina (1329–1334), *Cuadernos de Historia Econòmica de Cataluña,* 16 (1977), 11–54.
'Sevillian Medieval Nobility: Creation, Development and Character.' *Journal of Medieval History* 24:4 (1998), 367–80.
'Vino y fiscalidad en la edad media: El caso de los municipios Catalanes.' In *Actas del I simposio de la Asociación Internacional de Historia y Civilización de la vid y el vino, 1999.* Ed. Javier Maldonado Rosso. Madrid and Barcelona, 2001, 403–19.
Sánchez Martínez, Manuel, Antoni Furió, and Prim Bertran i Riogé. *Actes colloqui corona, municipis i fiscalitat a la baixa edat mitjana.* Lerida, 1996.
Sánchez Martínez, Manuel, and Pere Orti Gost. *Corts, parlaments i fiscalitat a Catalunya: Els capitols del donatiu (1288–1384).* Barcelona, 1997.
Sánchez Saus, Rafael. 'Los patriciados urbanos.' In *El mundo social de Isabel la Católica: La sociedad Castellana a finales del siglo XV.* Ed. Miguel Angel Ladero Quesada. Madrid, 2004, 143–55.
Santamaría, Alvaro. 'Los consells municipales de la Corona de Aragón mediado el siglo XIII. El sistema de cooptación.' *Anuario de historia del derecho español* 51 (1981), 291–364.
Sarasa, Esteban. *La sociedad en Aragón y Cataluña en el reinado de JaimeI (1213–1276).* Zaragoza, 2009.
Sarret Arbós, Joaquim. *La cequia de Manresa.* Manresa, 1906.
Historia de l'estat politic-social de Manresa. Monumenta Historica Civitatis Minorise, Vol. V. Manresa, 1925.
Historia de Manresa. Monumenta Historica Civitatis Minorise, Vol. I. Manresa, 1921.
Historia religiosa de Manresa: Iglesies i convents. Monumenta Historica Civitatis Minorise, Vol. IV. Manresa, 1924.
Schluchter, Wolfgang. *The Rise of Western Rationalism: Max Weber's Developmental History.* Berkeley, CA, 1985.
Schofield, Phillipp R. 'Credit and Debt in Medieval England: Introduction.' In *Credit and Debit in Medieval England, c.1180–c.1350.* Ed. Phillipp R. Schofield and N. J. Mayhew. Oxford, 2002, 1–18.
Scott, Tom. *The City-State in Europe, 1000–1600: Hinterland, Territory, Region.* Oxford, 2012.

Serrano Larrayoz, Fernando. '"Item perrexil, mostarda, lechugas et rauanosâ". Notas sobre la alimentación de mineros alemanes en Pamplona a finales del siglo XIV (1392).' *Anuario de Estudios Medievales* 38:1 (2008), 235–69.
Sesma Muñoz, José Ángel. 'Las ciudades en Aragón y la Cataluña interior: Población y flujos económicos (1150–1350).' In *La población de Aragón en la edad media, siglos XIII–XV: Estudios de demografía histórica*. Ed. J. Ángel Sesma Muñoz and Carlos Lallena Corbera. Zaragoza, 2004, 55–90.
'Fiscalidad y poder: La fiscalidad centralizada como instrumento de poder en la Corona de Aragón (siglo XIV).' *Espacio, Tiempo y Forma* 3:1 (1988), 447–63.
Huesca, ciudad mercado de ámbito internacional en la Baja Edad Media, según los registros de su aduana. Zaragoza, 2005.
'La población urbana en la Corona de Aragón (siglos XIV–XV).' In *Las sociedades urbanas en la España medieval: XXIX semana de Estudios medievales, Estella, 15 a 19 de Julio de 2002*. Pamplona, 2003, 151–93.
El tráfico mercantil por las aduanas de Ribagorza (1444–1450): Producción y comercio rural en Aragón a finales de la edad media. Zaragoza, 2010.
Sesma Muñoz, José Ángel. ed. *La Corona de Aragón en el centro de su historia (1208–1458): La monarquía Aragonesa y los reinos de la Corona*. Zaragoza, 2010.
Shatzmiller, Maya. *Her Day in Court: Women's Property Rights in Fifteenth-Century Granada*. Cambridge, MA, 2007.
'Women and Wage Labour in the Medieval Islamic West: Legal Issues in an Economic Context.' *Journal of the Economic and Social History of the Orient* 40:2 (1997), 174–206.
Shaw, Christine. *Popular Government and Oligarchy in Renaissance Italy*. Leiden, 2006.
Shaw, Diane. 'The Construction of the Private in Medieval London.' *Journal of Medieval and Early Modern Studies* (formerly *Journal of Medieval and Renaissance Studies)* 26:3 (1996), 447–66.
Shaw, David Gary. *The Creation of a Community: The City of Wells in the Middle Ages*. Oxford, 1993.
'Social Networks and the Foundations of Oligarchy in Medieval Towns.' *Urban History* 32:2 (2005), 200–22.
Shideler, John. *A Medieval Catalan Noble Family: The Montcadas, 1000–1230*. Berkeley, CA, 1984.
Shirk, Melanie. 'Royal Reaction to the Black Death in the Crown of Aragon, 1348–1351.' Unpub.Doctoral Dissertation, University of Kansas, 1975.
Smail, Daniel Lord. 'Common Violence: Vengeance and Inquisition in Fourteenth Century Marseille.' *Past and Present* 151 (1996), 28–59.
Imaginary Cartographies: Possession and Identity in Late Medieval Marseille. Ithaca, NY, 1999.
'Notaries, Courts, and the Legal Culture of Late Medieval Marseille.' In *Urban and Rural Communities in Medieval France: Provence and Languedoc, 1000–1500*. Ed. Kathryn Reyerson and John Drendel (The Medieval Mediterranean, 62). Leiden, 1998, 23–50.
Sobreques Vidal, Santiago, and Jaume Sobrequés Callicó. *La guerra civil Catalana del segle XV: Estudis sobre la crisi social i economica de la baixa edat mitjana*, 2 vols. Barcelona, 1973.

Soler Sala, Maria. 'Feudalisme i nucleació poblacional: Processos de concentració de l'hàbitat al Comtat de Barcelona Entre els segles X i XIII.' *Acta Historica et Archaeologica Mediaevalia* 23–4 (2003), 69–101.

Solórzano Telechea, Jesús Ángel. 'La organización interna de la oligarquía urbana y el ejercicio del poder en Santander durante la baja edad media: Linaje, familia y poder.' In *I encuentro de historia de Cantabria*. Santander, 1999, 575–97.

Santander en la edad media: Patrimonio, parentesco y poder. Santander, 2002.

'Violencia y conflictividad política en el siglo XV: El delito al servicio de la élite en las cuatro villas de la Costa de la Mar.' *Anuario de Estudios Medievales* 35:1 (2010), 159–84.

Solórzano Telechea, Jesús Ángel, and Beatriz Arízaga Bolumburu, eds. *La gobernanza de la ciudad europea enla edad media*. Logroño, 2011.

Spufford, Peter. *Handbook of Medieval Exchange*. London, 1986.

Stabel, Peter. 'Guilds in Medieval Flanders: Myths and Realities of Guild Life in an Export-oriented Environment.' *Journal of Medieval History* 30:2 (2004), 187–212.

Stabel, Peter. 'Markets and Retail in the Cities of the Late Medieval Low Countries: Economic Networks and Socio-cultural Display.' In *Fiere e mercati nella integrazione delle economie Europee secc. XIII–XVIII: Atti della trentaduesima settimana di studi, 8–12 Maggio 2000*. Ed. Simonetta Cavaciocchi. Florence, 2001, 797–817.

'Women at the Market: Gender and Retail in the Towns of Late Medieval Flanders.' In *Secretum scriptorum: Liber alumnorum Walter Prevenier*. Ed. Wim Blockmans, Marc Boone and Thérèse De Hemptinne, Leuven, 1999, 259–76.

Stasavage, David. *States of Credit: Size, Power, and the Development of European Polities*. Princeton, NJ, 2011.

Stephenson, Carl. *Borough and Town: A Study of Urban Origins in England*. Cambridge, MA, 1933.

Stuard, Susan Mosher. 'Dowry Inflation and Increments in Wealth in Medieval Ragusa (Dubrovnik).' *Journal of Economic History* 41:4 (1981), 795–812.

Gilding the Market: Luxury and Fashion in Fourteenth-Century Italy. Philadelphia, PA, 2006.

Swabey, Fiona. *Medieval Gentlewoman: Life in a Widow's Household in the Later Middle Ages*. London, 1999.

Swanson, Heather. *Medieval Artisans: An Urban Class in Late Medieval England*. London, 1989.

Medieval British Towns. Basingstoke, 1999.

'The Illusion of Economic Structure: Craft Guilds in Late Medieval English Towns.' *Past and Present: A Journal of Historical Studies* 121 (1988), 29–48.

Tabacco, Giovanni. *Egemonie sociali e strutture del potere nel medioevo Italiano*. Turin, 1974.

Tasis Marca, Rafael. *Pere el cerminoniós i els seus fills*. Barcelona, 1994.

Terpstra, Nicholas. *Lay Confraternities and Civic Religion in Renaissance Bologna*. Cambridge, 2002.

Thrupp, Sylvia. *The Merchant Class of Medieval London*. Chicago, IL, 1948; reprinted Ann Arbor, MI, 1989.

Tilly, Charles. *Coercion, Capital and European States: AD 990–1992*. Hoboken, NJ, 1992.

Tilly, Charles, and Wim P. Blockmans. *Cities and the Rise of States in Europe, A.D. 1000 to 1800*. Boulder, CO, 1994.

Tintó Sala, Margarita. 'Les cases gremials de Barcelona i el seu entorn urbà.' In *El món urbà a la Corona d'Aragó del 1137 als decrets de nova planta: XVII Congrés d'Història de la Corona d'Aragó / Congreso de Historia de la Corona de Aragón, Barcelona, Poblet, Lleida, 7 al 12 de Desembre de 2000*. Vol. II, Ed. Salvador Claramunt. Barcelona, 2003, 895–910.

Titone, Fabrizio. 'Aragonese Sicily as a Model of Late Medieval State Building.' *Viator* 44:1 (2013), 217–49.

'Élites di governo e "mastre" ad agrigento fra trecento e quattrocento.' *Anuario de Estudios Medievales* 32:2 (2002), 845–77.

Governments of the Universitates: Urban Communities of Sicily in the Fourteenth and Fifteenth Centuries. Turnhout, 2009.

Tittler, Robert, and Bridbury, A. R., 'Late Medieval Urban Prosperity: A Rejoinder.' *Economic History Review* 2nd ser. 37 (1984), 551–6.

To Figueras, Lluís. *Família i ereu a la Catalunya nord-oriental: (Segles X–XII)*. Barcelona, 1997.

'Servitude et mobilité paysanne: Les origines de la 'remença' Catalane (XIIe–XIIIe siècles).' *Mélanges de l'École Française de Rome: Moyen Age* 112:2 (2000), 827–65.

Tomás Faci, Guillermo. 'Distinción social en el seno de la baja nobleza Aragonesa: El palacio de los zapata de Calatayud en 1484.' *Anuario de Estudios Medievales* 39:2 (2009), 605–29.

Torras Serra, Marc. 'La carestia de Blat de 1374–1376 a Manresa.' *Miscel.lània d'Estudis Bagencs* 9 (1994), 99–138.

'Els consellers i altres càrrecs municipals de Manresa del segle XV.' *Butlletí Interior* 102 (2006), 329–42.

La crisi del segle XV a Manresa: Una aproximació a partir dels Llibres de Manifests. Barcelona, 1996.

'El deute públic a la ciutata de Manresa a la baixa edat mitjana.' In *Fiscalidad real y finanzas urbanas en la Cataluña medieval*. Ed. Manuel Sánchez Martínez. Barcelona 1999, 155–83.

Els privilegis del 'Llibre verd' de Manresa. Manresa, 1998.

Torras Serra, Marc, ed. *La crisi de l'edat mitjana a la Catalunya central*. Manresa, 1994.

Tracy, James D. *A Financial Revolution in the Habsburg Netherlands: Renten and Renteniers in the County of Holland, 1515–1565*. Berkeley, CA, 1985.

'On the Dual Origins of Long-term Urban Debt in Medieval Europe.' In *Urban Public Debts: Urban Government and the Market for Annuities in Western Europe (14th–18th Centuries)*. Ed. Marc Boone, Karel Davids, and Paul Janssens. Turnhout, 2003, 13–24.

Turull Rubinat, Max. *La configuració jurídica del municipi Baix medieval: Régim municipal i fiscalitat a Cervera entre 1182–1430*. Barcelona, 1990.

El gobierno de la ciudad medieval: Administración y finanzas en las ciudades medievales catalanas. Madrid, 2009.

'La hacienda municipal y la tributación directa en Cataluña durante la edad media: Planteamiento general,' *Revista de Hacienda Autónoma y Local* 22:64 (1992), 9–80.

'Intercanvi comercial, fira i mercat a Cervera entre 1136 i 1392.' *Miscel.lània Cerverina* 7 (1991), 19–39.

'El naixement de la fiscalitat municipal a Lleida, 1149–1289.' *Actes: Col.loqui corona, municipis i fiscalitat a la baixa edat mitjana.* Lerida, 1997, 219–32.

'Nuevas hipótesis sobre los orígenes de los consejos municipals in Cataluña, siglos XII–XIV, algunas reflexiones.' *Anuario de historia del derecho español* 72 (2002), 461–71.

El règim municipal de paeria: Cervera, 1331–1333: dinàmica social i politica. Lerida, 1986.

'Respostes de nobles i cavallers de la vegueria de Cervera per a la campanya de Sardenya de 1354–1355.' *Miscel.lània cerverina* 12 (1998), 131–4.

Turull Rubinat, Max, and Josep Hernando Delgado. 'Pràticha de la vegueria de Cervera: 1289–1301.' *Initium* 2 (1997), 731–9.

Turull Rubinat, Max, and Jordi Morelló Baget. 'Estructura y tipología de les "estimes-manifests" en Cataluña (siglos XIV–XV).' *Anuario de Estudios Medievales* 35:1 (2005), 271–326.

Udina Abelló, Antoni M. 'El braç reial a les corts Catalanes durant el regnat del Magnànim.' In *El món urbà a la Corona d'Aragó del 1137 als decrets de nova planta: XVII Congrés d'Història de la Corona d'Aragó / Congreso de Historia de la Corona de Aragón, Barcelona, Poblet, Lleida, 7 al 12 de Desembre de 2000.* Vol. III, Ed. Salvador Claramunt. Barcelona, 2003, 1013–21.

Ullman, Walter. *Medieval Foundations of Renaissance Humanism.* London, 1977.

Usher, Abbot Payton. *The Early History of Deposit Banking in Mediterranean Europe*, Vol. I. Cambridge, MA, 1943.

Vaca Lorenzo, Angel. 'La oligarquía urbana salmantina en la baja edad media. Caballeros y escuderos en Pugna por los cargos del Concejo (1390–1408).' *Anales de Historia Antigua, Medieval y Moderna: Revista del Instituto de Historia Antigua y Medieval (Universidad De Buenos Aires)* 31 (1998), 63–83.

Valdenebro Manrique, Raquel. *El castell i el poble de Talamanca.* Manresa, 1994.

'Les muralles de Manresa en el segle XIV.' *Miscel.lània d'Estudis Bagencs* 9 (1994), 163–77.

Valdeón Baruque, Julio. *Los conflictos sociales en el reino de Castilla en los siglos XIV y XV.* Madrid, 1975.

Valdivieso, Isabel del. 'Urban Growth and Royal Interventionism in Late Medieval Castile.' *Urban History* 24:2 (1997), 129–40.

Vela Aulesa, Carles. *Especiers i candelers a Barcelona a la baixa edat mitjana: Testaments, família i sociabilitat*, 2 vols. Barcelona, 2008.

Verdés Pijuan, Pere. 'Les finances municipals a Cervera (1338–1339).' In *Funcionament de les finances locals al Llarg de la història: Actes del III Congrès Internacional d'Història Local de Catalunya, Barcelona, 17–18 de Novembre de 1995.* Barcelona, 1996, 205–14.

Verhulst, Adriaan. 'The Origins of Towns in the Low Countries and the Pirenne Thesis.' *Past and Present* 122 (1989), 3–35.

Vicens Vives, Jaime. *An Economic History of Spain.* Princeton, NJ, 1969.

'Evolucion de la economia Catalana duranta la primera mitad del siglo XV.' *IV Congres d'Historia de la Corona d'Arago.* Palma, 1955.

Historia de los Remensas (en el siglo XV). Barcelona, 1978.

Juan II de Aragón, 1398–1479: Monarquía y revolución en la España del siglo XV. Barcelona, 1953.

Els trastàmares: El segle XV. Barcelona, 1961.

Viciano Navarro, Pau. 'Entre la comercio i el mercat: Els inversors en la gestió de la fiscalitat reial i municipal al país Valencia.' In *Corona, municipis i fiscalitat a la baixa edat mitjana: Col.loqui (Quaderns de l'Institut d'Estudis Ilerdencs, 13)*. Lerida, 1997, 603–22.

Vilar, Pierre. *La Catalogne dans l'Espagne moderne: Recherches sur les fondements économiques des structures nationales*. Paris, 1977. Also published as Vilar, Pierre, *Catalunya dins l'espanya moderna: Recerques sobre els fonaments économics de les estructures nacionals*. 3 vols. Barcelona, 1979.

'Le déclin catalan du bas Moyen Age: Hypothèses sur sa chronologie.' *Estudios de Historia Moderna* 6 (1956–9), 1–68.

'Quelques problèmes de démographie historique en Catalogne et en Espagne' (Communication faite à l'assemblée de la Société en juin 1964). *Annales de Démographie Historique* (1965), 2–31.

Vinyoles Vidal, Teresa-María. 'L'amor i la mort al segle XIV: Cartes de Dones.' *Miscel.lània de Textos Medievals* 8 (1996), 111–98.

Les Barcelonines a les darreries de l'edat mitjana, 1370–1410. Barcelona, 1976.

Vizcaino, Rafael Narbona. *Valencia, municipio medieval: Poder politico y luchas ciudadanas (1239–1418)*. Valencia, 1995.

Volckart, Oliver, and Nikolaus Wolf. 'Estimating Financial Integration in the Middle Ages: What Can We Learn from a TAR Model?' *Journal of Economic History* 66:1 (2006), 122–39.

Vose, Robin. *Dominicans, Muslims, and Jews in the Medieval Crown of Aragon*. Cambridge, 2009.

Vries, Jan de. 'The Industrial Revolution and the Industrious Revolution.' *The Journal of Economic History* 54:2 (1994), 249–70.

The Industrious Revolution: Consumer Behavior and the Household Economy, 1650 to the Present. Cambridge, 2008.

Vries, Peer. *State, Economy, and the Great Divergence: Great Britain and China, 1650s to 1850s*. London, 2015.

Waley, Daniel, and Trevor Dean. *The Italian City Republics*. 4th edn, Harlow and New York, 2010.

Weber, Max. *La ville*. Paris, 1982.

Wirtschaft und Gesellschaft. Siebeck, 1925.

Webster, Jill. 'Els framenors a Manresa.' *Miscel.lània d'Estudi Bagencs* 5 (1987), 127–37.

Webster, Jill, ed. *Francesc eiximenis: La societat Catalana al segle XIV*. Barcelona, 1967.

Wee, Herman van der. *The Growth of the Antwerp Market and the European Economy (Fourteenth–Sixteenth Centuries)*. The Hague, 1963.

West, Charles. *Reframing the Feudal Revolution: Political and Social Transformation Between Marne and Moselle, c.800–c.1100*. Cambridge, 2013.

Wilkinson, Louise J. 'The "Rules" of Robert Grosseteste Reconsidered: The Lady as Estate and Household Manager in Thirteenth-century England.' In *The Medieval Household in Christian Europe c. 850–c. 1550: Managing Power, Wealth, and the Body*. Ed. Cordelia Beattie, Anna Maslakovic and Sarah Rees Jones. Turnhout, 2003, 293–306.

Winer, Rebecca Lynn. *Women, Wealth and Community in Perpignan, c. 1250–1300: Christians, Jews and Enslaved Muslims in a Medieval Mediterranean Town*. Aldershot, 2006.

Wolff, Philippe. 'The 1391 Pogrom in Spain: Social Crisis or Not?' *Past and Present: A Journal of Historical Studies* 50 (1971), 4–18.

"L'Episode de Berenguer Oller à Barcelone en 1285: Essai d'interpretation sociale.' *Anuario de estudios medievales* 5 (1968), 207–22.

'Reflexions sur les troubles sociaux dans les pays de la C. A. du XIVème siècle.' *VIII Congreso de Historia de la Corona de Aragón*, Vol. I. Valencia, 1969, 95–102.

Wray, Shona Kelly. *Communities and Crisis: Bologna during the Black Death*. Leiden, 2009.

Zanden, J. L. van. *The Long Road to the Industrial Revolution: The European Economy in a Global Perspective, 1000–1800*. Leiden, 2009.

'The Skill Premium and the "Great Divergence".' *European Review of Economic History* 13 (2009), 120–30.

'Tracing the Beginning of the Kuznets Curve: Western Europe during the Early Modern Period.' *The Economic History Review* 48:4 (1995), 643–64.

Zorzi, Andrea. 'The Popolo.' In *Italy in the Age of the Renaissance, 1300–1550*. Ed. John M. Najemy. Oxford, 2004, 145–64.

Zuijderduijn, Jaco. *Medieval Capital Markets: Markets for Renten, State Formation and Private Investment in Holland (1300–1550)*. Leiden, 2009.

Zulaica Palacios, Fernando. 'Evolución de los precios y salarios aragoneses entre 1300–1430.' *Aragón en la edad media* 12 (1995), 123–52.

Fluctuaciones económicas en un período de crisis: Precios y salarios en Aragón en la baja edad media (1300–1430). Zaragoza, 1993.

INDEX